Reading the Buddha's Discourses in Pāli

Publisher's Acknowledgment

The publisher gratefully acknowledges the generous help of the Hershey Family Foundation in sponsoring the production of this book.

Reading the Buddha's Discourses in Pāli

A Practical Guide to the Language of the Ancient Buddhist Canon

TEXTS COLLECTED, TRANSLATED, AND EXPLAINED BY

Bhikkhu Bodhi

Wisdom

Wisdom Publications
199 Elm Street
Somerville, MA 02144 USA
wisdomexperience.org

Library of Congress Cataloging-in-Publication Data
Names: Bodhi, Bhikkhu compiler translator author of commentary.
Title: Reading the Buddha's discourses in Pāli: a practical guide to the language of the ancient Buddhist canon / texts collected, translated, and explained by Bhikkhu Bodhi.
Other titles: Tipiṭaka. Suttapiṭaka. Saṃyuttanikāya. Selections. English.
Description: Somerville, MA: Wisdom Publications, 2020. | Includes bibliographical references.
Identifiers: LCCN 2020014470 (print) | LCCN 2020014471 (ebook) | ISBN 9781614297000 (hardcover) | ISBN 9781614296973 (ebook)
Subjects: LCSH: Buddhist literature, Pali--Translations into English. | Buddhist literature, Pali. | Pali language—Readers—Buddhism.
Classification: LCC BQ1332.B36 E5 2020 (print) | LCC BQ1332.B36 (ebook) | DDC 294.3/82—dc23
LC record available at https://lccn.loc.gov/2020014470
LC ebook record available at https://lccn.loc.gov/2020014471

ISBN 978-1-61429-700-0 ebook ISBN 978-1-61429-697-3

24 23 22 21 20
5 4 3 2 1

Cover design by Graciela Galup. Interior design by Gopa & Ted2, Inc.

Printed on acid-free paper that meets the guidelines for permanence and durability of the Production Guidelines for Book Longevity of the Council on Library Resources.

Printed in Canada.

Contents

Preface

THE INTENTION BEHIND the present book is to help students of Early Buddhism learn to read the texts of the Pāli Canon in the ancient Indian language in which they have been preserved, the language known as Pāli. The book is based on a weekly course in Pāli that I have been conducting over the past several years at Chuang Yen Monastery in upstate New York. The course is meant for students who have completed the earlier courses I gave on the basics of Pāli grammar and the reading of the Buddha's discourses in Pāli, the former based on Lily de Silva's *Pāli Primer*, the latter on James Gair and W. S. Karunatillake's *A New Course in Reading Pāli*. In the subsequent weekly course that I developed we read and analyzed suttas from the major chapters of the Saṃyutta Nikāya. In each class I took a sutta (or portion of a longer sutta), explained the meaning of each word and the grammatical forms involved, and then gave a literal translation of each sentence, followed by a more natural English rendering.

Since most of the students were already familiar with Pāli grammar, I sometimes tested their knowledge by asking them to explain the grammatical forms to the other students. Some of the students had not studied Pāli grammar and had no desire to learn it, but participated because they wanted to become familiar with the terminology of the texts and to see how translations are constructed on the basis of the original Pāli. More than half the students participated online; several even joined from Germany. All the classes were recorded, and each week I made the recordings available to the students in the class as well as to others who would have liked to join but could not attend when the class was in progress.[1]

It occurred to me that the material I compiled during this course would

1. The class still continues, though at this point (late 2019) we have completed our study of selected suttas from the Saṃyutta Nikāya and have moved on to the *Mahāparinibbāna Sutta* of the Dīgha Nikāya.

make a suitable textbook for people who want to learn to read the suttas in the original language. Thus, as an experiment, I began taking a selection of the suttas that I taught, breaking them into short units of Pāli text, and writing down literal word-for-word (or phrase-by-phrase) translations, followed by more natural translations. As I proceeded, and tested the material with several friends, it became clear that such a book would serve the purpose I envisaged.

The present book, the result of that procedure, is intended for both types of students who participated in my weekly Pāli class: those who have already learned the basics of Pāli grammar and, having become acquainted with the style and terminology of the suttas, now want to progress further in their reading, and those who do not wish to study Pāli grammar but would like to gain as intimate an acquaintance with the language and idiom of the texts as is possible without studying the language grammatically.

One thing that this book is *not* intended to be is a Pāli primer. While I offer a brief overview of Pāli grammar and syntax, I do not provide detailed lessons in Pāli grammar in its own right. I presuppose that the reader is either already familiar with the basics of the grammar and will understand the explanations given or is not interested in the grammar as such. Those who want to learn Pāli grammar should turn to the books I used in the earlier two courses.

Nevertheless, to aid students in deciphering the grammar of the texts, I have added after each reading selection a section of grammatical explanations. These are not intended to cover every minute grammatical structure found in the text under consideration but to clarify points and principles that call for elucidation. As I progress from chapter to chapter, the grammatical explanations gradually diminish. They are intended to be progessive, the later ones building on earlier ones, and I assume that a diligent student who has become familiar with the grammatical structures and patterns explained in the earlier passages will know enough to understand what is taking place grammatically in the later passages. To avoid ambiguities, however, I occasionally repeat explanations that have come earlier and may even have gone to excess in explaining forms found in later passages that were already covered. Sometimes, however, it is better to say too much than too little.

To provide students with access to more ample explanations of the grammar, I have occasionally added references to two comprehensive Pāli grammars that I have relied on for clarification. One, available online, is Charles

Duroiselle's *A Practical Grammar of the Pāli Language*, originally published in Rangoon in 1906. My references to this grammar, however, cite the section numbers of the online edition rather than those in the printed edition of 1906. The other is Vito Perniola's *Pali Grammar*. Both grammars cover essentially the same territory, though occasionally one will treat a topic in more detail or in a more satisfactory way than the other. I have also on occasion referred to Steven Collins's *A Pali Grammar for Students*, Wilhelm Geiger's *A Pāli Grammar*, especially on phonology, A. K. Warder's *Introduction to Pali*, and William Dwight Whitney's *Sanskrit Grammar*.[2] Since Sanskrit and Pāli are closely related, principles that govern Sanskrit grammar are often applicable to Pāli as well.

As a preparation for the grammatical explanations attached to the individual readings, following the introduction I provide a very broad overview of Pāli grammar and another on Pāli syntax—which, while a branch of grammar, calls for special treatment. Separately, I also include a key to the terms used in the grammatical explanations. These include English terms used with specific reference to Pāli grammar, which are likely to be unfamiliar even to a well-educated reader. After all, apart from those familiar with the grammar of classical languages, not many people are likely to know offhand what an absolutive is or a locative absolute—a completely different kind of fish—or what an optative is or an aorist or a future passive participle.

As a supplement to the reading material, I include at the end of this volume a Pāli-English glossary organized according to the order of the Pāli alphabet. The glossary makes no pretense to be a complete Pāli dictionary. Rather, it collects virtually all the words used in the reading selections and offers only the meanings relevant to those passages. Many of the words have multiple meanings, but I have not included those not pertinent to the texts presented here. The meanings of most words can be determined from the literal translation, but if one has trouble correlating the Pāli word and the translation, one should look up the word in the glossary.

Whereas the grammatical explanations cite words in the inflected form in which they appear in the text, the glossary lists nouns, adjectives, and participles in their stem form, as they stand before they have been declined according to their case and number. Verbs are listed in the third-person sin-

2. Thomas Oberlies, *Pāli Grammar*, vol. 1, was published after the present book was already submitted to the publisher.

gular of the present tense, in the indicative mood. To give some examples: In the grammatical explanations to 1.3 (p. 95) we find *vitakke* explained as the plural accusative of the masculine noun *vitakka*. The latter, the stem, is the way this noun is listed in the glossary. Again, in the grammatical explanations we find the verb *vitakketha*, a second-person plural imperative of *vitakketi*, "thinks." The latter is the form listed in the glossary.

The suttas included in this anthology are all from the Saṃyutta Nikāya. For convenience, I have used as my basic source for the Pāli texts the electronic edition of the Chaṭṭha Saṅgāyana Tipiṭaka,[3] version 4.0, though occasionally I prefer a reading in either the PTS edition or the Sri Lankan Buddha Jayanti Sinhala-script edition. Since my purpose here is simply to present an acceptable version of the texts for translation and analysis, I have not attempted to construct a critical edition and thus my notes on preferred readings and alternatives are minimal.

Source references in the detailed table of contents and in the body of the book cite the chapter number of the Saṃyutta followed by the number of the sutta within that chapter. This is followed by the volume and page number of the Pali Text Society's Roman-script edition of the Saṃyutta. Thus SN 22:12; III 21 is Saṃyutta Nikāya, chapter 22, sutta 12, found in volume III, page 21, of the PTS edition. The numbering of suttas in the Saḷāyatana-saṃyutta (chapter 35) occasionally differs across the different editions of this volume, depending on whether the discourses in a group are considered a single sutta or separate suttas. In chapter 3 of this book I have used the numbering scheme of my translation of the Saṃyutta Nikāya, *The Connected Discourses of the Buddha*, which differs from that of the PTS edition of the Pāli text. Hence in the detailed list of contents and again in chapter 3, I give the sutta number of the PTS edition in brackets following my own number.

ACKNOWLEDGMENTS

I thank John Kelly, my long-term assistant in translation matters, who has proofread this work in several versions and offered useful suggestions for improving the presentation. Bryan Levman reviewed in detail the intro-

3. This was the version of the Pāli Canon compiled at the Sixth Buddhist Council, held in Myanmar in the mid-1950s. Despite its claim to authority, this version gives preference to Burmese readings over variants from other textual transmissions.

ductory chapters on Pāli grammar and sentence patterns, and the grammatical explanations in the body of the work, and offered abundant comments. Beatrice Chrystall kindly reviewed the introductory chapter on Pāli grammar and the grammatical explanations in the first two chapters and offered helpful comments. I am particularly thankful to the students who have joined this course over the past few years, especially the core group of about sixteen who have persisted with the class, either attending in person or participating over the internet.

For any errors in grammatical explanations I must take responsibility. Pāli grammar can be a thorny and difficult subject and on numerous points even specialists hold different opinions. If any reader discovers incorrect explanations on my part, I would appreciate learning about them for correction in future editions of this book. I can be reached through the publisher.

Abbreviations

Editions

Be	Burmese-script edition, Chaṭṭha Saṅgāyana Tipiṭaka, electronic version 4.0, Vipassana Research Institute
Ce	Sinhala-script edition, Buddha Jayanti Tripitaka Series
Ee	Roman-script edition, Pali Text Society

Texts in Pāli

AN	Aṅguttara Nikāya
Dhp	Dhammapada
DN	Dīgha Nikāya
It	Itivuttaka
It-a	Itivuttaka-aṭṭhakathā
MN	Majjhima Nikāya
Mp	Manorathapūraṇī (Aṅguttara Nikāya commentary)
Paṭis	Paṭisambhidāmagga
Paṭis-a	Paṭisambhidāmagga-aṭṭhakathā
Ps	Papañcasūdanī (Majjhima Nikāya commentary)
SN	Saṃyutta Nikāya
Sn	Suttanipāta
Spk	Sāratthapakāsinī (Saṃyutta Nikāya commentary)
Sv	Sumaṅgalavilāsinī (Dīgha Nikāya commentary)
Ud	Udāna
Vibh	Vibhaṅga
Vism	Visuddhimagga

Reference Works

DOP	*A Dictionary of Pāli* (see Cone 2001, 2010)
PED	*Pāli-English Dictionary* (see Rhy Davids and Stede 1999 [1921–25])
SED	*Sanskrit-English Dictionary* (see Monier-Williams 2003 [1899])

Other Abbreviations

absol.	absolutive
aor.	aorist
caus.	causative
f.	feminine
gen.	genitive
ifc	in fine compositi (at the end of a compound)
ind.	indeclinable
interrog.	interrogative
m.	masculine
m.f.	masculine, feminine
mfn.	masculine, feminine, neuter
m.n.	masculine, neuter
n.	neuter
neg.	negative
num.	number
p., pp.	page, pages
pl.	plural
pp	past participle
pron.	pronoun
PTS	Pali Text Society
sg.	singular
Skt	Sanskrit
vb.	verb
voc.	vocative
VRI	Vipassana Research Institute (Igatpuri, India)
*	word not listed in dictionary

Detailed Contents

General Introduction

Why Read Pāli?

Pāli is the language of the collection of texts regarded by the Theravāda Buddhist tradition as authoritative *buddhavacana*, "Word of the Buddha." This collection is commonly called the Pāli Canon, or the Pāli Tipiṭaka. The latter expression means "Three Baskets" or "Three Collections" (of Buddhist teachings)—namely, the Sutta Piṭaka (the collection of discourses), the Vinaya Piṭaka (the collection of monastic discipline), and the Abhidhamma Piṭaka (the collection of doctrinal treatises). Pāli falls within the broad category of Middle Indo-Aryan languages. It is descended from Vedic Sanskrit but shows the influence of other, more regional languages used in northern India.

The Theravāda tradition identifies Pāli with Māgadhī, the language of the state of Magadha, where the Buddha often stayed. Several of the Buddha's favorite resorts were located in Magadha, among them the Bamboo Grove near Rājagaha, mentioned in the suttas as the scene of many discourses. As the language of a powerful and influential kingdom, Māgadhī may well have spread to other states in northeast India and become a prestigious language distinguishing those who used it as persons of culture, somewhat in the way English is used by the educated elite today even in the countries of South Asia. However, while the Buddha himself may have spoken in Māgadhī when teaching in Magadha—and perhaps in other dialects when teaching in other states, such as Kosala—various features of Pāli indicate that it cannot be identified with Māgadhī as we know it from the earliest sources available to us, the edicts of King Aśoka.

Many scholars regard Pāli as a hybrid showing features of several Prakrit dialects used around the third century BCE, subjected to a partial process of Sanskritization. According to the eminent Indologist Oskar von Hinüber:

> Pāli has never been a spoken language neither in Magadha nor elsewhere. For it is possible to infer from linguistic peculiarities of this language that it has been created as some kind of *lingua franca* presumably used in a large area at a time considerably later than the Buddha. The evidence, on which these conclusions are based, are the inscriptions of Aśoka (3rd century BC), which allow [us] to draw a very rough linguistic map of northern India. This map shows that Pāli is rooted in a language spoken in western India far away from the home land of Buddhism. At the same time certain eastern features embedded in Pāli point to the fact that the texts have been recast from an earlier eastern version into their present western linguistic shape. Therefore, it is evident that the texts as found in the Theravāda canon, though the oldest Buddhist texts surviving, are the result of a lengthy and complicated development.[4]

While the language called "Pāli" is not identical with any that the Buddha himself would have spoken, it belongs to the same broad linguistic family as those he might have used and originates from the same conceptual matrix.[5] The canonical texts preserved in Pāli are not so much translations from more archaic originals into an altogether different language, as a translation from German into English would be, as they are "transfers" or renditions from one Middle Indo-Aryan dialect into another. This language thus reflects the thought-world that the Buddha inherited from the Indian culture into which he was born and captures the nuances of that thought-world without the intrusion of alien influences inevitable in even the best and most scrupulous translations. This contrasts with Chinese, Tibetan, or English translations of Indian Buddhist texts, which inevitably carry over nuances and connotations from those languages.

4. Von Hinüber 1996, 5. For a detailed discussion of the relation of Pāli to the regional dialects of northern India, see Norman 2006, 75–97.

5. In saying that Pāli is not identical with any language that the Buddha himself would have used, I am stating the position prevalent among scholars of Middle Indo-Aryan languages. Over the past few years, however, a debate over precisely this point has opened up, with some scholars (among them Richard Gombrich) maintaining that the Buddha did teach in Pāli or in a language extremely close to it.

On this basis we can infer that the language of the Pāli Canon, while likely not identical with the language or languages the Buddha spoke, would be so close as to provide an almost transparent window into the words and expressions he used. This is particularly true of the Sutta Piṭaka, the collection of discourses. The language of the Vinaya Piṭaka is more technical in a legalistic sense, and the manner of expression in the Abhidhamma Piṭaka more abstract and formulaic. If by some unexpected miracle transcripts of the original discourses should turn up in the exact language(s) in which they were delivered, one who knows Pāli well would be able to read them with perhaps 90 percent accuracy. Thus one reason for studying Pāli is that it is probably the Buddhist canonical language closest to the language or languages used by the Buddha himself. So if you want to get some idea of what the Buddha said in the language he used on his teaching rounds, then it would be helpful to learn to read the discourses in Pāli.

While the Pāli Canon belongs to a particular Buddhist school, now called the Theravāda, or "Doctrine of the Elders," the suttas or discourses preserved in this collection are not exclusively Theravāda Buddhist texts. They stem from the earliest period of Buddhist literary history, a period lasting roughly 150 years after the Buddha's death. The Pāli suttas have counterparts in the collections of other early Buddhist schools that correspond closely to the Pāli versions, differing mainly in details and arrangements but not in essential doctrine. Therefore the Pāli suttas, along with their counterparts, constitute the most ancient records available of the Buddha's teachings, taking us as close as possible to what the Buddha actually taught. To study these texts in Pāli therefore leads us to the very taproot of the Dhamma in a language very close to the original.[6]

A second reason for reading the texts in Pāli rather than in English translation is because words in that language are closely connected with one another in ways that cannot be easily captured in translation. For instance, in English the words "knowledge," "perception," "wisdom," "understanding," and "consciousness" have no etymological connection. These are the words most commonly used to render the Pāli words *ñāṇa*, *saññā*, *paññā*, *pariññā*, and *viññāṇa*. With a knowledge of Pāli, you would see that they are all based on the root *ñā*, meaning "to know," and thus beneath the surface are

6. For arguments on the authenticity of these texts, see Sujāto and Brahmāli 2014.

connected by the idea of knowing. In the formula for *paṭiccasamuppāda*, "dependent origination," the English word "dependent" looks utterly different from the word "condition" used to connect each pair of terms. Yet the Pāli word *paṭicca*, rendered "dependent," is an absolutive of the verb *pacceti*, "falls back on, relies on," and *paccaya* a noun derived from the same verb. A *paccaya* is "that on which something else falls back," hence "a condition." For instance, in the expression *jātipaccayā jarāmaraṇaṃ*, birth is posited as the *paccaya*, the condition, from which there arise old age and death.

Still a third reason for learning to read the suttas in Pāli is because any translation, even the most accurate, inevitably involves some degree of interpretation that reflects the understanding and preferences of the translator as well as the linguistic limits of the destination language. No language can fully capture the meanings and connotations of words in another language, and often any rendering of a term must be an inadequate makeshift. Take for example the word *dukkha*. We normally translate this as "suffering," and in certain contexts *dukkha* does mean suffering and painful feeling. But as the theme of the four noble truths, and thus the cornerstone of the Buddha's teaching, "suffering" hardly covers the many nuances and implications of *dukkha*. While for the sake of transparency I render *dukkha* as "suffering," in doing so I have to acknowledge that this rendering is unsatisfactory and in some respects even misleading.

Another example is the Pāli word *saṅkhārā*. This has been rendered by a bewildering variety of English words: formations, confections, activities, concoctions, preparations, fabrications, and still others. This diversity of renderings has come about because English lacks a concept that exactly corresponds to *saṅkhārā*. The word is derived from the verb *karoti*, "to make, to do, to act," with the prefix *sam*, which suggests the sense of "together." Thus *saṅkhārā* are things that act together in making other things, and also the things made by the convergence of several conditioning factors. Since *saṅkhārā* is often connected to *cetanā*, volition, I have rendered the word in its active sense as "volitional activities." But *saṅkhārā* in the passive sense does not have a necessary connection with volition; in that sense it is a designation for things made by a multiplicity of other things, and thus I render it "conditioned things." When one comes across an English translation with the expression "volitional activities" and again encounters "conditioned things," one would be unlikely to suspect that they represent the same word in Pāli. But if one can read the original, one will see that this is so.

The Ground Plan of This Book

Something should be said now about the passages from which the chapters in this book have been composed and the arrangement of the selections. The passages are all taken from the Saṃyutta Nikāya. I have restricted my selections to this source for two reasons. The first is to ensure that the suttas to be translated and explained preserve the fairly uniform terminology and highly structured mode of presentation typical of the Saṃyutta. To have introduced a great variety of words and styles by selecting material from all four major Nikāyas (and the more archaic sections of the Khuddaka Nikāya) might have overwhelmed students with limited time, thereby discouraging them from persisting with their attempts to learn the language.

But there is another reason I chose the Saṃyutta as the basis for my course and for this book. This reason pertains to the doctrinal rather than the linguistic side of the Buddhist canon. It seems that the major chapters of the Saṃyutta Nikāya, if rearranged, provide a systematic overview of the Buddha's teachings that mirrors the four noble truths. The system emerges from the order of the chapters found here. The first chapter contains selections from the Saccasaṃyutta (SN 56), the Connected Discourses on the Truths—that is, on the four noble truths—which are elsewhere described as the "special Dhamma teaching of the buddhas" (*buddhānaṃ sāmukkaṃsikā dhammadesanā*, for instance at DN I 110,6–7). The four truths serve as the most concise statement of the Buddha's core teaching, a "matrix" that generates all the other teachings and a framework into which most other teachings can fit.

The suttas in the Saccasaṃyutta seldom elaborate on the content of the four noble truths. For details we have to turn to other chapters in this collection. It is noteworthy that the Buddha's discourses are linked through a complex network of allusions and cross-references. A theme or topic treated briefly in one place may be elaborated elsewhere; a term used in one sutta may be analyzed in detail in another. Thus, for example, a sutta on the noble eightfold path (such as SN 45:8) defines "right mindfulness" as the four establishments of mindfulness, but for a fuller explanation of these we must consult another sutta (such as DN 22 or MN 10).

In accordance with this principle, we can see the four noble truths enunciated as a set in the Saccasaṃyutta to be pointing toward other chapters in the Saṃyutta Nikāya for more detailed treatment. The formula for the first noble truth states that the noble truth of suffering consists in the five clinging-aggregates (see p. 97). For a fuller explication of the five aggregates, and thus of the first noble truth, we would therefore turn to the Khandhasaṃyutta (SN 22). Thus I have taken a selection of suttas from the Khandhasaṃyutta to make up chapter 2, which I subtitle "the meaning of suffering in brief," echoing the words of the first discourse: *saṃkhittena pañcupādānakkhandhā dukkhā*.

Another sutta on the first noble truth (SN 56:14) identifies the first noble truth with the six internal sense bases. Since it is through the six sense bases that all the other phenomena included in the five aggregates arise—feeling, perception, volition, and consciousness—I have designated the sense bases "the channels through which suffering originates." Selected suttas from the Saḷāyatanasaṃyutta (SN 35) therefore make up chapter 3 of this book.

Many discourses state that craving is the origin of suffering, among them the Buddha's first discourse (SN 56:11) along with SN 56:13 and SN 56:14. Yet the designation of craving as the origin of suffering seems to be an oblique way of pointing to a process that is intricate and complex, involving the interplay of a multitude of factors. In the suttas, these factors are joined into a lengthy chain that lays bare the causal dynamics that underlie the round of birth and death and thus the genesis of *dukkha*. This chain is expressed by the formula of dependent origination, which usually consists of twelve terms linked by relations of conditionality. The chain situates craving in the middle; behind it lies ignorance, which thus serves as the most fundamental root of the series; and at the end comes old-age-and-death,[7] which can be seen as the epitome of existential distress. The chain occurs in two modes: a mode of origination, which corresponds to the truth of the origin of suffering, and a mode of cessation, which corresponds to the truth of the cessation of suffering. Suttas on dependent origination are collected in the Nidānasaṃyutta (SN 12), and a selection from this collection makes up chapter 4 of this book.

The fourth noble truth, according to the Buddha's first discourse, is the noble eightfold path, described as "the way to the cessation of suffering." However, while the eightfold path may be the most comprehensive formulation of the practice—including as it does cognitive, ethical, and meditative

7. Here, and throughout this book, I translate the Pāli *jarāmaraṇaṃ* (a dvanda compound of the singular type) as a hyphenated singular.

factors—it is not the only set of practices that the Buddha taught as the way to the goal of his teaching. Rather, he presented the path from different perspectives, governed by the needs and aptitudes of the people being instructed. The broadest of these lays out seven sets of factors that altogether contain thirty-seven principles. In texts of a later period these come to be called "the aids to enlightenment" (*bodhipakkhiyā dhammā*, literally, "factors on the side of enlightenment," or "wings to awakening," according to another translation). In the oldest sources, however, they are not yet collected under a single designation but are simply referred to as seven sets. These seven sets are the four establishments of mindfulness, the four right kinds of striving, the four bases for spiritual power, the five faculties, the five powers, the seven factors of enlightenment, and the noble eightfold path. Chapters on each of these have been brought together in the last volume of the Saṃyutta Nikāya, the Mahāvagga, the Great Division, which might have also been called the Maggavagga, the Division on the Path.

I have dedicated chapter 5 of this book to the path of practice. However, if I had attempted to include here suttas representing all seven groups, I would have strained the limits imposed on this book. I have therefore restricted my choice of suttas to three groups, which each becomes a distinct division of this chapter: the four establishments of mindfulness, the seven factors of enlightenment, and the noble eightfold path. Since the systematic cultivation of mindfulness might be called "the essential practice of the way to liberation," I begin with suttas from the Satipaṭṭhānasaṃyutta (SN 47). When mindfulness reaches a certain degree of maturity, it becomes the first of the seven factors of enlightenment, the starting point from which the other six factors emerge; thus suttas from the Bojjhaṅgasaṃyutta (SN 46) constitute the second section of this chapter. And when the seven factors of enlightenment reach their pinnacle, they bring into being the liberating eightfold path, the truly noble path, and thus suttas from the Maggasaṃyutta (SN 45) constitute the third section of this chapter.

The goal of the path is nibbāna. Nibbāna has already been indicated obliquely in the chapter on the four noble truths as the cessation of suffering—and in the chapter on dependent origination as the cessation of each of the links in the formula of dependent origination—but in those chapters it has not been shown in its own nature. To provide a fuller picture of the goal of the teaching, I have included, as chapter 6, a wide selection from the Asaṅkhatasaṃyutta (SN 43), the Connected Discourses on the

Unconditioned, which offers thirty-two epithets for the goal, with *nibbāna* being only one among them. Each of these is equated with the destruction of lust, the destruction of hatred, and the destruction of delusion.

Sources and Conventions

I have confined my selections to prose texts and have not included texts in verse. Pāli verse typically alters normal word order to fit the requirements of meter, and also uses archaic and rare forms intended to give an elevated tone to the composition. I believe that students should first become familiar with Pāli prose before venturing to read verse. To elucidate the special features of Pāli verse would have called for extensive explanations that would have added to the volume of this book.

In each chapter, each sutta is broken down into relatively self-contained units of several sentences. The units are treated in three ways: first, the text is given in Pāli; second, a literal translation is offered, word for word or phrase by phrase; and third, a translation is made into natural English. The "natural translations" are not intended to be polished literary compositions, and thus in preparing them I have adhered to the phrasing of the original more closely than I do in my published translations. Finally, at the end of each selection, I provide a set of grammatical explanations that cites the Pāli word or phrase to be commented on along with a translation of that word or phrase, followed by an elucidation of the grammatical structures and syntax involved in the statement. By comparing the literal translations with the corresponding portion in Pāli, and following closely the grammatical explanations, the student should be able to determine the meaning of each word and phrase and gain familiarity with the syntax of Pāli sentences and the distinctive idioms and style of expression in the Pāli suttas.

I have divided the longer suttas into numbered sections, to which I have given subtitles. The grammatical explanations to these suttas are also divided into sections with the corresponding numbers and subtitles. This will make it easier for the student to locate the words and phrases on which I am commenting.

In editing the Pāli text, I have provided the reader with more aids than most published versions would do. While Pāli includes a marker for the end of a quotation (*ti*), the older Asian editions do not use quotation marks, though the Chaṭṭha Saṅgāyana Tipiṭaka has inserted them. I have followed normal English style in my use of quotation marks.

Where words are joined by *sandhi* in the Pāli text, I usually insert an apostrophe to show where a vowel has been elided, unless there is some ambiguity. (*Sandhi* refers to the changes that letters undergo in their combinations and encounters with other letters.) In the literal translation I use a hyphen to divide the English words, showing where the Pāli text contains two (or more) words, not a single word. An example would be "what-and" to represent *katamañca* (a sandhi formation of *katamaṃ* + *ca*). Sometimes the Chaṭṭha Saṅgāyana Tipiṭaka edition joins words that are not actually joined by sandhi. In such cases, too, in the literal translation I have inserted a hyphen between the words. An example is at 3.2 (p. 227), where we find: *cakkhusmimpi nibbindati, rūpesupi nibbindati, cakkhuviññāṇepi nibbindati, cakkhusamphassepi nibbindati.* Here the first is a proper sandhi formation, where the copulative particle *pi* changes the *niggahīta -ṃ* of *cakkhusmiṃ* into the labial *-m*. The locatives *rūpesu*, *cakkhuviññāṇe*, and *cakkhusamphasse* are unaffected by the addition of *pi*, but because the Pāli text joins the words I represent them in the literal translation thus: "in forms-too is disenchanted, in eye-consciousness-too is disenchanted, in eye-contact-too is disenchanted."

Again, I have used hyphens in the literal translation to separate words making up compounds, which abound in Pāli; for example, *ariyasacca* is literally rendered "noble-truth," *dukkhasamudaya*, "suffering-origin." I have not, however, hyphenated the Pāli text except to divide long dvanda ("copulative") compounds into their constituents. For instance, in the five-part dvanda *soka-parideva-dukkha-domanass'upāyāsā*, the hyphens help the reader distinguish the individual words that enter into this long compound. Since the last two words are joined in sandhi by the elision of the last vowel in *domanassa*, I have used an apostrophe to show the elision.

In the grammatical explanations, I do not italicize the Pāli grammatical terms I employ but only the words from the text that are being explained. I make this distinction in order to avoid intimidating the student with an excess of italicized words. Following this rule will also help the student to clearly distinguish which Pāli words are grammatical terms and which are being cited from the text. Since English lacks exact counterparts for some of the fundamental concepts of Pāli grammar, I have found it preferable to use the Pāli terms rather than makeshift renderings. This is particularly the case with the compounds. It is better, I think, for students to become familiar with such terms for the compounds as *dvanda*, *kammadhāraya*, *tappurisa*, and *bahubbīhi* than to have to decipher such expressions as "copulative compound," "descriptive compound," "determinative compound," and "possessive compound," which are either inadequate or misleading (or both).

References to texts in the introduction and the grammatical explanations cite chapter and text number. For example, a citation 4.4 refers to chapter 4, text 4. If the text has been divided into sections, the last number refers to the section; thus 2.5.2 means chapter 2, text 5, section 2. In references to chapter 5, which has three divisions, the number after the chapter number indicates the division. Thus 5.1.5 means chapter 5, division 1, text 5, while 5.2.7.2 means chapter 5, division 2, text 7, section 2.

After completing the book, students who wish to further develop their reading knowledge of Pāli may try accessing a complete chapter of the Saṃyutta Nikāya (available at https://www.tipitaka.org/) and reading it through from start to finish, if necessary with a reliable English translation and a Pāli dictionary at hand. A compilation of several Pāli dictionaries, including the PTS's Pāli-English Dictionary, is available at https://palidictionary.appspot.com/.

A Very Brief Overview of Pāli Grammar

SINCE PĀLI GRAMMAR is a vast and complex subject, here I will offer only a very brief overview, focusing on the topics that prevail in the grammatical explanations following each reading. I have drawn most of my information from the grammars by Duroiselle, Perniola, Collins, and Geiger. I also consulted Warder and Wijesekera on particular points. I have not included the paradigms of noun and pronoun declensions and verb conjugations, which can be found in full in the above grammars.

THE ALPHABET

The Pāli alphabet consists of 42 letters divided into 8 vowels, 33 consonants, and a nasal sound called *niggahīta*.[8]

The 8 vowels are: *a, ā, i, ī, u, ū, e, o.*

The consonants are divided into the following groups:

Gutturals	*k*	*kh*	*g*	*gh*	*ṅ*
Palatals	*c*	*ch*	*j*	*jh*	*ñ*
Cerebrals	*ṭ*	*ṭh*	*ḍ*	*ḍh*	*ṇ*
Dentals	*t*	*th*	*d*	*dh*	*n*
Labials	*p*	*ph*	*b*	*bh*	*m*

Liquid consonants:	*r, l, ḷ, ḷh*
Semivowels:	*y, v*
Sibilant:	*s*
Aspirate:	*h*
Niggahīta:	*ṃ*

8. The number of letters differs among the grammars. Here I follow Perniola. Collins counts 40 letters; he omits *ḷh* as a distinct liquid and considers the *niggahīta* to be a mere nasalization of the three vowels *a, i,* and *u*. Duroiselle counts 41 by including the *niggahīta* as a separate letter but omitting *ḷh*.

As to pronunciation:[9]

a as in "cut"
ā as in "ah"
i as in "king"
ī as in "keen"
u as in "put"
ū as in "pool"
e as in "ate," but before a double consonant more as in "bed"
o as in "home," but before a double consonant pronounced more briskly, as in "goat"[10]

Of the vowels, *a*, *i*, and *u* are short; *ā*, *ī*, and *ū* are long, held twice the length of the short vowels. The vowels *e* and *o* are of variable length. They are long when they occur at the end of a syllable, as in *tesaṃ*, "to them," and *loko*, "world"; they are short when they are followed by a consonant with which they form a syllable, as in *mettā*, "loving-kindness," and *gotta*, "clan."[11] An *o* and an *e* always carry a stress; otherwise the stress falls on a long vowel—*ā*, *ī*, *ū*, or on a double consonant, or on an internal *ṃ*.

Among the consonants, the gutturals are articulated in the throat, the palatals with the tongue against the palate. The guttural *g* is always pronounced as in "good," the palatal *c* like the *ch* in "church," the nasal *ñ* usually like the *ny* in "canyon."[12] The cerebrals (also called retroflexes or linguils) are spoken with the tongue curled back, the dentals with the tongue against

9. Pāli is pronounced somewhat differently in the different Theravāda countries. I describe here the Sri Lankan pronunciation. Since Sinhala, the language of most Sri Lankan Buddhists, belongs to the Indo-Aryan family of languages, the Sri Lankan pronunciation likely corresponds more closely to the original North Indian pronunciation than that used in Myanmar, Thailand, and other countries of Southeast Asia.

10. Warder 4 says that before a double consonant, *o* is pronounced more like the *o* in "not" or "odd," but I have never heard Sri Lankan monks pronounce it that way. I have always heard it as simply a shorter articulation of the ordinary *o* sound.

11. See Geiger §1.

12. This is the pronunciation when a single *ñ* precedes a vowel, as in *ñāṇa* or *ñeyya*, and in the case of the double consonant *ññ*, as in *paññā*, but before a palatal consonant, such as *c* or *j*, as in *sañchinditvā* or *sañjāta*, *ñ* is pronounced like an ordinary *n* but with the tongue against the palate.

the upper teeth. The aspirates—*kh*, *gh*, *ch*, *jh*, *ṭh*, *ḍh*, *th*, *dh*, *ph*, *bh*—are single consonants each represented in Asian scripts by a single letter; they are pronounced with slightly more force than the non-aspirates. Thus *th* is pronounced as in "Thomas" (not as in "thin"); *ph* as in "puff" (not as in "phone"). Double consonants are always enunciated separately, for instance *dd* as in "mad dog," *gg* as in "big gun."

In Sri Lanka and other Theravāda Buddhist countries, the *niggahīta* is currently pronounced like *ng* in "sing," and in India like the *m* in "hum," but historically it may have been pronounced as a pure nasal vowel as in French *enfant*.[13] It sometimes occurs inside words (for instance, in *vaṃsa*, "lineage," and *paṃsu*, "dust"); but most often it comes at the end of words following the vowels *a*, *i*, and *u*, for instance in *rūpaṃ*, *sambodhiṃ*, and *avocuṃ*.

Sandhi

The word *sandhi*, which literally means "putting together," refers to the changes that letters undergo in their combinations and encounters with other letters. The ostensible purpose behind such changes is to enhance euphony. Thus sandhi might be thought of as the euphonic combination of letters and words. Some analogues of sandhi in English might be the change of *can* + *not* to *can't* and of *will* + *not* to *won't*, though in Pāli sandhi occurs in formal diction and not merely in colloquial speech.

Sandhi pertains to both the internal combination of letters within a word ("internal sandhi") and to the changes that letters undergo when two words meet ("external sandhi"). The rules governing sandhi in Pāli are complex, but whereas the rules of sandhi in Sanskrit are rigid and exact, sandhi in Pāli admits of many variations, probably stemming from the fact that Pāli is more directly rooted in colloquial languages and thus displays the variability of sound combinations characteristic of a spoken language.

The principles of sandhi are too involved to be explained in full in a short overview of Pāli grammar such as this, but students who wish to be able to read the texts with a fair degree of fluency should familiarize themselves with the modifications that letters and words undergo as a result of

13. Warder 4 calls it the "pure nasal" and describes it as "the humming sound produced when the mouth is closed but air escapes through the nose with voicing (vibration of the vocal cords); it is *m* without release (consequently without place of articulation except the nose)."

sandhi.[14] When we come to the readings, I will point out the more noteworthy instances of sandhi in the grammatical explanations attached to each reading, but here a few general principles may be noted.

Vowel sandhi

First, we'll take a quick look at vowel sandhi. When two short vowels of the same kind meet, a long vowel might replace them and the words will merge. This is most common with *a*. Thus *na* + *ahaṃ* > *nāhaṃ*; *na* + *ayaṃ* > *nāyaṃ*; *pana* + *aniccaṃ* > *panāniccaṃ*. But when *i* is followed by *i*, one is often elided, as with *cattāri* + *imāni* > *cattār'imāni*.[15] When different vowels meet, generally the preceding vowel is elided. Thus when *a* meets *ā*, the *a* may be elided, as in *uṭṭhāy'āsanā*. Similarly, *ca* + *eva* > *c'eva*; *na* + *eva* > *n'eva*; *tena* + *upasaṅkami* > *ten'upasaṅkami*; *hi* + *etaṃ* > *h'etaṃ*. Several instances of sandhi between vowels occur in the stock formula for non-self: *n'etaṃ mama, n'eso'hamasmi, na m'eso attā*.[16]

Some kinds of vowel sandhi can easily mislead an unwary reader and therefore should be recognized when they are encountered. When *me* and *ayaṃ* meet, the result is *myāyaṃ* (p. 355), and when *kho* and *ahaṃ* meet, the result is *khvāhaṃ* (p. 152); the meeting of *kho* and *ayaṃ* results in *khvāyaṃ* (p. 310). Each strong vowel is replaced by its respective semivowel (*e* by *y*, *o* by *v*) and the following initial *a-* is lengthened.[17]

To avoid hiatus when vowels meet, certain liaison consonants may be inserted between them: *t*, *d*, and *m* serve mainly in this role. Thus we find *ajjatagge* (p. 452), *yāvadeva* (p. 490), and *yena-m-idh'ekacce* (p. 245). The semivowel *y* may also be inserted between two vowels, such as *na* + *idaṃ* > *nayidaṃ* (p. 156).

14. Sandhi is discussed at length in Duroiselle §§14–50; Perniola §§5–23; Geiger §§66–74; and Collins 3–12. Warder 213–18 gives many useful examples of sandhi.

15. It is, of course, an open question which *i* is being elided, but since the final vowel of other numbers is elided in the encounter with *imāni* (for instance, *pañc'imāni*), we can assume here it is the final vowel of *cattāri*.

16. Without sandhi, this would be read *na etaṃ mama, na eso ahaṃ asmi, na me eso attā*.

17. The mutual interchange of certain vowels and their corresponding semivowels is called in Sanskrit *samprasāraṇa*. In Pāli *samprasāraṇa* may occur between *i-* and *e-* with *y-*, and between *u-* and *o-* with *v-*.

The prefix sam

The prefix *sam* may be modified in relation to the letter that follows it. When *sam* precedes a vowel, the labial nasal *m* is retained, as in *samaya*, *samādhi*, *samudaya*, and so forth. However, before a consonant belonging to the five consonant groups, the *-m* is usually changed by internal sandhi into the nasal pertaining to that group, respectively to *ṅ*, *ñ*, *ṇ*, and *n* for the gutturals, palatals, cerebrals, and dentals; thus *saṅkhārā*, *sañjānāti*, *saṇṭhāna*, and *sandiṭṭhika*.[18] Before a labial consonant *m* retains its own form, as in *samphassa* or *sambodha*. Before a consonant outside the five groups—that is, before *y*, *v*, *s*, and *h*—the final consonant of the prefix becomes a *niggahīta*. We thus find *saṃyojana*, *saṃvara*, *saṃsāra*, and *saṃhita*. Before *l*, *m* is assimilated; thus *sam* + *lekha* becomes *sallekha*, and *sam* + *līna* becomes *sallīna*. When encountering such words as *samudaya*, *saṅkhārā*, *sañjānāti*, *saṇṭhāna*, *sandiṭṭhika*, *samphassa*, and *sallekha*, one should realize that despite the differences in the first syllable, they are all modifications of *sam* determined by the rules of sandhi.

Palatalization

When, in word formation, a consonant is immediately followed by *-y-*, the consonant cluster usually changes by internal sandhi into a double palatal: *-cc-*, *-cch-*, *-jj-*, *-jjh-*, or *-ññ-*. This is common in verbs with an internal *-ya-*. For example, the verbal root *man*, "to think," belongs to the class of verbs that form their active indicative stem with *-ya-*; thus the third-person singular of this verb is *maññati*, "one thinks." Such palatalization is commonly seen in the forming of passive verbs with the *-ya-* insert. For instance, the passive based on the root *chid*, "to cut," would in the first instance be *chidyati*, but the consonant cluster *-dy-* is palatalized to yield *chijjati*, "is cut." The absolutive *nisadya* becomes *nisajja*. Palatalization also occurs in nouns. The noun that appears in Sanskrit as *pratyaya*, "condition," becomes in Pāli *paccaya*, with the *-ty-* cluster turned into *-cc-*. Whenever a word has an

18. It is possible, however, for the *niggahīta* to be used instead of the corresponding nasal, particularly before consonants of the guttural group. We thus find *saṃkhārā* as well as *saṅkhārā*, *saṃgha* as well as *saṅgha*.

internal *-cc-*, *-cch-*, *-jj-*, *-jjh-*, or *-ññ-*, this likely results from *-y-* being inserted into it. Further examples of palatalization will be noted below.

The niggahīta

In external sandhi, a *niggahīta* preceding a word beginning with a vowel may change into *m* and the words may be joined without hiatus, as if they form a single word. Thus *evaṃ* followed by *assa* becomes *evamassa*, *evaṃ* followed by *eva* becomes *evameva*, and *ayaṃ* followed by *eva* becomes *ayameva*.

When the *niggahīta* at the end of a word is followed by a consonant, it may change into the nasal corresponding to that consonant group. This is most common with conjunctions of monosyllabic words. For instance, *kiṃ* followed by *ca* turns into *kiñca*, *taṃ* followed by *ca* becomes *tañca*, and *taṃ* followed by *pi* turns into *tampi*.

When the *niggahīta* precedes the quotation marker *ti*,[19] it turns into *n*. An example occurs in the paragraph at the end of the first reading, where we find: *"idaṃ dukkhan"ti yogo karaṇīyo*.

When *ti* is preceded by any of the short vowels—*a*, *i*, or *u*—it causes that vowel to be lengthened. Thus in the phrase *"dīghassa addhuno accayenā"ti*, the final *-a* of *accayena* is lengthened. Again, in *"ariyasaccānī"ti vuccanti*, the *-i* at the end of *saccāni* is lengthened. And *-u* at the end of *bhikkhu* is lengthened thus: *"Siyā, bhikkhū"ti*. These are instances of external sandhi affecting vowels.

NOUNS

In dictionaries of Pāli, nouns and their qualifiers (such as adjectives and participles) are usually represented in their stem form, the noun (or modifier) as it stands before it has undergone declension. Declension is the addition of certain suffixes to the stems of nouns, their derivatives, and adjectives to determine their case and number. In the texts, nouns always appear in their declined forms, and thus it is imperative that the reader be able to determine a noun's stem from the way it appears after it has undergone declension.

Nouns and pronouns are of three genders: masculine, feminine, and neu-

19. Pāli *ti* is equivalent to Skt *iti*, with loss of the initial vowel. For this and other cases of the loss of an initial vowel, see Geiger §66.1.

ter. The masculine and feminine genders apply to inanimate objects and states as well as to people. Thus a tree is masculine *rukkha* and a river feminine *nadī*; dispassion is masculine *virāga* and liberation feminine *vimutti*. Knowledge is neuter *ñāṇa*, but wisdom is feminine *paññā* and enlightenment is masculine *sambodha*. Adjectives and verbal derivatives qualifying a noun will agree with the gender of that noun. There are two numbers, the singular and the plural. Pāli lacks the distinctive dual forms found in Sanskrit.

Nouns are distinguished into different classes by way of the termination of their stems. The stems of masculine and neuter nouns may end in the vowels *a*, *i*, *u*, and *ū*. The stems of feminine nouns may end in *ā*, *i*, *ī*, *u*, and *ū*. There are also nouns whose stems end in consonants. These include a class of neuter nouns that terminate in *-s* (among them *manas*, *cetas*, *tapas*, *tejas*, and *vayas*). There are stems that end in *-at*, *-vat*, and *-mat*,[20] and still others that end in *-in*, *-an*, and *-ar*. These can be declined in all three genders. Thus, on the basis of the stem *sīlavat*, a virtuous man is designated in the nominative as *sīlavā*, a virtuous woman as *sīlavatī*. The usual honorific for the Buddha, *bhagavā*, "one who has good fortune," belongs to this class. On the basis of the stem *brahmacārin*, a male celibate might be designated in the nominative as *brahmacārī*, a female celibate as *brahmacārinī*. But the nouns *attan*, *brahman* (as referring to the deity), and *rājan* are exclusively masculine; their nominative singular forms are, respectively, *attā*, *brahmā*, and *rājā*. The long final vowel should not be taken to mean that they are feminine.[21] Agent nouns whose stems end in *-ar* also form masculine nominatives with *-ā*. For instance, *satthar*, "the teacher," has *satthā* as its masculine nominative; *kattar*, "doer," has *kattā*. The relational words *pitar*, "father," and *mātar*, "mother," respectively, form masculine *pitā* and feminine *mātā*.

The case of a noun and its qualifiers governs its role in the syntax of a sentence. The case is shown by its suffixes, which function somewhat in the way prepositions do in English. Pāli has eight cases: the nominative, the accusative, the instrumental, the dative, the ablative, the genitive, the locative, and the vocative. Each case has multiple uses, as will become clear

20. These suffixes are also represented in their strong forms as *-ant*, *-vant*, and *-mant*. The suffix *-vat* or *-vant* is attached to stems that end in *-a*, *-mat* or *-mant* to stems that end in *-i* or *-u*.

21. Paradigms for the declensions of nouns of all these classes are in Duroiselle §§116–95; Perniola §§24–38; and Collins 52–60.

when we proceed to the reading passages and explain how the cases operate in specific sentences. Here I must confine myself to the principal uses for each, which may be briefly noted as follows.[22]

1. The *nominative* is used for the grammatical subject of a sentence, which may be active or passive. The nominative may denote the agent of a transitive or intransitive verb, or the subject in a sentence without a verb, such as an equational sentence that ascribes to the subject a quality represented by an adjective or participle, for instance: *rūpaṃ aniccaṃ*, "form [is] impermanent," or *dukkhaṃ ariyasaccaṃ anubuddhaṃ paṭividdhaṃ*, "the noble truth of suffering [has been] understood and penetrated."

2. The *accusative* is used for the direct object of transitive verbs and secondary objects in double accusatives with verbs of speaking. It is also used in certain adverbial expressions, for example in the expression with which many suttas begin, *ekaṃ samayaṃ*, "on one occasion."

3. The *instrumental* denotes the agent of passive verbs, the instrument of action, the cause or reason of an action or event, the qualities with which someone or something is endowed, persons who accompany the subject (usually with the indeclinable *saddhiṃ*), and the accompaniment of an action. It corresponds to the prepositions "by" and "with."

4. The *dative* shows the purpose of an action and an indirect object; it corresponds to the preposition "to," "for," or "for the sake of." However, the verbs of going and coming, *gacchati* and *āgacchati*, bear the sense, respectively, of "goes to" and "comes to," and thus they normally take their destination in the accusative; but in a few instances (mainly in verse) *gacchati* takes the destination in the dative. The dative may also be used to characterize a subject in a passive role, as the one *to whom* something occurs, such as a thought, as seen in the common expression *tassa etadahosi*, "this occurred to him."[23] The dative differs from the genitive only in the *-a* declension in the singular. In other declensions it is often hard to determine whether the case of a noun or its qualifiers is dative or genitive, and there is seldom need to draw such a distinction.[24]

22. These summaries of the uses of each case are drawn largely from Collins 18–19. Collins continues by illustrating each of these usages with examples from the suttas. See too Duroiselle §§594–602 and Perniola §§245–66. The fullest discussion is in Wijesekera 1993.

23. I here follow Wijesekera §97c, which describes this construction as "an idiomatic and popular usage" of the dative. However, Perniola §261 and Warder 56 take the noun and its qualifiers in such phrases to be the genitive.

24. This point is made by Collins 27. See too Wijesekera §138.

5. The *ablative* shows the place or cause from which an entity or action originates; it expresses causation, departure, separation, and point of origin, and corresponds to the prepositions "from" or "through" and often to "because of." It is also used in comparisons, when, for example, one thing is said to be better than another.

6. The *genitive* expresses a possessive or partitive relation between two nouns. It often corresponds to the preposition "of," showing that something belongs to someone, as with *rañño nāgā*, "the king's elephants." The genitive is occasionally used in the suttas with a sense that is closer to the instrumental than the possessive (see the explanation of *tumhākaṃ* on p. 105).

7. The *locative* denotes the location where an action or event occurs, corresponding to the prepositions "in," "on," and "at." It is also used to specify the time at which an event occurs, corresponding to the sense of "when," and for the objects of nouns signifying desire and knowledge; this latter usage is called "the locative of reference." Thus, where in English a person has "knowledge of suffering" and "lust for forms," in Pāli one has *dukkhe ñāṇaṃ* and *rūpesu rāgo*, "knowledge in regard to suffering" and "lust in relation to forms." A special use of the locative is in the absolute construction, which will be discussed below (see pp. 70–72).

8. The *vocative* is used to address someone (or a group of people). Thus the Buddha addresses his personal attendant with the vocative *Ānanda* and addresses the monks with *bhikkhave*. The monks address the Buddha with the vocative *bhante* and the brahmins address him as *bho Gotama*.

Pronouns

Pronouns undergo declension in the same way as nouns do. Pāli has personal, demonstrative, relative, interrogative, and indefinite pronouns. Personal pronouns correspond to the sense of "I" and "we," "you" (the singular and plural are distinct), "he" or "she," and "it," and their plurals "they" and "these" or "those." The first and second personal pronouns do not have gender. Third-person pronouns, when used both as personal and demonstrative pronouns, agree in number and gender with that to which they refer.[25]

Certain pronouns have enclitic forms—forms that occur only within a sentence or clause, not at the beginning of a sentence or clause. The enclitic

25. For paradigms of pronoun declensions see Duroiselle §§288–335; Perniola §§40–47; and Collins 61–69.

pronouns are *me* and *no*, respectively, the first-person singular and plural; and *te* and *vo*, the second-person singular and plural. The enclitic pronouns usually represent the dative, genitive, and instrumental, though occasionally they can also represent the accusative.[26]

Strictly speaking, a pronoun takes the place of a noun, so when a word in the form of a pronoun modifies a noun it should be called a "pronominal adjective" rather than a pronoun. But since the forms of the words are the same, for convenience most modern grammars speak of such pronominal adjectives as "pronouns" even when they modify a noun in the same sentence. I have adopted this convention in my grammatical explanations. The term "pronominal adjective" tends to be reserved for a class of adjectives declined like pronouns. These include *añña*, "other," *aññatara*, "a certain," *ekacca*, "some," *katama*, "which one," *para*, "other," and *sabba*, "all."[27]

Pronouns often occur in statements that pair a subordinate clause with the main clause; in such constructions the relative pronoun in the subordinate clause is completed by a demonstrative pronoun in the main clause. Generally, but not invariably, the relative clause precedes the main clause. Types of correlation between relative clauses and main clauses will be discussed more fully below (pp. 63–67).

VERBS

Voices and classes

All verbs in Pāli (as in Sanskrit) are ultimately derived from a root, from which a stem is formed by the addition of a prefix, suffix, or infix, by reduplication, or by lengthening of a vowel. Thus the root *gam*, meaning "to go," takes *gaccha* as its present stem, to which the other elements may be added. Adding *-mi* to the stem (with lengthening of the preceding vowel) results in the first-person singular *gacchāmi*, "I am going," but adding *-nti* yields the third-person plural *gacchanti*, "they are going."

Pāli verbs have two voices, the active and the middle, which differ with respect to the endings attached to their stems. In theory the active voice corresponds to a transitive verb, denoting an action that passes from a sub-

26. See Geiger §104 for the case occurrences of each enclitic form; see too Duroiselle §290 and Perniola §40, which partly differ in their ascription of cases to these forms.

27. See Duroiselle §353; Perniola §47; and Collins 61.

ject to an object, while the middle voice corresponds to an intransitive verb, one denoting an action that inheres in the subject. While this distinction is maintained fairly rigorously in Sanskrit, in Pāli the middle voice has largely faded into the background and the active voice prevails with virtually all verbs, whether used transitively or reflexively. The middle voice is confined mostly to verse, but occasionally surfaces in prose passages, especially in those with an elevated tone. A prose text with a poetic simile (p. 216) employs the middle-voice verbs *bhāsate*, *tapate*, and *virocate* instead of their active counterparts, *bhāsati*, *tapati*, and *virocati*. Middle-voice forms appear more often in the present participle, where they have shed their reflexive character and function in the same way as active participles. These will be discussed below.

Verbs belong to different classes, varying in number from seven to ten depending on the grammarian.[28] The classes are differentiated by the alterations the root undergoes to form its present stem. Verbs belonging to several of these classes are rare. For the purposes of this book it is not necessary to dissect the classes of verbs, but the student should be able to recognize the verbs behind their inflections.

Conjugation

The process of inflection to which a verb is subjected is called *conjugation*. The conjugation of a verb is divided into tenses, moods, and systems. Pāli has *three tenses*, distinguishing the verb temporally into the past (aorist), the present, and the future. A verb may occur in any of *four moods*: the indicative, used for normal statements of fact; the imperative, which expresses a command or a request; the optative, which expresses what should be done, would be done, or might happen, or to issue a polite request; and the conditional or hypothetical, which expresses a conditional relationship about a counterfactual matter. The *four systems* are the causative, the desiderative, the intensive, and the denominative. Of these, the only one that occurs with any degree of frequency in all tenses and moods is the causative. The other systems are rarely used apart from the present indicative active. Wherever

28. The ten classes of verbs based on Sanskrit grammar are explained by Perniola §§62–71. Other grammarians recognize seven classes, explained by Duroiselle §§370–79. Collins 76 compares the different schemes and shows that some grammars have eight and nine classes.

these occur, I point them out in the grammatical explanations attached to each reading.

The present indicative active is the form of the verb used when listing verbs in Pāli dictionaries. I use this form to list verbs in the glossary here. The present indicative aspect is formed by adding the primary personal endings to the stem of the present. Thus for the stem *labha-*, "gain," we have the singular first, second, and third persons *labhāmi*, *labhasi*, and *labhati*, and the corresponding plurals *labhāma*, *labhatha*, and *labhanti*.[29]

The aorist

The form of the verb that can be most confusing is the aorist, which is used primarily as the past tense.[30] The aorist is generally formed by prefixing the augment *a-* to the root or the stem and by adding the secondary personal endings either directly or by means of one of the suffixes, *-a*, *-s*, or *-is*.[31] Because of the phonological changes that take place when moving from Sanskrit to Pāli, these suffixes are not always apparent. Depending on how it is formed, there are four types of aorist: (1) the root aorist, (2) the *a*-aorist, (3) the *s*-aorist, and (4) the *is*-aorist.[32] While this diversity of types may be perplexing to the novice student of Pāli, once one becomes familiar with the ways of forming the aorist, aorist verbs are fairly easy to recognize.

In the readings in this volume we encounter perhaps only one instance of the root aorist. This is the verb *ahu* used when the Buddha describes his

29. See Perniola §73 for parallel conjugations of the present indicative of verbs belonging to other classes.

30. The aorist is also used with the prohibitive particle *mā*, "don't," to express a prohibition or negative command. See for example *evaṃ me rūpaṃ mā ahosī*, "Let my form not be thus" (p. 168).

31. The addition of the augment is common but not mandatory. The root aorist, which is of rare occurrence, always takes the augment; the a-aorist generally does not; the s-aorist formed from the verbal root and the extended s-aorist based on the a-aorist generally take the augment; the s-aorist formed from the stem of the present in *-e/-aya* generally does not take the augment. The is-aorist formed from the verbal root generally takes the augment. When the is-aorist is based on the present stem, the augment is optional, but forms without the augment are much more common.

32. On the rules for forming the aorist, see Perniola §§82–87 and Collins 87–89. Duroiselle, using a somewhat different terminology, recognizes three kinds of aorist and calls the a-aorist "the imperfect." Geiger §§160–70 cites many examples from the texts to illustrate the different types of aorists.

discovery of dependent origination (at p. 298): *tassa mayhaṃ, bhikkhave, yonisomanasikārā ahu paññāya abhisamayo*, "through thorough attention, monks, there *occurred* [*was*] for me a breakthrough by wisdom."[33]

A limited number of verbs commonly take the a-aorist. The root *vac* has the a-aorist in the third-person singular *avoca* and the third-person plural *avocuṃ*, which are both commonly found in the suttas. The a-aorist is also used with the verb meaning "to see." In the readings we find the first-person singular *addasaṃ* and the third-person singular *addasā*. Instances of the s-aorist and is-aorist are more frequent. I have specified instances of the other three aorists in the grammatical explanations, but not the commonplace is-aorist.

When an aorist with a prefix takes the a-augment, the augment is inserted between the prefix and the stem. Occasionally changes caused by the meeting of prefix and augment may obscure the identity of the verb. To identify the verb requires some familiarity with the rules of internal sandhi. An example is *udapādi*, an is-aorist of *uppajjati*, "arises," from the root *pad* (strengthened to *pād*), with the *-a-* augment inserted between the prefix *ud-* and the base. In *pāyāsi*, aorist of *payāti*, "departs," the short *-a-* of the prefix *pa-* merges with the augment to form *-ā-*.

Again, consider the verb *paṭijānāti*, "claims," based on the root *ñā* (= Skt *jñā*). This verb takes *paccaññāsiṃ* as its first-person singular s-aorist (p. 151). When the augment is inserted, the consonant *ñ-* is doubled to represent the lost *j-* of the Sanskrit. Before the augment the prefix *paṭi* turns to *paṭy*; then, to avoid a hard consonant conjunct *-ṭy-*, *paṭy* turns into the softer palatal *pacc*, which is then joined to the augment. A similar transformation takes place with the verb *abhijānāti*, where the first-person singular aorist is *abbhaññāsiṃ* (p. 151). In this instance, before the augment the original prefix *abhi* turns first into *abhy* and then into the more euphonic *abbh*.

The passive verb

Passive verbs are formed from active verbs by attaching the infix *-ya-* either to the root in its weak grade, directly or by means of the connecting vowel

33. The original root of this verb is *bhū*, which retains its integrity in Sanskrit, but in some verb forms in Pāli loses the initial *b-*, with the aspirate becoming an initial *h*. Thus where Sanskrit has the third-person singular indicative *bhavati*, Pāli usually has *hoti*, where we see the change of *bh* to *h* and the contraction of *ava* to *o*.

-i-/*-ī-*, or to the present stem by means of the connecting vowel *-i-*/*-ī-*. A passive verb often seen in the suttas is *paññāyati*, "is known, is discerned." The verb is the passive of *pajānāti*, "understands, knows," built on the root *ñā* with doubling of *ñ-* to represent the lost *j-* of the Sanskrit. An example with insertion of the vowel is *pahīyati* (p. 230). When *-ya-* is inserted to form a passive verb, the *-y-* may be assimilated to the preceding consonant or both consonants may be modified by sandhi, often through palatalization. In Sanskrit, *-ya-* would be preserved, but in Pāli assimilation or mutation is the rule. We thus find the passive verbs *vuccati*, "is said," *bhijjati*, "is broken," *vimuccati*, "is liberated," and *dissati*, "is seen."

The infinitive

The infinitive in Pāli is formed by addition of the suffix *-tuṃ* either to the strong form of the root, to the stem of the present by means of the connecting vowel *-i-*, or directly to the present stem in *-e* or *-o*. In function the infinitive is similar to the dative of purpose. The infinitive of a causal verb, *ujjāleti*, occurs in the question (p. 460) *Bhabbo nu kho so puriso parittaṃ aggiṃ ujjāletuṃ*, "Would that person be able to cause a small fire to blaze up?" The infinitive is used with the indeclinable *kallaṃ*, "fitting, proper," in the query (p. 169) *kallaṃ nu taṃ samanupassituṃ*, "Is it fitting to regard that [thus]?" The infinitive is also used with the indeclinable *alaṃ*, "enough, sufficient," in the statements (p. 319) *alameva . . . viriyaṃ ārabhituṃ*, "It is enough . . . to arouse energy," and *alameva appamādena sampādetuṃ*, "It is enough to strive with heedfulness."

PREFIXES

The meaning of a simple verb can be altered and enhanced by the addition of prefixes, which are also attached to nouns. The most common prefixes, with the nuances they suggest, are:

ati, "beyond, above"
adhi, "toward, up to"
anu, "along with, after"
abhi, "toward, facing, over, superior"
ava or *o*, "downward"

ā, "toward"
ud, "upward"
upa, "toward"
dur, "bad, wrong"
ni, "down, out"
nī or *nir*, "away, out"
pa, "toward"
paṭi or *pati*, "back to, opposite, sequential"
pari, "round, fully"
vi, "separate, distinctive"
sam, "together, complete"
su, "well, easy, very."[34]

To illustrate how a prefix can modify the meaning of a verb, let us take the root *ñā*, which yields the verb *jānāti*, "knows." The prefixed verb *abhijānāti* means "knows directly" or "knows in a superior way." The corresponding noun *abhiññā* comes to denote superior knowledge. *Anujānāti*, often used in the context of monastic discipline, means "allows" or "authorizes." *Pajānāti* is rendered "understands" or "discerns"; its corresponding noun *paññā* is usually translated as "wisdom." *Paṭijānāti* can mean "acknowledges" or "claims," and its noun *paṭiññā* is "a claim." *Parijānāti* might be rendered "fully understands," and its noun *pariññā*, "full understanding." *Vijānāti* suggests "distinctly knows." Its cognate noun *viññāṇa*, used for the six types of sensory consciousness, may originally have denoted some kind of distinct knowledge, but that nuance has faded into the background. *Sañjānāti* (from *sam* + *ñā*) has taken on the meaning "perceives." Its corresponding noun *saññā* is usually rendered "perception," but may have originally denoted a syncretic knowledge, a nuance lost by the time of the Nikāyas.

Two more examples may be briefly considered. The verb *gacchati* means "goes," but *upagacchati* "goes toward, approaches," *āgacchati* "comes," *vigacchati*, "vanishes," *nigacchati*, "undergoes, encounters," and *adhigacchati*, "finds, achieves." The prefixed verb *uppajjati* means "arises," but *āpajjati* means "enters upon, incurs," *paṭipajjati* "proceeds, practices," *vipajjati* "fails," and *sampajjati* "succeeds."

The above examples should show that one must be cautious about inter-

34. Here I largely follow Collins 125.

preting words with prefixes. While the meaning that emerges from the addition of the prefix is sometimes obvious (for instance, *abhikkamati* means "goes forward" and *paṭikkamati* "comes back"), often one cannot deduce the meaning of a verb simply by adding the nuance of the prefix to the meaning of the basic verb. It is thus advisable always to learn the meaning of a prefixed verb from a dictionary or glossary and to interpret it in context.

Participles

Participles are verbal derivatives qualifying or representing a subject. They are declined along with the noun they qualify or represent, agreeing with it in number, gender, and case. Participles can act as adjectives modifying a noun in the sentence, or they can stand in for the nouns themselves. There are three principal participles in Pāli, commonly found in the readings included here: the present participle, the past participle, and the future passive participle.[35]

The present participle

The present participle is used to describe an action performed by a subject or occurring to an object at roughly the same time as the action denoted by the main verb of the sentence. Verbs that have their stem in *-a*, such as *gacchati*, form the present participle by adding to the present stem either the suffix *-ant/-an* or the suffix *-anta*.[36] Participles formed with *-anta* are declined like the *-a* stems for masculine and neuter nouns, and like the *-ī* stems for feminine nouns. This model is more common in the commentaries. In the suttas, present participles formed with *ant/-an* prevail. Thus the nominative singular normally terminates in *-aṃ*, while the oblique cases in the singular, and the dative and genitive in the plural, use a weak form of the stem, such as *gacchat* (rather than the strong form, *gacchant*). Verbs that decline in *-e*

35. For the *present participle*, see Duroiselle §§439–48, Perniola §§94–95 and §277, and Collins 103–7; for the *past participle*, Duroiselle §§450–65, Perniola §§96–99 and §§278–83, and Collins 107–9; for the *future passive participle*, Duroiselle §§466–69, Perniola §100 and §§284–86, and Collins 110–12. There are also remnants of the perfect active participle (see Geiger §100.2) and a future active participle (see Geiger §193A).

36. I rely on Collins 103–5, who provides tables showing the declension of the present participles. Somewhat different accounts are given by Duroiselle and Perniola.

or *-o* form the present participle like verbs in *-a*, except for the nominative singular, which would have to use the strong form: for example, *desento* for the indicative *deseti* and *karonto* for the indicative *karoti*.

The use of the weak stem in the dative singular is illustrated by the statement (p. 106) *jānato passato āsavānaṃ khayo hoti*, "for one knowing, for one seeing, the destruction of the influxes occurs." The description of beings as *sandhāvantā saṃsarantā*, "running [and] roaming" (p. 115), uses the nominative plural built on the strong stem. The statement *anupādiyaṃ na paritassati, aparitassaṃ paccattaññeva parinibbāyati*, "not clinging, he does not thirst; not thirsting, he personally attains nibbāna" (p. 337), employs the nominative singular participles (in the negative) of the verbs *upādiyati* and *paritassati*.

The middle-voice present participle takes the ending *-māna*, which is added to the present stem. The ending is declined like ordinary nouns of the *-a*/*-ā* type. Verbs in *-e* change this to *-aya* and add the suffix. This form is no longer restricted in use to the reflexive sense but often functions just like the active present participle.

A few present participles take the middle-voice suffix *-āna*, which declines like a stem ending in *-a* or *-ā*. One example of this participle, in the masculine nominative, is the word *sampajāno* used in the formula for the establishment of mindfulness: *bhikkhu kāye kāyānupassī viharati ātāpī sampajāno satimā*, "a monk dwells contemplating the body in the body, ardent, clearly comprehending, mindful" (p. 382). Other participles formed in this way are *esāna*, "seeking," *sayāna*, "lying down," and *kubbāna*, "doing."

The middle-voice participle *ākaṅkhamāno* can be seen in its reflexive use in the proclamation about a noble disciple: *so ākaṅkhamāno attanā'va attānaṃ vyākareyya*, "wishing, he could even by himself declare himself" a stream-enterer (p. 325). But the middle voice participle is often used transitively. We see this in the statement *rūpaṃ . . . upādiyamāno baddho mārassa*, "one clinging to form . . . is bound by Māra" (p. 176), where the participle takes *rūpaṃ* as its object.[37] Another example of the transitive use of the middle-voice participle is seen in the assertion about certain monks, *anuttaraṃ yogakkhemaṃ patthayamānā viharanti*, "who dwell desiring the unsurpassed security from the bonds" (p. 389).

37. *Upādiyati*, the verb on which *upādiyamāno* is based, is originally a passive form but is always used in an active sense.

The middle-voice participle of the verb *atthi*, "to be," *samāna*, occurs in the declaration of the devas: *Aniccā'va kira, bho, mayaṃ samānā 'nicc'amhā'ti amaññimha*, "It seems, sir, that being actually impermanent, we thought: 'We're permanent'" (p. 185). Elsewhere we find the active-voice present participle of *atthi*; for instance in the following line (p. 235), *santaṃ* (joined by sandhi to *ca*) occurs as an accusative singular qualifying *rāgaṃ*: *santañca ajjhattaṃ rūpesu rāgaṃ . . . pajānāti*, "he understands the lust for forms existing internally."[38]

Passive forms of the present participle are created by attaching the suffix *-māna* to the present passive stem. When the Buddha falls ill, it is said that he endures the pains *avihaññamāno*, "without being distressed" (p. 399). Here the double consonant, *-ññ-*, results from the sandhi of *n* and *y*. A string of passive present participles in the locative case is seen in the following statement (p. 203): *evaṃ ācikkhiyamāne desiyamāne paññāpiyamāne paṭṭhapiyamāne vivariyamāne vibhajiyamāne uttānīkariyamāne*, "when it is being thus pointed out, taught, made known, established, disclosed, analyzed, and elucidated." The construction here is a locative absolute, which will be explained below in the chapter on sentence structure.

The present participle can occur in a sentence without an explicit noun that it qualifies. In this case, the participle may be referring to a subject already mentioned or may stand in for an implicit general "one." The following sentence (p. 148) includes four examples of the present participle, singular masculine in the nominative case, representing an implicit "one": *rūpañca . . . abhijānaṃ parijānaṃ virājayaṃ pajahaṃ bhabbo dukkhakkhayāya,* "one directly knowing form, fully understanding it, removing passion for it, abandoning it, is capable of the destruction of suffering." In the sentence cited above, *jānato passato āsavānaṃ khayo hoti*, the two dative singular participles occur in this role: "for one knowing, for one seeing." In another sentence cited above, the nominative participles *anupādiyaṃ* and *aparitassaṃ* represent *bhikkhu*, mentioned earlier in the passage.

38. *Santa* and its derivatives are also used in the sense of "good persons," as in Dhp 304: *Dūre santo pakāsenti, himavanto'va pabbato*, "the good shine at a distance, like the Himalaya mountains." The stem *sat* is joined with *purisa* to form *sappurisa*, "the good person."

The past participle

The past participle can function as an adjective or a noun, or it may take the place of the verb of the sentence. The past participle is also joined to other words to create compounds. It is usually formed by adding the suffix *-ta* directly to the root, or to the root by means of the connecting vowel *-i-*, or to the stem of the present by means of the connecting vowel *-i-*. Thus the root *bhū* forms the past participle *bhūta*, "become, was"; the root *bhās* forms *bhāsita*, "spoken." When the root ends in a consonant, the suffix may be modified according to the rules of sandhi. Adding *-ta* to the root *badh-*, "to bind," yields the past participle *baddha*, "bound." The root *labh-*, "to gain," has *laddha*, "gained," as its past participle. Common past participles formed with the connecting vowel include *vusita*, "lived," *vidita*, "known," *rakkhita*, "protected," *desita*, "taught," and *vedayita*, "felt."

The verb *passati*, meaning "to see," takes its past participle, *diṭṭha*, from a different root, *dis*.[39] The root *ṭhā*, "to stand," has *ṭhita* as its past participle. Some roots ending in *-m* or *-n* are weakened in the formation of the participle. For instance, the past participle of *gam* is *gata*, "gone"; of *han*, *hata*, "slain." The past participle of *karoti* is *kata*, "done, made."

Past participles can also be formed by adding the suffix *-na* to the verbal root. Common participles formed in this way include *khīṇa*, "destroyed," *jiṇṇa*, "aged, old," *tiṇṇa*, "crossed over, liberated," and *puṇṇa*, "filled." The verb *nisīdati* has *nisinna* as its past participle, *chindati* has *chinna*, and *bhindati*, *bhinna*. The past participle of *pajahati* is *pahīna*.

Past participles are declined like nouns of the *-a/-ā* class, agreeing with the nouns they modify in gender, case, and number. Though often called "past passive participles," they are not necessarily passive but can function passively, actively, or both. In the Buddha's declaration that he has understood and penetrated the noble truth of suffering, *dukkhaṃ ariyasaccaṃ anubuddhaṃ paṭividdhaṃ* (p. 103), the past participles *anubuddhaṃ* and *paṭividdhaṃ* qualifying *ariyasaccaṃ* are passive—neuter singular in agreement with *saccaṃ*. And so too with the past participles in the canonical

39. Besides the past participle, the root *dis* is the basis for certain aorists, such as *addasā*, certain forms of the future, such as *dakkhati*, the future passive participle *daṭṭhabba*, and the common nouns *diṭṭhi* and *dassana*. The root *pas* appears in such nouns as *vipassanā*, "insight," and *anupassanā*, "contemplation."

declaration of arahantship, *khīṇā jāti, vusitaṃ brahmacariyaṃ, kataṃ karaṇīyaṃ*, "finished [is] birth, the spiritual life [has been] lived, the task [has been] done" (p. 143). But in the statement *te jātisaṃvattanikesu saṅkhāresu abhiratā*, "they are delighted with volitional activities that lead to birth" (p. 124), the participle *abhiratā* is active, agreeing with *te*, "they," the deluded ascetics and brahmins. So too, when it is said of a monk who finds enjoyment in sensual pleasures, *anayaṃ āpanno vyasanaṃ āpanno*, "he has incurred misery, incurred disaster" (p. 253), the past participle has an active sense. Similarly with the description of a monk as *paṭisallānā vuṭṭhito*, "emerged from seclusion" (p. 256), the sense is active. And even the word *buddha*, originally a past participle, means one who has known (the truth), not one who has been known.

Several past participles function almost like active present participles. This is the case with *ṭhita* and *nisinna*, meaning, respectively, "standing" and "sitting," which describe what a person does after approaching the Buddha. The term of praise for the Sangha, *suppaṭipanno*, though built on the past participle of *paṭipajjati*, is best translated as "practicing well," as if it were a present participle. Again, in the Fire Sermon (p. 226), the past participle *āditta* has the active sense of "burning, blazing."

Past particles can function as adjectives in apposition to nouns, as when it is said (p. 88) *samāhito bhikkhu yathābhūtaṃ pajānāti*, "a concentrated monk understands [things] as they are." Of a monk who exercises sense restraint, it is said (p. 447) *tassa ṭhito ca kāyo hoti, ṭhitaṃ cittaṃ*, "his body is steady and his mind is steady."

Several past participles have been transformed into independent nouns. This is the case with *vedayita*, which comes to mean feeling; *bhāsita*, which comes to mean a statement; and *carita*, which comes to mean conduct, and in later literature, character or temperament.

Pāli includes several instances of an active past participle, a rare form. Active past participles are formed by adding the suffix *-vant* or *-āvin* to the passive past participle; they are declined like nouns or adjectives with the *-vant* and *-in* endings, respectively.[40] An example of the former is the stock description (p. 390) of an arahant as *vusitavā*, "one who has lived (the spiritual life)." An example of the latter is the description (p. 135) of a noble

40. This form is explained at Duroiselle §465; Perniola §99; Collins 107; and Geiger §198.

disciple as *abhisametāvino* (in the genitive), "one who has broken through," who has realized the four noble truths.

The future passive participle

The future passive participle (also known as the gerundive or potential participle) is used to express the ideas of necessity, obligation, fitness, probability, or possibility. It indicates that the particular action on which the participle is based should be done, must be done, or is worth doing. Future passive participles agree with the nouns they qualify in gender, number, and case, though they can also be used as simple adjectives or as impersonal passives to express necessity or to issue a polite command.

The future passive participle is formed: (1) by adding the ending -(*i*)*tabba* either to the root—usually strengthened—or to the present stem; (2) by adding the ending *-anīya* (sometimes *-aneyya*) to the root, usually strengthened; and (3) by adding the endings *-ya* or *-iya* to the root, usually strengthened. In participles of this third type, the ending may force a change in form through internal sandhi. Thus *bhid* + *ya* results in *bhejja*, "to be broken, fragile"; *bhuj* + *ya* results in *bhojja*, "to be eaten, edible." Again, *dā* + *iya* results in *deyya*, "what is to be given, a gift"; *ñā* + *iya* results in *ñeyya*, "what is to be known"; and *pā* + *iya* results in *peyya*, "what is to be drunk, a drink."

Classic examples of the future passive participle occur in the statement about the four tasks regarding the four noble truths (p. 110). Here it is said that the truth of suffering is *pariññeyyaṃ*, "to be fully understood"; the truth of its origin, *pahātabbaṃ*, "to be abandoned"; the truth of its cessation, *sacchikātabbaṃ*, "to be realized"; and the truth of the path, *bhāvetabbaṃ*, "to be developed." Each of these participles is a singular neuter nominative in agreement with the noun it qualifies, *saccaṃ*. Again, the aggregate of material form, it is said (p. 170), should be seen as non-self. The future participle for "should be seen," *daṭṭhabbaṃ*, is neuter nominative in agreement with *rūpaṃ*, but in relation to the feeling and perception aggregates the participle is feminine, *daṭṭhabbā*, in agreement with the feminine nouns *vedanā* and *saññā*. In the instruction that senior monks should encourage junior monks in meditation (p. 387), the future passive participle is based on causative forms of the corresponding verbs: *catunnaṃ satipaṭṭhānānaṃ bhāvanāya samādapetabbā nivesetabbā patiṭṭhāpetabbā*, "they [the junior monks] should be enjoined, settled, and established in the development of the four establishments of mindfulness."[41] The participles here are masculine plural nominatives, in agreement with *bhikkhū*.

The future passive participle is sometimes used without an explicit corresponding noun. We see this usage when the Buddha instructs the monks (p. 414) *Tasmātiha vo, bhikkhave, evaṃ sikkhitabbaṃ*. This would be literally rendered "Therefore by you, monks, thus should-be-trained," but more naturally, "Therefore, monks, you should train thus." Without a corresponding noun, *sikkhitabbaṃ*, a neuter nominative singular, serves almost as a surrogate noun, "that in which you are to train." A future passive participle of *karoti* also functions as a virtual noun in the stock declaration of arahantship (p. 143), *kataṃ karaṇīyaṃ*, "done [is] what-had-to-be-done," where *karaṇīyaṃ* has assumed the meaning of "task" or "duty." Another future passive participle of *karoti*, *kicca* (from *kit* + *ya*, with palatalization), takes on the meaning of "task, duty."

Many future passive participles have adjectival meanings unconnected with any verbal function; for example, the sound of a lute is described as *rajanīyo, kamanīyo, madanīyo, mucchanīyo, bandhanīyo* (p. 274). All are future passive participles meaning, respectively, "enticing, lovely, intoxicating, infatuating, captivating." In the stock description of an exchange of greetings between monks (p. 255) or between a wanderer and the Buddha (p. 444), the talk that occurs is described as *sammodanīyaṃ* and *sārāṇīyaṃ*. Both words are future passive participles with the acquired meanings of "friendly" and "cordial."

The future passive participle may occur with an optative from *atthi* as an auxiliary verb. An example of this is seen in a questionnaire on the four noble truths (p. 97), where in response to the question "What is the noble truth of suffering?" the Buddha says: *"Pañc'upādānakkhandhā'ti 'ssa vacanīyaṃ,"* "It should be said, 'The five clinging-aggregates.'" Since in this case the reply is impersonal, the third-person optative *assa* (abridged by sandhi to *'ssa*) is used in combination with the neuter singular participle *vacanīyaṃ*. But elsewhere, when the monks are told how to reply to a question from wandering ascetics, the instruction uses the optative auxiliary verb in the third-person plural and the participle in the masculine plural, *evamassu vacanīyā*,

41. The causative verbs on which the future participles are based are, respectively, *samādapeti*, *niveseti*, and *patiṭṭhāpeti*.

"they should be told thus" (p. 458). These forms are appropriate because they qualify the wanderers who are to be spoken to.

The future passive participle may be incorporated into a compound, as we see in the description of a fish that has swallowed the baited hook (p. 253), as *yathākāmakaraṇīyo bālisikassa*, "to be done with according to his desire by the fisherman." Analogously, a monk who delights in sense objects is *yathākāmakaraṇīyo pāpimato*, "to be done with according to his desire by the Evil One"—that is, by Māra.

Absolutives

The absolutive

Many Pāli grammars refer to this form as the gerund, but in recent scholarship the designation "absolutive" has prevailed.[42] The primary use of the absolutive is to express an action done by the subject of the sentence prior to the action denoted by the main verb; on occasion the action described by the absolutive may occur at the same time as the action denoted by the main verb. While in English consecutive actions performed by a subject in a single sentence are typically represented by finite verbs joined by commas, with "and" at the end, in Pāli a series of actions leading up to the main action is usually represented by absolutives. In English this construction would literally be translated as "having done X," but in practice it is usually more natural to render it as a finite verb followed by a comma or "and."

The absolutive is indeclinable, for which reason it is sometimes called an "indeclinable participle." It is formed in various ways: by adding the suffix *-tvā* directly to the root, to the root by means of the connecting vowel *-i-*, or to the present stem by means of *-i-*. Occasionally, for poetic effect, *-tvāna* or *-tūna* may be used; these endings do not appear in any of the readings included here, but we do occasionally find the irregular absolutive *disvāna*, "having seen."

Another suffix used to form the absolutive is *-ya*, which may be added

42. On this form, see Duroiselle §§470–72; Perniola §101 and §§288–90; and Collins 114–17. Duroiselle and Warder call this form the "gerund," and Perniola the "past gerund," but Geiger and Collins call it the "absolutive." K. R. Norman, in his influential body of work, consistently calls it the "absolutive." Collins 114 discusses the competing designations and concludes that "absolutive . . . is perhaps the least misleading term to use."

either to the root or to the stem of the present by means of *-i-*. In Sanskrit the strict rule prevails that *-tvā* is to be used for simple verbs and *-ya* for verbs with a prefix, but in Pāli this rule has virtually been discarded and many verbs form their absolutives in either way or in both ways.

When added to a vowel, the suffix *-ya* may cause a change in the vowel; thus the absolutive of *vineti* (from *vi* + *nī*) is *vineyya*, and the absolutive of *abhibhavati* (from *abhi* + *bhū*) is *abhibhuyya*. When added directly to certain consonants, *-ya* may be assimilated to the consonant or the consonant conjunct may be modified, so that the absolutive may not be readily apparent. I discuss a few examples just below.

A stock passage with which many suttas open provides a clear illustration of the use of the absolutive. The text begins when an inquirer has approached the Buddha. It continues thus: *Upasaṅkamitvā bhagavantaṃ abhivādetvā ekamantaṃ nisīdi*, "Having approached, having paid homage to the Blessed One, he sat down to one side." In this passage there is a clear sequence of three successive actions, the first two described by absolutives of the *-tvā* type, the last by the aorist *nisīdi*. In the following (p. 399) we see an absolutive with *-tvā* followed by one with *-ya*: *Atha kho bhagavā taṃ ābādhaṃ viriyena paṭipaṇāmetvā jīvitasaṅkhāraṃ adhiṭṭhāya vihāsi*, "Then the Blessed One, having suppressed (*paṭipaṇāmetvā*) that illness by means of energy, having determined (*adhiṭṭhāya*) the life condition, lived on."

When absolutives are formed by adding *-ya* to a consonant, the combination may obscure the word's status as an absolutive. For instance, in *abhisamecca*, "having realized" (an absolutive of *abhisameti*, p. 128), palatalization has taken place whereby the dental *-t-* followed by *-ya* has resulted in *-cca*. In the simile of the lotus (p. 203), it is said of the lotus that has grown beneath the water, *udakā accuggamma ṭhāti*, "having risen from the water, it stands." Here the ablative *udakā* is followed by an absolutive based on the root *gam* (of the verb *gacchati*) with two prefixes, and with *-y-* assimilated to the preceding nasal consonant. The same kind of assimilation occurs when it is said of the Buddha's style of teaching (p. 311): *ubho ante anupagamma majjhena tathāgato dhammaṃ deseti*, "without approaching both extremes, the Tathāgata teaches the Dhamma by the middle." Here *anupagamma* is a negative absolutive of *upagacchati*, "approaches."

The absolutive need not designate an action that occurs prior to the main action of the sentence but on occasion can describe an action concurrent with the main action. In the phrase found in the *satipaṭṭhāna* formula

(p. 382), *vineyya loke abhijjhādomanassaṃ*, "having removed longing and dejection in regard to the world," the absolutive describes an action that may occur along with the activity of "contemplating the body in the body" and so forth. Again, when it is said (p. 216), *ādicco . . . sabbaṃ ākāsagataṃ tamagataṃ abhivihacca bhāsate ca tapate ca virocate ca*, "the sun . . . having dispersed all darkness throughout space, shines and beams and radiates," this does not mean that the sun first dispels darkness and then shines; rather, its act of shining is precisely what dispels the darkness.

Many absolutives are regularly used in the suttas in an adverbial sense. The absolutive *paṭicca*, another example of *-cca* palatalization, literally means "having relied on, having fallen back on," but has acquired the sense of "in dependence on." The word occurs with this function in the term *paṭicca-samuppāda*, "dependent origination"—that is, "origination in dependence on." It is also seen in the stock passage on the arising of consciousness (p. 232) thus: *cakkhuñca paṭicca rūpe ca uppajjati cakkhuviññāṇaṃ*, "in dependence on the eye and forms, eye-consciousness arises." The absolutive of *ārabhati*, "begins, undertakes," *ārabbha* (< *ārabhya*), takes on the sense of "concerning, with reference to," as when Ānanda (at p. 401) asks the Buddha to say something *bhikkhusaṅghaṃ ārabbha*, "concerning the monastic sangha." The absolutive *upādāya*, from the verb *upādiyati*, "clings," is used in an adverbial sense in the expression *anukampaṃ upādāya*, "out of compassion" (p. 416). An absolutive of *āgacchati*, "comes," *āgamma*, has the special sense of "relying on, depending on," as in the statement (p. 470) *mamañhi ānanda kalyāṇamittaṃ āgamma*, "by relying on me as a good friend, Ānanda." The absolutive *upanidhāya* has come to mean "compared with" (see p. 135). Two other absolutives, *nissāya* and *patiṭṭhāya*, are used jointly in an adverbial function to mean "based on" and "established in," as when it is said (p. 422) that a monk develops the enlightenment factors *sīlaṃ nissāya sīle patiṭṭhāya*, "based on good behavior, established in good behavior."[43]

Compounds

Pāli contains a large number of compounds (*samāsa*), words formed by joining together two or more words in such a way that the combination

43. For additional examples of the adverbial use of the absolutive, see Collins 126–27.

functions as a single unit.[44] The first member of a compound may be a noun, an adjective, a pronoun, a numeral, an adverb, or a verbal form. The last member may be a noun, a past participle, or a future passive participle. As a general rule, only the last member of the compound is declined while the preceding members remain in their stem form. There are, however, a few exceptions to this rule, compounds in which the first member retains its case ending or inflected form.

Pāli has six types of compounds: *dvanda*, *kammadhāraya*, *tappurisa*, *bahubbīhi*, adverbial, and syntactical. For the first four I use the Pāli names, which are more precise than any English equivalent, and clearer once one becomes familiar with them. Since the ways of forming compounds included under each type are numerous, I will explain only the most important instances of each, which I will illustrate with examples from the readings.

Dvanda, *the copulative compound*

A dvanda compound is made up of two or more words that, used separately, would be joined by the conjunction *ca*, "and." There are two kinds of dvanda compounds. One, known as *itaritara*, is declined as a plural and takes the gender and case of the last member. The other, known as *samāhāra*, takes the form of a collective singular; it is usually neuter though occasionally declined in accordance with the gender of the last member.

An example of the former type is *candimasuriyā* (p. 120), "moon and sun," where the two nouns, *candimā* and *suriya*, are joined into a dvanda treated as a nominative plural. A more complex compound of this type occurs at the end of the formula for dependent origination (p. 294), where five types of suffering are joined into a five-member dvanda declined as a masculine plural: *soka-parideva-dukkha-domanass'upāyāsā*, "sorrow, lamentation, pain, dejection, and misery." The plural dvanda in the genitive case is seen in one of the epithets of the Buddha, *satthā devamanussānaṃ* (p. 184), where the compound of *deva* and *manussa* is declined as a genitive masculine plural. A plural dvanda in the locative feminine (p. 184) joins together various localities: *gāma-nigama-rājadhānīsu*, "in the villages, towns, and royal cities."

Just below, in the same passage, we encounter a collective singular type

44. For more on compounds, see Duroiselle §§539–57; Perniola §§124–42; and Collins 129–39.

of dvanda, *muttakarīsaṃ*, "urine and feces," a neuter singular in the accusative case. Again, the collective singular dvanda is illustrated by a compound that merges four types of vegetation into a neuter singular (p. 161): *tiṇa-kaṭṭha-sākhā-palāsaṃ*, "grass, logs, branches, and foliage." Still other examples are *abhijjhādomanassaṃ*, "longing and dejection," in the *satipaṭṭhāna* formula (p. 382) and *thīnamiddhaṃ* and *uddhaccakukkuccaṃ* among the five hindrances.[45]

While most collective singular dvandas are declined as neuters, we occasionally encounter compounds of this type that are declined in the gender of their last member. This is the case with *chandarāgo*, "desire and lust" (p. 190), declined as a masculine singular.

Dvanda compounds may be joined to other words to form more complex compounds. For instance, craving, as the second noble truth, is said to be *nandirāgasahagatā*, "accompanied by delight and lust" (p. 98). Here, *nandirāga* is a dvanda in a more complex compound that is overall a tappurisa (see below). The same holds for the standard epithet for the Buddha as *vijjācaraṇasampanno*, where *vijjā* and *caraṇa* form a dvanda within this tappurisa. When the Buddha is called the noble one "in this population with its ascetics and brahmins, with its devas and humans" (p. 109), the Pāli, *sassamaṇabrāhmaṇiyā pajāya sadevamanussāya*, embeds two dvandas, *samaṇabrāhmaṇa* and *devamanussa*, within separate bahubbīhi compounds in the locative singular describing *pajāya*, the population.

Kammadhāraya, *the descriptive determinative compound*

The kammadhāraya compound is made up of two members, with the first modifying the second as an attributive adjective, a noun, or an adverb. The second member of the compound may be a noun, an adjective, or a past participle. If the members of the compound were separated out in the sentence, they would both have the same case and number (unless the first were an adverb). If the first member were an adjective, it would also have the same gender as the second member; if the first member were a noun, it would have its own gender.

Since there are many subordinate types of kammadhārayas,[46] we must

45. For the genitive singulars of these, see p. 426.

46. Perniola §129 lists five types, Duroiselle §546 lists nine.

limit our examples to those most often found in the readings included in this volume. The simplest type of kammadhāraya is one in which an adjective modifies a noun. This would be analogous to the English word "blackbird." A simple example is *mahāsamudda*, "the great ocean," where *mahā* modifies *samudda*. Another is *puthujjana*, a common person or "worldling," where *puthu*, "widespread," qualifies *jana*, person. *Ariyasacca*, if understood as "truth that is noble" (p. 108), can be taken as a kammadhāraya with an adjective modifying a noun.

Numerals can also be considered adjectives modifying a noun. Such compounds are given a distinct name, *digu*, or numerical compounds. Thus *saḷāyatana*, "sixfold sense base," is classified as a numerical kammadhāraya. The locative *cātummahāpatha*, "a crossroads," is a more complex numerical kammadhāraya, with both the number *catur*, "four," and *mahā* modifying *patha*, "road."

Kammadhārayas can also be composed from two nouns joined in apposition. The factors of dependent origination are kammadhārayas of this type; for instance, *avijjāpaccayā* is "through the condition that is ignorance," and so for the others. Similarly, *satisambojjhaṅga* is a kammadhāraya composed of two nouns, "the enlightenment factor that is mindfulness," and so for the other factors of enlightenment.[47] The three fires (at p. 226) would fall under this category. Although we translate *rāgaggi, dosaggi, mohaggi* as "the fire of lust, the fire of hatred, the fire of delusion," grammatically the compounds should be resolved as "the fire that is lust" and so forth.

Kammadhārayas can consist of an adverb and a noun. Each of the factors of the noble eightfold path belongs to this category; for instance, *sammādiṭṭhi*, "right view," is a compound of the adverb *sammā* and the noun *diṭṭhi*. Other examples of the adverb-noun kammadhāraya are *musāvāda*, "false speech," and *punabbhava*, "again-existence, renewed existence."

Kammadhārayas can consist of an adverb and an adjective. The compounds describing the sound of a lute (p. 274) are of this type. Here the sound (*saddo*) is described as *evaṃrajanīyo evaṃkamanīyo evaṃmadanīyo evaṃmucchanīyo evaṃbandhanīyo*, "so enticing, so lovely, so intoxicating, so infatuating, so captivating," where the adverb *evaṃ* qualifies five future passive participles used as adjectives. The epithet of the Buddha,

47. But *bojjhaṅga* itself is a tappurisa compound, a factor *for* enlightenment or a factor *of* enlightenment.

sammāsambuddho, is a kammadhāraya that joins the adverb *sammā* to the past participle *sambuddho* used as a noun.

Kammadhāraya compounds can be integrated into more complex compounds. For instance, *sakkāyapariyāpannā*, "included in the personal-collection" (p. 185), is a tappurisa compound, but it includes *sakkāya*, a kammadhāraya meaning literally "an existent body."

A kammadhāraya may also include another compound as a subordinate member. An example is *cakkhusamphassapaccayā*, "with eye-contact as condition" (p. 224), where *cakkhusamphassa*, "eye-contact," is a tappurisa compound, "contact at the eye," that has been incorporated into a kammadhāraya to be resolved as "through the condition that is eye-contact."

Tappurisa, *the dependent determinative compound*

The tappurisa compound is made up of two members, with the first dependent on the second. The first member may be a noun or pronoun in any case except the nominative or vocative; the second member may be a noun, an adjective, or a past participle. The whole compound may be used as a noun or an adjective, and occasionally as an adverb. The case ending of the first member is usually elided, though there are a few atypical tappurisas in which the case ending of the first member is preserved.

Tappurisas are distinguished into different types according to the case of the first member. Thus there are accusative tappurisas, instrumental tappurisas, ablative tappurisas, genitive tappurisas, and locative tappurisas. These case designations must be distinguished from the case of the tappurisa compound itself, which is determined by its role in the syntax of the sentence. Some examples of tappurisas in English would be a bookcase (= a case for books, according to Pāli grammar a dative tappurisa), a waterfall (= a cascade of water, a genitive tappurisa), and heartfelt (= felt in the heart, a locative tappurisa).

In the expression *kāyagatā sati*, "mindfulness directed to the body" (p. 283), *kāyagatā*, literally "body-gone," is an accusative tappurisa composed from a noun and a past participle; it functions as an adjective describing *sati*. Other accusative tappurisas appearing here are *pāraṅgato*, "gone beyond," describing an arahant (p. 251), and *gāmagato* and *araññagato*, "gone to the village" and "gone to the forest," describing a monk (p. 280).

An example of the instrumental tappurisa is *paññāvimutti*, "liberation by wisdom," composed of two nouns, the first instrumental in relation to the second. Another instrumental tappurisa is the expression *attaguttā attarakkhitā*, "self-guarded, self-protected," occurring in the parable of the acrobats (p. 410); the compounds can be resolved as "guarded by oneself" and "protected by oneself."

The description of the Buddha as *bhikkhusaṅghaparivuto*, "surrounded by the sangha of monks" (p. 188), is an instrumental tappurisa within which is nested a genitive tappurisa—namely, *bhikkhusaṅgha*. The case of the entire compound is nominative. The Buddha is also described as *dasabalasamannāgato*, "endowed with the ten powers" (p. 318), a complex instrumental tappurisa (*samannāgata* takes its concomitants in the instrumental) with the prior member, *dasabala*, a numerical kammadhāraya. Its case here is nominative.

The most populous subclass of tappurisas is the genitive type. Examples include *dukkhasamudaya*, "the origin of suffering," *dukkhanirodha*, "the cessation of suffering," *rāgakkhaya*, *dosakkhaya*, *mohakkhaya*—the destruction of lust, the destruction of hatred, the destruction of delusion—and many others. Compounds that take a large number as their last member, such as *sata* or *sahassa*, "a hundred" or "a thousand," are considered tappurisas.[48]

The three kinds of craving— *kāmataṇhā, bhavataṇhā, vibhavataṇhā*—are locative tappurisas. While in English we translate these compounds as "craving for sensual pleasures, craving for existence, craving for non-existence," Pāli words for desire take their object in the locative case. Words for views also take their object in the locative; thus *sakkāyadiṭṭhi*, the view of a self existing in relation to the five aggregates, can be classified as a locative tappurisa.[49] The series of three terms used to describe each of the enlightenment factors, *vivekanissitaṃ virāganissitaṃ nirodhanissitaṃ*, "based on seclusion, based on dispassion, based on cessation" (p. 422), can be understood as locative tappurisas made up of a noun and a past participle.

The word for enlightenment factor, *bojjhaṅga*, should probably be seen as a dative tappurisa, "factor for enlightenment," an interpretation that seems to be supported by the explanation in the suttas (see p. 442). The commentaries, however, treat the compound as a genitive tappurisa, "the factors of

48. For an example with *vassa*, years, see p. 131.

49. The Mahāniddesa commentary (VRI, Niddı-a I 162) defines it in such a way: *sati khandhapañcakasaṅkhāte kāye diṭṭhī ti sakkāyadiṭṭhi.*

enlightenment," the factors that constitute the enlightenment event. An instance of an ablative tappurisa is *yogakkhema*, "security from bondage." Another would be the description of a monk as *saddhāpabbajita*, "gone forth out of faith" (p. 319), where *saddhā* seems to be a causal ablative in relation to the act of going forth.

Occasionally the prior member of a tappurisa may retain its case ending. An example is *manasikāra*, usually translated as "attention," a compound of the locative *manasi*, "in the mind," and *kāra*, "action." Another example is *kālaṃkata*, a compound of the accusative and a past participle. It literally means "time-done," but serves as a euphemism for "dead."

Bahubbīhi, *the relative or attributive compound*

The bahubbīhi is not a different kind of compound but a compound of any of the preceding types used as an adjective to describe a noun external to itself. Because these compounds necessarily refer to something outside themselves, they are said to be "exocentric."[50] The noun so described may be present only implicitly, understood from the context, in which case the bahubbīhi does service for the absent noun. A bahubbīhi must end in a noun; it is declined like the noun it qualifies and must agree with it in gender, number, and case. This means that a feminine noun at the end of a bahubbīhi, used to describe a masculine noun, will become masculine in gender, and vice versa. A neuter noun will take on the gender of the noun it describes, as when a monk with a well-developed mind is described as *subhāvitacitto*.

Some examples in English might shed light on the bahubbīhi compound. When we speak of a laptop computer, the word "laptop" does not refer to the top of the lap but to a computer compact enough to fit on one's lap. "Laptop" is then an adjective describing the computer. If we drop the word "computer," the context will still make it clear that the word "laptop" refers to the machine, not to the top of my lap. If we call a girl a "redhead," we are using this word to designate the girl by the color of her hair, not to refer to the girl as a head that is red.

A good example of bahubbīhis derived from kammadhāraya compounds can be seen in the description of beings caught in saṃsāra as *avijjānīvaraṇā*

50. Collins 135.

taṇhāsaṃyojanā, "having ignorance as a hindrance [and] craving as a fetter" (p. 115). On their own the two compounds, *avijjānīvaraṇa* and *taṇhāsaṃyojana*, are kammadhārayas, "the hindrance that is ignorance" and "the fetter that is craving," but in this sentence they function as adjectives describing *sattā*, beings.

A bahubbīhi based on a tappurisa is seen in the expression *āmisacakkhu maccho*, "a fish with an eye for bait" (p. 253). The compound *āmisacakkhu* on its own is a dative tappurisa, "an eye for bait," but here it serves as an adjective describing the fish. Once the fish falls for the bait, it is described as *maccho gilitabaliso*, "a fish that has swallowed the hook," where *gilitabaliso* is a bahubbīhi composed of a past participle and a noun. Similarly, when it is said of the Buddha that he is *suvimuttacitto*, "well liberated in mind" (p. 260), the entire compound is a bahubbīhi, with the neuter noun *citta* at the end of the compound becoming a masculine in agreement with *bhagavā*.

Bahubbīhis can be constructed from an adverb and a noun, creating a kammadhāraya compound employed as an adjective to describe an external subject. An example is seen when someone wishes *Evaṃrūpo siyaṃ anāgatamaddhānaṃ . . . evaṃviññāṇo siyaṃ anāgatamaddhānaṃ*, "May I be of such form in the future . . . may I be of such consciousness in the future" (p. 191). Each of the nouns designating the aggregates is here transformed into the masculine singular nominative to agree with the implicit subject, the first-person pronoun *ahaṃ*.

A bahubbīhi can be created from a compound of a pronoun and a noun. This is commonly done with the demonstrative pronoun *taṃ* (which may take the form *tad* before a vowel). Thus it is said of a certain tree: *so . . . mahārukkho tadāhāro tadupādāno ciraṃ dīghamaddhānaṃ tiṭṭheyya*; "that great tree, with that [sap] as nutriment, with that [sap] as sustenance, would stand for a very long time" (p. 346). Here *tadāhāro* and *tadupādāno* are bahubbīhis derived from kammadhārayas: the sap itself is the nutriment and sustenance.

Interrogative bahubbīhi compounds can be formed with interrogative pronouns, as seen in the following inquiry, where the interrogative compounds function as adjectives in agreement with *dukkhaṃ*, the noun they are describing: *idaṃ nu kho dukkhaṃ kiṃnidānaṃ kiṃsamudayaṃ kiṃjātikaṃ kiṃpabhavaṃ*; "Now this suffering: what is its cause, what is its origin, what is its genesis, what is its source?" (p. 334). Another example occurs when a visitor asks the Buddha: *Bhavaṃ pana gotamo kimānisaṃso viharati*, "But for what benefit does Master Gotama live?" (p. 444). Here the interrogative *kimānisaṃso* describes *bhavaṃ gotamo*.

Bahubbīhis are also found when the prefix *sa*-, "with, accompanied by," is added to a noun used to qualify another noun. An example is the description of the "ocean of the eye" (p. 251) as *saūmiṃ sāvaṭṭaṃ sagāhaṃ sarakkhasaṃ*, "with waves, with whirlpools, with sharks, with demons," where each of the words beginning with *sa*- is a bahubbīhi, agreeing with *cakkhusamuddaṃ*, a masculine accusative. Similarly, negating a noun with the prefix *vīta*-, "devoid of," turns it into a bahubbīhi, as when the Satipaṭṭhāna Sutta section on contemplation of mind speaks of *cittaṃ*, the mind, as *vītarāgaṃ*, *vītadosaṃ*, *vītamohaṃ*, "devoid of lust, devoid of hatred, devoid of delusion."

Compounds of nouns can be turned into bahubbīhis by the addition of certain suffixes, particularly *-ka*, *-ika*, *-iya*, and *-in*. Thoughts about the four noble truths are said to be *ādibrahmacariyakā*, "pertinent to the fundamentals of the spiritual life." Here the suffix *-kā* enables the compound to function as an adjective describing *vitakkā*. The path itself is described as *aṭṭhaṅgiko*, a bahubbīhi composed of the numeral *aṭṭha*, "eight," and *aṅga*, "factor," given an adjectival function in relation to the noun *maggo* by the masculine suffix *-iko*.

Bahubbīhi compounds can be built on combinations of other compounds. For example, it is said of the cultivation of the path factors (p. 487): *bhikkhu sammāsamādhiṃ bhāveti rāgavinayapariyosānaṃ dosavinayapariyosānaṃ mohavinayapariyosānaṃ*, "a monk develops right concentration, which has as its culmination the removal of lust, which has as its culmination the removal of hatred, which has as its culmination the removal of delusion." Each of the three bahubbīhis describing right concentration—for instance, *rāgavinayapariyosānaṃ*—contains an internal genitive tappurisa (*rāgavinaya*) joined into a kammadhāraya (which equates *pariyosāna* with *rāgavinaya*), yet the complex compound describes an exocentric subject, *sammāsamādhi*, and is thus a bahubbīhi. Another example is seen when the Buddha describes himself with a four-term bahubbīhi as *vijjāvimuttiphalānisaṃso*, "one who has the fruit and benefit of clear knowledge and liberation" (p. 445). This complex compound contains two subordinate dvanda compounds joined in a genitive tappurisa relationship, but as a whole it functions as an adjective qualifying *tathāgato* and is thus a bahubbīhi.

*Adverbial compounds (*avyāyibhāvasamāsa*)*

Adverbial compounds are of two kinds: those that have a prefix as initial member and those that have an indeclinable as initial member. The compounds generally are indeclinable and assume the form of the accusative singular ending in the *niggahīta*. Sometimes, however, the case ending is retained.

Adverbial compounds with a prefix as initial member include *ajjhattaṃ*, "internally," and *paccattaṃ*, "personally." The former is from *adhi* + *attan*, the latter from *paṭi* + *attan*. Duroiselle (at §549) lists several others, among them *anuvassaṃ*, "every year," *upanagaraṃ*, "near the city," and *paṭisotaṃ*, "against the stream."[51] *Anupubbena*, "gradually," is an example of such a compound with an instrumental suffix.

An adverbial compound with an indeclinable as initial member is *yathābhūtaṃ*, "as it really is," where *yathā* is an adverb of manner ("as, in accordance with") joined to *bhūtaṃ*, "real, actual, factual." This compound describes how one should understand the four noble truths, the five aggregates, and so forth. Again, in the simile of the grass in Jeta's Grove, we find *yathāpaccayaṃ*, "as one wishes" (p. 161). Still another adverbial compound occurs in the simile of the stick thrown *uparivehāsaṃ*, "into the air" (p. 115), an adverbial compound that joins the indeclinable *upari* and *vehāsa*, "the air, the sky."

Syntactical compounds

This class of compounds is derived from Western scholarship. Perniola (§142) explains the syntactical compound as "two or more independent words . . . joined together owing to the fact that they have often been used together in a sentence."[52] Perhaps Norman's definition of this kind of compound is more precise: "that [kind of compound] where some components retain the syntactical form they would have had in a non-compounded statement."[53] Perniola cites as examples several compounds that join an absolutive

51. Collins 134 gives still other examples.

52. Collins 136–37 distinguishes four types of syntactical compounds, but we need not dwell on the details.

53. Norman 1993, 218.

and a noun: *paṭiccasamuppāda*, "dependent origination," *aveccappasādena*, "with confirmed confidence" (p. 327), and *saṃkheyyakāro*, "acting after reflecting."[54] A syntactical compound joining an absolutive to a past participle is *paṭiccasamuppanne*, "dependently originated," a qualification of *dhamme* (p. 314).

Another syntactical compound is the epithet of the Dhamma, *ehipassiko*, literally, "a come-see thing" (p. 234), which joins two second-person imperatives, *ehi* and *passa*, with the adjectival suffix *-iko*. Perniola classifies *asmimāna*, "the conceit 'I am'" (see p. 215), and *ahaṅkāra*, "I-making," as syntactical compounds; to these we should add *mamaṅkāra*, "mine-making" (see p. 181).

Indeclinables

Indeclinables (*nipāta*) are words not subject to declension. These include adverbs, prepositions, conjunctions, and interjections.[55] I can mention only a few of the most important examples under each category.

Adverbs

Adverbs can be distinguished into several classes as follows:

1. *Adverbs of time*: *atha*, "then," *yadā*, "when," *tadā*, "then," *yato*, "since," *tato*, "thereupon, then," *yāva*, "as long as," *tāva*, "for so long," *ajja*, "today," *idāni/dāni*, "now," *etarahi*, "now, presently," *puna*, "again," *kadāci karahaci*, "at some time, ever."
2. *Adverbs of place*: *idha*, "here," *yattha*, "where," *tattha/tatra*, "there," *aññatra*, "elsewhere, apart from," *uddhaṃ*, "above," *adho*, "below."
3. *Adverbs of manner*: *evaṃ*, "thus," *tathā*, "thus," *sammā*, "rightly, properly," *micchā*, "wrongly," *sādhukaṃ*, "well," *sukhaṃ*, "happily," *dukkhaṃ*, "painfully."
4. *Adverbs of quantity, extent, and degree*: *yāvatā*, "as far as," *tāvatā*, "so far," *ettāvatā*, "to such an extent, in such a way," *bhiyyoso*, "greatly."
5. *Adverbs of cause or reason*: *tena*, "hence," *tasmā*, *tato*, "therefore," *tatonidānaṃ*, "because of that, on that account."

54. Norman mentions even more at 1993, 219–20.

55. I here draw mostly from Perniola §§103–7.

6. *Adverbial particles*: *api*, "even, perhaps," *pi*, "although," *kira*, "indeed," *iti*, "thus," *alaṃ*, "enough," *nūna*, "perhaps, certainly," *nu*, an interrogative particle, *sudaṃ*, a connective particle, and *kho*, an exclamatory particle. Perhaps in this class we should include *eva*, which stresses the term it qualifies or posits it as in some way exclusive. *Eva* always follows immediately after the word it emphasizes.

Combinations of particles are often used to mark a transition in a narrative or to establish a connection between sentences. These include *atha kho*, "then," *ca pana*, "and, further," and *puna caparaṃ*, "furthermore." *Kho pana* has a connective function but is virtually untranslatable.

In my discussion of the absolutive, I mentioned several examples of that form that are used with an adverbial function (see p. 35). Declined nouns too are sometimes used adverbally. The cases used most often in this way are the accusative and the instrumental.

Accusative adverbs include *addhānaṃ*, "a period of time," *dīgharattaṃ*, "for a long time," *āyatiṃ*, "in the future," *bhūtapubbaṃ*, "in the past" (see p. 409), *ekaṃ samayaṃ*, "on one occasion," *ajjhattaṃ*, "internally," and *kāmaṃ*, "willingly" (see p. 319).

Examples of the instrumental adverb are *accayena*, "after, with the passage of," *saṃkhittena*, "briefly, in brief," *vitthārena*, "in detail," *antarena*, "in between," and *yebhuyyena*, "mostly, generally." The pairing of *yena* and *tena* to indicate direction might also be considered instrumental adverbs of place. In such a construction the destination, whether a person or a place, occurs in the nominative, as in *yena bhagavā ten'upasaṅkami*, "he approached the Blessed One."

There are a few adverbs based on the suffix *-so*, originally an ablative. These include *yoniso*, "thoroughly, carefully," *bhiyyoso*, "even more," and *sabbaso*, "entirely." The first is often joined with the noun *manasikāra* to form *yoniso manasikāra*, "thorough (or careful) attention."

Conjunctions

Conjunctions are another class of indeclinables. Coordinative conjunctions include *ca*, "and," *pi*, "and, also," *vā*, "or," and *udāhu*, "or." *Ca* is used not only in the copulative sense of "and" but in the disjunctive sense of "but." Subordinative conjunctions include *sace*, *ce*, and *yadi*, all meaning "if," and *yathā*, "as." When *ca* and *vā* are used as conjunctions, they usually occur after each noun or adjective that they qualify. Thus where in English one might say, "The cat and the mouse are playing in the hall," in Pāli one would generally say, "The cat-and the mouse-and are playing in the hall." Similarly for disjunction, one would say, "The boy-or the girl-or should answer the question."

Interjections

Finally, interjections, which intensify the emotional tone of an utterance, include *vata*, "indeed, alas," *sādhu*, "good, please," *taggha*, "certainly," and *nūna*, "perhaps, surely."

Common Sentence Patterns in the Nikāyas

SENTENCE PATTERNS in the Nikāyas are as varied as in any language, and therefore any system for classifying such patterns will necessarily be to some extent simplistic and inadequate. Sentences may state facts (rightly or wrongly), express wishes or preferences, issue commands and prohibitions, or ask questions. Sentence types may partly overlap, and it is often uncertain whether a sequence of words constitutes a complete sentence in itself or functions as a unit within a larger sentence. If a sentence is understood as a grammatically independent group of words, then a sentence in Pāli may contain units that can be extracted from the larger grammatical structure in which they are embedded and regarded as sentences in themselves. Thus it is hard, even at times impossible, to draw fixed and impenetrable boundaries between sentence types.

Nevertheless, to arrive at a broad picture of Pāli syntax, we might distinguish sentences into three main types: the simple, the compounded, and the complex. Sentences may be further distinguished into those containing a verb and those without a verb. A verb may be transitive or intransitive. A transitive verb designates an action that passes from a subject to an object, needing an object to complete the sense. An example in English would be "The boy hit the ball." An intransitive verb designates an action that inheres in the subject itself, for example, "The boy laughed." Again, a verb might assert simply that something exists ("There is a dog in the house") or does not exist ("There is no cat in the house").

The principal type of sentence in Pāli without a verb is the equational sentence, a sentence that equates the subject—a noun or pronoun—with another noun, or which describes the subject by means of an adjective, a participle functioning as an adjective, or a compound functioning as an adjective.

In a sentence containing a transitive verb and an object, the word order according to the typical Pāli grammar is: (1) subject, (2) object, and (3) verb.

On this model, words qualifying the subject or object come before the subject and object, respectively; a negation of the action (by the particle *na* or *no*) immediately precedes the verb; and nouns in indirect cases come before the direct object. While this model may serve as an ideal type, in the Nikāyas such stipulations of syntax are honored more in the breach than in the observance. As the product of a process of oral transmission recording actual dialogues and discourses, the Pāli of the Nikāyas reflects patterns of living speech. Sentence structure in the Nikāyas is thus extremely fluid and variable, even in the narrative portions. For this reason the governing principles of Pāli syntax must be seen as broad generalities rather than as rigid and inflexible rules.

In the following section I will attempt to highlight some of the common patterns of sentence structure in the Pāli of the Nikāyas, drawing most of my examples from the texts included in this collection. While I will be covering the most prominent syntactical patterns, this overview will necessarily be incomplete, though forms passed over here, when they occur in a particular sutta included in the chapters below, will be explained in the grammatical explanations attached to that sutta. Because I want my renderings to mirror more closely the syntactical features under discussion, my translations in the account to follow will sometimes differ slightly from those in the anthology itself.

Simple Verbal Sentences

The following two sentences conform closely to the standard model of a sentence with a transitive verb and object:

> *Tatra kho bhagavā bhikkhū āmantesi.*
>
> There the Blessed One addressed the monks.

> *"Atha kho so, bhikkhave, rājā vā rājamahāmatto vā taṃ nagaraṃ māpeyya."*
>
> "Then, monks, that king or the king's chief minister would build up that city."

In the first (p. 102), *bhagavā* is the nominative subject, *bhikkhū* the object, and *āmantesi* the aorist verb, a third-person singular in agreement with *bhagavā*. The second sentence (p. 357), though still simple in structure, is slightly more complex since it contains two subjects joined by *vā*, the particle of disjunction, and two demonstrative pronouns, the first, *so*, qualifying the subject, *rājā* (and *rājamahāmatto*), and the other, *taṃ*, qualifying the object, *nagaraṃ*. Since either subject is masculine singular, the verb *māpeyya* is third-person singular in the optative mood, describing an imaginery situation. The sentence also includes the vocative *bhikkhave*, used to address the monks. In direct speech in Pāli, the use of the vocative is extremely common, occurring in almost every sentence. This feature may strike the modern reader of English as quaint, but it seems to have been characteristic of formal discourse in the Buddha's time. Since multiple repetitions of the vocative would be grating to a reader of modern English, in my translations I usually retain the vocative only in the first portion of a passage and in the conclusion.

The following sentence (p. 445) follows the same pattern, with the nominative subject taking an accusative object. Here the subject is described by two past participles that follow the subject and function as adjectives; the accusative object is a dvanda compound of the singular type:

> *"Satta kho, kuṇḍaliya, bojjhaṅgā bhāvitā bahulīkatā vijjāvimuttiṃ paripūrenti."*
>
> "The seven enlightenment factors, Kuṇḍaliya, developed and cultivated, fulfill clear knowledge and liberation."

Contrary to the stipulation in standard Pāli grammars that the verb comes last, in the Nikāyas we occasionally find the verb coming at the beginning of a sentence. This is done, it seems, either for emphasis or for elegance of expression. The following (p. 264) is a transitive sentence that begins with the verb *addasā*, an aorist of **dassati*.[56] The subject is *bhagavā* and the object *dārukkhandhaṃ*, a log, described by the adjective *mahantaṃ*, "large," and again by a clause with the present participle *vuyhamānaṃ*, accusative singular in agreement with *dārukkhandhaṃ*.

56. The verb does not occur in the active present, having been displaced by *passati*, from a different root.

> *Addasā kho bhagavā mahantaṃ dārukkhandhaṃ gaṅgāya nadiyā sotena vuyhamānaṃ.*
>
> The Blessed One saw a large log being swept along by the stream of the Ganges River.

The following sentence (p. 457) opens with an intransitive verb, the aorist *vuṭṭhahi*, with *mahākassapo* as the subject, and a closing ablative construction dependent on the verb:

> *Vuṭṭhahi c'āyasmā mahākassapo tamhā ābādhā.*
>
> And the Venerable Mahākassapa recovered from that affliction.

Verbs that assert or deny existence often come at the beginning of a sentence, as here (p. 425, p. 236):

> *"Atthi, bhikkhave, subhanimittaṃ."*
>
> "There is, monks, a beautiful object."
>
> *"Natthi me ajjhattaṃ rūpesu rāgo."*[57]
>
> "There does not exist for me internally lust for forms."

A verb may even occur in the middle of a sentence, with an object following it, here described by an accusative phrase in agreement with the object (p. 356):

> *"Seyyathāpi, bhikkhave, puriso araññe pavane caramāno passeyya purāṇaṃ maggaṃ purāṇañjasaṃ pubbakehi manussehi anuyātaṃ."*
>
> "Suppose, monks, a man wandering in a forest grove would see an ancient path, an ancient road, traveled along by people in the past."

57. This statement actually occurs as a direct quotation within a larger, more complex sentence, but it can be extracted and treated as a grammatically complete sentence.

We occasionally encounter sentences that completely invert normal word order, such as the following, which often comes near the end of a sutta, with the sequence: object-verb-subject:

> *Idamavoca bhagavā.*
>
> This the Blessed One said.

Another illustration of structural variability is seen in the declaration of discipleship, which opens with the accusative object *upāsakaṃ*, qualified by accusatives (*pāṇupetaṃ*, *gataṃ*) following the subject and verb. The verb *dhāretu*, a third-person singular imperative, is used to make a polite request (p. 452):

> *"Upāsakaṃ maṃ bhavaṃ gotamo dhāretu ajjatagge pāṇupetaṃ saraṇaṃ gataṃ."*
>
> "Let Master Gotama consider me a lay disciple who from today, [as long as he is] endowed with life, has gone for refuge."

In the following sentence (p. 232), the nominative subject, *cakkhuviññāṇaṃ*, occurs last, preceded by the intransitive verb *uppajjati*. The absolutive *paṭicca*, here used adverbally to mean "in dependence on," takes its objects in the accusative; one accusative, *cakkhuṃ*, precedes the absolutive; the other, *rūpe*, follows it:

> *"Cakkhuñca paṭicca rūpe ca uppajjati cakkhuviññāṇaṃ."*
>
> "In dependence on the eye and forms, eye-consciousness arises."

Simple sentences in the Nikāyas may take a passive verb in the present indicative. A simple sentence of this type, with the subject implicit, occurs in the stock account of the attainment of liberation (p. 143):

> *"Virāgā vimuccati."*
>
> "Through dispassion [he] is liberated."

The following sentence (p. 472) begins with an accusative of purpose, followed by the main clause, which has the verb *vussati*, "is lived," passive of *vasati*:

> *"Dukkhassa kho, āvuso, pariññatthaṃ bhagavati brahmacariyaṃ vussati."*
>
> "For the purpose of full understanding of suffering, friends, the spiritual life is lived under the Blessed One."

The passive *vuccati*, "is called, is said," is often used to identify a subject (usually a pronoun) with a predicate, and thus the sentences in which it occurs come close to being equational in character, as the following example illustrates (p. 97):

> *"Idaṃ vuccati, bhikkhave, 'dukkhaṃ ariyasaccaṃ.'"*
>
> "This is called, monks, the 'noble truth of suffering.'"

Passive constructions with the past participle and future passive particle are even more common in the Nikāyas, as we will see below.

Sentences that issue commands and prohibitions are generally simple in structure. These can be recognized in their use of the imperative form of a verb. For example, when the Buddha intends to explain a point to the monks, he issues a command using two second-person imperative plurals (*suṇātha, manasikarotha*), with the subject implicit (p. 164):

> *"Tena hi, bhikkhave, suṇātha, sādhukaṃ manasikarotha."*
>
> "Well then, monks, listen [and] attend well."

Here is a direct command with the second-person imperative singular (p. 357):

> *"Taṃ, bhante, nagaraṃ māpehi."*
>
> "Build up that city, sire."

Polite commands (or requests) often use the third-person imperative. We saw an example just above, when a man asks the Buddha to accept him as a lay disciple. Here is how a monk asks the Buddha for a teaching (p. 175):

> *"Sādhu me, bhante, bhagavā saṃkhittena dhammaṃ desetu."*
>
> "Please, Bhante, let the Blessed One briefly teach me the Dhamma."

The polite imperative is also used when a person addresses a command to himself, as when a monk makes the following determination (p. 319):[58]

> *"Kāmaṃ taco ca nahāru ca aṭṭhi ca avasissatu, sarīre upasussatu maṃsalohitaṃ."*

> "Willingly, let [only] my skin, sinews, and bones remain; let the flesh and blood in my body dry up."

Negative commands, or prohibitions, usually include the prohibitive particle *mā* in place of *na*. Often the verb occurs in the aorist form, though with a prohibitive rather than a past sense. Here is an example (p. 395):

> *"Tasmātiha, bhikkhave, mā agocare carittha paravisaye."*

> "Therefore, monks, do not wander into what is not your range, into the domain of others."

But prohibitions may also use the imperative, as in the following (p. 94), where the verb *vitakketha* is a second-person plural imperative of *vitakketi*, "thinks":

> *"Mā, bhikkhave, pāpake akusale vitakke vitakketha."*

> "Monks, do not think bad unwholesome thoughts."

Equational Sentences

Equational sentences identify the subject with a predicate without the mediation of a finite verb, though the verb *hoti* or its equivalent may be tacitly understood. The two terms of an equational sentence may both be nouns, as in the following sentence (p. 232) that defines contact as the meeting of a sense faculty, an object, and the corresponding consciousness:

> *"Tiṇṇaṃ saṅgati phasso."*

> "The meeting of the three [is] contact."

58. We might also note the use of a singular verb, *avasissatu*, with several subjects. Perhaps the singular verb is used because the three subjects here are each a grammatical singular.

The following more elaborate equational sentence (p. 469) identifies the noun, *brahmacariyaṃ*, the spiritual life (qualified by *idaṃ*, this, and *sakalaṃ*, whole), with three other nouns, *kalyāṇamittatā*, *kalyāṇasahāyatā*, and *kalyāṇasampavaṅkatā*, which are more or less synonymous, indicating good friendship:

> *"Sakalamev'idaṃ, ānanda, brahmacariyaṃ, yadidaṃ kalyāṇamittatā kalyāṇasahāyatā kalyāṇasampavaṅkatā."*

> "This whole spiritual life, Ānanda, [is] this: good friendship, good companionship, good comradeship."

In the next sentence (p. 108) the predicate consists entirely of adjectives without any verb or verbal surrogate:

> *"Imāni kho, bhikkhave, cattāri ariyasaccāni tathāni avitathāni anaññathāni."*

> "These four noble truths, monks, [are] real, not unreal, not otherwise."

An equational sentence may describe a noun with a past participle, which performs the function of a verb. Here is an extremely simple example (p. 226):

> *"Sabbaṃ, bhikkhave, ādittaṃ."*

> "All, monks, [is] ablaze."[59]

The following sentence (p. 103) uses two past participles to describe what has been done regarding the first noble truth:

> *"Tayidaṃ dukkhaṃ ariyasaccaṃ anubuddhaṃ paṭividdhaṃ."*

> "This noble truth of suffering, monks, [has been] understood [and] penetrated."

And here the Buddha, in his advanced years, describes himself—denoted by the first-person pronoun *ahaṃ*—with a series of adjectives, most of which are past participles (p. 402):

59. Although grammatically *ādittaṃ* is a past participle, as used here it almost carries the sense of a present participle.

> *"Etarahi kho panāhaṃ, ānanda, jiṇṇo vuddho mahallako addhagato vayoanuppatto."*
>
> "Now, Ānanda, I [am] old, aged, elderly, reached the end of my journey, arrived at [the end of] life."

The future passive participle, which indicates something that should be done, might be done, or is worth doing, can also serve as the predicate of a noun in an equational sentence, again with a verbal function. The following is an illustration (p. 176):

> *"Imassa kho, bhikkhu, mayā saṃkhittena bhāsitassa evaṃ vitthārena attho daṭṭhabbo."*
>
> "It is in such a way, monk, that the meaning of what was stated by me in brief should be seen in detail."

Equational sentences of this type may include a finite auxiliary verb, as in the following (p. 458), where *assu*, the third-person plural optative of *atthi*, reinforces the optative sense of *vacanīyā*:

> *"Evaṃvādino, bhikkhave, aññatitthiyā paribbājakā evamassu vacanīyā."*
>
> "Wanderers of other sects, monks, who speak thus should be told thus."

Again, equational sentences in the Nikāyas may be constructed with the subject described by means of a compound or series of compounds. Here is an example in which the predicates describing a beverage are tappurisa compounds (p. 368):

> *"Ayaṃ te, ambho purisa, āpānīyakaṃso vaṇṇasampanno gandhasampanno rasasampanno."*
>
> "Good man, this goblet for you [is filled with a beverage] having a fine color, fragrance, and flavor."

In this discourse on dependent origination, the words describing *saṅkhārā* are bahubbīhi compounds, all masculine plural in agreement with their subject (p. 336):

"Saṅkhārā avijjānidānā avijjāsamudayā avijjājātikā avijjā-pabhavā."

"Volitional activities [have] ignorance as cause, ignorance as origin, ignorance as genesis, ignorance as source."

In a parallel passage where the subject is the masculine noun *upadhi*, "acquisition," the same series of compounds is used in the masculine singular (p. 363): *Upadhi taṇhānidāno taṇhāsamudayo taṇhājātiko taṇhāpabhavo*; "Acquisition has craving as cause, craving as origin, craving as genesis, craving as source."

Sentences of a simple structure can be found in the Nikāyas that do not fit neatly into the mold of either the verbal type or the equational type. In such sentences an action can be suggested by the case relation between the nouns. An example is seen in the formula for dependent origination (p. 294), where the ablative *-paccayā* places the antecedent term (*avijjā*, etc.) in the role of condition in relation to the consequent term (*saṅkhārā*, etc.). A verb, *hoti* or *uppajjati*, may be understood:

"Avijjāpaccayā, bhikkhave, saṅkhārā."

"With ignorance as condition, monks, volitional activities [occur]."

A similar structure is used in the corresponding formula for cessation, where the ablative *-nirodhā* indicates that the cessation of the condition causes the cessation of the next term in the series, thus (p. 301):

"Avijjānirodhā saṅkhāranirodho."

"With the cessation of ignorance [there is] cessation of volitional activities."

In the opening declaration of the Satipaṭṭhāna-saṃyutta (p. 382) the meaning of the statement is governed by the dative clauses that follow the initial nominative subject, without any verb:

"Ekāyano ayaṃ, bhikkhave, maggo sattānaṃ visuddhiyā . . . nibbānassa sacchikiriyāya, yadidaṃ cattāro satipaṭṭhānā."

"This one-way path, monks, [is] for the purification of beings . . .

for the realization of nibbāna, that is, the four establishments of mindfulness."

Compound Sentences

While in English grammar a compound sentence is understood to be a sentence that consists of two or more independent clauses, I use the expression here, in relation to Pāli, to designate a sentence that consists of two or more clauses of parallel grammatical structure even when they are not strictly independent. The clauses might be joined by particles of conjunction (*ca*, *pi*), disjunction (*vā*), or negation (*na*), or they may simply follow one another in a series without a connecting particle.

Since the Nikāyas make frequent use of itemized groups of terms, a compound sentence might consist of little more than a list, often proposed as the answer to a question. An example occurs when the Buddha opens a discourse by stating that there are four noble truths, asks what they are, and then answers himself (p. 92):

> *"Dukkhaṃ ariyasaccaṃ, dukkhasamudayaṃ ariyasaccaṃ, dukkhanirodhaṃ ariyasaccaṃ, dukkhanirodhagāminī paṭipadā ariyasaccaṃ."*
>
> "The noble truth of suffering, the noble truth of the origin of suffering, the noble truth of the cessation of suffering, the noble truth of the way leading to the cessation of suffering."

The following (pp. 110–11) is a more elaborate compound sentence in which each truth is qualified by a future passive participle assigning to the truth a particular task that the practitioner must take up to fulfill the aim of the teaching:

> *"Dukkhaṃ, bhikkhave, ariyasaccaṃ pariññeyyaṃ; dukkhasamudayaṃ ariyasaccaṃ pahātabbaṃ; dukkhanirodhaṃ ariyasaccaṃ sacchikātabbaṃ; dukkhanirodhagāminī paṭipadā ariyasaccaṃ bhāvetabbaṃ."*
>
> "The noble truth of suffering, monks, is to be fully understood; the noble truth of the origin of suffering is to be abandoned; the noble truth of the cessation of suffering is to be realized; the

noble truth of the way leading to the cessation of suffering is to be developed."

The following compound sentence (p. 120) conjoins three parallel clauses with different nominative plural subjects and the same verb, *paññāyanti*, a passive plural of *pajānāti*:

> *"Atha rattindivā paññāyanti, māsaddhamāsā paññāyanti, utusaṃvaccharā paññāyanti."*
>
> "Then nights and days are discerned, months and fortnights are discerned, seasons and years are discerned."

In the following sentence (p. 215) the nominative subject, qualified by two past participles (*bhāvitā bahulīkatā*), remains constant in each subordinate clause in which the object is a different defilement:

> *"Aniccasaññā bhāvitā bahulīkatā sabbaṃ kāmarāgaṃ pariyādiyati, sabbaṃ rūparāgaṃ pariyādiyati, sabbaṃ bhavarāgaṃ pariyādiyati, sabbaṃ avijjaṃ pariyādiyati, sabbaṃ asmimānaṃ samūhanati."*
>
> "Perception of the impermanent, developed and cultivated, eliminates all sensual lust, eliminates all lust for form, eliminates all lust for existence, eliminates all ignorance, demolishes all conceit 'I am.'"

In contrast, in the next compound sentence (p. 299) the same intransitive verb is repeated in each clause but the nominative subject changes:

> *"'Samudayo, samudayo'ti kho me, bhikkhave, pubbe ananussutesu dhammesu cakkhuṃ udapādi, ñāṇaṃ udapādi, paññā udapādi, vijjā udapādi, āloko udapādi."*
>
> "'Origin, origin'—thus, monks, in regard to things unheard before, the eye arose in me, knowledge arose, wisdom arose, clear knowledge arose, light arose."

Compound sentences often use the conjunctive particle *ca* to connect the clauses. In such sentences *ca* may be used in relation to each clause including the first, not only between items, as in English. In fact, the double *ca* occurs more frequently than the single *ca*.[60] The following sentence (p. 410) joins three phrases by *ca*, which in relation to the first enters into sandhi with *eva*, as is common at the beginning of a series connected by *ca*.[61] The subject is the first-person plural pronoun *mayaṃ*, described by two tappurisa compounds; the actions in the three parallel clauses are designated by three verbs in the future tense:

> *"Evaṃ mayaṃ attaguttā attarakkhitā sippāni c'eva dassessāma, lābhañca lacchāma, sotthinā ca caṇḍālavaṃsā orohissāmā."*

> "Thus self-guarded and self-protected, we will display our skills, and will gain a profit, and will safely descend from the bamboo pole."

The following compound sentence (p. 460) joins five parallel clauses having a single subject, different objects, and variable verbs:

> *"So tattha allāni c'eva tiṇāni pakkhipeyya, allāni ca gomayāni pakkhipeyya, allāni ca kaṭṭhāni pakkhipeyya, udakavātañca dadeyya, paṃsukena ca okireyya."*

> "He would throw wet grass upon it, and would throw wet cow dung, and would throw wet sticks, and would give it a wet wind, and would sprinkle it with soil."

Conjunction may also be performed by the particle *pi*, which, like *ca*, usually occurs after each conjoined item. In the following sentence (p. 438) there are two different objects, *kāyo* and *cittaṃ*, both of which undergo the action denoted by the same verb:

> *"Pītimanassa kāyopi passambhati, cittampi passambhati."*

> "For one with a mind of rapture, the body becomes tranquil and the mind becomes tranquil."

60. See p. 47.

61. Similarly, in a list of negations, the initial negative particle *na* is usually joined with *eva* to form *n'eva*.

The following sentence (p. 142) consists of a series of clauses joined by *pi*. The subject occurs only at the beginning, but the verb is repeated each time with a different locative object:

> *"Sutavā ariyasāvako rūpasmimpi nibbindati, vedanāyapi nibbindati, saññāyapi nibbindati, saṅkhāresupi nibbindati, viññāṇasmimpi nibbindati."*

> "The learned noble disciple becomes disenchanted with form, disenchanted with feeling, disenchanted with perception, disenchanted with volitional activities, disenchanted with consciousness."

Compound sentences can be formed with the disjunctive particle *vā* and the negative particle *na*. In the following sentence (p. 161) the different clauses, each with its own verb, are linked by the disjunctive particle:

> *"Amhe jano harati vā ḍahati vā yathāpaccayaṃ vā karoti."*

> "People are taking us, or burning us, or doing [with us] as they wish."

The following sentence, on the four ways of regarding the aggregates as self, is of the disjunctive type (p. 194). It has a single subject, *puthujjano*, with the verb *samanupassati* stated only in the first clause but implicitly extending to each of the other three clauses, and with the disjunctive particle *vā* omitted from the first alternative but necessarily implied by the rest of the sentence:

> *"Idha, bhikkhu, assutavā puthujjano . . . rūpaṃ attato samanupassati, rūpavantaṃ vā attānaṃ, attani vā rūpaṃ, rūpasmiṃ vā attānaṃ."*

> "Here, monk, an unlearned worldling . . . regards form as self, or self as possessing form, or form as in self, or self as in form."

The following (p. 120) is a compound sentence of negation, with a series of clauses joined by the negative particle *na*, the first in sandhi with *eva*:

> *"N'eva tāva rattindivā paññāyanti, na māsaddhamāsā paññāyanti, na utusaṃvaccharā paññāyanti."*

"For just so long nights and days are not discerned, months and fortnights are not discerned, seasons and years are not discerned."

Complex Sentences

A complex sentence has a primary independent clause and one or more dependent clauses. Complex sentences can be constructed from relative clauses, conditionals, absolutives, and absolutes; they can also be composed by embedding direct speech into a larger sentence and by the use of a simile. Although I discussed several of these forms earlier, here I will explore them further, citing additional examples.

Relative clause and main clause correlation

The most common type of complex sentence joins a relative clause (also called a bound clause) to the main clause. In the following example (p. 145) the relative clause with *yo* qualifying *hetu* and *paccayo* is correlated with the main clause, which represents the two nouns with the demonstrative pronoun *so*:

> *"Yopi hetu yopi paccayo rūpassa uppādāya, sopi anicco."*
>
> "That which is the cause, that which is the condition, for the arising of form—that too is impermanent."

In the above sentence the relative and demonstrative pronouns are of the same case, here the nominative. The structure of a sentence, however, may require a change of case between the relative pronoun and the demonstrative, as here (p. 283):

> *"Yadā kho te, bhikkhave, chappāṇakā jhattā assu kilantā, atha kho yo nesaṃ pāṇakānaṃ balavataro assa, tassa te anuvatteyyuṃ anuvidhāyeyyuṃ vasaṃ gaccheyyuṃ."*
>
> "When, monks, those six animals would be weakened and fatigued, then they would follow whichever of those animals is strongest, would submit to it, would come under its control."

In the above, the masculine relative pronoun *yo* is nominative in the second dependent clause, but is correlated with the dative (or genitive) *tassa* in the main clause. The pronoun *te*, qualifying the six animals, remains the same in both the first and third clauses, but becomes genitive plural (*nesaṃ*) in the second clause.

If a relative pronoun qualifying a noun in one gender is correlated with a demonstrative qualifying a noun of a different gender, each takes the gender of the noun it qualifies. In the following sentence (p. 497), the masculine relative pronoun *yo* in the relative clause is in agreement with *-khayo*, which is masculine, but in the main clause its corollary is the neuter *idaṃ*, which agrees with the neuter noun *asaṅkhataṃ*:

> *"Yo, bhikkhave, rāgakkhayo dosakkhayo mohakkhayo, idaṃ vuccati, bhikkhave, 'asaṅkhataṃ.'"*
>
> "The destruction of lust, the destruction of hatred, the destruction of delusion: this is called, monks, the 'unconditioned.'"

When a relative pronoun is conjoined with a series of nouns of different genders, it agrees with the first noun in the series. Thus in the next sentence (p. 242), since *saṅgati* is feminine, the relative pronoun *yā* is of the feminine gender, even though the following two nouns are masculine; but in the main clause the demonstrative *ayaṃ* is masculine, in agreement with the noun it qualifies, *-samphasso*:

> *"Yā kho, bhikkhave, imesaṃ tiṇṇaṃ dhammānaṃ saṅgati sannipāto samavāyo, ayaṃ vuccati 'cakkhusamphasso.'"*
>
> "The meeting, encounter, concurrence of these three things is called 'eye-contact.'"

Pronouns can be generalized either by repetition or by adding *koci, kāci, kiñci, keci*, etc., to the relative clause. Statements that begin with a generalization in the relative clause are often completed in the main clause by the pronominal adjective *sabba*, suitably declined. Thus in the following (p. 91) we find a generalization made about ascetics and brahmins expressed by *ye hi keci samaṇā vā brāhmaṇā vā* completed by *sabbe te* in the main clause:

> *"Ye hi keci, bhikkhave, etarahi samaṇā vā brāhmaṇā vā yathābhūtaṃ abhisambujjhanti, sabbe te cattāri ariyasaccāni yathābhūtaṃ abhisambujjhanti."*

"Whatever ascetics or brahmins now, monks, are fully enlightened [to things] as they really are, they are all fully enlightened to the four noble truths as they really are."

The following sentence (p. 170) employs a similar construction when giving directions about the contemplation of form, with *yaṃ kiñci rūpaṃ* completed by *sabbaṃ rūpaṃ* in the main clause:

"Yaṃ kiñci rūpaṃ atītānāgatapaccuppannaṃ ajjhattaṃ vā bahiddhā vā oḷārikaṃ vā sukhumaṃ vā hīnaṃ vā paṇītaṃ vā yaṃ dūre santike vā, sabbaṃ rūpaṃ: 'N'etaṃ mama, n'eso'hamasmi, na m'eso attā'ti evametaṃ yathābhūtaṃ sammappaññāya daṭṭhabbaṃ."

"Whatever form there is, whether past, future, or present, internal or external, gross or subtle, inferior or superior, far or near, all form should be seen as it really is with correct wisdom thus: 'This is not mine, this I am not, this is not my self.'"

Although the relative clause usually precedes the main clause, occasionally, for emphasis, the sequence may be inverted, as the following illustrates (p. 459), with the demonstrative *taṃ* of the initial main clause correlated with the relative *yo* of the dependent clause:

"Nāhaṃ taṃ, bhikkhave, passāmi . . . yo imesaṃ pañhānaṃ veyyākaraṇena cittaṃ ārādheyya aññatra tathāgatena vā tathāgatasāvakena vā ito vā pana sutvā."

"I do not see anyone, monks, . . . who could satisfy the mind with an answer to these questions apart from the Tathāgata or a disciple of the Tathāgata or one who has heard it from here."

The correlation between relative clause and main clause is not restricted to units that contain pronouns but extends to other pairs coupled as relative and demonstrative. Thus the pair *yasmā* and *tasmā* is used to express causation or logical entailment (p. 240):

"Yasmā ca kho, ānanda, suññaṃ attena vā attaniyena vā, tasmā 'suñño loko'ti vuccati."

"Because, Ānanda, it is empty of self and of what belongs to self, therefore it is said: 'The world is empty.'"

The pair *yato* and *atha* expresses temporal relationships (p. 121):

"Yato ca kho, bhikkhave, tathāgato loke uppajjati . . . atha mahato ālokassa pātubhāvo hoti mahato obhāsassa."

"But, monks, when the Tathāgata arises in the world . . . then there is the manifestation of great light, of great radiance."

More precise temporal relationships can be expressed by still another pair, *yasmiṃ* and *tasmiṃ*, used to qualify *samaye* (p. 458):

"Yasmiṃ, bhikkhave, samaye līnaṃ cittaṃ hoti, akālo tasmiṃ samaye passaddhisambojjhaṅgassa bhāvanāya."

"On whichever occasion, monks, the mind is sluggish, on that occasion it is not the time to develop the enlightenment factor of tranquility."

Relations between extensions in time are expressed by the pair *yāva* (and *yāvakīva*) and *tāva* (p. 151):

"Yāvakīvañcāhaṃ, bhikkhave, imesaṃ pañcannaṃ upādānakkhandhānaṃ evaṃ assādañca assādato, ādīnavañca ādīnavato, nissaraṇañca nissaraṇato, yathābhūtaṃ nābbhaññāsiṃ, n'eva tāvāhaṃ, bhikkhave, sadevake loke . . . 'anuttaraṃ sammāsambodhiṃ abhisambuddho'ti paccaññāsiṃ."

"So long, monks, as I did not directly know as it really is, in regard to these five clinging-aggregates, the enjoyment as the enjoyment, the danger as the danger, and the escape as the escape, for so long, monks, in the world with its devas . . . I did not claim: 'I have been enlightened to the unsurpassed perfect enlightenment.'"

Relations of place may be expressed by the pair *yattha* and *tattha* (p. 413):

"Yatth'eva naṃ thokampi chaḍḍessasi, tatth'eva te siro pātessati."

"Wherever you spill even a little, just there he will fell your head."

Relations of manner may be expressed by the pair *yathā* and *tathā* (SN IV 95,1–2):

> *"Yathā vo bhagavā vyākareyya tathā naṃ dhāreyyātha."*
>
> "As the Blessed One answers you, in just that way you should remember it."

Such relations may be generalized by repetition, as in the following (MN I 57,1–2):

> *"Yathā yathā vā pan'assa kāyo paṇihito hoti tathā tathā naṃ pajānāti."*
>
> "Or in whatever way one's body is disposed, in just that way one knows it."

Conditional sentences

Conditional sentences are of two main types, those expressing a conditional relationship of genuine possibility and those expressing a conditional relationship in which the antecedent is counterfactual. The latter type are also called "hypothetical sentences."

In a conditional sentence the antecedent (the condition) is generally signaled by the word *sace* or the enclitic (internal) form *ce*, both meaning "if."[62] But such sentences can also be constructed without such a word, with the conditional mood conveyed by the verbs and the context. In conditionals of genuine possibility the verbs in both the antecedent clause and the consequent clause may occur in the present, the future, or optative. In the following they are both optative (p. 474):

> *"Sace vo, bhikkhave, aññatitthiyā paribbājakā evaṃ puccheyyuṃ . . . evaṃ puṭṭhā tumhe, bhikkhave, tesaṃ aññatitthiyānaṃ paribbājakānaṃ evaṃ vyākareyyātha. . . ."*
>
> "If, monks, wanderers belonging to other sects would ask you thus . . . being asked thus, monks, you should answer those wanderers belonging to other sects thus. . . ."

62. Occasionally the conditional may be indicated by the word *yadi*, though in the Nikāyas *yadi* is used more often to express alternatives, for example at MN I 36, *yadi nīlakāya yadi pītakāya yadi lohitakāya yadi mañjiṭṭhakāya*, "whether blue or yellow or red or purple."

In the following (p. 264) the antecedent occurs in both the present and future tense and the consequent in the future tense, indicating inevitability:

> *"Sace so, bhikkhave, dārukkhandho na orimaṃ tīraṃ upagacchati, na pārimaṃ tīraṃ upagacchati . . . na antopūti bhavissati, evaṃ hi so, bhikkhave, dārukkhandho samuddaninno bhavissati samuddapoṇo samuddapabbhāro."*
>
> "If, monks, that log does not approach the near bank, does not approach the far bank . . . if it will not become inwardly rotten, in such a case, monks, that log will slant toward the ocean, slope toward the ocean, incline toward the ocean."

In a hypothetical sentence the counterfactual antecedent is signaled by the conditional form of the verb, usually *abhavissa*, and the consequent by the optative. The false hypothesis is then generally countered by a statement with the *yasmā-tasmā* structure. Here is an example (p. 156):

> *"No ce'daṃ, bhikkhave, rūpassa assādo abhavissa, nayidaṃ sattā rūpasmiṃ sārajjeyyuṃ. Yasmā ca kho, bhikkhave, atthi rūpassa assādo, tasmā sattā rūpasmiṃ sārajjanti."*
>
> "If, monks, there were no enjoyment in form, beings would not become attached to form. But because there is enjoyment in form, beings become attached to form."

The absolutive

The absolutive can be used to create complex sentences in which subordinate clauses are linked together in a sequence of actions that is completed by the main clause. Thus when a monk finishes his conversation with the Buddha, he might engage in a series of actions described by absolutives, as here (p. 177), where four absolutives are formed with the *-tvā* suffix and one with the *-ya* suffix:

> *Atha kho so bhikkhu bhagavato bhāsitaṃ abhinanditvā anumoditvā uṭṭhāy'āsanā bhagavantaṃ abhivādetvā padakkhiṇaṃ katvā pakkāmi.*

> Then, having delighted [and] having rejoiced in the Blessed One's statement, having risen from his seat, having paid homage to the Blessed One, having circumambulated him, that monk departed.

For rhetorical effect, absolutives can be chained together in a repetitive pattern with a group of related items, as in the following (p. 125):

> *"Te jātisaṃvattanikepi saṅkhāre abhisaṅkharitvā, jarāsaṃvattanikepi saṅkhāre abhisaṅkharitvā, maraṇasaṃvattanikepi saṅkhāre abhisaṅkharitvā, soka-parideva-dukkha-domanass'upāyāsasaṃvattanikepi saṅkhāre abhisaṅkharitvā, jātipapātampi papatanti, jarāpapātampi papatanti, maraṇapapātampi papatanti, soka-parideva-dukkha-domanass'upāyāsapapātampi papatanti."*

> "Having generated volitional activities that lead to birth, having generated volitional activities that lead to old age, having generated volitional activities that lead to death, having generated volitional activities that lead to sorrow, lamentation, pain, dejection, and misery, they fall down the precipice of birth, they fall down the precipice of old age, they fall down the precipice of death, they fall down the precipice of sorrow, lamentation, pain, dejection, and misery."

By means of the absolutive, paragraphs can be constructed in which the finite verb of the preceding sentence is turned into an absolutive flowing into the action in the main clause of the next sentence, denoted by its own finite verb. Thus a series of actions can be strung together in such a way that each new sentence echoes the last action of the preceding sentence. This is exemplified in the following passage (p. 183), where the autonomous grammatical units can be treated either as separate sentences or as parts of a single long sentence. Here I use both kinds of punctuation:

> *"Sīho, bhikkhave, migarājā sāyanhasamayaṃ āsayā nikkhamati. Āsayā nikkhamitvā vijambhati; vijambhitvā samantā catuddisā anuviloketi; samantā catuddisā anuviloketvā tikkhattuṃ sīhanādaṃ nadati. Tikkhattuṃ sīhanādaṃ naditvā gocarāya pakkamati."*

"The lion, monks, the king of beasts, in the evening comes out from his lair. Having come out from his lair, he stretches; having stretched, he surveys the four directions all around; having surveyed the four directions all around, he roars a lion's roar three times. Having roared a lion's roar three times, he departs for his feeding ground."

The locative absolute

The locative absolute is a construction used in a sentence to represent a subordinate clause with a subject *different from* the subject of the main clause, performing an action or undergoing a process different from that of the main clause. In such a construction the subject of the subordinate clause—usually a noun or pronoun—is set in the locative case, and the subordinate subject's action or process is represented by a past participle or present participle also in the locative case, as are any other modifiers of the subordinate subject. The past participle is generally used when the subordinate activity precedes the action of the main clause, the present participle when the two occur more or less concurrently.

The distinction between the absolutive and the locative absolute should be carefully noted. Both may be used to describe an action that occurs prior to the main action of the sentence. If the prior action is done by the subject of the main verb, the absolutive of that action is used; if the prior action is done by someone or something else, the locative absolute with the past participle is used.

The following statement (p. 171; see too p. 228) uses the locative absolute with the present participle to describe a situation in which the subordinate action (the discourse being spoken) occurs concurrently with the action described in the main clause (the liberation of the monks' minds):

Imasmiñca pana veyyākaraṇasmiṃ bhaññamāne pañcavaggiyānaṃ bhikkhūnaṃ anupādāya āsavehi cittāni vimucciṃsu.

And while this discourse was being spoken, through non-clinging the minds of the monks of the group of five were liberated from the influxes.

The locative subject of the subordinate clause here is *imasmiṃ veyyākaraṇasmiṃ*, "this discourse"; the process undergone by this subject is described by the passive present participle in the locative case, *bhaññamāne*, "being spoken." In the main clause, the subject, *cittāni*, the minds (of the monks), is nominative plural, and the process the subject undergoes is specified by the aorist passive verb, *vimucciṃsu*, "were liberated."

The following sentence (p. 117) has a locative absolute construction with the past participle:

> *"Āditte, bhante, cele vā sīse vā, tass'eva celassa vā sīsassa vā nibbāpanāya adhimatto chando ca vāyāmo ca ussāho ca ussoḷhī ca appaṭivānī ca sati ca sampajaññañca karaṇīyaṃ."*
>
> "When, Bhante, one's turban or head is ablaze, extraordinary desire, effort, zeal, enthusiasm, persistence, mindfulness, and clear comprehension should be practiced for the extinguishing of that [fire on one's] turban or head."

The abstract statement of the principle of conditionality includes a locative absolute in both its positive and negative formulations: positively, *imasmiṃ sati idaṃ hoti*, "this existing, that occurs," and negatively, *imasmiṃ asati idaṃ na hoti*, "this not existing, that does not occur." Here *sati* is the locative singular present participle of *atthi*.[63] The locative absolute recurs in statements that flesh out the process of origination and cessation thus (p. 334): *Jātiyā sati jarāmaraṇaṃ hoti; jātiyā asati jarāmaraṇaṃ na hoti*, "When there is birth, old-age-and-death occurs; when there is no birth, old-age-and-death does not occur." It should be noted that the masculine singular locative present participles *asati* and *sati* are used even when the locative subjects they qualify are feminine nouns, here *jāti* and later in the formula *taṇhā*, *vedanā*, and *avijjā*; this is probably done simply to maintain uniformity. Again, the singulars *asati* and *sati* are used even when the corresponding locative noun is the plural *saṅkhāresu* (see p. 340).

Occasionally the locative absolute of a verb or verbs may be used without an explicit subject, but with the adverb of manner *evaṃ* taking the place of the subject. The most common examples are *evaṃ sante*, "such being [the case]," and *evaṃ vutte*, "when such was said." We also see this in the clause

63. Needless to say, this *sati* has nothing to do with the word usually translated as "mindfulness."

evaṃ ācikkhiyamāne desiyamāne paññāpiyamāne paṭṭhapiyamāne vivariyamāne vibhajiyamāne uttānīkariyamāne, "when it is being thus pointed out, taught, made known, established, disclosed, analyzed, and elucidated" (see p. 202). Here the implicit subject is already clear from the context.

Besides the locative absolute, the Nikāyas occasionally employ a genitive absolute, which appears much less often. No occurrences of the genitive absolute are found in the reading passages in this volume, but an example is at MN I 13,36–37: *Āyasmā Sāriputto acirapakkantassa bhagavato bhikkhū āmantesi*, "Not long after the Blessed One had left, the Venerable Sāriputta addressed the monks." The genitive absolute often, but not always, has the nuance of "despite" or "although," as when the Buddha describes his renunciation (at MN I 163,27–31): *So kho ahaṃ . . . akāmakānaṃ mātāpitūnaṃ assumukhānaṃ rudantānaṃ . . . agārasmā anagāriyaṃ pabbajiṃ*, "Though my mother and father were unwilling, weeping with tearful faces . . . I went forth from home to homelessness."

Embedded direct speech

Whereas English generally uses indirect statements to indicate something that is known or thought (for example, "He knew that the cat was in the house," "She thought she should visit her mother"), the Nikāyas usually convey the idea of knowing a fact or thinking a thought by embedding direct quotations in the sentence. In this way, the texts can construct sentences of varying degrees of complexity within a relatively simple overarching pattern. In the following sentence (p. 88) a direct quotation represents the object of understanding:

> *"'Idaṃ dukkhan'ti yathābhūtaṃ pajānāti."*
>
> "He understands as it really is: 'This is suffering.'"

The same idea can be stated in the optative mood, as here (p. 89) with the future passive participle:

> *"'Idaṃ dukkhan'ti yogo karaṇīyo."*
>
> "An exertion should be made [to understand]: 'This is suffering.'"

We see a sentence of greater complexity in the instructions for contemplating the aggregates as non-self, where a three-phrase direct quotation is used (p. 170):

> *"Tasmātiha, bhikkhave, yaṃ kiñci rūpaṃ . . . sabbaṃ rūpaṃ: 'N'etaṃ mama, n'eso'hamasmi, na m'eso attā'ti evametaṃ yathābhūtaṃ sammappaññāya daṭṭhabbaṃ."*
>
> "Therefore, monks, whatever form [there is] . . . all form should be seen as it really is with correct wisdom thus: 'This [is] not mine, this I am not, this [is] not my self.'"

Another statement with the object of understanding indicated by a quotation is as follows (p. 235), where the direct object of the verb, modified by a present participle, occurs in the accusative case (*santaṃ . . . rāgaṃ*), while the actual content of understanding is expressed as direct speech:

> *"Santañca ajjhattaṃ rūpesu rāgaṃ 'atthi me ajjhattaṃ rūpesu rāgo'ti pajānāti."*
>
> "And he understands the lust for forms existing internally thus, 'There exists for me internally lust for forms.'"

Similes

The Buddha's discourses make ample use of similes to illustrate the teachings. Extended similes might consist of many sentences, in which case they amount almost to parables.[64] But shorter similes, which abound throughout the texts, might be expressed by a single sentence that is fairly complex in structure. Similes, whether concise or extended, typically open with the word *seyyathāpi*, "just as." They usually employ optative forms of the verb and use the expression *evameva*, "just so," to introduce the application of the simile to the point being illustrated. Here is a typical example (p. 488):

> *"Seyyathāpi, bhikkhave, gaṅgā nadī pācīnaninnā pācīnapoṇā pācīnapabbhārā, evameva kho, bhikkhave, bhikkhu ariyaṃ*

64. Examples included in this volume are the similes of the lion's roar (p. 183), the six animals (p. 282, p. 285), the ancient city (p. 356), and the two acrobats (p. 409).

> *aṭṭhaṅgikaṃ maggaṃ bhāvento ariyaṃ aṭṭhaṅgikaṃ maggaṃ bahulīkaronto nibbānaninno hoti nibbānapoṇo nibbānapabbhāro."*
>
> "Just as, monks, the Ganges River slants to the east, slopes to the east, inclines to the east, just so, a monk developing the noble eightfold path, cultivating the noble eightfold path, slants to nibbāna, slopes to nibbāna, inclines to nibbāna."

The following passage (p. 451) weaves together four similes, all in a single sentence, to express appreciation for the teaching. It will be observed that the last simile employs embedded direct speech:

> *"Seyyathāpi, bho gotama, nikkujjitaṃ vā ukkujjeyya, paṭicchannaṃ vā vivareyya, mūḷhassa vā maggaṃ ācikkheyya, andhakāre vā telapajjotaṃ dhāreyya, 'Cakkhumanto rūpāni dakkhantī'ti, evameva bhotā gotamena anekapariyāyena dhammo pakāsito."*
>
> "Just as, Master Gotama, one would turn upright what had been overturned, or would reveal what was concealed, or would point out the path to one who is lost, or would hold up an oil lamp in the darkness, [thinking,] 'Those with eyes will see forms,' just so the Dhamma has been revealed in many ways by Master Gotama."

The Subject in a Passive Role

While English generally inclines to representing the subject of a sentence in an active role, as the agent of the action, Pāli often features the logical subject—the agent of an action, observation, or thought—in a passive role relative to the grammatical subject of the sentence.[65] The logical subject becomes *one to whom* a thought occurs, *one to whom* an event happens, *one to*

65. "Logical subject" refers to the subject of a sentence other than in a grammatical (or "syntactic") sense. Sentences with a logical subject (as well as a grammatical subject) usually have a passive verb. For example, in the sentence "The burglar was arrested by the policeman," the grammatical subject is "the burglar" but the logical subject (the doer of the action referred to, the arresting) is the policeman. (Definition and example taken from https://www.quora.com/What-is-meant-by-logical-subject-in-grammar-Is-the-book-the-logical-subject-in-The-book-sells-easily-Whats-the-difference-between-a-syntactic-subject-and-a-logical-subject.)

whom an object appears, with the thought, the event, or the object becoming the grammatical subject. A simple example is the following phrase introducing a thought, which would then be formulated in direct speech (p. 399):

Atha kho bhagavato etadahosi. . . .

Then this occurred to the Blessed One. . . .

In the following (p. 106), instead of saying that one who knows and sees the four noble truths attains the destruction of the influxes, the destruction of the influxes functions as the grammatical subject occurring to the actual agent—represented by two dative present participles—as if the agent were passively undergoing the attainment:[66]

"'Idaṃ dukkhan'ti, bhikkhave, jānato passato āsavānaṃ khayo hoti."

"It is, monks, for one knowing and seeing, 'This is suffering,' that the destruction of the influxes occurs."

And again, with two main clauses (p. 230):

"Cakkhuṃ kho, bhikkhu, aniccato jānato passato avijjā pahīyati, vijjā uppajjati."

"For one knowing and seeing the eye as impermanent, monk, ignorance is abandoned and clear knowledge arises."

Sentences conforming to this model can be made more complex by qualifying the subject more extensively, as in the following (p. 149), where the Buddha describes himself as engaging in a certain course of reflection before his enlightenment:

"Pubbeva me, bhikkhave, sambodhā anabhisambuddhassa bodhisattass'eva sato etadahosi. . . ."

"Before the enlightenment, monks, while I was just a bodhisatta, not fully enlightened, this occurred to me. . . ."

66. Wijesekera §95 calls these datives of possession.

The following sentence (p. 206) describes how something appears to a subject, the dative *tassa*, qualified by three present participles, the last of which is further modified by an adverb. The object of investigation of the subordinate clause—the accusative pronoun *taṃ*—becomes the grammatical subject of the main clause, and the act of appearing is expressed in three ways with the same optative verb (*khāyeyya*) qualified by three accusatives functioning adverbally:

> *"Tassa taṃ passato nijjhāyato yoniso upaparikkhato rittakaññeva khāyeyya, tucchakaññeva khāyeyya, asārakaññeva khāyeyya."*[67]

> "As he is seeing it, pondering it, thoroughly investigating it, it would appear just void, it would appear just hollow, it would appear just insubstantial."

The predilection for passive modes of expression makes use of still other grammatical forms. I will give only three examples. Here is the first (p. 420):

> *"Anāgāmiphalaṃ tayā, gahapati, vyākataṃ."*

> "The fruit of a non-returner, householder, has been declared by you."

In this sentence, instead of saying, in the active voice (as we would say in normal English), "You have declared the fruit of a non-returner," the speaker uses the nominative *anāgāmiphalaṃ* to represent the grammatical subject, which is the logical object; the second-person instrumental pronoun *tayā* stands for the agent, which is the logical subject; and the past passive participle *vyākataṃ* describes the action, also nominative in agreement with the grammatical subject.

The second is a resolution that the monks are advised to make to practice mindfulness of the body (p. 286). Again, it casts the logical object as the grammatical subject, *kāyagatā sati*, in the nominative case; it represents the agent with the first-person plural instrumental pronoun *no*; and it qualifies the grammatical subject with a string of past participles (or their derivatives) functioning as adjectives, nominatives in agreement with the subject. The

67. The *-ññ-* in the three adverbs results from sandhi with *eva*; that is, *rittakaṃ* + *eva* > *rittakaññeva*. And so for the other two.

resolution to practice in this way is shown by the use of the future verb *bhavissati*:

> *"Kāyagatā sati no bhāvitā bhavissati bahulīkatā yānīkatā vatthukatā anuṭṭhitā paricitā susamāraddhā."*
>
> "Mindfulness directed to the body will be developed and cultivated by us, made a vehicle, made a basis, stabilized, repeated, and well undertaken."

Finally, the following is an instruction the Buddha gives to senior monks on how they should train junior monks (p. 387). The objects of the action, the junior monks, occur as the grammatical subjects of the sentence and thus are in the nominative case, while the logical subjects, the monks being addressed (presumably elders), are referred to with the enclitic pronoun *vo*, "by you," and the actions to be performed by them are described by future passive participles.

> *"Ye te, bhikkhave, bhikkhū navā acirapabbajitā adhunāgatā imaṃ dhammavinayaṃ, te vo, bhikkhave, bhikkhū catunnaṃ satipaṭṭhānānaṃ bhāvanāya samādapetabbā nivesetabbā patiṭṭhāpetabbā."*
>
> "Monks, those monks who are juniors, not long gone forth, recently come to this Dhamma and discipline, should be enjoined, settled, and established by you in the development of the four establishments of mindfulness."

Interrogative Sentences

Interrogative sentences are usually recognizable by the presence of interrogative words, which generally (but not invariably) come at the very beginning of the sentence posing a question. Interrogative words often begin with the consonant *k-*, and several correspond to relative and demonstrative words. Thus *kattha*, "Where?" is the interrogative corresponding to *yattha* and *tattha*; *kathaṃ*, "How?" corresponds to *yathā* and *tathā*; *kuto*, "How? From where?" corresponds to *yato* and *tato*; *kasmā*, "Why?" corresponds to *yasmā* and *tasmā*; *kadā*, "When?" corresponds to *yadā* and *tadā*; and *kittāvatā*, "In what way? To what extent?" corresponds to *ettāvatā*.

The most common interrogative word is *kiṃ*, "What?" a neuter that corresponds to *yaṃ* and *taṃ*. The word also has masculine and feminine forms, in the nominative *ko* and *kā*, respectively; it is declined like a pronoun. Another common interrogative is *katama*, "What? Which?" which is also declined like a pronoun.

Some examples of interrogative sentences may be briefly noted.

With *katama*:

> *"Katame ca, bhikkhave, pariññeyyā dhammā?"* (masculine plural nominative)
>
> "And what, monks, are things to be fully understood?" (p. 146)
>
> *"Katamā ca, bhikkhave, pariññā?"* (feminine singular nominative)
>
> "And what, monks, is full understanding?" (p. 147)
>
> *"Katamesaṃ tasmiṃ samaye bojjhaṅgānaṃ akālo bhāvanāya?"* (masculine plural genitive)
>
> "Of which factors of enlightenment is it not the time for development on that occasion?" (p. 458)

With *kasmā*:

> *"Kasmā c'etaṃ, bhikkhave, mayā anakkhātaṃ?"*
>
> "And why, monks, have I not expounded this?" (p. 112)

With *kuto*:

> *"Aniccasambhūtaṃ, bhikkhave, rūpaṃ kuto niccaṃ bhavissati?"*
>
> "When form, monks, has originated from what is impermanent, how could it be permanent?" (p. 145)

With *kattha*:

> *"Taṇhā panāyaṃ kattha uppajjamānā uppajjati, kattha nivisamānā nivisati?"*

"When this craving is arising, where does it arise? When it is settling down, where does it settle?" (p. 364)

With *kathaṃ*:

"Kathaṃ nu kho, bhante, sakkāyadiṭṭhi hoti?"

"How, Bhante, does the view of the personal-collection occur?" (p. 194)

"Kathaṃ nu kho, bhante, jānato kathaṃ passato avijjā pahīyati?"

"For one knowing how, Bhante, for one seeing how, is ignorance abandoned?" (p. 230)

"Kittāvatā nu kho, bhante, sandiṭṭhiko dhammo hoti?"

"In what way, Bhante, is the Dhamma directly visible?" (p. 234)

Interrogative sentences can also be constructed by the use of certain interrogative particles. The most common of these is *nu*, which may be combined with other words in such conjuncts as *nu kho* or *api nu* or *api nu kho*. The first is often found in sentences with an interrogative, as we saw in several of the above examples. The second, *api nu*, often occurs when the Buddha begins a question by asking the monks, *taṃ kiṃ maññatha*? "What do you think?" Here are some examples of the second and third types:

"Taṃ kiṃ maññatha, bhikkhave, api nu so mahājanakāyo gaṅgaṃ nadiṃ pacchāninnaṃ kareyya pacchāpoṇaṃ pacchāpabbhāraṃ?"

"What do you think, monks, can that great crowd of people make the Ganges River slant to the west, slope to the west, incline to the west?" (p. 490)

"Api nu kho kāṇo kacchapo . . . yuge gīvaṃ paveseyya?"

"Would that blind turtle . . . insert its neck into that yoke?" (p. 131)

"Jātinirodhā api nu kho jarāmaraṇaṃ paññāyetha?"

"With the cessation of birth, would old-age-and-death be discerned?" (p. 340)

Key to Grammatical Terms Used in This Book

ablative: the case of nouns and their modifiers expressing causation, departure, separation, and point of origin.

absolutive: a verbal derivative used to express an action, or a series of consecutive actions, done by the subject of the sentence prior to the action denoted by the main verb.

accusative: the case of nouns and their modifiers used principally for the direct object of transitive verbs and secondary objects in double accusatives with verbs of speech, also in certain adverbial expressions.

adverbial compound: a compound that functions adverbially; it is generally indeclinable and in the form of the accusative singular ending in the *niggahīta*, though sometimes with the case ending retained.

aorist: the past tense of a verb.

bahubbīhi: a compound ending in a noun used as an adjective to describe or represent a noun external to itself; it is declined like the noun it qualifies and agrees with it in gender, number, and case.

case: the form of a noun and its qualifiers that governs its role in the syntax of a sentence.

causative: a form of the verb that expresses its role in causing the action denoted by the primary verb to take place.

compound: a word formed by joining together two or more words in such a way that the combination of words functions as a single unit.

conditional: a form of the verb that expresses a conditional relationship about a counterfactual matter—that is, "if such [which is not the case] were the case."

dative: the case of nouns and their modifiers that may express the destination of movement, an indirect object, and the purpose of an action.

dvanda: a copulative compound, made up of two or more words that, used separately, would be joined by the conjunction *ca*.

enclitic: the form of a word, especially the pronouns *me*, *no*, *te*, and *vo*, that occurs only within a sentence or clause, never at the beginning of a sentence or clause.

future passive participle: a verbal derivative used to express the ideas of necessity, obligation, or fitness, indicating that a certain action should be done, must be done, or is worth doing.

gender: the classification of nouns and their modifiers as masculine, feminine, or neuter.

genitive: the case of nouns and their modifiers that may express a possessive or partitive relation between two nouns, corresponding to the preposition "of" or possessive forms of nouns and pronouns.

imperative: the mood of a verb used to issue a command or make a request.

indeclinable: a word that is not subject to declination by way of case, number, and gender.

infinitive: a form of the verb not specified for any person, number, or tense, usually used with the sense of "to do [the action signified by the verb]."

instrumental: the case of nouns and their modifiers that may express the agent of passive verbs, the instrument of action, the cause or reason of an action or event, the qualities with which someone or something is endowed, persons who accompany the subject, and the accompaniment of an action.

interrogative: a sentence (or part of speech) that poses a question.

itaritara: a dvanda compound in which the joined terms constitute a plural and take the gender and case of the last member.

kammadhāraya: a descriptive determinative compound, a compound made up of two members, with the first modifying the second as an attributive adjective, a noun, or an adverb.

locative: the case of nouns and their modifiers that expresses location and position in space and time; it is also used for the object referred to by nouns of desire and knowledge.

locative absolute: a construction used to show a situation with a subordinate subject and action/event, distinct from the main subject and its action/event in the primary clause; the subordinate subject along with the terms that qualify it and its action/event, represented by either the past participle or present participle, all occur in the locative case.

middle voice: the form of a verb and present participle originally used to denote an action that accrues only to the subject (as contrasted with an action that passes from a subject to an object), but in Pāli confined mostly to verse and elevated prose, without necessarily signifying an action that inheres only in the subject.

niggahīta: the pure nasal sound attached to certain vowels, represented by *-ṃ*.

nominative: the case of a noun and its modifiers used to represent the grammatical subject of a sentence.

number: the determination of nouns, their modifiers, verbs, and verbal derivatives by way of the distinction of singular or plural.

optative: the form of a verb that expresses what should be done, can be done, or might happen.

past participle: a verbal derivative based on an action that has already occurred whose effect continues; it can function as an adjective or a noun, or it may take the place of the verb of the sentence. Some past participles (such as *nisinna*, *ṭhita*, and *paṭipanna*) function almost as present participles.

person: the determination of pronouns and verbs as referring to oneself and those in one's group (first person), another person or persons whom one is addressing (second person), or another person, persons, or things to whom or to which one is referring (third person).

present participle: a verbal derivative used to describe an action performed by a subject or occurring to an object at roughly the same time as the action denoted by the main verb of the sentence; in English it corresponds to forms ending in *-ing*.

prohibitive: a sentence (or part of speech) that forbids an action.

samāhāra: a dvanda in which the joined terms constitute a neuter singular; some, however, take the case ending of the last term, for instance, *chandarāgo* and *lābhasakkārasiloko*.

sandhi: the changes that letters undergo in their combinations and encounters with other letters, both within a word and when words meet.

syntactical compound: a compound of two or more words joined together, in which some components retain the syntactical form they would have had in a non-compounded statement.

tappurisa: a dependent determinative compound, a compound made up of two members with the first dependent on the second.

vocative: the case of a noun as it is used to address someone or a group of people.

1. The Four Noble Truths: The Matrix of the Teaching

Introduction

The four noble truths are generally regarded as the most concise formulation of the Buddha's program of liberation. The Buddha's chief disciple, Sāriputta, declared as much in an often-quoted statement: "Just as the footprints of all other animals that walk can fit into the footprint of an elephant, which is declared chief with respect to size, so whatever wholesome teachings there are can all fit into the four noble truths" (MN 28, I 184,26–30). The four noble truths were so central to the Buddha's exposition of the Dhamma that the compilers of the Saṃyutta Nikāya devoted an entire chapter to suttas on this topic, and indeed the four truths might be seen as the implicit framework of the entire Saṃyutta Nikāya, as shown in the general introduction.

The Buddha revealed the four noble truths in his first discourse, thereby "setting in motion the wheel of the Dhamma." It was upon learning these truths that his first disciples, the five monks, attained the "eye of the Dhamma," marking the entry to the liberating path. The Buddha spent his teaching career proclaiming and expounding the four truths. He would begin his standard discourse to newcomers with a talk on generosity and morality, and only when he knew that the minds of his listeners were sufficiently ripe would he speak about the truths. According to 1.10, the things that the Buddha directly knew were many, like the leaves in a forest grove, but the things he expounded were few, like the leaves he took up in his hand. These few things were suffering, its origin, its cessation, and the path.

The first discourse, the *Dhammacakkappavattana Sutta*, provides formal explanations of the four noble truths. Most of these explanations are also included in 1.4, which differs from those in the first discourse only by offering a more concise definition of the first truth. Omitting the detailed manifestations of *dukkha* that begin with birth, this sutta explains the first truth simply by way of the five clinging-aggregates, which in the first discourse are said to encapsulate the truth of suffering "in brief." Text **1.9** assigns specific tasks to each of the four truths, in this respect also echoing the middle portion of the first discourse. Thus the truth of suffering is to be fully understood; the truth of its origin, craving, is to be abandoned; the truth of its cessation, the eradication of craving, is to be realized; and the truth of the way, the noble eightfold path, is to be developed.

The four noble truths served the Buddha not only as a teaching device but as the objects of cultivation and realization. When describing his own attainment of enlightenment, he brings the exposition to its climax by declaring that in the last watch of the night: "When my concentrated mind was purified, bright, unblemished, rid of imperfection, malleable, wieldy, steady, and attained to imperturbability, I directed it to knowledge of the destruction of the influxes. I directly knew as it actually is: 'This is suffering, this its origin, this its cessation, this the way leading to its cessation.'" With the arising of this insight, "Ignorance was banished and clear knowledge arose, darkness was banished and light arose," and his mind was liberated from the influxes.[68]

In several suttas the Buddha generalizes from his own experience to highlight the centrality of the four noble truths to the attainment of enlightenment and liberation throughout all periods of time, thus universalizing their significance. Text **1.2** states that all those who attain full enlightenment do so by becoming fully enlightened to the four noble truths. The verb found in this passage, *abhisambujjhati*, seems to be used solely in relation to a buddha's enlightenment (in contrast to that of his disciples); thus the text is implicitly saying that all buddhas—past, future, and present—become enlightened to these same four truths. Other suttas not included here reinforce this point in relation to disciples. SN 56:3 says that all those who rightly go forth into the homeless life do so for the purpose of realizing the four noble truths as they really are, and SN 56:4 says that all those who have rightly gone forth and realized things as they really are, realize the four noble truths as they really are.

Lack of knowledge of the four noble truths is the blind spot that keeps

68. The passage occurs in MN I 23 and elsewhere in MN. It is also at AN IV 178–79, which compares the process of realization to a chick breaking out from its shell.

us bound to the round of birth and death. Because we have not seen these truths, we run pointlessly from one existence to the next, passing through the repetitive cycle of birth, aging, and death, and then new birth. Just as a stick thrown into the air falls sometimes on its bottom, sometimes on its top, so sentient beings who have not seen the four truths, being hindered by ignorance and fettered by craving, migrate up and down among the multiple realms of existence (**I.11**). It is because we have not penetrated the four noble truths, **I.5** tells us, that we have roamed through the "long journey" of saṃsāra, and it is with the penetration of these truths that the journey comes to an end. Even seekers dedicated to the pursuit of liberation fail to achieve their aim if they do not understand the four truths. According to **I.15**, those ascetics and brahmins who do not understand these truths "generate volitional activities" that lead to birth, old age, and death, and by doing so they fall down "the deep precipice" of birth, old age, and death, meeting anguish and misery.

The purpose of the Buddha's appearance in the world—indeed, the reason for the appearance of any buddha—is to proclaim the four noble truths. So long as a buddha has not appeared, says **I.14**, the world is enveloped in spiritual darkness, like the world before the sun and moon have appeared. But when a buddha arises, there is "the explaining, teaching, proclaiming, establishing, disclosing, analyzing, and elucidation of the four noble truths." Just as it is impossible to construct the upper story of a house without having first constructed the lower story, so **I.16** says, without breaking through to these truths it is impossible to make an end of suffering.

For this reason, the Buddha constantly presses his disciples to make an effort to realize the four noble truths. Each of the discourses in the Saccasaṃyutta ends with the injunction: "Therefore an exertion should be made [to understand]: 'This is suffering' . . . 'This is the way leading to the cessation of suffering.'" He instructs the monks not to indulge in thoughts connected with sensuality, ill will, and harmfulness, but to think instead about the four noble truths (**I.2**). They are not only to reflect on the truths, but to develop concentration as a basis for seeing them with direct vision (**I.1**). He insists they undertake this task with a compelling sense of urgency, just as a person whose turban or hair were on fire would make an urgent effort to extinguish the flames (see **I.12**).

The initial vision of the four noble truths brings the attainment of stream-entry. Those who see the four noble truths through this initial breakthrough become "accomplished in view" (*diṭṭhisampanna*) and will migrate at most through seven more lives, as stated in 1.18. But for the Buddha even the attainment of stream-entry is insufficient. The final goal of the path is the extinction of the influxes, the defilements of sensual craving, craving for existence, and ignorance. This, too, according to 1.6, is attained only by those who see the four noble truths. Having made the initial breakthrough, the texts say, one should not pause until one can declare, like the Buddha: "Craving for existence has been cut off; the conduit to existence has been destroyed; now there is no more renewed existence" (1.5).

1. Samādhisutta

Concentration (SN 56:1; V 414)

"Samādhiṃ, bhikkhave, bhāvetha. Samāhito, bhikkhave, bhikkhu yathābhūtaṃ pajānāti.

"Concentration, monks, develop. Concentrated, monks, a monk as-really-is understands.

"Monks, develop concentration. A concentrated monk, monks, understands [things] as they really are.

"Kiñca yathābhūtaṃ pajānāti? 'Idaṃ dukkhan'ti yathābhūtaṃ pajānāti, 'ayaṃ dukkhasamudayo'ti yathābhūtaṃ pajānāti, 'ayaṃ dukkhanirodho'ti yathābhūtaṃ pajānāti, 'ayaṃ dukkhanirodhagāminī paṭipadā'ti yathābhūtaṃ pajānāti.

"What-and as-really-is understands? 'This suffering' as-really-is understands. 'This suffering-origin' as-really-is understands. 'This suffering-cessation' as-really-is understands. 'This suffering-cessation-going way' as-really-is understands.

"And what does he understand as it really is? He understands as it really is: 'This is suffering.' He understands as it really is: 'This is the origin of suffering.' He understands as it really is: 'This is the cessation of suffering.' He understands as it really is: 'This is the way leading to the cessation of suffering.'

"Samādhiṃ, bhikkhave, bhāvetha. Samāhito, bhikkhave, bhikkhu yathābhūtaṃ pajānāti.

"Concentration, monks, develop. Concentrated, monks, a monk as-really-is understands.

"Monks, develop concentration. A concentrated monk, monks, understands [things] as they really are.

"Tasmātiha, bhikkhave, 'idaṃ dukkhan'ti yogo karaṇīyo, 'ayaṃ dukkhasamudayo'ti yogo karaṇīyo, 'ayaṃ dukkhanirodho'ti yogo karaṇīyo, 'ayaṃ dukkhanirodhagāminī paṭipadā'ti yogo karaṇīyo"ti.

"Therefore, monks, 'This suffering' exertion should-be-made; 'This suffering-origin' exertion should-be-made; 'This suffering-cessation' exertion should-be-made; 'This suffering-cessation-going way' exertion should-be-made."

"Therefore, monks, an exertion should be made [to understand]: 'This is suffering.' An exertion should be made [to understand]: 'This is the origin of suffering.' An exertion should be made [to understand]: 'This is the cessation of suffering.' An exertion should be made [to understand]: 'This is the way leading to the cessation of suffering.'"

Grammatical explanations

samādhiṃ: "concentration"; singular accusative of the masculine noun *samādhi*, the object of the verb *bhāvetha*.

bhikkhave: a vocative plural of *bhikkhu*, monk; the other vocative plural, generally used at the beginning of a discourse to call attention, is *bhikkhavo*.[69]

bhāvetha: second-person plural imperative of *bhāveti*, "develops." The verb, a causative of *bhavati*, "comes to be," literally means "brings into being."

samāhito: "concentrated"; the past participle of the passive verb *samādhiyati*, from which the noun *samādhi* is also derived. It here functions

69. Geiger (§82.5) describes *bhikkhave* as "a Māgadhism [a vestige of the language of Magadha] which has penetrated into the literary language from the popular speech."

as an adjective agreeing in gender, number, and case with the subject, *bhikkhu*.

bhikkhu: "monk"; a masculine singular noun in the nominative case.

yathābhūtaṃ: "as it really is"; an indeclinable adverbial compound (see p. 44) describing *the manner* in which one understands. It is composed of *yathā*, "as, in accordance with," and *bhūtaṃ*, the past participle of *bhavati*: "what has come to be, what is real."

pajānāti: "understands"; a third-person singular verb, in the present indicative. The verb is composed of the prefix *pa-* added to *jānāti*, "knows." Here it is in agreement with *bhikkhu*. In the following sentences, though no subject is mentioned, *bhikkhu* is implicit in the verb itself. Often in Pāli sentences a subject is not mentioned when it is clear from the context.

kiñca: the interrogative pronoun *kiṃ*, "what," followed by *ca*, "and." By sandhi, *-ṃ* is changed to *-ñ*, the palatal nasal corresponding to the palatal *ca* (see p. 16).

idaṃ: "this"; a neuter singular nominative pronoun in agreement with *dukkhaṃ*.

dukkhaṃ: "suffering"; a neuter singular noun in the nominative case. In other contexts *dukkha* functions as an adjective, as in *dukkhā vedanā*, "painful feeling," but here, as the subject of the four noble truths, it is a noun. *Idaṃ dukkhaṃ* is an equational sentence, with *idaṃ* as the subject and *dukkhaṃ* the predicate; hence no verb is needed.

ti: the marker for the end of a direct quotation or an emphatic statement. Before *ti*, short vowels are lengthened and *-ṃ* changes to *-n*, the corresponding dental nasal.

ayaṃ: "this"; a masculine singular nominative pronoun, in agreement with *samudayo*.

dukkhasamudayo: "origin of suffering"; a genitive tappurisa compound (see p. 39) in the nominative case. The compound is made up of *dukkha* and the masculine singular noun *samudayo*, "origin."

dukkhanirodho: "cessation of suffering"; another genitive tappurisa in the nominative case made up of *dukkha* and the masculine singular noun *nirodho*, "cessation."

ayaṃ: The pronoun *ayaṃ*, "this," can be either masculine or feminine, depending on the noun it qualifies. Here it is feminine singular nominative in agreement with *paṭipadā*.

dukkhanirodhagāminī: "going to the cessation of suffering." This is a complex accusative tappurisa compound in the nominative case, qualifying *paṭipadā*. It is made up of *dukkhanirodha*, a genitive tappurisa, and the suffix *-gāminī* (feminine singular of *-gāmin*), "going to, leading to," which takes *dukkhanirodha* as its object in an accusative relationship.[70]

paṭipadā: "way, practice"; a feminine singular noun in the nominative case.

tasmātiha: ind. "therefore," often followed by an imperative (or, as here, a future passive participle suggesting a command). It is probably derived from Vedic Skt *tasmāt*, "therefore," and *iha*, "here, in this case."

yogo: "exertion, effort"; a masculine singular in the nominative case.

karaṇīyo: "should be done, should be made"; a future passive participle (see pp. 31–33) based on the verb *karoti*, "does, makes." It is here masculine singular nominative in agreement with *yogo*.

2. Samaṇabrāhmaṇasutta

Ascetics and Brahmins (SN 56:5; V 416–17)

"Ye hi keci, bhikkhave, atītamaddhānaṃ samaṇā vā brāhmaṇā vā yathābhūtaṃ abhisambujjhiṃsu, sabbe te cattāri ariyasaccāni yathābhūtaṃ abhisambujjhiṃsu. Ye hi keci, bhikkhave, anāgatamaddhānaṃ samaṇā vā brāhmaṇā vā yathābhūtaṃ abhisambujjhissati, sabbe te cattāri ariyasaccāni yathābhūtaṃ abhisambujjhissanti. Ye hi keci, bhikkhave, etarahi samaṇā vā brāhmaṇā vā yathābhūtaṃ abhisambujjhanti, sabbe te cattāri ariyasaccāni yathābhūtaṃ abhisambujjhanti.

"Whatever, monks, past period ascetics or brahmins or as-really-is were fully-enlightened, all those the four noble-truths as-really-is were fully-enlightened. Whatever, monks, future period ascetics or brahmins as-really-is will be fully-enlightened, all those four noble-truths as-really-is will be fully-enlightened. Whatever, monks, now ascetics or brahmins as-really-is are fully-enlightened, all those four noble-truths as-really-is are fully-enlightened.

"Whatever ascetics or brahmins in the past, monks, were fully enlightened [to things] as they really are, they were all fully enlightened to the four

70. For examples of the accusative tappurisa functioning as an adjective in relation to another noun, see Duroiselle §545(i); Perniola §134; and Whitney §1265.

noble truths as they really are. Whatever ascetics or brahmins in the future, monks, will be fully enlightened [to things] as they really are, they will all be fully enlightened to the four noble truths as they really are. Whatever ascetics or brahmins now, monks, are fully enlightened [to things] as they really are, they are all fully enlightened to the four noble truths as they really are.

"Katamāni cattāri? Dukkhaṃ ariyasaccaṃ, dukkhasamudayaṃ ariyasaccaṃ, dukkhanirodhaṃ ariyasaccaṃ, dukkhanirodhagāminī paṭipadā ariyasaccaṃ. Ye hi keci bhikkhave, atītamaddhānaṃ samaṇā vā brāhmaṇā vā . . . anāgatamaddhānaṃ samaṇā vā brāhmaṇā vā . . . etarahi samaṇā vā brāhmaṇā vā yathābhūtaṃ abhisambujjhanti, sabbe te imāni cattāri ariyasaccāni yathābhūtaṃ abhisambujjhanti.

"What four? Suffering noble-truth, suffering-origin noble-truth, suffering-cessation noble-truth, suffering-cessation-going way noble-truth. Whatever, monks, past period ascetics or brahmins . . . future period ascetics or brahmins . . . now ascetics or brahmins as-really-is are fully-enlightened, all those these four noble-truths as-really-is are fully-enlightened.

"What four? The noble truth of suffering, the noble truth of the origin of suffering, the noble truth of the cessation of suffering, the noble truth of the way leading to the cessation of suffering. Whatever ascetics or brahmins in the past . . . Whatever ascetics or brahmins in the future . . . Whatever ascetics or brahmins now are fully enlightened [to things] as they really are, they are all fully enlightened to these four noble truths as they really are.

"Tasmātiha, bhikkhave, 'idaṃ dukkhan'ti yogo karaṇīyo, 'ayaṃ dukkhasamudayo'ti yogo karaṇīyo, 'ayaṃ dukkhanirodho'ti yogo karaṇīyo, 'ayaṃ dukkhanirodhagāminī paṭipadā'ti yogo karaṇīyo"ti.

"Therefore, monks, 'This suffering' exertion should-be-made; 'This suffering-origin' exertion should-be-made; 'This suffering-cessation' exertion should-be-made; 'This suffering-cessation-going way' exertion should-be-made."

"Therefore, monks, an exertion should be made [to understand]: 'This is suffering.' An exertion should be made [to understand]: 'This is the origin of suffering.' An exertion should be made [to understand]: 'This is the cessation of suffering.' An exertion should be made [to understand]: This is the way leading to the cessation of suffering.'"[71]

Grammatical explanations

ye hi keci: "whatever," a general pronoun. *Ye* is a relative pronoun, masculine plural in the nominative case; *hi*, a mere emphatic; *keci*, an indefinite pronoun. The general pronoun extends to all instances of the noun it qualifies, here *samaṇā* and *brāhmaṇā*. It is correlated with *sabbe te*, "all those," where *te* is the demonstrative pronoun and *sabbe* a pronominal adjective qualifying *te* (see p. 20).

atītam: "past"; a past participle of *acceti*, "goes by, elapses." It is here used as an adjective qualifying *addhānaṃ*; through sandhi with the following vowel, *-ṃ* becomes *-m*.

addhānaṃ: "period of time"; an accusative of *addhan*, "an extent [of space or time]." Accusatives are used adverbially to represent a period of time (Duroiselle §598,viii; Perniola §247h).[72]

samaṇā . . . brāhmaṇā: "ascetics [or] brahmins"; the subjects of the relative clause, masculine plurals in the nominative case.

vā: "or," a disjunctive particle. In Pāli, the copulative particles *ca* or *pi* and the disjunctive particle *vā* are usually repeated after each term in the series.

abhisambujjhiṃsu, abhisambujjhissanti, abhisambujjhanti: These are respectively the aorist (past), future, and present tense forms of the verb *abhisambujjhati*, here third-person plurals. The primary verb is *bujjhati*, "understands, becomes enlightened to, awakens to," with two prefixes, *abhi* and *sam*, which respectively suggest superiority and completeness. *Abhisambujjhati* is used only in relation to the perfect enlightenment of a buddha.

sabbe te: "all those"; a pronominal expression completing the relative pronoun *ye hi keci* that opens the sentence.

cattāri: the number "four" in the accusative neuter plural.

71. From this point on I omit the "*tasmātiha*" peroration that concludes each of the suttas that follow.

72. The electronic Buddhanet version of Duroiselle has a typographical error, with the number of the section on the accusative given as 538. This should be corrected to 598.

ariyasaccāni: "noble truths"; the compound can be understood as either a kammadhāraya consisting of an adjective and a noun, "truths that are noble," or a genitive tappurisa, "truths of the noble one." In support of the former, see p. 108; in support of the latter, p. 109. As the object of *abhisambujjhiṃsu*, the compound is a plural accusative.

katamāni: the interrogative pronominal adjective "what?" in the neuter plural nominative (Duroiselle §342; Perniola §43).

anāgatam: "future," literally, "not yet come." *Āgata* is a past participle of *āgacchati*, "comes," negated by the prefix *an-*.

etarahi: "now, at present."

dukkhaṃ ariyasaccaṃ . . . dukkhanirodhagāminī paṭipadā ariyasaccaṃ: There is a disparity between the grammatical construction of the first three truths and the fourth. In the first three, the name of the truth takes on the gender of *saccaṃ*, as is evident in the second and third truths, where the masculine nouns *samudaya* and *nirodha* form neuter compounds, presumably because they function as bahubbīhis qualifying neuter *ariyasaccaṃ*. However, in the fourth truth *paṭipadā* occurs as a feminine, its own proper gender, qualified by a compound ending in *-gāminī*, a feminine termination.

3. Vitakkasutta

Thought (SN 56:7; V 417–18)

"Mā, bhikkhave, pāpake akusale vitakke vitakketha, seyyathīdaṃ: kāmavitakkaṃ, vyāpādavitakkaṃ, vihiṃsāvitakkaṃ. Taṃ kissa hetu? N'ete, bhikkhave, vitakkā atthasaṃhitā nādibrahmacariyakā na nibbidāya na virāgāya na nirodhāya na upasamāya na abhiññāya na sambodhāya na nibbānāya saṃvattanti.

"Do not, monks, bad unwholesome thoughts think, that is, sensual-desire-thought, ill-will-thought, harming-thought. That for what reason? Not these, monks, thoughts good-connected, not-basis-spiritual-life, not to disenchantment, not to dispassion, not to cessation, not to peace, not to direct-knowledge, not to enlightenment, not to nibbāna lead.

"Monks, do not think bad unwholesome thoughts—that is, sensual thought, thought of ill will, thought of harming. For what reason? These thoughts, monks, are unbeneficial; they do not pertain to the basis for the spiritual life; they do not lead to disenchantment, to dispassion, to cessation, to peace, to direct knowledge, to enlightenment, to nibbāna.

"Vitakkentā ca kho tumhe, bhikkhave, 'idaṃ dukkhan'ti vitakkeyyātha, 'ayaṃ dukkhasamudayo'ti vitakkeyyātha, 'ayaṃ dukkhanirodho'ti vitakkeyyātha, 'ayaṃ dukkhanirodhagāminī paṭipadā'ti vitakkeyyātha. Taṃ kissa hetu? Ete, bhikkhave, vitakkā atthasaṃhitā ete ādibrahmacariyakā ete nibbidāya virāgāya nirodhāya upasamāya abhiññāya sambodhāya nibbānāya saṃvattanti."

"Thinking, but, you, monks, 'This suffering' should think; 'This suffering-origin' should think; 'This suffering-cessation' should think; 'This suffering-cessation-going way' should think. That for what reason? These, monks, thoughts good-connected, these basis-spiritual-life, these to disenchantment, to dispassion, to cessation, to peace, to direct-knowledge, to enlightenment, to nibbāna lead."

"When you think, monks, you should think: 'This is suffering'; you should think: 'This is the origin of suffering'; you should think: 'This is the cessation of suffering'; you should think: 'This is the way leading to the cessation of suffering.' For what reason? These thoughts, monks, are beneficial; they pertain to the basis for the spiritual life; they lead to disenchantment, to dispassion, to cessation, to peace, to direct knowledge, to enlightenment, to nibbāna."

Grammatical explanations

mā: a prohibitive particle, "do not," used with an imperative or aorist verb. Here the verb *vitakketha* is a second-person plural imperative of *vitakketi*, "thinks."

pāpake: "bad, evil"; an adjective qualifying *vitakke*.

akusale: "unwholesome, unskillful"; another adjective qualifying *vitakke*.

vitakke: "thoughts"; a masculine plural in the accusative case as the object of *vitakketha*.

seyyathīdaṃ: an indeclinable meaning "that is, as follows, namely," usually introducing a set of terms.[73]

73. According to Geiger (§105.2), *se* is a Māgadhi form preserved in Pāli.

kāmavitakkaṃ: "sensual thought"; a tappurisa compound of *kāma*, "desire, sensuality, sensual pleasure," and *vitakka*, "thought"; as the object of *vitakketha*, it is in the accusative case singular.[74]

vyāpādavitakkaṃ, vihiṃsāvitakkaṃ: "thought of ill will, thought of harming"; also tappurisa compounds constructed like *kāmavitakkaṃ*.

taṃ: an impersonal pronoun, "that," representing the matter being interrogated.

kissa hetu: an idiomatic expression used when asking about the reason for a statement. The commentaries gloss this with *kiṃkāraṇā* or *kena kāraṇena*, "For what reason?"

n'ete: a sandhi formation of *na ete*, "not these."

atthasaṃhitā: "beneficial"; an instrumental tappurisa compound composed of *attha*, "good, benefit, meaning," and *saṃhitā*, a past participle meaning "connected with, endowed with." The compound, which functions as an adjective, is masculine plural nominative in agreement with *vitakkā*.

ādibrahmacariyakā: "pertaining to the basis for the spiritual life"; a bahubbīhi compound composed of *ādi*, "beginning, basis," and *brahmacariya*, "the spiritual life, the holy life,"[75] with the suffix *-kā* turning the compound into an adjective qualifying *vitakkā*.

nibbidāya, virāgāya, nirodhāya, upasamāya, abhiññāya, sambodhāya, nibbānāya: "to disenchantment, to dispassion, to cessation, to peace, to direct knowledge, to enlightenment, to nibbāna." These are datives of purpose (Duroiselle §597,vi; Perniola §259a).

saṃvattanti: "lead to, conduce to"; a third-person plural verb in the present tense.

vitakkentā: "thinking"; a present participle of *vitakketi*, masculine plural nominative.

74. It-a II 93 explains this compound as "thought connected with sensuality," and says it is "thought associated with the defilement of sensuality that occurs in relation to sensual objects" (*kāmavitakko ti kāmapaṭisaṃyutto vitakko, so hi kilesakāmasahito hutvā vatthukāmesu pavattati*). Parallel explanations are given of *vyāpādavitakka* and *vihiṃsāvitakka*.

75. I follow the commentaries, which confirm taking *ādi* as "beginning, starting point." Ps III 355,21–22 says: *Ādibrahmacariyakānī ti maggabrahmacariyassa ādibhūtāni, pubbabhāgapaṭipattibhūtāni* ("*Pertaining to the basis for the spiritual life*: the things that are the starting point of the spiritual life of the path, the things that constitute the preliminary practice").

ca: here used in the disjunctive sense, as meaning "but" rather than "and." See DOP *ca*[2] 2.

kho: According to DOP, this indeclinable "emphasizes the preceding word(s), but is often merely expletive." Here, following *ca*, it reinforces the disjunctive sense of "but." Elsewhere, especially in the expression *atha kho*, it "marks a change of subject or a further stage in a narrative" (DOP).

vitakkeyyātha: "should think"; a second-person plural verb in the optative.

4. Khandhasutta

Aggregates (SN 56:13; V 425–26)

"Cattār'imāni, bhikkhave, ariyasaccāni. Katamāni cattāri? Dukkhaṃ ariyasaccaṃ, dukkhasamudayaṃ ariyasaccaṃ, dukkhanirodhaṃ ariyasaccaṃ, dukkhanirodhagāminī paṭipadā ariyasaccaṃ.

"Four these, monks, noble-truths. What four? Suffering noble-truth, suffering-origin noble-truth, suffering-cessation noble-truth, suffering-cessation-going way noble-truth.

"There are, monks, these four noble truths. What four? The noble truth of suffering, the noble truth of the origin of suffering, the noble truth of the cessation of suffering, the noble truth of the way leading to the cessation of suffering.

"Katamañca, bhikkhave, dukkhaṃ ariyasaccaṃ? 'Pañc'upādānakkhandhā'ti 'ssa vacanīyaṃ, seyyathīdaṃ: rūpupādānakkhandho, vedanupādānakkhandho, saññupādānakkhandho, saṅkhārupādānakkhandho, viññāṇupādānakkhandho. Idaṃ vuccati, bhikkhave, 'dukkhaṃ ariyasaccaṃ.'

"What-and, monks, the suffering noble-truth? 'Five-clinging-aggregates' should be said, that is, the form-clinging-aggregate, the feeling-clinging-aggregate, the perception-clinging-aggregate, the volitional-activities-clinging-aggregate, the consciousness-clinging-aggregate. This is called, monks, the 'suffering noble-truth.'

"And what, monks, is the noble truth of suffering? 'The five clinging-aggregates,' it should be said—that is, the form clinging-aggregate, the feeling clinging-aggregate, the perception clinging-aggregate, the volitional activities clinging-aggregate, the consciousness clinging-aggregate. This is called, monks, the 'noble truth of suffering.'

"Katamañca, bhikkhave, dukkhasamudayaṃ ariyasaccaṃ? Yāyaṃ taṇhā ponobhavikā nandirāgasahagatā tatratatrābhinandinī, seyyathīdaṃ: kāmataṇhā, bhavataṇhā, vibhavataṇhā. Idaṃ vuccati, bhikkhave, 'dukkhasamudayaṃ ariyasaccaṃ.'

"What-and, monks, the suffering-origin noble-truth? Which-this craving again-existence-causing, delight-lust-accompanied, there-there-delighting, that is, sensual-pleasure-craving, existence-craving, non-existence-craving. This is called, monks, the 'suffering-origin noble-truth.'

"And what, monks, is the noble truth of the origin of suffering? It is this craving causing renewed existence, accompanied by delight and lust, delighting here and there—that is, craving for sensual pleasures, craving for existence, craving for non-existence. This is called, monks, the 'noble truth of the origin of suffering.'

"Katamañca, bhikkhave, dukkhanirodhaṃ ariyasaccaṃ? Yo tassāyeva taṇhāya asesavirāganirodho cāgo paṭinissaggo mutti anālayo. Idaṃ vuccati, bhikkhave, 'dukkhanirodhaṃ ariyasaccaṃ.'

"What-and, monks, the suffering-cessation noble-truth? Which of that-same craving without-remainder-fading-cessation, giving-up, relinquishment, freedom, non-attachment. This is called, monks, the 'suffering-cessation noble-truth.'

"And what, monks, is the noble truth of the cessation of suffering? It is the remainderless fading away and cessation of that same craving, its giving up, relinquishment, freedom [from it], non-attachment. This is called, monks, the 'noble truth of the cessation of suffering.'

"Katamañca, bhikkhave, dukkhanirodhagāminī paṭipadā ariya-saccaṃ? Ayameva ariyo aṭṭhaṅgiko maggo, seyyathīdaṃ: sammā-diṭṭhi sammāsaṅkappo sammāvācā sammākammanto sammā-ājīvo sammāvāyāmo sammāsati sammāsamādhi. Idaṃ vuccati, bhikkhave, 'dukkhanirodhagāminī paṭipadā ariyasaccaṃ.' Imāni kho, bhikkhave, cattāri ariyasaccāni."

"What-and, monks, the suffering-cessation-going way noble-truth? This-just noble eightfold path, that is: right-view, right-intention, right-speech, right-action, right-livelihood, right-effort, right-mindfulness, right-concentration. This is called, monks, the 'suffering-cessation-going way noble-truth.' These, monks, the four noble truths."

"And what, monks, is the noble truth of the way leading to the cessation of suffering? It is just this noble eightfold path—that is, right view, right intention, right speech, right action, right livelihood, right effort, right mindfulness, right concentration. This is called, monks, the 'noble truth of the way leading to the cessation of suffering.' These, monks, are the four noble truths."

Grammatical explanations

cattār'imāni: *cattāri*, "four," and *imāni*, the pronoun "these," with an *-i* dropping off on account of sandhi. Both are neuter plural nominatives qualifying *saccāni*, truths. In the Nikāyas, opening statements about numerical sets usually place the number before the pronoun, as here, probably for emphasis. Note that both the nominative and accusative plural of neuter nouns ending in *-a* terminate in *-āni*, and thus the case of the noun must be determined from the context. In equational sentences like this Pāli does not require a verb, but in translation we should add "there are."

katamañca: a sandhi formation of *katamaṃ*, "what?" and *ca*, "and." *Katamaṃ* is neuter singular nominative in agreement with *saccaṃ*. The copulative *ca*, it seems, links the expositions of each of the four truths.

pañc'upādānakkhandhā: "five clinging-aggregates"; a numerical compound of *pañca*, "five," and *upādānakkhandhā*, a genitive tappurisa compound in the nominative masculine plural. The commentaries explain that the *upādānakkhandhā* are the aggregates that serve as "the objective domain of clinging."[76] For more on the relationship between *upādāna* and *khandhā*, see p. 190.

'ssa vacanīyaṃ = assa vacanīyaṃ: The initial vowel *a-* is elided on account of sandhi with the preceding *ti*. *Assa* is the third-person singular optative of *atthi*, hence "should be," here used as an auxiliary verb in relation to *vacanīyaṃ*, a future passive participle of *vuccati*, "is said." The optative auxiliary verb and the future passive participle in combination mean "should be said." The suttas often use the construction *ti 'ssa vacanīyaṃ* when explaining how to reply to a question about the teaching.

idaṃ: the neuter singular nominative pronoun, "this," qualifying *dukkhaṃ ariyasaccaṃ*.

vuccati: "is called"; a passive verb based on the root *vac*. The present active verb *vatti* (Skt *vakti*) is not found in the suttas, but the a-aorists *avoca* and *avocuṃ* are common.

yāyaṃ: a sandhi of *yā*, "which," a relative pronoun, and *ayaṃ*, "this." *Yā* and *ayaṃ* are feminine as qualifying *taṇhā*, craving; they are correlated with the demonstrative pronoun *idaṃ*, which is neuter because it qualifies *ariyasaccaṃ* (see p. 64).

ponobhavikā: "causing renewed existence"; a bahubbīhi compound derived from *punabbhava*, "renewed existence," composed of the adverb *puna(r)*, "again," and the noun *bhava*, "existence." In forming the compound, the first vowel of *puna(r)* is strengthened (*u* > *o*) and *-ar* becomes *o*.[77] Because *pono* ends in the heavy syllable *-no*, the *bh* in *bhava* is not duplicated as it is in *punabbhava*. The suffix *-ikā* enables the compound to serve as an adjective qualifying *taṇhā*. The Saṃyutta commentary (Spk II 264,7) glosses *ponobhavikā* with *punabbhavanibbattikā*, "productive of renewed existence."

nandirāgasahagatā: "accompanied by delight and lust"; a complex instrumental tappurisa compound (Duroiselle §554) describing *taṇhā*. It includes a dvanda (see p. 36) made up of *nandi*, "delight," and *rāga*, "lust," with the suffix *-sahagatā*, "going along with, accompanying." As modifying *taṇhā*, the compound is feminine singular.

76. *Upādānānaṃ gocarā khandhā upādānakkhandhā* (Abhidhammatthasaṅgaha-ṭīkā, VRI 201). On the distinction between *khandhā* and *upādānakkhandhā*, see SN 22:48 (III 47–48) and Spk II 270.

77. On the change of *-ar*, *-as* to *-o*, see Geiger §66.2.

tatratatrābhinandinī: "delighting here and there"; a complex bahubbīhi, with *tatratatra* a dvanda meaning "in various objects" or "in various realms" (Perniola §127a). *Abhinandinī*, "delighting," is based on the neuter noun *abhinandana*, with the feminine suffix *-inī* facilitating its adjectival function as modifying *taṇhā*.

kāmataṇhā, bhavataṇhā, vibhavataṇhā: "craving for sensual pleasures, craving for existence, craving for non-existence"; three locative tappurisa compounds enumerating the kinds of craving, which takes its objects in the locative case. The Dīgha commentary defines them thus: "*Sensual craving* is a name for lust for the five objects of sensual pleasure. *Craving for existence* is a designation for lust that has arisen as a yearning for existence—that is, lust for existence in the form and formless realms accompanied by the eternalist view—and attachment to jhāna. *Craving for non-existence* is a designation for lust accompanied by the annihilationist view."[78]

yo: a relative pronoun qualifying *-nirodho*, hence nominative masculine singular; it is correlated with the neuter *idaṃ*, which qualifies *ariyasaccaṃ*.

tassāyeva: *tassā* is a feminine demonstrative pronoun in the genitive case, qualifying *taṇhāya*, with *eva* an emphatic indicating that the cessation of *dukkha* depends on the cessation of "that same" craving spoken of in the second noble truth. The semivowel *-y-* is inserted for euphony.

asesavirāganirodho: "the remainderless fading away and cessation"; a complex kammadhāraya compound with *asesa*, "remainderless" (negation of *sesa*, "remainder"), modifying both *virāga*, "fading away," and *nirodho*, "cessation." *Virāga* occurs in the suttas in two senses: fading away and dispassion. The former is more apt here. The Saṃyutta commentary explains: "All these terms are synonyms for nibbāna. Since it is in dependence on nibbāna that craving fades away and ceases without remainder, nibbāna is called the 'remainderless fading away and cessation of that same craving.'"[79]

78. Sv III 800,5–9: *Kāme taṇhā kāmataṇhā, pañcakāmaguṇikarāgass'etaṃ nāmaṃ. Bhave taṇhā bhavataṇhā, bhavapatthanāvasena uppannassa sassatadiṭṭhisahagatassa rūpārūpabhavarāgassa ca jhānanikantiyā c'etaṃ adhivacanaṃ. Vibhave taṇhā vibhavataṇhā, ucchedadiṭṭhisahagatarāgass'etaṃ adhivacanaṃ.*

79. Spk III 800,35: *Sabbāni nibbānavevacanān'eva. Nibbānaṃ hi āgamma taṇhā asesā virajjati nirujjhati, tasmā taṃ "tassāyeva taṇhāya asesavirāganirodho"ti vuccati.*

cāgo paṭinissaggo mutti anālayo: "giving up, relinquishment, freedom [from it], non-attachment"; four additional terms signifying the elimination of craving, all nominative singulars.

ayameva: the masculine nominative pronoun *ayaṃ* followed by the emphatic *eva*, with change from *-ṃ* to *-m* due to sandhi with the vowel.

aṭṭhaṅgiko: "eightfold"; a bahubbīhi built on a numerical compound (Duroiselle §551; Perniola §138d), composed of *aṭṭha*, "eight," and *aṅga*, "factor," with the suffix *-iko* facilitating its function as an adjective qualifying *maggo*.

sammādiṭṭhi: "right view." For definitions of the eight path factors, see pp. 477–81. All the terms for the path factors are kammadhāraya compounds composed of the adverb *sammā* and the noun denoting the specific factor.

5. Koṭigāmasutta

Koṭigāma (SN 56:21; V 431–42)

Ekaṃ samayaṃ bhagavā vajjīsu viharati koṭigāme. Tatra kho bhagavā bhikkhū āmantesi: "Catunnaṃ, bhikkhave, ariyasaccānaṃ ananubodhā appaṭivedhā evamidaṃ dīghamaddhānaṃ sandhāvitaṃ saṃsaritaṃ mamañc'eva tumhākañca.

One occasion the Blessed One among the Vajjis was dwelling at Koṭigāma. There the Blessed One the monks addressed: "Of four, monks, noble-truths through non-understanding, through non-penetration, thus-this long-journey run roamed of me-and of you-and.

On one occasion the Blessed One was dwelling among the Vajjis at Koṭigāma. There the Blessed One addressed the monks thus: "Monks, it is because of not understanding and not penetrating the four noble truths that you and I have run and roamed through this long journey [of saṃsāra].

"Katamesaṃ catunnaṃ? Dukkhassa, bhikkhave, ariyasaccassa ananubodhā appaṭivedhā evamidaṃ dīghamaddhānaṃ sandhāvitaṃ saṃsaritaṃ mamañc'eva tumhākañca. Dukkhasamudayassa ariyasaccassa . . . Dukkhanirodhassa ariyasaccassa . . . Dukkhanirodhagāminiyā paṭipadāya

ariyasaccassa ananubodhā appaṭivedhā evamidaṃ dīghamaddhānaṃ sandhāvitaṃ saṃsaritaṃ mamañc'eva tumhākañca.

"Of what four? Of suffering, monks, noble-truth through non-understanding, through non-penetration, thus-this long-journey run roamed of me-and of you-and. Of suffering-origin noble-truth . . . of suffering-cessation noble-truth . . . of suffering-cessation-going way noble-truth through non-understanding, through non-penetration, thus-this long-journey run roamed of me-and of you-and.

"What four? It is, monks, because of not understanding and not penetrating the noble truth of suffering that you and I have run and roamed through this long journey [of saṃsāra]. It is because of not understanding and not penetrating the noble truth of the origin of suffering . . . the noble truth of the cessation of suffering . . . the noble truth of the way leading to the cessation of suffering that you and I have run and roamed through this long jouney [of saṃsāra].

"Tayidaṃ, bhikkhave, dukkhaṃ ariyasaccaṃ anubuddhaṃ paṭividdhaṃ, dukkhasamudayaṃ ariyasaccaṃ anubuddhaṃ paṭividdhaṃ, dukkhanirodhaṃ ariyasaccaṃ anubuddhaṃ paṭividdhaṃ, dukkhanirodhagāminī paṭipadā ariyasaccaṃ anubuddhaṃ paṭividdhaṃ. Ucchinnā bhavataṇhā, khīṇā bhavanetti, natthi dāni punabbhavo"ti.

"That-this, monks, suffering noble-truth understood penetrated, suffering-origin noble-truth understood penetrated, suffering-cessation noble-truth understood penetrated, suffering-cessation-going way noble-truth understood penetrated. Cut-off existence-craving; destroyed existence-conduit; there is not now again-existence."

"This noble truth of suffering, monks, has been understood and penetrated. This noble truth of the origin of suffering has been understood and penetrated. This noble truth of the cessation of suffering has been understood and penetrated. This noble truth of the way leading to the cessation of suffering has been understood and penetrated. Craving for existence has been cut off; the conduit to existence has been destroyed; now there is no renewed existence."

Grammatical explanations

ekaṃ samayaṃ: "one occasion, one time"; an accusative used adverbially for a period of time.

bhagavā: "the Blessed One," the Buddha; the nominative singular of *bhagavat*, a possessive noun meaning literally "one who possesses (*-vat*) fortune (or excellence)."

Vajjīsu: the name of the people of the Vajji confederacy, here a locative plural.

viharati: "lives, dwells"; a third-person singular verb used as a historical present (Duroiselle §611,vi; Perniola §271d).

Koṭigāme: the name of a village in the Vajji country, here locative singular.

tatra: "there"; an indeclinable indicating place.

kho: a mere particle, when used with *atha* or *tatra* indicates the continuation of a narrative.

āmantesi: "addressed"; a third-person singular aorist of *āmanteti*.

bhikkhū: the plural accusative.

catunnaṃ: genitive plural of *cattāri*, "four," in agreement with *ariyasaccānaṃ*.

ananubodhā: "through non-understanding"; negation of *anubodhā*, a masculine singular noun in the ablative case, indicating cause, reason, or motive (Duroiselle §600,xi; Perniola §257e).

appaṭivedhā: "through non-penetration"; a negation of *paṭivedha*, a masculine singular noun in the ablative case. When prefixed by the negative *a-*, the initial *p* is doubled through the influence of the *-r-* in the Skt prefix *prati*, which is eliminated in Pāli.

evam: "thus"; *evaṃ* with *-ṃ* changed to *-m* in sandhi with the following vowel.

idaṃ: a neuter singular pronoun, "this," in the nominative case qualifying the noun that follows.

dīghamaddhānaṃ: "long journey"; an adjective, *dīghaṃ*, followed by a singular noun, *addhānaṃ*, a nominative functioning as the passive grammatical subject. The logical subjects of the sentence are represented by the genitive pronouns that follow, the actions by the past participles. See pp. 74–75.

sandhāvitaṃ: a past participle of the verb *sandhāvati*, "runs along," qualifying *addhānaṃ*.

saṃsaritaṃ: a past participle of the verb *saṃsarati*, "roams," also qualifying *addhānaṃ*. It is from this verb that the noun *saṃsāra* is derived.

mamañc'eva: a sandhi formation of *mamaṃ* and *c'eva* (see below). *Mamaṃ* is a euphonic form of *mama*, "of me," with *-ṃ* changed to palatal *-ñ* before palatal *ca*; the pronoun is a singular genitive here referring to the Buddha himself.

c'eva: "and." The addition of *eva* to the initial *ca* is typical in conjunctions and in series of negations; it is merely stylistic and does not imply either emphasis or exclusivity.

tumhākañca: a sandhi formation of *tumhākaṃ* and *ca*, "and." *Tumhākaṃ* is a plural genitive pronoun, "of you," referring to the monks. The two pronouns—*mamaṃ* and *tumhākaṃ*—are instances of the "subjective genitive," the genitive used to represent the agent of the action, often with an instrumental sense (see Wijesekera §142, Duroiselle §596; Perniola §260b). The Dīgha commentary to a corresponding passage actually glosses *mamaṃ* and *tumhākaṃ* with their corresponding instrumentals.[80] The actions are represented by the two past participles, *sandhāvitaṃ* and *saṃsaritaṃ*. The syntax is almost the converse of that used in modern English. Whereas a normal English sentence would represent the agents as the active subjects and the "long journey" as the object—as I render it in the natural translation—the Pāli makes *dīghamaddhānaṃ* the grammatical subject, while the logical subject or effective agents, the persons who run and roam through this long journey, occur in the genitive. For similar instances, see pp. 75–77.

tayidaṃ: "that this"; a sandhi of *taṃ* and *idaṃ*, with the *-ṃ* dropping out and the semivowel *-y-* inserted for euphony (see Geiger §72.2). In English *tayidaṃ* has the sense of an emphatic "this."

anubuddhaṃ: "understood"; the past participle of *anubujjhati*, nominative neuter as qualifying *ariyasaccaṃ*.

paṭividdhaṃ: "penetrated"; the past participle of *pativijjhati*, also nominative neuter as qualifying *ariyasaccaṃ*.

ucchinnā: "cut off"; the past participle of *ucchindati*, feminine nominative in agreement with *bhavataṇhā*, "craving for existence."

khīṇā: "destroyed, worn away"; the past participle of *khīyati*, "is destroyed, is worn away," also feminine nominative in agreement with *netti*.

bhavanetti: "the conduit to existence." *Netti* (from the verb *neti*) is "that which leads," in this case, to *bhava*, existence. The compound is a dative tappurisa.

80. See Sv II 543,3: *Mamañceva tumhākañcā ti mayā ca tumhehi ca.*

natthi (= *na* + *atthi*): "there is not."
dāni: abridgment of *idāni* (Skt *idānīṃ*), "now."[81]
punabbhavo: "renewed existence"; a kammadhāraya with the adverb *puna(r)* modifying the noun *bhavo*. The *-rbh-* cluster of Skt *punarbhava* is represented in Pāli by doubling of the consonant, *-bbh*.

6. Āsavakkhayasutta

Destruction of the Influxes (SN 56:25; V 434)

"Jānato'haṃ, bhikkhave, passato āsavānaṃ khayaṃ vadāmi, no ajānato apassato. Kiñca, bhikkhave, jānato passato āsavānaṃ khayo hoti? 'Idaṃ dukkhan'ti, bhikkhave, jānato passato āsavānaṃ khayo hoti. 'Ayaṃ dukkha-samudayo'ti jānato passato āsavānaṃ khayo hoti. 'Ayaṃ dukkhanirodho'ti jānato passato āsavānaṃ khayo hoti. 'Ayaṃ dukkhanirodhagāminī paṭi-padā'ti jānato passato āsavānaṃ khayo hoti. Evaṃ kho, bhikkhave, jānato evaṃ passato āsavānaṃ khayo hoti."

"For one-knowing, I, monks, for one-seeing, of the influxes destruction, say, not for one-not-knowing, for one-not-seeing. What-and, monks, for one-knowing, for one-seeing, of the influxes destruction occurs? 'This suffering,' monks, for one-knowing, for one-seeing, of the influxes destruction occurs. 'This suffering-origin,' for one-knowing, for one-seeing, of the influxes destruction occurs. 'This suffering-cessation,' for one-knowing, for one-seeing, of the influxes destruction occurs. 'This suffering-cessation-going way,' for one-knowing, for one-seeing, of the influxes destruction occurs. Thus, monks, for one-knowing, thus for-one seeing, of the influxes destruction occurs."

"Monks, I say that the destruction of the influxes occurs for one knowing, for one seeing, not for one not knowing, not seeing. For one knowing what, monks, for one seeing what, does the destruction of the influxes occur? It is, monks, for one knowing and seeing, 'This is suffering,' that the destruction of the influxes occurs. It is for one knowing and seeing, 'This is the origin of suffering,' that the destruction of the influxes occurs. It is for one knowing and seeing, 'This is the cessation of suffering,' that the destruction of the

81. Geiger §66.1 cites other instances where an initial vowel of the Skt word has been lost in Pāli.

influxes occurs. It is for one knowing and seeing, 'This is the way leading to the cessation of suffering,' that the destruction of the influxes occurs. It is, monks, for one knowing thus, for one seeing thus, that the destruction of the influxes occurs."

Grammatical explanations

jānato: "for one knowing"; the masculine singular present participle of the verb *jānāti*. *Passato*: "for one seeing"; the present participle of the verb *passati*. I take the case in both instances to be dative, of the type Wijesekera §95 calls "datives of possession," with the sense: "one who knows and sees thus *has* the destruction of the influxes." Other grammarians, however, take the case in such constructions to be genitive. Parallel constructions are at 2.11, 2.15, 3.3, and 4.4.

'haṃ: the first-person singular pronoun *ahaṃ*, "I," with elision of the initial vowel because of sandhi with the preceding vowel.

āsavānaṃ: genitive plural of *āsava*, "influx," derived from the verb *āsavati*, "flows (in or out)." The word has also been translated as taint, canker, effluent, contaminant, and intoxicant. The term suggests the way that certain defilements "flow into" the mind or "flow out" through the sense faculties toward their objects. The Nikāyas mention three *āsavas*: *kāmāsava*, "the influx of sensuality"; *bhavāsava*, "the influx of [craving for] existence"; and *avijjāsava*, "the influx of ignorance." The Abhidhamma adds a fourth, *diṭṭhāsava*, "the influx of views." These have likely been designated *āsavas* because they are the most primordial defilements obscuring cognition and holding beings in bondage to the cycle of rebirths.[82]

khayaṃ: "destruction," here accusative singular, as object of the verb *vadāmi*,

82. The Majjhima commentary (Ps I 61,13–18) explains: "They are called *āsavas* because they flow. What is meant is that they stream out through the eye . . . through the mind. Or they flow up to [the stage of] change-of-lineage, or they flow up to the highest realm of existence. They are also called *āsavas* because they have been long fermented, like certain wines, which are called *āsavas* in that they have been long fermented." (*Tattha āsavantī ti* ***āsavā****, cakkhutopi . . . manatopi sandanti pavattantī ti vuttaṃ hoti. Dhammato yāva gotrabhuṃ okāsato yāva bhavaggaṃ savantīti vā āsavā, ete dhamme etañca okāsaṃ anto karitvā pavattantī ti attho. . . . Cirapārivāsiyaṭṭhena madirādayo āsavā, āsavā viyā ti pi āsavā.*)

"(I) say." Just below the nominative singular, *khayo*, is the grammatical subject of the verb *hoti*.

no ajānato apassato: "not for one not knowing, not seeing"; a negation (by *no*) of two negative present participles in the dative case.

7. Tathasutta

Real (SN 56:27; V 435)

"Cattār'imāni, bhikkhave, ariyasaccāni. Katamāni cattāri? Dukkhaṃ ariyasaccaṃ, dukkhasamudayaṃ ariyasaccaṃ, dukkhanirodhaṃ ariyasaccaṃ, dukkhanirodhagāminī paṭipadā ariyasaccaṃ. Imāni kho, bhikkhave, cattāri ariyasaccāni tathāni avitathāni anaññathāni; tasmā 'ariyasaccānī'ti vuccanti."

"Four these, monks, noble-truths. What four? Suffering noble-truth, suffering-origin noble-truth, suffering-cessation noble-truth, suffering-cessation-going way noble-truth. These, monks, four noble-truths real, not-unreal, not-otherwise; therefore 'noble-truths' are called."

"There are, monks, these four noble truths. What four? The noble truth of suffering, the noble truth of the origin of suffering, the noble truth of the cessation of suffering, the noble truth of the way leading to the cessation of suffering. These four noble truths, monks, are real, not unreal, not otherwise; therefore they are called 'noble truths.'"

Grammatical explanations

tathāni avitathāni anaññathāni: "real, not unreal, not otherwise." All three terms are neuter plural adjectives in agreement with *ariyasaccāni*. *Tathā* is originally an adverb of manner, "thus," turned into an adjective. The four truths are *tathāni*, "real, actual," because they accord with reality. *Avitathāni* is the negation (by the prefix *a-*) of an absence (by the prefix *vi-*), thus a double negation meaning "not devoid of reality, not unreal." *Anaññathāni* is another negation of an adjective based on an adverb, *aññathā*, "otherwise," hence meaning "not otherwise," not other than the way things are.

tasmā "ariyasaccānī"ti vuccanti: "therefore they are called 'noble truths.'"

On this explanation, *ariyasacca* is a kammadhāraya compound, "a truth that is noble."

8. Lokasutta
The World (SN 56:28; V 435)

"Cattār'imāni, bhikkhave, ariyasaccāni. . . . Sadevake loke samārake sabrahmake, sassamaṇabrāhmaṇiyā pajāya sadevamanussāya, tathāgato ariyo; tasmā 'ariyasaccānī'ti vuccanti."

"Four these, monks, noble-truths. . . . In with-devas world, with-Māra, with-Brahmā, in with-ascetics-brahmins population, with-devas-humans, the Tathāgata the noble one; therefore 'noble-truths' are called."

"There are, monks, these four noble truths. . . . In the world with its devas, with Māra, with Brahmā, in this population with its ascetics and brahmins, with its devas and humans, the Tathāgata is the noble one; therefore they are called 'noble truths.'"

Grammatical explanations

sadevake loke samārake sabrahmake: "in the world with its devas, with Māra, with Brahmā." *Loke* is a masculine noun in the locative case, preceded and followed by adjectives constructed by prefixing *sa-*, "together with," respectively, to *deva, māra*, and *brahmā*, and adding the suffix *-ka*, which becomes *-ke* as modifying the locative singular *loke*. We find here a common syntactical pattern in Pāli: when a series of adjectives (including adjectival compounds and present participles) modifies a noun, the first precedes the noun and the others follow it. This might be represented as M1 N M2 M3 . . . , where N represents the noun and M the modifiers.

sassamaṇabrāhmaṇiyā pajāya sadevamanussāya: "in this population with its ascetics and brahmins, with its devas and humans." *Pajāya* is the singular locative of the feminine noun *pajā*, "the created order, the population." It is first described by the bahubbīhi *sassamaṇabrāhmaṇiyā*, built on the dvanda compound *samaṇabrāhmaṇa* with prefix *sa-*. The double *-ss-* occurs through the influence of the *-śr-* cluster in Skt *śramaṇa*. The compound is turned into an adjective by the suffix *-iyā*, a feminine singular locative in agreement with *pajāya*. *Sadevamanussāya* is a bahubbīhi formed by prefixing *sa-* to the dvanda *devamanussa*, which takes a feminine locative termination agreeing with *pajāya*.

tathāgato: untranslated; an honorific designation of the Buddha, explained by the commentaries as meaning (among other things) "thus come" (*tathā āgato*)—that is, come in the way the previous buddhas have come—and "thus gone" (*tathā gato*), gone to nibbāna by cultivating the factors of the noble path.[83] The word is a kammadhāraya compound composed of an adverb and a past participle.

tasmā "ariyasaccānī"ti vuccanti: "therefore they are called 'noble truths.'" On this explanation, *ariyasacca* is a tappurisa compound, "a truth of the noble one"—that is, of the Buddha.

9. Pariññeyyasutta

To Be Fully Understood (SN 56:29; V 436)

"Cattār'imāni, bhikkhave, ariyasaccāni. . . . Imesaṃ kho, bhikkhave, catunnaṃ ariyasaccānaṃ atthi ariyasaccaṃ pariññeyyaṃ; atthi ariyasaccaṃ pahātabbaṃ; atthi ariyasaccaṃ sacchikātabbaṃ; atthi ariyasaccaṃ bhāvetabbaṃ.

"Four these, monks, noble-truths. . . . Of these, monks, four noble-truths there is a noble-truth to-be-fully-understood; there is a noble-truth to-be-abandoned; there is a noble-truth to-be-realized; there is a noble-truth to-be-developed.

"Monks, there are these four noble truths. . . . Of these four noble truths, monks, there is a noble truth to be fully understood; there is a noble truth to be abandoned; there is a noble truth to be realized; there is a noble truth to be developed.

"Katamañca, bhikkhave, ariyasaccaṃ pariññeyyaṃ? Dukkhaṃ, bhikkhave, ariyasaccaṃ pariññeyyaṃ; dukkhasamudayaṃ ariyasaccaṃ pahātabbaṃ;

83. For a translation of the long commentarial explanation of *tathāgata*, see Bodhi 2007, 317–30.

dukkhanirodhaṃ ariyasaccaṃ sacchikātabbaṃ; dukkhanirodhagāminī paṭipadā ariyasaccaṃ bhāvetabbaṃ."

"What-and, monks, the noble-truth to-be-fully-understood? Suffering, monks, noble-truth to-be-fully-understood; suffering-origin noble-truth to-be-abandoned; suffering-cessation noble-truth to-be-realized; suffering-cessation-going way noble-truth to-be-developed."

"And what, monks, is the noble truth that is to be fully understood? The noble truth of suffering is to be fully understood; the noble truth of the origin of suffering is to be abandoned; the noble truth of the cessation of suffering is to be realized; the noble truth of the way leading to the cessation of suffering is to be developed."

Grammatical explanations

imesaṃ: "of these"; a neuter plural genitive used in apposition to *catunnaṃ ariyasaccānaṃ*.

atthi: "there is."

pariññeyyaṃ: "to be fully understood"; a future passive participle from the verb *parijānāti*, based on the root *ñā* with prefix *pari*.

pahātabbaṃ: "to be abandoned"; a future passive participle from the verb *pajahati*, based on the root *hā* with prefix *pa*.

sacchikātabbaṃ: "to be realized"; a future passive participle from the verb *sacchikaroti*. The verb is based on *karoti*, "to do, to make," + *saccha*, "with one's own eyes," with change of *-a-* to *-i-* before *karoti*.

bhāvetabbaṃ: "to be developed"; a future passive participle from the verb *bhāveti* (see p. 89).

The four future passive participles, neuter singulars in agreement with *saccaṃ*, indicate the four tasks to be performed with respect to the four noble truths. When these tasks are completed, the four truths are described by their respective past participles (as at SN V 422): *pariññātaṃ, pahīnaṃ, sacchikataṃ*, and *bhāvitaṃ*, "fully understood, abandoned, realized, developed."

10. Siṃsapāvanasutta
The Siṃsapa Grove (SN 56:31; V 437–38)

Ekaṃ samayaṃ bhagavā kosambiyaṃ viharati siṃsapāvane. Atha kho bhagavā parittāni siṃsapāpaṇṇāni pāṇinā gahetvā bhikkhū āmantesi: "Taṃ kiṃ maññatha, bhikkhave, katamaṃ nu kho bahutaraṃ: yāni vā mayā parittāni siṃsapāpaṇṇāni pāṇinā gahitāni yāni vā upari[84] *siṃsapāvane"ti?*

One occasion the Blessed One at Kosambī was dwelling, in a siṃsapā-grove. Then the Blessed One a few siṃsapā-leaves with hand having taken, the monks addressed: "That what do you think, monks, which more: which or by me few siṃsapā-leaves with hand taken, which or above in the siṃsapā-grove?"

On one occasion the Blessed One was dwelling at Kosambī in a siṃsapā grove. Then the Blessed One took a few siṃsapā leaves with his hand and addressed the monks: "What do you think about this, monks, which is more numerous: these few siṃsapā leaves that I have taken with my hand or those above in the siṃsapā grove?"

"Appamattakāni, bhante, bhagavatā parittāni siṃsapāpaṇṇāni pāṇinā gahitāni; atha kho etān'eva bahutarāni yadidaṃ upari siṃsapāvane"ti.

"Trifling, Bhante, by the Blessed One few siṃsapā-leaves with hand taken; but these indeed more, that is, above in the siṃsapā-grove."

"Bhante, the siṃsapā leaves that the Blessed One has taken in his hand are few, but those above in the siṃsapā grove are indeed more numerous."

"Evameva kho, bhikkhave, etadeva bahutaraṃ yaṃ vo mayā abhiññāya anakkhātaṃ. Kasmā c'etaṃ, bhikkhave, mayā anakkhātaṃ? Na h'etaṃ, bhikkhave, atthasaṃhitaṃ nādibrahmacariyakaṃ na nibbidāya na virāgāya na nirodhāya na upasamāya na abhiññāya na sambodhāya na nibbānāya saṃvattati; tasmā taṃ mayā anakkhātaṃ.

84. I here follow Ce and Ee. Be has *yadidaṃ upari*, which seems less satisfactory. But *yadidaṃ upari* is appropriate just below, in the reply of the monks.

"Just-so, monks, this-indeed more which to you by me having directly known not-expounded. Why and this, monks, by me not-expounded? Not because this, monks, good-connected, not-basis-spiritual-life, not to disenchantment, not to dispassion, not to cessation, not to peace, not to direct-knowledge, not to enlightenment, not to nibbāna leads; therefore that by me not-expounded.

"So too, monks, that which I have directly known but have not expounded to you is more numerous. And why, monks, have I not expounded this? Because this is unbeneficial; this does not pertain to the basis for the spiritual life; it does not lead to disenchantment, to dispassion, to cessation, to peace, to direct knowledge, to enlightenment, to nibbāna. Therefore I have not expounded it.

"Kiñca, bhikkhave, mayā akkhātaṃ? 'Idaṃ dukkhan'ti, bhikkhave, mayā akkhātaṃ; 'ayaṃ dukkhasamudayo'ti mayā akkhātaṃ; 'ayaṃ dukkhanirodho'ti mayā akkhātaṃ; 'ayaṃ dukkhanirodhagāminī paṭipadā'ti mayā akkhātaṃ. Kasmā c'etaṃ, bhikkhave, mayā akkhātaṃ? Etaṃ hi, bhikkhave, atthasaṃhitaṃ etaṃ ādibrahmacariyakaṃ etaṃ nibbidāya virāgāya nirodhāya upasamāya abhiññāya sambodhāya nibbānāya saṃvattati; tasmā taṃ mayā akkhātaṃ."

"What-and, monks, by me expounded? 'This suffering,' monks, by me expounded. 'This suffering-origin' by me expounded; 'This suffering-cessation' by me expounded; 'This suffering-cessation-going way' by me expounded. Why and this, monks, by me expounded? This because, monks, good-connected, this basis-spiritual-life, this to disenchantment, to dispassion, to cessation, to peace, to direct-knowledge, to enlightenment, to nibbāna leads; therefore that by me expounded."

"And what, monks, have I expounded? I have expounded: 'This is suffering'; I have expounded: 'This is the origin of suffering'; I have expounded: 'This is the cessation of suffering'; I have expounded: 'This is the way leading to the cessation of suffering.' And why, monks, have I expounded this? Because this is beneficial; this pertains to the basis for the spiritual life; this leads to disenchantment, to dispassion, to cessation, to peace, to direct knowledge, to enlightenment, to nibbāna. Therefore I have expounded this."

Grammatical explanations

kosambiyaṃ: "at Kosambī"; a feminine noun designating the city, here in the locative case.

siṃsapāvane: "in a siṃsapā grove"; a genitive tappurisa compound in the locative case ("a grove of siṃsapā trees").

parittāni: "few, small, limited"; a neuter plural adjective in the accusative case qualifying *siṃsapāpaṇṇāni*.

siṃsapāpaṇṇāni: "siṃsapā leaves"; a genitive tappurisa compound ("leaves of a siṃsapā tree"), neuter plural in the accusative case as the object of *gahetvā*.

pāṇinā: "with the hand"; an instrumental singular of *pāṇi*.

gahetvā: "having taken"; an absolutive of the verb *gaṇhāti*.

taṃ kiṃ maññatha: "what do you think about this?" The pronoun *taṃ* is the object, *kiṃ* an interrogative meaning "what?" and *maññatha* the second person plural interrogative of *maññati*.

katamaṃ: The interrogative "what?" is here neuter singular as qualifying *bahutaraṃ*, an impersonal subject.

nu: an interrogative particle, indicating that the sentence poses a question.

bahutaraṃ: "more," *bahu*, "much," with the comparative suffix *-tara*. The gender is neuter.

yāni: the relative pronoun in the neuter plural qualifying *-paṇṇāni*. The *vā* after each occurrence of *yāni* establishes a disjunction between *mayā parittāni siṃsapāpaṇṇāni pāṇinā gahitāni* (the few siṃsapā leaves the Buddha has taken up in his hand) and *upari siṃsapāvane* (those above in the siṃsapā grove).

mayā: "by me"; the instrumental of the first-person singular pronoun.

gahitāni: "taken"; the past participle of *gaṇhāti*, here neuter plural as qualifying *siṃsapāpaṇṇāni*, the nominative grammatical subject of the sentence.

upari: "above"; an indeclinable.

appamattakāni: "trifling, insignificant"; a bahubbīhi compound composed of *appa*, "little," and *-matta*, "amount," with the adjectival suffix *-kāni* (from *-ka*), a neuter plural qualifying *siṃsapāpaṇṇāni*.

bhante: respectful vocative used as an address for the Buddha, and also by junior monks when addressing senior monks and by laypeople when addressing monks.

atha kho: often this serves to indicate the continuation of a narrative, but in this context, as introducing a comparison, it is best rendered "but rather."

etān'eva bahutarāni: "just these are more numerous." The final vowel of *etāni* is elided through sandhi with the initial vowel of *eva*, an emphatic particle.

yadidaṃ (= *yaṃ* + *idaṃ*): an adverbial expression meaning "that is, namely."[85]

evameva: "just so, in the same way," a sandhi of *evaṃ* and *eva*.

etadeva (= *etaṃ* + *eva*): the neuter pronoun "this" with emphatic *eva*.

vo: "to you"; an enclitic (internal) pronoun, second-person plural in the dative case. On this type of pronoun, see pp. 19–20.

abhiññāya: "having directly known"; an absolutive of *abhijānāti*.

anakkhātaṃ: "not expounded"; a negation (*an-*) of the past participle *akkhātaṃ*.

kasmā: "why?"; an interrogative.

atthasaṃhitaṃ . . . saṃvattati: see p. 96.

tasmā: "therefore"; the demonstrative used adverbally, correlated with *kasmā*.

11. Daṇḍasutta

The Stick (SN 56:33; V 439–40)

"Seyyathāpi, bhikkhave, daṇḍo uparivehāsaṃ khitto sakimpi mūlena nipatati, sakimpi aggena nipatati, evameva kho, bhikkhave, avijjānīvaraṇā sattā taṇhāsaṃyojanā sandhāvantā saṃsarantā sakimpi asmā lokā paraṃ lokaṃ gacchanti, sakimpi parasmā lokā imaṃ lokaṃ āgacchanti. Taṃ kissa hetu? Adiṭṭhattā, bhikkhave, catunnaṃ ariyasaccānaṃ. Katamesaṃ catunnaṃ? Dukkhassa ariyasaccassa . . . dukkhanirodhagāminiyā paṭipadāya ariyasaccassa."

"Just as, monks, a stick up-air thrown, once-also by bottom falls, once-also by top falls, just-so, monks, ignorance-hindrance beings craving-fetter running

85. Geiger §72.1 cites *yad* and *etad* as instances of the restoration of an original *-d-* to avoid hiatus.

roaming, once-also from this world to the other world go, once-also from the other world to this world come. That for what reason? Because of not-seenness, monks, of the four noble-truths. Of what four? Of the suffering noble-truth . . . of the suffering-cessation-going way noble-truth."

"Just as, monks, a stick, thrown up into the air, sometimes falls on its bottom and sometimes falls on its top, just so, monks, beings who have ignorance as a hindrance and craving as a fetter, running and roaming, sometimes go from this world to the other world, and sometimes come from the other world to this world. For what reason? Because, monks, of not having seen the four noble truths. What four? The noble truth of suffering . . . the noble truth of the way leading to the cessation of suffering."

Grammatical explanations

seyyathāpi (= *seyyathā* + *pi*): "just as, suppose"; an indeclinable used to introduce a simile or analogy, completed by *evameva*, which introduces the application of the simile to the message.

uparivehāsaṃ: an adverbial compound composed of *upari*, "above, upward," and *vehāsa*, "the air, the sky," describing *the manner* in which the stick has been thrown. It is an indeclinable in the form of the accusative.

sakiṃ: an indeclinable meaning "once"; followed by *pi*, *-ṃ* changes by sandhi to *-m*, the labial nasal corresponding to the labial consonant *p-*.

mūlena, *aggena*: instrumentals of *mūla* and *agga*, "bottom" and "top."

avijjānīvaraṇā, *taṇhāsaṃyojanā*: "who have ignorance as a hindrance and craving as a fetter"; two bahubbīhi compounds describing *sattā*, "beings" (see pp. 41–42).

sandhāvantā saṃsarantā: "running [and] roaming"; present participles from the verbs *sandhāvati* and *saṃsarati*, here plural nominatives describing *sattā*.

asmā: "from this"; ablative of *ayaṃ* (Duroiselle §305; Perniola §41), qualifying *lokā*.

parasmā: the ablative of *para*, "other, another, far," a pronominal adjective declined like a pronoun (Duroiselle §353; Perniola §47).

adiṭṭhattā: "because of not having seen." The neuter suffix *-tta* (Skt *-tva*) is added to the past participle *diṭṭha*, "seen," turning the participle into an abstract noun, *diṭṭhatta*, "seen-ness." The prefix *a-* negates the noun.

Adiṭṭhattā, the ablative, is here used in the causal sense (Duroiselle §600,xi; Perniola §257e).

12. Celasutta

The Turban (SN 56:34; V 440)

"Āditte, bhikkhave, cele vā sīse vā, kimassa karaṇīyan"ti?

"Ablaze, monks, turban or head or, what should-be-done?"

"If, monks, one's turban or head were ablaze, what should be done?"

"Āditte, bhante, cele vā sīse vā, tass'eva celassa vā sīsassa vā nibbāpanāya adhimatto chando ca vāyāmo ca ussāho ca ussoḷhī ca appaṭivānī ca sati ca sampajaññañca karaṇīyan"ti.

"Ablaze, Bhante, turban or head or, of that just turban or head or for extinguishing extraordinary desire and effort and zeal and enthusiasm and persistence and mindfulness and clear-comprehension should be done."

"If, Bhante, one's turban or head were ablaze, extraordinary desire, effort, zeal, enthusiasm, persistence, mindfulness, and clear comprehension should be practiced for the extinguishing of that [fire on one's] turban or head."

"Ādittaṃ, bhikkhave, celaṃ vā sīsaṃ vā ajjhupekkhitvā amanasikaritvā anabhisametānaṃ catunnaṃ ariyasaccānaṃ yathābhūtaṃ abhisamayāya adhimatto chando ca vāyāmo ca ussāho ca ussoḷhī ca appaṭivānī ca sati ca sampajaññañca karaṇīyaṃ."

"Ablaze, monks, turban or head or, having observed equanimously, not having attended, of unbroken-through four noble-truths as-really-is for breakthrough, extraordinary desire and effort and zeal and enthusiasm and courage and mindfulness and clear-comprehension should be done."

"If, monks, one's turban or head were ablaze, having observed this equanimously, not having attended to it, so long as the four noble truths have not been realized (broken through to), one should practice extraordinary desire, effort, zeal, enthusiasm, courage, mindfulness, and clear comprehension for the realizing of them (for breaking through to them) as they really are."

Grammatical explanations

āditte . . . cele vā sīse vā: "one's turban or head were ablaze." The construction is a locative absolute (see p. 71), where the secondary subject is *cele sīse*, the turban [or] head, and the secondary action is *āditte*, ablaze. Normally the locative absolute with the locative of the past participle is used to state "when X has occurred" or "when Y did X," but since the situation described here is purely hypothetical—it being highly unlikely that one's turban or head would actually be ablaze—in translation it makes better sense to use "if" than "when."

kimassa karaṇīyaṃ: "what should be done?" This is the main clause. *Kimassa* results from the sandhi of *kiṃ* and *assa*, the latter an optative auxiliary verb paired with *karaṇiyaṃ*, a future passive participle. On this construction, see p. 32.

tass'eva: the genitive demonstrative *tassa* qualifying *celassa* and *sīsassa*, with *eva* adding emphasis.

nibbāpanāya: a dative of *nibbāpana*, "extinguishing," from the causative verb *nibbāpeti*, "extinguishes."

ādittaṃ . . . celaṃ vā sīsaṃ vā: an accusative construction indicating the objects of the two absolutives, *ajjhupekkhitvā* and *amanasikaritvā*.

ajjhupekkhitvā: an absolutive of *ajjhupekkhati*, "observes equanimously." The phonetic development is *adhi* + *upekkhati* > *adhyupekkhati* > *ajjhupekkhati*.

amanasikaritvā: a negative absolutive of *manasikaroti*, "attends to." See p. 34.

anabhisametānaṃ: "not been realized (not been broken through to)"; a negation of the past participle *abhisameta* (from *abhisameti*, "realizes, comprehends, breaks through to"); the form is plural genitive in apposition to *ariyasaccānaṃ*.

abhisamayāya: "for realizing"; the dative of the noun *abhisamaya*, also from *abhisameti*.

adhimatto: "extraordinary"; an adjective from *adhi*, "superior" + *matta*, "amount." The word qualifies each term in this series but takes the masculine gender of the first term, *chando*.

appaṭivānī: a negation of the feminine *paṭivānī*, "turning away, discouragement." Hence I render it "persistence." The double consonant *-pp-* is due to the influence of Skt *prati-*.

karaṇīyaṃ: "should be done." Although this future passive participle applies to all the preceding nominative nouns, it takes the neuter gender of the last term, *sampajaññaṃ*.

13. Suriyasutta—1

The Sun—1 (SN 56:37; V 442)

"Suriyassa, bhikkhave, udayato etaṃ pubbaṅgamaṃ etaṃ pubbanimittaṃ, yadidaṃ aruṇuggaṃ. Evameva kho, bhikkhave, bhikkhuno catunnaṃ ariyasaccānaṃ yathābhūtaṃ abhisamayāya etaṃ pubbaṅgamaṃ etaṃ pubbanimittaṃ, yadidaṃ sammādiṭṭhi."

"Of the sun, monks, rising, this the forerunner, this the sign, which this: the dawn-rise. Just so, monks, for a monk, of four noble-truths as-really-are for breakthrough, this the forerunner, this the sign, which-this: right view."

"This, monks, is the forerunner, this is the sign, of the rising of the sun—that is, the start of the dawn. Just so, monks, for a monk, this is the forerunner, this is the sign, for the breakthrough to the four noble truths as they really are—that is, right view."

Grammatical explanations

suriyassa . . . udayato: "of the rising of the sun"; a masculine singular noun in the genitive case followed by the corresponding present participle of the verb *udeti*.

pubbaṅgamaṃ: "forerunner"; a kammadhāraya compound of *pubba*, "before," and *gamaṃ*, "going," with *-ṃ* inserted for euphony becoming *-ṅ-* before the guttural consonant *g-*.

pubbanimittaṃ: "sign"; more literally, "foresign," a kammadhāraya compound of *pubba* and *nimitta*.

yadidaṃ: see p. 115.

aruṇuggaṃ: "start of the dawn"; a genitive tappurisa compound. *Aruṇa*, originally a reddish-brown color, comes to mean dawn. *Aruṇugga* is the time when the sky just begins to turn reddish brown.

14. Suriyasutta—2

The Sun—2 (SN 56:38; V 442–43)

"Yāvakīvañca, bhikkhave, candimasuriyā loke n'uppajjanti, n'eva tāva mahato ālokassa pātubhāvo hoti mahato obhāsassa. Andhatamaṃ tadā hoti andhakāratimisā. N'eva tāva rattindivā paññāyanti, na māsaddhamāsā paññāyanti, na utusaṃvaccharā paññāyanti.

"So long as and, monks, moon-sun in the world not arise, not just for so long of great light manifestation is, of great radiance. Blind-darkness then is, darkness-gloom. Not for so long night-day are discerned, not months-fortnights are discerned, not seasons-years are discerned.

"So long, monks, as the sun and moon do not arise in the world, for just so long there is no manifestation of great light and great radiance, but then there is blind darkness, darkness and gloom. For just so long nights and days are not discerned, months and fortnights are not discerned, seasons and years are not discerned.

"Yato ca kho, bhikkhave, candimasuriyā loke uppajjanti, atha mahato ālokassa pātubhāvo hoti mahato obhāsassa. N'eva andhakāratamaṃ tadā hoti na andhakāratimisā. Atha rattindivā paññāyanti, māsaddhamāsā paññāyanti, utusaṃvaccharā paññāyanti.

"When but, monks, moon-sun in the world arise, then of great light manifestation is, of great radiance. Not blind-darkness then is, not darkness-gloom. Then night-day are discerned, months-fortnights are discerned, seasons-years are discerned.

"But, monks, when the sun and moon arise in the world, then there is the manifestation of great light and great radiance. Then there is no blinding darkness, no darkness and gloom. Then nights and days are discerned, months and fortnights are discerned, seasons and years are discerned.

"Evameva kho, bhikkhave, yāvakīvañca tathāgato loke n'uppajjati arahaṃ sammāsambuddho, n'eva tāva mahato ālokassa pātubhāvo hoti mahato obhāsassa. Andhatamaṃ tadā hoti andhakāratimisā. N'eva tāva catunnaṃ

ariyasaccānaṃ ācikkhaṇā hoti desanā paññāpanā paṭṭhapanā vivaraṇā vibhajanā uttānīkammaṃ.

"Just so, monks, so long as the Tathāgata in the world not arise, the arahant, the perfectly-enlightened one, not for so long of great light manifestation is, of great radiance. Blind-darkness then is, darkness-gloom. Not for so long of four noble-truths explaining is, teaching, conveying, establishing, disclosing, analyzing, elucidation.

"So too, monks, so long as the Tathāgata does not arise in the world, the arahant, the perfectly enlightened one, for just so long there is no manifestation of great light and great radiance, but then there is blinding darkness, darkness and gloom. For just so long there is no explaining, teaching, conveying, establishing, disclosing, analyzing, and elucidation of the four noble truths.

"Yato ca kho, bhikkhave, tathāgato loke uppajjati arahaṃ sammāsambuddho, atha mahato ālokassa pātubhāvo hoti mahato obhāsassa. N'eva andhatamaṃ tadā hoti na andhakāratimisā. Atha kho catunnaṃ ariyasaccānaṃ ācikkhaṇā hoti desanā paññāpanā paṭṭhapanā vivaraṇā vibhajanā uttānīkammaṃ."

"When but, monks, the Tathāgata in the world arises, the arahant, the perfectly-enlightened one, then of great light manifestation is, of great radiance. Not blind-darkness then is, not darkness-gloom. Then of four noble-truths explaining is, teaching, making known, establishing, disclosing, analyzing, elucidation."

"But, monks, when the Tathāgata arises in the world, the arahant, the perfectly enlightened one, then there is the manifestation of great light and great radiance. Then there is no blinding darkness, no darkness and gloom. Then there is the explaining, teaching, making known, establishing, disclosing, analyzing, and elucidation of the four noble truths."

Grammatical explanations

yāvakīvaṃ: "so long as"; an indeclinable indicating extent in time.
candimasuriyā: "moon and sun"; a nominative dvanda compound of the plural type (see p. 36).

n'uppajjanti = *na uppajjanti*: "do not arise"; a third-person plural indicative.

tāva: "for so long"; the demonstrative counterpart of *yāva*.

mahato ālokassa: "of great light"; *ālokassa*, a singular genitive noun in relation to *pātubhāvo*, with *mahato* qualifying *ālokassa*.

pātubhāvo: "manifestation"; the nominative subject of the main clause of the sentence. The word is a kammadhāraya compound composed of the indeclinable *pātur*, "visible, open, manifest," and *bhāva*, "state, condition."

mahato obhāsassa: "of great radiance"; another genitive singular. This kind of sentence structure is typical of the suttas: the main expression, here *mahato ālokassa pātubhāvo*, precedes the verb *hoti*, while the nearly synonymous expression, *mahato obhāsassa* (also dependent on *pātubhāvo*), follows the verb.

andhatamaṃ: a kammadhāraya compound composed of *andha*, "blind," and *tamaṃ*, "darkness"—a neuter singular in the nominative case.

tadā: "then"; an indeclinable indicating time.

andhakāratimisā: another dvanda compound of the plural type, feminine nominative, composed of *andhakāra*, darkness (literally, "making blind"), and *timisā*, also meaning darkness.

n'eva (= *na* + *eva*): "not" at the beginning of a series.

rattindivā: "nights and days"; a plural dvanda composed of *ratti*, night, and *diva*, day; this compound, like those that follow, is masculine nominative.

paññāyanti: "are known, are discerned"; a third-person plural passive verb.

māsaddhamāsā: "months and fortnights"; a plural dvanda of *māsa*, month, and *addhamāsa*, half-month.

utusaṃvaccharā: "seasons and years"; a plural dvanda of *utu*, season, and *saṃvacchara*, year.

yato: "when."

ca: used here in the disjunctive sense, "but" rather than "and." See DOP *ca*[2] 2. The following *kho* is a mere emphatic.

tathāgato: It cannot be determined here whether the text is speaking about buddhas in general ("a tathāgata") or specifically about the present buddha. Either interpretation is feasible.

arahaṃ: "worthy one"; a masculine nominative, from the stem *arahat*, here used to refer to the Buddha. The other masculine nominative, *arahā*, is used to describe a liberated monk.

sammāsambuddho: "the perfectly enlightened one." *Sammāsambuddho* is a kammadhāraya compound of the adverb *sammā*, "right(ly), perfect(ly), complete(ly)," and the past participle *sambuddha*, a prefixed form of *buddha*, "enlightened, awakened," used as a noun.

ācikkhaṇā: "pointing out." This noun and those that follow are nominatives. All but the last are feminine, and all but the last are action nouns (with the *-ana-* insert typical of an action noun). The first noun precedes the verb *hoti*, while the others, near-synonyms, follow. This is another typical Pāli syntactical feature, similar to the construction where the first modifier precedes the noun and the subsequent modifiers follow it (see p. 122).

desanā: "teaching"; based on the verb *deseti*, "teaches, expounds."

paññāpanā: "making known"; based on *paññāpeti*, "makes known," causative of *pajānāti*, "understands, knows."

paṭṭhapanā: "establishing"; based on *paṭṭhapeti*, "establishes, sets forth."

vivaraṇā: "disclosing"; based on *vivarati*, "opens up, discloses."

vibhajanā: "analyzing"; based on *vibhajati*, "divides up, analyzes."

uttānīkammaṃ: "elucidation"; a verbal compound composed of *uttāna*, "clear, evident," and *kamma*, "action," hence "making clear, making evident." Before *kamma*, the final *-a* is changed to *-ī* (Duroiselle §557).

15. Papātasutta

The Precipice (SN 56:42; V 448–50)

[*The Buddha leads the monks to a place on Mount Vulture's Peak called Paṭibhānakūṭa—"Inspiration Peak." One monk sees a steep precipice off Paṭibhānakūṭa and asks the Buddha whether there is any steeper precipice. The Buddha replies as follows.*]

[1. Those who fall down the precipice]

"Ye hi keci, bhikkhave, samaṇā vā brāhmaṇā vā 'idaṃ dukkhan'ti yathābhūtaṃ nappajānanti, 'ayaṃ dukkhasamudayo'ti yathābhūtaṃ nappajānanti, 'ayaṃ dukkhanirodho'ti yathābhūtaṃ nappajānanti, 'ayaṃ dukkhanirodhagāminī paṭipadā'ti yathābhūtaṃ nappajānanti, te jātisaṃvattanikesu saṅkhāresu abhiramanti, jarāsaṃvattanikesu saṅkhāresu abhiramanti, maraṇasaṃvattanikesu saṅkhāresu abhiramanti,

soka-parideva-dukkha-domanass'upāyāsasaṃvattanikesu saṅkhāresu abhiramanti.

"Those who, monks, ascetics or brahmins or 'This suffering' as-really-is not-understand, 'This suffering-origin' as-really-is not-understand, 'This suffering-cessation' as-really-is not-understand, 'This suffering-cessation-going way' as-really-is not-understand: they in birth-leading-to volitional-activities delight, in old age-leading-to volitional-activities delight, in death-leading-to volitional-activities delight, in sorrow-lamentation-pain-dejection-misery-leading-to volitional-activities delight.

"Those ascetics and brahmins, monks, who do not understand as it really is: 'This is suffering'; who do not understand as it really is: 'This is the origin of suffering'; who do not understand as it really is: 'This is the cessation of suffering'; who do not understand as it really is: 'This is the way leading to the cessation of suffering': they delight in volitional activities that lead to birth; they delight in volitional activities that lead to old age; they delight in volitional activities that lead to death; they delight in volitional activities that lead to sorrow, lamentation, pain, dejection, and misery.

"Te jātisaṃvattanikesu saṅkhāresu abhiratā, jarāsaṃvattanikesu saṅkhāresu abhiratā, maraṇasaṃvattanikesu saṅkhāresu abhiratā, soka-parideva-dukkha-domanass'upāyāsasaṃvattanikesu saṅkhāresu abhiratā, jāti-saṃvattanikepi saṅkhāre abhisaṅkharonti, jarāsaṃvattanikepi saṅkhāre abhisaṅkharonti, maraṇasaṃvattanikepi saṅkhāre abhisaṅkharonti, soka-parideva-dukkha-domanass'upāyāsasaṃvattanikepi saṅkhāre abhisaṅkharonti.

"They in birth-leading-to volitional-activities delighted, in old age-leading-to volitional-activities delighted, in death-leading-to volitional-activities delighted, in sorrow-lamentation-pain-dejection-misery-leading-to volitional-activities delighted, birth-leading-to too volitional-activities generate, old age-leading-to too volitional-activities generate, death-leading-to too volitional-activities generate, sorrow-lamentation-pain-dejection-misery-leading-to too volitional-activities generate.

"Delighted with volitional activities that lead to birth, delighted with volitional activities that lead to old age, delighted with volitional activities that lead to death, delighted with volitional activities that lead to sorrow, lamentation, pain, dejection, and misery, they generate volitional activities that lead to birth; they generate volitional activities that lead to old age; they generate volitional activities that lead to death; they generate volitional activities that lead to sorrow, lamentation, pain, dejection, and misery.

"Te jātisaṃvattanikepi saṅkhāre abhisaṅkharitvā, jarāsaṃvattanikepi saṅkhāre abhisaṅkharitvā, maraṇasaṃvattanikepi saṅkhāre abhisaṅkharitvā, soka-parideva-dukkha-domanass'upāyāsasaṃvattanikepi saṅkhāre abhisaṅkharitvā, jātipapātampi papatanti, jarāpapātampi papatanti, maraṇapapātampi papatanti, soka-parideva-dukkha-domanass'upāyāsapapātampi papatanti.

"They birth-leading-to too volitional-activities having generated, old age-leading-to too volitional-activities having generated, death-leading-to too volitional-activities having generated, sorrow-lamentation-pain-dejection-misery-leading-to too volitional-activities having generated, the birth-precipice too fall down, the old age-precipice too fall down, the death-precipice too fall down, the sorrow-lamentation-pain-dejection-misery-precipice too fall down.

"Having generated volitional activities that lead to birth, having generated volitional activities that lead to old age, having generated volitional activities that lead to death, having generated volitional activities that lead to sorrow, lamentation, pain, dejection, and misery, they fall down the precipice of birth; they fall down the precipice of old age; they fall down the precipice of death; they fall down the precipice of sorrow, lamentation, pain, dejection, and misery.

"Te na parimuccanti jātiyā jarāya maraṇena sokehi paridevehi dukkhehi domanassehi upāyāsehi. 'Na parimuccanti dukkhasmā'ti vadāmi.

"They not are freed from birth, from old age, from death, from sorrows, from lamentations, from pains, from dejections, from miseries. 'Not are freed from suffering,' I say.

"They are not freed from birth, from old age, from death, from sorrow, from lamentation, from pain, from dejection, from misery. 'They are not freed from suffering,' I say.

[2. Those who do not fall down the precipice]

"Ye ca kho keci, bhikkhave, samaṇā vā brāhmaṇā vā 'idaṃ dukkhan'ti yathābhūtaṃ pajānanti . . . 'ayaṃ dukkhanirodhagāminī paṭipadā'ti yathābhūtaṃ pajānanti, te jātisaṃvattanikesu saṅkhāresu nābhiramanti. . . . Te jātisaṃvattanikesu saṅkhāresu anabhiratā . . . jātisaṃvattanikepi saṅkhāre nābhisaṅkharonti. . . . Te jātisaṃvattanikepi saṅkhāre anabhisaṅkharitvā . . . jātipapātampi nappapatanti, jarāpapātampi nappapatanti, maraṇapapātampi nappapatanti, soka-parideva-dukkha-domanass'upāyāsapapātampi nappapatanti.

"Those who but, monks, ascetics or brahmins or 'This suffering' as-really-is understand . . . 'This suffering-cessation-going way' as-really-is understand, they in birth-leading-to volitional-activities not delight. . . . They in birth-leading-to volitional-activities not delighted . . . birth-leading-to too volitional-activities not generate. . . . They birth-leading-to too volitional-activities not having generated . . . the birth-precipice too not-fall down, the old-age-precipice too not-fall down, the death-precipice too not-fall down, the sorrow-lamentation-pain-dejection-misery-precipice too not-fall down.

"But, monks, those ascetics or brahmins who understand as it really is: 'This is suffering' . . . who understand as it really is: 'This is the way leading to the cessation of suffering': they do not delight in volitional activities that lead to birth. . . . Not delighted with volitional activities that lead to birth, they do not generate volitional activities that lead to birth. . . . Not having generated volitional activities that lead to birth . . . they do not fall down the precipice of birth; they do not fall down the precipice of old age; they do not fall down the precipice of death; they do not fall down the precipice of sorrow, lamentation, pain, dejection, and misery.

"Te parimuccanti jātiyā jarāya maraṇena sokehi paridevehi dukkhehi domanassehi upāyāsehi. 'Parimuccanti dukkhasmā'ti vadāmi."

"They are freed from birth, from old age, from death, from sorrows, from lamentations, from pains, from dejections, from miseries. 'They are freed from suffering,' I say."

"They are freed from birth, from old age, from death, from sorrow, from lamentation, from pain, from dejection, from misery. 'They are freed from suffering,' I say."

Grammatical explanations

ye hi keci: see p. 93.

nappajānanti (= *na* + *pajānanti*): "do not understand," with the *-p-* doubled on account of the *-r-* in Skt *prajānanti*, lost in Pāli.

jātisaṃvattanikesu: "leading to birth"; a bahubbīhi compound qualifying *saṅkhāresu*, hence locative plural. *Saṃvattanika* is an adjective from *saṃvattati*, "leads to." In the following clauses *jāti* is replaced by *jarā* and *maraṇa*. In the last clause, *soka-parideva-dukkha-domanass'upāyāsa* is a five-term dvanda, with vowel sandhi between *domanassa* and *upāyāsa*.

saṅkhāresu: "volitional activities," here locative plural. The word *saṅkhārā* occurs in several major contexts in the suttas, with a different nuance in each. *Saṅkhārā* are things—or, more accurately, processes—that act in unison to create other things, but they are equally the things created by the combined activity of other things. Here the word refers to the second link in the chain of dependent origination, activities that create kamma; the first term of the formula, ignorance (*avijjā*), is represented by not understanding the four noble truths (see the definition of *avijjā* at SN II 4,11–14).

te: the third-person plural subject "they," signifying *samaṇā* and *brāhmaṇā*.

abhiramanti: "delight"; a third-person plural indicative verb, agreeing with *te*.

abhiratā: "delighted in"; the past participle of *abhiramanti*, third-person plural nominative, in agreement with *te*. Here it is used in an active sense.

jātisaṃvattanikepi saṅkhāre: "they generate volitional activities that lead to birth." Here *saṅkhāre* is plural accusative as the object of the verb *abhisaṅkharonti*, which takes its cognate noun as its own object. To preserve idiomatic English, I have used a verb unrelated to the noun. A translator who wants to mirror the style of the Pāli might render it "they construct constructions" or "they fabricate fabrications."

saṅkhāre abhisaṅkharitvā: "having generated volitional activities"; the accusative plural of the noun followed by an absolutive of *abhisaṅkharonti*.

jātipapātampi papatanti: "they fall down the precipice of birth." This is another example of a verb taking a cognate noun as its own accusative object.

parimuccanti: "are freed"; a prefixed third-person plural form of the verb *muccati*, passive of *muñcati*, "sets free."

nappapatanti (= *na* + *papatanti*): "do not fall down"; with consonant duplication *-pp-* (see p. 127).

jātiyā, etc.: Normally, *parimuccati* goes with the ablative case; thus the nouns here must be ablatives. *Maraṇena* is likely an ablative in the form of an instrumental.

dukkhasmā: This is clearly an ablative. The quotation marker *ti* is for special emphasis.

16. Kūṭāgārasutta

Peaked House (SN 56:44; V 452–53)

"Yo hi, bhikkhave, evaṃ vadeyya, 'Ahaṃ dukkhaṃ ariyasaccaṃ yathābhūtaṃ anabhisamecca . . . dukkhanirodhagāminiṃ paṭipadaṃ ariyasaccaṃ yathābhūtaṃ anabhisamecca sammā dukkhass'antaṃ karissāmī'ti, n'etaṃ ṭhānaṃ vijjati.

"Who indeed, monks, thus would say, 'I suffering noble-truth as-really-is not having broken-through . . . suffering-cessation-going way noble-truth as-really-is not having broken through, completely of suffering end will make,' not this case exists.

"If, monks, one would say thus, 'Without having broken through the noble truth of suffering as it really is . . . without having broken through the noble truth of the way leading to the cessation of suffering as it really is, I will completely make an end of suffering,' there is no possibility of this.

"Seyyathāpi, bhikkhave, yo evaṃ vadeyya, 'Ahaṃ kūṭāgārassa heṭṭhimaṃ gharaṃ akaritvā uparimaṃ gharaṃ āropessāmī'ti, n'etaṃ ṭhānaṃ vijjati, evameva kho, bhikkhave, yo evaṃ vadeyya, 'Ahaṃ dukkhaṃ ariyasaccaṃ yathābhūtaṃ anabhisamecca . . . dukkhanirodhagāminiṃ paṭipadaṃ ariyasaccaṃ yathābhūtaṃ anabhisamecca sammā dukkhassantaṃ karissāmī'ti, n'etaṃ ṭhānaṃ vijjati.

"Suppose, monks, who thus would say, 'I of a peaked house the lower level not having built, the upper level will set up,' not this case exists. Just so, monks, who thus would say, 'I suffering noble truth as-really-is not having broken-through . . . suffering-cessation-going way noble truth as-really-is not having broken through, completely of suffering end will make,' not this case exists.

"Suppose, monks, someone would say thus: 'Without having built the lower story of a peaked house, I will set up the upper story'; there is no possibility of this. Just so, monks, though someone would say thus: 'Without having broken through the noble truth of suffering as it really is . . . without having broken through the noble truth of the way leading to the cessation of suffering as it really is, I will completely make an end of suffering,' there is no possibility of this.

"Yo ca kho, bhikkhave, evaṃ vadeyya, 'Ahaṃ dukkhaṃ ariyasaccaṃ yathābhūtaṃ abhisamecca . . . dukkhanirodhagāminiṃ paṭipadaṃ ariyasaccaṃ yathābhūtaṃ abhisamecca sammā dukkhass'antaṃ karissāmī'ti, ṭhānametaṃ vijjati.

"Who but, monks, thus would say, 'I suffering noble truth as-really-is having broken-through . . . suffering-cessation-going way as-really-is noble truth having broken through, completely of suffering end will make,' case this exists.

"But, monks, if one would say thus, 'Having broken through the noble truth of suffering as it really is . . . having broken through the noble truth of the way leading to the cessation of suffering as it really is, I will completely make an end of suffering,' there is this possibility.

"Seyyathāpi, bhikkhave, yo evaṃ vadeyya, 'Ahaṃ kūṭāgārassa heṭṭhimaṃ gharaṃ karitvā uparimaṃ gharaṃ āropessāmī'ti, ṭhānametaṃ vijjati, evameva kho, bhikkhave, yo evaṃ vadeyya: 'Ahaṃ dukkhaṃ ariyasaccaṃ yathābhūtaṃ abhisamecca . . . dukkhanirodhagāminiṃ paṭipadaṃ ariyasaccaṃ yathābhūtaṃ abhisamecca sammā dukkhass'antaṃ karissāmī'ti, ṭhānametaṃ vijjati."

"Suppose, monks, who thus would say: 'I of a peaked house the lower story having built, the upper story will set up,' case this exists. Just so, monks, who thus would say, 'I suffering noble truth as-really-is having broken-through . . .

suffering-cessation-going way noble truth as-really-is having broken through, completely of suffering end will make,' case this exists."

"Suppose, monks, one would say: 'Having built the lower story of a peaked house, I will set up the upper story'; there is this possibility. Just so, monks, if one would say thus: 'Having broken through the noble truth of suffering as it really is . . . having broken through the noble truth of the way leading to the cessation of suffering as it really is, I will completely make an end of suffering,' there is this possibility."

Grammatical explanations

yo: the relative pronoun "who"; in this sentence there is no corresponding demonstrative. Rather, the relative clause is correlated with the declaration *n'etaṃ ṭhānaṃ vijjati*, in which the subject *etaṃ* is not the demonstrative corresponding to *yo*. The construction is idiomatic.

hi: a mere emphatic.

vadeyya: "would say"; the third-person singular optative in a hypothetical sense.

anabhisamecca: "not having broken through, not having realized"; a negative absolutive of *abhisameti*, with palatalization of the final consonant cluster. The modifications are as follows: *abhisamet* + *ya* > *abhisametya* > *abhisamecca* (see Geiger §55; Duroiselle §§73–74). The absolutive is negated by the prefix *an-*.

n'etaṃ ṭhānaṃ vijjati: literally, "this case does not exist"—that is, "there is no possibility of this"—a common idiom in the suttas used to express impossibility.

kūṭāgārassa: "of a peaked house"; the compound is in the genitive case.

gharaṃ: Usually this means "house," but here, as part of a house, it seems to be intended in the sense of a level or story.

akaritvā: a negative absolutive of *karoti*.

āropessāmi: a first-person singular future of *āropeti*, "sets up, puts on to," a causative of *āruhati*, "to ascend, to rise," with strengthening of *-u-* to *-o-* and insertion of the causative suffix *āpe*.[86]

86. See Duroiselle §§492–93 and Perniola §90d.

ṭhānametaṃ vijjati: literally, "this case exists"—that is, "there is this possibility"—the positive counterpart of *n'etaṃ ṭhānaṃ vijjati*, with the *-ṃ* in *ṭhānaṃ* becoming *-m* before the vowel.

17. Chiggaḷayugasutta

Yoke with a Hole (SN 56:47; V 455–56)

"Seyyathāpi, bhikkhave, puriso mahāsamudde ekacchiggaḷaṃ yugaṃ pakkhipeyya. Tatrāpi'ssa kāṇo kacchapo. So vassasatassa vassasatassa accayena sakiṃ sakiṃ ummujjeyya. Taṃ kiṃ maññatha, bhikkhave, api nu kho kāṇo kacchapo vassasatassa vassasatassa accayena sakiṃ sakiṃ ummujjanto amusmiṃ ekacchiggaḷe yuge gīvaṃ paveseyyā"ti?

"Suppose, monks, a man into the great-ocean a one-holed yoke would throw. There too would be a blind turtle. He of years-hundred of years-hundred with passage once once would emerge. That what do you think, monks, the blind turtle of years-hundred of years-hundred with passage once once emerging, in that one-holed yoke neck would insert?"

"Suppose, monks, a man would throw a yoke with a single hole into the great ocean, and there was a blind turtle that would come to the surface once every hundred years. What do you think, monks, would that blind turtle, coming to the surface once every hundred years, insert its neck into that yoke with a single hole?"

"Yadi nūna, bhante, kadāci karahaci dīghassa addhuno accayenā"ti.

"If surely, Bhante, sometimes ever, of long time with passage."

"If ever, Bhante, surely it would be with the passage of a long time."

"Khippataraṃ kho so, bhikkhave, kāṇo kacchapo vassasatassa vassasatassa accayena sakiṃ sakiṃ ummujjanto amusmiṃ ekacchiggaḷe yuge gīvaṃ paveseyya, na tvevāhaṃ, bhikkhave, sakiṃ vinipātagatena bālena manussattaṃ vadāmi.

"More quickly that, monks, blind turtle of years-hundred of years-hundred with passage once once emerging, in that one-holed yoke neck would insert, not indeed I, monks, once by lower-realm-gone fool human-state say.

"I say, monks, that blind turtle, coming to the surface once every hundred years, would more quickly insert its neck into that yoke with a single hole than the fool who has gone once to the lower world [would regain] the human state.

"Taṃ kissa hetu? Na h'ettha, bhikkhave, atthi dhammacariyā samacariyā kusalakiriyā puññakiriyā. Aññamaññakhādikā ettha, bhikkhave, vattati dubbalakhādikā. Taṃ kissa hetu? Adiṭṭhattā, bhikkhave, catunnaṃ ariyasaccānaṃ. Katamesaṃ catunnaṃ? Dukkhassa ariyasaccassa . . . dukkhanirodhagāminiyā paṭipadāya ariyasaccassa."

"That for what reason? Not because here, monks, is dhamma-conduct, righteous-conduct, wholesome-doing, merit-doing. Other-other-devouring here, monks, occurs, weak-devouring. That for what reason? Because of not-seen-ness, monks, of the four noble-truths. Of what four? Of the suffering noble truth . . . of the suffering-cessation-going way noble truth."

"For what reason? Because here, monks, there is no Dhamma conduct, no righteous conduct, no wholesome activity, no meritorious activity. Here mutual devouring occurs, the devouring of the weak. For what reason? Because, monks, of not having seen the four noble truths. What four? The noble truth of suffering . . . the noble truth of the way leading to the cessation of suffering."

Grammatical explanations

mahāsamudde: "in the great ocean"; a kammadhāraya compound of the adjective *mahat* and *samudde*, a singular locative.

ekacchiggaḷaṃ: "having one hole"; a numerical bahubbīhi compound (Duroiselle §551; Perniola §138d) describing *yugaṃ*, based on a numerical kammadhāraya.

yugaṃ: "yoke"; a neuter noun in the accusative case.

pakkhipeyya: "would throw"; a third-person singular optative of *pakkhipati*, used to describe an imaginary situation.

tatrāpi: "there too," the vowel being lengthened through sandhi.

'ssa = assa: "would be, might be"; a third-person singular optative of *atthi*. The initial *a-* is elided on account of sandhi with preceding *pi*.

kāṇo: "blind," in one eye or both; an adjective describing *kaccapo*, a turtle.

vassasatassa: "a hundred years"; here a singular genitive. The higher numerals—such as *sata*, hundred, *sahassa*, thousand, and *satasahassa*, a hundred thousand—often occur as neuter substantives following the noun they modify. Compounds of this type are considered genitive tappurisas; in this case it is as if the sense is "a hundred of years." The repetition of the compound indicates that the event occurs at repeated intervals.

accayena: "after, with the passage of"; the instrumental used adverbially (see p. 46). It belongs with *vassasatassa vassasatassa*, in the sense of "with the repeated passage of centuries."

sakiṃ: "once"; an indeclinable repeated to show that the event takes place at intervals.

ummujjeyya: "would emerge"; a third-person singular optative of *ummujjati*.

api nu kho: an interrogative expression, not really translatable, indicating that a question is being posed.

amusmiṃ: "in that"; a neuter locative pronoun agreeing with *yuge* (Duroiselle §310; Perniola §41).

gīvaṃ: "neck"; a neuter accusative noun, object of *paveseyya*.

paveseyya: "would insert"; an optative of *paveseti*, causative of *pavisati*, "enters."

yadi: "if," establishing a hypothetical.

nūna: a particle that imbues a statement with a tone either of affirmation or doubt, "surely" or "perhaps." Here, together with *yadi*, it suggests certainty.

kadāci karahaci: the two words jointly express the idea of "at some time."

dīghassa addhuno: "of a long extent of time"; an adjective and a noun (genitive of *addhan*) in a genitive construction with *accayena*, "with the passage of."

khippataraṃ: the comparative of *khippa*, "quickly," here the adverb "more quickly." The suffix *-tara* gives an adjective or adverb the comparative sense.

tvevāhaṃ (= *tu eva ahaṃ*): *Tu* is an enclitic particle, "however, but, rather," sometimes used as a mere expletive. The personal pronoun *ahaṃ*, the subject of this clause, is completed by the verb *vadāmi* at the end.

vinipātagatena: "gone to the lower world"; a tappurisa compound qualifying *bālena*. *Vinipāta* is a designation for the lower realms of rebirth.

bālena: "a fool"; a masculine noun in the instrumental case.

manussattaṃ: "human status." *Manussa* is a human being; the neuter suffix *-tta* creates an abstract noun "human-ness" (see p. 116). *Manussattaṃ* is the accusative object of *vadāmi*.

vadāmi: "I say." This first-person present indicative verb is connected syntactically with the pronoun *ahaṃ* occurring just above; it is negated by the *na* at the beginning of this clause.

h'ettha (= *hi ettha*): "because here."

dhammacariyā, etc.: "Dhamma conduct." These four compounds, all feminine singulars, are nominative subjects of *atthi*, which is negated by the *na* at the beginning of the sentence.

aññamaññakhādikā: "the eating of one another"; a tappurisa compound, feminine singular, functioning as the nominative subject of the verb *vattati*.

dubbalakhādikā: "the eating of the weak"; a tappurisa compound parallel to *aññamaññakhādikā*. The first noun, functioning as subject, precedes the verb, while the second noun, again as subject, follows the verb.

adiṭṭhattā: as at p. 116.

18. Sinerupabbatarājasutta

Sineru, King of Mountains (SN 56:49; V 457–58)

"Seyyathāpi, bhikkhave, puriso sinerussa pabbatarājassa satta muggamattiyo pāsāṇasakkharā upanikkhipeyya. Taṃ kiṃ maññatha, bhikkhave, katamaṃ nu kho bahutaraṃ: yā vā satta muggamattiyo pāsāṇasakkharā upanikkhittā, yo vā sinerupabbatarājā"ti?

"Suppose, monks, a man of Sineru the mountain-king seven mung-bean-size gravel-grains would place-beside. That what do you think, monks, which more: which or seven mung-bean-size gravel-grains placed, which or Sineru-mountain-king?"

"Suppose, monks, a man would place beside Sineru, the king of mountains, seven gravel grains the size of mung beans. What do you think, monks, which is more: the seven gravel grains the size of mung beans that have been placed [there] or Sineru, the king of mountains?"

"Etadeva, bhante, bahutaraṃ, yadidaṃ sinerupabbatarājā. Appamattikā satta muggamattiyo pāsāṇasakkharā upanikkhittā. Saṅkhampi na upenti, upanidhampi na upenti, kalabhāgampi na upenti sinerupabbatarājānaṃ upanidhāya satta muggamattiyo pāsāṇasakkharā upanikkhittā"ti.

"This-indeed, Bhante, more, which this, Sineru-mountain-king. Trifling seven mung-bean-size gravel-grains placed. Calculation even not approach, comparison even not approach, fraction even not approach, Sineru-mountain-king having compared, seven mung-bean-size gravel-grains placed."

"This indeed is more, Bhante—that is, Sineru, the king of mountains. The seven gravel grains the size of mung beans are trifling. Compared to Sineru, the king of mountains, the seven gravel grains the size of mung beans placed [there] are not even calculable, do not even bear comparison, do not amount even to a fraction."

"Evameva kho, bhikkhave, ariyasāvakassa diṭṭhisampannassa puggalassa abhisametāvino etadeva bahutaraṃ dukkhaṃ yadidaṃ parikkhīṇaṃ pariyādinnaṃ; appamattakaṃ avasiṭṭhaṃ. Saṅkhampi na upeti, upanidhampi na upeti, kalabhāgampi na upeti, purimaṃ dukkhakkhandhaṃ parikkhīṇaṃ pariyādinnaṃ upanidhāya yadidaṃ sattakkhattuparamatā, yo 'idaṃ dukkhan'ti yathābhūtaṃ pajānāti, 'ayaṃ dukkhasamudayo'ti yathābhūtaṃ pajānāti, 'ayaṃ dukkhanirodho'ti yathābhūtaṃ pajānāti, 'ayaṃ dukkhanirodhagāminī paṭipadā'ti yathābhūtaṃ pajānāti."

"Just so, monks, of a noble disciple, a view-accomplished person, one who has broken-through, this indeed more suffering, that is, destroyed eliminated; trifling has remained. Calculation even not approaches, comparison even not approaches, fraction even not approaches, former suffering-mass destroyed eliminated having compared, that is, seven-times-maximum, one who 'This suffering' as-really-is understands; 'this suffering-origin' as-really-is understands; 'this suffering-cessation' as-really-is understands; 'this suffering-cessation-going way' as-really-is understands."

"Just so, monks, for a noble disciple, a person accomplished in view, one who has broken through, the suffering that has been destroyed and eliminated is more, while that which remains is trifling. Compared to the former mass of suffering that has been destroyed and eliminated, the latter is not even calculable, does not even bear comparison, does not amount even to a fraction, because there is a maximum of seven more times [seven more lives, in the case of] one who understands as it really is: 'This is suffering'; who understands as it really is: 'This is the origin of suffering'; who understands as it really is: 'This is the cessation of suffering'; who understands as it really is: 'This is the way leading to the cessation of suffering.'"

Grammatical explanations

sinerussa pabbatarājassa: "Sineru, the king of mountains." Sineru is the name of the mountain, followed by its epithet. Both are masculine genitives, which, according to DOP, suggests that the grains are placed beside the mountain rather than on top of it (in which case the locative would have been used). Just below the two terms are compounded, with *sinerupabbatarājā* the nominative and *sinerupabbatarājānaṃ* the accusative.

satta: "seven," qualifying *pāsāṇasakkharā*.

muggamattiyo: "the size of mung beans." The compound is feminine plural in agreement with *pāsāṇasakkharā*; the ending *-iyo* turns *muggamattā* into a bahubbīhi.

pāsāṇasakkharā: "pieces of gravel"; feminine plural in the accusative case. In the question that follows, *satta muggamattiyo pāsāṇasakkharā* is nominative.

upanikkhipeyya: "would place"; a third-person singular optative of *upanikkhipati*.

katamaṃ nu kho bahutaraṃ: see p. 114.

upanikkhittā: "placed"; the past participle of *upanikkhipati*, here a feminine plural nominative.

appamattikā: "trifling"; see p. 114. The compound is here feminine plural qualifying *pāsāṇasakkharā*.

saṅkhampi, *upanidhampi*: "calculation, comparison," feminine singulars in the accusative case; the *pi* after each is a copulative.

kalabhāgampi: "a fraction"; a masculine singular accusative, again followed by *pi*.

upanidhāya: an absolutive of *upanidhāti*, used adverbially to mean "compared with," taking an accusative object.

ariyasāvakassa: "a noble disciple," here singular dative or genitive. The compound can be understood either as a kammadhāraya, "a disciple who is noble," or a tappurisa, "a disciple of the noble ones."

diṭṭhisampannassa puggalassa: "a person accomplished in view (or endowed with view)"; one who possesses the experiential right view of the four noble truths, at minimum a stream-enterer.

abhisametāvino: "broken through, realized"; an active past participle (see pp. 30–31) in the dative or genitive singular, signifying a person who has arrived at *abhisamaya*, the "breakthrough" or realization; the corresponding verb is *abhisameti*.

parikkhīṇaṃ pariyādinnaṃ: "destroyed and eliminated"; two past participles used almost as synonyms, qualifying *dukkhaṃ*.

avasiṭṭhaṃ: "what remains"; a past participle of *avasissati*; also qualifying *dukkhaṃ*.

purimaṃ dukkhakkhandhaṃ: "the former mass of suffering"; an accusative in relation to *upanidhāya*. *Dukkhakkhandhaṃ* is a genitive tappurisa compound.

sattakkhattuparamatā: a compound of *satta*, "seven," *khattuṃ*, a suffix meaning "times," and the feminine singular abstract noun *paramatā*, "maximum, at most." The sense is: "(since) there is a maximum of seven more births." While *paramatā* looks like a feminine nominative, it is probably a truncated feminine instrumental in the causal sense, representing *paramatāya*, "because there is a maximum. . . ."[87]

87. See Geiger §27.2 for other examples of final feminine *-āya* being truncated to *-ā*.

2. The Five Aggregates: The Meaning of Suffering in Brief

Introduction

In his first discourse the Buddha declared, "In brief, the five clinging-aggregates are suffering" (*saṃkhittena pañcupādānakkhandhā dukkhā*), but on that occasion he did not explain what is meant by the five aggregates nor did he analyze them at length. For clarification of this matter, one must turn to the Khandhasaṃyutta (SN 22), which serves almost as an extended commentary on that expression. The word *khandha* itself has multiple meanings, among them a mass (of firewood or water), the trunk of a tree, the torso of the body, or the shoulder of an elephant. But in the context of the Buddha's teaching, the word refers to five groups into which the Buddha classified the constituents of experience: material form, feeling, perception, volitional activities, and consciousness.

Each aggregate can be seen as a broad category comprising all manifestations of that particular aggregate. Thus, in **2.13**, when a monk asks the Buddha how the designation "aggregates" applies to the aggregates, he replies: "Whatever form there is, whether past, future, or present, internal or external, gross or subtle, inferior or superior, far or near: this is called the 'form aggregate.'" And so for the other four aggregates. Thus each aggregate includes every instance of the particular factor that gives its name to the category. These instances are distinguished in eleven ways: by a triad referring to time, a dyad referring to situation (one's own or that of others), two dyads referring to quality, and another dyad referring to location.

The content of the five aggregates is specified in SN 22:56 (III 58–61), a text not included in the present collection. The Buddha there explains that the aggregate of form (*rūpakkhandha*)—that is, material substance—comprises the four great elements and the form derived from the four great elements. The aggregate of feeling includes the six kinds of feeling: feeling born of eye-contact, feeling born of ear-contact, feeling born of nose-contact, feeling born of tongue-contact, feeling born of body-contact, and feeling born of mind-contact. The aggregate of perception consists of the six kinds of perception: perception of visible forms, perception of sounds, perception of odors, perception of tastes, perception of tactile objects, and perception of mental objects. The aggregate of volitional activities comprises the six kinds of volition: volition regarding visible forms, volition regarding sounds, volition regarding odors, volition regarding tastes, volition regarding tactile objects, and volition regarding mental objects. And the aggregate of consciousness comprises the six kinds of consciousness: eye-consciousness, ear-consciousness, nose-consciousness, tongue-consciousness, body-consciousness, and mind-consciousness.

The special attention that the Buddha gives to the aggregates stems from the fact that these aggregates are the primary bases for the false sense of personal identity. They are designated "clinging-aggregates" because they serve as the objects of clinging. While clinging can occur in diverse ways, the most insidious type of clinging, for the Buddhist texts, is the misconception of the aggregates as being "mine," "I," and "my self." These misconceptions are reinforced by the enjoyment provided by the aggregates. As **2.5** states, each of the aggregates yields a certain measure of enjoyment deriving from the pleasure and joy that arise from it. To ensure that this enjoyment continues, the ordinary person—spoken of in the texts as the "unlearned worldling"—mistakenly takes the aggregates to be "I" and "mine."

For the Buddha, however, these notions are the products of distorted cognition. Under their sway, the worldling posits a concrete self existing in some definite relation to the five aggregates. The self is seen either as identical with one or another of the aggregates, as possessing them, as contained within them, or as containing them within itself. This is what the suttas call *sakkāyadiṭṭhi*, a term hard to translate but which is rendered here as "the view of the personal-collection." The aggregates are "the personal-collection" (*sakkāya*), the objective basis of the view, and the view is the notion that there is a self existing in some specific relation to the aggregates.

Just as a dog bound to a post keeps on running around the post, so, according to SN 22:100 (III 150–51), having adopted a view of self, the worldling keeps on revolving around the five aggregates, unable to find release. The Buddha realizes the real nature of the five aggregates—which are called "world-phenomena in the world"—and then "he points them out, teaches them, makes them known, establishes them, discloses, analyzes, and elucidates them" (**2.14**). As the pioneer and discoverer of the path, the Buddha first gains release from bondage to the five aggregates himself, then he guides others to release. Those who follow his teaching and practice as instructed become "liberated by wisdom," also winning release from the aggregates (**2.8**). In sounding his message of liberation, the Buddha's proclamation is like a lion's roar. As the lion's roar fills all the other animals with fear and dread, so the Buddha's teaching that the five aggregates undergo origination and dissolution extends throughout the world system, filling even the deities in the celestial realms with the shocking realization that they too are impermanent (**2.12**).

To break the false identification with the five aggregates, the Buddha says that under examination all these constituents of our being, which we cling to and identify with, turn out to be non-self (*anattā*), not our true identity. The texts offer various approaches to the realization of the non-self nature of the aggregates. The well-known "Discourse on the Non-Self Characteristic" (**2.9**) proposes two arguments for dispelling the identification of the aggregates as a self. The first proceeds from the recognition that each aggregate is subject to affliction. Being bound by processes beyond our control—processes of change and decay—the aggregates cannot be made to conform to our wishes, which should be possible if they were truly our self, truly "I" and "mine." The second argument begins with the empirical observation that the aggregates are all impermanent. Being impermanent, they are also *dukkha*, defective and unsatisfactory. And since they all turn out to be impermanent, *dukkha*, and subject to change, they are not fit to be regarded as "mine" or "I" or "my self."

While the three-step sequence from impermanence to suffering to non-self is the usual procedure the Buddha offers for cutting off identification with the aggregates, other texts offer more compressed strategies. Some proceed straight from the impermanence of the aggregates to the destruction of the defilements. Thus **2.16** maintains that perception of the aggregates as impermanent "eliminates all sensual lust, eliminates all lust for form, eliminates all lust for existence, eliminates all ignorance, demolishes all conceit 'I am.'" Others, such as **2.11**, suggest that one can directly contemplate the five aggregates as non-self, without proceeding through the preliminary steps. Text **2.15** exposes the intrinsic emptiness of the five aggregates, comparing them, respectively, to a lump of foam, bubbles on the surface of water, a mirage, a plantain trunk, and a magical illusion. While these appear solid to the untrained eye, on inspection they turn out to be void, hollow, and insubstantial. So too, when the aggregates are closely investigated with insight, they turn out to be void, hollow, and insubstantial.

No matter which approach is taken, the culmination is always the same. By seeing into the non-self nature of the aggregates, one becomes disenchanted. And then, "being disenchanted, one becomes dispassionate. Through dispassion one is liberated. In regard to what is liberated, the knowledge occurs thus: 'Liberated.' One understands: 'Finished is birth, the spiritual life has been lived, what had to be done has been done, there is no further for this state of being.'"

1. Aniccasutta

Impermanent (SN 22:12; III 21)

"Rūpaṃ, bhikkhave, aniccaṃ, vedanā aniccā, saññā aniccā, saṅkhārā aniccā, viññāṇaṃ aniccaṃ.

"Form, monks, impermanent, feeling impermanent, perception impermanent, volitional-activities impermanent, consciousness impermanent.

"Form, monks, is impermanent, feeling is impermanent, perception is impermanent, volitional activities are impermanent, consciousness is impermanent.

"Evaṃ passaṃ, bhikkhave, sutavā ariyasāvako rūpasmimpi nibbindati, vedanāyapi nibbindati, saññāyapi nibbindati, saṅkhāresupi nibbindati, viññāṇasmimpi nibbindati.

"Thus seeing, monks, the learned noble-disciple in regard to form-too is disenchanted, in regard to feeling-too is disenchanted, in regard to perception-too is disenchanted, in regard to volitional-activities-too is disenchanted, in regard to consciousness-too is disenchanted.

"Thus seeing, monks, the learned noble disciple becomes disenchanted with form, disenchanted with feeling, disenchanted with perception, disenchanted with volitional activities, disenchanted with consciousness.

"Nibbindaṃ virajjati. Virāgā vimuccati. Vimuttasmiṃ vimuttamiti ñāṇaṃ hoti. 'Khīṇā jāti, vusitaṃ brahmacariyaṃ, kataṃ karaṇīyaṃ, nāparaṃ itthattāyā'ti pajānātī"ti.

"Being disenchanted, becomes dispassionate. Through dispassion is liberated. In liberated, 'liberated' thus knowledge occurs. 'Finished birth, lived the spiritual-life, done what-is-to-be-done, not-further for such-a-state,' understands."

"Being disenchanted, he becomes dispassionate. Through dispassion he is liberated. In regard to what is liberated, the knowledge occurs thus: 'Liberated.' He understands: 'Finished is birth, the spiritual life has been lived, what had to be done has been done, there is no further for this state of being.'"

Grammatical explanations

rūpaṃ: "form," a neuter noun in the nominative case. The word has two primary senses: (1) *material form*, the first of the five aggregates, intended here; and (2) a *visible object*, the first of the six sense objects. Occasionally the word also occurs as the second part of a compound, meaning "nature," as in *piyarūpa*, "a pleasant nature" (see p. 374).

aniccaṃ: "impermanent," a negation (*a-*) of permanent (*nicca*), here neuter nominative in agreement with *rūpaṃ*. It is also neuter following *viññāṇaṃ*. Following *vedanā* and *saññā* it is feminine singular, and following *saṅkhārā* it is masculine plural. Since the statement merely predicates the quality to the noun, a verb is not necessary.

evaṃ passaṃ: "thus seeing." *Passaṃ* is a masculine singular nominative present participle of *passati*; it is here in agreement with the subject, *ariyasāvako*. On the declension of the present participle, see Duroiselle §§439–440 and §219–26; Perniola §§94–95.

sutavā: "learned, instructed"; masculine nominative of *sutavat*, in agreement with *ariyasāvako*. The word is an adjective composed of *suta*, "learning" (a noun derived from the past participle), and the possessive suffix *-vat*. On the declension of substantives ending in *-vat*, see Duroiselle §§229–30; Perniola §34.

rūpasmiṃ: "in regard to form"; a singular locative, with *-ṃ* changing to *-m* before the labial consonant *pi*.

nibbindati: "becomes disenchanted with, repelled by, disgusted with"; a third-person singular indicative verb, with the locative *rūpasmiṃ* as its object. The verb is composed of the prefix *nir-* and *vindati*, "finds, knows." In Pāli, the sandhi of *r* + *v* results in *-bb-*, as seen too in Pāli *nibbāna* for Skt *nirvāṇa*.

vedanāya, etc.: locatives of the respective aggregates.

nibbindaṃ: a present participle of *nibbindati*, masculine singular nominative in agreement with *ariyasāvako*.

virajjati: "becomes dispassionate"; a third-person singular verb in the present indicative.

virāgā: "through dispassion"; the case is ablative, in the sense of cause.

vimuccati: "is liberated"; a passive verb in the third-person singular.

vimuttasmiṃ: "in regard to what is liberated"; a locative of the past participle *vimutta*. Since *vimuttasmiṃ* can be either neuter or masculine, the subject of the participle could be either *cittaṃ*, "mind," or *so*, "he," the noble disciple. It is possible, but uncertain, that *vimuttasmiṃ* is a locative absolute past participle without a corresponding locative subject, in which case it would bear the meaning "when liberated."

vimuttamiti ñāṇaṃ hoti: *Iti* following *vimuttam* serves as a quotation marker, highlighting the object of knowledge. Again, it is ambiguous whether the object of this knowledge is the mind or the person. The past participle *vimuttaṃ* is neuter, which would agree with *cittaṃ*, "mind," but up to this point the sutta has been speaking about the *ariyasāvaka*, a person. I have replicated the ambiguity by simply using "liberated" without specifying whether the word refers to the mind or the person. In either case, since the mind and the person are inseparable, the choice is insignificant.

khīṇā: "finished, destroyed, ended"; a past participle of *khiṇāti* qualifying the feminine noun *jāti*.

vusitaṃ: "lived"; a past participle of *vasati* qualifying the neuter noun *brahmacariyaṃ*.

kataṃ karaṇīyaṃ: "what had to be done has been done"; a past participle, *kataṃ*, "done," followed by the future passive participle, *karaṇīyaṃ*, used as a noun, "what should be done," that is, a duty or task.

nāparaṃ (= *na aparaṃ*): "not further, no more."

itthattāya: dative of the abstract noun *itthatta*, formed from *ittha*, "thus," and the abstract suffix *-tta* (Skt *-tva*). DOP defines *itthatta* as "the state of being thus; existence in this form; existence here." The word sometimes refers to the human realm or the sense-sphere realm in contrast to other realms, sometimes (as here) to all existence within saṃsāra.

2. Sahetu-aniccasutta

Impermanent with Cause (SN 22:18; III 23)

"Rūpaṃ, bhikkhave, aniccaṃ. Yopi hetu yopi paccayo rūpassa uppādāya, sopi anicco. Aniccasambhūtaṃ, bhikkhave, rūpaṃ kuto niccaṃ bhavissati?

"Form, monks, impermanent. Which-too the cause, which-too the condition, of form for arising—that-too impermanent. Impermanent-originated, monks, form, how permanent will be?

"Form, monks, is impermanent. The cause and condition for the arising of form is also impermanent. How, monks, could form, which has originated from what is impermanent, be permanent?

"Vedanā aniccā. . . . Saññā aniccā. . . . Saṅkhārā aniccā. . . . Viññāṇaṃ aniccaṃ. Yopi hetu yopi paccayo viññāṇassa uppādāya, sopi anicco. Aniccasambhūtaṃ, bhikkhave, viññāṇaṃ kuto niccaṃ bhavissati?"

"Feeling impermanent. . . . Perception impermanent. . . . Volitional-activities impermanent. . . . Consciousness impermanent. Which-too the cause, which-too the condition, of consciousness for arising—that-too impermanent. Impermanent-originated, monks, consciousness, how permanent will be?"

"Feeling is impermanent. . . . Perception is impermanent. . . . Volitional activities are impermanent. . . . Consciousness is impermanent. The cause and condition for the arising of consciousness is also impermanent. How, monks, could consciousness, which has originated from what is impermanent, be permanent?"

Grammatical explanations

yo: the relative pronoun, here masculine singular as qualifying *hetu* and *paccayo*. It is completed in the main clause by the demonstrative pronoun *so*.

hetu: "cause"; *paccayo*: "condition." While later systems of Buddhist thought distinguish between *hetu* as a primary cause and *paccaya* as a supporting condition, the suttas use the two words almost synonymously.

uppādāya: "for the arising"; a dative of purpose.

aniccasambhūtaṃ: "originating [from] the impermanent"; an ablative tappurisa compound, used as an adjective in apposition to *rūpaṃ*. In the compound *anicca* functions as a noun, "what is impermanent," ablative in sense. *Sambhūta* is the past participle of *sambhavati*, "originates, comes to be."

kuto: "how?"; an interrogative.

bhavissati: the future of *bhavati*, here showing possibility—"could be"—rather than future status, "will be." See Perniola §274c.

3. Pariññasutta

Full Understanding (SN 22:23; III 26)

"Pariññeyye ca, bhikkhave, dhamme desessāmi pariññañca. Taṃ suṇātha. Katame ca, bhikkhave, pariññeyyā dhammā? Rūpaṃ, bhikkhave, pariññeyyo dhammo, vedanā pariññeyyo dhammo, saññā pariññeyyo dhammo, saṅkhārā pariññeyyo dhammo, viññāṇaṃ pariññeyyo dhammo. Ime vuccanti, bhikkhave, pariññeyyā dhammā.

"To-be-fully-understood and, monks, things I will teach, full understanding-and. That listen. What and, monks, to-be-fully-understood things? Form, monks, to-be-fully-understood thing, feeling to-be-fully-understood thing, perception to-be-fully-understood thing, volitional-activities to-be-fully-understood thing, consciousness to-be-fully-understood thing. These are called, monks, 'to-be-fully-understood things.'

"I will teach you, monks, things to be fully understood, and full understanding. Listen to that. And what, monks, are things to be fully understood? Form, monks, is a thing to be fully understood, feeling is a thing to be fully understood, perception is a thing to be fully understood, volitional activities are things to be fully understood, consciousness is a thing to be fully understood. These are called, monks, 'things to be fully understood.'

"Katamā ca, bhikkhave, pariññā? Yo, bhikkhave, rāgakkhayo dosakkhayo mohakkhayo: ayaṃ vuccati, bhikkhave, 'pariññā'"ti.

"What and, monks, full-understanding? Which, monks, lust-destruction, hatred-destruction, delusion-destruction: this is called, monks, 'full-understanding.'"

"And what, monks, is full understanding? The destruction of lust, the destruction of hatred, the destruction of delusion: this, monks, is called 'full understanding.'"

Grammatical explanations

pariññeyye: "to be fully understood"; a future passive participle of *parijānāti*, used as an adjective describing *dhamme*; hence it is a plural accusative in agreement with *dhamme*. Just below it occurs as singular nominative in agreement with *dhammo*.

dhamme: here in the general sense of "things"; a masculine plural in the accusative case, as object of *desessāmi*. On the multiple meanings of *dhamma*, see Glossary.

desessāmi: "will teach"; the first-person singular future of *deseti*.

pariññaṃ: "full understanding"; a feminine singular in the accusative case. In the suttas *pariññā* is considered an achievement of the arahant, though the commentaries explain *pariññā* as already beginning at the stage of deep insight.[88]

suṇātha: "listen"; as addressed to the monks, a second-person plural imperative.

saṅkhārā pariññeyyo dhammo: Although *saṅkhārā* is a masculine plural, *pariññeyyo dhammo* is singular, perhaps for consistency with the parallel clauses.

ime vuccanti, bhikkhave, pariññeyyā dhammā: "these are called, monks, things to be fully understood." The pronoun *ime* is plural masculine nominative agreeing with *dhammā*.

rāgakkhayo, etc.: "the destruction of lust," etc. These are genitive tappurisa compounds, each in the masculine singular nominative.

88. On the commentarial scheme of three kinds of *pariññā*, see Vism 606–7.

4. Abhijānasutta

Directly Knowing (SN 22:24; III 26–27)

"Rūpaṃ, bhikkhave, anabhijānaṃ aparijānaṃ avirājayaṃ appajahaṃ abhabbo dukkhakkhayāya. Vedanaṃ anabhijānaṃ . . . Saññaṃ anabhijānaṃ . . . Saṅkhāre anabhijānaṃ . . . Viññāṇaṃ anabhijānaṃ aparijānaṃ avirājayaṃ appajahaṃ abhabbo dukkhakkhayāya.

"Form, monks, not-directly-knowing, not-fully-understanding, not-removing-passion, not-abandoning, incapable for suffering-destruction. Feeling not-directly-knowing . . . Perception not-directly-knowing . . . Volitional-activities not-directly-knowing . . . Consciousness not-directly-knowing, not-fully-understanding, not-removing-passion, not-abandoning, incapable for suffering-destruction.

"One not directly knowing form, monks, not fully understanding it, not removing passion for it, not abandoning it, is incapable of the destruction of suffering. One not directly knowing feeling . . . One not directly knowing perception . . . One not directly knowing volitional activities . . . One not directly knowing consciousness, not fully understanding it, not removing passion for it, not abandoning it, is incapable of the destruction of suffering.

"Rūpañca kho, bhikkhave, abhijānaṃ parijānaṃ virājayaṃ pajahaṃ bhabbo dukkhakkhayāya. Vedanaṃ abhijānaṃ . . . Saññaṃ abhijānaṃ . . . Saṅkhāre abhijānaṃ . . . Viññāṇaṃ abhijānaṃ parijānaṃ virājayaṃ pajahaṃ bhabbo dukkhakkhayāyā"ti.

"Form but, monks, directly-knowing, fully-understanding, removing-passion, abandoning, capable for suffering-destruction. Feeling directly-knowing . . . Perception directly-knowing . . . Volitional-activities directly-knowing . . . Consciousness directly-knowing, fully-understanding, removing-passion, abandoning, capable for suffering-destruction."

"But one directly knowing form, monks, fully understanding it, removing passion for it, abandoning it, is capable of the destruction of suffering. One directly knowing feeling . . . One directly knowing perception . . . One directly knowing volitional activities . . . One directly knowing consciousness, fully understanding it, removing passion for it, abandoning it, is capable of the destruction of suffering."

Grammatical explanations

abhijānaṃ: "directly knowing"; a present participle of *abhijānāti*, in the masculine singular nominative, with the subject "one" inherent in the participle. The present participles that follow are likewise all masculine singular nominatives. In the suttas *abhijānāti* (and its derivatives) signifies a more elementary level of knowledge than *parijānāti*. The former already occurs at the stage of the trainee (*sekha*) while the latter marks the attainment of arahantship.[89]

parijānaṃ: "fully understanding"; a present participle of *parijānāti*.

virājayaṃ: "removing passion"; a present participle of *virājeti*, a causative of *virajjati*, "to become dispassionate." While the indicative verb suggests a process that occurs naturally, the causative implies deliberate effort; hence I use "removing passion" to convey this nuance.

pajahaṃ: "abandoning"; a present participle of *pajahati*.

bhabbo: "capable"; a masculine singular nominative describing the subject "one." It is an idiomatic use of the future passive participle of *bhavati* (*bhav* + *ya* > *bhavya* > *bhabba*), with a dative designating what one is capable (or incapable) of.

dukkhakkhayāya: "for the destruction of suffering"; a tappurisa compound in the dative case.

5. Assādasutta—1

Enjoyment—1 (SN 22:26; III 27–28)

[1. The three perspectives]

"Pubbeva me, bhikkhave, sambodhā anabhisambuddhassa bodhisattass'eva sato etadahosi: 'Ko nu kho rūpassa assādo, ko ādīnavo, kiṃ nissaraṇaṃ?

89. On this, see MN I 4, which says that the trainee (*sekha*) directly knows earth as earth (*sopi pathaviṃ pathavito abhijānāti*) but must proceed further to fully understand it (*pariññeyyaṃ tassa*). Only the arahant is said to have fully understood earth and the other bases of misconception (*pariññātaṃ tassa*).

Ko vedanāya assādo, ko ādīnavo, kiṃ nissaraṇaṃ? Ko saññāya assādo, ko ādīnavo, kiṃ nissaraṇaṃ? Ko saṅkhārānaṃ assādo, ko ādīnavo, kiṃ nissaraṇaṃ? Ko viññāṇassa assādo, ko ādīnavo, kiṃ nissaraṇan'ti?

"Before-indeed to me, monks, from enlightenment, to an unenlightened bodhisatta just being, this-occurred: 'What of form the enjoyment, what the danger, what the escape? What of feeling the enjoyment, what the danger, what the escape? What of perception the enjoyment, what the danger, what the escape? What of volitional-activities the enjoyment, what the danger, what the escape? What of consciousness the enjoyment, what the danger, what the escape?'

"Before the enlightenment, monks, while I was just a bodhisatta, not fully enlightened, this occurred to me: 'What is the enjoyment in form, what is the danger, what is the escape? What is the enjoyment in feeling, what is the danger, what is the escape? What is the enjoyment in perception, what is the danger, what is the escape? What is the enjoyment in volitional activities, what is the danger, what is the escape? What is the enjoyment in consciousness, what is the danger, what is the escape?'

"Tassa mayhaṃ, bhikkhave, etadahosi: 'Yaṃ kho rūpaṃ paṭicca uppajjati sukhaṃ somanassaṃ, ayaṃ rūpassa assādo. Yaṃ rūpaṃ aniccaṃ dukkhaṃ vipariṇāmadhammaṃ, ayaṃ rūpassa ādīnavo. Yo rūpasmiṃ chandarāgavinayo chandarāgappahānaṃ, idaṃ rūpassa nissaraṇaṃ. Yaṃ vedanaṃ paṭicca . . . Yaṃ saññaṃ paṭicca . . . Yaṃ saṅkhāre paṭicca . . . Yaṃ viññāṇaṃ paṭicca uppajjati sukhaṃ somanassaṃ, ayaṃ viññāṇassa assādo. Yaṃ viññāṇaṃ aniccaṃ dukkhaṃ vipariṇāmadhammaṃ, ayaṃ viññāṇassa ādīnavo. Yo viññāṇasmiṃ chandarāgavinayo chandarāgappahānaṃ, idaṃ viññāṇassa nissaraṇaṃ.'

"To that to me, monks, this occurred: 'Which form in dependence on arises pleasure joy, this of form the enjoyment. Which form impermanent, suffering, change-subject-to, this of form the danger. Which in regard to form desire-lust-removal, desire-lust-abandoning, this of form the escape. Which feeling in dependence on . . . Which perception in dependence on . . . Which volitional-activities in dependence on . . . Which consciousness in dependence on arises pleasure joy, this of consciousness the enjoyment. Which consciousness impermanent, suffering, change-subject-to, this of form the danger. Which in regard to consciousness desire-lust-removal, desire-lust-abandoning, this of form the escape.'

"This occurred to me, monks: 'The pleasure and joy that arise in dependence on form: this is the enjoyment in form. That form is impermanent, suffering, and subject to change: this is the danger in form. The removal of desire-and-lust, the abandonment of desire-and-lust, in regard to form: this is the escape from form. The pleasure and joy that arise in dependence on feeling . . . . in dependence on perception . . . in dependence on volitional activities . . . . in dependence on consciousness: this is the enjoyment in consciousness. That consciousness is impermanent, suffering, and subject to change: this is the danger in consciousness. The removal of desire-and-lust, the abandonment of desire-and-lust, in regard to consciousness: this is the escape from consciousness.'

[2. The proclamation of enlightenment]

"Yāvakīvañcāhaṃ, bhikkhave, imesaṃ pañcannaṃ upādānakkhandhānaṃ evaṃ assādañca assādato, ādīnavañca ādīnavato, nissaraṇañca nissaraṇato, yathābhūtaṃ nābbhaññāsiṃ, n'eva tāvāhaṃ, bhikkhave, sadevake loke samārake sabrahmake, sassamaṇabrāhmaṇiyā pajāya sadevamanussāya, 'anuttaraṃ sammāsambodhiṃ abhisambuddho'ti paccaññāsiṃ.

"So-long-as-and-I, monks, of these five clinging-aggregates thus the enjoyment-and as the enjoyment, the danger-and as the danger, the escape-and as the escape, as-really-is not directly-knew, not so-long-I, monks, in with-devas world with-Māra with-Brahmā, in with-ascetics-brahmins population, with-devas-humans, 'Unsurpassed perfect-enlightenment enlightened' claimed.

"So long, monks, as I did not directly know as it really is, in regard to these five clinging-aggregates, the enjoyment as the enjoyment, the danger as the danger, and the escape as the escape, for so long, monks, in the world with its devas, Marā, and Brahmā, in the population with its ascetics and brahmins, its devas and humans, I did not claim: 'I have been enlightened to the unsurpassed perfect enlightenment.'

"Yato ca khvāhaṃ, bhikkhave, imesaṃ pañcannaṃ upādānakkhandhānaṃ evaṃ assādañca assādato, ādīnavañca ādīnavato, nissaraṇañca nissaraṇato, yathābhūtaṃ abbhaññāsiṃ, athāhaṃ, bhikkhave, sadevake loke samārake sabrahmake, sassamaṇabrāhmaṇiyā pajāya sadevamanussāya, 'anuttaraṃ sammāsambodhiṃ abhisambuddho'ti paccaññāsiṃ. Ñāṇañca pana me dassanaṃ udapādi: 'Akuppā me cetovimutti; ayam antimā jāti; natthi dāni punabbhavo'"ti.

"When but I, monks, of these five clinging-aggregates thus the enjoyment-and as the enjoyment, the danger-and as the danger, the escape-and as the escape, as-really-is directly-knew, then I, monks, in with-devas world with-Māra with-Brahmā, in with-ascetics-brahmins population, with-devas-humans, 'Unsurpassed perfect-enlightenment enlightened' claimed. Knowledge-and for me vision arose: 'Unshakable my mind-liberation; this last birth; there-is-not now again-existence.'"

"But when, monks, I directly knew as it really is, in regard to these five clinging-aggregates, the enjoyment as the enjoyment, the danger as the danger, and the escape as the escape, then, monks, in the world with its devas, Marā, and Brahmā, in the population with its ascetics and brahmins, its devas and humans, I claimed: 'I have been enlightened to the unsurpassed perfect enlightenment.' And the knowledge and vision arose for me: 'Unshakable is my liberation of mind; this is my final birth; now there is no renewed existence.'"

Grammatical explanations

[1. The three perspectives]
pubbeva: "in the past, before, prior to, previous to."[90] This might be resolved *pubbe* + *eva* or *pubbaṃ* + *eva*, with elision of *-ṃ* before *eva*.
me: the enclitic (internal) personal first-person pronoun. The pronoun

90. Ps I 113,15 glosses the expression occurring at MN I 17,6 thus: *pubbeva sambodhā ti sambodhato pubbeva.* Spk II 21,2–3 glosses the same expression at SN II 5,10 thus: *pubbeva sambodhā ti sambodho vuccati catūsu maggesu ñāṇaṃ, tato pubbeva* ("The knowledge in the four paths is called 'enlightenment'; prior to that"). *Sambodhato* and *tato* are ablatives, which shows that *pubbe/pubbaṃ* can take the ablative of the corresponding noun. SED, under *pūrva*, says that the indeclinable *pūrvaṃ* can function as a preposition with the ablative.

is part of the dative (or perhaps genitive) construction with *bodhisattass'eva sato*, not the possessive of *sambodhā*.[91]

sambodhā: The word for "enlightenment" is here in the ablative case relative to *pubbeva*.

anabhisambuddhassa . . . etadahosi: "while I was just a bodhisatta, not fully enlightened, this occurred to me." In the present sentence *me* represents the passive dative subject, described as *anabhisambuddhassa bodhisattassa*, "an unenlightened bodhisatta," with *eva* added for emphasis. *Sato* is the present participle of *atthi*, masculine singular dative in agreement with *bodhisattassa*. On this use of the dative, Wijesekera §97c says: "An idiomatic and popular usage is the dative of the person with the verb *hoti* (usually the aorist *ahosi*) used impersonally to mean 'it occurred to. . . .'"[92] Since dative and genitive forms are often identical, other grammarians (among them Warder and Perniola) explain the case in such constructions as genitive.

ko, kiṃ: These are interrogatives, their gender agreeing with the nouns they qualify.

nu kho: the interrogative particle *nu*, with *kho* a mere expletive. Neither is translatable but they give the sentence an interrogative flavor.

assādo, ādīnavo, nissaraṇaṃ: "enjoyment, danger, escape." This triad occurs in relation to several doctrinal sets mentioned in the Nikāyas. Here it is the five aggregates, elsewhere the four elements (SN II 170), the twelve sense bases (SN IV 7), sensual pleasures, form, and feeling (MN I 85–90), and even the world (AN I 258–59).

tassa mayhaṃ . . . etadahosi: "This occurred to me"; another example of the construction referred to just above in which the thinker serves as the passive subject of the thought. The grammatical subject is *etad* (< *etaṃ*), "this," indicating the thought; the datives *tassa mayhaṃ*, "to me," represent the bodhisatta, the thinker. The use of a third-person pronoun followed by a first-person pronoun has a strengthening function.[93]

91. Proof of this is at MN I 17,6, where we find: *Mayhampi kho, brāhmaṇa, pubbeva sambodhā anabhisambuddhassa bodhisattass'eva sato etadahosi.* Here there is no *me* between *pubbeva* and *sambodhā*, but instead the proper dative *mayham* at the beginning of the sentence. Thus in the present clause *me* must be a dative in agreement with the other datives, not a possessive genitive.

92. I am thankful to Beatrice Chrystall for calling my attention to this passage.

93. See Geiger §106.1.

yaṃ kho rūpaṃ paṭicca uppajjati sukhaṃ somanassaṃ: "The pleasure and joy that arise in dependence on form." Here *yaṃ* qualifies *sukhaṃ somanassaṃ* and is completed by *ayaṃ* in the main clause. *Paṭicca*, "dependent on," absolutive of *pacceti*, is used adverbially; it takes its object (*rūpaṃ* and the other aggregates) in the accusative. In the phrase *uppajjati sukhaṃ somanassaṃ* normal word order is inverted, with the verb *uppajjati* preceding its subjects, *sukhaṃ somanassaṃ*, probably for emphasis.

ayaṃ rūpassa assādo: "this is the enjoyment in form." While *ayaṃ*, "this," refers back to *sukhaṃ somanassaṃ*, both neuters, its gender is masculine in agreement with *assādo*.

yaṃ rūpaṃ aniccaṃ dukkhaṃ vipariṇāmadhammaṃ: "That form is impermanent, suffering, and subject to change." *Yaṃ* here introduces a reason, somewhat like "since" or "because."[94] *Vipariṇāmadhammaṃ*, "subject to change," is a bahubbīhi compound describing *rūpaṃ*. At the end of bahubbīhi compounds *-dhamma* is commonly used in the sense of "subject to" or "having the nature of."

chandarāgavinayo chandarāgappahānaṃ: "the removal of desire-and-lust, the abandonment of desire-and-lust"; two genitive tappurisa compounds built upon the dvanda *chandarāga*.

idaṃ rūpassa nissaraṇaṃ: "this is the escape from form." While in English the object of "escape" takes the preposition "from" (for instance, "escape from danger"), in Pāli the noun *nissaraṇa* takes its dependent word in the genitive; however, the corresponding verb, *nissarati*, takes its object in the ablative (see p. 157).

[2. The proclamation of enlightenment]

yāvakīvañcāhaṃ (= *yāvakīvaṃ* + *ca* + *ahaṃ*): On *yāvakīvaṃ*, see p. 121.

pañcannaṃ: genitive of *pañca*, "five," in relation to *upādānakkhandhānaṃ*.

assādañca assādato, etc.: *Assādaṃ*, *ādīnavaṃ*, and *nissaraṇaṃ* are the objects of *abbhaññāsiṃ*; in each case, *-ṃ* is replaced by *-ñ* in sandhi with *ca*. The ablative suffix *-to*, used with nouns or adjectives in relation to acts of perception, knowledge, and understanding, often has the sense of "as"—that is, perceiving, knowing, or understanding something in a

94. On this use of the relative pronoun, see SED under *yad* (844b): "*yad* also = . . . since, because."

particular way, "as X." In this passage, *assādato* has the sense of "as enjoyment." And so *ādīnavato* and *nissaraṇato*, respectively, mean "as danger" and "as escape." Wijesekera calls this form "the ablative of viewpoint" (§133), Perniola calls it the ablative of limitation (§257d). For another example, see Dhp 12: *sārañca sārato ñatvā asārañca asārato*, "having known the essential as essential, and the inessential as inessential."

yathābhūtaṃ nābbhaññāsiṃ: *Abbhaññāsiṃ* is the first-person s-aorist of *abhijānāti* (Duroiselle §§418–24; Perniola §220), with the *a-* augment. Before the augment the prefix *abhi* undergoes the following modifications: *abhi* + *a* > *abhya* > *abbha*. Following the augment, *-ñ-*, the initial consonant of the base, is doubled, representing the lost *-j-* of Skt *ajñāsiṣaṃ*. The statement is a negation, with *na* joined in sandhi to the initial vowel of the verb.

n'eva (= *na* + *eva*): an emphatic negation of the verb *paccaññāsiṃ* at the end of the sentence.

tāvāhaṃ (= *tāva* + *ahaṃ*): *tāva*, "for so long," the correlative of *yāvakīva*.

sadevake . . . sadevamanussāya: see p. 109.

n'eva tāvāhaṃ . . . "anuttaraṃ sammāsambodhiṃ abhisambuddho"ti paccaññāsiṃ: "for so long I did not claim: 'I have been enlightened to the unsurpassed perfect enlightenment.'" Since the verb *abhisambujjhati* often takes *anuttaraṃ sammāsambodhiṃ* as its own object, I have assumed that *anuttaraṃ sammāsambodhiṃ abhisambuddho* forms a complete utterance, which is the claim that the Buddha *did not* make at this point (as *n'eva tāvāhaṃ* indicates). *Anuttaraṃ sammāsambodhiṃ* is an accusative, but in actuality the Buddha does not become enlightened to enlightenment itself (which would be redundant), but *through* the enlightenment he becomes enlightened to the four noble truths.

paccaññāsiṃ: another s-aorist based on the root *ñā*. The indicative is *paṭijānāti*, "admits, acknowledges, claims." The prefix *paṭi* before the *-a-* augment undergoes palatalization as follows: *paṭi* + *a* > *paṭya* > *pacca*. The corresponding noun is *paṭiññā*, a claim or promise.

yato ca khvāhaṃ: This begins the positive counterpart, with *ca* being used in the disjunctive sense, "but." *Khvāham* is a sandhi of *kho* and *ahaṃ* (see Duroiselle §27; Geiger §71c).

ñāṇañca pana me dassanaṃ udapādi: "and the knowledge and vision arose for me." *Ca pana* is just a connective, "and." *Ñāṇaṃ* and *dassanaṃ* are used almost synonymously as a single nominative subject, knowledge and vision. The singular verb *udapādi* is an is-aorist of *uppajjati*, "arises," from the root *pad* (strengthened to *pād*), with the *-a-* augment inserted between the prefix *ud-* and the base.

akuppā: a negative future passive participle of *kuppati*, "is shaken," from *a* + *kupya*, with assimilation of *-y-* to the preceding consonant. The gender is feminine in agreement with *cetovimutti*.

natthi dāni punabbhavo: see p. 106.

6. Assādasutta—3

Enjoyment—3 (SN 22:28; III 29–31)

[1. Attachment, disenchantment, escape]

"No ce'daṃ, bhikkhave, rūpassa assādo abhavissa, nayidaṃ sattā rūpasmiṃ sārajjeyyuṃ. Yasmā ca kho, bhikkhave, atthi rūpassa assādo, tasmā sattā rūpasmiṃ sārajjanti.

"Not if this, monks, of form enjoyment were, not-this beings in regard to form would become attached. Because but, monks, there is of form enjoyment, therefore beings in regard to form become attached.

"If, monks, there were no enjoyment in form, beings would not become attached to form. But because there is enjoyment in form, beings become attached to form.

"No ce'daṃ, bhikkhave, rūpassa ādīnavo abhavissa, nayidaṃ sattā rūpasmiṃ nibbindeyyuṃ. Yasmā ca kho, bhikkhave, atthi rūpassa ādīnavo, tasmā sattā rūpasmiṃ nibbindanti.

"Not if this, monks, of form danger were, not-this beings in regard to form would become disenchanted. Because but, monks, there is of form danger, therefore beings in regard to form become disenchanted.

"If there were no danger in form, beings would not become disenchanted with form. But because there is danger in form, beings become disenchanted with form.

"No ce'daṃ, bhikkhave, rūpassa nissaraṇaṃ abhavissa, nayidaṃ sattā rūpasmā nissareyyuṃ. Yasmā ca kho, bhikkhave, atthi rūpassa nissaraṇaṃ, tasmā sattā rūpasmā nissaranti.

"Not if this, monks, of form escape were, not-this beings from form would escape. Because but, monks, there is of form escape, therefore beings from form escape.

"If there were no escape from form, beings would not escape from form. But because there is an escape from form, beings escape from form.

"No ce'daṃ, bhikkhave, vedanāya . . . sannāya . . . saṅkhārānaṃ . . . viññāṇassa assādo abhavissa, nayidaṃ sattā viññāṇasmiṃ sārajjeyyuṃ. Yasmā ca kho, bhikkhave, atthi viññāṇassa assādo, tasmā sattā viññāṇasmiṃ sārajjanti. No ce'daṃ, bhikkhave, viññāṇassa ādīnavo abhavissa, nayidaṃ sattā viññāṇasmiṃ nibbindeyyuṃ. Yasmā ca kho, bhikkhave, atthi viññāṇassa ādīnavo, tasmā sattā viññāṇasmiṃ nibbindanti. No ce'daṃ, bhikkhave, viññāṇassa nissaraṇaṃ abhavissa, nayidaṃ sattā viññāṇasmā nissareyyuṃ. Yasmā ca kho, bhikkhave, atthi viññāṇassa nissaraṇaṃ, tasmā sattā viññāṇasmā nissaranti.

"Not if this, monks, of feeling . . . of perception . . . of volitional-activities . . . of consciousness enjoyment were, not-this beings in regard to consciousness would become attached. Because but, monks, there is of consciousness enjoyment, therefore beings in regard to consciousness become attached. Not if this, monks, of consciousness danger were, not-this beings in regard to consciousness would become disenchanted. Because but, monks, there is of consciousness danger, therefore beings in regard to consciousness become disenchanted. Not if this, monks, of consciousness escape were, not-this beings from consciousness would escape. Because but, monks, there is of consciousness escape, therefore beings from consciousness escape.

"If, monks, there were no enjoyment in feeling . . . in perception . . . in volitional activities . . . in consciousness, beings would not become attached to consciousness. But because there is enjoyment in consciousness, beings become attached to consciousness. If there were no danger in consciousness, beings would not become disenchanted with consciousness. But because there is danger in consciousness, beings become disenchanted with consciousness. If there were no escape from consciousness, beings would not escape from consciousness. But because there is an escape from consciousness, beings escape from consciousness.

[2. How beings attain release]

"Yāvakīvañca, bhikkhave, sattā imesaṃ pañcannaṃ upādānakkhandhānaṃ assādañca assādato, ādīnavañca ādīnavato, nissaraṇañca nissaraṇato, yathābhūtaṃ nābbhaññiṃsu, n'eva tāva, bhikkhave, sattā sadevakā lokā samārakā sabrahmakā, sassamaṇabrāhmaṇiyā pajāya sadevamanussāya, nissaṭā visaṃyuttā vippamuttā vimariyādīkatena cetasā vihariṃsu.

"So-long-as-and, monks, beings of these five clinging-aggregates the enjoyment-and as enjoyment, the danger-and as danger, the escape-and as escape, as-really-is not-directly-knew, not so long, monks, beings in with-devas world, with-Māra, with-Brahmā, in with-ascetics-brahmins population, with-devas-humans, released, detached, freed, with unboundary-made mind dwelled.

"So long, monks, as beings have not directly known as it really is, in regard to these five clinging-aggregates, the enjoyment as enjoyment, the danger as danger, and the escape as escape, for so long, monks, in the world with its devas, Māra, and Brahmā, in the population with its ascetics and brahmins, its devas and humans, beings did not dwell released, detached, freed, with mind made without a boundary.

"Yato ca kho, bhikkhave, sattā imesaṃ pañcannaṃ upādānakkhandhānaṃ assādañca assādato, ādīnavañca ādīnavato, nissaraṇañca nissaraṇato, yathābhūtaṃ abbhaññiṃsu, atha, bhikkhave, sattā sadevakā lokā samārakā sabrahmakā, sassamaṇabrāhmaṇiyā pajāya sadevamanussāya, nissaṭā visaṃyuttā vippamuttā vimariyādīkatena cetasā viharanti."

"When but, monks, beings of these five clinging-aggregates the enjoyment-and as enjoyment, the danger-and as danger, the escape-and as escape as-really-is directly-knew, then, monks, beings in with-devas world, with-Māra, with-Brahmā, in with-ascetics-brahmins population, with-devas-humans, released, detached, freed, with unboundary-made mind dwell."

"But when, monks, beings have directly known as it really is, in regard to these five clinging-aggregates, the enjoyment as enjoyment, the danger as danger, and the escape as escape, then, monks, in the world with its devas, Māra, and Brahmā, in the population with its ascetics and brahmins, its devas and humans, beings dwell released, detached, freed, with mind made without a boundary."

Grammatical explanations

[1. Attachment, disenchantment, escape]

no ce'daṃ: emphatic negative particle *no*, "not," followed by *ce*, the conditional "if," which in turn is followed by neuter *idaṃ*, "this," with the initial vowel elided by sandhi. *Idaṃ* here does not qualify *assādo* (in which case the masculine *ayaṃ* would be needed) but serves as an indeclinable representing the situation to be described.[95]

abhavissa: the conditional (or hypothetical) form of *bhavati*, here third-person singular (Duroiselle §615; Perniola §81).

nayidaṃ: a sandhi of *na* and *idaṃ*, with *-y-* inserted for euphony. The neuter *idaṃ* again is probably an indeclinable pointing to the entire consequence that follows.

sārajjeyyuṃ: "would become attached"; the third-person plural of *sārajjati*, in the optative. The present indicative plural is just below. The verb takes its object in the locative case.

yasmā: "because," introducing a reason; the word is correlated with *tasmā* just below, introducing the consequence.

ca kho: The context requires the disjunctive sense of "but" rather than "and."

nibbindeyyuṃ: "would become disenchanted"; the third-person plural of *nibbindati*, in the optative. The present indicative plural is just below. This verb, too, takes its object in the locative case.

nissareyyuṃ: "would escape"; the third-person plural of *nissarati* in the optative. The present indicative plural is just below. While the noun *nissaraṇaṃ* takes the object of escape in the genitive (*rūpassa nissaraṇaṃ*), the corresponding verb takes its object in the ablative (*rūpasmā nissareyyuṃ*).

95. SED gives, as a possible meaning for *idam* used as an indeclinable, "in this manner," and this seems to be the usage intended here. See SED 2. *idam*.

[2. How beings attain release]

sadevakā lokā . . . pajāya sadevamanussāya: These expressions, along with their qualifiers, are all ablatives in relation to *nissaṭā visaṃyuttā vippamuttā*. See p. 109.

nissaṭā visaṃyuttā vippamuttā: "released, detached, freed"; these are past participles qualifying *sattā*.

vimariyādīkatena cetasā vihariṃsu: The verb is a third-person plural aorist of *viharati*. The phrase shows, with the instrumental, the manner in which these beings did not dwell. *Cetasā* is instrumental of *cetas*, a Vedic form preserved in Pāli, which occurs mainly in two oblique cases, instrumental (*cetasā*) and genitive (*cetaso*), as well as in compounds as *ceto*. *Vimariyādīkatena*, "made without a boundary," describing *cetasā*, is an accusative tappurisa: made (*kata*) without (*vi*) boundary (*mariyādā*). In the compound with *-kata*, the final vowel of *mariyādā* is changed to *ī* (Duroiselle §557).

7. Natumhākaṃsutta

Not Yours (SN 22:33; III 33–34)

"Yaṃ, bhikkhave, na tumhākaṃ, taṃ pajahatha. Taṃ vo pahīnaṃ hitāya sukhāya bhavissati. Kiñca, bhikkhave, na tumhākaṃ? Rūpaṃ, bhikkhave, na tumhākaṃ, taṃ pajahatha. Taṃ vo pahīnaṃ hitāya sukhāya bhavissati. Vedanā na tumhākaṃ . . . Saññā na tumhākaṃ . . . Saṅkhārā na tumhākaṃ . . . Viññāṇaṃ na tumhākaṃ, taṃ pajahatha. Taṃ vo pahīnaṃ hitāya sukhāya bhavissati.

"Which, monks, not yours, that abandon. That by you abandoned for welfare for happiness will be. What-and, monks, not yours? Form, monks, not yours, that abandon. That by you abandoned for welfare for happiness will be. Feeling not yours . . . Perception not yours . . . Volitional-activities not yours . . . Consciousness not yours, that abandon. That by you abandoned for welfare for happiness will be.

"Whatever, monks, is not yours, abandon it. That being abandoned by you will be for your welfare and happiness. And what, monks, is not yours? Form, monks, is not yours: abandon it. That being abandoned by you will be for your welfare and happiness. Feeling is not yours . . . Perception is not yours . . . Volitional activities are not yours . . . Consciousness is not yours: abandon it. That being abandoned by you will be for your welfare and happiness.

"Seyyathāpi, bhikkhave, yaṃ imasmiṃ jetavane tiṇa-kaṭṭha-sākhā-palāsaṃ taṃ jano hareyya vā ḍaheyya vā yathāpaccayaṃ vā kareyya. Api nu tumhākaṃ evamassa: 'Amhe jano harati vā ḍahati vā yathāpaccayaṃ vā karotī'"ti?

"Suppose, monks, which in this Jeta-grove grass-logs-branches-foliage, that people would take or would burn or according-to-wish or would do. Is it the case that to you thus would occur: 'Us people are taking or burning or according-to-wish or are doing'?"

"Suppose, monks, people would take the grass, logs, branches, and foliage in this Jeta's Grove, or burn them, or do with them as they wish. Would it occur to you thus: 'People are taking us, or burning us, or doing with us as they wish'?"

"No h'etaṃ, bhante. Taṃ kissa hetu? Na hi no etaṃ, bhante, attā vā attaniyaṃ vā"ti.

"Not indeed this, Bhante. That for what reason? Not because our this, Bhante, self or self's belonging or."

"Surely not, Bhante. For what reason? Because, Bhante, that is not our self or what belongs to our self."

"Evameva kho, bhikkhave, rūpaṃ na tumhākaṃ, taṃ pajahatha. Taṃ vo pahīnaṃ hitāya sukhāya bhavissati . . . Viññāṇaṃ na tumhākaṃ, taṃ pajahatha. Taṃ vo pahīnaṃ hitāya sukhāya bhavissatī"ti.

"Just-so, monks, form not yours, that abandon. That by you abandoned for welfare for happiness will be . . . Consciousness not yours, that abandon. That by you abandoned for welfare for happiness will be."

"Just so, monks, form is not yours: abandon it. That being abandoned by you will be for your welfare and happiness . . . Consciousness is not yours: abandon it. That being abandoned by you will be for your welfare and happiness."

Grammatical explanations

yaṃ: "whatever"; an indefinite pronoun, correlated with *taṃ* just below.
tumhākaṃ: "yours"; a second-person plural pronoun in the genitive case.
pajahatha: "abandon"; the second-person plural imperative of *pajahati*.
vo: an enclitic second-person plural pronoun, here instrumental, "by you." On the enclitic pronouns, see pp. 19–20.
pahīnaṃ: "abandoned"; the past participle of *pajahati*, here neuter as qualifying the indefinite neuter *taṃ*.
hitāya sukhāya: "for welfare, for happiness"; datives of purpose.
bhavissati: "will be"; third-person singular future of *bhavati*.
yaṃ: This relative term, singular neuter nominative, agrees with *tiṇa-kaṭṭha-sākhā-palāsaṃ*, a dvanda compound of the collective singular type; it is correlated with the demonstrative *taṃ* just below, an accusative object of *hareyya* and the other actions.
jano: "people"; a singular noun, which can refer to either a single person or a group of people.
hareyya vā ḍaheyya vā yathāpaccayaṃ vā kareyya: "would take, or burn, or do as they wish." The verbs are all optatives. *Yathāpaccayaṃ* is an adverbial compound. My rendering follows the commentaries.[96]
api nu: "Is it the case?" An indeclinable formation expressing doubt or a question.
attā: nominative of *attan*, "self, oneself," always a masculine singular noun.
attaniyaṃ: "what belongs to the self"; an adjective being used here as a neuter noun.

8. Sammāsambuddhasutta

The Perfectly Enlightened One (SN 22:58; III 65–66)

"Tathāgato, bhikkhave, arahaṃ sammāsambuddho rūpassa nibbidā virāgā nirodhā anupādā vimutto 'sammāsambuddho'ti vuccati. Bhikkhupi, bhikkhave, paññāvimutto rūpassa nibbidā virāgā nirodhā anupādā vimutto 'paññāvimutto'ti vuccati.

96. Ps II 119,6–7 glosses *yathāpaccayaṃ vā kareyya* with *yathā yathā iccheyya tathā tathā kareyya*, "one might do [with it] as one wishes."

"The Tathāgata, monks, the arahant, the perfectly-enlightened one, of form through disenchantment, through dispassion, through cessation, not having clung liberated, 'perfectly-enlightened one' is called. A monk-too, monks, wisdom-liberated, of form through disenchantment, through dispassion, through cessation, not having clung liberated, 'wisdom-liberated' is called.

"The Tathāgata, monks, the arahant, the perfectly enlightened one, being liberated by non-clinging through disenchantment with form, through dispassion, through cessation, is called 'a perfectly enlightened one.' A monk liberated by wisdom, monks, being also liberated by non-clinging through disenchantment with form, through dispassion, through cessation, is called 'liberated by wisdom.'

"Tathāgato, bhikkhave, arahaṃ sammāsambuddho vedanāya . . . saññāya. . . saṅkhārānaṃ . . . viññāṇassa nibbidā virāgā nirodhā anupādā vimutto 'sammāsambuddho'ti vuccati. Bhikkhupi, bhikkhave, paññāvimutto vedanāya . . . saññāya. . . saṅkhārānaṃ . . . viññāṇassa nibbidā virāgā nirodhā anupādā vimutto 'paññāvimutto'ti vuccati.

"The Tathāgata, monks, the arahant, the perfectly-enlightened one, of feeling . . . of perception . . . of volitional-activities . . . of consciousness through disenchantment, through dispassion, through cessation, not having clung liberated, 'perfectly-enlightened one' is called. A monk-too, monks, wisdom-liberated, of feeling . . . of perception . . . of volitional activities . . . of consciousness through disenchantment, through dispassion, through cessation, not having clung liberated, 'wisdom-liberated' is called.

"The Tathāgata, the arahant, the perfectly enlightened one, being liberated by non-clinging through disenchantment with feeling . . . with perception . . . with volitional activities . . . with consciousness, through dispassion, through cessation, is called 'a perfectly enlightened one.' A monk liberated by wisdom, monks, being also liberated by non-clinging through disenchantment with feeling . . . with perception . . . with volitional activities . . . with consciousness, through dispassion, through cessation, is called 'liberated by wisdom.'

"Tatra kho, bhikkhave, ko viseso, ko adhippāyo, kiṃ nānākaraṇaṃ, tathāgatassa arahato sammāsambuddhassa paññāvimuttena bhikkhunā"ti?

"There, monks, what the distinction, what the disparity, what the difference of the Tathāgata, the arahant, the perfectly-enlightened one, with a wisdom-liberated monk?"

"There, monks, what is the distinction, what is the disparity, what is the difference between the Tathāgata, the arahant, the perfectly enlightened one, and a monk liberated by wisdom?"

"Bhagavaṃmūlakā no, bhante, dhammā bhagavaṃnettikā bhagavaṃpaṭisaraṇā. Sādhu vata, bhante, bhagavantaññeva paṭibhātu etassa bhāsitassa attho. Bhagavato sutvā bhikkhū dhāressantī"ti.

"The Blessed One-rooted for us, Bhante, teachings, the Blessed One-guided, the Blessed One-recourse. Please indeed, Bhante, the Blessed One-himself let dawn of this statement the meaning. Of the Blessed One having heard, the monks will retain."

"Bhante, for us teachings are rooted in the Blessed One, guided by the Blessed One, take recourse in the Blessed One. Please, Bhante, let the Blessed One clear up the meaning of this statement. Having heard it from him, the monks will retain it in mind."

"Tena hi, bhikkhave, suṇātha, sādhukaṃ manasikarotha, bhāsissāmī"ti. — "Evaṃ, bhante"ti kho te bhikkhū bhagavato paccassosuṃ. Bhagavā etadavoca:

"In that case, monks, listen, well attend, I will speak." — "Yes, Bhante," those monks to the Blessed One replied. The Blessed One this-said:

"In that case, monks, listen and attend well, I will speak." — "Yes, Bhante," the monks replied to the Blessed One. The Blessed One said this:

"Tathāgato, bhikkhave, arahaṃ sammāsambuddho anuppannassa maggassa uppādetā, asañjātassa maggassa sañjanetā, anakkhātassa maggassa akkhātā,

maggaññū maggavidū maggakovido. Maggānugā ca, bhikkhave, etarahi sāvakā viharanti pacchāsamannāgatā. Ayaṃ kho, bhikkhave, viseso, ayaṃ adhippāyo, idaṃ nānākaraṇaṃ tathāgatassa arahato sammāsambuddhassa paññāvimuttena bhikkhunā"ti.

"The Tathāgata, monks, the arahant, the perfectly-enlightened one, of unarisen path the originator, of unproduced path the producer, of undeclared path the declarer, path-knower, path-finder, path-expert. Path-followers and, monks, now disciples dwell later-possessed of. This, monks, the distinction, this the disparity, this the difference of the Tathāgata, the arahant, the perfectly-enlightened one, with a wisdom-liberated monk."

"The Tathāgata, monks, the arahant, the perfectly enlightened one, is the originator of the [previously] unarisen path, the producer of the [previously] unproduced path, the one who declares the [previously] undeclared path; he is the path-knower, the path-finder, the path-expert. And his disciples now dwell as path-followers and become possessed of it later. This, monks, is the distinction, this is the disparity, this is the difference between the Tathāgata, the arahant, the perfectly enlightened one, and a monk liberated by wisdom."

Grammatical explanations

tathāgato arahaṃ sammāsambuddho: see p. 110.

nibbidā virāgā nirodhā: While *virāgā* and *nirodhā* are the expected ablatives of the masculine nouns *virāga* and *nirodha*, the expected ablative of feminine *nibbidā* would be *nibbidāya*. *Nibbidā* here is probably best seen as a feminine ablative truncated for uniformity of diction.[97]

anupādā vimutto: The commentaries explain *anupādā* as a truncated absolutive.[98] For stylistic reasons, however, I find it more convenient to translate it as if it were a truncated instrumental noun.

paññāvimutto: "liberated by wisdom"; an instrumental tappurisa. Else-

97. On truncated forms of absolutives and feminine nouns where *-āya* is changed to *-ā*, see Geiger §27.2.

98. See preceding note, as well as Duroiselle §472 (a) and Perniola §101d.1. Ps III 198,7–8 glosses the expression thus: *catūhi upādānehi kañci dhammaṃ anupādiyitvā vimutto* ("liberated without having clung to anything with the four kinds of clinging").

where (for example, at MN I 477–78), the *paññāvimutta* arahant is contrasted with the *ubhatobhāgavimutta* arahant—"one liberated in both respects"—on the basis of their attainments in concentration. The one liberated in both respects gains the formless attainments, while the wisdom-liberated arahant lacks them. Here, however, *paññāvimutta* seems to be used as a designation for any arahant disciple.

viseso, adhippāyo, nānākaraṇaṃ: "distinction, disparity, difference"; three near-synonyms each preceded by the interrogative that corresponds to its gender.

bhagavaṃmūlakā: "rooted in the Blessed One"; a bahubbīhi compound of *bhagavaṃ* and *mūla*, "root," with the suffix *-kā* making it an adjective describing *dhammā*.

no: "for us, our"; an enclitic (internal) pronoun, first-person plural in the dative (or genitive).

bhagavaṃnettikā bhagavaṃpaṭisaraṇā: two more bahubbīhis describing *dhammā*. While the first adds *-kā* to form an adjective, the second functions as an adjective simply by joining the two nouns.

sādhu: Often the word means "good," but in this context, used with the imperative, it functions as a polite way of making a request, somewhat like "please." Sentences of this form, requesting an explanation from the Buddha, are frequent in the Nikāyas.

vata: an indeclinable that merely adds an emphatic tone to the request.

bhagavantaññeva paṭibhātu etassa bhāsitassa attho: This is a peculiar idiom hard to translate literally. *Bhagavantaññeva* is *bhagavantaṃ*, the accusative of *bhagavat*, with emphatic *eva*. The verb *paṭibhātu* is a third-person singular imperative, based on the root *bhā*, "to shine," with the prefix *paṭi*. The grammatical subject is *attho*, the "meaning" of *etassa bhāsitassa*, the statement spoken by the Buddha. Thus the monks are asking, via the imperative, for the meaning of the statement to "shine upon" the Blessed One—that is, to occur to him. "Let the Blessed One clear up the meaning of this statement" is a very free rendition of the sense.

bhagavato: a genitive, though here with an ablative sense, "from the Blessed One."

dhāressanti: "retain in mind"; a third-person plural verb in the future tense.

tena hi: "well then, in that case."

suṇātha: "listen"; the second-person plural imperative.

sādhukaṃ manasikarotha: "attend well"; an adverb "well" followed by a verbal compound in which the first member retains its inflected form, *manasi*, the locative of *manas*. Here the verb is a second-person plural imperative.

bhāsissāmi: "I will speak"; a first-person singular in the future tense.

paccassosuṃ: "replied"; the third-person plural of the s-aorist of *paṭisuṇāti*, with the *-a-* augment inserted between the prefix *paṭi* and *assosuṃ*. On the modifications, see the note on *paccaññāsiṃ* (p. 155).

etadavoca: *etad* (= *etaṃ*) joined by sandhi to the aorist *avoca*, "said."

uppādetā, sañjanetā, akkhātā: "originator, producer, declarer"; nominative singular agent nouns with their stem in *-ar* (Duroiselle §163; Perniola §37).

maggaññū: "a path-knower"; a tappurisa compound of *magga*, path, and *-ññū* (from root *ñā*), "one who knows" (Duroiselle §218). The second member is described by Warder (92) as a "bound form" or dependent word, a word that can appear only at the end of a compound and cannot be used independently. For other examples, see Perniola §135. *Maggavidū* is almost identical in meaning, but with *-vidū*, another bound form, from the root *vid*.

maggānugā: "path-followers"; a tappurisa compound composed of *magga* and *anugā*, describing *sāvakā*.

pacchāsamannāgatā: another compound describing *sāvakā*, composed of the indeclinable *pacchā*, "afterward," and the past participle *samannāgatā*, "possessing."

9. Anattalakkhaṇasutta

The Non-Self Characteristic (SN 22:59; III 66–68)

[1. The argument from affliction]

Ekaṃ samayaṃ bhagavā bārāṇasiyaṃ viharati isipatane migadāye. Tatra kho bhagavā pañcavaggiye bhikkhū āmantesi: "Bhikkhavo"ti.—"Bhadante"ti te bhikkhū bhagavato paccassosuṃ. Bhagavā etadavoca:

One occasion the Blessed One at Bārāṇasī was dwelling in Isipatana in the deer-park. There the Blessed One the five-group monks addressed: "Monks!"—"Venerable One," those monks to the Blessed One replied. The Blessed One this-said:

On one occasion the Blessed One was dwelling at Bārāṇasī in Isipatana, in the deer park. There the Blessed One addressed the monks of the group of five thus: "Monks!"—"Venerable One!" those monks replied to the Blessed One. The Blessed One said this:

"Rūpaṃ, bhikkhave, anattā. Rūpañca h'idaṃ, bhikkhave, attā abhavissa, nayidaṃ rūpaṃ ābādhāya saṃvatteyya, labbhetha ca rūpe: 'Evaṃ me rūpaṃ hotu, evaṃ me rūpaṃ mā ahosī'ti. Yasmā ca kho, bhikkhave, rūpaṃ anattā, tasmā rūpaṃ ābādhāya saṃvattati, na ca labbhati rūpe: 'Evaṃ me rūpaṃ hotu, evaṃ me rūpaṃ mā ahosī.'

"Form, monks, non-self. Form-and because this, monks, self were, not-this form to affliction would lead, it would be possible and in regard to form: 'Thus my form let be; thus my form not let be.' Because but, monks, form non-self, therefore form to affliction leads, not and it is possible in regard to form: 'Thus my form let be; thus my form not let be.'

"Form, monks, is non-self. For if, monks, form were self, this form would not lead to affliction, and it would be possible [to get one's way] in regard to form thus: 'Let my form be thus; let my form not be thus.' But because form is non-self, form therefore leads to affliction, and it is not possible [to get one's way] in regard to form thus: 'Let my form be thus; let my form not be thus.'

"Vedanā anattā . . . Saññā anattā . . . Saṅkhārā anattā . . . Viññāṇaṃ anattā. Viññāṇañca h'idaṃ, bhikkhave, attā abhavissa, nayidaṃ viññāṇaṃ ābādhāya saṃvatteyya, labbhetha ca viññāṇe: 'Evaṃ me viññāṇaṃ hotu, evaṃ me viññāṇaṃ mā ahosī'ti. Yasmā ca kho, bhikkhave, viññāṇaṃ anattā, tasmā viññāṇaṃ ābādhāya saṃvattati, na ca labbhati viññāṇe: 'Evaṃ me viññāṇaṃ hotu, evaṃ me viññāṇaṃ mā ahosī'ti.

"Feeling non-self . . . Perception non-self . . . Volitional-activities non-self . . . Consciousness non-self. Consciousness-and because this, monks, self were, not-this consciousness to affliction would lead, it would be possible and in regard to consciousness: 'Thus my consciousness let be; thus my consciousness not let be.' Because but, monks, consciousness non-self, therefore consciousness to affliction leads, not and it is possible in regard to consciousness: 'Thus my consciousness let be; thus my consciousness not let be.'

"Feeling is non-self... Perception is non-self... Volitional activities are non-self... Consciousness is non-self. For if, monks, consciousness were self, this consciousness would not lead to affliction, and it would be possible [to get one's way] in regard to consciousness thus: 'Let my consciousness be thus; let my consciousness not be thus.' But because consciousness is non-self, consciousness leads to affliction, and it is not possible [to get one's way] in regard to consciousness thus: 'Let my consciousness be thus; let my consciousness not be thus.'

[2. The argument from impermanence]

"Taṃ kiṃ maññatha, bhikkhave, rūpaṃ niccaṃ vā aniccaṃ vā"ti?—"Aniccaṃ, bhante." "Yaṃ panāniccaṃ dukkhaṃ vā taṃ sukhaṃ vā"ti?—"Dukkhaṃ, bhante."—"Yaṃ panāniccaṃ dukkhaṃ vipariṇāma-dhammaṃ, kallaṃ nu taṃ samanupassituṃ: 'Etaṃ mama, eso'hamasmi, eso me attā'"ti?—"No h'etaṃ, bhante."

"That what do you think, monks, form permanent or impermanent or?"—"Impermanent, Bhante."—"What but-impermanent, suffering or that happiness or?"—"Suffering, Bhante."—"What but-impermanent, suffering, change-subject-to, fitting is it that to regard: 'This mine, this I-am, this my self'?"—"Not indeed this, Bhante."

"What do you think, monks, is form permanent or impermanent?"—"Impermanent, Bhante."—"But is that which is impermanent suffering or happiness?"—"Suffering, Bhante."—"But is it fitting to regard that which is impermanent, suffering, and subject to change thus: 'This is mine, this I am, this is my self'?"—"Surely not, Bhante."

"Vedanā . . . Saññā . . . Saṅkhārā . . . Viññāṇaṃ niccaṃ vā aniccaṃ vā"ti?—"Aniccaṃ, bhante."—"Yaṃ panāniccaṃ dukkhaṃ vā taṃ sukhaṃ vā"ti?—"Dukkhaṃ, bhante."—"Yaṃ panāniccaṃ dukkhaṃ vipariṇāma-dhammaṃ, kallaṃ nu taṃ samanupassituṃ: 'Etaṃ mama, eso'hamasmi, eso me attā'"ti?—"No h'etaṃ, bhante."

"Feeling . . . Perception . . . Volitional-activities . . . Consciousness permanent or impermanent or?"—"Impermanent, Bhante."—"What but-impermanent, suffering or that happiness or?"—"Suffering, Bhante."—"What but-impermanent, suffering, change-subject-to, fitting is it that to regard: 'This mine, this I-am, this my self'?"—"Not indeed this, Bhante."

"Is feeling . . . Is perception . . . Are volitional activities . . . Is consciousness permanent or impermanent?"—"Impermanent, Bhante."—"But is that which is impermanent suffering or happiness?"—"Suffering, Bhante."—"But is it fitting to regard that which is impermanent, suffering, and subject to change thus: 'This is mine, this I am, this is my self'?"—"Surely not, Bhante."

"Tasmātiha, bhikkhave, yaṃ kiñci rūpaṃ atītānāgatapaccuppannaṃ ajjhattaṃ vā bahiddhā vā oḷārikaṃ vā sukhumaṃ vā hīnaṃ vā paṇītaṃ vā yaṃ dūre santike vā, sabbaṃ rūpaṃ: 'N'etaṃ mama, n'eso'hamasmi, na m'eso attā'ti evametaṃ yathābhūtaṃ sammappaññāya daṭṭhabbaṃ.

"Therefore, monks, whatever form past-future-present, internal or external or, gross or subtle or, inferior or superior or, which far near or, all form: 'Not this mine, not this I am, not my this self,' thus this as-really-is with correct-wisdom should-be-seen.

"Therefore, monks, whatever form there is, whether past, future, or present, internal or external, gross or subtle, inferior or superior, far or near, all form should be seen as it really is with correct wisdom thus: 'This is not mine, this I am not, this is not my self.'

"Yā kāci vedanā . . . Yā kāci saññā . . . Ye keci saṅkhārā . . . Yaṃ kiñci viññāṇaṃ atītānāgatapaccuppannaṃ ajjhattaṃ vā bahiddhā vā oḷārikaṃ vā sukhumaṃ vā hīnaṃ vā paṇītaṃ vā yaṃ dūre santike vā, sabbaṃ viññāṇaṃ: 'N'etaṃ mama, n'eso'hamasmi, na m'eso attā'ti evametaṃ yathābhūtaṃ sammappaññāya daṭṭhabbaṃ.

"Whatever feeling . . . Whatever perception . . . Whatever volitional-activities . . . Whatever consciousness past-future-present, internal or external or, gross or subtle or, inferior or superior or, which far near or, all consciousness: 'Not this mine, not this I-am, not my this self,' thus this as-really-is with correct-wisdom should-be-seen.

"Whatever feeling there is . . . Whatever perception there is . . . Whatever volitional activities there are . . . Whatever consciousness there is, whether past, future, or present, internal or external, gross or subtle, inferior or superior, far or near, all consciousness should be seen as it really is with correct wisdom thus: 'This is not mine, this I am not, this is not my self.'

"Evaṃ passaṃ, bhikkhave, sutavā ariyasāvako rūpasmimpi nibbindati, vedanāyapi nibbindati, saññāyapi nibbindati, saṅkhāresupi nibbindati, viññāṇasmimpi nibbindati. Nibbindaṃ virajjati. Virāgā vimuccati. Vimuttasmiṃ vimuttamiti ñāṇaṃ hoti. 'Khīṇā jāti, vusitaṃ brahmacariyaṃ, kataṃ karaṇīyaṃ, nāparaṃ itthattāyā'ti pajānātī"ti.

"Thus seeing, monks, learned noble-disciple in regard to form-too is disenchanted, in regard to feeling-too is disenchanted, in regard to perception-too is disenchanted, in regard to volitional-activities-too is disenchanted, in regard to consciousness-too is disenchanted. Being disenchanted, becomes dispassionate. Through dispassion is liberated. In liberated 'liberated' thus knowledge occurs. 'Finished birth, lived the spiritual-life, done what-is-to-be-done, not-further for such-a-state,' understands."

"Seeing thus, monks, the learned noble disciple becomes disenchanted with form, disenchanted with feeling, disenchanted with perception, disenchanted with volitional activities, disenchanted with consciousness. Being disenchanted, he becomes dispassionate. Through dispassion he is liberated. In regard to what is liberated, the knowledge occurs thus: 'Liberated.' He understands: 'Finished is birth, the spiritual life has been lived, what had to be done has been done, there is no further for this state of being.'"

[3. Conclusion]
Idamavoca bhagavā. Attamanā pañcavaggiyā bhikkhū bhagavato bhāsitaṃ abhinanduṃ. Imasmiñca pana veyyākaraṇasmiṃ bhaññamāne pañcavaggiyānaṃ bhikkhūnaṃ anupādāya āsavehi cittāni vimucciṃsu.

This-said the Blessed One. Elated, the five-group monks the Blessed One's statement delighted in. While this-and discourse was being spoken, of the five-group monks, without having clung, from influxes minds were liberated.

This is what the Blessed One said. Elated, the monks of the group of five delighted in the Blessed One's statement. And while this discourse was being spoken, through non-clinging the minds of the monks of the group of five were liberated from the influxes.

Grammatical explanations

[1. The argument from affliction]

bārāṇasiyaṃ: "at Bārāṇasī"; a feminine noun designating the city, here in the locative case.

isipatane migadāye: "in Isipatana, in the deer park"; two compounds in the locative case indicating the specific place where the discourse takes place.

pañcavaggiye bhikkhū: "the monks of the group of five"; the recipients of the teaching, a masculine plural in the accusative case as the object of the s-aorist *āmantesi*. The *pañcavaggiyā bhikkhū* were the Buddha's first five monastic disciples. *Pañcavaggiye* is a bahubbīhi compound, masculine plural accusative, qualifying *bhikkhū*. It is composed of *pañca*, "five," and *vagga*, "group," with the adjectival suffix *-iya* (here accusative plural *-iye*).

bhikkhavo: a plural vocative of *bhikkhu*, generally used when the Buddha initially calls the monks to attention.

bhadante: a vocative used by the monks when initially responding to the Buddha; *bhante* is the contracted form.

rūpaṃ, bhikkhave, anattā: "form, monks, is non-self." *Anattā* is a negative of *attan*, in the nominative case (Duroiselle §154).[99] The present sentence

99. The Pāli grammarians consider negatives formed with *a-* and *an-* to be kammadhāraya compounds (Duroiselle §546 [8]). However, when a negative is set in apposition to a noun, the negative becomes a bahubbīhi. An example is at SN III 56,22, in the sentence *anattaṃ rūpaṃ "anattā rūpan"ti yathābhūtaṃ nappajānāti*, where *anattaṃ* is a bahubbīhi functioning as an adjective qualifying *rūpaṃ*, while *anattā* is a kammadhāraya descriptive of *rūpaṃ*.

simply predicates *anattā* of *rūpaṃ*, but *anattā* retains its own status as a negative noun; it is not an adjective qualifying *rūpaṃ*.

abhavissa: the conditional (or hypothetical) form of *bhavati*, here third-person singular; see p. 68.

nayidaṃ = *na* + *idaṃ*, with *-y-* inserted for euphony (Duroiselle §28; Geiger §72.2).

ābādhāya: "to affliction"; a masculine dative, the object of the optative verb, *saṃvatteyya*.

labbhetha ca rūpe: "it would be possible [to get one's way] in regard to form." *Labbhetha* is a passive third-person singular in the middle-voice optative (see Perniola §78 for the active middle voice and §89 for the passive). The active indicative is *labhati*, "gains, obtains." The expression *labbhetha rūpe* implies that if form were the self, one would have such control over form—and the other aggregates—that one could govern them with one's will. Just below, in the expression *na ca labbhati rūpe*, the verb occurs as a passive indicative (*labhyati* > *labbhati*).

mā ahosi: "let my form not be thus." *Mā*, the prohibitive particle, is generally (but not invariably) used with an aorist, here *ahosi*. In such constructions the aorist *does not* refer to a past action but to a prohibited action (Duroiselle §612,iii; Perniola §273b). The prohibition here is against form being subject to affliction.

ca kho: used in the disjunctive sense, as "but" or "however" rather than "and."

[2. The argument from impermanence]

yaṃ panāniccaṃ dukkhaṃ vā taṃ sukhaṃ vā: "But is that which is impermanent suffering or happiness?" Here, the relative *yaṃ* qualifies *aniccaṃ*, "what is impermanent." *Pana* is a conjunction, "but," and *taṃ*, "that," the demonstrative correlated with *yaṃ*, points to the subject about which the question is posed: "Is that suffering or happiness (unpleasurable or pleasurable)?"

kallaṃ nu taṃ samanupassituṃ: *Kallaṃ*, "proper, fitting, suitable," occurs with the infinitive, *samanupassituṃ*, "to regard, to consider" (from the verb *passati*, with two prefixes, *sam* and *anu*). The interrogative particle *nu* indicates that the sentence poses a question.

etaṃ mama, eso'hamasmi, eso me attā: "This is mine, this I am, this is my self." In this stock expression, the pronoun in the first phrase, *etaṃ*, is neuter because it is an independent subject, while in the following two phrases the pronoun *eso* is masculine because in each clause it qualifies a masculine subject, respectively, *ahaṃ* and *attā*.[100]

tasmātiha: see p. 91.

yaṃ kiñci rūpaṃ: "whatever form, any form whatever." This indefinite relative expression (Duroiselle §325; Perniola §44) is followed by a description of *rūpaṃ* in eleven ways—as past, future, and present, and so forth—culminating in the universalization, *sabbaṃ rūpaṃ*, "all form." The indefinite relatives preceding each of the five aggregates agree with the gender and number of the corresponding noun; they are neuter singular in the case of *rūpaṃ* and *viññāṇaṃ*, feminine singular in the case of *vedanā* and *saññā*, and masculine plural in the case of *saṅkhārā*.

yaṃ dūre santike vā: "far or near"; here *dūre* and *santike* are locatives used in an adverbial sense.

sammappaññāya: "with correct wisdom"; a kammadhāraya compound composed of the adverb *sammā* and *paññāya*, the instrumental of *paññā*.

daṭṭhabbaṃ: "should be seen"; a future passive participle of **dassati* here in agreement with *rūpaṃ*.[101]

evaṃ passaṃ, etc.: see pp. 143–45.

[3. Conclusion]

idamavoca bhagavā: *idamavoca* is a sandhi formation of *idaṃ*, "this," and *avoca*, "said," an aorist; the normal word order is inverted, with the subject *bhagavā* placed last, presumably for elegance of expression.

bhāsitaṃ: a past participle of *bhāsati*, here functioning as a noun, "what was stated, a statement."

abhinanduṃ: "delighted in"; a third-person plural aorist taking its object in the accusative.

imasmiñca pana veyyākaraṇasmiṃ bhaññamāne: "and while this discourse was being spoken"; a locative absolute construction (see pp. 70–71), with *imasmiṃ veyyākaraṇasmiṃ* as the subject and *bhaññamāne* a passive present participle of the verb *bhaṇati*, "to speak."

pañcavaggiyānaṃ bhikkhūnaṃ: a genitive plural.

100. As an ancient Indian document, the sutta presupposes that the person engaging in this reflection is male. If a female were reflecting, presumably the text would read *esā'hamasmi*.

101. On **dassati*, see p. 51, note 56.

anupādāya: a negative absolutive of the verb *upādiyati*. However, to avoid awkwardness in translation, I have rendered it as if it were a negative action noun, "through non-clinging."
āsavehi: "from the influxes"; an ablative plural.
vimucciṃsu: "were liberated"; the third-person plural is-aorist of *vimuccati*.

10. Upādiyamānasutta

One Clinging (SN 22:63; III 73–74)

Atha kho aññataro bhikkhu yena bhagavā ten'upasaṅkami. Upasaṅkamitvā bhagavantaṃ abhivādetvā ekamantaṃ nisīdi. Ekamantaṃ nisinno kho so bhikkhu bhagavantaṃ etadavoca: "Sādhu me, bhante, bhagavā saṃkhittena dhammaṃ desetu yamahaṃ bhagavato dhammaṃ sutvā eko vūpakaṭṭho appamatto ātāpī pahitatto vihareyyan"ti.

Then a certain monk where the Blessed One, there approached. Having approached, the Blessed One having paid homage to, one-side sat down. One-side seated, that monk to the Blessed One this-said: "Please to me, Bhante, the Blessed One briefly the Dhamma let teach which-I of the Blessed One the Dhamma having heard, alone, withdrawn, heedful, ardent, resolute might dwell."

Then a certain monk approached the Blessed One. Having approached, he paid homage to the Blessed One and sat down to one side. Seated to one side, that monk said this to the Blessed One: "Please, Bhante, let the Blessed One briefly teach me the Dhamma, so that, having heard the Dhamma from the Blessed One, I might dwell alone, withdrawn, diligent, ardent, and resolute."

"Upādiyamāno kho, bhikkhu, baddho mārassa; anupādiyamāno mutto pāpimato"ti.

"Aññātaṃ bhagavā! Aññātaṃ sugatā!"ti.

"Yathākathaṃ pana tvaṃ, bhikkhu, mayā saṃkhittena bhāsitassa vitthārena atthaṃ ājānāsī"ti?

"One clinging, monk, bound of Māra; one not-clinging, freed of the Evil One."

"Understood, Blessed One! Understood, Fortunate One!"

"In what way but you, monk, by me briefly spoken in detail meaning understand?"

"One clinging, monk, is bound to Māra; one not clinging is freed from the Evil One."

"Understood, Blessed One! Understood, Fortunate One!"

"In what way, monk, do you understand in detail the meaning of what was briefly stated by me?"

"Rūpaṃ kho, bhante, upādiyamāno baddho mārassa; anupādiyamāno mutto pāpimato. Vedanaṃ . . . Saññaṃ . . . Saṅkhāre . . . Viññāṇaṃ upādiyamāno baddho mārassa; anupādiyamāno mutto pāpimato. Imassa khvāhaṃ, bhante, bhagavatā saṃkhittena bhāsitassa evaṃ vitthārena atthaṃ ājānāmī"ti.

"Form, Bhante, one clinging to, bound of Māra; one not-clinging, freed of the Evil One. Feeling . . . Perception . . . Volitional-activities . . . Consciousness one clinging to, bound of Māra; one not-clinging, freed of the Evil One. Of this I, Bhante, by the Blessed One briefly stated thus in detail the meaning understand."

"One clinging to form, Bhante, is bound by Māra; one not clinging is freed from the Evil One. One clinging to feeling . . . to perception . . . to volitional activities . . . to consciousness is bound by Māra; one not clinging is freed from the Evil One. It is in such a way, Bhante, that I understand in detail the meaning of what was briefly stated by the Blessed One."

"Sādhu sādhu, bhikkhu! Sādhu kho tvaṃ, bhikkhu, mayā saṃkhittena bhāsitassa vitthārena atthaṃ ājānāsi. Rūpaṃ kho, bhikkhu, upādiyamāno baddho mārassa; anupādiyamāno mutto pāpimato. Vedanaṃ . . . Saññaṃ . . . Saṅkhāre . . . Viññāṇaṃ upādiyamāno baddho mārassa; anupādiyamāno mutto pāpimato. Imassa kho, bhikkhu, mayā saṃkhittena bhāsitassa evaṃ vitthārena attho daṭṭhabbo"ti.

"Good, good, monk! Good you, monk, by me briefly spoken in detail the meaning understand. Form, monk, one clinging to, bound of Māra; one not-clinging, freed of the Evil One. Feeling . . . Perception . . . Volitional-activities . . . Consciousness one clinging to, bound of Māra; one not-clinging, freed of the Evil One. Of this, monk, by me briefly stated thus in detail meaning should be seen."

"Good, good, monk! It is good that you understand in detail the meaning of what was stated by me in brief. One clinging to form, monk, is bound by Māra; one not clinging is freed from the Evil One. One clinging to feeling . . . to perception . . . to volitional activities . . . to consciousness is bound by Māra; one not clinging is freed from the Evil One. It is in such a way that the meaning of what was stated by me in brief should be seen in detail."

Atha kho so bhikkhu bhagavato bhāsitaṃ abhinanditvā anumoditvā uṭṭhāy'āsanā bhagavantaṃ abhivādetvā padakkhiṇaṃ katvā pakkāmi.

Then that monk, the Blessed One's statement having delighted in, having rejoiced in, having risen from the seat, to the Blessed One having paid homage, circumambulation having done, departed.

Then that monk, having delighted and rejoiced in the Blessed One's statement, rose from his seat, and, after paying homage to the Blessed One, having circumambulated him, he departed.

Atha kho so bhikkhu eko vūpakaṭṭho appamatto ātāpī pahitatto viharanto nacirass'eva yass'atthāya kulaputtā sammadeva agārasmā anagāriyaṃ pabbajanti tadanuttaraṃ brahmacariyapariyosānaṃ diṭṭhe'va dhamme sayaṃ abhiññā sacchikatvā upasampajja viharati. "Khīṇā jāti, vusitaṃ brahmacariyaṃ, kataṃ karaṇīyaṃ, nāparaṃ itthattāyā"ti abbhaññāsi. Aññataro ca pana so bhikkhu arahataṃ ahosīti.

Then that monk alone, withdrawn, heedful, ardent, resolute dwelling, not long indeed of which for sake of family-sons rightly from home to homelessness go forth, that-unsurpassed spiritual-life-goal in present-life by himself having directly known, having realized, having entered, dwelled. "Finished birth, lived the spiritual-life, done what-is-to-be-done, not-further for such-a-state," directly knew. A certain one and that monk of the arahants was.

Then, dwelling alone, withdrawn, heedful, ardent, and resolute, that monk, in no long time, by realizing it for himself with direct knowledge, in this present life entered and dwelled in that unsurpassed goal of the spiritual life for the sake of which young people rightly go forth from the household life into homelessness. He directly knew: "Finished is birth, the spiritual life has been lived, what had to be done has been done, there is no further for this state of being." And that monk became one of the arahants.

Grammatical explanations

aññataro: "a certain one"; a pronominal adjective (Duroiselle §353; Perniola §47) qualifying *bhikkhu*.

yena bhagavā ten'upasaṅkami: Here the instrumentals *yena* and *tena* might be considered adverbs of place, the destination approached by the monk. See p. 46.

upasaṅkamitvā bhagavantaṃ abhivādetvā ekamantaṃ nisīdi. See p. 34. *Ekamantaṃ*, literally "one end," in this context means "to one side." The case is accusative, used adverbally.

nisinno: "seated"; the past participle of *nisīdati*, but functioning almost as a present participle, "sitting." It is masculine nominative in agreement with *bhikkhu*.

sādhu: see p. 166.

me: the enclitic (internal) pronoun, "to me, for me," here dative (or genitive).

saṃkhittena: an instrumental functioning as an adverb, "briefly."

yam: the relative in apposition to *dhammaṃ*, with *-ṃ* changed to *-m* by sandhi with *ahaṃ*. Alternatively, *yam* may be the relative pronoun functioning adverbially to introduce the following clause: "so that . . . I might dwell."[102]

eko vūpakaṭṭho appamatto ātāpī pahitatto vihareyyaṃ: "I might dwell alone, withdrawn, diligent, ardent, and resolute." The verb is a singular first-person optative. The adjectives are all masculine singular nominatives describing the aspiring monk. *Eko*, which often represents the numeral "one," here means "alone." *Vūpakaṭṭho* is a past participle functioning as an adjective; *appamatto*, a negative of *pamatto*, "heedless, negligent"; *ātāpī* (stem *ātāpin*), the possessive of *ātāpa*, "ardor," a synonym of *viriya*,

102. This suggestion was made to me by Beatrice Chrystall.

energy. *Pahitatto* is a bahubbīhi compound composed of *pahita*, likely the past participle of *padahati*, "strives," and *atta*, "self."[103]

upādiyamāno: "clinging"; a middle-voice present participle of *upādiyati* (Duroiselle §447; Perniola §95); the subject "one" is implicit in the participle. Although *upādiyati* appears passive in form (with the passive insert *-iy-*), it always bears an active sense.

mārassa: grammatically a genitive, but probably used in an instrumental sense.[104]

pāpimato: grammatically a genitive of *pāpimat*, but probably used in an ablative sense. See note 104 for the commentarial explanation of the genitive.

aññātaṃ: "understood." Two homonyms of *aññāta* should be distinguished: (1) the negative of the past participle *ñāta*, "known," thus "unknown," representing Skt *ajñāta*; and (2) the past participle of *ājānāti*, "understands," representing Skt *ājñāta*, with shortening of the initial vowel and duplication of the nasal *-ñ-*. Here it is the latter. The second-person singular, *ājānāsi*, and first-person singular, *ājānāmi*, occur just below.

vitthārena: "in detail"; the opposite of *saṃkhittena*. Again, the instrumental is used adverbially. The contrast between *saṃkhittena* and *vitthārena*, the "brief statement" and the "detailed account," is common in both the Nikāyas and the commentaries.

imassa: the demonstrative belongs with *bhāsitassa*.

khvāhaṃ: a sandhi of *kho* and *ahaṃ*.

daṭṭhabbo: "should be seen"; a future passive participle occurring in apposition to *attho*.

uṭṭhāy'āsanā (= *uṭṭhāya āsanā*): "rose from his seat"; an absolutive followed by an ablative.

103. *Pahita* is a homonym that can be the past participle of either *pahiṇati*, "sends," or *padahati*, "strives." The commentaries take it in the former sense but modern scholars understand it in the latter sense. PED expressly says that Buddhaghosa has wrongly derived it from *peseti*.

104. In relation to the same statement occurring at SN IV 202,19, the commentary (Spk III 73,9–12) explains the genitive thus: "*Bound of Māra*: bound by Māra's bondage; or this is the genitive case in an instrumental sense. *Freed of Māra*: freed from the bondage of Māra; or this is just the genitive case in an instrumental sense. The meaning is: freed from bondage by Māra, by the bondage of defilements." (*Baddho mārassā ti mārabandhanena baddho. Karaṇatthe vā etaṃ sāmivacanaṃ, kilesamārena baddhoti attho. Mutto pāpimato ti mārassa bandhanena mutto. Karaṇattheyeva vā idaṃ sāmivacanaṃ, pāpimatā kilesabandhanena muttoti attho.*)

padakkhiṇaṃ katvā: "having circumambulated"; the practice of circling a revered person or object (such as a shrine or bodhi tree) with the right side inward.

pakkāmi: a third-person singular aorist of *pakkamati*, "leaves, departs."

nacirass'eva: "not long after"; *cira*, meaning a long time, is negated by *na*, with emphatic *eva*.

yass'atthāya kulaputtā sammadeva agārasmā anagāriyaṃ pabbajanti: "for the sake of which young people rightly go forth from the household life into homelessness." The dative *atthāya* is often used with a genitive *yassa* to indicate that "for the sake of which" something is done. Here *yassa* refers to *tadanuttaraṃ brahmacariyapariyosānaṃ*.

tadanuttaraṃ brahmacariyapariyosānaṃ: "that unsurpassed goal of the spiritual life." *Tad* is a demonstrative (= *taṃ*) in agreement with neuter *pariyosānaṃ*, with an original *-d-* restored to avoid hiatus (see Geiger §72.1). *Anuttaraṃ*, "unsurpassed," qualifies *brahmacariya-pariyosānaṃ*,[105] a genitive tappurisa in the accusative case; the latter is the object of the absolutives *abhiññā sacchikatvā upasampajja*. The commentaries consistently explain "the spiritual life" as the path, and "the goal of the spiritual life" as the fruit of arahantship.[106]

diṭṭhe'va dhamme: literally, "in this seen state itself"—that is, "in this present life."

abhiññā sacchikatvā upasampajja viharati: a string of three absolutives followed by *viharati* used as a historical present. *Abhiññā* is a truncated absolutive of *abhiññāya*;[107] *upasampajja*, an absolutive formed by palatalization of *upasampadya*. To avoid awkwardness, I translate *abhiññā* as if it were a truncated instrumental and *upasampajja* as if it were a finite verb.

abbhaññāsi: "directly knew"; see p. 155.

arahataṃ: a plural genitive of *arahant*. The sense is that he became one (*aññataro*) of this select group.

105. *Brahmacariya* is itself either a kammadhāraya compound (= "holy conduct") or a genitive tappurisa (= "the conduct of Brahmā").

106. For instance, at Sv II 363,28–30: *Brahmacariyapariyosānan ti maggabrahmacariyassa pariyosānabhūtaṃ arahattaphalaṃ*.

107. See p. 165, note 97.

11. Rādhasutta
Rādha (SN 22:71; III 79–80)

Atha kho āyasmā rādho yena bhagavā ten'upasaṅkami. Upasaṅkamitvā bhagavantaṃ abhivādetvā ekamantaṃ nisīdi. Ekamanataṃ nisinno kho āyasmā rādho bhagavantaṃ etadavoca: "Kathaṃ nu kho bhante jānato kathaṃ passato imasmiñca saviññāṇake kāye bahiddhā ca sabbanimittesu ahaṅkāra-mamaṅkāra-mānānusayā na hontī"ti?

Then the Venerable Rādha where the Blessed One, there approached. Having approached, the Blessed One having paid homage to, one-side sat down. One-side seated, the Venerable Rādha to the Blessed One this-said: "How, Bhante, for one knowing, how for one seeing, in regard to this-and with-consciousness body, externally and in regard to all-objects, I-making-mine-making-conceit-tendencies not occur?"

Then the Venerable Rādha approached the Blessed One. Having approached, he paid homage to the Blessed One and sat down to one side. Seated to one side, the Venerable Rādha said this to the Blessed One: "How, Bhante, does one know, how does one see, so that I-making, mine-making, and tendencies to conceit do not occur in regard to this body with consciousness and in regard to all external objects?"

"Yaṃ kiñci, rādha, rūpaṃ atītānāgatapaccuppannaṃ ajjhattaṃ vā bahiddhā vā oḷārikaṃ vā sukhumaṃ vā hīnaṃ vā paṇītaṃ vā yaṃ dūre santike vā, sabbaṃ rūpaṃ, 'n'etaṃ mama, n'eso'hamasmi, na m'eso attā'ti evametaṃ yathābhūtaṃ sammappaññāya passati. Yā kāci vedanā . . . Yā kāci saññā . . . Ye keci saṅkhārā . . . Yaṃ kiñci viññāṇaṃ atītānāgatapaccuppannaṃ . . . yaṃ dūre santike vā, sabbaṃ viññāṇaṃ, 'n'etaṃ mama, n'eso'hamasmi, na m'eso attā'ti evametaṃ yathābhūtaṃ sammappaññāya passati.

"Whatever, Rādha, form past-future-present, internal or external or, gross or subtle or, inferior or superior or, which far near or, all form: 'Not this mine, not this I am, not my this self,' thus this as-really-is with correct-wisdom sees. Any feeling . . . Any perception . . . Any volitional-activities . . . Any consciousness past-future-present, internal or external or, gross or subtle or, inferior or superior or, which far near or, all consciousness: 'Not this mine, not this I am, not my this self,' thus this as-really-is with correct-wisdom sees.

"Whatever form there is, Rādha, whether past, future, or present, internal or external, gross or subtle, inferior or superior, far or near—one sees all form as it really is with correct wisdom thus: 'This is not mine, this I am not, this is not my self.' Whatever feeling there is . . . Whatever perception there is . . . Whatever volitional activities there are . . . Whatever consciousness there is, whether past, future, or present, internal or external, gross or subtle, inferior or superior, far or near—one sees all consciousness as it really is with correct wisdom thus: 'This is not mine, this I am not, this is not my self.'

"Evaṃ kho, rādha, jānato evaṃ passato imasmiñca saviññāṇake kāye bahiddhā ca sabbanimittesu ahaṅkāra-mamaṅkāra-mānānusayā na hontī"ti. . . . Aññataro ca panāyasmā rādho arahataṃ ahosī ti.

"Thus, Rādha, for one knowing, thus for one seeing, in regard to this-and with-consciousness body, externally and in regard to all-objects, I-making-mine-making-conceit-tendencies not occur.". . . A certain one and the Venerable Rādha of the arahants was.

"For one knowing thus, Rādha, for one seeing thus, I-making, mine-making, and tendencies to conceit do not occur in regard to this body with consciousness and in regard to all external objects.". . . And the Venerable Rādha became one of the arahants.

Grammatical explanations

āyasmā: "venerable," a respectful designation for a monk—but not restricted in use to monks—composed of *āyus*, "life," and the possessive suffix *-mat*. The Skt is *āyuṣmat*; the Pāli has assimilation of *u* to *a*.

kathaṃ nu kho bhante jānato kathaṃ passato: "How, Bhante, does one know, how does one see. . . ?" The case of the two present participles is dative. See p. 107.

imasmiṃ: a singular locative qualifying *kāye*.

saviññāṇake: a bahubbīhi compound composed of *sa-*, "together with," and *viññāṇa*, "consciousness," with suffix *-ka* converting the compound into an adjective; *saviññāṇake* is here locative singular qualifying *kāye*.

sabbanimittesu: a kammadhāraya compound, plural locative, composed of *sabba*, "all," and *nimittesu*. *Nimitta* has several meanings: object, mark (of concentration), cause, etc. As contrasted with "this body together with consciousness," it likely designates external objects of cognition.

ahaṅkāra-mamaṅkāra-mānānusayā: "I-making, mine-making, and tendencies to conceit." This is a complex dvanda compound of the plural type. It includes three internal compounds. The first two are syntactical compounds (see p. 45), the third a tappurisa. The Aṅguttara commentary (at Mp II 206,8–9) resolves it thus: *ahaṅkāradiṭṭhi ca mamaṅkārataṇhā ca mānānusayo ca* ("the view that is I-making; the craving that is mine-making; and the tendency to conceit").

evaṃ kho, rādha, jānato evaṃ passato: "For one knowing thus, Rādha, for one seeing thus."

12. Sīhasutta

The Lion (SN 22:78; III 84–86)

"Sīho, bhikkhave, migarājā sāyanhasamayaṃ āsayā nikkhamati. Āsayā nikkhamitvā vijambhati; vijambhitvā samantā catuddisā anuviloketi; samantā catuddisā anuviloketvā tikkhattuṃ sīhanādaṃ nadati. Tikkhattuṃ sīhanādaṃ naditvā gocarāya pakkamati.

"The lion, monks, beast-king evening-time from lair comes out. From lair having come out, stretches; having stretched, all-around four-directions surveys; all-around four-directions having surveyed, three-times lion-roar roars. Three-times lion-roar having roared, for feeding-ground departs.

"The lion, monks, the king of beasts, in the evening comes out from his lair. Having come out, he stretches; having stretched, he surveys the four directions all around; having surveyed the four directions all around, he roars a lion's roar three times. Having roared a lion's roar three times, he departs for his feeding ground.

"Ye hi keci, bhikkhave, tiracchānagatā pāṇā sīhassa migarañño nadato saddaṃ suṇanti, yebhuyyena bhayaṃ saṃvegaṃ santāsaṃ āpajjanti. Bilaṃ bilāsayā pavisanti; dakaṃ dakāsayā pavisanti; vanaṃ vanāsayā pavisanti; ākāsaṃ pakkhino bhajanti.

"Those indeed which, monks, animal-gone creatures, of lion beast-king roaring sound hear, mostly fear, sense-of-urgency, terror acquire. Hole hole-lair-ones enter; water water-lair-ones enter; woods woods-lair-ones enter; sky birds resort to.

"Those animals that hear the sound of the lion, the king of beasts, as he is roaring, for the most part acquire fear, a sense of urgency, and terror. Those who live in holes enter holes; those who live in the water enter the water; those who live in the woods enter the woods; the birds resort to the sky.

"Yepi te, bhikkhave, rañño nāgā gāma-nigama-rājadhānīsu, daḷhehi varattehi baddhā, tepi tāni bandhanāni sañchinditvā sampadāletvā bhītā muttakarīsaṃ cajamānā yena vā tena vā palāyanti. Evaṃmahiddhiko kho, bhikkhave, sīho migarājā tiracchānagatānaṃ pāṇānaṃ, evaṃmahesakkho, evaṃmahānubhāvo.

"Which-even those, monks, king's bull-elephants in village-town-royal-cities, by strong thongs bound, they-too those bonds having burst, having split, frightened, urine-feces discharging, by this way or by that way or flee. So-powerful, monks, the lion beast-king of animal-gone creatures, so-commanding, so-mighty.

"Even the king's bull elephants, bound by strong thongs in the villages, towns, and royal cities, having burst and split those bonds, frightened, discharging urine and feces, flee here and there. So powerful, monks, is the lion, the king of beasts, over the animals, so commanding, so mighty.

"Evameva kho, bhikkhave, yadā tathāgato loke uppajjati arahaṃ sammāsambuddho vijjācaraṇasampanno sugato lokavidū anuttaro purisadammasārathi satthā devamanussānaṃ buddho bhagavā, so dhammaṃ deseti: 'Iti rūpaṃ, iti rūpassa samudayo, iti rūpassa atthaṅgamo; iti vedanā . . . iti saññā . . . iti saṅkhārā . . . iti viññāṇaṃ, iti viññāṇassa samudayo, iti viññāṇassa atthaṅgamo'ti.

"Just so, monks, when the Tathāgata in the world arises, the arahant, the perfectly-enlightened one, clear-knowledge-conduct-accomplished, fortunate, world-knower, unsurpassed persons-to-be-tamed-trainer, teacher of devas-humans, enlightened one, blessed one, he the Dhamma teaches: 'Such form, such of form origin, such of form passing; such feeling . . . such perception . . . such volitional-activities . . . such consciousness, such of consciousness origin, such of consciousness passing.'

"So too, monks, when the Tathāgata arises in the world, an arahant, perfectly enlightened, accomplished in clear knowledge and conduct, fortunate, knower of the world, unsurpassed trainer of persons to be tamed, teacher of devas and humans, the Enlightened One, the Blessed One, he teaches the Dhamma thus: 'Such is form, such its origin, such its passing away; such is feeling . . . such is perception . . . such are volitional activities . . . such is consciousness, such its origin, such its passing away.'

"Yepi te, bhikkhave, devā dīghāyukā vaṇṇavanto sukhabahulā uccesu vimānesu ciraṭṭhitikā, tepi tathāgatassa dhammadesanaṃ sutvā yebhuyyena bhayaṃ saṃvegaṃ santāsaṃ āpajjanti:

"Which-even those, monks, devas, long-lived, beautiful, happiness-abounding, in tall palaces long-dwelling, they-too Tathāgata's Dhamma-teaching having heard, mostly fear, sense-of-urgency, terror acquire:

"Even, monks, those devas that are long-lived, beautiful, abounding in happiness, dwelling for a long time in tall palaces, when they hear the Tathāgata's Dhamma teaching, they too for the most part acquire fear, a sense of urgency, and terror:

'Aniccā'va kira, bho, mayaṃ samānā "nicc'amhā"ti amaññimha. Addhuvā'va kira, bho, mayaṃ samānā "dhuv'amhā"ti amaññimha. Asassatā'va kira, bho, mayaṃ samānā "sassat'amhā"ti amaññimha. Mayampi kira, bho, aniccā addhuvā asassatā sakkāyapariyāpannā'ti. Evaṃmahiddhiko kho, bhikkhave, tathāgato sadevakassa lokassa, evaṃmahesakkho, evaṃmahānubhāvo"ti.

'Impermanent indeed, it seems, sir, we being, "Permanent we are" thought. Not-lasting indeed, it seems, sir, we being, "Lasting we are" thought. Non-eternal indeed, it seems, sir, we being, "Eternal we are" thought. We-too, it seems, sir, impermanent, not-lasting, non-eternal, personal-collection-included.' So-powerful, monks, the Tathāgata of with-devas world, so-commanding, so-mighty."

'It seems, sir, that being actually impermanent, we thought: "We're permanent." It seems, sir, that being actually not lasting, we thought: "We're lasting." It seems, sir, that being actually non-eternal, we thought: "We're eternal." It seems, sir, that we are impermanent, not lasting, non-eternal, included in the personal-collection.' So powerful, monks, is the Tathāgata over this world together with its devas, so commanding, so mighty."

Grammatical explanations

sāyanhasamayaṃ: a kammadhāraya compound with two nouns in apposition: *sāyanha*, "evening," and *samaya*, "occasion, time." The case is accusative used adverbially to denote a period of time (Duroiselle §538,viii; Perniola §250b).

samantā: "all around"; an ablative with an adverbial function.

catuddisā: "the four directions"; a feminine plural in the accusative.

tikkhattuṃ: "three times"; *ti*, "three," joined with *-khattuṃ*, a "multiplicative adverb" (Duroiselle §285; Perniola §54b).

sīhanādaṃ nadati: "he roars a lion's roar." Here the verb *nadati* takes an object cognate with itself in the accusative case. *Sīhanādaṃ* is a genitive tappurisa compound.

tiracchānagatā pāṇā: a compound of *tiracchāna*, "animal," and *gatā*, "gone," qualifying *pāṇā*, "creatures." I translate the entire expression simply as "animals."

sīhassa migarañño nadato: the noun followed by the corresponding present participle of *nadati*, in the singular genitive. *Rañño* is the singular genitive of *rājan*.

yebhuyyena: "mostly, for the most part"; an instrumental functioning as an adverb.

bilāsayā, dakāsayā, vanāsayā: three bahubbīhi compounds built upon kammadhārayas, each composed of the place where the animal dwells (*bila*; *daka* [= *udaka*], *vana*) and *āsaya*, a lair. The bahubbīhis are plural nominatives denoting the different kinds of animals.

gāma-nigama-rājadhānīsu: "in the villages, towns, [and] royal cities": a plural dvanda compound in the locative case.

yena vā tena vā palāyanti: "flee here and there." The instrumentals are used here adverbially to show direction of movement (Duroiselle §599,v; Perniola §256c).

evaṃmahiddhiko: "so powerful"; a bahubbīhi compound qualifying *sīho migarājā*, masculine singular in the nominative case. It is composed of *evaṃ*, indicating manner; *mahā*, "great"; and *iddhi*, "power," with the suffix *-iko*. *Evaṃmahesakkho* and *evaṃmahānubhāvo* are parallel bahubbīhis with almost the same meaning.

tiracchānagatānaṃ pāṇānaṃ: "over creatures that are animals." Wijesekera (§144e) writes with regard to this use of the genitive: "With substantives and adjectives denoting *mastery* and *power* it [the genitive] takes a slightly different turn of meaning and can be rendered by the English *over*."[108]

arahaṃ, etc.: a series of nine epithets describing *tathāgato*.[109]

sugato: literally, "well gone," but used elsewhere to mean "fortunate" as opposed to *duggata*, "unfortunate."

anuttaro purisadammasārathi: "unsurpassed trainer of persons to be tamed." *Anuttaro* qualifies the following genitive tappurisa compound, which nests a kammadhāraya, *purisadamma*, with inversion of the normal word order. The latter is composed of the noun *purisa*, "persons," and the future passive participle *damma* (< *damya*, with consonant assimilation), "tamable," qualifying *purisa*.

satthā devamanussānaṃ: "teacher of devas and humans." The nominative preceding the plural genitive is an "elegant" inversion of normal word order, which would be *devamanussānaṃ satthā*.

dīghāyukā vaṇṇavanto sukhabahulā uccesu vimānesu ciraṭṭhitikā: "long-lived, beautiful, abounding in happiness, dwelling for a long time in tall palaces." All are descriptions of *devā*. *Dīghāyukā* is a bahubbīhi composed of *dīgha*, "long," and *āyu*, "life," with the suffix *-kā*, masculine plural nominative; *vaṇṇavanto* is from *vaṇṇa*, "beauty," with the possessive suffix *-vanto*, also masculine plural nominative; *sukhabahulā* is from *sukha*, "happiness, pleasure," and *bahulā*, "abounding in, devoted to." *Uccesu vimānesu* is locative plural, and *ciraṭṭhitikā* is another bahubbīhi composed of *cira*, "long," and *ṭhiti*, "duration," again with the suffix *-kā*.

108. I am thankful to Bryan Levman for this reference.

109. For a detailed analysis of these nine virtues (*navaguṇa*) according to the commentarial method, see Vism 198–212.

aniccā'va kira, bho, mayaṃ samānā 'nicc'amhā'ti amaññimha: "It seems, sir, that we are actually impermanent, [though] we thought: 'We're permanent.'" The polite vocative *bho*, "sir," suggests the devas are speaking to one another. *Aniccā*, "impermanent," is followed by the emphatic *va* (from *eva*); *samānā*, "being," is a middle-voice present participle of the verb *atthi*, plural nominative. Both qualify *mayaṃ*, "we," the subject of *amaññimha*, a first-person plural aorist of *maññati*, "thinks."

addhuvā'va kira, bho . . . asassatā'va kira, bho: These two sentences are constructed in the same way as the previous one, only substituting "not lasting" and "non-eternal."

sakkāyapariyāpannā: "included in the personal-collection." This tappurisa compound is composed of the noun *sakkāya*, itself a kammadhāraya compound, and the past participle *pariyāpanna*. It is almost impossible to find a satisfactory English rendering for *sakkāya*, a kammadhāraya compound of *sat*, "existing, real," and *kāya*, "body" in the sense of a collection. The suttas explain *sakkāya* as a term for the five clinging-aggregates.[110] The commentaries occasionally take *sakkāya* to signify the entire round of existence with its three planes.[111]

sadevakassa lokassa: "over this world together with its devas." For this use of the genitive, see the above comment on *tiracchānagatānaṃ pāṇānaṃ*.

13. Puṇṇamasutta

Full Moon (SN 22:82; III 100–104)

[1. The request for clarification]

Ekaṃ samayaṃ bhagavā sāvatthiyaṃ viharati pubbārāme migāramātupāsāde mahatā bhikkhusaṅghena saddhiṃ. Tena kho pana samayena bhagavā tadahuposathe pannarase puṇṇāya puṇṇamāya rattiyā bhikkhusaṅghaparivuto ajjhokāse nisinno hoti.

One occasion the Blessed One at Sāvatthī was dwelling in the Eastern-Park, in Migāra-mother's-mansion, with great monk-sangha together. By that occasion the Blessed One, on that-day-uposatha, on the fifteenth, on a full full-moon night, monk-saṅgha-surrounded, in the open seated was.

110. For instance, SN III 159,10: *Katamo ca, bhikkhave, sakkāyo? Pañcupādānakkhandhā ti 'ssa vacanīyaṃ.*

111. Mp III 404,25: *Sakkāyo ti tebhūmakavaṭṭaṃ.*

On one occasion the Blessed One was dwelling at Sāvatthī in the Eastern Park, in Migāra mother's mansion, together with a great monastic sangha. On that occasion the Blessed One—on that uposatha day, the fifteenth, a full-moon night—was seated out in the open surrounded by the monastic sangha.

Atha kho aññataro bhikkhu uṭṭhāy'āsanā ekaṃsaṃ uttarāsaṅgaṃ karitvā yena bhagavā ten'añjaliṃ paṇāmetvā bhagavantaṃ etadavoca: "Puccheyyāhaṃ, bhante, bhagavantaṃ kiñcideva desaṃ, sace me bhagavā okāsaṃ karoti pañhassa veyyākaraṇāyā"ti.

"Tena hi tvaṃ, bhikkhu, sake āsane nisīditvā puccha yadākaṅkhasī"ti.

"Evaṃ, bhante"ti kho so bhikkhu bhagavato paṭissutvā sake āsane nisīditvā bhagavantaṃ etadavoca:

Then a certain monk, having risen from a seat, one-shoulder upper-robe having made, where the Blessed One, there joined-palms having saluted, to the Blessed One this-said: "Would ask-I, Bhante, the Blessed One a particular point, if to me the Blessed One opportunity makes of question for answering."

"In that case you, monk, in own seat having sat, ask what-you wish."

"Yes, Bhante," that monk to the Blessed One having replied, in own seat having sat, to the Blessed One this-said.

Then a certain monk, having risen from his seat, having arranged his upper robe over one shoulder, having saluted the Blessed One with joined palms, said this to the Blessed One: "Bhante, I would ask the Blessed One about a particular point, if the Blessed One does me the favor of answering my question."

"In that case, monk, having sat down in your own seat, ask what you wish."

"Yes, Bhante," that monk replied to the Blessed One, sat in his own seat, and said this to the Blessed One:

[2. The five aggregates and desire]

"Ime nu kho, bhante, pañcupādānakkhandhā, seyyathīdaṃ: rūpupādānakkhandho, vedanupādānakkhandho, saññupādānakkhandho, saṅkhārupādānakkhandho, viññāṇupādānakkhandho"ti?

"Ime kho pana, bhikkhu, pañcupādānakkhandhā, seyyathīdaṃ: rūpupādānakkhandho . . . viññāṇupādānakkhandho"ti.

"These, Bhante, the five-clinging-aggregates, that is: the form-clinging-aggregate, the feeling-clinging-aggregate, the perception-clinging-aggregate, the volitional-activities-clinging-aggregate, the consciousness-clinging-aggregate?"

"These, monk, the five-clinging-aggregates, that is: the form-clinging-aggregate . . . the consciousness-clinging-aggregate."

"Are these, Bhante, the five clinging-aggregates—that is, the form clinging-aggregate, the feeling clinging-aggregate, the perception clinging-aggregate, the volitional activities clinging-aggregate, the consciousness clinging-aggregate?"

"Those, monk, are the five clinging-aggregates—that is, the form clinging-aggregate . . . the consciousness clinging-aggregate."

"Sādhu, bhante"ti kho so bhikkhu bhagavato bhāsitaṃ abhinanditvā anumoditvā bhagavantaṃ uttariṃ pañhaṃ apucchi: "Ime kho pana, bhante, pañcupādānakkhandhā kiṃmūlakā"ti?

"Ime kho, bhikkhu, pañcupādānakkhandhā chandamūlakā"ti.

"Good, Bhante," that monk the Blessed One's statement having delighted in, having rejoiced in, the Blessed One a further question asked: "These but, Bhante, five-clinging-aggregates what-rooted?"

"These, monk, five-clinging-aggregates desire-rooted."

Saying, "Good, Bhante," having delighted and rejoiced in the Blessed One's statement, that monk asked a further question: "But, Bhante, in what are these five clinging-aggregates rooted?"

"These five clinging-aggregates, monk, are rooted in desire."

"Sādhu, bhante"ti kho so bhikkhu . . . uttariṃ pañhaṃ apucchi: "Taññeva nu kho, bhante, upādānaṃ te pañcupādānakkhandhā udāhu aññatra pañcahi upādānakkhandhehi upādānan"ti?

"Na kho, bhikkhu, taññeva upādānaṃ te pañcupādānakkhandhā nāpi aññatra pañcahi upādānakkhandhehi upādānaṃ, api ca yo tattha chandarāgo taṃ tattha upādānan"ti.

"Good, Bhante," that monk . . . a further question asked: "That-itself, Bhante, clinging those five-clinging-aggregates, or else apart from the five clinging-aggregates clinging?"

"Not, monk, that-itself clinging those five-clinging-aggregates, not-too apart from the five clinging-aggregates clinging, but rather which there desire-lust that there the clinging."

Saying, "Good, Bhante," . . . that monk asked a further question: "Bhante, is that clinging itself those five clinging-aggregates, or is there clinging apart from the five clinging-aggregates?"

"Monk, that clinging itself is not those five clinging-aggregates, nor is there clinging apart from the five clinging-aggregates. But rather the desire-and-lust there [in relation to them], that is the clinging there."

"Sādhu, bhante"ti kho so bhikkhu . . . uttariṃ pañhaṃ apucchi: "Siyā pana, bhante, pañcupādānakkhandhesu chandarāgavemattatā"ti?

"Siyā, bhikkhū"ti bhagavā avoca: "Idha, bhikkhu, ekaccassa evaṃ hoti: 'Evaṃrūpo siyaṃ anāgatamaddhānaṃ, evaṃvedano siyaṃ anāgatam-addhānaṃ, evaṃsañño siyaṃ anāgatamaddhānaṃ, evaṃsaṅkhāro siyaṃ anāgatamaddhānaṃ, evaṃviññāṇo siyaṃ anāgatamaddhānan'ti. Evaṃ kho, bhikkhu, siyā pañcupādānakkhandhesu chandarāgavemattatā"ti.

"Good, Bhante," that monk . . . a further question asked: "Could there be, Bhante, in the five-clinging-aggregates desire-lust-diversity?"

"There could be, monk," the Blessed One said: "Here, monk, to someone such occurs: 'Such-form may I be future-time, such-feeling may I be future-time, such-perception may I be future-time, such-volitional-activities may I be future-time, such-consciousness may I be future-time.' Thus, monk, there could be in the five-clinging-aggregates desire-lust-diversity."

Saying, "Good, Bhante," that monk asked a further question: "Bhante, could there be diversity in the desire-and-lust for the five clinging-aggregates?"

"There could be, monk," the Blessed One said. "Here, monk, it occurs to someone: 'May I have such form in the future, may I have such feeling in the future, may I have such perception in the future, may I have such volitional activities in the future, may I have such consciousness in the future!' Thus, monk, there can be diversity in the desire-and-lust for the five clinging-aggregates."

[3. Designating and describing the aggregates]
"Sādhu, bhante"ti kho so bhikkhu . . . uttariṃ pañhaṃ apucchi: "Kittāvatā nu kho, bhante, khandhānaṃ khandhādhivacanan"ti?

"Yaṃ kiñci, bhikkhu, rūpaṃ atītānāgatapaccuppannaṃ ajjhattaṃ vā bahiddhā vā oḷārikaṃ vā sukhumaṃ vā hīnaṃ vā paṇītaṃ vā yaṃ dūre santike vā, ayaṃ vuccati 'rūpakkhandho.' Yā kāci vedanā . . . Yā kāci saññā . . . Ye keci saṅkhārā . . . Yaṃ kiñci viññāṇaṃ atītānāgatapaccuppannaṃ ajjhattaṃ vā bahiddhā vā oḷārikaṃ vā sukhumaṃ vā hīnaṃ vā paṇītaṃ vā yaṃ dūre santike vā, ayaṃ vuccati 'viññāṇakkhandho.' Ettāvatā kho, monk, khandhānaṃ khandhādhivacanan"ti.

"Good, Bhante," that monk . . . a further question asked: "In what way, Bhante, of the aggregates aggregates-designation?"

"Whatever, monk, form past-future-present, internal or external or, gross or subtle or, inferior or superior or, which far near or: this is called the 'form-aggregate.' Whatever feeling past-future-present . . . Whatever perception past-future-present . . . Whatever volitional-activities past-future-present . . . Whatever consciousness past-future-present, internal or external or, gross or subtle or, inferior or superior or, which far near or: this is called the 'consciousness-aggregate.' In this way, monk, of the aggregates aggregates-designation. "

Saying, "Good, Bhante," that monk asked a further question: "In what way, Bhante, does the designation 'aggregates' apply to the aggregates?"

"Whatever form there is, monk, whether past, future, or present, internal or external, gross or subtle, inferior or superior, far or near: this is called the 'form aggregate.' Whatever feeling there is, whether past, future, or present . . . Whatever perception there is, whether past, future, or present . . . Whatever volitional activities there are, whether past, future, or present . . . Whatever consciousness there is, whether past, future, or present, internal or external, gross or subtle, inferior or superior, far or near: this is called the 'consciousness aggregate.' It is in this way, monk, that the designation 'aggregates' applies to the aggregates."

"Sādhu, bhante"ti kho so bhikkhu . . . uttariṃ pañhaṃ apucchi: "Ko nu kho, bhante, hetu ko paccayo rūpakkhandhassa paññāpanāya? Ko hetu ko paccayo vedanākkhandhassa paññāpanāya? Ko hetu ko paccayo saññākkhandhassa

paññāpanāya? Ko hetu ko paccayo saṅkhārakkhandhassa paññāpanāya? Ko hetu ko paccayo viññāṇakkhandhassa paññāpanāyā"ti?

"Good, Bhante," that monk . . . a further question asked: "What, Bhante, the cause, what the condition, of the form-aggregate for the making known? What the cause, what the condition, of the feeling-aggregate for the making known? What the cause, what the condition, of the perception-aggregate for the making known? What the cause, what the condition, of the volitional-activities-aggregate for the making known? What the cause, what the condition, of the consciousness-aggregate for the making known?"

Saying, "Good, Bhante," that monk asked a further question: "What is the cause and condition, Bhante, for the making known of the form aggregate? What is the cause and condition for the making known of the feeling aggregate? What is the cause and condition for the making known of the perception aggregate? What is the cause and condition for the making known of the volitional activities aggregate? What is the cause and condition for the making known of the consciousness aggregate?"

"Cattāro kho, bhikkhu, mahābhūtā hetu, cattāro mahābhūtā paccayo, rūpakkhandhassa paññāpanāya. Phasso hetu, phasso paccayo, vedanākkhandhassa paññāpanāya. Phasso hetu, phasso paccayo, saññākkhandhassa paññāpanāya. Phasso hetu, phasso paccayo, saṅkhārakkhandhassa paññāpanāya. Nāmarūpaṃ hetu, nāmarūpaṃ paccayo, viññāṇakkhandhassa paññāpanāyā"ti.

"The four, monk, great-elements the cause, the four great-elements the condition, of the form-aggregate for the making known. Contact the cause, contact the condition, of the feeling-aggregate for the making known. Contact the cause, contact the condition, of the perception-aggregate for the making known. Contact the cause, contact the condition, of the volitional-activities-aggregate for the making known. Name-form the cause, name-form the condition, of the consciousness-aggregate for the making known."

"The four great elements, monk, are the cause and condition for the making known of the form aggregate. Contact is the cause and condition for the making known of the feeling aggregate. Contact is the cause and condition for the making known of the perception aggregate. Contact is the cause and condition for the making known of the volitional activities aggregate. Name-and-form is the cause and condition for the making known of the consciousness aggregate."

[4. The view of the personal-collection]

"Sādhu, bhante"ti kho so bhikkhu . . . uttariṃ apucchi: "Kathaṃ nu kho, bhante, sakkāyadiṭṭhi hotī"ti?

"Idha, bhikkhu, assutavā puthujjano ariyānaṃ adassāvī ariyadhammassa akovido ariyadhamme avinīto, sappurisānaṃ adassāvī sappurisadhammassa akovido sappurisadhamme avinīto, rūpaṃ attato samanupassati, rūpavantaṃ vā attānaṃ, attani vā rūpaṃ, rūpasmiṃ vā attānaṃ. Vedanaṃ . . . Saññaṃ . . . Saṅkhāre . . . Viññāṇaṃ attato samanupassati, viññāṇavantaṃ vā attānaṃ; attani vā viññāṇaṃ, viññāṇasmiṃ vā attānaṃ. Evaṃ kho, bhikkhu, sakkāyadiṭṭhi hotī"ti.

"Good, Bhante," that monk . . . a further question asked: "How, Bhante, personal-collection-view occurs?"

"Here, monk, an unlearned worldling, of noble ones not-seer, of noble-ones-Dhamma not-skilled, in noble-ones-Dhamma not-trained, of good persons not-seer, of good-persons-Dhamma not-skilled, in good-persons-Dhamma not-trained, form as self regards, form-possessing or self, in self or form, in form or self. Feeling . . . Perception . . . Volitional-activities . . . Consciousness as self regards, consciousness-possessing or self, in self or consciousness, in consciousness or self. Thus, monk, personal-collection-view occurs."

Saying, "Good, Bhante," that monk asked a further question: "How, Bhante, does the view of the personal-collection occur?"

"Here, monk, an unlearned worldling, who is not a seer of noble ones, who is unskilled in the noble ones' Dhamma, who is untrained in the noble ones' Dhamma, who is not a seer of good persons, who is unskilled in the good persons' Dhamma, who is untrained in the good persons' Dhamma, regards form as self, or self as possessing form, or form as in self, or self as in form. He regards feeling as self . . . perception as self . . . volitional activities as self . . . consciousness as self, or self as possessing consciousness, or consciousness as in self, or self as in consciousness. That is how the view of the personal-collection occurs."

"Kathaṃ pana, bhante, sakkāyadiṭṭhi na hotī"ti?

"Idha, bhikkhu, sutavā ariyasāvako ariyānaṃ dassāvī ariyadhammassa kovido ariyadhamme suvinīto, sappurisānaṃ dassāvī sappurisadhammassa kovido sappurisadhamme suvinīto na rūpaṃ attato samanupassati, na rūpavantaṃ vā attānaṃ, na attani vā rūpaṃ, na rūpasmiṃ vā attānaṃ. Na vedanaṃ . . . Na saññaṃ . . . Na saṅkhāre . . . Na viññāṇaṃ attato samanupassati, na viññāṇavantaṃ vā attānaṃ; na attani vā viññāṇaṃ, na viññāṇasmiṃ vā attānaṃ. Evaṃ kho, bhikkhu, sakkāyadiṭṭhi na hotī"ti.

"How but, Bhante, personal-collection-view not occurs?"

"Here, monk, a learned noble-disciple, of noble ones seer, of noble-ones-Dhamma skilled, in noble-ones-Dhamma trained, of good-persons seer, of good-persons-Dhamma skilled, in good-persons-Dhamma trained, not form as self regards, not form-possessing or self, not in self or form, not in form or self. Not feeling . . . Not perception . . . Not volitional-activities . . . Not consciousness as self regards, not consciousness-possessing or self, not in self or consciousness, not in consciousness or self. Thus, monk, personal-collection-view not occurs."

"But, Bhante, how does the view of the personal-collection not occur?"

"Here, monk, an instructed noble disciple, who is a seer of the noble ones, who is skilled in the noble ones' Dhamma, who is trained in the noble ones' Dhamma, who is a seer of good persons, who is skilled in the good persons' Dhamma, who is trained in the good persons' Dhamma, does not regard form as self, or self as possessing form, or form as in self, or self as in form. He does not regard feeling as self . . . perception as self . . . volitional activities as self . . . consciousness as self, or self as possessing consciousness, or consciousness as in self, or self as in consciousness. That is how the view of the personal-collection does not occur."[112]

Grammatical explanations

[1. The request for clarification]

migāramātupāsāde: "in Migāra mother's mansion"; a genitive tappurisa compound with an internal genitive tappurisa (*migāramātu*, "the

112. The remaining sections of this sutta open with questions whose answers correspond to 2.5, 2.11, and 2.9.3.

mother of Migāra"). The residence was located in the Eastern Park, to the east of the city of Sāvatthī.

mahatā bhikkhusaṅghena saddhiṃ: "together with a great monastic sangha." *Mahatā* is the masculine singular instrumental of *mahat*, here qualifying *bhikkhusaṅghena*, a tappurisa compound. The compound actually means "a sangha of monks," but I translate it as "the monastic sangha" for the purpose of gender inclusiveness. *Saddhiṃ*, "together," is an indeclinable taking nouns and their qualifiers in the instrumental case (Duroiselle §599,x; Perniola §255). The instrumental usually precedes *saddhiṃ* (as here), but occasionally follows it (see p. 226).

tena kho pana samayena: "on that occasion." *Tena samayena* is an instrumental used to express time (Duroiselle §599,ix; Perniola §253f); *kho pana* connects the sentence with its predecessor. The expression refers back to the occasion mentioned in the preceding sentence, indicated by *ekaṃ samayaṃ*.

tadahuposathe pannarase: "on that uposatha day, the fifteenth." These are locatives indicating that the discussion to follow occurs on the *uposatha*, the monastic observance day—on this occasion, the fifteenth of the fortnight. The full-moon *uposatha* always falls on the fifteenth; the new-moon *uposatha* may fall on the fourteenth or the fifteenth. DOP, under *aha(n)*, takes *tadahu* to mean "that day, that very day."

puṇṇāya puṇṇamāya rattiyā: literally, "on a full full-moon night." The terms are all locatives, with both *puṇṇāya* and *puṇṇamāya* qualifying the feminine locative *rattiyā*. There seems to be a redundancy in the use of both adjectives to describe *rattiyā*.

bhikkhusaṅghaparivuto: "surrounded by the monastic sangha"; a complex instrumental tappurisa compound describing the Buddha, composed of *bhikkhusaṅgha* and the past participle, *parivuto*, "surrounded."

ajjhokāse (*adhi* + *okāse* > *adhyokāse* > *ajjhokāse*): "out in the open." The prefix *adhi* may have the effect of turning *okāsa*, "open space," into a locative, but DOP lists *ajjhokāse* as an indeclinable.

nisinno hoti: a combination of a past participle and the present finite verb *hoti* in an auxiliary role. The combination indicates a continuous action occurring in the past.

ekaṃsaṃ: "one shoulder"; a numerical compound used adverbially to indicate the manner in which the robe is arranged.

yena bhagavā ten'añjaliṃ paṇāmetvā: "having saluted the Blessed One with joined palms." The *yena . . . tena* construction here is similar to that used when someone approaches the Buddha. *Añjali* is the traditional Indian gesture of respect.

puccheyyāhaṃ: "I would ask"; a sandhi formation of optative *puccheyyaṃ* and *ahaṃ*.

sace me okāsaṃ karoti pañhassa veyyākaraṇāya: "if the Blessed One does me the favor of answering my question." *Okāsa* is used here in a different sense from the above, where it means "open space." As opportunity, *okāsa* goes with the dative of purpose, *veyyākaraṇāya*, "for answering, to answer."

tena hi: a common adverbial expression, meaning "in that case, well then."

puccha: "ask"; the second-person singular imperative of *pucchati*.

paṭissutvā: "having replied"; the absolutive of *paṭissuṇāti*.

[2. The five aggregates and desire]

pañcupādānakkhandhā: see pp. 99–100.

apucchi: a third-person singular aorist of *pucchati*, "asks," with the *a-* augment.

kiṃmūlakā: an interrogative bahubbīhi compound composed of *kiṃ*, "what?" and *mūla*, "root," with the adjectival suffix *-kā*, agreeing with *pañcupādānakkhandhā*.

chandamūlakā: "rooted in desire." The answer too is a bahubbīhi, with *chanda* in place of *kiṃ*.

taññeva (= *taṃ* + *eva*): "that same," qualifying *upādānaṃ*. The question proposes two alternatives, separated by the indeclinable *udāhu*, "or else." One, signaled by *taññeva*, posits identity between *upādāna* and the *pañcupādānakkhandhā*; the other posits *upādāna* as existing *aññatra*, elsewhere, apart from the *pañcupādānakkhandhā*.[113]

api ca: "but rather."

yo tattha chandarāgo: "the desire-and-lust there." The relative *yo* agrees with *chandarāgo* and is correlated with the demonstrative *taṃ*, which qualifies *upādānaṃ*. *Chandarāgo* is a dvanda compound composed of two virtually synonymous terms and thus functions grammatically as a singular. *Tattha* is apparently used here in a locative sense representing the objects of *chandarāgo*. As pointed out earlier, nouns signifying desire often take their objects in the locative, to be read "desire in regard to X."

113. *Aññatra* takes the term it refers to in the instrumental case—or perhaps the ablative, since in both cases the masculine plural ending of this class of nouns is the same.

siyā: "could there be," a third-person singular optative of *atthi*.

ekaccassa evaṃ hoti: "to someone such occurs"; an idiomatic way of saying "someone thinks," with the logical subject in the dative. See p. 75.

evaṃrūpo: a bahubbīhi composed of the adverb *evaṃ* and the noun *rūpa*, qualifying the implicit subject *ahaṃ*, indicated by the first-person optative verb *siyaṃ*. *Evaṃvedano . . . evaṃviññāṇo* are similarly composed. The gender of each compound becomes masculine singular to match the subject, *ahaṃ*.

anāgatamaddhānaṃ: "in the future"; the accusative used to indicate a period of time. See p. 93.

[3. Designating and describing the aggregates]

kittāvatā: "how much? how far? in what way? to what extent?"

khandhānaṃ khandhādhivacanaṃ: The questioner is in effect asking: "Why are the aggregates called 'aggregates'?" And the answer shows that each *khandha* is a category comprising all instances of its defining characteristic.

paññāpanāya: the dative of *paññāpana*, "making known."[114]

cattāro: the number four, in the masculine nominative, agreeing with *mahābhūtā*.

mahābhūtā: the primary material elements. The compound is a kammadhāraya of *mahā*, "great," and *bhūta*, the past participle of *bhavati* functioning as a noun, "entity." Since the sentence establishes a relationship of identity between *mahābhūtā* and *hetu*, and again between *mahābhūtā* and *paccaya*, no verb is required. The same holds for the other four aggregates and their respective cause and condition.

[4. The view of the personal-collection]

sakkāyadiṭṭhi: "the view of the personal-collection." This is a locative tappurisa compound, "a view in regard to the personal-collection."[115]

114. Wijesekera §107e calls this an *adnominal* use of the dative, explaining: "The logical justification for the dative with these [that is, with *hetu* and *paccaya*] seems to lie in the fact that the notion implied is one of *aim*, denoting as it does *that* to which the cause leads. The same nuance is expressed by the English idioms 'the reason for' and 'the cause for.'"

115. See p. 40.

assutavā puthujjano: "the unlearned worldling"; the stock canonical description of the ordinary person attached to the world. *Puthujjana* is a kammadhāraya compound composed of *puthu*, "common" (or "distinct"),[116] and *jana*, person. The *puthujjana* is usually described as *assutavat*, devoid of (*a*-) the learning (*suta*) that comes from hearing the Dhamma; *assutavā* is the masculine nominative. The worldling also lacks (*a*-) sight (*dassana*) of the noble ones, hence is described as *adassāvī*, the nominative of *adassāvin*.

rūpaṃ attato samanupassati, rūpavantaṃ vā attānaṃ, attani vā rūpaṃ, rūpasmiṃ vā attānaṃ: This formula posits four alternative ways of relating the self to each aggregate. The verb *samanupassati* takes either the aggregate or the self as its object. The first alternative is by way of identity, with the suffix *-to* establishing that the object, *rūpaṃ*, is viewed "as the self" (*attato*).[117] The second takes the self to be *rūpavantaṃ*, where the suffix *-vantaṃ* denotes possession. The third sees the object *rūpaṃ* existing *attani*, a locative, "in the self," while the fourth sees the object *attānaṃ* existing *rūpasmiṃ*, a locative, "in form."

sutavā ariyasāvako: This passage should be construed in all ways as the opposite of the passage on the *puthujjana*.

14. Pupphasutta

Flowers (SN 22:94; III 138–40)

[1. Not disputing with the world]

"Nāhaṃ, bhikkhave, lokena vivadāmi; loko'va mayā vivadati. Na, bhikkhave, dhammavādī kenaci lokasmiṃ vivadati. Yaṃ, bhikkhave, natthisammataṃ loke paṇḍitānaṃ, ahampi taṃ 'natthī'ti vadāmi. Yaṃ, bhikkhave, atthisammataṃ loke paṇḍitānaṃ, ahampi taṃ 'atthī'ti vadāmi.

"Not-I, monks, with the world dispute; the world indeed with me disputes. Not, monks, a Dhamma-speaker with anyone in the world disputes. Which,

116. Pāli *puthu* can represent two different Skt words: *pṛthak*, "apart or separately or different from," or *pṛthu*, "copious, numerous, manifold." The commentaries, playing upon both meanings of *puthu*, give various derivations of *puthujjana*. See for instance Ps I 20–21.

117. On this use of the ablative, see pp. 154–55.

monks, not-exists-agreed in the world of wise ones, I-too that 'not exists' say. Which, monks, exists-agreed in the world of wise ones, I-too that 'exists' say.

"I, monks, do not dispute with the world; the world, indeed, disputes with me. A speaker of the Dhamma does not dispute with anyone in the world. That, monks, which is agreed upon as not existing by the wise in the world, I too say of that: 'It does not exist.' That which is agreed upon as existing by the wise in the world, I too say of that: 'It exists.'

"Kiñca, bhikkhave, natthisammataṃ loke paṇḍitānaṃ, yamahaṃ 'natthī'ti vadāmi? Rūpaṃ, bhikkhave, niccaṃ dhuvaṃ sassataṃ avipariṇāma-dhammaṃ natthisammataṃ loke paṇḍitānaṃ; ahampi taṃ 'natthī'ti vadāmi. Vedanā . . . Saññā . . . Saṅkhārā . . . Viññāṇaṃ niccaṃ dhuvaṃ sassataṃ avipariṇāmadhammaṃ natthisammataṃ loke paṇḍitānaṃ; ahampi taṃ 'natthī'ti vadāmi. Idaṃ kho, bhikkhave, natthisammataṃ loke paṇḍitānaṃ; ahampi taṃ 'natthī'ti vadāmi.

"What-and, monks, not-exists-agreed in the world of wise ones, which-I 'not exists' say? Form, monks, permanent, lasting, eternal, not-change-subject, not-exists-agreed in the world of wise ones; I-too that 'not exists' say. Feeling . . . Perception . . . Volitional-activities . . . Consciousness permanent, lasting, eternal, not-change-subject, not-exists-agreed in the world of wise ones; I-too that 'not exists,' say. This, monks, not-exists-agreed in the world of wise ones; I too that 'not exists' say.

"And what is it, monks, that is agreed upon by the wise in the world as not existing, of which I too say: 'It does not exist'? Form that is permanent, lasting, eternal, not subject to change, is agreed upon by the wise in the world as not existing; I too say of that: 'It does not exist.' Feeling . . . Perception . . . Volitional activities . . . Consciousness that is permanent, lasting, eternal, not subject to change, is agreed upon by the wise in the world as not existing; I too say of that: 'It does not exist.' This, monks, is what the wise in the world have agreed upon as not existing, of which I too say: 'It does not exist.'

"Kiñca, bhikkhave, atthisammataṃ loke paṇḍitānaṃ, yamahaṃ 'atthī'ti vadāmi? Rūpaṃ, bhikkhave, aniccaṃ dukkhaṃ vipariṇāmadhammaṃ atthisammataṃ loke paṇḍitānaṃ; ahampi taṃ 'atthī'ti vadāmi. Vedanā . . . Saññā. . . Saṅkhārā. . . Viññāṇaṃ aniccaṃ dukkhaṃ vipariṇāma-dhammaṃ atthisammataṃ loke paṇḍitānaṃ; ahampi taṃ 'atthī'ti vadāmi. Idaṃ kho, bhikkhave, atthisammataṃ loke paṇḍitānaṃ; ahampi taṃ 'atthī'ti vadāmi.

"What-and, monks, exists-agreed in the world of wise ones, which-I 'exists' say? Form, monks, impermanent, suffering, change-subject, exists-agreed in the world of wise ones; I-too that 'exists' say. Feeling . . . Perception . . . Volitional-activities . . . Consciousness impermanent, suffering, change-subject, exists-agreed in world of wise ones; I-too that 'exists' say. This, monks, exists-agreed in the world of wise ones; I too that 'exists' say.

"And what is it, monks, that is agreed upon by the wise in the world as existing, of which I too say: 'It exists'? Form that is impermanent, suffering, subject to change, is agreed upon by the wise in the world as existing; I too say of that: 'It exists.' Feeling . . . Perception . . . Volitional activities . . . Consciousness that is permanent, suffering, subject to change, is agreed upon by the wise in the world as existing; I too say of that: 'It exists.' This, monks, is what is agreed upon by the wise in the world as existing, of which I too say: 'It exists.'

[2. World-phenomena in the world]
"Atthi, bhikkhave, loke lokadhammo, taṃ tathāgato abhisambujjhati abhisameti. Abhisambujjhitvā abhisametvā taṃ ācikkhati deseti paññāpeti paṭṭhapeti vivarati vibhajati uttānīkaroti.

"There is, monks, in the world a world-phenomenon that the Tathāgata awakens to, breaks through to. Having awakened to, having broken through to, that points out, teaches, makes known, establishes, discloses, analyzes, elucidates.

"There is, monks, a world-phenomenon in the world to which the Tathāgata has awakened and broken through. Having awakened to it, having broken through to it, he points it out, teaches it, makes it known, establishes it, discloses it, analyzes it, and elucidates it.

"Kiñca, bhikkhave, loke lokadhammo, taṃ tathāgato abhisambujjhati abhisameti, abhisambujjhitvā abhisametvā ācikkhati deseti paññāpeti paṭṭhapeti vivarati vibhajati uttānīkaroti? Rūpaṃ, bhikkhave, loke lokadhammo taṃ tathāgato abhisambujjhati abhisameti. Abhisambujjhitvā abhisametvā ācikkhati deseti paññāpeti paṭṭhapeti vivarati vibhajati uttānīkaroti.

"What-and, monks, in the world a world-phenomenon that the Tathāgata awakens to, breaks through to, having awakened to, having broken through to, points out, teaches, makes known, establishes, discloses, analyzes, elucidates? Form, monks, in the world a world-phenomenon that the Tathāgata awakens to, breaks through to. Having awakened to, having broken through to, that points out, teaches, makes known, establishes, discloses, analyzes, elucidates.

"And what is that world-phenomenon in the world to which the Tathāgata has awakened and broken through, and which, having awakened to it, having broken through to it, he points out, teaches, makes known, establishes, discloses, analyzes, and elucidates? Form, monks, is a world-phenomenon in the world to which the Tathāgata has awakened and broken through. Having awakened to it, having broken through to it, he points it out, teaches, makes known, establishes, discloses, analyzes, and elucidates it.

"Yo, bhikkhave, tathāgatena evaṃ ācikkhiyamāne desiyamāne paññāpiyamāne paṭṭhapiyamāne vivariyamāne vibhajiyamāne uttānīkariyamāne na jānāti na passati, tamahaṃ, bhikkhave, bālaṃ puthujjanaṃ andhaṃ acakkhukaṃ ajānantaṃ apassantaṃ kinti karomi?

"One who, monks, by the Tathāgata thus being pointed out, being taught, being made known, being established, being disclosed, being analyzed, being elucidated, not knows, not sees, that-I, monks, foolish worldling, blind, sightless, not-knowing, not-seeing, how I do?

"When it is being thus pointed out, taught, made known, established, disclosed, analyzed, and elucidated by the Tathāgata, if anyone does not know and see, how can I do anything with that foolish worldling who is blind, sightless, one who does not know, who does not see?

"Vedanā . . . Saññā . . . Saṅkhārā . . . Viññāṇaṃ, bhikkhave, loke loka-dhammo taṃ tathāgato abhisambujjhati abhisameti. Abhisambujjhitvā abhisametvā ācikkhati deseti paññāpeti paṭṭhapeti vivarati vibhajati uttānīkaroti.

"Feeling . . . Perception . . . Volitional-activities . . . Consciousness, monks, in the world a world-phenomenon that the Tathāgata awakens to, breaks through to. Having awakened to, having broken through to, that points out, teaches, makes known, establishes, discloses, analyzes, elucidates.

"Feeling . . . Perception . . . Volitional activities . . . Consciousness, monks, is a world-phenomenon in the world to which the Tathāgata has awakened and broken through. Having awakened to it, having broken through to it, he points it out, teaches, makes known, establishes, discloses, analyzes, and elucidates it.

"Yo, bhikkhave, tathāgatena evaṃ ācikkhiyamāne desiyamāne paññāpiya-māne paṭṭhapiyamāne vivariyamāne vibhajiyamāne uttānīkariyamāne na jānāti na passati, tamahaṃ, bhikkhave, bālaṃ puthujjanaṃ andhaṃ acakkhukaṃ ajānantaṃ apassantaṃ kinti karomi?

"One who, monks, by the Tathāgata thus when being pointed out, when being taught, when being made known, when being established, when being disclosed, when being analyzed, when being elucidated, not knows, not sees, that-I, monks, foolish worldling, blind sightless, not-knowing, not-seeing, how I do?

"When it is being thus pointed out, taught, made known, established, disclosed, analyzed, and elucidated by the Tathāgata, if someone does not know and see, how can I do anything with that foolish worldling who is blind, sightless, one who does not know, who does not see?

[3. The simile of the lotus]

"Seyyathāpi, bhikkhave, uppalaṃ vā padumaṃ vā puṇḍarīkaṃ vā udake jātaṃ udake saṃvaḍḍhaṃ udakā accuggamma ṭhāti anupalittaṃ udakena; evameva kho, bhikkhave, tathāgato loke jāto loke saṃvaḍḍho lokaṃ abhibhuyya viharati anupalitto lokenā"ti.

"Just as, monks, a blue lotus or a red lotus or a white lotus or, in the water born, in the water grown, from the water having risen, stands untainted by water, just so, monks, the Tathāgata in the world born, in the world grown, the world having overcome, dwells untainted by the world."

"Monks, just as a blue lotus or a red lotus or a white lotus is born in the water and grown up in the water, but having risen from the water, it stands untainted by the water, so too the Tathāgata was born in the world and grew up in the world, but having overcome the world, he dwells untainted by the world."

Grammatical explanations

[1. Not disputing with the world]

nāhaṃ: a sandhi formation of *na* and *ahaṃ*.

kenaci: "with anyone"; the instrumental of the general pronoun *koci*.

natthisammataṃ: "agreed upon as not existing"; a compound of *natthi*, "not exists," and *sammataṃ*, "agreed upon," a past participle.[118] With *yaṃ*, the compound functions as a noun and the grammatical subject of the relative clause.

paṇḍitānaṃ: "by the wise"; a plural genitive used with an instrumental sense.

ahampi taṃ "natthī"ti vadāmi: "I too say of that: 'It does not exist.'" In this main clause *taṃ*, the accusative object of *vadāmi*, refers back to the nominative *yaṃ natthisammataṃ* of the preceding relative clause.

yaṃ, bhikkhave, atthisammataṃ: "that which is agreed upon as existing." This sentence should be construed in the same way, but with *atthisammataṃ*, a compound of "exists" and "agreed upon," as the subject.

[2. World-phenomena in the world]

atthi, bhikkhave, loke lokadhammo, taṃ tathāgato abhisambujjhati abhisameti: The nominative subject of the first clause is *lokadhammo*. In the

118. The compound might be considered a syntactical compound whose first member involves an implicit *ti*, the marker for a direct quotation. It would thus be resolved: "*natthī*"*ti sammataṃ*, "[what is] agreed 'there is not.'" In the typology proposed by Collins 136–37, it would fit into his type (iii).

second clause, *lokadhammo* is represented by the accusative pronoun *taṃ*, which becomes the object of the two verbs, *abhisambujjhati abhisameti*. On *abhisambujjhati*, see p. 93; on *abhisameti*, see p. 118.

abhisambujjhitvā abhisametvā: "having awakened to it, having broken through to it"; absolutives of the above two verbs. We earlier encountered a different absolutive of *abhisameti*, *abhisamecca*, formed with the *-ya* suffix (see p. 130). It is not unusual for verbs to form their absolutives in different ways.

ācikkhati deseti paññāpeti paṭṭhapeti vivarati vibhajati uttānīkaroti: a series of near-synonymous verbs. The corresponding sequence of nouns is at p. 121.

yo . . . na jānāti na passati: "if someone does not know and see." The sentence is not conditional but declarative, but I use the conditional "if" to preserve the syntax of the Pāli, with the relative clause preceding the main clause. The relative clause has the person as subject; in the main clause, the person becomes the accusative object: *taṃ . . . bālaṃ puthujjanaṃ*. A more natural translation would omit the relative clause as already entailed by the main clause thus: "When it is being thus pointed out . . . elucidated by the Tathāgata, how can I do anything with that foolish worldling who is blind, sightless, one who does not know, who does not see?"

evaṃ ācikkhiyamāne desiyamāne paññāpiyamāne paṭṭhapiyamāne vivariyamāne vibhajiyamāne uttānīkariyamāne: an extended locative absolute built on present participles. The indeclinable *evaṃ*, representing the *manner* in which these principles are being taught, occupies the position usually taken by the locative noun or pronoun. There are other examples of this kind of locative absolute in the suttas, the most common being: *evaṃ sante*, "such being [the case]," and *evaṃ vutte*, "such being said." Perhaps here the locative nouns representing the five aggregates, that is, *rūpe* through *viññāṇe*, should be understood as occurring with each series of locative present participles.

[3. The simile of the lotus]

uppalaṃ, padumaṃ, puṇḍarīkaṃ: three kinds of lotus flowers, distinguished by color. *Paduma* (Skt *padma*) is also a general term for all types of lotus flowers.

udakā accuggamma: "having risen from the water"; an ablative followed by an absolutive based on the verb *gacchati*, from the root *gam* with two prefixes, *ati*, implying "above, beyond," and *ud*, implying "upward." The modifications are as follows: *ati* + *ud* > *atyud* > *accud* + *gam* > *accuggam* + *ya* > *accuggamya* > *accuggamma*.[119]

ṭhāti anupalittaṃ udakena: "stands untainted by the water." The finite verb *ṭhāti* is an alternative to *tiṭṭhati*, formed by adding the suffix directly to the root *ṭhā*. *Anupalittaṃ* is the past participle of *upalippati* (passive of *upalimpati*), "is defiled, is tainted," negated by *an-* and of neuter gender in agreement with the nouns *uppalaṃ*, etc. The word order, with the instrumental following the participle, is irregular, probably for poetic effect.

abhibhuyya: "having overcome"; an absolutive of *abhibhavati*, based on the root: *abhibhū* + *ya* > *abhibhuyya*.

viharati anupalitto lokena: "dwells untainted by the world"; again, the normal word order is inverted, mirroring the word order of the simile.

15. Pheṇapiṇḍūpamasutta

Simile of the Lump of Foam (SN 22:95; III 140–42)

[1. Form]

Ekaṃ samayaṃ bhagavā ayojjhāyaṃ viharati gaṅgāya nadiyā tīre. Tatra kho bhagavā bhikkhū āmantesi: "Seyyathāpi, bhikkhave, ayaṃ gaṅgā nadī mahantaṃ pheṇapiṇḍaṃ āvaheyya. Tamenaṃ cakkhumā puriso passeyya nijjhāyeyya yoniso upaparikkheyya. Tassa taṃ passato nijjhāyato yoniso upaparikkhato rittakaññeva khāyeyya, tucchakaññeva khāyeyya, asārakaññeva khāyeyya. Kiṃ hi siyā, bhikkhave, pheṇapiṇḍe sāro?

One occasion the Blessed One at Ayojjhā was dwelling, of Ganges River on the bank. There the Blessed One the monks addressed: "Suppose, monks, this Ganges River a great foam-lump would carry along. That-this an eye-possessing man would see, would ponder, thoroughly would investigate. To him that seeing, pondering, thoroughly investigating, void-just would appear, hollow-just would appear, insubstantial-just would appear. What for could be, monks, in foam-lump substance?

119. The modifications of the consonant clusters here are as follows: *-ty-* > *-cc-*; *-dg-* > *-gg-*; and *-my-* > *-mm-*.

On one occasion the Blessed One was dwelling at Ayojjhā on the bank of the Ganges River. There the Blessed One addressed the monks: "Suppose, monks, this Ganges River would carry along a great lump of foam. A clear-sighted man would see this, ponder it, and thoroughly investigate it. As he is seeing it, pondering it, and thoroughly investigating it, it would appear to him to be just void, it would appear just hollow, it would appear just insubstantial. For what substance could there be in a lump of foam?

"Evameva kho, bhikkhave, yaṃ kiñci rūpaṃ atītānāgatapaccuppannaṃ ajjhattaṃ vā bahiddhā vā oḷārikaṃ vā sukhumaṃ vā hīnaṃ vā paṇītaṃ vā yaṃ dūre santike vā, taṃ bhikkhu passati nijjhāyati yoniso upaparikkhati. Tassa taṃ passato nijjhāyato yoniso upaparikkhato rittakaññeva khāyati, tucchakaññeva khāyati, asārakaññeva khāyati. Kiṃ hi siyā, bhikkhave, rūpe sāro?

"Just so, monks, whatever form past-future-present, internal or external or, gross or subtle or, inferior or superior or, which far near or, that a monk sees, ponders, thoroughly investigates. To him that seeing, pondering, thoroughly investigating, void-just would appear, hollow-just would appear, insubstantial-just would appear. What for could be, monks, in form substance?

"So too, monks, whatever form there is, whether past, future, or present, internal or external, gross or subtle, inferior or superior, far or near: a monk sees it, ponders it, and thoroughly investigates it. As he is seeing it, pondering it, and thoroughly investigating it, it would appear to him to be just void, it would appear just hollow, it would appear just insubstantial. For what substance could there be in form?

[2. Feeling]

"Seyyathāpi, bhikkhave, saradasamaye thullaphusitake deve vassante udake udakabubbuḷaṃ uppajjati c'eva nirujjhati ca. Tamenaṃ cakkhumā puriso passeyya nijjhāyeyya yoniso upaparikkheyya. Tassa taṃ passato nijjhāyato yoniso upaparikkhato rittakaññeva khāyeyya, tucchakaññeva khāyeyya, asārakaññeva khāyeyya. Kiṃ hi siyā, bhikkhave, udakabubbuḷe sāro?

"Suppose, monks, in autumn-time, when the big-drops sky raining, on the water a water-bubble arises and ceases and. That-this an eye-possessing man would see, would ponder, thoroughly would investigate. To him that seeing, pondering, thoroughly investigating, void-just would appear, hollow-just would appear, insubstantial-just would appear. What for could be, monks, in water-bubble substance?

"Suppose, monks, in the autumn, when the sky is raining with big raindrops falling, a water bubble arises and ceases on the water. A clear-sighted man would see this, ponder it, and thoroughly investigate it. As he is seeing it, pondering it, and thoroughly investigating it, it would appear to him to be just void, it would appear just hollow, it would appear just insubstantial. For what substance could there be in a water bubble?

"Evameva kho, bhikkhave, yā kāci vedanā atītānāgatapaccuppannā ajjhattaṃ vā bahiddhā vā oḷārikaṃ vā sukhumaṃ vā hīnaṃ vā paṇītaṃ vā yaṃ dūre santike vā, taṃ bhikkhu passati nijjhāyati yoniso upaparikkhati. Tassa taṃ passato nijjhāyato yoniso upaparikkhato rittakaññeva khāyati, tucchakaññeva khāyati, asārakaññeva khāyati. Kiṃ hi siyā, bhikkhave, vedanāya sāro?

"Just so, monks, whatever feeling past-future-present, internal or external or, gross or subtle or, inferior or superior or, which far near or, that a monk sees, ponders, thoroughly investigates. To him that seeing, pondering, thoroughly investigating, void-just would appear, hollow-just would appear, insubstantial-just would appear. What for could be, monks, in feeling substance?

"So too, monks, whatever feeling there is, whether past, future, or present, internal or external, gross or subtle, inferior or superior, far or near: a monk sees it, ponders it, and thoroughly investigates. As he is seeing it, pondering it, and thoroughly investigating it, it would appear to him to be just void, it would appear just hollow, it would appear just insubstantial. For what substance could there be in feeling?

[3. Perception]

"Seyyathāpi, bhikkhave, gimhānaṃ pacchime māse ṭhite majjhanhike kāle marīcikā phandati. Tamenaṃ cakkhumā puriso passeyya nijjhāyeyya yoniso upaparikkheyya. Tassa taṃ passato nijjhāyato yoniso upaparikkhato

rittakaññeva khāyeyya, tucchakaññeva khāyeyya, asārakaññeva khāyeyya. Kiṃ hi siyā, bhikkhave, marīcikāya sāro?

"Suppose, monks, of summer in last month, when stood mid-day time, a mirage shimmers. That-this an eye-possessing man would see, would ponder, thoroughly would investigate. To him that seeing, pondering, thoroughly investigating, void-just would appear, hollow-just would appear, insubstantial-just would appear. What for could be, monks, in a mirage substance?

"Suppose, monks, in the last month of the hot season, at midday, a mirage shimmers. A clear-sighted man would see this, ponder it, and thoroughly investigate it. As he is seeing it, pondering it, and thoroughly investigating it, it would appear to him to be just void, it would appear just hollow, it would appear just insubstantial. For what substance could there be in a mirage?

"Evameva kho, bhikkhave, yā kāci saññā atītānāgatapaccuppannā ajjhattaṃ vā bahiddhā vā oḷārikaṃ vā sukhumaṃ vā hīnaṃ vā paṇītaṃ vā yaṃ dūre santike vā, taṃ bhikkhu passati nijjhāyati yoniso upaparikkhati. Tassa taṃ passato nijjhāyato yoniso upaparikkhato rittakaññeva khāyati, tucchakaññeva khāyati, asārakaññeva khāyati. Kiṃ hi siyā, bhikkhave, saññāya sāro?

"Just so, monks, whatever perception past-future-present, internal or external or, gross or subtle or, inferior or superior or, which far near or, that a monk sees, ponders, thoroughly investigates. To him that seeing, pondering, thoroughly investigating, void-just would appear, hollow-just would appear, insubstantial-just would appear. What for could be, monks, in perception substance?

"So too, monks, whatever perception there is, whether past, future, or present, internal or external, gross or subtle, inferior or superior, far or near: a monk sees it, ponders it, and thoroughly investigates it. As he is seeing it, pondering it, and thoroughly investigating it, it would appear to him to be just void, it would appear just hollow, it would appear just insubstantial. For what substance could there be in perception?

[4. Volitional activities]

"Seyyathāpi, bhikkhave, puriso sāratthiko sāragavesī sārapariyesanaṃ caramāno tiṇhaṃ kuṭhāriṃ ādāya vanaṃ paviseyya. So tattha passeyya mahantaṃ kadalikkhandhaṃ ujuṃ navaṃ akukkukajātaṃ. Tamenaṃ mūle chindeyya; mūle chetvā agge chindeyya; agge chetvā pattavaṭṭiṃ vinibbhujeyya. So tassa pattavaṭṭiṃ vinibbhujanto pheggumpi nādhigaccheyya, kuto sāraṃ? Tamenaṃ cakkhumā puriso passeyya nijjhāyeyya yoniso upaparikkheyya. Tassa taṃ passato nijjhāyato yoniso upaparikkhato rittakaññeva khāyeyya, tucchakaññeva khāyeyya, asārakaññeva khāyeyya. Kiṃ hi siyā, bhikkhave, kadalikkhandhe sāro?

"Suppose, monks, a man heartwood-needing, heartwood-seeking, heartwood-search wandering, a sharp axe having taken, a woods would enter. He there would see a large plaintain-trunk, straight, fresh, without shoots. That-this at the root would cut; at the root having cut, at the top would cut; at the top having cut, the coil would unroll. He its coil unrolling softwood even not would find, how then heartwood? That-this an eye-possessing man would see, would ponder, thoroughly would investigate. To him that seeing, pondering, thoroughly investigating, void-just would appear, hollow-just would appear, insubstantial-just would appear. What for could be, monks, in plantain-trunk substance?

"Suppose, monks, a man needing heartwood, seeking heartwood, wandering on a search for heartwood, would take a sharp axe and enter a woods. There he would see a large plantain trunk, straight, fresh, without an inflorescence. He would cut it down at the root; having cut it down at the root, he would cut it off at the crown; having cut it off at the crown, he would unroll the coil. As he unrolls the coil, he would not find even softwood, how then heartwood? A clear-sighted man would see this, ponder it, and thoroughly investigate it. As he is seeing it, pondering it, and thoroughly investigating it, it would appear to him to be just void, it would appear just hollow, it would appear just insubstantial. For what substance could there be in a plantain trunk?

"Evameva kho, bhikkhave, ye keci saṅkhārā atītānāgatapaccuppannā ajjhattaṃ vā bahiddhā vā oḷārikaṃ vā sukhumaṃ vā hīnaṃ vā paṇītaṃ vā yaṃ dūre santike vā, taṃ bhikkhu passati nijjhāyati yoniso upaparikkhati. Tassa taṃ passato nijjhāyato yoniso upaparikkhato rittakaññeva khāyati,

tucchakaññeva khāyati, asārakaññeva khāyati. Kiṃ hi siyā, bhikkhave, saṅkhāresu sāro?

"Just so, monks, whatever volitional-activities past-future-present, internal or external or, gross or subtle or, inferior or superior or, which far near or, that a monk sees, ponders, thoroughly investigates. To him that seeing, pondering, thoroughly investigating, void-just would appear, hollow-just would appear, insubstantial-just would appear. What for could be, monks, in volitional-activities substance?

"So too, monks, whatever volitional activities there are, whether past, future, or present, internal or external, gross or subtle, inferior or superior, far or near: a monk sees them, ponders them, and thoroughly investigates them. As he is seeing them, pondering them, and thoroughly investigating them, they would appear to him to be just void, they would appear just hollow, they would appear just insubstantial. For what substance could there be in volitional activities?

[5. Consciousness]

"Seyyathāpi, bhikkhave, māyākāro vā māyākārantevāsī vā catummahāpathe māyaṃ vidaṃseyya. Tamenaṃ cakkhumā puriso passeyya nijjhāyeyya yoniso upaparikkheyya. Tassa taṃ passato nijjhāyato yoniso upaparikkhato rittakaññeva khāyeyya, tucchakaññeva khāyeyya, asārakaññeva khāyeyya. Kiṃ hi siyā, bhikkhave, māyāya sāro?

"Suppose, monks, a magician or a magician-apprentice or at a crossroads a magical-illusion would display. That-this an eye-possessing man would see, would ponder, thoroughly would investigate. To him that seeing, pondering, thoroughly investigating, void-just would appear, hollow-just would appear, insubstantial-just would appear. What for could be, monks, in a magical-illusion substance?

"Suppose, monks, a magician or a magician's apprentice would display a magical illusion at a crossroads. A clear-sighted man would see this, ponder it, and thoroughly investigate it. As he is seeing it, pondering it, and thoroughly investigating it, it would appear to him to be just void, it would appear just hollow, it would appear just insubstantial. For what substance could there be in a magical illusion?

"Evameva kho, bhikkhave, yaṃ kiñci viññāṇaṃ atītānāgatapaccuppannaṃ ajjhattaṃ vā bahiddhā vā oḷārikaṃ vā sukhumaṃ vā hīnaṃ vā paṇītaṃ vā yaṃ dūre santike vā, taṃ bhikkhu passati nijjhāyati yoniso upaparikkhati. Tassa taṃ passato nijjhāyato yoniso upaparikkhato rittakaññeva khāyati, tucchakaññeva khāyati, asārakaññeva khāyati. Kiṃ hi siyā, bhikkhave, viññāṇe sāro?

"Just so, monks, whatever consciousness past-future-present, internal or external or, gross or subtle or, inferior or superior or, which far near or, that a monk sees, ponders, thoroughly investigates. To him that seeing, pondering, thoroughly investigating, void-just would appear, hollow-just would appear, insubstantial-just would appear. What for could be, monks, in consciousness substance?

"So too, monks, whatever consciousness there is, whether past, future, or present, internal or external, gross or subtle, inferior or superior, far or near: a monk sees it, ponders it, and thoroughly investigates it. As he is seeing it, pondering it, and thoroughly investigating it, it would appear to him to be just void, it would appear just hollow, it would appear just insubstantial. For what substance could there be in consciousness?

[6. Liberation]

"Evaṃ passaṃ, bhikkhave, sutavā ariyasāvako rūpasmimpi nibbindati, vedanāyapi nibbindati, saññāyapi nibbindati, saṅkhāresupi nibbindati, viññāṇasmimpi nibbindati. Nibbindaṃ virajjati. Virāgā vimuccati. Vimuttasmiṃ vimuttamiti ñāṇaṃ hoti. 'Khīṇā jāti vusitaṃ brahmacariyaṃ kataṃ karaṇīyaṃ nāparaṃ itthattāyā'ti pajānātī"ti.

"Thus seeing, monks, the learned noble-disciple in form-too is disenchanted, in feeling-too is disenchanted, in perception-too is disenchanted, in volitional-activities-too is disenchanted, in consciousness-too is disenchanted. Being disenchanted, becomes dispassionate. Through dispassion is liberated. In liberated 'liberated' thus knowledge occurs. 'Finished birth, lived the spiritual-life, done what-is-to-be-done, not-further for such-a-state,' understands."

"Thus seeing, monks, the learned noble disciple becomes disenchanted with form, disenchanted with feeling, disenchanted with perception, disenchanted with volitional activities, disenchanted with consciousness. Being disenchanted, he becomes dispassionate. Through dispassion he is liberated. In regard to what is liberated, the knowledge occurs thus: 'Liberated.' He understands: 'Finished is birth, the spiritual life has been lived, what had to be done has been done, there is no further for this state of being.'"

Grammatical explanations

[1. Form]

ayojjhāyaṃ viharati gaṅgāya nadiyā tīre: "was dwelling at Ayojjhā on the bank of the Ganges River." The line mentions two places where the Buddha was dwelling, both in the locative, with the verb *viharati* between them. The first is Ayojjhā (modern Ayodhya), *ayojjhāyaṃ* being a feminine locative; and the second, the bank of the Ganges River, with *gaṅgāya nadiyā* a feminine genitive and *tīre* the locative of a neuter noun.

tamenaṃ (= *taṃ enaṃ*). The use of two adjacent pronouns to designate the same entity is for emphasis: "just this one" or "this very one" (Geiger §106.1).

cakkhumā: literally, "possessing eyes," the masculine singular nominative of *cakkhumat*, used to mean one of good sight; here it qualifies *puriso*.

yoniso: an ablative of *yoni*, "down to its origin or foundation" (PED), used as an adverb to mean "thoroughly, orderly, wisely, properly, judiciously."

tassa taṃ passato nijjhāyato yoniso upaparikkhato: "as he is seeing it, pondering it, and thoroughly investigating it." The pronoun *tassa* represents the subject to whom the lump of foam appears; the actions he performs are described by the present participles *passato*, *nijjhāyato*, and *upaparikkhato*. These are all masculine singular datives of the type "found with verbs of *manifestation* and *meeting*" (Wijesekera §97b). *Taṃ*, signifying the lump of foam, is the accusative object of the participles, but it also becomes the implicit grammatical subject of the verb *khāyeyya* (optative of *khāyati*), "would appear." The three words beginning with *rittakaṃ*, each emphasized by *eva*, indicate *how* the lump appears; perhaps they should be understood as adverbs of manner. The modifications are as follows: *rittakaṃ + eva > rittakaṃyeva > rittakaññeva*. The same construction is employed in the application of the simile, which describes *how* the monk investigates the corresponding aggregate.

sāro: "substance"; the word originally denoted the heartwood of a tree, but its meaning was broadened to cover the core of anything—a substance, substantial value. The adjective *asāraka*, which occurs just above in the phrase *asārakañneva khāyati*, signifies the absence of a core, lack of substance.

[2. Feeling]

thullaphusitake deve vassante: "when the sky is raining with big raindrops falling"; a locative absolute construction, with *deve*, the sky, as the locative subject described by the compound *thullaphusitake*, "[composed of] large drops." The action is represented by *vassante*, the locative present participle of *vassati*, rains.

udake: This is not part of the locative absolute construction but an independent locative meaning "on [the surface of] the water."

[3. Perception]

gimhānaṃ pacchime māse: "in the last month of the hot season." *Gimhānaṃ*, a plural of *gimhā*, is the summer, perhaps standing for *gimhānaṃ māsānaṃ*, "of the hot months." *Pacchime māse* is a locative signifying a period of time.

ṭhite majjhanhike kāle: literally, "when the midday time is standing." This too is a locative absolute, with *kāle*, "time," the subject, described by the adjective *majjhanhike*, composed of *majjha*, "middle," and *aha*, "day" (with the nasal inserted for euphony), and the adjectival suffix *-ike* in agreement with *kāle*. The action is indicated by the past participle *ṭhite*, "stood," used with a present sense.

[4. Volitional activities]

sāratthiko sāragavesī: "needing heartwood, seeking heartwood"; two bahubbīhis describing *puriso*. *Sāratthiko* is composed of *sāra*, "heartwood, substance," and *attha*, "need," with the suffix *-iko* in agreement with *puriso*. *Sāragavesī* is a compound of *sāra* and *gavesī* (the masculine nominative of *gavesin*), "seeking."[120]

sārapariyesanaṃ caramāno: "wandering on a search for heartwood"; the masculine nominative present participle of *carati*, "walks, wanders," in

120. *Gavesin* itself is originally a compound of *go*, "cow," and *esin*, "seeking," but by the time of the Nikāyas it had come to mean simply "seeking."

the middle voice, taking the act of searching, *pariyesanaṃ*, as its object. *Sārapariyesanaṃ* is a tappurisa compound (probably a dative tappurisa).

ujuṃ navaṃ akukkukajātaṃ: "straight, fresh, without an inflorescence"; three adjectives describing *kadalikkhandhaṃ*. The exact meaning of *kukkukajātaṃ* is uncertain but I take it to be the "terminal inflorescence."[121]

[5. Consciousness]

catummahāpathe: a numerical kammadhāraya compound of *catur*, "four," *mahā*, "great," and *patha*, "path, road," here in the locative.

vidaṃseyya: optative of *vidaṃseti*, which PED defines as "to make appear, to show," derived from *vi* + *daṃseti* < *dasseti*.

16. Aniccasaññāsutta

Perception of the Impermanent (SN 22:102; III 155–57)

"Aniccasaññā, bhikkhave, bhāvitā bahulīkatā sabbaṃ kāmarāgaṃ pariyādiyati, sabbaṃ rūparāgaṃ pariyādiyati, sabbaṃ bhavarāgaṃ pariyādiyati, sabbaṃ avijjaṃ pariyādiyati, sabbaṃ asmimānaṃ samūhanati.

"Impermanent-perception, monks, developed cultivated, all sensual-lust eliminates, all form-lust eliminates, all existence-lust eliminates, all ignorance eliminates, all 'I-am'-conceit demolishes.

"Perception of the impermanent, monks, developed and cultivated, eliminates all sensual lust, eliminates all lust for form, eliminates all lust for existence, eliminates all ignorance, demolishes all conceit 'I am.'

"Seyyathāpi, bhikkhave, saradasamaye kassako mahānaṅgalena kasanto sabbāni mūlasantānakāni sampadālento kasati, evameva kho, bhikkhave, aniccasaññā bhāvitā bahulīkatā sabbaṃ kāmarāgaṃ pariyādiyati, sabbaṃ

121. According to http://bananaplants.net/banananinfo.html: "Banana is a tropical herbaceous plant consisting of an underground corm and a trunk (pseudostem) comprised of concentric layers of leaf sheaths. At 10 to 15 months after the emergence of a new plant, its true stem rapidly grows up through the center and emerges as a terminal inflorescence which bears fruit." The *kukkuka* is probably the "terminal inflorescence."

rūparāgaṃ pariyādiyati, sabbaṃ bhavarāgaṃ pariyādiyati, sabbaṃ avijjaṃ pariyādiyati, sabbaṃ asmimānaṃ samūhanati. . . .

"Just as, monks, in autumn-time a plowman with a great-plow plowing all root-filaments splitting plows, just so, monks, impermanent-perception developed cultivated, all sensual-lust eliminates, all form-lust eliminates, all existence-lust eliminates, all ignorance eliminates, all 'I-am'-conceit demolishes. . . .

"Just as, monks, in the autumn a plowman, plowing with a great plow, splits apart all root filaments as he plows, just so, monks, perception of the impermanent, developed and cultivated, eliminates all sensual lust, eliminates all lust for form, eliminates all lust for existence, eliminates all ignorance, demolishes all conceit 'I am.' . . .

"Seyyathāpi, bhikkhave, yā kāci tārakarūpānaṃ pabhā, sabbā tā candimappabhāya kalaṃ nāgghanti soḷasiṃ, candappabhā tāsaṃ aggamakkhāyati, evameva kho, bhikkhave, aniccasaññā . . . sabbaṃ asmimānaṃ samūhanati.

"Just as, monks, whatever of star-forms the radiance, all those of moon-radiance a portion not-worth sixteenth, moon-radiance of them chief-is declared, just so, monks, impermanent-perception . . . all 'I-am'-conceit demolishes.

"Just as, monks, whatever radiance there is of the stars, all that is not worth a sixteenth portion of the radiance of the moon, [such that] the radiance of the moon is declared chief among them, just so, monks, perception of the impermanent . . . demolishes all conceit 'I am.'

"Seyyathāpi, bhikkhave, saradasamaye viddhe vigatavalāhake deve ādicco nabhaṃ abbhussukkamāno[122] *sabbaṃ ākāsagataṃ tamagataṃ abhivihacca bhāsate ca tapate ca virocate ca; evameva kho, bhikkhave, aniccasaññā bhāvitā bahulīkatā sabbaṃ kāmarāgaṃ pariyādiyati, sabbaṃ rūparāgaṃ pariyādiyati, sabbaṃ bhavarāgaṃ pariyādiyati, sabbaṃ avijjaṃ pariyādiyati, sabbaṃ asmimānaṃ samūhanati.*

122. This is the reading in Ce and Ee; Be has *abbhussakkamāno*.

"Just as, monks, in autumn-time when clear rid-clouds sky, sun firmament rising, all space-gone darkness-gone having dispersed, shines and beams and radiates and, just so, monks, impermanent-perception, developed cultivated, all sensual-lust eliminates, all form-lust eliminates, all existence-lust eliminates, all ignorance eliminates, all 'I-am'-conceit demolishes.

"Just as, monks, in autumn, when the sky is clear, rid of clouds, the sun, rising through the firmament, having dispersed all darkness throughout space, shines and beams and radiates, just so, monks, perception of the impermanent, developed and cultivated, eliminates all sensual lust, eliminates all lust for form, eliminates all lust for existence, eliminates all ignorance, demolishes all conceit 'I am.'

"Kathaṃ bhāvitā ca, bhikkhave, aniccasaññā kathaṃ bahulīkatā sabbaṃ kāmarāgaṃ pariyādiyati . . . sabbaṃ asmimānaṃ samūhanati? 'Iti rūpaṃ, iti rūpassa samudayo, iti rūpassa atthaṅgamo; iti vedanā . . . iti saññā . . . iti saṅkhārā . . . iti viññāṇaṃ, iti viññāṇassa samudayo, iti viññāṇassa atthaṅgamo'ti. Evaṃ bhāvitā kho, bhikkhave, aniccasaññā evaṃ bahulīkatā sabbaṃ kāmarāgaṃ pariyādiyati, sabbaṃ rūparāgaṃ pariyādiyati, sabbaṃ bhavarāgaṃ pariyādiyati, sabbaṃ avijjaṃ pariyādiyati, sabbaṃ asmimānaṃ samūhanatī"ti.

"How developed and, monks, impermanent-perception, how cultivated, all sensual-lust eliminates . . . all 'I-am'-conceit demolishes? 'Such form, such of form origin, such of form passing-away; such feeling . . . such perception . . . such volitional-activities . . . such consciousness, such of consciousness origin, such of consciousness passing-away.' Thus developed, monks, impermanent-perception, thus cultivated, all sensual-lust eliminates, all form-lust eliminates, all existence-lust eliminates, all ignorance eliminates, all 'I-am'-conceit demolishes."

"And how, monks, is perception of the impermanent developed, how is it cultivated, so that it eliminates all sensual lust . . . demolishes all conceit 'I am'? 'Such is form, such its origin, such its passing away; such is feeling . . . such is perception . . . such are volitional activities . . . such is consciousness, such its origin, such its passing away.' When, monks, perception of the impermanent is thus developed, thus cultivated, it eliminates all sensual lust, eliminates all lust for form, eliminates all lust for existence, eliminates all ignorance, demolishes all conceit 'I am.'"

Grammatical explanations

aniccasaññā: This tappurisa compound is usually rendered "perception of impermanence," but grammatically *anicca* is not an abstract noun but either an adjective descriptive of a noun, "impermanent," or a substantive, "the impermanent"; here the latter is intended. The commentary explains: "*Perception of the impermanent* is the perception that has arisen in one who develops [the idea] 'impermanent, impermanent.'"[123]

bhāvitā bahulīkatā: "developed [and] cultivated"; two past participles often joined together as near-synonyms. *Bhāvita* is from *bhāveti*: see p. 89; *bahulīkatā* is from *bahulīkaroti*, literally, "makes abundant."

kāmarāgaṃ, rūparāgaṃ, bhavarāgaṃ: *Kāmarāga* can be taken as lust for sensual pleasures or desire for existence in the sense-sphere realm; *rūparāga* as desire for existence in the form realm or attachment to jhāna; and *bhavarāga* as desire for any kind of existence.

sabbaṃ asmimānaṃ samūhanati: "demolishes all conceit 'I am.'" *Asmimāna* is the most fundamental conceit, which manifests in the notion, "I am." Perniola (§142c) classifies *asmimāna* as a syntactical compound. The verb *samūhanati* is from *sam* + *ud* + *hanati*, where *hanati* (or *hanti*) means "strikes, kills, destroys." See DOP and PED under *ūhanati*.

kassako mahānaṅgalena kasanto sabbāni mūlasantānakāni sampadālento kasati: "a plowman, plowing with a great plow, splits apart all root filaments as he plows." The subject is *kassako*, which takes the finite verb *kasati*; between the subject and verb are two subordinate clauses with present participles agreeing with *kassako*. The first, *mahānaṅgalena kasanto*, shows the means of plowing, a great plow, in the instrumental; the second, *mūlasantānakāni sampadālento*, shows the effect of his plowing, "splitting apart all root filaments," with a plural accusative as the object.

yā kāci: an indefinite relative, "whatever," correlated with *sabbā tā*, "all those"; the pronouns qualify *pabhā*, "radiance," a feminine plural.

nāgghanti (= *na* + *agghanti*): "not worth."

123. Spk III 331,21–23: *Aniccasaññā ti aniccaṃ aniccan ti bhāventassa uppannasaññā.*

kalaṃ . . . soḷasiṃ: *kalaṃ*, a portion or fraction, qualified by *soḷasiṃ*, "sixteenth."

aggamakkhāyati: "is declared chief," a sandhi formation of *aggaṃ* and *akkhāyati*.

saradasamaye: "in autumn time," a kammadhāraya with *sarada* and *samaye* in apposition.

viddhe vigatavalāhake deve: a locative absolute, with *deve*, "sky," as the subject, described as *viddhe*, "clear," and *vigatavalāhake*, "rid of clouds," the latter a bahubbīhi composed of the past participle *vigata*, "gone away, rid of," and *valāhaka*, "cloud."

nabhaṃ abbhussukkamāno: The Saṃyutta commentary (Spk I 125,25) glosses this as meaning "ascending in the sky" (*ākāsaṃ abhilaṅghanto*) and says it refers to "the tender state of the sun" (*taruṇasuriyabhāvo*), the sun early in the morning.

ākāsagataṃ tamagataṃ: "all darkness throughout space." I take *-gataṃ* to be used differently in the compounds *ākāsagataṃ* and *tamagataṃ*, with *ākāsagataṃ* an accusative tappurisa functioning as an adjective qualifying *tamagataṃ*, a noun in the accusative case. The latter, qualified by the adjective, is the object of the absolutive *abhivihacca*. DOP (p. 5a) ascribes to the suffix *-gata* the meaning "belonging to."[124] A more literal rendering of the expression than the one I offered would thus be: "whatever pertains to the darkness that is contained in space" or "whatever kind of darkness there is situated in space."[125]

abhivihacca: "having dispersed"; an absolutive of *abhivihanati*, occurring only in this stock expression.

bhāsate ca tapate ca virocate ca: "shines and beams and radiates." These are middle-voice forms of the present tense, third-person singular of the three verbs (see Duroiselle §357, §381; Perniola §74, §210b). The middle voice in Pāli has largely lost its reflective sense. It is used primarily for poetic elegance and is more frequent in verse than in prose (see Geiger §120).

124. At MN I 435,32–33 we find: *yadeva tattha hoti rūpagataṃ vedanāgataṃ saññāgataṃ saṅkhāragataṃ viññāṇagataṃ*, "whatever exists there pertaining to form, pertaining to feeling, pertaining to perception, pertaining to volitional activities, pertaining to consciousness."

125. In the gloss at Ps II 377,20 *-gataṃ* in *tamagataṃ* is dropped as superfluous: *ākāsagataṃ tamaṃ*.

3. The Six Sense Bases: The Channels through which Suffering Originates

Introduction

The six sense bases, explored in detail in chapter 35 of the Saṃyutta Nikāya, are another structure, complementary to the five aggregates, that the Buddha uses to explore the nature of suffering. The six internal sense bases are the sensory faculties through which we gain access to the world. Since all conditioned experience is included in the noble truth of suffering, the six bases may be called "the channels through which suffering originates." A discourse in the Saccasaṃyutta (at SN V 426,7–8), in fact, concisely defines the noble truth of suffering as the six internal sense bases.

The six internal bases are paired with their corresponding external bases, making twelve bases in all: the eye and visible forms, the ear and sounds, the nose and odors, the tongue and tastes, the body and tactile objects, and the mind and mental objects. The pairs of bases are called "bases" because each serves as the platform for the arising of the corresponding type of consciousness. Thus eye-consciousness arises in dependence on the eye and visible forms, ear-consciousness in dependence on the ear and sounds, and each of the other types of consciousness in dependence on its respective internal and external bases.

The exact referent of the mind-base has been a matter of uncertainty. The commentaries, following the Abhidhamma, identify the mind-base with consciousness in its entirety. However, since the mind (*mano*) is said to be the base for the arising of mind-consciousness, it seems unlikely that the commentarial interpretation reflects the original intention of the suttas, which treat the mind-base as analogous to the material sense bases in relation to their corresponding types of consciousness. All that can be said with certainty, on the authority of the suttas themselves, is that the mind is viewed as an internal base for mind-consciousness, the interior consciousness that takes purely mental objects.

Whereas the scheme of the five aggregates seems to have been advanced primarily to show the objective range for the deluded notions of "mine," "I," and "self," the six sense bases have a closer connection with craving. This can be seen in the formula of dependent origination, which will be dealt with in the next chapter. The meeting of the sense base, object, and consciousness is called "contact," and with contact as condition there arises feeling (see 3.4), which in turn conditions craving. Eliminating craving thus requires, as a preliminary step, that we change our attitude toward sense objects and the feelings they engender, curbing our habitual responses and instead viewing feelings from a stance of detached observation.

To disengage ourselves from craving requires that we explore the origin of feelings. Instead of simply responding to each and every feeling like an automaton, driven by the desire to find new sources of pleasure and avoid the feelings of pain that accompany distress and anxiety, we are instructed to see how feeling is merely a conditioned state that arises through a complex process involving the paired sense bases, consciousness, and contact. On some occasions, simply discerning the conditioned genesis of feeling is sufficient to induce disenchantment with the entire cascade of events by which feeling comes to be. As 3.4 states, seeing how feeling arises on the basis of sensory contact, "one becomes disenchanted with the eye, disenchanted with forms, disenchanted with eye-consciousness, disenchanted with eye-contact, disenchanted with whatever feeling arises with eye-contact as condition."

Feeling can be either pleasant, painful, or neutral—that is, neither painful nor pleasant. Each of these feelings is correlated with one of the three root defilements. Pleasant feeling is the trigger for lust, painful feeling for hatred, and neutral feeling for delusion. As long as lust, hatred, and delusion consume the mind, the entire field of sense experience, right down to the internal and external sense bases, blazes with the fires of lust, hatred, and delusion, with the fires of birth, old age, and death—the theme of the famous "Fire Sermon" (3.2).

Craving thrives because we take the feelings we enjoy to be permanent and thus tacitly assume we can go on enjoying them forever. When seen rightly, however, all the constituents of sensory experience turn out to be impermanent. Whereas the suttas on the five aggregates emphasize the absence of a self among the aggregates, and thus the contemplation of the aggregates as being non-self, the suttas on the six sense bases emphasize the contemplation of impermanence. The internal sense bases, their objects, the corresponding types of consciousness, and the contacts are said to be "impermanent, changing, and becoming otherwise" (3.7). The same is true for the feeling, perception, and volition that arise through contact. When one contemplates the impermanence of feelings, the associated contacts, and the sense bases through which those contacts originate, ignorance is abandoned and clear knowledge arises (3.3).

Each of the sense faculties is naturally drawn to its corresponding object. Normally, we rejoice when we gain the objects of desire, but in doing so we set ourselves up for a fall; for when those objects cease and perish, our delight vanishes and we plunge into dejection and anguish. Delight in sense objects obstructs the path to nibbāna, the final goal of the spiritual life; by dispelling delight one dwells happily and attains nibbāna (3.8). Agreeable sense objects are described as "six hooks for the misery of beings," and those who delight in these objects have "swallowed the bait of Māra" and come under his control (3.11). Those who do not delight in sense objects escape Māra's control.

The problem of bondage and suffering created by the six pairs of sense bases does not lie in the sense bases themselves, but in the craving that arises through their interaction. Text 3.12 tells us that just as, when a black ox and a white ox are yoked together by a single harness, what binds them together is the harness, so the eye is not the fetter of forms nor forms the fetter of the eye, but the desire-and-lust that arises in dependence on them is the fetter. The Buddha himself has eyes and sees forms with his eyes, but having eradicated craving, he is liberated in mind. This sets the task for the disciple as well: to remove craving and thereby win liberation of mind.

The six senses are compared to six kinds of animals (3.15). Just as these animals, if released, will rush toward their respective habitats, so each of the senses, without the exercise of restraint and self-control, will run toward its respective object. But if the animals are tied to a post or pillar, though they pull in different directions, eventually they will settle down and become still. Similarly, when the senses are tied to a strong pillar, they too will settle down. That pillar, the Buddha says, is mindfulness of the body.

1. Pahānasutta

Abandoning (SN 35:24; IV 15–16)

"Sabbappahānāya vo, bhikkhave, dhammaṃ desessāmi. Taṃ suṇātha. Katamo ca, bhikkhave, sabbappahānāya dhammo? Cakkhuṃ, bhikkhave, pahātabbaṃ, rūpā pahātabbā, cakkhuviññāṇaṃ pahātabbaṃ, cakkhusamphasso pahātabbo, yampidaṃ cakkhusamphassapaccayā uppajjati vedayitaṃ sukhaṃ vā dukkhaṃ vā adukkhamasukhaṃ vā tampi pahātabbaṃ.

"For all-abandoning to you, monks, the Dhamma I will teach. That listen to. What and, monks, for all-abandoning the Dhamma? The eye, monks, to-be-abandoned, forms to-be-abandoned, eye-consciousness to-be-abandoned, eye-contact to-be-abandoned, which-too-this through eye-contact-condition arises·feeling pleasant or painful or neither-painful-nor-pleasant or, that-too to-be-abandoned.

"I will teach you, monks, the Dhamma for the abandoning of all. Listen to that. And what, monks, is the Dhamma for the abandoning of all? The eye is to be abandoned, forms are to be abandoned, eye-consciousness is to be abandoned, eye-contact is to be abandoned, whatever feeling arises with eye-contact as condition—whether pleasant or painful or neither-painful-nor-pleasant—that too is to be abandoned.

"Sotaṃ pahātabbaṃ . . . Ghānaṃ pahātabbaṃ . . . Jivhā pahātabbā . . . Kāyo pahātabbo . . . Mano pahātabbo, dhammā pahātabbā, manoviññāṇaṃ pahātabbaṃ, manosamphasso pahātabbo, yampidaṃ manosamphassapaccayā uppajjati vedayitaṃ sukhaṃ vā dukkhaṃ vā adukkhamasukhaṃ vā tampi pahātabbaṃ. Ayaṃ kho, bhikkhave, sabbappahānāya dhammo"ti.

"The ear to-be-abandoned . . . The nose to-be-abandoned . . . The tongue to-be-abandoned . . . The body to-be-abandoned . . . The mind to-be-abandoned, mental-objects to-be-abandoned, mind-consciousness to-be-abandoned, mind-contact to-be-abandoned, which-too-this through mind-contact-condition arises feeling pleasant or painful or neither-painful-nor-pleasant or, that-too to-be-abandoned. This, monks, for all-abandoning the Dhamma."

"The ear is to be abandoned . . . The nose is to be abandoned . . . The tongue is to be abandoned . . . The body is to be abandoned . . . The mind is to be abandoned, mental objects are to be abandoned, mind-consciousness is to be abandoned, mind-contact is to be abandoned, whatever feeling arises with mind-contact as condition—whether pleasant or painful or neither-painful-nor-pleasant—that too is to be abandoned. This, monks, is the Dhamma for the abandoning of all."

Grammatical explanations

sabbappahānāya: "for the abandoning of all"; a genitive tappurisa compound in the dative case, indicating the purpose of this teaching.

vo: "to you"; the enclitic (internal) pronoun, second-person plural in the dative case.

dhammaṃ desessāmi: "I will teach the Dhamma": the first-person singular of the verb *deseti*, here in the future tense, taking *dhammaṃ* as an accusative object.

katamo: an interrogative in agreement with *dhammo*, the nominative subject of the question.

pahātabbaṃ: "to be abandoned"; the future passive participle of *pajahati*, neuter singular in agreement with *cakkhuṃ*. With *rūpā* the participle becomes masculine plural, with *cakkhusamphasso* masculine singular, and so forth.

yampidaṃ (= *yaṃ pi idaṃ*): The relative *yaṃ* qualifies *vedayitaṃ* and is correlated with the demonstrative *tam* just below.

cakkhuviññāṇaṃ, *cakkhusamphasso*: "eye-consciousness, eye-contact." Both are tappurisa compounds.[126]

cakkhusamphassapaccayā: "with eye-contact as condition." This is probably a kammadhāraya compound with an internal tappurisa: "eye-consciousness that is a condition." The case is ablative in the causal sense.

uppajjati vedayitaṃ sukhaṃ vā dukkhaṃ vā adukkhamasukhaṃ vā: The normal word order is inverted, probably for emphasis, with the verb *uppajjati*, "arises," preceding its subject, *vedayitaṃ*. Originally a past participle, *vedayitaṃ* serves as a neuter noun, "what-is-felt," synonymous

126. Spk II 17,17–18 explains *cakkhuviññāṇaṃ* as "consciousness at the eye or consciousness arisen through the eye" (*cakkhumhi viññāṇaṃ, cakkhuto vā jātaṃ viññāṇan*); hence it is either a locative tappurisa or an ablative tappurisa. Spk II 16,21 takes *cakkhusamphasso* to be a locative tappurisa, "contact at the eye" (*cakkhumhi samphasso*).

with *vedanā*. The terms that follow—*sukhaṃ*, *dukkhaṃ*, and *adukkhamasukhaṃ*—are the three feeling tones, pleasant, painful, and neither-painful-nor-pleasant, agreeing in gender with neuter *vedayitaṃ*.

tampi pahātabbaṃ: "that too is to be abandoned." This is the main clause, with *tam* the demonstrative correlated with *yam* above.

sotaṃ pahātabbaṃ: "the ear is to be abandoned," etc. All should be construed in accordance with the section on *cakkhuṃ*.

2. Ādittasutta

Burning (SN 35:28; IV 19–20)

Ekaṃ samayaṃ bhagavā gayāyaṃ viharati gayāsīse saddhiṃ bhikkhusahassena. Tatra kho bhagavā bhikkhū āmantesi: "Sabbaṃ, bhikkhave, ādittaṃ. Kiñca, bhikkhave, sabbaṃ ādittaṃ? Cakkhuṃ, bhikkhave, ādittaṃ, rūpā ādittā, cakkhuviññāṇaṃ ādittaṃ, cakkhusamphasso āditto, yampidaṃ cakkhusamphassapaccayā uppajjati vedayitaṃ sukhaṃ vā dukkhaṃ vā adukkhamasukhaṃ vā tampi ādittaṃ.

One occasion the Blessed One at Gayā was dwelling, at Gayā-head, together with monks-thousand. There the Blessed One the monks addressed: "All, monks, burning. What-and, monks, all burning? The eye, monks, burning, forms burning, eye-consciousness burning, eye-contact burning, which-too-this through eye-contact-condition arises feeling pleasant or painful or neither-painful-nor-pleasant or, that too burning.

On one occasion the Blessed One was dwelling at Gayā, at Gayā's Head, together with a thousand monks. There the Blessed One addressed the monks: "Monks, all is burning. And what, monks, is the all that is burning? The eye is burning, forms are burning, eye-consciousness is burning, eye-contact is burning, and whatever feeling arises with eye-contact as condition—whether pleasant or painful or neither-painful-nor-pleasant—that too is burning.

"Kena ādittaṃ? 'Rāgagginā, dosagginā, mohagginā ādittaṃ, jātiyā jarāya maraṇena sokehi paridevehi dukkhehi domanassehi upāyāsehi ādittan'ti vadāmi. . . .

"With what burning? 'With lust-fire, with hatred-fire, with delusion-fire burning, with birth, with old age, with death, with sorrows, with lamentations, with pains, with dejections, with miseries burning,' I say. . . .

"Burning with what? 'Burning with the fire of lust, with the fire of hatred, with the fire of delusion; burning with birth, old age, and death; with sorrow, lamentation, pain, dejection, and misery,' I say. . . .

"Mano āditto, dhammā ādittā, manoviññāṇaṃ ādittaṃ, manosamphasso āditto, yampidaṃ manosamphassapaccayā uppajjati vedayitaṃ sukhaṃ vā dukkhaṃ vā adukkhamasukhaṃ vā tampi ādittaṃ. Kena ādittaṃ? 'Rāgagginā, dosagginā, mohagginā ādittaṃ, jātiyā jarāya maraṇena sokehi paridevehi dukkhehi domanassehi upāyāsehi ādittan'ti vadāmi.

"The mind burning, mental objects burning, mind-consciousness burning, mind-contact burning, which-too-this through mind-contact-condition arises feeling pleasant or painful or neither-painful-nor-pleasant or, that-too burning. With what burning? 'With lust-fire, with hatred-fire, with delusion-fire burning, with birth, with old age, with death, with sorrows, with lamentations, with pains, with dejections, with miseries burning,' I say.

"The mind is burning, mental objects are burning, mind-consciousness is burning, mind-contact is burning, and whatever feeling arises with mind-contact as condition—whether pleasant or painful or neither-painful-nor-pleasant—that too is burning. Burning with what? 'Burning with the fire of lust, with the fire of hatred, with the fire of delusion; burning with birth, old age, and death; with sorrow, lamentation, pain, dejection, and misery,' I say.

"Evaṃ passaṃ, bhikkhave, sutavā ariyasāvako cakkhusmimpi nibbindati, rūpesupi nibbindati, cakkhuviññāṇepi nibbindati, cakkhusamphassepi nibbindati, yampidaṃ cakkhusamphassapaccayā uppajjati vedayitaṃ sukhaṃ vā dukkhaṃ vā adukkhamasukhaṃ vā tasmimpi nibbindati . . . yampidaṃ manosamphassapaccayā uppajjati vedayitaṃ sukhaṃ vā dukkhaṃ vā adukkhamasukhaṃ vā tasmimpi nibbindati.

"Thus seeing, monks, the learned noble-disciple in the eye-too is disenchanted, in forms-too is disenchanted, in eye-consciousness-too is disenchanted, in eye-contact-too is disenchanted, which-too-this through eye-contact-condition arises feeling pleasant or painful or neither-painful-nor-pleasant or, in that-too is disenchanted . . . which-too-this through mind-contact-condition arises feeling pleasant or painful or neither-painful-nor-pleasant, in that-too is disenchanted.

"Seeing thus, monks, the learned noble disciple becomes disenchanted with the eye, disenchanted with forms, disenchanted with eye-consciousness, disenchanted with eye-contact, disenchanted with whatever feeling arises with eye-contact as condition—whether pleasant or painful or neither-painful-nor-pleasant . . . disenchanted with whatever feeling arises with mind-contact as condition—whether pleasant or painful or neither-painful-nor-pleasant.

"Nibbindaṃ virajjati. Virāgā vimuccati. Vimuttasmiṃ vimuttamiti ñāṇaṃ hoti. 'Khīṇā jāti, vusitaṃ brahmacariyaṃ, kataṃ karaṇīyaṃ, nāparaṃ itthattāyā'ti pajānātī"ti.

"Being disenchanted, becomes dispassionate. Through dispassion is liberated. In liberated 'liberated' thus knowledge occurs. 'Finished birth, lived the spiritual-life, done what-is-to-be-done, not-further for such-a-state,' understands."

"Being disenchanted, he becomes dispassionate. Through dispassion he is liberated. In regard to what is liberated, the knowledge occurs thus: 'Liberated.' He understands: 'Finished is birth, the spiritual life has been lived, what had to be done has been done, there is no more for this state of being.'"

Idamavoca bhagavā. Attamanā te bhikkhū bhagavato bhāsitaṃ abhinanduṃ. Imasmiñca pana veyyākaraṇasmiṃ bhaññamāne tassa bhikkhusahassassa anupādāya āsavehi cittāni vimucciṃsū ti.

This-said the Blessed One. Elated, those monks the Blessed One's statement delighted in. While this and discourse was being spoken, of the monks-thousand without having clung, from influxes minds were liberated.

This is what the Blessed One said. Elated, those monks delighted in the Blessed One's statement. And while this discourse was being spoken, the minds of the thousand monks were liberated from the influxes by non-clinging.

Grammatical explanations

gayāyaṃ . . . gayāsīse: two locatives indicating where the Buddha was living. The first, a feminine locative, designates the general area, "at Gayā"; the second, a neuter locative, designates the specific place, "at Gayā's Head."

saddhiṃ: "together [with]"; see p. 196. Here the instrumental connected with *saddhiṃ* follows it, contrary to normal word order.

bhikkhusahassena: "with a thousand monks." The case is instrumental. As is common in Pāli, the numeral *sahassaṃ*, "thousand," occurs as a neuter substantive following the noun it modifies, here *bhikkhu*. For another example, see p. 131.

sabbaṃ: a neuter noun, the nominative subject, "all."

ādittaṃ: the past participle of *ādippati*, "burns, blazes, shines," functioning as an adjective, "ablaze," or even as a present participle, "burning, blazing."

kena: "with what?"; the instrumental of the interrogative *kiṃ*.

rāgagginā, dosagginā, mohagginā: "with the fire of lust, with the fire of hatred, with the fire of delusion." These are kammadhāraya compounds ending in the instrumental of the masculine noun *aggi*: "the fire that is lust," etc. The nouns that follow—*jātiyā*, etc.—are also instrumentals, each in its respective gender and number.

evaṃ passaṃ, etc.: see pp. 143–44.

idamavoca bhagavā, etc.: This is constructed on the same pattern as the conclusion of **2.9**. It includes the same kind of locative absolute (see p. 171), but with *tassa bhikkhusahassassa*, "of the thousand monks," instead of *pañcavaggiyānaṃ bhikkhūnaṃ*, "the monks of the group of five."

3. Avijjāpahānasutta

Abandoning Ignorance (SN 35:53; IV 30–31)

Atha kho aññataro bhikkhu yena bhagavā ten'upasaṅkami. Upasaṅkamitvā bhagavantaṃ abhivādetvā ekamantaṃ nisīdi. Ekamantaṃ nisinno kho so bhikkhu bhagavantaṃ etadavoca: "Kathaṃ nu kho, bhante, jānato kathaṃ passato avijjā pahīyati, vijjā uppajjatī"ti?

Then a certain monk where the Blessed One, there approached. Having approached, the Blessed One having paid homage to, one-side sat down. One-side seated, that monk to the Blessed One this-said: "How, Bhante, for one knowing, for one seeing, ignorance is abandoned, clear-knowledge arises?"

Then a certain monk approached the Blessed One. Having approached, he paid homage to the Blessed One and sat down to one side. Seated to one side, that monk said this to the Blessed One: "How, Bhante, does one know, how does one see, so that ignorance is abandoned and clear knowledge arises?"

"Cakkhuṃ kho, bhikkhu, aniccato jānato passato avijjā pahīyati, vijjā uppajjati. Rūpe aniccato jānato passato avijjā pahīyati, vijjā uppajjati. Cakkhuviññāṇaṃ aniccato jānato passato avijjā pahīyati, vijjā uppajjati. Cakkhusampassaṃ aniccato jānato passato avijjā pahīyati, vijjā uppajjati. Yampidaṃ cakkhusamphassapaccayā uppajjati vedayitaṃ sukhaṃ vā dukkhaṃ vā adukkhamasukhaṃ vā tampi aniccato jānato passato avijjā pahīyati, vijjā uppajjati. . . .

"The eye, monk, as impermanent for one knowing, for one seeing, ignorance is abandoned, clear-knowledge arises. Forms as impermanent for one knowing, for one seeing, ignorance is abandoned, clear-knowledge arises. Eye-consciousness as impermanent for one knowing, for one seeing, ignorance is abandoned, clear-knowledge arises. Eye-contact as impermanent for one knowing, for one seeing, ignorance is abandoned, clear-knowledge arises. Which-too-this through eye-contact-condition arises feeling pleasant or painful or neither-painful-nor-pleasant or, that-too as impermanent for one knowing, for one seeing, ignorance is abandoned, clear-knowledge arises. . . .

"For one knowing and seeing the eye as impermanent, monk, ignorance is abandoned and clear knowledge arises. For one knowing and seeing forms as impermanent, ignorance is abandoned and clear knowledge arises. For one knowing and seeing eye-consciousness as impermanent, ignorance is abandoned and clear knowledge arises. For one knowing and seeing eye-contact as impermanent, ignorance is abandoned and clear knowledge arises. For one knowing and seeing as impermanent whatever feeling arises with eye-contact as condition—whether pleasant or painful or neither-painful-nor-pleasant—ignorance is abandoned and clear knowledge arises. . . .

"Manaṃ aniccato jānato passato avijjā pahīyati, vijjā uppajjati. Dhamme aniccato jānato passato avijjā pahīyati, vijjā uppajjati. Manoviññāṇaṃ aniccato jānato passato avijjā pahīyati, vijjā uppajjati. Manosamphassaṃ aniccato jānato passato avijjā pahīyati, vijjā uppajjati. Yampidaṃ manosamphassapaccayā uppajjati vedayitaṃ sukhaṃ vā dukkhaṃ vā adukkham-asukhaṃ vā tampi aniccato jānato passato avijjā pahīyati, vijjā uppajjati. Evaṃ kho, bhikkhu, jānato evaṃ passato avijjā pahīyati, vijjā uppajjatī"ti.

"The mind as impermanent for one knowing, for one seeing, ignorance is abandoned, clear-knowledge arises. Mental-objects as impermanent for one knowing, for one seeing, ignorance is abandoned, clear-knowledge arises. Mind-consciousness as impermanent for one knowing, for one seeing, ignorance is abandoned, clear-knowledge arises. Mind-contact as impermanent for one knowing, for one seeing, ignorance is abandoned, clear-knowledge arises. Which-too-this through mind-contact-condition arises feeling pleasant or painful or neither-painful-nor-pleasant or, that-too as impermanent for one knowing, for one seeing, ignorance is abandoned, clear-knowledge arises. Thus, monk, for one knowing, for one seeing, ignorance is abandoned, clear-knowledge arises."

"For one knowing and seeing the mind as impermanent, ignorance is abandoned and clear knowledge arises. For one knowing and seeing mental objects as impermanent, ignorance is abandoned and clear knowledge arises. For one knowing and seeing mind-consciousness as impermanent, ignorance is abandoned and clear knowledge arises. For one knowing and seeing mind-contact as impermanent, ignorance is abandoned and clear knowledge arises. For one knowing and seeing as impermanent whatever feeling arises with mind-contact as condition—whether pleasant or painful or neither-painful-nor-pleasant—ignorance is abandoned and clear knowledge arises. For one knowing thus, monk, for one seeing thus, ignorance is abandoned and clear knowledge arises."

Grammatical explanations

atha kho aññataro bhikkhu, etc.: see p. 178.

kathaṃ nu kho bhante jānato kathaṃ passato: "How, Bhante, does one know, how does one see. . . ?" On this construction, see the note on *jānato* at p. 107.

pahīyati: "is abandoned"; a third-person singular passive of *pajahati*.

cakkhuṃ kho, bhikkhu, aniccato jānato passato: On the significance of the ablative suffix *-to* in *aniccato*, see pp. 154–55.

4. Sabbupādānapariññāsutta

The Full Understanding of All Clinging (SN 35:60; IV 32–33)

"Sabbupādānapariññāya vo, bhikkhave, dhammaṃ desessāmi. Taṃ suṇātha. Katamo ca, bhikkhave, sabbupādānapariññāya dhammo? Cakkhuñca paṭicca rūpe ca uppajjati cakkhuviññāṇaṃ. Tiṇṇaṃ saṅgati phasso. Phassapaccayā vedanā. Evaṃ passaṃ, bhikkhave, sutavā ariyasāvako cakkhusmimpi nibbindati, rūpesupi nibbindati, cakkhuviññāṇepi nibbindati, cakkhusamphassepi nibbindati, vedanāyapi nibbindati. Nibbindaṃ virajjati. Virāgā vimuccati. Vimokkhā 'pariññātaṃ me upādānan'ti pajānāti. . . .

"For all-clinging-full-understanding to you, monks, the Dhamma I will teach. That listen to. What and, monks, for all-clinging-full-understanding the Dhamma? The eye-and in dependence on forms and arises eye-consciousness. Of the three meeting contact. Through contact-condition, feeling. Thus seeing, monks, the learned noble-disciple in the eye-too is disenchanted, in forms-too is disenchanted, in eye-consciousness-too is disenchanted, in eye-contact-too is disenchanted, in feeling-too is disenchanted. Being disenchanted, becomes dispassionate. Through dispassion is liberated. Through emancipation 'fully-understood by me clinging,' understands. . . .

"I will teach you, monks, the Dhamma for the full understanding of all clinging. Listen to that. And what, monks, is the Dhamma for the full understanding of all clinging? In dependence on the eye and forms, eye-consciousness arises. The meeting of the three is contact. With contact as condition, feeling [comes to be]. Seeing thus, monks, the learned noble disciple becomes disenchanted with the eye, disenchanted with forms, disenchanted with eye-consciousness, disenchanted with eye-contact, disenchanted with feeling. Being disenchanted, he becomes dispassionate. Through dispassion [the mind] is liberated. Through emancipation he understands: 'Clinging has been fully understood by me.' . . .

"Manañca paṭicca dhamme ca uppajjati manoviññāṇaṃ. Tiṇṇaṃ saṅgati phasso. Phassapaccayā vedanā. Evaṃ passaṃ, bhikkhave, sutavā ariyasāvako manasmimpi nibbindati, dhammesupi nibbindati, manoviññāṇepi nibbindati, manosamphassepi nibbindati, vedanāyapi nibbindati. Nibbindaṃ virajjati. Virāgā vimuccati. Vimokkhā 'pariññātaṃ me upādānan'ti pajānāti. Ayaṃ kho, bhikkhave, sabbupādānapariññāya dhammo"ti.

"The mind-and in dependence on mental objects and arises mind-consciousness. Of the three meeting contact. Through contact-condition, feeling. Thus seeing, monks, the learned noble-disciple in the mind-too is disenchanted, in mental objects-too is disenchanted, in mind-consciousness-too is disenchanted, in mind-contact-too is disenchanted, in feeling-too is disenchanted. Being disenchanted, becomes dispassionate. Through dispassion is liberated. Through emancipation 'fully-understood by me clinging,' understands. This, monks, for all-clinging-full-understanding the Dhamma."

"In dependence on the mind and mental objects, mind-consciousness arises. The meeting of the three is contact. With contact as condition, feeling [comes to be]. Seeing thus, the learned noble disciple becomes disenchanted with the mind, disenchanted with mental objects, disenchanted with mind-consciousness, disenchanted with mind-contact, disenchanted with feeling. Being disenchanted, he becomes dispassionate. Through dispassion [the mind] is liberated. Through emancipation he understands: 'Clinging has been fully understood by me.' This, monks, is the Dhamma for the full understanding of all clinging."

Grammatical explanations

sabbupādānapariññāya: "for the full understanding of all clinging." Overall, the compound is a genitive tappurisa in the dative case.

paṭicca: see p. 154. *Cakkhuviññāṇaṃ* is the subject of the absolutive *paṭicca* and the finite verb *uppajjati*. *Paṭicca* takes two objects in the accusative case, *cakkhuṃ* and *rūpe*, the eye and visible forms, representing the internal and external sense bases.

tiṇṇaṃ saṅgati phasso: "the meeting of the three is contact." *Tiṇṇaṃ*, the neuter genitive of *tīṇi*, "three," refers to the eye, forms, and eye-consciousness. Since the sentence merely equates *phasso* with *tiṇṇaṃ saṅgati*, a verb is not needed.

phassapaccayā vedanā: "with contact as condition, feeling." On compounds formed with the ablative *paccayā* as the second member, see the explanation of *cakkhusamphassapaccayā* (p. 225). A verb *hoti*, "comes to be," is implicit.

vimokkhā: "through emancipation"; an ablative of the masculine noun *vimokkha*, used in the causal sense. In relation to ultimate liberation, it is unusual for *vimokkha* to be used as the noun derived from *vimuccati* rather than the more common *vimutti*. *Vimokkha* is more often used as the designation for a set of eight meditative attainments (see, for example, AN IV 306).

pariññātaṃ me upādānaṃ: "clinging has been fully understood by me." The past participle *pariññātaṃ* agrees with *upādānaṃ*; *me* is the enclitic pronoun, either instrumental or genitive with an instrumental sense, equivalent to *mayā*, "by me."

5. Upavāṇasutta

Upavāṇa (SN 35:70; IV 41–43)

[1. When lust is present]

Atha kho āyasmā upavāṇo yena bhagavā ten'upasaṅkami. . . . Ekamantaṃ nisinno kho āyasmā upavāṇo bhagavantaṃ etadavoca: "'Sandiṭṭhiko dhammo, sandiṭṭhiko dhammo'ti, bhante, vuccati. Kittāvatā nu kho, bhante, sandiṭṭhiko dhammo hoti, akāliko ehipassiko opanayiko paccattaṃ veditabbo viññūhī"ti?

Then the Venerable Upavāṇa where the Blessed One, there approached. . . . One-side seated, the Venerable Upavāṇa to the Blessed One this-said: "'A directly-visible Dhamma, a directly-visible Dhamma,' Bhante, is said. In what way, Bhante, directly-visible Dhamma is, not-temporal, a come-see-thing, applicable, personally to-be-understood by the wise?"

Then the Venerable Upavāṇa approached the Blessed One. . . . Seated to one side, the Venerable Upavāṇa said this to the Blessed One: "It is said, Bhante, 'a directly visible Dhamma, a directly visible Dhamma.' In what way, Bhante, is the Dhamma directly visible, immediate, asking one to come and see, applicable, to be personally understood by the wise?"

"Idha pana, upavāṇa, bhikkhu cakkhunā rūpaṃ disvā rūpappaṭisaṃvedī ca hoti rūparāgappaṭisaṃvedī ca, santañca ajjhattaṃ rūpesu rāgaṃ 'atthi me ajjhattaṃ rūpesu rāgo'ti pajānāti. Yaṃ taṃ, upavāṇa, bhikkhu cakkhunā rūpaṃ disvā rūpappaṭisaṃvedī ca hoti rūparāgappaṭisaṃvedī ca, santañca ajjhattaṃ rūpesu rāgaṃ 'atthi me ajjhattaṃ rūpesu rāgo'ti pajānāti, evampi kho, upavāṇa, sandiṭṭhiko dhammo hoti akāliko ehipassiko opanayiko paccattaṃ veditabbo viññūhī ti. . . .

"Here, Upavāṇa, a monk with the eye a form having seen, form-experiencer and is, form-lust-experiencer and, existing-and internally in forms lust, 'There is for me internally in forms lust,' understands. Since that, Upavāṇa, a monk with the eye a form having seen, form-experiencer and is, form-lust-experiencer and, existing-and internally in forms lust, 'There is for me internally in forms lust,' understands, in such a way too, Upavāṇa, directly-visible Dhamma is, not-temporal, a come-see-thing, applicable, personally to-be-understood by the wise. . . .

"Here, Upavāṇa, having seen a form with the eye, a monk is one who experiences the form and one who experiences lust for the form, and he understands the lust for forms existing internally thus, 'There exists for me internally lust for forms.' Since, Upavāṇa, having seen that form with the eye, the monk is one who experiences the form and who experiences lust for the form, and he understands the lust for forms existing internally thus, 'There exists for me internally lust for forms,' in such a way, Upavāṇa, the Dhamma is directly visible, immediate, asking one to come and see, applicable, to be personally understood by the wise. . . .

"Puna caparaṃ, upavāṇa, bhikkhu manasā dhammaṃ viññāya dhammappaṭisaṃvedī ca hoti dhammarāgappaṭisaṃvedī ca, santañca ajjhattaṃ dhammesu rāgaṃ 'atthi me ajjhattaṃ dhammesu rāgo'ti pajānāti. Yaṃ taṃ, upavāṇa, bhikkhu manasā dhammaṃ viññāya dhammappaṭisaṃvedī ca hoti dhammarāgappaṭisaṃvedī ca, santañca ajjhattaṃ dhammesu rāgaṃ 'atthi me ajjhattaṃ dhammesu rāgo'ti pajānāti, evampi kho, upavāṇa, sandiṭṭhiko dhammo hoti . . . paccattaṃ veditabbo viññūhī.

"Again, further, Upavāṇa, a monk with the mind a mental-object having cognized, mental-object-experiencer and is, mental-object-lust-experiencer and, existing-and internally in mental-objects lust, 'There is for me internally in mental-objects lust,' understands. Since that, Upavāṇa, a monk with the mind a mental-object having cognized, mental-object-experiencer and is, mental-object-lust-experiencer and, existing-and internally in mental-objects lust, 'There is for me internally in mental-objects lust,' understands, in such a way too, Upavāṇa, directly-visible Dhamma is . . . personally to-be-understood by the wise.

"Again, Upavāṇa, having cognized a mental object with the mind, a monk is one who experiences the mental object and one who experiences lust for the mental object, and he understands the lust for mental objects existing internally thus, 'There exists for me internally lust for mental objects.' Since, Upavāṇa, having cognized that mental object with the mind, a monk is one who experiences the mental object and one who experiences lust for the mental object, and he understands the lust for mental objects existing internally thus, 'There exists for me internally lust for mental objects,' in such a way too, Upavāṇa, the Dhamma is directly visible . . . to be personally understood by the wise.

[2. When lust is absent]

"Idha pana, upavāṇa, bhikkhu cakkhunā rūpaṃ disvā rūpappaṭisaṃvedī ca hoti, no ca rūparāgappaṭisaṃvedī. Asantañca ajjhattaṃ rūpesu rāgaṃ 'natthi me ajjhattaṃ rūpesu rāgo'ti pajānāti. Yaṃ taṃ, upavāṇa, bhikkhu cakkhunā rūpaṃ disvā rūpappaṭisaṃvedī kho hoti, no ca rūparāgappaṭisaṃvedī, asantañca ajjhattaṃ rūpesu rāgaṃ 'natthi me ajjhattaṃ rūpesu rāgo'ti pajānāti, evampi kho, upavāṇa, sandiṭṭhiko dhammo hoti, akāliko ehipassiko opanayiko paccattaṃ veditabbo viññūhī. . . .

"Here but, Upavāṇa, a monk with the eye a form having seen, form-experiencer and is, not and form-lust-experiencer, not-existing-and internally in forms lust, 'There is not for me internally in forms lust,' understands. Since that, Upavāṇa, a monk with the eye a form having seen, form-experiencer is, not and form-lust-experiencer, not-existing-and internally in forms lust, 'There is not for me internally in forms lust,' understands, in such a way too, Upavāṇa, directly-visible Dhamma is, not-temporal, a come-see-thing, applicable, personally to-be-understood by the wise. . . .

"But here, Upavāṇa, having seen a form with the eye, a monk is one who experiences the form but does not experience lust for the form, and he understands there is no lust for forms existing internally thus, 'There does not exist for me internally lust for forms.' Since, Upavāṇa, having seen that form with the eye, the monk is one who experiences the form but does not experience lust for the form, and he understands there is no lust for forms existing internally thus, 'There does not exist for me internally lust for forms,' in such a way too, Upavāṇa, the Dhamma is directly visible, immediate, asking one to come and see, applicable, to be personally understood by the wise. . . .

"Puna caparaṃ, upavāṇa, bhikkhu manasā dhammaṃ viññāya dhammappaṭisaṃvedī kho hoti, no ca dhammarāgappaṭisaṃvedī, asantañca ajjhattaṃ dhammesu rāgaṃ 'natthi me ajjhattaṃ dhammesu rāgo'ti pajānāti. Yaṃ taṃ, upavāṇa, bhikkhu manasā dhammaṃ viññāya dhammappaṭisaṃvedī kho hoti, no ca dhammarāgappaṭisaṃvedī, asantañca ajjhattaṃ dhammesu rāgaṃ 'natthi me ajjhattaṃ dhammesu rāgo'ti pajānāti, evampi kho, upavāṇa, sandiṭṭhiko dhammo hoti, akāliko ehipassiko opanayiko paccattaṃ veditabbo viññūhī"ti.

"Again, further, Upavāṇa, a monk with the mind a mental-object having cognized, mental-object-experiencer is, not and mental-object-lust-experiencer, not-existing-and internally in mental-objects lust, 'There is not for me internally in mental-objects lust,' understands. Since that, Upavāṇa, a monk with the mind a mental-object having cognized, mental-object-experiencer is, not and mental-object-lust-experiencer, not-existing-and internally in mental-objects lust, 'There is not for me internally in mental-objects lust,' understands, in such a way too, Upavāṇa, directly-visible Dhamma is, not-temporal, a come-see-thing, applicable, personally to-be-understood by the wise."

"Again, Upavāṇa, having cognized a mental object with the mind, a monk is one who experiences the mental object but does not experience lust for the mental object, and he understands there is no lust for mental objects existing internally thus, 'There does not exist for me internally lust for mental objects.' Since, Upavāṇa, having cognized that mental object with the mind, the monk is one who experiences the mental object but does not experience lust for the mental object, and he understands there is no lust for mental objects existing internally thus, 'There does not exist for me internally lust for mental objects,' in such a way too, Upavāṇa, the Dhamma is directly visible, immediate, asking one to come and see, applicable, to be personally understood by the wise."

Grammatical explanations

[1. When lust is present]

sandiṭṭhiko: "directly visible"; the first in a series of epithets for *dhammo*, with the others following the noun. *Sandiṭṭhiko* is based on *diṭṭha*, "seen," with prefix *sam-* and suffix *-iko*, which turns the word into an adjective. *Akāliko* is based on *kāla*, time, negated by the prefix *a-* and with the suffix *-iko*; thus "not involving [a lapse of] time, immediate." *Ehipassiko* is composed of two second-person imperatives, *ehi*, "come," and *passa*, "see," again with the suffix *-iko*; Perniola (§142c) considers this a syntactical compound. *Opanayiko*, a derivative of *upanaya*, means "fit for taking to oneself, fit for making use of, deserving to be used" (DOP). In the phrase *paccattaṃ veditabbo viññūhi*, "to be personally understood by the wise," the future passive participle, *veditabbo*, qualifies *dhammo*. *Paccattaṃ* is an adverbial compound, from *paṭi* + *attan* (> *paṭyattaṃ* > *paccattaṃ*), "for oneself, by oneself," and *viññūhi* is the plural instrumental of *viññū*, "a wise person."

rūpappaṭisaṃvedī: "one who experiences form"; an accusative tappurisa compound qualifying *bhikkhu*, with *rūpa* in an accusative relationship to *paṭisaṃvedī*, "one who experiences," based on the verb *paṭisaṃvedeti*, "experiences."

rūparāgappaṭisaṃvedī, "who experiences lust for form"; a complex accusative tappurisa compound, with *rūparāga* a subordinate locative tappurisa in an accusative relationship to *paṭisaṃvedeti*.[127]

santañca ajjhattaṃ rūpesu rāgaṃ 'atthi me ajjhattaṃ rūpesu rāgo'ti pajānāti: "he understands the lust for forms existing internally thus, 'There exists for me internally lust for forms.'" The verb *pajānāti* takes *rāgaṃ* as its object. *Rāgaṃ* is qualified by *santaṃ*, the present participle of *atthi*, "exists"; it is a masculine singular in the accusative case, in agreement with *rāgaṃ*. *Ajjhattaṃ* is an indeclinable from *adhi* + *attan* (> *adhyattaṃ* > *ajjhattaṃ*). Words for desire in Pāli, such as *rāga*, take their object in the locative case (here *rūpesu*). The direct quotation (beginning *atthi me*) expresses the monk's awareness of the internal lust for forms. Constructions with *atthi me* often have the sense of "I have."

yaṃ taṃ . . . bhikkhu cakkhunā rūpaṃ disvā: "Since, Upavāṇa, having seen that form with the eye, the monk. . . ." I take *yaṃ* here to bear the sense of "since, because" (see SED under *yad*, p. 844b), with *taṃ* qualifying *rūpaṃ*. *Disvā* is an absolutive, "having seen."

puna caparaṃ: "furthermore, again."

manasā dhammaṃ viññāya: *Manasā* is instrumental of *manas*, *viññāya* the absolutive of *vijānāti*.

[2. When lust is absent]

asantañca ajjhattaṃ rūpesu rāgaṃ 'natthi me ajjhattaṃ rūpesu rāgo'ti pajānāti: "and he understands there is no lust for forms existing internally thus, 'There does not exist for me internally lust for forms.'" This should be construed as the opposite of the sentence beginning *santañca ajjhattaṃ rūpesu rāgaṃ*, with *asantaṃ* the negative present participle qualifying *rāgaṃ*, the accusative object of the verb *pajānāti*.

127. *Rūparāga* is a locative tappurisa because *rūpa* takes the position of a locative *rūpesu* relative to *rāga*.

6. Suññalokasutta

Empty World (SN 35:85; IV 54)

Atha kho āyasmā ānando . . . bhagavantaṃ etadavoca: "'Suñño loko, suñño loko'ti, bhante, vuccati. Kittāvatā nu kho, bhante, 'suñño loko'ti vuccatī"ti?

Then the Venerable Ānanda . . . to the Blessed One this-said: "'Empty world, empty world,' Bhante, is said. In what way, Bhante, 'empty world' is said?"

Then the Venerable Ānanda . . . said this to the Blessed One: "It is said, Bhante: 'The world is empty, the world is empty.' In what way, Bhante, is it said: 'The world is empty'?"

"Yasmā ca kho, ānanda, suññaṃ attena vā attaniyena vā tasmā 'suñño loko'ti vuccati. Kiñca, ānanda, suññaṃ attena vā attaniyena vā? Cakkhu kho, ānanda, suññaṃ attena vā attaniyena vā. Rūpā suññā attena vā attaniyena vā. Cakkhuviññāṇaṃ suññaṃ attena vā attaniyena vā. Cakkhusamphasso suñño attena vā attaniyena vā. . . .

"Because and, Ānanda, empty with self or with what-belongs-to-self or, therefore 'empty world' is said. What-and, Ānanda, empty with self or with what-belongs-to-self or? The eye, Ānanda, empty with self or with what-belongs-to-self or. Forms empty with self or with what-belongs-to-self or. Eye-consciousness empty with self or with what-belongs-to-self or. Eye-contact empty with self or with what-belongs-to-self or. . . .

"Because, Ānanda, it is empty of self and of what belongs to self, it is therefore said: 'The world is empty.' And what, Ānanda, is empty of self and of what belongs to self? The eye, Ānanda, is empty of self and of what belongs to self. Forms are empty of self and of what belongs to self. Eye-consciousness is empty of self and of what belongs to self. Eye-contact is empty of self and of what belongs to self. . . .

"Yampidaṃ manosamphassapaccayā uppajjati vedayitaṃ sukhaṃ vā dukkhaṃ vā adukkhamasukhaṃ vā tampi suññaṃ attena vā attaniyena vā. Yasmā ca kho, ānanda, suññaṃ attena vā attaniyena vā, tasmā 'suñño loko'ti vuccatī"ti.

"Which-too-this through mind-contact-condition arises feeling pleasant or painful or neither-painful-nor-pleasant or, that-too empty with self or with what-belongs-to-self or. Because and, Ānanda, empty with self or with what-belongs-to-self or, therefore 'empty world' is said."

"Whatever feeling arises with mind-contact as condition—whether pleasant or painful or neither-painful-nor-pleasant—that too is empty of self and of what belongs to self. Because, Ānanda, it is empty of self and of what belongs to self, it is therefore said: 'The world is empty.'"

Grammatical explanations

suñño loko: "the world is empty." Whereas in English we would normally use "of" to indicate deficiency or absence, in Pāli the adjective *suñña* takes the quality of which something is empty in the instrumental case, that is, "empty with respect to."

attena vā attaniyena vā: "of self and of what belongs to self." The instrumental *attena* is based on the assimilation of *attan* to masculine nouns of the *-a* type; the usual instrumental of *attan* is *attanā*. *Attaniya* is derived from *attan*, with the suffix *-iya* indicating "related to, belonging to." It here functions as a neuter noun, "that which belongs to self."

cakkhu . . . suññaṃ, rūpā suññā: "the eye . . . is empty, forms are empty." *Suñña* agrees in gender and number with the entity said to be empty.

7. Dvayasutta
Dyads (SN 35:93; IV 67–69)

"Dvayaṃ, bhikkhave, paṭicca viññāṇaṃ sambhoti. Kathañca, bhikkhave, dvayaṃ paṭicca viññāṇaṃ sambhoti?

"Dyad, monks, in dependence on consciousness comes-to-be. How-and, monks, dyad in dependence on consciousness comes-to-be?

"Consciousness, monks, comes to be in dependence on a dyad. And how, monks, does consciousness come to be in dependence on a dyad?

"Cakkhuñca paṭicca rūpe ca uppajjati cakkhuviññāṇaṃ. Cakkhu aniccaṃ vipariṇāmi aññathābhāvi. Rūpā aniccā vipariṇāmino aññathābhāvino. Itth'etaṃ dvayaṃ calañc'eva vyathañca[128] *aniccaṃ vipariṇāmi aññathābhāvi.*

"The eye-and in dependence on, forms and, arises eye-consciousness. The eye impermanent, changing, otherwise-becoming. Forms impermanent, changing, otherwise-becoming. Thus this dyad moving-and tottering-and, impermanent, changing, otherwise-becoming.

"In dependence on the eye and forms, eye-consciousness arises. The eye is impermanent, changing, becoming otherwise. Forms are impermanent, changing, becoming otherwise. Thus this dyad is moving and tottering, impermanent, changing, becoming otherwise.

"Cakkhuviññāṇaṃ aniccaṃ vipariṇāmi aññathābhāvi. Yopi hetu yopi paccayo cakkhuviññāṇassa uppādāya, sopi hetu sopi paccayo anicco vipariṇāmī aññathābhāvī. Aniccaṃ kho pana, bhikkhave, paccayaṃ paṭicca uppannaṃ cakkhuviññāṇaṃ kuto niccaṃ bhavissati?

"Eye-consciousness impermanent, changing, otherwise-becoming. Which-too cause, which-too condition, of eye-consciousness for arising, that-too cause, that-too condition, impermanent, changing, otherwise-becoming. Impermanent, monks, condition in dependence on arisen eye-consciousness, how permanent will be?

"Eye-consciousness is impermanent, changing, becoming otherwise. The cause and condition for the arising of eye-consciousness too is impermanent, changing, becoming otherwise. When, monks, eye-consciousness has arisen in dependence on an impermanent condition, how could it be permanent?

"Yā kho, bhikkhave, imesaṃ tiṇṇaṃ dhammānaṃ saṅgati sannipāto samavāyo, ayaṃ vuccati 'cakkhusamphasso.' Cakkhusamphassopi anicco vipariṇāmī aññathābhāvī. Yopi hetu yopi paccayo cakkhusamphassassa uppādāya, sopi hetu sopi paccayo anicco vipariṇāmī aññathābhāvī. Aniccaṃ

128. On my preference for reading *vyathaṃ* here, see p. 244.

kho pana, bhikkhave, paccayaṃ paṭicca uppanno cakkhusamphasso kuto nicco bhavissati?

"Which, monks, of these three things the meeting, the encounter, the concurrence, this is called 'eye-contact.' Eye-contact-too impermanent, changing, otherwise-becoming. Which-too cause, which-too condition, of eye-contact for arising, that-too cause, that-too condition, impermanent, changing, otherwise-becoming. Impermanent, monks, condition in dependence on arisen eye-contact, how permanent will be?

"The meeting, the encounter, the concurrence of these three things, monks, is called 'eye contact.' Eye contact too is impermanent, changing, becoming otherwise. The cause and condition for the arising of eye contact too is impermanent, changing, becoming otherwise. When, monks, eye contact has arisen in dependence on a condition that is impermanent, how could it be permanent?

"Phuṭṭho, bhikkhave, vedeti, phuṭṭho ceteti, phuṭṭho sañjānāti. Itth'etepi dhammā calā c'eva vyathā ca aniccā vipariṇāmino aññathābhāvino. . . .

"Contacted, monks, one feels, contacted one wills, contacted one perceives. Thus these-too things moving and tottering and, impermanent, changing, otherwise-becoming. . . .

"Contacted, monks, one feels, contacted one wills, contacted one perceives. Thus these things too are moving and tottering, impermanent, changing, becoming otherwise. . . .

"Manañca paṭicca dhamme ca uppajjati manoviññāṇaṃ. Mano anicco vipariṇāmī aññathābhāvī. Dhammā aniccā vipariṇāmino aññathābhāvino. . . . Phuṭṭho, bhikkhave, vedeti, phuṭṭho ceteti, phuṭṭho sañjānāti. Itth'etepi dhammā calā c'eva vyathā ca aniccā vipariṇāmino aññathābhāvino. Evaṃ kho, bhikkhave, dvayaṃ paṭicca viññāṇaṃ sambhotī"ti.

"The mind-and in dependence on, mental objects and arises mind-consciousness. The mind impermanent, changing, otherwise-becoming. Mental objects impermanent, changing, otherwise-becoming. . . . Contacted, monks, one feels, contacted one wills, contacted one perceives. Thus these-too things moving and tottering and, impermanent, changing, otherwise-becoming. In such a way, monks, dyad in dependence on consciousness comes-to-be."

"In dependence on the mind and mental objects, mind-consciousness arises. The mind is impermanent, changing, becoming otherwise. Mental objects are impermanent, changing, becoming otherwise. . . . Contacted, monks, one feels, contacted one wills, contacted one perceives. Thus these things too are moving and tottering, impermanent, changing, becoming otherwise. In such a way, monks, consciousness comes to be in dependence on a dyad."

Grammatical explanations

sambhoti: "comes to be"; a contracted form of *sambhavati* (on the contraction *ava* > *o*, see Geiger §26.2).

aniccaṃ vipariṇāmi aññathābhāvi: "impermanent, changing, becoming otherwise"; three adjectives, here neuter nominatives in agreement with *cakkhu*. *Aññathābhāvi* is composed of *aññathā* and *bhāva*, with the suffix *-in* enabling the compound to serve as an adjective. Just below the terminations change in accordance with the gender and number of the qualified nouns.

itth'etaṃ dvayaṃ calañc'eva vyathañca: "thus this dyad is moving and tottering." *Calaṃ* is an adjective derived from the verb *calati*, "moves, shakes," suggesting instability and transience. While Ce and Ee read the second adjective as *vyayaṃ* (from the verb *veti*), *vyathaṃ* cited as a variant in Ce (and the Be variant *byathaṃ*), from the verb *vyathati*, has the support of the commentary.[129]

saṅgati sannipāto samavāyo: "the meeting, the encounter, the concurrence"; three synonyms used to explain *phassa*.

phuṭṭho: the past participle of *phusati*, "touches, makes contact," corresponding to *phassa*.

129. VRI at Spk III 26 (= Ee II 380,19–20) reads: *Calañc'eva byathañcā ti attano sabhāvena asaṇṭhahanato calati ceva byathati ca* ("*Moving and tottering*: It moves and totters because of its own inherent instability"). Ce has here *vyathañca* and *vyathati*. SED ascribes to the verbal root *vyath* the meaning "to tremble, waver, come to naught, fail."

vedeti, ceteti, sañjānāti: "feels, wills (intends), perceives"; the verbs corresponding to the nouns *vedanā*, *cetanā*, and *saññā*. Since *saṅkhārā* is defined as the six types of *cetanā* (at SN III 60,25–28), this can be taken as an allusion to the middle three aggregates: the *vedanākkhandha*, the *saññākkhandha*, and the *saṅkhārakkhandha*.

8. Sakkapañhasutta

Sakka's Questions (SN 35:118; IV 101–2)

[1. Why beings do not attain nibbāna]

Ekaṃ samayaṃ bhagavā rājagahe viharati gijjhakūṭe pabbate. Atha kho sakko devānamindo yena bhagavā ten'upasaṅkami. Upasaṅkamitvā bhagavantaṃ abhivādetvā ekamantaṃ aṭṭhāsi. Ekamantaṃ ṭhito kho sakko devānamindo bhagavantaṃ etadavoca:

One occasion the Blessed One at Rājagaha was dwelling on Vulture-Peak Mountain. Then Sakka of devas-lord where the Blessed One, there approached. Having approached, the Blessed One having paid homage to, one-side stood. One-side stood, Sakka of devas-lord to the Blessed One this-said:

On one occasion the Blessed One was dwelling at Rājagaha on Vulture Peak Mountain. Then Sakka, lord of the devas, approached the Blessed One. Having approached, having paid homage to the Blessed One, he stood to one side. As he stood to one side, he said this to the Blessed One:

"Ko nu kho, bhante, hetu, ko paccayo yena-m-idh'ekacce sattā diṭṭhe'va dhamme no parinibbāyanti? Ko pana, bhante, hetu, ko paccayo yena-m-idh'ekacce sattā diṭṭhe'va dhamme parinibbāyantī"ti?

"What, Bhante, the cause, what the condition, by which here some beings in-present-life not attain-nibbāna? What but, Bhante, the cause, what the condition, by which here some beings in-present-life attain-nibbāna?"

"What, Bhante, is the cause, what is the reason, why some beings here do not attain nibbāna in this present life? And what, Bhante, is the cause, what is the reason, why some beings here attain nibbāna in this present life?"

"Santi kho, devānaminda, cakkhuviññeyyā rūpā iṭṭhā kantā manāpā piyarūpā kāmūpasaṃhitā rajanīyā. Tañce bhikkhu abhinandati abhivadati ajjhosāya tiṭṭhati, tassa taṃ abhinandato abhivadato ajjhosāya tiṭṭhato tannissitaṃ viññāṇaṃ hoti tadupādānaṃ. Saupādāno, devānaminda, bhikkhu no parinibbāyati. . . .

"There are, of devas-lord, eye-cognizable forms, wished-for, desired, agreeable, pleasing-nature, sensuality-connected, enticing. That-if a monk delights in, welcomes, having held stands, for him that delighting in, welcoming, having held standing, that-dependent consciousness is, that-clinging. With-clinging, of devas-lord, a monk not attains-nibbāna. . . .

"There are, lord of the devas, forms cognizable by the eye that are wished for, desired, agreeable, of a pleasing nature, connected with sensuality, enticing. If a monk delights in them, welcomes them, and remains holding them, as he is delighting in them, welcoming them, and remains holding to them, his consciousness is dependent on them, with them as clinging (fuel). A monk with clinging (fuel) does not attain nibbāna. . . .

"Santi kho, devānaminda, manoviññeyyā dhammā iṭṭhā kantā manāpā piyarūpā kāmūpasaṃhitā rajanīyā. Tañce bhikkhu abhinandati abhivadati ajjhosāya tiṭṭhati, tassa taṃ abhinandato abhivadato ajjhosāya tiṭṭhato tannissitaṃ viññāṇaṃ hoti tadupādānaṃ. Saupādāno, devānaminda, bhikkhu no parinibbāyati. Ayaṃ kho, devānaminda, hetu, ayaṃ paccayo yena-m-idh'ekacce sattā diṭṭh'eva dhamme no parinibbāyanti.

"There are, of devas-lord, mind-cognizable mental-objects, wished-for, desired, agreeable, pleasing-nature, sensuality-connected, enticing. That-if a monk delights in, welcomes, having held stands, for him that delighting in, welcoming, having held standing, that-dependent consciousness is, that-clinging. With-clinging, of devas-lord, a monk not attains-nibbāna. This, of devas-lord, the cause, this the condition, by which here some beings in-present-life not attain-nibbāna.

"There are, lord of the devas, mental objects cognizable by the mind that are wished for, desired, agreeable, of a pleasing nature, connected with sensuality, enticing. If a monk delights in them, welcomes them, and remains holding to them, as he is delighting in them, welcoming them, and remains holding to them, his consciousness is dependent on them, with them as clinging (fuel). A monk with clinging (fuel) does not attain nibbāna. This is the cause, lord of the devas, this is the reason, why some beings here do not attain nibbāna in this present life.

[2. How beings attain nibbāna]

"Santi ca kho, devānaminda, cakkhuviññeyyā rūpā . . . manoviññeyyā dhammā iṭṭhā kantā manāpā piyarūpā kāmūpasaṃhitā rajanīyā. Tañce bhikkhu nābhinandati nābhivadati nājjhosāya tiṭṭhati, tassa taṃ anabhinandato anabhivadato anajjhosāya tiṭṭhato na tannissitaṃ viññāṇaṃ hoti na tadupādānaṃ. Anupādāno, devānaminda, bhikkhu parinibbāyati. Ayaṃ kho, devānaminda, hetu, ayaṃ paccayo yena-m-idh'ekacce sattā diṭṭh'eva dhamme parinibbāyantī"ti.

"There are, of devas-lord, eye-cognizable forms . . . mind-cognizable mental-objects, wished-for, desired, agreeable, pleasing-nature, sensuality-connected, enticing. That-if a monk not delights in, not welcomes, not having held stands, for him that not delighting in, not welcoming, not having held standing, not that-dependent consciousness is, not that-clinging. Without-clinging, of devas-lord, a monk attains-nibbāna. This, of devas-lord, the cause, this the condition, by which here some beings in-present-life attain-nibbāna."

"There are, lord of the devas, forms cognizable by the eye . . . mental objects cognizable by the mind that are wished for, desired, agreeable, of a pleasing nature, connected with sensuality, enticing. If a monk does not delight in them, does not welcome them, and does not remain holding to them, as he is not delighting in them, not welcoming them, and does not remain holding to them, his consciousness is not dependent on them, does not have them as clinging (fuel). A monk without clinging (fuel) attains nibbāna. This is the cause, lord of the devas, this is the reason, why some beings here attain nibbāna in this present life."

Grammatical explanations

rājagahe viharati gijjhakūṭe pabbate: "was dwelling at Rājagaha on Vulture Peak Mountain." The nouns are locatives naming the city where the Buddha was dwelling and the specific place near that city. The commentaries explain that the mountain was called "Vulture Peak" because vultures lived on its peak, or because its peak was shaped like a vulture.

sakko devānamindo: Sakka is the proper name of this deity, *devānaminda*, "lord of the devas," an epithet composed of *devānaṃ*, plural genitive, and *inda*, "lord, ruler," with *-ṃ* changed to *-m* in sandhi with *inda*.

yena-m-idh'ekacce: The instrumental pronoun *yena* indicates causation, "because of which." Duroiselle (§532) calls this a "case-form adverb." The *-m-* is inserted as a liaison consonant bridging the two vowels. The final vowel of *idha* is elided in sandhi with *ekacce*, "some," qualifying *sattā*, "beings."

diṭṭhe'va dhamme: see p. 180.

parinibbāyanti: "attain nibbāna." It is uncertain whether the question pertains to the extinguishing of defilements (called in the commentaries *kilesaparinibbāna*) or liberation from repeated birth and death (called *khandhaparinibbāna*). Both could be intended.

tañce: *Ce* is an enclitic (internal) conditional particle, "if." Since *rūpā* is plural, the accusative pronoun representing *rūpā* should also be plural. While *tañ* (= *taṃ* in sandhi with *ce*) appears to be singular, Geiger points out (at §78.3a) that "there is an accusative plural in *-aṃ* [corresponding to the Skt masculine plural suffix *-ān*], with the *-n* becoming *-ṃ* and the consequent shortening of *ā* > *a* before *ṃ*." The same applies to *taṃ* in the immediate sequel.

ajjhosāya tiṭṭhati: "remains holding"; an idiomatic construction composed of an absolutive and a finite verb, literally meaning "having held, one stands."

tassa taṃ abhinandato abhivadato ajjhosāya tiṭṭhato: For convenience I translate "as he is delighting in them, welcoming them, and remains holding to them," but the three present participles are datives qualifying *tassa*.

tannissitaṃ viññāṇaṃ hoti tadupādānaṃ: "consciousness is dependent on them, with them as clinging (fuel)." *Tannissitaṃ* is a tappurisa compound of *taṃ*, "that" (meaning the forms, or perhaps the attachment to the forms), and *nissitaṃ*, "dependent"; *tadupādānaṃ* is a bahubbīhi composed of *taṃ* and *upādānaṃ*, which here suggests that "clinging" is the "fuel" that keeps the flame of consciousness burning. Both compounds describe *viññāṇaṃ*, the subject of *hoti*.

saupādāno = *sa* + *upādāno*: "with clinging"; a bahubbīhi describing *bhikkhu*.
anupādāno: "without clinging"; the negative bahubbīhi, also describing *bhikkhu*.

9. Rūpārāmasutta

Delight in Forms (SN 35:136; IV 126–27)

"Rūpārāmā, bhikkhave, devamanussā rūparatā rūpasammuditā. Rūpavipariṇāmavirāganirodhā dukkhaṃ,[130] *bhikkhave, devamanussā viharanti. Saddārāmā . . . Gandhārāmā . . . Rasārāmā . . . Phoṭṭhabbārāmā . . . Dhammārāmā, bhikkhave, devamanussā dhammaratā dhammasammuditā. Dhammavipariṇāmavirāganirodhā dukkhaṃ, bhikkhave, devamanussā viharanti.*

"Forms-delight-in, monks, devas-humans, forms-delighted-in, forms-rejoiced-in. Through forms-change-fading-cessation painfully, monks, devas-humans dwell. . . . Sounds-delight-in . . . Odors-delight-in . . . Tastes-delight-in . . . Tactiles-delight-in . . . Mental-objects-delight-in, monks, devas-humans, mental-objects-delighted-in, mental-objects-rejoiced-in. Through mental-objects-change-fading-cessation painfully, monks, devas-humans dwell.

"Devas and humans, monks, delight in forms, are delighted with forms, rejoice in forms. With the change, fading away, and cessation of forms, monks, devas and humans dwell painfully. Devas and humans delight in sounds . . . delight in odors . . . delight in tastes . . . delight in tactile objects . . . delight in mental objects, are delighted with mental objects, rejoice in mental objects. With the change, fading away, and cessation of mental objects, monks, devas and humans dwell painfully.

"Tathāgato ca kho, bhikkhave, arahaṃ sammāsambuddho rūpānaṃ samudayañca atthaṅgamañca assādañca ādīnavañca nissaraṇañca yathābhūtaṃ

130. I have amended the text's *dukkhā* to *dukkhaṃ* here and just below. It seems that what is needed is an adverb corresponding to *viharanti* rather than an adjective modifying *devamanussā*. Similarly, in the next section, I have amended the text's *sukho* to *sukhaṃ*. See SN II 29,1–5 (here at p. 320), where we find similar sentences with the expected readings *dukkhaṃ* and *sukhaṃ*.

viditvā na rūpārāmo na rūparato na rūpasammudito. Rūpavipariṇāmavirāganirodhā sukhaṃ, bhikkhave, tathāgato viharati. Saddānaṃ . . . Gandhānaṃ . . . Rasānaṃ . . . Phoṭṭhabbānaṃ . . . Dhammānaṃ samudayañca atthaṅgamañca assādañca ādīnavañca nissaraṇañca yathābhūtaṃ viditvā na dhammārāmo, na dhammarato, na dhammasammudito. Dhammavipariṇāmavirāganirodhā sukhaṃ, bhikkhave, tathāgato viharati."

"The Tathāgata but, monks, the arahant, the perfectly-enlightened one, of forms the origin-and passing-away-and enjoyment-and danger-and escape-and as-really-is having known, not forms-delight-in, not forms-delighted-in, not forms-rejoiced-in. Through forms-change-fading-cessation happily, monks, the Tathāgata dwells. Of sounds . . . Of odors . . . Of tastes . . . Of tactiles . . . Of mental-objects origin-and passing away-and enjoyment-and danger-and escape-and as-really-is having known, not mental-objects-delight-in, not mental-objects-delighted-in, not mental-objects-rejoiced-in. Through mental-objects-change-fading-cessation happily, monks, the Tathāgata dwells."

"But, monks, the Tathāgata, the arahant, the perfectly enlightened one, having known as they really are the origin and the passing away, the enjoyment, the danger, and the escape in the case of forms, does not delight in forms, is not delighted with forms, does not rejoice in forms. With the change, fading away, and cessation of forms, monks, the Tathāgata dwells happily. Having known as they really are the origin and the passing away, the enjoyment, the danger, and the escape in the case of sounds . . . odors . . . tastes . . . tactile objects . . . mental objects, the Tathāgata does not delight in mental objects, is not delighted with mental objects, does not rejoice in mental objects. With the change, fading away, and cessation of mental objects, monks, the Tathāgata dwells happily."

Grammatical explanations

rūpārāmā, rūparatā, rūpasammuditā: "delight in forms, are delighted with forms, rejoice in forms." The first is a bahubbīhi compound; the other two are tappurisas ending in past participles. All three function as adjectives describing *devamanussā*.

rūpavipariṇāmavirāganirodhā: "with the change, fading away, and cessation of forms"; a complex genitive tappurisa in the ablative case. The final member is a three-part dvanda made up of *vipariṇāma*, *virāga*, and *nirodha*.

viditvā: an absolutive of *vindati*, a verb seldom used in the indicative. In the suttas the indicative *pajānāti* describes a presently occurring act of understanding. A completed act of understanding is indicated by the past participle *vidita* or, as preliminary to some other event or condition, by the absolutive *viditvā*.

10. Samuddasutta

The Ocean (SN 35:228 [187]; IV 157)

"'Samuddo, samuddo'ti, bhikkhave, assutavā puthujjano bhāsati. N'eso, bhikkhave, ariyassa vinaye samuddo. Mahā eso, bhikkhave, udakarāsi mahā udakaṇṇavo.

"'The ocean, the ocean,' monks, the unlearned worldling says. Not this, monks, of the noble one in the discipline the ocean. Great this, monks, water-mass, great water-flood.

"'The ocean, the ocean,' monks, the unlearned worldling says. This, monks, is not the ocean in the discipline of the noble one. This, monks, is a great mass of water, a great flood of water.

"Cakkhu, bhikkhave, purisassa samuddo, tassa rūpamayo vego. Yo taṃ rūpamayaṃ vegaṃ sahati, ayaṃ vuccati, bhikkhave, 'atari cakkhusamuddaṃ saūmiṃ sāvaṭṭaṃ sagāhaṃ sarakkhasaṃ.' Tiṇṇo pāraṅgato thale tiṭṭhati brāhmaṇo. . . .

"The eye, monks, a person's ocean, its forms-consisting current. One who that forms-consisting current endures, he is called, monks, 'crossed eye-ocean with-waves, with-whirlpools, with-sharks, with-demons.' Crossed, beyond-gone, on high-ground stands the brahmin. . . .

"The eye, monks, is a person's ocean, its current consisting of forms. One who endures that current consisting of forms is called, monks, '[one who has] crossed the ocean of the eye with its waves, with its whirlpools, with its sharks, with its demons.' Crossed, gone beyond, the brahmin stands on high ground. . . .

"Mano, bhikkhave, purisassa samuddo, tassa dhammamayo vego. Yo taṃ dhammamayaṃ vegaṃ sahati, ayaṃ vuccati, bhikkhave, 'atari manosamuddaṃ saūmiṃ sāvaṭṭaṃ sagāhaṃ sarakkhasaṃ.' Tiṇṇo pāraṅgato thale tiṭṭhati brāhmaṇo"ti.

"The mind, monks, a person's ocean, its mind-objects-consisting current. One who that mind-objects-consisting current endures, he is called, monks, 'crossed mind-ocean with-waves, with-whirlpools, with-sharks, with-demons.' Crossed, beyond-gone, on high-ground stands the brahmin."

"The mind, monks, is a person's ocean, its current consisting of mental objects. One who endures that current consisting of mental objects is called, monks, '[one who has] crossed the ocean of the mind with its waves, with its whirlpools, with its sharks, with its demons.' Crossed, gone beyond, the brahmin stands on high ground."

Grammatical explanations

n'eso: a sandhi of *na* and *eso*, the latter modifying *samuddo*.

mahā eso, bhikkhave, udakarāsi: "This, monks, is a great mass of water." The adjective *mahā* is placed first for emphasis.

tassa rūpamayo vego: "its current consisting of forms." The tappurisa compound *rūpamayo* qualifies *vego*, with the suffix *-maya* meaning "made of" (as here) or "made by."

cakkhusamuddaṃ: a kammadhāraya compound that can be resolved as "the eye that is an ocean." It is the accusative object of *atari*.

saūmiṃ sāvaṭṭaṃ sagāhaṃ sarakkhasaṃ: "with waves, with whirlpools, with sharks, with demons." These are bahubbīhis qualifying *cakkhusamuddaṃ*; see p. 43.

tiṇṇo pāraṅgato thale tiṭṭhati brāhmaṇo: "Crossed, gone beyond, the brahmin stands on high ground." *Tiṇṇo* is the past participle of *tarati*, "crosses," and *pāraṅgato* an accusative tappurisa; both are in agreement with *brāhmaṇo*, the subject of the sentence, which has probably been put last for emphasis.

11. Bālisikopamasutta

The Simile of the Fisherman (SN 35:230 [189]; IV 158–59)

"Seyyathāpi, bhikkhave, bālisiko āmisagatabalisaṃ gambhīre udakarahade pakkhipeyya. Tamenaṃ aññataro āmisacakkhu maccho gileyya. Evaṃ hi so, bhikkhave, maccho gilitabaliso bālisikassa, anayaṃ āpanno vyasanaṃ āpanno yathākāmakaraṇīyo bālisikassa.

"Suppose, monks, a fisherman a bait-gone-hook into deep water-pool would throw. That-this a certain bait-eye fish would swallow. Thus indeed that, monks, fish swallowed-hook of the fisherman, misery has incurred, disaster has incurred, according-to-desire-to-be-done-with of the fisherman.

"Suppose, monks, a fisherman would throw a baited hook into a pool of deep water. A certain fish with an eye for bait would swallow it. Thus, monks, the fish that has swallowed the hook of the fisherman has incurred misery, has incurred disaster, to be done with by the fisherman as he desires.

"Evameva kho, bhikkhave, chayime balisā lokasmiṃ anayāya sattānaṃ, vyābādhāya pāṇinaṃ. Katame cha? Santi, bhikkhave, cakkhuviññeyyā rūpā . . . sotaviññeyyā saddā . . . ghānaviññeyyā gandhā . . . jivhāviññeyyā rasā . . . kāyaviññeyyā phoṭṭhabbā . . . manoviññeyyā dhammā iṭṭhā kantā manāpā piyarūpā kāmūpasaṃhitā rajanīyā.

"Just so, monks, six-these hooks in the world for the misery of beings, for the harm of living beings. What six? There are, monks, eye-cognizable forms . . . ear-cognizable sounds . . . nose-cognizable odors . . . tongue-cognizable tastes . . . body-cognizable tactiles . . . mind-cognizable mental objects, wished-for, desired, agreeable, pleasing-nature, sensuality-connected, enticing.

"Just so, monks, these six hooks in the world are for the misery of beings, for the harm of living beings. What six? There are, monks, forms cognizable by the eye . . . sounds cognizable by the ear . . . odors cognizable by the nose . . . tastes cognizable by the tongue . . . tactiles cognizable by the body . . . mental objects cognizable by the mind that are wished for, desired, agreeable, of a pleasing nature, connected with sensuality, enticing.

"Tañce bhikkhu abhinandati abhivadati ajjhosāya tiṭṭhati, ayaṃ vuccati, bhikkhave, 'bhikkhu gilitabaliso mārassa,' anayaṃ āpanno vyasanaṃ āpanno yathākāmakaraṇīyo pāpimato.

"Those-if a monk delights in, welcomes, having held stands, he is called, monks, 'a monk swallowed-bait of Māra,' misery has incurred, disaster has incurred, according-to-desire-to-be-done-with of the Evil One.

"If a monk delights in them, welcomes them, and remains holding to them, he is called, monks, 'a monk who has swallowed the bait of Māra,' who has incurred misery, has incurred disaster, to be done with by the Evil One as he desires.

"Santi ca, bhikkhave, cakkhuviññeyyā rūpā . . . manoviññeyyā dhammā iṭṭhā kantā manāpā piyarūpā kāmūpasaṃhitā rajanīyā. Tañce bhikkhu nābhinandati nābhivadati nājjhosāya tiṭṭhati, ayaṃ vuccati, bhikkhave, 'bhikkhu na gilitabaliso mārassa,' abhedi balisaṃ, paribhedi balisaṃ, na anayaṃ āpanno na vyasanaṃ āpanno na yathākāmakaraṇīyo pāpimato."

"There are, monks, eye-cognizable forms . . . mind-cognizable mental objects, wished-for, desired, agreeable, pleasing-nature, sensuality-connected, enticing. Those-if a monk not-delights in, not-welcomes, not-having held stands, he is called, monks, 'a monk not swallowed-bait of Māra, broke the hook, destroyed the hook,' not misery has incurred, not disaster has incurred, not according-to-desire-to-be-done-with of the Evil One."

"There are, monks, forms cognizable by the eye . . . mental objects cognizable by the mind that are wished for, desired, agreeable, of a pleasing nature, connected with sensuality, enticing. If a monk does not delight in them, does not welcome them, and does not remain holding to them, he is called, monks, 'a monk who has not swallowed the bait of Māra, who broke the hook, who destroyed the hook,' who has not incurred misery, not incurred disaster, who is not to be done with by the Evil One as he desires."

Grammatical explanations

bālisiko (Be: *bāḷisiko*): from *balisa* (Be: *baḷisa*), a fishhook; thus a *bālisika* is "one who uses a fishhook," a fisherman.

āmisagatabalisaṃ: literally, "bait-gone-hook," with *āmisagata* qualifying *balisaṃ*—an idiomatic way of saying "a baited hook."

āmisacakkhu: "with an eye for bait"; a bahubbīhi compound describing *maccho*, the fish.

gilitabaliso: "swallowed the bait"; another bahubbīhi describing *maccho*. The placement of *bālisikassa* after the compound is another inversion of normal word order, probably for special effect.

yathākāmakaraṇīyo: "to be done with as he desires"; a kammadhāraya compound constructed from the adverb *yathākāma* joined to a future passive participle, *karaṇīyo*, describing *maccho*. Again, the placement of *bālisikassa* after the compound is probably for emphasis.

chayime ("six these") = *cha* + *ime*, with the semivowel *-y-* inserted for euphony.

anayāya sattānaṃ, vyābādhāya pāṇinaṃ: "for the misery of beings, for the harm of living beings"; each is a dative followed by a plural genitive.

tañce bhikkhu abhinandati: For *tañ* with a plural sense, see p. 248.

pāpimato: the singular genitive of *pāpimat*, with an instrumental sense, "by the Evil One."

abhedi balisaṃ, paribhedi balisaṃ: "who broke the hook, who destroyed the hook." Each expression consists of an aorist of *bhedeti* (causative of *bhindati*, "breaks")—the second with a prefix—followed by the accusative.

12. Koṭṭhikasutta

Koṭṭhika (SN 35:232 [191]; IV 162–65)

[1. What is the fetter?]

Ekaṃ samayaṃ āyasmā ca sāriputto āyasmā ca mahākoṭṭhiko bārāṇasiyaṃ viharanti isipatane migadāye. Atha kho āyasmā mahākoṭṭhiko sāyanhasamayaṃ paṭisallānā vuṭṭhito yen'āyasmā sāriputto ten'upasaṅkami. Upasaṅkamitvā āyasmatā sāriputtena saddhiṃ sammodi. Sammodanīyaṃ kathaṃ sārāṇīyaṃ vītisāretvā ekamantaṃ nisīdi. Ekamantaṃ nisinno kho āyasmā mahākoṭṭhiko āyasmantaṃ sāriputtaṃ etadavoca: "Kiṃ nu kho, āvuso sāriputta, cakkhu rūpānaṃ saṃyojanaṃ, rūpā cakkhussa saṃyojanaṃ . . . mano dhammānaṃ saṃyojanaṃ, dhammā manassa saṃyojanan"ti?

One occasion the Venerable and Sāriputta, the Venerable and Mahākoṭṭhika, at Bārāṇasī were dwelling, in Isipatana in the deer-park. Then the Venerable Mahākoṭṭhika evening-time from seclusion emerged, where the Venerable Sāriputta, there approached. Having approached, with the Venerable Sāriputta together greeted. Greetings talk cordial having concluded, one-side sat. One-side seated, the Venerable Mahākoṭṭhika to the Venerable Sāriputta this-said: "What, friend Sāriputta, eye of forms the fetter, forms of eye the fetter . . . mind of mental-objects the fetter, mental-objects of mind the fetter?"

On one occasion the Venerable Sāriputta and the Venerable Mahākoṭṭhika were dwelling at Bārāṇasī in Isipatana, in the deer park. Then, in the evening, the Venerable Mahākoṭṭhita emerged from seclusion and approached the Venerable Sāriputta. Having approached, he exchanged greetings with the Venerable Sāriputta. When they had concluded their greetings and cordial talk, he sat down to one side. Seated to one side, the Venerable Mahākoṭṭhita said this to the Venerable Sāriputta: "How is it, friend Sāriputta, is the eye the fetter of forms [or] are forms the fetter of the eye? . . . Is the mind the fetter of mental objects [or] are mental objects the fetter of the mind?"

"Na kho, āvuso koṭṭhika, cakkhu rūpānaṃ saṃyojanaṃ, na rūpā cakkhussa saṃyojanaṃ, yañca tattha tadubhayaṃ paṭicca uppajjati chandarāgo taṃ tattha saṃyojanaṃ. . . . Na mano dhammānaṃ saṃyojanaṃ, na dhammā manassa saṃyojanaṃ, yañca tattha tadubhayaṃ paṭicca uppajjati chandarāgo taṃ tattha saṃyojanaṃ.

"Not, friend Koṭṭhika, the eye of forms the fetter, not forms of the eye the fetter, which-but there those-both in dependence on arises desire-lust, that there the fetter. . . . Not the mind of mental-objects the fetter, not mental-objects of the mind the fetter, which-but there those-both in dependence on arises desire-lust, that there the fetter.

"Friend Koṭṭhita, the eye is not the fetter of forms nor are forms the fetter of the eye, but the desire-and-lust that arises there in dependence on both of these: that is the fetter there. . . . The mind is not the fetter of mental objects nor are mental objects the fetter of the mind, but the desire-and-lust that arises there in dependence on both of these: that is the fetter there.

[2. The simile of the ox]

"Seyyathāpi, āvuso, kāḷo ca balivaddo odāto ca balivaddo ekena dāmena vā yottena vā saṃyuttā assu. Yo nu kho evaṃ vadeyya, 'Kāḷo balivaddo odātassa balivaddassa saṃyojanaṃ, odāto balivaddo kāḷassa balivaddassa saṃyojanan'ti, sammā nu kho so vadamāno vadeyyā"ti?

"Suppose, friend, a black and ox, a white and ox, by one harness or yoke or yoked-together were. One who thus would say, 'The black ox of the white ox the fetter, the white ox of the black ox the fetter,' rightly he speaking would speak?"

"Suppose, friend, a black ox and a white ox were yoked together by a single harness or yoke. If one were to say, 'The black ox is the fetter of the white ox; the white ox is the fetter of the black ox,' would one speaking thus speak rightly?"

"No h'etaṃ, āvuso. Na kho, āvuso, kāḷo balivaddo odātassa balivaddassa saṃyojanaṃ, na odāto balivaddo kāḷassa balivaddassa saṃyojanaṃ, yena ca kho te ekena dāmena vā yottena vā saṃyuttā taṃ tattha saṃyojanaṃ."

"Not indeed this, friend. Not, friend, the black ox of the white ox the fetter, not the white ox of the black ox the fetter, by which but they one harness or yoke or yoked-together, that there the fetter."

"No indeed, friend. The black ox, friend, is not the fetter of the white ox, nor is the white ox the fetter of the black ox, but rather the single harness or yoke by which the two are yoked together: that is the fetter there."

"Evameva kho, āvuso, na cakkhu rūpānaṃ saṃyojanaṃ, na rūpā cakkhussa saṃyojanaṃ, yañca tattha tadubhayaṃ paṭicca uppajjati chandarāgo taṃ tattha saṃyojanaṃ. . . . Na mano dhammānaṃ saṃyojanaṃ, na dhammā manassa saṃyojanaṃ, yañca tattha tadubhayaṃ paṭicca uppajjati chandarāgo taṃ tattha saṃyojanaṃ.

"Just so, friend, not the eye of forms the fetter, not forms of the eye the fetter, which-but there those-both in dependence on arises desire-lust, that there the fetter. . . . Not the mind of mental-objects the fetter, not mental-objects of the mind the fetter, which-but there those-both in dependence on arises desire-lust, that there the fetter.

"So too, friend, the eye is not the fetter of forms nor are forms the fetter of the eye, but the desire-and-lust that arises there in dependence on both of these: that is the fetter there.... The mind is not the fetter of mental objects nor are mental objects the fetter of the mind, but the desire-and-lust that arises there in dependence on both of these: that is the fetter there.

[3. A supportive counter-argument]

"Cakkhu vā, āvuso, rūpānaṃ saṃyojanaṃ abhavissa, rūpā vā cakkhussa saṃyojanaṃ, nayidaṃ brahmacariyavāso paññāyetha sammā dukkhakkhayāya. Yasmā ca kho, āvuso, na cakkhu rūpānaṃ saṃyojanaṃ, na rūpā cakkhussa saṃyojanaṃ, yañca tattha tadubhayaṃ paṭicca uppajjati chandarāgo taṃ tattha saṃyojanaṃ, tasmā brahmacariyavāso paññāyati sammā dukkhakkhayāya....

"The eye or, friend, of forms the fetter would be, forms or of the eye the fetter, not this spiritual-life-living would be discerned complete for suffering-destruction. Since but, friend, not the eye of forms the fetter, not forms of the eye the fetter, which-but there those-both in dependence on arises desire-lust, that there the fetter, therefore spiritual-life-living is discerned complete for suffering-destruction. . . .

"If, friend, the eye were the fetter of forms or if forms were the fetter of the eye, this living of the spiritual life would not be discerned for the complete destruction of suffering. But since the eye is not the fetter of forms nor are forms the fetter of the eye—but the desire-and-lust that arises there in dependence on both is the fetter there—the living of the spiritual life is discerned for the complete destruction of suffering...

"Mano vā, āvuso, dhammānaṃ saṃyojanaṃ abhavissa, dhammā vā manassa saṃyojanaṃ, nayidaṃ brahmacariyavāso paññāyetha sammā dukkhakkhayāya. Yasmā ca kho, āvuso, na mano dhammānaṃ saṃyojanaṃ, na dhammā manassa saṃyojanaṃ, yañca tattha tadubhayaṃ paṭicca uppajjati

chandarāgo taṃ tattha saṃyojanaṃ, tasmā brahmacariyavāso paññāyati sammā dukkhakkhayāya.

"The mind or, friend, of mental-objects the fetter would be, mental-objects or of the mind the fetter, not-this spiritual-life-living would be discerned complete for suffering-destruction. Since but, friend, not the mind of mental-objects the fetter, not mental-objects of the mind the fetter, which-but there those-both in dependence on arises desire-lust, that there the fetter, therefore spiritual-life-living is discerned complete for suffering-destruction.

"If the mind were the fetter of mental objects or if mental objects were the fetter of the mind, this living of the spiritual life would not be discerned for the complete destruction of suffering. But since the mind is not the fetter of mental objects nor are mental objects the fetter of the mind—but the desire-and-lust that arises there in dependence on both is the fetter there—the living of the spiritual life is discerned for the complete destruction of suffering.

[4. Another method]

"Iminā p'etaṃ, āvuso, pariyāyena veditabbaṃ yathā na cakkhu rūpānaṃ saṃyojanaṃ, na rūpā cakkhussa saṃyojanaṃ, yañca tattha tadubhayaṃ paṭicca uppajjati chandarāgo taṃ tattha saṃyojanaṃ . . . na mano dhammānaṃ saṃyojanaṃ, na dhammā manassa saṃyojanaṃ, yañca tattha tadubhayaṃ paṭicca uppajjati chandarāgo taṃ tattha saṃyojanaṃ.

"By this too this, friend, by method can-be-understood how not the eye of forms the fetter, not forms of the eye the fetter, which-but there those-both in dependence on arises desire-lust, that there the fetter . . . not the mind of mental-objects the fetter, not mental-objects of the mind the fetter, which-but there those-both in dependence on arises desire-lust, that there the fetter.

"In this way too, friend, it can be understood how the eye is not the fetter of forms nor forms the fetter of the eye, but the desire-and-lust that arises there in dependence on both is the fetter there . . . how the mind is not the fetter of mental objects nor mental objects the fetter of the mind, but the desire-and-lust that arises there in dependence on both: that is the fetter there.

"Saṃvijjati kho, āvuso, bhagavato cakkhu. Passati bhagavā cakkhunā rūpaṃ. Chandarāgo bhagavato natthi. Suvimuttacitto bhagavā. Saṃvijjati kho, āvuso, bhagavato sotaṃ. Suṇāti bhagavā sotena saddaṃ. Chandarāgo bhagavato natthi. Suvimuttacitto bhagavā. Saṃvijjati kho, āvuso, bhagavato ghānaṃ. Ghāyati bhagavā ghānena gandhaṃ. Chandarāgo bhagavato natthi. Suvimuttacitto bhagavā. Saṃvijjati kho, āvuso, bhagavato jivhā. Sāyati bhagavā jivhāya rasaṃ. Chandarāgo bhagavato natthi. Suvimuttacitto bhagavā. Saṃvijjati kho, āvuso, bhagavato kāyo. Phusati bhagavā kāyena phoṭṭhabbaṃ. Chandarāgo bhagavato natthi. Suvimuttacitto bhagavā. Saṃvijjati kho, āvuso, bhagavato mano. Vijānāti bhagavā manasā dhammaṃ. Chandarāgo bhagavato natthi. Suvimuttacitto bhagavā.

"There exists, friend, of the Blessed One the eye. Sees the Blessed One with the eye a form. Desire-lust for the Blessed One there is not; well-liberated-mind the Blessed One. There exists, friend, of the Blessed One the ear. Hears the Blessed One with the ear a sound. Desire-lust for the Blessed One there is not; well-liberated-mind the Blessed One. There exists, friend, of the Blessed One the nose. Smells the Blessed One with the nose an odor. Desire-lust for the Blessed One there is not; well-liberated-mind the Blessed One. There exists, friend, of the Blessed One the tongue. Tastes the Blessed One with the tongue a taste. Desire-lust for the Blessed One there is not; well-liberated-mind the Blessed One. There exists, friend, of the Blessed One the body. Feels the Blessed One with the body a tactile-object. Desire-lust for the Blessed One there is not; well-liberated-mind the Blessed One. There exists, friend, of the Blessed One the mind. Cognizes the Blessed One with the mind a mental-object. Desire-lust for the Blessed One there is not; well-liberated-mind the Blessed One.

"There exists, friend, in the Blessed One the eye, the Blessed One sees a form with the eye, but for the Blessed One there is no desire-and-lust; the Blessed One is well liberated in mind. There exists in the Blessed One the ear, the Blessed One hears a sound with the ear, but for the Blessed One there is no desire-and-lust; the Blessed One is well liberated in mind. There exists in the Blessed One the nose, the Blessed One smells an odor with the nose, but for the Blessed One there is no desire-and-lust; the Blessed One is well liberated in mind. There exists in the Blessed One the tongue, the Blessed One experiences a taste with the tongue, but for the Blessed One there is no desire-and-lust; the Blessed One is well liberated in mind. There exists in the Blessed One the body, the Blessed One feels a tactile object with the body, but for the Blessed One there is no desire-and-lust; the Blessed One is well liberated in mind. There exists in the Blessed One the mind, the Blessed One cognizes a mental object with the mind, but for the Blessed One there is no desire-and-lust; the Blessed One is well liberated in mind.

"Iminā kho etaṃ, āvuso, pariyāyena veditabbaṃ yathā na cakkhu rūpānaṃ saṃyojanaṃ, na rūpā cakkhussa saṃyojanaṃ, yañca tattha tadubhayaṃ paṭicca uppajjati chandarāgo taṃ tattha saṃyojanaṃ . . . na mano dhammānaṃ saṃyojanaṃ, na dhammā manassa saṃyojanaṃ; yañca tattha tadubhayaṃ paṭicca uppajjati chandarāgo taṃ tattha saṃyojanan"ti.

"By this this, friend, by method can-be-understood how not the eye of forms the fetter, not forms of the eye the fetter, which-but there those-both in dependence on arises desire-lust, that there the fetter . . . not the mind of mental-objects the fetter, not mental-objects of the mind the fetter, which-but there those-both in dependence on arises desire-lust, that there the fetter."

"In this way, friend, it can be understood how the eye is not the fetter of forms nor forms the fetter of the eye, but the desire-and-lust that arises there in dependence on both is the fetter there . . . how the mind is not the fetter of mental objects nor mental objects the fetter of the mind, but the desire-and-lust that arises there in dependence on both: that is the fetter there."

Grammatical explanations

[1. What is the fetter?]

sāyanhasamayaṃ: see p. 186.

paṭisallānā vuṭṭhito: "emerged from seclusion"; an ablative followed by a past participle agreeing with the nominative subject, *mahākoṭṭhiko*.

āyasmatā sāriputtena saddhiṃ sammodi: "he exchanged greetings with the Venerable Sāriputta." In this stock formula, the verb *sammodi*, a third-person singular aorist, is accompanied by the indeclinable *saddhiṃ*, "together with," taking the instrumental case of the person greeted.

sammodanīyaṃ kathaṃ sārāṇīyaṃ vītisāretvā: "When they had concluded their greetings and cordial talk." *Kathaṃ*, the feminine accusative of *kathā*, "talk," is the object of the absolutive, *vītisāretvā*, "having concluded." The two words describing *kathaṃ*, *sammodanīyaṃ* and *sārāṇīyaṃ*, are future passive participles functioning as adjectives. On *sārāṇīya*, PED says "the question of derivation is still unsettled" and offers several theories.

kiṃ nu kho: Here the interrogative formation does not directly pose a question but shows that the speaker is inquiring about alternatives. In each pair of alternatives, the verb *hoti* should be understood.

yañca tattha tadubhayaṃ paṭicca uppajjati chandarāgo: The relative *yañ* (*yaṃ* before *ca*) is problematic since in relation to *chandarāgo* the masculine *yo* would have been expected. It is possible that *yaṃ* here is an example of the general or "empty" relative, serving merely as a marker of a relative clause.[131] Alternatively, *yaṃ* may have entered this passage through the influence of the *Satipaṭṭhāna Sutta*, where we find *yañca tadubhayaṃ paṭicca uppajjati saṃyojanaṃ*. There *yaṃ* qualifies *saṃyojanaṃ*, so the neuter is to be expected, but here it seems the pronoun should be masculine in agreement with *chandarāgo*. *Tadubhayaṃ* is an accusative object of the absolutive *paṭicca*; it is a sandhi of *taṃ* and *ubhayaṃ*, "both of them," that is, both the eye and forms. *Chandarāgo* is the nominative subject of the verb *uppajjati*, which precedes it by inversion of the normal word order. *Chandarāgo* is a dvanda, with the two components so close in meaning that the compound is declined as a nominative singular. The commentaries explain *chanda* as "weak lust" and *rāga* as "strong lust."[132]

taṃ tattha saṃyojanaṃ: "that there [is] the fetter." *Taṃ*, which here modifies *saṃyojanaṃ*, is the demonstrative correlate of *yaṃ* in the relative clause.

[2. The simile of the ox]

ekena dāmena vā yottena vā: "by a single harness or yoke"; an instrumental construction, with *ekena* qualifying both *dāmena* and *yottena*.

saṃyuttā assu: "were yoked together"; a past participle followed by the third-person plural optative of *atthi* functioning as an auxiliary verb; the optative is used because this is an imaginary example.

131. On this use of *yaṃ*, see Warder 291.

132. Mp IV 190,1–3: *Chandarāgo ti evaṃ . . . dubbalarāgo ca balavarāgo ca uppajjati.*

nu kho: Although this interrogative phrase occurs twice in the sentence, it seems the second occurrence would be sufficient.

sammā nu kho so vadamāno vadeyya: "would one thus speaking speak rightly?" This stock phrase uses forms of the verb *vadati* twice. The middle-voice present participle *vadamāno* belongs with the statement that is quoted, while *vadeyya*, "would speak," qualified by *sammā*, "rightly," poses the question whether the statement is correct.

yena ca kho te ekena dāmena vā yottena vā saṃyuttā taṃ tattha saṃyojanaṃ: The relative instrumental *yena* qualifies *ekena dāmena yottena* and is correlated with the nominative *taṃ saṃyojanaṃ*. The connective *ca kho* is used in the disjunctive sense, "but rather."

[3. A supportive counter-argument]

abhavissa: the conditional (or hypothetical) form of *bhavati*, here third-person singular. See p. 68 and p. 159. The conditional *abhavissa* is also implicit in the next clause, *rūpā vā cakkhussa saṃyojanaṃ*.

nayidaṃ: a sandhi of *na* and *idaṃ*, with *-y-* inserted for euphony. The demonstrative *idaṃ* "this" does not agree in gender with *-vāso*, the noun it qualifies.

paññāyetha: "would be discerned"; a third-person singular optative of *paññāyati* in the middle voice, here negated by *na*.

sammā dukkhakkhayāya: "for the complete destruction of suffering." *Dukkhakkhayāya* is a genitive tappurisa in the dative case highlighting the purpose of *brahmacariyavāso*, a genitive tappurisa in the nominative. On *brahmacariya*, see p. 180, note 105.

yasmā . . . tasmā: This indicates the actual situation, in contrast to the hypothetical proposed by the preceding sentence.

[4. Another method]

iminā p'etaṃ, āvuso, pariyāyena veditabbaṃ: "in this way too, friend, it can be understood." The demonstrative *iminā* qualifies *pariyāyena*. The sandhi formation *p'etaṃ* should be resolved into *pi etaṃ*, where *etaṃ*, the pronoun indicating the point being conveyed, belongs with *veditabbaṃ*, "can be understood."

saṃvijjati kho, āvuso, bhagavato cakkhu: "there exists, friend, in the Blessed One the eye." The verb is placed first for emphasis.

passati bhagavā cakkhunā rūpaṃ: "the Blessed One sees a form with the eye"; another inversion of normal word order with the verb coming first.

suvimuttacitto: "well liberated in mind"; a bahubbīhi qualifying *bhagavā*.

13. Dārukkhandhopamasutta

The Simile of the Log (SN 35:241 [200]; IV 179–81)

[1. The log on the Ganges]

Ekaṃ samayaṃ bhagavā kosambiyaṃ viharati gaṅgāya nadiyā tīre. Addasā kho bhagavā mahantaṃ dārukkhandhaṃ gaṅgāya nadiyā sotena vuyhamānaṃ. Disvāna bhikkhū āmantesi: "Passatha no tumhe, bhikkhave, amuṃ mahantaṃ dārukkhandhaṃ gaṅgāya nadiyā sotena vuyhamānan"ti? — "Evaṃ, bhante."

One occasion the Blessed One at Kosambī was dwelling, of Ganges River on the bank. Saw the Blessed One a great wooden-log of the Ganges River by the stream being swept along. Having seen, the monks he addressed: "See you, monks, that great wooden-log of the Ganges River by the stream being swept along?" — "Yes, Bhante."

On one occasion the Blessed One was dwelling at Kosambī on the bank of the Ganges River. The Blessed One saw a great log being swept along by the stream of the Ganges River. Having seen this, he addressed the monks: "Do you see, monks, that great log being swept along by the stream of the Ganges River?" — "Yes, Bhante."

"Sace so, bhikkhave, dārukkhandho na orimaṃ tīraṃ upagacchati, na pārimaṃ tīraṃ upagacchati, na majjhe saṃsīdissati, na thale ussīdissati, na manussaggāho gahessati, na amanussaggāho gahessati, na āvaṭṭaggāho gahessati, na antopūti bhavissati, evaṃ hi so, bhikkhave, dārukkhandho samuddaninno bhavissati samuddapoṇo samuddapabbhāro. Taṃ kissa hetu? Samuddaninno, bhikkhave, gaṅgāya nadiyā soto samuddapoṇo samuddapabbhāro.

"If that, monks, wooden-log not the near bank approaches, not the far bank approaches, not in the middle will sink, not on high ground will be cast-up, not human-grasp will grab, not non-human grasp will grab, not whirlpool-grasp will grab, not inward-rotten will become, thus indeed that, monks, wooden-log ocean-slanting will be, ocean-sloping, ocean-inclining. That for what reason? Ocean-slanting, monks, of the Ganges river the stream, ocean-sloping, ocean-inclining.

"If, monks, that log does not approach the near bank, does not approach the far bank, will not sink in the middle, will not be cast up on high ground; if humans will not grab it, if non-humans will not grab it, if whirlpools will not grab it, if it will not become inwardly rotten, in such a case, monks, that log will slant toward the ocean, slope toward the ocean, incline toward the ocean. For what reason? Because, monks, the stream of the Ganges River slants toward the ocean, slopes toward the ocean, inclines toward the ocean.

[2. Instruction to the monks]

"Evameva kho, bhikkhave, sace tumhepi na orimaṃ tīraṃ upagacchatha, na pārimaṃ tīraṃ upagacchatha, na majjhe saṃsīdissatha, na thale ussīdissatha, na manussaggāho gahessati, na amanussaggāho gahessati, na āvaṭṭaggāho gahessati, na antopūtī bhavissatha, evaṃ tumhe, bhikkhave, nibbānaninnā bhavissatha nibbānapoṇā nibbānapabbhārā. Taṃ kissa hetu? Nibbānaninnā, bhikkhave, sammādiṭṭhi nibbānapoṇā nibbānapabbhārā"ti.

"Just so, monks, if you-too not the near bank approach, not the far bank approach, not in the middle will sink, not on high ground will be cast-up, not human-grasp will grab, not non-human grasp will grab, not whirlpool-grasp will grab, not inward-rotten will become, thus you, monks, nibbāna-slanting will be, nibbāna-sloping, nibbāna-inclining. That for what reason? Nibbāna-slanting, monks, right view, nibbāna-sloping, nibbāna-inclining."

"Just so, monks, if you too do not approach the near bank, do not approach the far bank, will not sink in the middle, will not be cast up on high ground; if humans will not grab you, if non-humans will not grab you, if whirlpools will not grab you, if you will not become inwardly rotten, in such a case, monks, you will slant toward nibbāna, slope toward nibbāna, incline toward nibbāna. For what reason? Because, monks, right view slants toward nibbāna, slopes toward nibbāna, inclines toward nibbāna."

[3. The monk's questions]
Evaṃ vutte, aññataro bhikkhu bhagavantaṃ etadavoca: "Kiṃ nu kho, bhante, orimaṃ tīraṃ, kiṃ pārimaṃ tīraṃ, ko majjhe saṃsādo, ko thale ussādo, ko manussaggāho, ko amanussaggāho, ko āvaṭṭaggāho, ko antopūtibhāvo"ti?

Such said, a certain monk to the Blessed One this-said: "What, Bhante, the near bank, what the far bank, what in the middle sinking, what on high ground cast-up, what human-grasp, what non-human-grasp, what whirlpool-grasp, what inward-rottenness?"

When such was said, a certain monk said to the Blessed One: "What, Bhante, is the near bank, what is the far bank, what is sinking in the middle, what is being cast up on high ground, what is the human grasp, what is the non-human grasp, what is the grasp of a whirlpool, what is inward rottenness?"

"'Orimaṃ tīran'ti kho, bhikkhu, chann'etaṃ ajjhattikānaṃ āyatanānaṃ adhivacanaṃ. 'Pārimaṃ tīran'ti kho, bhikkhu, chann'etaṃ bāhirānaṃ āyatanānaṃ adhivacanaṃ. 'Majjhe saṃsādo'ti kho, bhikkhu, nandīrāgass'etaṃ adhivacanaṃ. 'Thale ussādo'ti kho, bhikkhu, asmimānass'etaṃ adhivacanaṃ.

"'The near bank,' monk, of the six this internal sense-bases a designation. 'The far bank,' monk, of the six this external sense-bases a designation. 'In the middle sinking,' monk, of delight-lust this a designation. 'On high ground cast-up,' monk, of 'I am'-conceit this a designation.

"'The near bank,' monk: this is a designation for the six internal sense bases. 'The far bank,' monk: this is a designation for the six external sense bases. 'Sinking in the middle,' monk: this is a designation for delight and lust. 'Being cast up on high ground,' monk: this is a designation for the conceit 'I am.'

"Katamo ca, bhikkhu, manussaggāho? Idha, bhikkhu, gihīhi saṃsaṭṭho viharati sahanandī sahasokī, sukhitesu sukhito, dukkhitesu dukkhito, uppannesu kiccakaraṇīyesu attanā tesu yogaṃ āpajjati. Ayaṃ vuccati, bhikkhu, 'manussaggāho.'

"What and, monk, the human-grasp? Here, monk, with laypeople bonded dwells, together-delighting, together-sorrowing, among the happy happy, among the miserable miserable, in arisen duties-tasks by himself in those exertion incurs. This is called, monks, the 'human-grasp.'

"And what, monk, is the human grasp? Here, monk, [a monk] dwells bonded with laypeople, delighting together, sorrowing together, happy when they are happy, miserable when they are miserable; when duties and tasks have arisen [for those laypeople], he exerts himself in them. This is called, monks, the 'human grasp.'

"Katamo ca, bhikkhu, amanussaggāho? Idha, bhikkhu, ekacco aññataraṃ devanikāyaṃ paṇidhāya brahmacariyaṃ carati: 'Iminā'haṃ sīlena vā vatena vā tapena vā brahmacariyena vā devo vā bhavissāmi devaññataro vā'ti. Ayaṃ vuccati, bhikkhu, 'amanussaggāho.' 'Āvaṭṭaggāho'ti kho, bhikkhu, pañcann'etaṃ kāmaguṇānaṃ adhivacanaṃ.

"What and, monk, the non-human grasp? Here, monk, someone a certain deva-company having wished, the spiritual-life lives: 'By this I good-behavior or by observance or by austerity or by spiritual-life or, a deva or will become a deva-certain one or.' This is called, monk, the 'non-human grasp.' 'The whirlpool-grasp,' monk, of the five this sensual-pleasure-objects a designation.

"And what, monk, is the non-human grasp? Here, monk, someone lives the spiritual life, having wished for [rebirth into] a certain company of devas: 'By this good behavior or observance or austerity or spiritual life I will become a deva or a certain one among the devas.' This is called, monk, the 'non-human grasp.' 'The whirlpool grasp,' monk: this is a designation for the five objects of sensual pleasure.

"Katamo ca, bhikkhu, antopūtibhāvo? Idha, bhikkhu, ekacco dussīlo hoti pāpadhammo asucisaṅkassarasamācāro paṭicchannakammanto assamaṇo samaṇapaṭiñño abrahmacārī brahmacāripaṭiñño antopūti avassuto kasambujāto. Ayaṃ vuccati, bhikkhu, 'antopūtibhāvo'"ti.

"What and, monk, inward-rottenness? Here, monk, someone bad-behavior is, evil-nature, impure-suspect-behavior, concealed-action, not-ascetic ascetic-claim, not-celibate celibate-claim, inwardly-rotten, corrupt, rubbish-become. This is called, monk, 'inward-rottenness.'"

"And what, monk, is inward rottenness? Here, monk, someone is of bad behavior, of an evil nature, of impure suspect behavior, concealed in his action, not an ascetic but claiming to be an ascetic, not celibate but claiming to be celibate, inwardly rotten, corrupt, become rubbish. This is called, monk, 'inward rottenness.'"

[4. The cowherd Nanda]

Tena kho pana samayena nando gopālako bhagavato avidūre ṭhito hoti. Atha kho nando gopālako bhagavantaṃ etadavoca: "Ahaṃ kho, bhante, na orimaṃ tīraṃ upagacchāmi, na pārimaṃ tīraṃ upagacchāmi, na majjhe saṃsīdissāmi, na thale ussīdissāmi, na maṃ manussaggāho gahessati, na amanussaggāho gahessati, na āvaṭṭaggāho gahessati, na antopūti bhavissāmi. Labheyyāhaṃ, bhante, bhagavato santike pabbajjaṃ, labheyyaṃ upasampadan"ti.

By that occasion Nanda the cowherd of the Blessed One not-far stood was. Then Nanda the cowherd to the Blessed One this-said: "I, Bhante, not near bank approach, not far bank approach, not in the middle will sink, not on high ground will be cast-up, not me human-grasp will grab, not non-human grasp will grab, not whirlpool-grasp will grab, not inward-rotten will become. Would obtain-I, Bhante, of the Blessed One in the presence the going-forth, would obtain ordination."

Now on that occasion the cowherd Nanda was standing not far from the Blessed One. Then the cowherd Nanda said this to the Blessed One: "Bhante, I do not approach the near bank, I do not approach the far bank, I will not sink in the middle, I will not be cast up on high ground; humans will not grab me, non-humans will not grab me, a whirlpool will not grab me, I will not become inwardly rotten. Bhante, I would obtain the going forth in the presence of the Blessed One; I would obtain ordination."

"Tena hi tvaṃ, nanda, sāmikānaṃ gāvo niyyādehī"ti.

"Gamissanti, bhante, gāvo vacchagiddhiniyo"ti.

"Niyyādeh'eva tvaṃ, nanda, sāmikānaṃ gāvo"ti.

"In that case you, Nanda, to the owners the cows return."
"Will go, Bhante, the cows calves-longing-for."
"Return indeed you, Nanda, to the owners the cows."

"In that case, Nanda, return the cows to the owners."
"The cows will go, Bhante, longing for their calves."
"Return the cows to the owners, Nanda."

Atha kho nando gopālako sāmikānaṃ gāvo niyyādetvā yena bhagavā ten'upasaṅkami. Upasaṅkamitvā bhagavantaṃ etadavoca: "Niyyāditā, bhante, sāmikānaṃ gāvo. Labheyyāhaṃ, bhante, bhagavato santike pabbajjaṃ, labheyyaṃ upasampadan"ti.

Then Nanda the cowherd to the owners the cows having returned, where the Blessed One, there he approached. Having approached, to the Blessed One this-said: "Returned, Bhante, to the owners the cows. Would obtain I, Bhante, of the Blessed One in presence the going-forth, would obtain ordination."

Then the cowherd Nanda, having returned the cows to the owners, approached the Blessed One. Having approached, he said this to the Blessed One: "Bhante, the cows have been returned to the owners. Bhante, I would obtain the going forth in the presence of the Blessed One; I would obtain ordination."

Alattha kho nando gopālako bhagavato santike pabbajjaṃ, alattha upasampadaṃ. Acirūpasampanno ca pan'āyasmā nando eko vūpakaṭṭho appamatto ātāpī pahitatto viharanto nacirass'eva yass'atthāya kulaputtā sammadeva agārasmā anagāriyaṃ pabbajanti tadanuttaraṃ brahmacariyapariyosānaṃ diṭṭhe'va dhamme sayaṃ abhiññā sacchikatvā upasampajja viharati. "Khīṇā jāti, vusitaṃ brahmacariyaṃ, kataṃ karaṇīyaṃ, nāparaṃ itthattāyā"ti abbhaññāsi. Aññataro ca panāyasmā nando arahataṃ ahosī ti.

Obtained Nanda the cowherd of the Blessed One in the presence the going-forth, obtained ordination. Not-long-ordained and, the Venerable Nanda alone, withdrawn, heedful, ardent, resolute dwelling, not long indeed of which for sake of family-sons rightly from home to homelessness go forth, that-unsurpassed spiritual-life-goal in-present-life by himself having directly known, having realized, having entered, dwelled. "Finished birth, lived the spiritual-life, done what-is-to-be-done, not-further for such-a-state," directly knew. A certain one and the Venerable Nanda of the arahants was.

The cowherd Nanda obtained the going forth in the presence of the Blessed One; he obtained ordination. And not long after he was ordained, dwelling alone, withdrawn, heedful, ardent, and resolute, the Venerable Nanda, in no long time, by realizing it for himself with direct knowledge, in this present life entered and dwelled in that unsurpassed goal of the spiritual life for the sake of which young people rightly go forth from the household life into homelessness. He directly knew: "Finished is birth, the spiritual life has been lived, what had to be done has been done, there is no further for this state of being." And the Venerable Nanda became one of the arahants.

Grammatical explanations

[1. The log on the Ganges]

kosambiyaṃ viharati gaṅgāya nadiyā tīre: "was dwelling at Kosambī on the bank of the Ganges River." See p. 213.

addasā: a third-person singular a-aorist of **dassati*, "sees."[133]

vuyhamānaṃ: "being swept along"; a passive present participle of *vuyhati*, passive of *vahati*, "carries, conveys, bears," with metathesis (transposition of letters) *-hy-* > *-yh-* (see Geiger §49.1).

disvāna: an absolutive of **dassati*, more elegant than the usual *disvā*.

passatha: the second-person plural imperative of *passati*.

no: equivalent to *nu*, the interrogative particle.[134]

amuṃ: masculine singular accusative of the demonstrative pronoun *asu* (Duroiselle §308; Perniola §41), "that," in agreement with *dārukhandhaṃ*.

sace: the conditional "if," an indeclinable. The conditional here takes the verbs in the future tense both in the antecedent and the consequent.

upagacchati: Since the verbs to follow are of the future tense, this verb too, though present tense in form, seems to be used in a future sense.

na manussaggāho gahessati: a construction in which a noun, *gāha*, is paired

133. See p. 51, note 56.

134. Spk II 139,19; Mp IV 65,4: *Passatha no ti passatha nu.*

with its cognate verb *gahessati*, future of *gaṇhāti*. To avoid awkwardness, I render it in accordance with normal English diction: "if humans will not grab it." And so for the following clauses.

antopūti: a kammadhāraya compound consisting of the adverb *anto*, "inside, inwardly," and the adjective *pūti*, "rotten" (see Perniola §132). It is a masculine nominative in agreement with *dārukkhandho*.

samuddaninno samuddapoṇo samuddapabbhāro: "slant toward the ocean, slope toward the ocean, incline toward the ocean." The three compounds function as adjectives in agreement with *dārukkhandho*, and just below with *soto*.

[2. Instruction to the monks]

upagacchatha, saṃsīdissatha, ussīdissatha, bhavissatha: Since the subject of these verbs is the second-person plural *tumhe*, referring to the monks, the verbs are second-person plurals. Again, *upagacchatha* seems to be a present form used with a future sense.

nibbānaninnā nibbānapoṇā nibbānapabbhārā: The three compounds are here masculine plurals agreeing with *tumhe*, and just below, feminine singulars agreeing with *sammādiṭṭhi*.

[3. The monk's questions]

ko majjhe saṃsādo, ko thale ussādo: "what is sinking in the middle, what is being cast up on high ground?" The nominatives correspond to the verbs *saṃsīdati* and *ussīdati*.

antopūtibhāvo: "inward rottenness." At the end of a compound *bhāva*, "state" or "condition," turns an adjective or concrete noun into an abstract noun. It thus functions somewhat like *-ness* or *-ship* in English—for example, "softness" or "ownership."

chann'etaṃ ajjhattikānaṃ āyatanānaṃ adhivacanaṃ: "this is a designation for the six internal sense bases." *Chann'etaṃ* is a sandhi of *channaṃ* and *etaṃ*, where *channaṃ*, the genitive of *cha*, "six," qualifies *ajjhattikānaṃ āyatanānaṃ*, and the nominative *etaṃ* qualifies *adhivacanaṃ*.

asmimāna: see p. 218.

sahanandī sahasokī: "delighting together, sorrowing together"; compounds describing the monk, consisting of the indeclinable *saha*, "together with," and either *nandī*, "delighting," or *sokī*, "sorrowing"—the adjectival forms of *nanda* and *soka*.

sukhitesu sukhito, dukkhitesu dukkhito: "happy when they are happy, miserable when they are miserable." The nominatives qualify the monk, the locative plurals the laypeople. The locative plurals may be locative absolutes, with the subject *tesu* understood, but they may also be simple locatives, "among those who are happy," and "among those who are miserable."

uppannesu kiccakaraṇīyesu: "in arisen duties and tasks." Both *kicca* and *karaṇīya*, future passive participles of *karoti*, can be used as nouns, as I have done here.

attanā tesu yogaṃ āpajjati: "he exerts himself in them," or, more literally, "on his own he undertakes exertion in them." The instrumental, *attanā*, is often used in the sense of "on one's own, by oneself, on one's own initiative."

paṇidhāya: absolutive of *paṇidahati*, "wishes, aspires for."

imināhaṃ: a sandhi of *iminā* and *ahaṃ*. *Iminā* qualifies *sīlena* and the following terms.

devo vā bhavissāmi devaññataro vā: "I will become a deva or a certain one among the devas." The two alternatives seem redundant, but the commentaries explain *devo* to mean a powerful deity and *devaññataro* "one among the less powerful deities."[135]

pañcann'etaṃ kāmaguṇānaṃ adhivacanaṃ: "this is a designation for the five objects of sensual pleasure." The genitive *pañcannaṃ* qualifies *kāmaguṇānaṃ*, and *etaṃ* qualifies *adhivacanaṃ*. The commentaries explain *kāmaguṇa* thus: "*Kāma* has the meaning of what is to be desired; *guṇa*, the meaning of binding."[136]

pāpadhammo: "of an evil nature"; a bahubbīhi compound describing the person (*ekacco*), with *-dhamma* in the sense of "character, nature."

asucisaṅkassarasamācāro: "of impure suspect behavior"; another bahubbīhi describing the person. The derivation of *saṅkassara* is obscure, but the Saṃyutta commentary explains *saṅkassarasamācāro* as meaning "behavior to be remembered with suspicion by others."[137]

135. See for example Ps II 69,15–17: *Devo vā bhavissāmī ti mahesakkhadevo vā bhavissāmi. Devaññataro vāpi appesakkhadevesu vā aññataro.*

136. Sv II 403,8 and Ps II 55,31 both say: *Kāmaguṇā ti kāmayitabbaṭṭhena kāmā, bandhanaṭṭhena guṇā.*

137. Spk III 42,10–12: *Parehi saṅkāya saritabbasamācāro.*

paṭicchannakammanto: "concealed in his action"; still a third bahubbīhi, signifying that this person hides his evil actions.

samaṇapaṭiñño, brahmacāripaṭiñño: Both are bahubbīhis indicating that this person makes false claims to be, respectively, an ascetic and a celibate.

avassuto: "corrupt." The word is derived from the verb *savati*, "flows" (from which *āsava* is also derived), with prefix *ava-* suggesting a downward direction. Perhaps the sense is that the person is "oozing" or "leaking" with defilements.

kasambujāto: a compound of *kasambu*, "rubbish," and *-jāta*, "having such a nature."

[4. The cowherd Nanda]

upagacchāmi, saṃsīdissāmi, ussīdissāmi: The verbs here are first-person forms. Again, *upagacchāmi* is a present-tense form, but used with a future sense.

labheyyāhaṃ: a sandhi of *labheyyaṃ* and *ahaṃ*. *Labheyyaṃ* is the first-person singular optative used to make a polite request.

pabbajjaṃ, upasampadaṃ: two accusatives, the objects of *labheyyaṃ*. These are two stages in monastic ordination. *Pabbajjā*, "the going forth," is the initial entry upon the homeless life; *upasampadā* is full admission into the monastic community.

niyyādehi: "give back, return"; the second-person singular imperative of *niyyādeti*.[138]

vacchagiddhiniyo: "longing [for] calves"; an accusative tappurisa compound describing the cows, *gāvo*, plural of *go*. *Giddha* is greed; *giddhin*, "greedy for, longing for," is the stem form, and *giddhiniyo* its feminine plural, taking its object *vaccha* as an implicit accusative.

niyyāditā: the past participle of *niyyādeti*, plural in agreement with *gāvo*.

alattha: a third-person singular aorist of *labhati*.

acirūpasampanno: "not long after he was ordained"; a compound of *acira* and *upasampanno*, with lengthening of *-u-* through sandhi.

eko vūpakaṭṭho appamatto ātāpī pahitatto viharanto: For this and the following, see pp. 178–79.

138. I follow here the reading of Ee.

14. Vīṇopamasutta

The Simile of the Lute (SN 35:246 [205]; IV 195–98)

[*In the first part of this discourse, the Buddha urges monks and nuns*[139] *to restrain the mind whenever "desire or lust or hatred or delusion or aversion" arise toward any sense object. Having illustrated the training of the mind with the simile of a bull that has to be beaten so that it does not eat the barley growing in a barley field, he continues:*] *"Evameva kho, bhikkhave, yato kho bhikkhuno chasu phassāyatanesu cittaṃ udājitaṃ*[140] *hoti sudājitaṃ, ajjhattameva santiṭṭhati sannisīdati ekodi hoti samādhiyati.*

"Just so, monks, when of a monk in the six contact-bases the mind disciplined is, well disciplined, internally indeed is composed, settles down, unified becomes, is concentrated.

"Just so, monks, when a monk's mind is disciplined, well disciplined, in regard to the six bases of contact, it becomes internally composed, settles down, becomes unified, is concentrated.

"Seyyathāpi, bhikkhave, rañño vā rājamahāmattassa vā vīṇāya saddo assutapubbo assa. So vīṇāya saddaṃ suṇeyya. So evaṃ vadeyya: 'Ambho, kissa nu kho eso saddo evaṃrajanīyo evaṃkamanīyo evaṃmadanīyo evaṃmucchanīyo evaṃbandhanīyo'ti?

"Suppose, monks, of a king or of a king-great-minister or, of a lute the sound not-heard-before would be. He of a lute the sound would hear. He thus would say: 'Hey, of what this sound so-enticing, so-lovely, so-intoxicating, so-infatuating, so-captivating?'

"Suppose, monks, a king or a king's chief minister had never before heard the sound of a lute. He would hear the sound of a lute. He would say thus: 'Hey, of what is this the sound, which is so enticing, so lovely, so intoxicating, so infatuating, so captivating?'

139. *Yassa kassaci, bhikkhave, bhikkhussa vā bhikkhuniyā vā* . This is one of the very few suttas in the major chapters of SN where bhikkhunīs are expressly mentioned.

140. I adopt here the reading found in DOP, which defines it as "driven out; scared (away); disciplined, trained."

"Tamenaṃ evaṃ vadeyyuṃ: 'Esā, kho, bhante, vīṇā nāma yassā eso saddo evaṃrajanīyo evaṃkamanīyo evaṃmadanīyo evaṃmucchanīyo evaṃbandhanīyo'ti. So evaṃ vadeyya: 'Gacchatha me, bho, taṃ vīṇaṃ āharathā'ti. Tassa taṃ vīṇaṃ āhareyyuṃ.

"That-him thus they would tell: 'This, sire, a "lute" called, whose this sound so-enticing, so-lovely, so-intoxicating, so-infatuating, so-captivating.' He thus would say: 'Go to me, men, that lute bring.' To him that lute they would bring.

"They would tell him: 'This, sire, is what is called a "lute," whose sound is so enticing, so lovely, so intoxicating, so infatuating, so captivating.' He would say thus: 'Go, men, bring that lute to me.' They would bring that lute to him.

"Tamenaṃ evaṃ vadeyyuṃ: 'Ayaṃ kho sā, bhante, vīṇā yassā eso saddo evaṃrajanīyo evaṃkamanīyo evaṃmadanīyo evaṃmucchanīyo evaṃbandhanīyo'ti. So evaṃ vadeyya: 'Alaṃ me, bho, tāya vīṇāya. Tameva me saddaṃ āharathā'ti.

"That-him thus they would tell: 'This that, sire, lute whose this sound so-enticing, so-lovely, so-intoxicating, so-infatuating, so-captivating.' He thus would say: 'Enough for me, men, with that lute. That-itself to me sound bring.'

"They would tell him: 'This, sire, is that lute whose sound is so enticing, so lovely, so intoxicating, so infatuating, so captivating.' He would say: 'Enough for me with that lute, men. Bring me that sound itself.'

"Tamenaṃ evaṃ vadeyyuṃ: 'Ayaṃ kho, bhante, vīṇā nāma anekasambhārā mahāsambhārā. Anekehi sambhārehi samāraddhā vadati, seyyathīdaṃ: doṇiñca paṭicca cammañca paṭicca daṇḍañca paṭicca upadhāraṇe ca paṭicca tantiyo ca paṭicca koṇañca paṭicca purisassa ca tajjaṃ vāyāmaṃ paṭicca. Evāyaṃ, bhante, vīṇā nāma anekasambhārā mahāsambhārā. Anekehi sambhārehi samāraddhā vadatī'ti.

"That-him thus they would tell: 'This, sire, lute called numerous-components, great-components. With numerous components played it speaks, that is: the belly-and in dependence on, the parchment-and in dependence on, the arm-and in dependence on, the support and in dependence on, the strings and in dependence on, the plectrum-and in dependence on, of a person and appropriate effort in dependence on. Thus-this, sire, lute called numerous-components, great-components. With numerous components played it speaks.'

"They would tell him: 'This lute, sire, is made up of numerous components, of a great many components.[141] When played upon with its numerous components, it makes music—that is, in dependence on the belly, the parchment, the arm, the support,[142] the strings, the plectrum, and a person's appropriate effort. Thus, sire, this lute is made up of numerous components, of a great many components. When played upon with its numerous components, it makes music.'

"So taṃ vīṇaṃ dasadhā vā satadhā vā phāleyya. Dasadhā vā satadhā vā taṃ phāletvā sakalikaṃ sakalikaṃ kareyya. Sakalikaṃ sakalikaṃ karitvā agginā ḍaheyya. Agginā ḍahitvā masiṃ kareyya. Masiṃ karitvā mahāvāte vā opuneyya nadiyā vā sīghasotāya pavāheyya. So evaṃ vadeyya: 'Asatī kirāyaṃ, bho, vīṇā nāma yath'ev'ayaṃ kiñci vīṇā nāma. Ettha ca mahājano ativelaṃ pamatto palaḷito'ti.

"He that lute tenfold or a hundred-fold or would split. Tenfold or a hundred-fold or that having split, splinter splinter would make. Splinter splinter having made, with fire would burn. With fire having burned, ash would make. Ash having made, in a great-wind or would winnow, of by river or swift-current would have-carried-off. He thus would say: 'Non-existing, indeed, this, men, "lute" called, as just this anything "lute" called. Here and the multitude extremely heedless confused.'

"He would split the lute into ten pieces or a hundred pieces. Having split it into ten pieces or a hundred pieces, he would reduce these to splinters. Having reduced these to splinters, he would burn them in a fire and reduce

141. For a discussion of the parts of the old Indian *vīṇā*, see Coomaraswamy 1930. I have based my renderings of the parts of the instrument on this article.

142. My rendering is speculative. Coomaraswamy does not list this part, but under the terms whose sense "is not so clear" he lists a part called in Skt *upastaraṇa*. In Pāli this would be *upattharaṇa*, a word otherwise not known. On *upastaraṇa* Coomaraswamy says: "I cannot offer any suggestion."

them to ashes. Having reduced them to ashes, he would winnow the ashes in a strong wind or have them carried off by a river with a swift current. Then he would say: 'Non-existing indeed, men, is this [thing] called a "lute," as well as anything else called a "lute." The multitude are extremely heedless and confused about this!'

"Evameva kho, bhikkhave, bhikkhu rūpaṃ samanvesati yāvatā rūpassa gati, vedanaṃ samanvesati yāvatā vedanāya gati, saññaṃ samanvesati yāvatā saññāya gati, saṅkhāre samanvesati yāvatā saṅkhārānaṃ gati, viññāṇaṃ samanvesati yāvatā viññāṇassa gati. Tassa rūpaṃ samanvesato yāvatā rūpassa gati, vedanaṃ samanvesato . . . saññaṃ . . . saṅkhāre . . . viññāṇaṃ samanvesato yāvatā viññāṇassa gati, yampi'ssa taṃ hoti 'ahan'ti vā 'maman'ti vā 'asmī'ti vā tampi tassa na hotī"ti.

"Just so, monks, a monk form investigates as far as of form the range, feeling investigates as far as of feeling the range, perception investigates as far as of perception the range, volitional-activities investigates as far as of volitional-activities the range, consciousness investigates as far as of consciousness the range. For him form investigating as far as of form the range, feeling . . . perception . . . volitional-activities . . . consciousness investigating as far as of consciousness the range, which-even-to him that occur 'I' or 'mine' or 'I am' or, that-even-to him not occur."

"So too, monks, a monk investigates form as far as there is the range of form, he investigates feeling as far as there is the range of feeling, he investigates perception as far as there is the range of perception, he investigates volitional activities as far as there is the range of volitional activities, he investigates consciousness as far as there is the range of consciousness. As he is investigating form as far as there is the range of form . . . consciousness as far as there is the range of consciousness, those [notions of] 'I' or 'mine' or 'I am' that occurred to him do not occur to him."

Grammatical explanations

chasu phassāyatanesu: the locative of *cha*, "six," qualifying *phassāyatanesu*, "bases of contact," a genitive tappurisa compound in the locative plural.

rañño vā rājamahāmattassa vā vīṇāya saddo assutapubbo assa: "a king or a king's chief minister had never before heard the sound of a lute." The agents—*rañño* and *rājamahāmattassa*—are genitives with an instrumental sense in relation to the grammatical subject, *saddo*, "sound" (see Wijesekera §142). The kammadhāraya compound *assutapubbo* is composed of *assuta*, "unheard," a negative past participle, and *pubba*, "before, previously." It is masculine singular nominative in agreement with *saddo*. The optative verb *assa* indicates this is a hypothetical example.

ambho: (PED) "part. of exclamation, employed: (1) to draw attention = look here, hey! hallo!; (2) to mark reproach and anger = you silly, you rascal."

kissa: an interrogative pronoun, "of what," singular neuter in the genitive case.

evaṃrajanīyo: This and the following compounds are kammadhārayas used as adjectives qualifying *saddo*. Each is composed of *evaṃ*, an adverb of manner, and a future passive participle.

vadeyyuṃ: "would say"; the third-person plural of *vadati*, in the optative. The subject is not explicitly mentioned, but it is obviously the king's attendants who are speaking to him. The same applies to the following third-person plural optative verbs.

nāma: an indeclinable used in two ways: (1) as meaning "by name, called," the use relevant here; and (2) as a marker of emphasis.[143]

yassā: the relative genitive pronoun, feminine as standing for *vīṇā*.

gacchatha: "go"; the second-person plural imperative.

āharatha: "bring"; again, the second-person plural imperative.

alaṃ: "away with, no need for," with the instrumental, *tāya vīṇāya* (see Duroiselle §599,xiii; Perniola §254d).

anekasambhārā mahāsambhārā: "of numerous components, of a great many components"; both are bahubbīhis, feminine singulars agreeing with *vīṇā*.

doṇiñca paṭicca: "in dependence on the belly"; the absolutive *paṭicca* taking the accusative object; so too for each of the following components.

evāyaṃ: a sandhi of *evaṃ* and *ayaṃ*.

dasadhā, satadhā: The suffix *-dhā* is used to create numerical adverbs cor-

143. For examples of this second usage, see DOP *nāma*[2].

responding to "-fold" or "times" (Duroiselle §281; Perniola 54d). The forms are indeclinables.

sakalikaṃ sakalikaṃ kareyya: "would reduce these to splinters." The repetition of *sakalikaṃ*, accusative of feminine *sakalikā*, suggests repeatedly dividing the fragments of the lute to make a multitude of splinters.

nadiyā vā sīghasotāya pavāheyya: "have them carried off by a river with a swift current." *Sīghasotāya* is a bahubbīhi compound describing *nadiyā*, the feminine instrumental of *nadī*; it is not a tappurisa compound with *nadiyā* as a genitive.

asatī kirāyaṃ, bho, vīṇā nāma: The commentary explains *asatī* as "mean, a poor thing,"[144] but as the negative present participle of *atthi*, "is" (here feminine singular agreeing with *vīṇā*), it could also mean "nonexistent." Possibly the text has been corrupted, but the point the king seems to be making is that, because one cannot find the lovely sound inside the lute, the lute itself is worthless and deceptive. *Kirāyaṃ* = *kira* + *ayaṃ*, where *kira* is an emphatic, "indeed," and *ayaṃ* the demonstrative qualifying *vīṇā*.

yath'ev'ayaṃ kiñci vīṇā nāma: The commentary explains this obscure utterance to mean that the king is saying that any other stringed instrument too is worthless.[145]

rūpaṃ samanvesati yāvatā rūpassa gati: "investigates form as far as there is the range of form." This seems to be an idiomatic way of saying that he investigates form in all its modes and varieties; and so for the other aggregates. *Yāvatā* is an indeclinable, "as far as, to the extent that."[146] *Gati* has various meanings, among them "movement, path, destination, sphere (of movement), destiny, realm of rebirth," and so forth.

tassa rūpaṃ samanvesato: In this construction the agent, the monk, is represented by the dative pronoun *tassa* and the action by the dative present participle *samanvesato*, taking *rūpaṃ*, an accusative, as its object.

yampi'ssa taṃ hoti "ahan"ti vā "maman"ti vā "asmī"ti vā tampi tassa na hoti: "those [notions of] 'I' or 'mine' or 'I am' that occurred to him do not occur to him." The pronouns *yaṃ* and *taṃ* both refer to the three

144. Spk III 67,8–9: *Asatī kirāyan ti asatī kira ayaṃ vīṇā, lāmikā ti attho. Asatī ti lāmakādhivacanametaṃ.*

145. Spk III 67,13–14: *Yath'eva pana aññampi tantibaddhaṃ lāmakamevā ti attho.*

146. Perniola (§103.4) classifies it as "an adverb of extent."

notions *ahaṃ*, *mamaṃ*, and *asmi*, which, according to the commentary, respectively correspond to wrong view, craving, and conceit.[147] The use of the demonstrative pronoun *taṃ* after the relative *yaṃ* gives the general meaning "whoever, whatever" (Geiger §106b). The dative *'ssa* (= *assa*), "to him," refers to the monk and is in agreement with *tassa* of the previous clause. The sense is that since he has successfully investigated the full range of the five aggregates, the notions of *ahaṃ*, *mamaṃ*, and *asmi* that formerly occurred to him no longer occur to him.

15. Chappāṇakopamasutta

The Simile of the Six Animals (SN 35:247 [206]; IV 198–200)

[1. A village thorn]

"Seyyathāpi, bhikkhave, puriso arugatto pakkagatto saravanaṃ paviseyya. Tassa kusakaṇṭakā c'eva pāde vijjheyyuṃ, sarapattāni ca gattāni vilikheyyuṃ. Evaṃ hi so, bhikkhave, puriso bhiyyosomattāya tatonidānaṃ dukkhaṃ domanassaṃ paṭisaṃvediyetha.

"Suppose, monks, a man wound-limbs festered-limbs, reeds-woods would enter. Of him kusa-thorns and feet would pierce, reed-leaves and limbs would scratch. Thus indeed that, monks, man to greater-extent on-that-account pain dejection would experience.

"Suppose, monks, a man with wounded limbs, with festering limbs, would enter a woods of sharp reeds. The kusa thorns would pierce his feet and the reed blades would scratch his limbs. Thus, monks, to a greater extent the man would on that account experience pain and dejection.

"Evameva kho, bhikkhave, idh'ekacco bhikkhu gāmagato vā araññagato vā labhati vattāraṃ: 'Ayaṃ so āyasmā evaṃkārī evaṃsamācāro asucigāmakaṇṭako'ti. Taṃ 'kaṇṭako'ti iti viditvā saṃvaro ca asaṃvaro ca veditabbo.

"Just so, monks, here some monk village-gone or forest-gone or, gains a speaker: 'This that venerable one thus-acting thus-behavior impure-village-

147. Spk III 68,15–16: *Yadetaṃ rūpādīsu ahan ti vā maman ti vā asmī ti vā evaṃ niddiṭṭhaṃ diṭṭhitaṇhāmānaggāhattayaṃ.*

thorn.' Him 'a thorn' thus having known, restraint and non-restraint and should-be-understood.

"Just so, monks, here some monk, gone to the village or gone to the forest, would get one who speaks of him thus: 'This venerable one, acting in such a way, behaving in such a way, is an impure village thorn.' Having known him thus as 'a thorn,' restraint and non-restraint should be understood.

[2. Non-restraint]

"Kathañca, bhikkhave, asaṃvaro hoti? Idha, bhikkhave, bhikkhu cakkhunā rūpaṃ disvā piyarūpe rūpe adhimuccati, appiyarūpe rūpe vyāpajjati. Anupaṭṭhitakāyassati ca viharati parittacetaso, tañca cetovimuttiṃ paññāvimuttiṃ yathābhūtaṃ nappajānāti yatth'assa te uppannā pāpakā akusalā dhammā aparisesā nirujjhanti. . . .

"How-and, monks, non-restraint occurs? Here, monks, a monk with the eye a form having seen, in regard to a pleasant-nature form is intent, in regard to an unpleasant-nature form is annoyed. Not-established-body-mindfulness and dwells, limited-mind, that-and mind-liberation wisdom-liberation as-really-is not understands, where for him those arisen bad unwholesome qualities without-remainder cease. . . .

"And how, monks, does non-restraint occur? Here, monks, having seen a form with the eye, a monk is intent upon a pleasant form and annoyed by an unpleasant form. He dwells without having established mindfulness of the body, with a limited mind, and he does not understand as it really is that liberation of mind, liberation by wisdom, where for him those arisen bad unwholesome qualities cease without remainder. . . .

"Manasā dhammaṃ viññāya piyarūpe dhamme adhimuccati, appiyarūpe dhamme vyāpajjati, anupaṭṭhitakāyassati ca viharati parittacetaso, tañca cetovimuttiṃ paññāvimuttiṃ yathābhūtaṃ nappajānāti yatth'assa te uppannā pāpakā akusalā dhammā aparisesā nirujjhanti.

"With the mind a mental-object having cognized, in regard to a pleasant-nature mental-object is intent, in regard to an unpleasant-nature mental-object is annoyed, not-established-body-mindfulness and dwells, limited-mind, that-

and mind-liberation wisdom-liberation as-really-is not understands, where for him those arisen bad unwholesome qualities without-remainder cease.

"Having cognized a mental object with the mind, a monk is intent upon a pleasant mental object and annoyed by an unpleasant mental object. He dwells without having established mindfulness of the body, with a limited mind, and he does not understand as it really is that liberation of mind, liberation by wisdom, where for him those arisen bad unwholesome qualities cease without remainder.

[3. The simile for non-restraint]
"Seyyathāpi, bhikkhave, puriso chappāṇake gahetvā nānāvisaye nānāgocare daḷhāya rajjuyā bandheyya. Ahiṃ gahetvā daḷhāya rajjuyā bandheyya. Suṃsumāraṃ gahetvā daḷhāya rajjuyā bandheyya. Pakkhiṃ gahetvā daḷhāya rajjuyā bandheyya. Kukkuraṃ gahetvā daḷhāya rajjuyā bandheyya. Siṅgālaṃ gahetvā daḷhāya rajjuyā bandheyya. Makkaṭaṃ gahetvā daḷhāya rajjuyā bandheyya. Daḷhāya rajjuyā bandhitvā majjhe gaṇṭhiṃ karitvā ossajjeyya.

"Suppose, monks, a man six-animals having caught, different-domains different-feeding-grounds, with a strong rope would bind. A snake having caught, with a strong rope would bind. A crocodile having caught, with a strong rope would bind. A bird having caught, with a strong rope would bind. A dog having caught, with a strong rope would bind. A jackal having caught, with a strong rope would bind. A monkey having caught, with a strong rope would bind. With a strong rope having bound, in the middle a knot having made, would let-go.

"Suppose, monks, a man would catch six animals that had different domains and different feeding grounds, and he would bind them with a strong rope. Having caught a snake, he would bind it with a strong rope. Having caught a crocodile, he would bind it with a strong rope. Having caught a bird, he would bind it with a strong rope. Having caught a dog, he would bind it with a strong rope. Having caught a jackal, he would bind it with a strong rope. Having caught a monkey, he would bind it with a strong rope. Having bound them with a strong rope, having made a knot in the middle, he would let go.

"Atha kho, te, bhikkhave, chappāṇakā nānāvisayā nānāgocarā sakaṃ sakaṃ gocaravisayaṃ āviñjeyyuṃ. Ahi āviñjeyya 'vammikaṃ pavekkhāmī'ti, suṃsumāro āviñjeyya 'udakaṃ pavekkhāmī'ti, pakkhī āviñjeyya 'ākāsaṃ ḍessāmī'ti, kukkuro āviñjeyya 'gāmaṃ pavekkhāmī'ti, siṅgālo āviñjeyya 'sīvathikaṃ pavekkhāmī'ti, makkaṭo āviñjeyya 'vanaṃ pavekkhāmī'ti.

"Then those, monks, six-animals, different-domains different-feeding-grounds, own own feeding-ground-domain would pull. The snake would pull, 'An anthill I will enter'; the crocodile would pull, 'Water I will enter'; the bird would pull, 'The sky I will fly'; the dog would pull, 'A village I will enter'; the jackal would pull, 'A charnel ground I will enter'; the monkey would pull, 'The woods I will enter.'

"Then, monks, those six animals that had different domains and different feeding grounds would each pull toward their own feeding ground and domain. The snake would pull, [thinking]: 'I will enter an anthill'; the crocodile would pull, [thinking]: 'I will enter the water'; the bird would pull, [thinking]: 'I will fly to the sky'; the dog would pull, [thinking]: 'I will enter a village'; the jackal would pull, [thinking]: 'I will enter a charnel ground'; the monkey would pull, [thinking]: 'I will enter the woods.'

"Yadā kho te, bhikkhave, chappāṇakā jhattā assu kilantā, atha kho yo nesaṃ pāṇakānaṃ balavataro assa, tassa te anuvatteyyuṃ anuvidhāyeyyuṃ vasaṃ gaccheyyuṃ.

"When those, monks, six-animals weakened would be, fatigued, then which of those animals the stronger would be, of it those would follow along, would submit to, control would go.

"When, monks, those six animals would be weakened and fatigued, then they would follow whichever of those animals is strongest; they would submit to it and come under its control.

"Evameva kho, bhikkhave, yassa kassaci bhikkhuno kāyagatā sati abhāvitā abahulīkatā, taṃ cakkhu āviñjati manāpiyesu rūpesu, amanāpiyā rūpā paṭikūlā honti . . . mano āviñjati manāpiyesu dhammesu, amanāpiyā dhammā paṭikūlā honti. Evaṃ kho, bhikkhave, asaṃvaro hoti.

"Just so, monks, for whichever monk body-gone mindfulness undeveloped uncultivated, him the eye pulls into agreeable forms, disagreeable forms repulsive are . . . the mind pulls into agreeable mental-objects, disagreeable mental-objects repulsive are. Thus, monks, non-restraint occurs.

"Just so, monks, when for any monk mindfulness directed to the body is undeveloped and uncultivated, the eye pulls him toward agreeable forms and disagreeable forms are repulsive . . . the mind pulls him toward agreeable mental objects and disagreeable mental objects are repulsive. Thus, monks, non-restraint occurs.

[4. Restraint]
"Kathañca, bhikkhave, saṃvaro hoti? Idha, bhikkhave, bhikkhu cakkhunā rūpaṃ disvā piyarūpe rūpe nādhimuccati, appiyarūpe rūpe na vyāpajjati. Upaṭṭhitakāyassati ca viharati appamāṇacetaso, tañca cetovimuttiṃ paññāvimuttiṃ yathābhūtaṃ pajānāti yatth'assa te uppannā pāpakā akusalā dhammā aparisesā nirujjhanti. . . .

"How-and, monks, restraint occurs? Here, monks, a monk with the eye a form having seen, in regard to a pleasant-nature form not is intent, in regard to an unpleasant-nature form not is annoyed. Established-body-mindfulness and dwells, measureless-mind, that-and mind-liberation wisdom-liberation as-really-is understands, where for him those arisen bad unwholesome qualities without-remainder cease. . . .

"And how, monks, does restraint occur? Here, monks, having seen a form with the eye, a monk is not intent upon a pleasant form and is not annoyed by an unpleasant form. He dwells with mindfulness of the body established, with a measureless mind, and he understands as it really is that liberation of mind, liberation by wisdom, where for him those arisen bad unwholesome qualities cease without remainder. . . .

"Manasā dhammaṃ viññāya piyarūpe dhamme nādhimuccati, appiyarūpe dhamme na vyāpajjati, upaṭṭhitakāyassati ca viharati appamāṇacetaso, tañca cetovimuttiṃ paññāvimuttiṃ yathābhūtaṃ pajānāti yatth'assa te uppannā pāpakā akusalā dhammā aparisesā nirujjhanti.

"With the mind a mental-object having cognized, in regard to a pleasant-nature mental-object not is intent, in regard to an unpleasant-nature mental-object not is annoyed. Established-body-mindfulness and dwells measureless-mind, that-and mind-liberation wisdom-liberation as-really-is understands, where for him those arisen bad unwholesome qualities without-remainder cease.

"Having cognized a mental object with the mind, a monk is not intent upon a pleasant mental object and is not annoyed by an unpleasant mental object. He dwells with mindfulness of the body established, with a measureless mind, and he understands as it really is that liberation of mind, liberation by wisdom, where for him those arisen bad unwholesome qualities cease without remainder.

[5. The simile for restraint]
"Seyyathāpi, bhikkhave, puriso chappāṇake gahetvā nānāvisaye nānāgocare daḷhāya rajjuyā bandheyya. Ahiṃ gahetvā daḷhāya rajjuyā bandheyya . . . Makkaṭaṃ gahetvā daḷhāya rajjuyā bandheyya. Daḷhāya rajjuyā bandhitvā daḷhe khīle vā thambhe vā upanibandheyya. Atha kho te, bhikkhave, chappāṇakā nānāvisayā nānāgocarā sakaṃ sakaṃ gocaravisayaṃ āviñjeyyuṃ. Ahi āviñjeyya 'vammikaṃ pavekkhāmī'ti . . . makkaṭo āviñjeyya 'vanaṃ pavekkhāmī'ti.

"Suppose, monks, a man six-animals having caught, different-domains different-feeding-grounds, with a strong rope would bind. A snake having caught, with a strong rope would bind. . . . A monkey having caught, with a strong rope would bind. With a strong rope having bound, to a strong post or pillar or would tie. Then those, monks, six-animals, different-domains different-feeding-grounds, own own feeding-ground-domain would pull. The snake would pull, 'An ant hill I will enter' . . . the monkey would pull, 'The woods I will enter.'

"Suppose, monks, a man would catch six animals that had different domains and different feeding grounds, and he would bind them with a strong rope. Having caught a snake, he would bind it with a strong rope. . . . Having caught a monkey, he would bind it with a strong rope. Having bound them with a strong rope, he would tie it to a strong post or pillar. Then, monks, those six animals that had different domains and different feeding grounds would each pull toward their own feeding ground and domain. The snake would pull, [thinking]: 'I will enter an anthill' . . . the monkey would pull, [thinking]: 'I will enter the woods.'

"Yadā kho te, bhikkhave, chappāṇakā jhattā assu kilantā, atha tameva khīlaṃ vā thambhaṃ vā upatiṭṭheyyuṃ upanisīdeyyuṃ upanipajjeyyuṃ.

"When those, monks, six animals weakened would be, fatigued, then that-same post or pillar or would stand-near, would sit-near, would lie-down-near.

"When, monks, those six animals are weakened and fatigued, then they would stand near that same post or pillar; they would sit near it; they would lie down near it.

"Evameva kho, bhikkhave, yassa kassaci bhikkhuno kāyagatā sati bhāvitā bahulīkatā, taṃ cakkhu nāviñjati manāpiyesu rūpesu, amanāpiyā rūpā nappaṭikūlā honti . . . mano nāviñjati manāpiyesu dhammesu, amanāpiyā dhammā nappaṭikūlā honti. Evaṃ kho, bhikkhave, saṃvaro hoti.

"Just so, monks, for whichever monk body-gone mindfulness developed cultivated, him the eye not-pulls in agreeable forms, disagreeable forms not repulsive are . . . the mind not-pulls in agreeable mental-objects, disagreeable mental-objects not repulsive are. Thus, monks, restraint occurs.

"Just so, monks, when for any monk mindfulness directed to the body is developed and cultivated, the eye does not pull him toward agreeable forms and disagreeable forms are not repulsive . . . the mind does not pull him toward agreeable mental objects and disagreeable mental objects are not repulsive. Thus, monks, restraint occurs.

"'Daḷhe khīle vā thambhe vā'ti kho, bhikkhave, kāyagatāya satiyā etaṃ adhivacanaṃ. Tasmātiha vo, bhikkhave, evaṃ sikkhitabbaṃ: 'Kāyagatā sati no bhāvitā bhavissati bahulīkatā yānīkatā vatthukatā anuṭṭhitā paricitā susamāraddhā'ti. Evaṃ hi kho, bhikkhave, sikkhitabban"ti.

"'To a strong post or pillar or,' monks, of body-gone mindfulness this a designation. Therefore by you, monks, thus should-be-trained: 'Body-gone mindfulness by us developed will be, cultivated, vehicle-made, basis-made, stabilized, repeated, well undertaken.' Thus indeed, monks, should-be-trained."

"'A strong post or pillar,' monks: this is a designation for mindfulness directed to the body. Therefore, monks, you should train thus: 'Mindfulness directed to the body will be developed and cultivated by us, made a vehicle, made a basis, stabilized, repeated, and well undertaken.' Thus indeed, monks, you should train."

Grammatical explanations

[1. A village thorn]

arugatto pakkagatto: "with wounded limbs, with festering limbs"; two bahubbīhis describing *puriso*.

bhiyyosomattāya: "to a greater extent, even more so"; an indeclinable in the form of a dative.

tatonidānaṃ: an indeclinable meaning "because of that." This seems to be a syntactical compound in which an ablative, *tato*, has been compounded with the noun *nidāna*, meaning "cause."

paṭisaṃvediyetha: "would experience"; a third-person singular optative in the middle voice. Although the verb has the appearance of a passive, it is an active form based on *paṭisaṃvediyati*, a variant on *paṭisaṃvedeti*.

gāmagato araññagato: "gone to the village or gone to the forest"; two tappurisas describing *bhikkhu*, the nominative subject of the sentence.

vattāraṃ: "one who speaks"; a singular accusative of the agent noun *vattar*, declined on the model of *satthar* (Duroiselle §163; Perniola §37). It is the object of the verb *labhati*.

asucigāmakaṇṭako: "an impure village thorn"; an odd expression, not found elsewhere, perhaps similar to "a thorn in the side."

taṃ "kaṇṭako"ti iti viditvā saṃvaro ca asaṃvaro ca veditabbo: "Having known him thus as 'a thorn,' restraint and non-restraint should be understood." Here the subject of the absolutive is unclear. I would have expected: *taṃ "kaṇṭako"ti iti viditvā saṃvarañca asaṃvarañca jāneyya*, "Having understood him to be 'a thorn,' one should know restraint and non-restraint." Possibly the text has been corrupted.[148]

148. Levman suggests (in a personal communication) the possibility that *saṃvaro ca asaṃ-*

[2. Non-restraint]

piyarūpe rūpe, appiyarūpe rūpe: "[in relation to] a pleasant form, [in relation to] an unpleasant form." These are singular locatives in relation to the two verbs, *adhimuccati* and *vyāpajjati*, which suggest, respectively, liking and disliking.[149]

anupaṭṭhitakāyassati parittacetaso: "without having established mindfulness of the body, with a limited mind"; two bahubbīhis, singular nominatives in agreement with *bhikkhu*. The first is a negative (*an-*) of one who has established (*upaṭṭhita*) mindfulness of the body (*kāyassati*); the second is composed of *paritta*, "limited," and *cetas*, "mind."

cetovimuttiṃ paññāvimuttiṃ: "liberation of mind, liberation by wisdom." I translate on the understanding that the former is a genitive tappurisa and the latter an instrumental tappurisa. The Saṃyutta commentary explains *cetovimutti* as the concentration of the fruit (of arahantship) and *paññāvimutti* as the wisdom of the fruit.[150]

yatth'assa: *yattha* followed by the dative pronoun *assa*. *Yattha*, "where," refers to the *cetovimuttiṃ paññāvimuttiṃ* of the previous clause, and *assa*, "for him," to the monk.

aparisesā: "without remainder"; an adjective in agreement with *dhammā*.

[3. The simile for non-restraint]

chappāṇake: a sandhi of *cha*, "six," and *pāṇake*, "animals," in the plural accusative.

nānāvisaye nānāgocare: "having different domains and different feeding grounds"; two bahubbīhis describing *chappāṇake*.

daḷhāya rajjuyā: "with a strong rope"; the instrumental of the feminine noun *rajju*, with the adjective *daḷhāya* in agreement.

sakaṃ sakaṃ: The repetition shows that each animal heads for its own domain.

pavekkhāmi: "I will enter"; a first-person singular future of *pavesati*.

---

varo ca veditabbo should be in quotes, representing the speaker's chastisement of the monk, "You should know the difference between restraint and non-restraint."

149. While in form the expressions may also have been taken to be plural accusatives, the use of the singular *rūpaṃ disvā* just above suggests that *rūpe* here is also singular.

150. Spk II 399,25: *Cetovimuttin ti phalasamādhiṃ. Paññāvimuttin ti phalapaññaṃ.*

jhattā assu kilantā: "would be weakened and fatigued." *Assu* is the third-person plural optative of *atthi*, preceded and followed by past participles functioning as adjectives.

nesaṃ: a third-person plural genitive pronoun, equivalent to *tesaṃ* (Duroiselle §295).

balavataro assa: The possessive *balavat*, "strong, possessing strength," with the comparative suffix *-tara*, followed by the singular optative verb.

tassa te anuvatteyyuṃ, anuvidhāyeyyuṃ, vasaṃ gaccheyyuṃ: "they would follow it, submit to it, come under its control." The pronoun *tassa* refers to the strongest animal; *te*, the third-person plural nominative pronoun, to the other animals, the subject of the verbs.

kāyagatā sati abhāvitā abahulīkatā: "mindfulness directed to the body is undeveloped and uncultivated." *Sati* is a feminine noun; *kāyagatā*, literally "body-gone," a tappurisa describing *sati*.[151]

taṃ cakkhu āviñjati manāpiyesu rūpesu: "the eye pulls him toward agreeable forms." Here, *taṃ* is an accusative pronoun referring to the monk, and *cakkhu* the nominative subject of the verb *āviñjati*; *manāpiyesu rūpesu* is locative plural.

amanāpiyā rūpā paṭikūlā honti: "disagreeable forms are repulsive": the nominative subject *amanāpiyā rūpā* described by the adjective *paṭikūlā* with the verb *honti*.

[5. The simile for restraint]

tameva khīlaṃ vā thambhaṃ vā upatiṭṭheyyuṃ, upanisīdeyyuṃ, upanipajjeyyuṃ: The subject is *chappāṇakā*, "the six animals," and the three optative verbs take their object, *tameva khīlaṃ vā thambhaṃ vā*, "that same post or pillar," in the accusative. The sense of "near" is already implied by the prefix *upa-* of the verbs.

tasmātiha: see p. 91.

vo, bhikkhave, evaṃ sikkhitabbaṃ: "Thus indeed, monks, you should train." A construction in which the agent, the monks, is represented by the enclitic pronoun, *vo*, instrumental in sense ("by you"), and the action enjoined is represented by the future passive participle *sikkhitabbaṃ*, a neuter singular. In translation it is necessary to use the active voice.

151. Perniola (at §135g) discusses tappurisas ending in *-gata*.

yānīkatā vatthukatā: "made a vehicle, made a basis." These are tappurisas (probably of the accusative type) formed from the nouns *yāna* and *vatthu*, each conjoined with the past participle *katā*. All the words in this string are feminine nominatives qualifying *sati*.

4. Dependent Origination: The Origination and Cessation of Suffering

Introduction

Dependent origination (*paṭiccasamuppāda*), the subject of chapter 12 in the Saṃyutta Nikāya, can be viewed as an expanded version of the second and third noble truths. The teaching shows in greater detail the chain of conditions responsible for the origination of suffering and how, with the elimination of the underlying conditions, all the factors responsible for suffering are brought to an end. The chain of conditions, in their paired relationships, is said to be a natural law. As 4.5 declares, whether or not buddhas appear in the world, this sequence of conditions—called "specific conditionality"—persists as a fixed principle, stable and invariable. The task of a buddha is to fully comprehend it and then to explain it and make it clear to others. Until a buddha appears this sequence of conditions is enveloped in darkness. A buddha alone can fully fathom it and expound it to the world.

Several suttas in this collection show the realization of dependent origination to have been the great discovery the Buddha made on the night of his enlightenment. One text included here, 4.2, states this with respect to the present buddha, Gotama; the preceding suttas in that series relate the same narrative about his six predecessors. The discernment of each link binding conditions together is here said to have come about through a process of "thorough attention" culminating in "a breakthrough by wisdom." The discernment of the entire chain, in the orders of both origination and cessation, marked the gaining of the eye of knowledge. In 4.11, the Buddha declares that, after seeing how consciousness and name-and-form cease together, he had discovered the path to enlightenment.

Dependent origination is usually represented by a sequence of twelve factors in which each factor arises in dependence on its predecessor and ceases with the ceasing of its predecessor. When ignorance, the most fundamental condition, comes to an end, the entire series also ends, bringing "the cessation of this whole mass of suffering." The individual factors are formally defined in SN 12:2 (II 2–4), but the suttas themselves do not explain precisely how the factors operate in unison. This ambiguity has led to the emergence of different interpretations of the formula, but the prevalent interpretation holds that the series shows the causal dynamics that sustain the round of rebirths known as saṃsāra.

This interpretation takes the twelve terms of the formula to be spread out over three lives. The explanation goes like this: Because of fundamental *ignorance*, one engages in various *volitional activities*—bodily, verbal, or purely mental—that nurture *consciousness* and propel it into a new existence. The new existence begins when consciousness, arriving at a new embodiment, brings forth a fresh assemblage of bodily and mental phenomena, designated *name-and-form*. As name-and-form matures, the *six sense bases* take shape and become operative. When these bases encounter their corresponding objects, *contact* occurs. Contact gives rise to *feeling*—pleasant, painful, and neutral feelings—and in an untrained person, feeling triggers *craving*, a desire to obtain pleasant objects and avoid pain. When one obtains the objects of desire, one relishes them and holds to them tightly; this is *clinging*. Through clinging, one engages in a fresh round of volitional activities, which plant the seeds for a new *existence*. That new existence begins with *birth*, and once birth takes place, there follows *old age and death* and all the other manifestations of *dukkha* encountered in the course of existence.

As stated, the twelve-factored formula is a simplified representation of a complex process that involves overlapping and intersecting lines of conditionality. To convey this point, the exegetical tradition (beginning perhaps with the Paṭisambhidāmagga) explains that when ignorance and volitional activities are present, craving, clinging, and the karmically active phase of existence are also present. Thus these five "propulsive" conditions function in unison to bring forth consciousness and name-and-form, which arise at the initial moment of the new existence and continue to evolve in uninterrupted interplay through the entire course of life. From their interplay, the six sense bases, contact, and feeling are drawn out to show the conditions for a new wave of craving, and when craving arises, ignorance necessarily underlies it. Thus ignorance and craving jointly function as the roots of the round. These feed into clinging, the volitional activities, and the karmically active phase of existence, which bring into being new aggregations of consciousness and name-and-form, starting the process of existence anew.

Dependent origination can be seen to offer a perspective on non-self that complements the analytic approach provided by the five aggregates. The formula shows how the sequence of rebirths occurs without an underlying subject, a substantial self passing through the successive stages of life and migrating from one existence to the next. In the Buddha's time, philosophers and contemplatives were divided into two opposed camps. One camp, the eternalists, affirmed rebirth. They held that the core of the person was a substantial self that persisted through the cycle of rebirths and attained liberation, preserving its unchanging identity. The other camp, the annihilationists, denied the existence of a substantial self that survived bodily death. They asserted that with the breakup of the body, all conscious experience comes to an end and thus that at death the living being is utterly annihilated. Dependent origination, as **4.4** demonstrates, served the Buddha as a "teaching by the middle." It avoids the extreme that "all exists," a statement of eternalism, by showing how the sequence of rebirths is possible without a self persisting through the process. And it avoids the extreme that "all does not exist," the claim of the annihilationists, by showing that so long as the conditions that drive the process of becoming remain operative, the series of conditions continues from one life to the next.

The suttas selected here are noteworthy not only for the various angles they present on dependent origination, but also for their similes. Thus **4.8** uses the simile of the clay pot to illustrate the arahant's attainment of final nibbāna. The simile of the great tree, in **4.9**, illustrates the two sides of dependent origination with the sustenance and destruction of the tree. In **4.10** the Buddha compares the ever-fickle mind to a monkey that roams through a forest by grabbing and releasing one branch after another. In **4.11** he compares his discovery of the noble eightfold path to a man wandering through a forest who comes across an ancient path leading to an ancient city, which he restores to its previous glory. And **4.12** employs the simile of the poisoned beverage to demonstrate how those ascetics who lack insight and nurture craving remain bound to the round of birth and death, while those who acquire insight and abandon craving are like the person who rejects the poisoned beverage.

1. Paṭiccasamuppādasutta

Dependent Origination (SN 12:1; II 1–2)

[1. Origination]

"Paṭiccasamuppādaṃ vo, bhikkhave, desessāmi. Taṃ suṇātha, sādhukaṃ manasikarotha, bhāsissāmī"ti. — "Evaṃ, bhante"ti kho te bhikkhū bhagavato paccassosuṃ. Bhagavā etadavoca:

"Dependent-origination to you, monks, I will teach. That listen to, well attend, I will speak." — "Yes, Bhante," those monks to the Blessed One replied. The Blessed One this-said:

"I will teach you, monks, dependent origination. Listen to that and attend well. I will speak." — "Yes, Bhante," those monks replied to the Blessed One. The Blessed One said this:

"Katamo ca, bhikkhave, paṭiccasamuppādo? Avijjāpaccayā, bhikkhave, saṅkhārā; saṅkhārapaccayā viññāṇaṃ; viññāṇapaccayā nāmarūpaṃ; nāmarūpapaccayā saḷāyatanaṃ; saḷāyatanapaccayā phasso; phassapaccayā vedanā; vedanāpaccayā taṇhā; taṇhāpaccayā upādānaṃ; upādānapaccayā bhavo; bhavapaccayā jāti; jātipaccayā jarāmaraṇaṃ soka-parideva-dukkha-domanass'upāyāsā sambhavanti. Evametassa kevalassa dukkhakkhandhassa samudayo hoti. Ayaṃ vuccati, bhikkhave, 'paṭiccasamuppādo.'

"What and, monks, dependent-origination? Through ignorance-condition, monks, volitional-activities; through volitional-activities-condition, consciousness; through consciousness-condition, name-form; through name-form-condition, six-sense-base; through six-sense-base-condition, contact; through contact-condition, feeling; through feeling-condition, craving; through craving-condition, clinging; through clinging-condition, existence; through existence-condition, birth; through birth-condition, old-age-death, sorrow-lamentation-pain-dejection-misery come-to-be. Thus-of this whole suffering-mass origin is. This is called, monks, 'dependent-origination.'

"And what, monks, is dependent origination? With ignorance as condition, monks, volitional activities [occur]; with volitional activities as condition, consciousness; with consciousness as condition, name-and-form;

with name-and-form as condition, the six sense bases; with the six sense bases as condition, contact; with contact as condition, feeling; with feeling as condition, craving; with craving as condition, clinging; with clinging as condition, existence; with existence as condition, birth; with birth as condition, old-age-and-death, sorrow, lamentation, pain, dejection, and misery come to be. Such is the origin of this whole mass of suffering. This, monks, is called 'dependent origination.'

[2. Cessation]

"Avijjāya tveva asesavirāganirodhā saṅkhāranirodho; saṅkhāranirodhā viññāṇanirodho; viññāṇanirodhā nāmarūpanirodho; nāmarūpanirodhā saḷāyatananirodho; saḷāyatananirodhā phassanirodho; phassanirodhā vedanānirodho; vedanānirodhā taṇhānirodho; taṇhānirodhā upādānanirodho; upādānanirodhā bhavanirodho; bhavanirodhā jātinirodho; jātinirodhā jarāmaraṇaṃ soka-parideva-dukkha-domanass'upāyāsā nirujjhanti. Evametassa kevalassa dukkhakkhandhassa nirodho hotī"ti.

"Of ignorance, but-indeed, through remainderless-fading-cessation, volitional-activities-cessation; through volitional-activities-cessation, consciousness-cessation; through consciousness-cessation, name-form-cessation; through name-form-cessation, six-sense-base-cessation; through six-sense-base-cessation, contact-cessation; through contact-cessation, feeling-cessation; through feeling-cessation, craving-cessation; through craving-cessation, clinging-cessation; through clinging-cessation, existence-cessation; through existence cessation, birth-cessation; through birth-cessation, old-age-death, sorrow-lamentation-pain-dejection-misery cease. Thus-of this whole suffering-mass cessation is."

"But with the remainderless fading away and cessation of ignorance [there occurs] cessation of volitional activities; with the cessation of volitional activities, cessation of consciousness; with the cessation of consciousness, cessation of name-and-form; with the cessation of name-and-form, cessation of the six sense bases; with the cessation of the six sense bases, cessation of contact; with the cessation of contact, cessation of feeling; with the cessation of feeling, cessation of craving; with the cessation of craving, cessation of clinging; with the cessation of clinging, cessation of existence; with the cessation of existence, cessation of birth; with the cessation of birth, old-age-and-death, sorrow, lamentation, pain, dejection, and misery cease. Such is the cessation of this whole mass of suffering."

Idamavoca bhagavā. Attamanā te bhikkhū bhagavato bhāsitaṃ abhinandun ti.

This-said the Blessed One. Elated, those monks the Blessed One's statement delighted in.

This is what the Blessed One said. Elated, those monks delighted in the Blessed One's statement.

Grammatical explanations

[1. Origination]

paṭiccasamuppādaṃ . . . etadavoca: On the terms used in this stock opening passage, see pp. 166–67. *Paṭiccasamuppāda* is taken to be a syntactical compound (see Perniola §142a), with *paṭicca* as the absolutive of *pacceti*, "comes back to, falls back on," joined to the noun *samuppāda*, "origination."[152] The common translation of *paṭiccasamuppāda* as "interdependent co-arising" (and its variants) is, strictly speaking, inaccurate. While certain pairs of factors in the formula may be mutually dependent, the word *paṭicca* itself does not imply mutuality but the dependence of one factor upon the other. Further, *samuppāda* does not imply simultaneous arising. While certain factors arise simultaneously (for instance, contact and feeling), others, such as feeling and craving, may be separated by a temporal gap.

avijjāpaccayā . . . saṅkhārā: The Saṃyutta commentary explains *avijjāpaccayā* as a kammadhāraya compound consisting of two nouns joined in apposition—that is, ignorance which itself is a condition.[153] The case of *paccayā* is ablative, and thus the compound might also have been ren-

152. See p. 35.

153. Spk II 10,3–4: "It is ignorance and a condition, so it is the ignorance-condition; through that ignorance-condition volitional activities come to be" (*avijjā ca sā paccayo cā ti avijjāpaccayo; tasmā avijjāpaccayā saṅkhārā sambhavantī ti*).

dered "because of ignorance." While the plural verb *sambhavanti* occurs only at the end of the series, the verb can be understood as implicit in each clause.[154]

nāmarūpaṃ: "name-and-form"; a dvanda compound of the collective singular type (see pp. 36–37).

saḷāyatanaṃ: "six sense bases"; a numerical compound of the collective singular type, made up of *cha*, "six," and *āyatanaṃ*, "sense base."[155]

jarāmaraṇaṃ: "old-age-and-death"; another dvanda compound of the collective singular type.

soka-parideva-dukkha-domanass'upāyāsā: "sorrow, lamentation, pain, dejection, and misery"; a five-term dvanda compound of the plural type (see p. 36), with vowel sandhi between *domanassa* and *upāyāsa*.

etassa kevalassa dukkhakkhandhassa: "of this whole mass of suffering"; the demonstrative *etassa* and adjective *kevalassa* both qualify *dukkhakkhandhassa*, a genitive tappurisa in the genitive case.

[2. Cessation]

avijjāya tveva: The Saṃyutta commentary glosses this with *avijjāya tu eva*, where *avijjāya* is the singular feminine genitive, *tu* means "but," and *eva* adds emphasis.[156]

asesavirāganirodhā: "remainderless fading away and cessation"; a complex compound in the ablative case. The Saṃyutta commentary glosses it: "Through the remainderless cessation by means of the path, which is designated 'fading away' (or 'dispassion')."[157] This takes *virāga* as an implicit instrumental and *asesa* as qualifying *nirodhā*. It is possible, however, to take *virāga* and *nirodha* as parallel terms (as I do in the translation), with both, or perhaps just *virāga*, qualified by *asesa*.

154. Vism 527,29–31 says: "And the words 'come to be' should be construed with all the terms, not only with those beginning with sorrow" (*na kevalañca sokādīh'eva, atha kho sabbapadehi sambhavanti-saddassa yojanā kātabbā*).

155. In the compound *cha* becomes *saḷ* through the influence of Skt *ṣaḍ*. Perniola (§9) cites *saḷāyatanaṃ* as an example of "restoring a Skt final consonant which drops when it is final of a word, and reappears in combination."

156. Spk II 10,9.

157. Spk II 10,9–10: *Virāgasaṅkhātena maggena asesanirodhā.*

2. Gotamasutta

Gotama (SN 12:10; II 10–11)

[1. Origination]

"Pubbeva me, bhikkhave, sambodhā anabhisambuddhassa bodhisattass'eva sato etadahosi: 'Kiccham̧ vatāyam̧ loko āpanno jāyati ca jīyati ca mīyati ca cavati ca upapajjati ca. Atha ca pan'imassa dukkhassa nissaraṇam̧ nappajānāti jarāmaraṇassa. Kudāssu nāma imassa dukkhassa nissaraṇam̧ paññāyissati jarāmaraṇassā'ti?

"Before-just to me, monks, from enlightenment, to an unenlightened bodhisatta just being, this-occurred: 'Trouble indeed-this world fallen, is born and ages and dies and passes away and is reborn and. But of this suffering escape not-understands, of old-age-death. When-now of this suffering escape will be discerned, of old-age-death'?

"Before the enlightenment, monks, while I was just a bodhisatta, not fully enlightened, this occurred to me: 'Alas, this world has fallen into trouble; it is born, grows old, and dies, it passes away and is reborn, yet it does not understand the escape from this suffering, from old-age-and-death. When now will an escape be discerned from this suffering, from old-age-and-death?'

"Tassa mayham̧, bhikkhave, etadahosi: 'Kimhi nu kho sati jarāmaraṇam̧ hoti; kim̧paccayā jarāmaraṇan'ti? Tassa mayham̧, bhikkhave, yoniso-manasikārā ahu paññāya abhisamayo: 'Jātiyā kho sati jarāmaraṇam̧ hoti; jātipaccayā jarāmaraṇan'ti.

"To that to me, monks, this-occurred: 'When what exists, old-age-death occurs? Through what-condition old-age-death?' To that to me, monks, through thorough-attention was by wisdom a breakthrough: 'When birth exists, old-age-death occurs; through birth-condition, old-age-death.'

"Then, monks, this occurred to me: 'When what exists does old-age-and-death occur? Through what condition is there old-age-and-death?' Then, monks, through thorough attention, there was for me a breakthrough by wisdom: 'When there is birth, old-age-and-death occurs; with birth as condition, old-age-and-death [occurs].'

"Tassa mayhaṃ, bhikkhave, etadahosi: 'Kimhi nu kho sati jāti hoti . . . bhavo . . . upādānaṃ . . . taṇhā . . . vedanā . . . phasso . . . saḷāyatanaṃ . . . nāmarūpaṃ . . . viññāṇaṃ . . . saṅkhārā honti; kiṃpaccayā saṅkhārā'ti? Tassa mayhaṃ, bhikkhave, yonisomanasikārā ahu paññāya abhisamayo: 'Avijjāya kho sati saṅkhārā honti; avijjāpaccayā saṅkhārā'ti.

"To that to me, monks, this-occurred: 'When what exists, birth occurs . . . existence . . . clinging . . . craving . . . feeling . . . contact . . . six-sense-base . . . name-form . . . consciousness . . . volitional-activities occur? Through what-condition volitional-activities?' To that to me, monks, through thorough-attention was by wisdom a breakthrough: 'When ignorance exists, volitional-activities occur; through ignorance-condition, volitional-activities.'

"Then, monks, this occurred to me: 'When what exists does birth occur . . . existence . . . clinging . . . craving . . . feeling . . . contact . . . the six sense bases . . . name-and-form . . . consciousness . . . do volitional activities occur? Through what condition are there volitional activities?' Then, monks, through thorough attention, there was for me a breakthrough by wisdom: 'When there is ignorance, volitional activities occur; with ignorance as condition, volitional activities [occur].'

"Iti h'idaṃ avijjāpaccayā saṅkhārā; saṅkhārapaccayā viññāṇaṃ. . . . Evametassa kevalassa dukkhakkhandhassa samudayo hoti. 'Samudayo, samudayo'ti kho me, bhikkhave, pubbe ananussutesu dhammesu cakkhuṃ udapādi, ñāṇaṃ udapādi, paññā udapādi, vijjā udapādi, āloko udapādi.

"Thus indeed this: through ignorance-condition, volitional-activities; through volitional-activities consciousness. . . . Thus-of this whole suffering-mass origin is. 'Origin, origin,' to me, monks, in the past in unheard things the eye arose, knowledge arose, wisdom arose, clear-knowledge arose, light arose.

"Thus this indeed [is so]: With ignorance as condition, volitional activities [occur]; with volitional activities as condition, consciousness. . . . Such is the origin of this whole mass of suffering. 'Origin, origin'—thus, monks, for me, in regard to things unheard before, the eye arose, knowledge arose, wisdom arose, clear knowledge arose, light arose.

[2. Cessation]

"Tassa mayhaṃ, bhikkhave, etadahosi: 'Kimhi nu kho asati jarāmaraṇaṃ na hoti; kissa nirodhā jarāmaraṇanirodho'ti? Tassa mayhaṃ, bhikkhave, yonisomanasikārā ahu paññāya abhisamayo: 'Jātiyā kho asati jarāmaraṇaṃ na hoti; jātinirodhā jarāmaraṇanirodho'ti.

"To that to me, monks, this-occurred: 'When what not existing, old-age-death not occurs? Of what through cessation, old-age-death-cessation?' To that to me, monks, through thorough-attention was by wisdom a breakthrough: 'When birth not existing, old-age-death does not occur; through birth-cessation, old-age-death-cessation.'

"Then, monks, this occurred to me: 'When what does not exist do old-age-and-death not occur? With the cessation of what [is there] the cessation of old-age-and-death?' Then, monks, through thorough attention, there was for me a breakthrough by wisdom: 'When there is no birth, old-age-and-death do not occur; with the cessation of birth [there is] cessation of old-age-and-death.'

"Tassa mayhaṃ, bhikkhave, etadahosi: 'Kimhi nu kho asati jāti na hoti . . . bhavo. . . upādānaṃ. . . taṇhā . . . vedanā . . . phasso . . . saḷāyatanaṃ . . . nāmarūpaṃ . . . viññāṇaṃ . . . saṅkhārā na honti; kissa nirodhā saṅkhāranirodho'ti? Tassa mayhaṃ, bhikkhave, yonisomanasikārā ahu paññāya abhisamayo: 'Avijjāya kho asati saṅkhārā na honti; avijjānirodhā saṅkhāranirodho'ti.

"To that to me, monks, this occurred: 'When what not existing, birth not occurs . . . existence . . . clinging . . . craving . . . feeling . . . contact . . . six-sense-bases . . . name-form . . . consciousness . . . volitional-activities do not occur? Of what through cessation, volitional-activities-cessation?' To that to me, monks, through thorough-attention was by wisdom a breakthrough: 'When ignorance not existing, volitional-activities not occur, through ignorance-cessation volitional-activities-cessation.'

"Then, monks, this occurred to me: 'When what does not exist does birth not occur . . . existence . . . clinging . . . craving . . . feeling . . . contact . . . the six sense bases . . . name-and-form . . . consciousness . . . volitional activities not occur? With the cessation of what [is there] cessation of volitional activities?' Then, monks, through thorough attention, there was for me a breakthrough by wisdom: 'When there is no ignorance, volitional activities do not occur; with the cessation of ignorance [there is] cessation of volitional activities.'

"Iti h'idaṃ avijjānirodhā saṅkhāranirodho; saṅkhāranirodhā viññāṇanirodho. . . . Evametassa kevalassa dukkhakkhandhassa nirodho hoti. 'Nirodho, nirodho'ti kho me, bhikkhave, pubbe ananussutesu dhammesu cakkhuṃ udapādi, ñāṇaṃ udapādi, paññā udapādi, vijjā udapādi, āloko udapādī"ti.

"Thus indeed this: through ignorance-cessation, volitional-activities cessation; through volitional-activities-cessation, consciousness-cessation. . . . Thus-of this whole suffering-mass cessation is. 'Cessation, cessation,' to me, monks, in the past in unheard things the eye arose, knowledge arose, wisdom arose, clear-knowledge arose, light arose."

"Thus this indeed [is so]: With the cessation of ignorance [there is] cessation of volitional activities; with the cessation of volitional activities, cessation of consciousness. . . . Such is the cessation of this whole mass of suffering. 'Cessation, cessation'—thus, monks, for me, in regard to things unheard before, the eye arose, knowledge arose, wisdom arose, clear knowledge arose, light arose."

Grammatical explanations

pubbeva me, bhikkhave, sambodhā: see pp. 152–53.

kicchaṃ: "trouble"; the accusative object of *āpanno*, the past participle of *āpajjati*, "enters upon, falls into."

vatāyaṃ: the exclamatory particle *vata* joined to *ayaṃ*.

jāyati ca jīyati ca mīyati: "is born and ages and dies"; the verbs are passive forms.

imassa dukkhassa nissaraṇaṃ nappajānāti jarāmaraṇassa: "it does not understand the escape from this suffering, from old-age-and-death." On *nissaraṇa* as taking the genitive, see p. 154. Placed after the verb, *jarāmaraṇassa* highlights the *dukkha* referred to before the verb.

kudāssu nāma: *Kudā* is an interrogative equivalent in sense to *kadā*, "when?"

Su (from Vedic *svid*; *ssu* in sandhi) is an interrogative particle and *nāma* a mere emphatic.[158]

tassa mayhaṃ: see p. 153.

kimhi nu kho sati: "when what exists"; an interrogative locative absolute, with the locative interrogative pronoun *kimhi* as the subject agreeing with *sati*, the locative present participle of *atthi*, "is." *Nu* is a mere interrogative particle.

kiṃpaccayā: "through what condition"; an interrogative kammadhāraya compound in the ablative case.

yonisomanasikārā: "through thorough attention"; the adverb *yoniso*, "thorough(ly), careful(ly)," joined to *manasikārā*, a tappurisa compound in which the first member preserves its case ending (see Duroiselle §545; Perniola §134). The case is ablative, indicating causation.

ahu: a root aorist of *hoti* (Duroiselle §413; Perniola §83; Geiger §160.3), equivalent in sense to the s-aorist *ahosi*. For emphasis the verb precedes its subject.

paññāya abhisamayo: "a breakthrough by wisdom"; the instrumental *paññāya* indicates the means to *abhisamayo*, breakthrough or realization.

jātiyā kho sati: "when there is birth" or "there being birth"; a locative absolute, with *jātiyā* the locative subject and *sati* the locative present participle of *atthi*.

h'idaṃ: the emphatic particle *hi* and the neuter pronoun *idaṃ*, referring to the entire series, joined by sandhi.

me: "for me"; the enclitic first-person pronoun, probably dative.

ananussutesu dhammesu: "in regard to things unheard"; a locative plural, where *ananussutesu* is a negative of *anussutesu* and *dhammesu* the things or teachings qualified by *ananussutesu*. *Anussuta* is a prefixed form of *suta*, "heard," and usually implies "heard through oral transmission," oral transmission (*anussava*) being the claim to the authority of the Vedas made by the brahmins.

udapādi: see p. 23.

158. Spk II 21,20 glosses with *katarasmiṃ nu kho kāle*, "at what time?"

3. Moḷiyaphaggunasutta

Moḷiyaphagguna (SN 12:12, II 12–14)

[1. The four kinds of nutriment]

"Cattāro'me, bhikkhave, āhārā bhūtānaṃ vā sattānaṃ ṭhitiyā sambhavesīnaṃ vā anuggahāya. Katame cattāro? Kabaliṅkāro āhāro oḷāriko vā sukhumo vā, phasso dutiyo, manosañcetanā tatiyā, viññāṇaṃ catutthaṃ. Ime kho, bhikkhave, cattāro āhārā bhūtānaṃ vā sattānaṃ ṭhitiyā sambhavesīnaṃ vā anuggahāyā"ti.

"Four these, monks, nutriments of come-to-be or beings for persistence, existence-approaching or for assistance. What four? Edible nutriment coarse or subtle or, contact second, mind-volition third, consciousness fourth. These, monks, four nutriments of come-to-be or beings for persistence, existence-approaching or for assistance."

"There are, monks, these four nutriments for the persistence of beings that have come to be or for the assistance of those approaching [a new] existence. What four? Edible nutriment coarse or subtle, contact second, mental volition third, and consciousness fourth. These, monks, are the four nutriments for the persistence of beings that have come to be or for the assistance of those approaching [a new] existence."

[2. Who consumes consciousness?]

Evaṃ vutte āyasmā moḷiyaphagguno bhagavantaṃ etadavoca: "Ko nu kho, bhante, viññāṇāhāraṃ āhāretī"ti?

Thus said, the Venerable Moḷiyaphagguna to the Blessed One this-said: "Who, Bhante, consciousness-nutriment consumes?"

When such was said, the Venerable Moḷiyaphagguna said this to the Blessed One: "Who, Bhante, consumes the consciousness nutriment?"

"No kallo pañho"ti bhagavā avoca: "'Āhāretī'ti ahaṃ na vadāmi. 'Āhāretī'ti cāhaṃ vadeyyaṃ, tatr'assa kallo pañho: 'Ko nu kho, bhante, āhāretī'ti? Evaṃ cāhaṃ na vadāmi. Evaṃ maṃ avadantaṃ yo evaṃ puccheyya, 'Kissa nu kho, bhante, viññāṇāhāro'ti? Esa kallo pañho. Tatra

kallaṃ veyyākaraṇaṃ: 'Viññāṇāhāro āyatiṃ punabbhavābhinibbattiyā paccayo. Tasmiṃ bhūte sati saḷāyatanaṃ, saḷāyatanapaccayā phasso'"ti.

"Not a proper question," the Blessed One said. "'Consumes,' I not say. 'Consumes,' if I would say, there would be a proper question: 'Who, Bhante, consumes?' Thus but I not say. Thus me not-saying, one thus should ask: 'For what, Bhante, consciousness-nutriment?' This a proper question. There the proper answer: 'Consciousness-nutriment for future again-existence-production a condition. When that come-to-be being existing, the six-sense-base; through the six-sense-base-condition, contact.'"

"Not a proper question," the Blessed One said: "I do not say: '[Someone] consumes.' If I would say, '[Someone] consumes,' in that case it would be a proper question: 'Who, Bhante, consumes?' But I do not say thus. Since I do not say thus, one should ask me: 'For what, Bhante, is the consciousness-nutriment [a condition]?' This is a proper question. The proper answer there is: 'The consciousness-nutriment is a condition for the production of renewed existence in the future. When there is that which has come-to-be, [there are] the six sense bases; with the six sense bases as condition, [there is] contact.'"

[3. From contact to clinging]
"Ko nu kho, bhante, phusatī"ti? — "No kallo pañho"ti bhagavā avoca. "'Phusatī'ti ahaṃ na vadāmi. 'Phusatī'ti cāhaṃ vadeyyaṃ, tatr'assa kallo pañho: 'Ko nu kho, bhante, phusatī'ti? Evaṃ cāhaṃ na vadāmi. Evaṃ maṃ avadantaṃ yo evaṃ puccheyya, 'Kiṃpaccayā nu kho, bhante, phasso'ti? Esa kallo pañho. Tatra kallaṃ veyyākaraṇaṃ: 'Saḷāyatanapaccayā phasso; phassapaccayā vedanā'"ti.

"Who, Bhante, contacts?" — "Not a proper question," the Blessed One said. "'Contacts,' I not say. 'Contacts,' if-I would say, there would be a proper question: 'Who, Bhante, contacts?' Thus but-I not say. Thus me not-saying, one thus should ask: 'Through what condition, Bhante, contact?' This a proper question. There the proper answer: 'Through the six-sense-base-condition, contact; through contact-condition, feeling.'"

"Who, Bhante, contacts?" — "Not a proper question," the Blessed One said. "I do not say: '[Someone] contacts.' If I would say, '[Someone] contacts,' there would be a proper question: 'Who, Bhante, contacts?' But I do not say thus. Since I do not say thus, one should ask me: 'Through what condition, Bhante, [is there] contact?' This is a proper question. The proper answer there is: 'With the six sense bases as condition [there is] contact; with contact as condition [there is] feeling.'"

"Ko nu kho, bhante, vediyatī"ti? — "No kallo pañho"ti bhagavā avoca. "'Vediyatī'ti ahaṃ na vadāmi. 'Vediyatī'ti cāhaṃ vadeyyaṃ, tatr'assa kallo pañho: 'Ko nu kho, bhante, vediyatī'ti? Evaṃ cāhaṃ na vadāmi. Evaṃ maṃ avadantaṃ yo evaṃ puccheyya, 'Kiṃpaccayā nu kho, bhante, vedanā'ti? Esa kallo pañho. Tatra kallaṃ veyyākaraṇaṃ: 'Phassapaccayā vedanā; vedanāpaccayā taṇhā'"ti.

"Who, Bhante, feels?" — "Not a proper question," the Blessed One said. "'Feels,' I not say. 'Feels,' if-I would say, there would be a proper question: 'Who, Bhante, feels?' Thus but-I not say. Thus me not-saying, one thus should ask: 'Through what condition, Bhante, feeling?' This a proper question. There the proper answer: 'Through contact-condition, feeling; through feeling-condition, craving.'"

"Who, Bhante, feels?" — "Not a proper question," the Blessed One said. "I do not say: '[Someone] feels.' If I would say, '[Someone] feels,' there would be a proper question: 'Who, Bhante, feels?' But I do not say thus. Since I do not say thus, one should ask me: 'Through what condition, Bhante, [is there] feeling?' This is a proper question. The proper answer there is: 'With contact as condition [there is] feeling; with feeling as condition [there is] craving.'"

"Ko nu kho, bhante, tasatī"ti? — "No kallo pañho"ti bhagavā avoca. "'Tasatī'ti ahaṃ na vadāmi. 'Tasatī'ti cāhaṃ vadeyyaṃ, tatr'assa kallo pañho: 'Ko nu kho, bhante, tasatī'ti? Evaṃ cāhaṃ na vadāmi. Evaṃ maṃ avadantaṃ yo evaṃ puccheyya, 'Kiṃpaccayā nu kho, bhante, taṇhā'ti? Esa kallo pañho. Tatra kallaṃ veyyākaraṇaṃ: 'Vedanāpaccayā taṇhā; taṇhā-paccayā upādānan'"ti.

"Who, Bhante, craves?" — "Not a proper question," the Blessed One said: "'Craves,' I not say. 'Craves,' if-I would say, there would be a proper question: 'Who, Bhante, craves?' Thus but-I not say. Thus me not-saying, one thus should ask: 'Through what condition, Bhante, craving?' This a proper question. There the proper answer: 'Through feeling-condition, craving; through craving-condition, clinging.'"

"Who, Bhante, craves?" — "Not a proper question," the Blessed One said. "I do not say: '[Someone] craves.' If I would say, '[Someone] craves,' there would be a proper question: 'Who, Bhante, craves?' But I do not say thus. Since I do not say thus, one should ask me: 'Through what condition, Bhante, [is there] craving?' This is a proper question. The proper answer there is: 'With feeling as condition [there is] craving; with craving as condition [there is] clinging.'"

"Ko nu kho, bhante, upādiyatī"ti? — "No kallo pañho"ti bhagavā avoca. "'Upādiyatī'ti ahaṃ na vadāmi. 'Upādiyatī'ti cāhaṃ vadeyyaṃ, tatr'assa kallo pañho: 'Ko nu kho, bhante, upādiyatī'ti? Evaṃ cāhaṃ na vadāmi. Evaṃ maṃ avadantaṃ yo evaṃ puccheyya, 'Kiṃpaccayā nu kho, bhante, upādānan'ti? Esa kallo pañho. Tatra kallaṃ veyyākaraṇaṃ: 'Taṇhāpaccayā upādānaṃ; upādānapaccayā bhavo'ti. . . . Evametassa kevalassa dukkhakkhandhassa samudayo hoti.

"Who, Bhante, clings?" — "Not a proper question," the Blessed One said. "'Clings,' I not say. 'Clings,' if-I would say, there would be a proper question: 'Who, Bhante, clings?' Thus but-I not say. Thus me not-saying, one thus should ask: 'Through what condition, Bhante, clinging?' This a proper question. There the proper answer: 'Through craving-condition, clinging; through clinging-condition, existence. . . .' Thus-of this whole suffering-mass origin is.

"Who, Bhante, clings?" — "Not a proper question," the Blessed One said. "I do not say: '[Someone] clings.' If I would say, '[Someone] clings,' there would be a proper question: 'Who, Bhante, clings?' But I do not say thus. Since I do not say thus, one should ask me: 'Through what condition, Bhante, [is there] clinging?' This is a proper question. The proper answer there is: 'With craving as condition [there is] clinging; with clinging as condition [there is] existence. . . .' Such is the origin of this whole mass of suffering.

[4. Cessation]
"Channaṃ tveva, phagguna, phassāyatanānaṃ asesavirāganirodhā phassanirodho; phassanirodhā vedanānirodho; vedanānirodhā taṇhānirodho; taṇhānirodhā upādānanirodho; upādānanirodhā bhavanirodho; bhavanirodhā jātinirodho; jātinirodhā jarāmaraṇaṃ soka-parideva-dukkha-domanass'upāyāsā nirujjhanti. Evametassa kevalassa dukkhakkhandhassa nirodho hotī"ti.

"Of six but-indeed, Phagguna, of contact-bases through without-remainder-fading-cessation, contact-cessation; through contact-cessation, feeling-cessation; through feeling-cessation, craving-cessation; through craving-cessation, clinging-cessation; through clinging-cessation, existence-cessation; through existence cessation, birth-cessation; through birth-cessation, old-age-death, sorrow-lamentation-pain-dejection-misery cease. Thus-of this whole suffering-mass cessation is."

"But, Phagguna, with the remainderless fading away and cessation of the six bases of contact, [there is] cessation of contact; with the cessation of contact, cessation of feeling; with the cessation of feeling, cessation of craving; with the cessation of craving, cessation of clinging; with the cessation of clinging, cessation of existence; with the cessation of existence, cessation of birth; with the cessation of birth, old-age-and-death, sorrow, lamentation, pain, dejection, and misery cease. Such is the cessation of this whole mass of suffering."

Grammatical explanations

[1. The four kinds of nutriment]

cattāro'me: *cattāro*, the masculine nominative for "four," joined by sandhi to the masculine nominative pronoun *ime* qualifying *āhārā*. The inversion of number and pronoun (as against *ime cattāro*) is typical at the beginning of a discourse.

bhūtānaṃ vā sattānaṃ ṭhitiyā sambhavesīnaṃ vā anuggahāya: In this disjunction, *ṭhitiyā* is a dative of purpose of the feminine noun *ṭhiti*, "persistence, duration," *anuggahāya* a dative of purpose of the masculine noun *anuggaha*, "assistance, help." Each stands in relation to the masculine plural genitive *sattānaṃ*, "beings," which in the first clause is qualified by the past participle *bhūtānaṃ*, "come to be," and in the second by *sambhavesīnaṃ*, "approaching existence." The commentary explains this as a compound of *sambhava*, "existence, origination," and *esin*, "seeking,"[159] but Geiger (§193A) considers it an instance of the rare future active participle.[160]

kabaḷiṅkāro (Be: *kabaḷīkāro*) *āhāro*: "edible nutriment."[161]

dutiyo, tatiyā, catutthaṃ: These ordinal numbers, qualifying the other three types of nutriment, agree with the gender of their respective subject—masculine, feminine, and neuter.

[2. Who consumes consciousness?]

evaṃ vutte: "when such was said"; a locative absolute, where *evaṃ* is an adverb of manner representing what was said and *vutte* is the locative past participle.

ko: an interrogative pronoun, the subject of the verb *āhāreti*; *viññāṇāhāraṃ* is the accusative object. The commentary identifies *viññāṇāhāra* here with the rebirth-linking consciousness (*paṭisandhicitta*). The Buddha's response indicates that Moḷiyaphagguna is presupposing a self as the subject of the act of consuming. The same assumption underlies each of the following questions, which the Buddha rejects by disallowing the formulation of the question and proposing instead a new formulation by way of conditionality.

āhāreti: "consumes." The verb takes its cognate noun, *āhāraṃ*, as its object; the subject "someone" is implicit in the verb.

cāhaṃ: probably a sandhi of *ce* and *ahaṃ*, though as below it could be a sandhi of *ca* and *ahaṃ*, with the conditional relationship entailed by the optative verbs, *vadeyyaṃ*, "would say," and *assa*, "would be," used because the situation is hypothetical.

assa: a third-person optative of *atthi*, with *pañho* as the subject.

cāhaṃ: here, a sandhi of *ca* and *ahaṃ*, with *ca* used in the disjunctive sense of "but" rather than "and."

159. The commentarial gloss is at Spk II 23,9: *Sambhavesino ti ye sambhavaṃ jātiṃ nibbattiṃ esanti gavesanti* ("They seek, search out, existence, birth, production").

160. See too Collins 109–10.

161. The expression literally means "food made into a ball," referring to the Indian custom of rolling the rice and condiments together into a ball (*kabala*) with the fingers and then placing the ball into the mouth.

maṃ avadantaṃ: *Maṃ*, the accusative object of *puccheyya*, is qualified by *avadantaṃ*, the negative of the accusative present participle of *vadati*, "speaks, says."

kissa nu kho, bhante, viññāṇāhāro: It seems that in order to make sense of the question, the word *paccayo* needs to be added, reading: *Kissa nu kho, bhante, viññāṇāhāro paccayo*?, "For what, Bhante, is the consciousness-nutriment a condition?"[162]

āyatiṃ: an accusative of the feminine *āyati*, "future," used adverbially.

punabbhavābhinibbattiyā: "the production of renewed existence"; a genitive tappurisa compound of *punabbhava*, "again-existence" (see p. 100), and the feminine noun *abhinibbatti*, "production."

tasmiṃ bhūte sati: This rare expression is a locative absolute. *Tasmiṃ* is a locative demonstrative and *bhūte* the locative past participle of *bhavati*; here it functions as a noun qualified by *tasmiṃ* and *sati*, the locative present participle of *atthi*. The commentary says that *bhūte* stands for *nāmarūpa*, which is the condition for *saḷāyatana*.[163]

[3. From contact to clinging]

ko nu kho, bhante, phusati: "Who, Bhante, contacts?" Again, with the interrogative *ko*, Phagguna assumes a self as the subject of the experience. The rest should be construed in accordance with the previous section, and so for the passages to follow.

[4. Cessation]

channaṃ . . . phassāyatanānaṃ: "of the six bases of contact." *Channaṃ* is genitive of *cha*, "six," qualifying *phassāyatanānaṃ*, a genitive plural.

162. Spk II 31,8–9 recognizes this in its paraphrase: "*Bhante, ayaṃ viññāṇāhāro katamassa dhammassa paccayo" ti attho*. The Buddha's reply to his own question also includes *paccayo*.

163. Spk II 31,14–16: *Tasmiṃ punabbhavābhinibbattisaṅkhāte nāmarūpe jāte sati saḷāyatanaṃ hoti* ("When that name-and-form, designated 'the production of renewed existence,' has arisen, there is the sixfold base").

4. Kaccānagottasutta

Kaccānagotta (SN 12:15; II 16–17)

Atha kho āyasmā kaccānagotto yena bhagavā ten'upasaṅkami. Upasaṅkamitvā bhagavantaṃ abhivādetvā ekamantaṃ nisīdi. Ekamantaṃ nisinno kho āyasmā kaccānagotto bhagavantaṃ etadavoca: "'Sammādiṭṭhi sammādiṭṭhī'ti, bhante, vuccati. Kittāvatā nu kho, bhante, sammādiṭṭhi hotī"ti?

Then the Venerable Kaccānagotta where the Blessed One, there approached. Having approached, the Blessed One having paid homage to, one-side sat down. One-side seated, the Venerable Kaccānagotta to the Blessed One this-said: "'Right-view, right-view,' Bhante, is said. In what way, Bhante, right-view occurs?"

Then the Venerable Kaccānagotta approached the Blessed One. Having approached, he paid homage to the Blessed One and sat down to one side. Seated to one side, the Venerable Kaccānagotta said this to the Blessed One: "Bhante, it is said, 'right view, right view.' In what way, Bhante, does right view occur?"

"Dvayanissito khvāyaṃ, kaccāna, loko yebhuyyena, atthitañc'eva natthitañca. Lokasamudayaṃ kho, kaccāna, yathābhūtaṃ sammappaññāya passato yā loke natthitā sā na hoti. Lokanirodhaṃ kho, kaccāna, yathābhūtaṃ sammappaññāya passato yā loke atthitā sā na hoti.

"Dyad-dependent this, Kaccāna, world mostly, it-exists-ness-and it-does-not-exist-ness-and. World-origin, Kaccāna, as-really-is with correct-wisdom for one seeing, which in regard to the world 'it-does-not-exist-ness,' that not occurs. World-cessation, Kaccāna, as-really-is with correct-wisdom for one seeing, which in regard to the world 'it-exists-ness,' that not occurs.

"This world, Kaccāna, for the most part is dependent upon a dyad—upon [the notions of] 'existence' and 'non-existence.' But, Kaccāna, for one seeing the world's origin as it really is with correct wisdom, [the notion of] 'non-existence' does not occur in regard to the world. And for one seeing the world's cessation as it really is with correct wisdom, [the notion of] 'existence' does not occur in regard to the world.

"Upay'upādānābhinivesavinibaddho[164] *khvāyaṃ, kaccāna, loko yebhuyyena. Tañcāyaṃ upay'upādānaṃ cetaso adhiṭṭhānaṃ abhinivesānusayaṃ na upeti na upādiyati nādhiṭṭhāti 'attā me'ti. 'Dukkhameva uppajjamānaṃ uppajjati, dukkhaṃ nirujjhamānaṃ nirujjhatī'ti na kaṅkhati na vicikicchati. Aparapaccayā ñāṇamev'assa ettha hoti. Ettāvatā kho, kaccāna, sammādiṭṭhi hoti.*

"Involvement-clinging-adherence-bound this, Kaccāna, world mostly. That-but-this one involvement-clinging, of mind standpoint, adherence-tendency not approaches, not clings, not stands-upon, 'Self of me.' 'Suffering-only arising arises, suffering ceasing ceases,' not perplexed, not doubts. Not-other-dependent-on knowledge-indeed to him here occurs. To this extent, Kaccāna, right view occurs.

"This world, Kaccāna, is for the most part bound by involvement, clinging, and adherence. But this one does not approach, does not cling, does not stand upon that involvement, clinging, mental standpoint, adherence, and tendency, 'My self.' He is not perplexed and does not doubt that what arises is only suffering arising, that what ceases is suffering ceasing. Without dependence on others knowledge about this occurs to him. It is in this way, Kaccāna, that right view occurs.

"'Sabbaṃ atthī'ti kho, kaccāna, ayameko anto. 'Sabbaṃ natthī'ti ayaṃ dutiyo anto. Ete te, kaccāna, ubho ante anupagamma majjhena tathāgato dhammaṃ deseti: 'Avijjāpaccayā saṅkhārā; saṅkhārapaccayā viññāṇaṃ. . . . Evametassa kevalassa dukkhakkhandhassa samudayo hoti. Avijjāya tveva asesavirāganirodhā saṅkhāranirodho; saṅkhāranirodhā viññāṇanirodho . . . evametassa kevalassa dukkhakkhandhassa nirodho hotī'"ti.

"'All exists,' Kaccāna, this-one end. 'All not exists,' this second end. These those, Kaccāna, both ends not having approached, by the middle the Tathāgata the Dhamma teaches: 'Through ignorance-condition, volitional-activities; through volitional-activities consciousness. . . . Thus-of this whole suffering-mass origin is. Of ignorance, but-indeed, through remainderless-fading-

164. I adopt the reading of Ce with the past participle *vinibaddho*. Be and Ee have the noun *vinibandho*.

cessation, volitional-activities cessation; through volitional-activities-cessation, consciousness-cessation. . . . Thus-of this whole suffering-mass cessation is.'"

"'All exists': Kaccāna, this is one extreme. 'All does not exist': this is the second extreme. Not having approached both these extremes, the Tathāgata teaches the Dhamma by the middle: 'With ignorance as condition, volitional activities [occur]; with volitional activities as condition, consciousness. . . . Such is the origin of this whole mass of suffering. But with the remainderless fading away and cessation of ignorance [there occurs] cessation of volitional activities; with the cessation of volitional activities, cessation of consciousness. . . . Such is the cessation of this whole mass of suffering.'"

Grammatical explanations

dvayanissito: "dependent upon a dyad"; a tappurisa compound in the nominative case qualifying *loko*; it is composed of the noun *dvaya* and the past participle *nissito*, "dependent." The tappurisa is probably of the accusative type.

khvāyaṃ: a sandhi of *kho* and *ayaṃ*.

atthitañc'eva natthitañca: The two feminine abstract nouns—*atthitā* and *natthitā*—are here accusatives in relation to *nissito*. They are formed from the verbs *atthi* and *natthi*, respectively, with the feminine suffix *-tā* turning them into abstract nouns. Hence what is being rejected by this statement is not the existence and non-existence of things as such, but the *abstract* concepts of "existence" and "non-existence," which the commentary correlates with the views of eternalism and annihilationism. Compare the present sutta with SN 22:94 (at pp. 199–201), in which the Buddha says that he affirms that certain things exist (*atthi*) and denies that other things exist (*natthi*).

passato: "for one seeing"; the singular dative of the present participle of *passati*. On this use of the dative, see pp. 74–75.

yā loke natthitā sā na hoti: "[the notion of] 'non-existence' does not occur in regard to the world." The relative *yā* and the demonstrative *sā* are here correlated.

upay'upādānābhinivesavinibaddho: "bound by involvement, clinging, and adherence." On the reading adopted here, this is a complex tappurisa compound qualifying *loko*, composed of a three-part dvanda (*upaya*, *upādāna*, and *abhinivesa*) and the past participle *vinibaddho*. There is vowel sandhi of *upaya* and *upādāna* and of *upādāna* and *abhinivesa*.

yebhuyyena: "for the most part, mostly"; an instrumental used adverbially.

tañcāyaṃ: a sandhi of *taṃ*, *ca*, and *ayaṃ*. The accusative *taṃ* qualifies each of the accusative nouns (*upay'upādānaṃ*, *adhiṭṭhānaṃ*, *abhinivesānusayaṃ*). The pronoun *ayaṃ* refers to the person with right view.

upay'upādānaṃ cetaso adhiṭṭhānaṃ abhinivesānusayaṃ na upeti na upādiyati nādhiṭṭhāti: "does not approach, does not cling, does not stand upon that involvement, clinging, mental standpoint, adherence, and tendency." Three of the nouns are the objects of their corresponding verbs (in the negative): *upayaṃ* of *upeti*, *upādānaṃ* of *upādiyati*, *adhiṭṭhānaṃ* of *adhiṭṭhāti*. *Upay'upādānaṃ* and *abhinivesānusayaṃ* are dvandas.

'attā me'ti: "my self"; the idea of self as the object of the ordinary person's involvement, clinging, adherence, and standpoint.

dukkhameva uppajjamānaṃ uppajjati: "what arises is only suffering arising." *Dukkhaṃ* is the subject of both the present participle and the finite verb, with *eva* serving an exclusionary function. So too in *dukkhaṃ nirujjhamānaṃ nirujjhati*. Here *dukkha* bears the broad sense it has in the first noble truth—not as experiential suffering, but as the unsatisfactory nature of conditioned existence.

aparapaccayā: "not dependent on others"; a negative tappurisa in the ablative case. A common variant reading is *aparappaccayā*. The expression describes the knowledge of a *sekha*; see too MN I 491,6.

ñāṇamev'assa ettha hoti: "knowledge about this occurs to him." The first part can be resolved *ñāṇaṃ eva assa*, where *assa* is the dative pronoun representing the person of right view. *Ettha*, "here," denotes the facts about the arising and ceasing of *dukkha*.

ayameko: a sandhi of *ayaṃ* and *eko*.

ete te . . . ubho ante: "both these extremes"; accusatives, objects of *anupagamma*. *Ubho* is the remnant in Pāli of the old dual form in Skt, *ubhau*.

anupagamma: a negative absolutive of *upagacchati*, from *upagamya* with assimilation of *-y-* to the preceding consonant.

majjhena: "by the middle." This is not the "middle way," which is the noble eightfold path, but a middle way of teaching that avoids the two extremes of eternalism and annihilationism.

5. Paccayasutta

Conditions (SN 12:20; II 25–26)

"Paṭiccasamuppādañca vo, bhikkhave, desessāmi paṭiccasamuppanne ca dhamme. Taṃ suṇātha, sādhukaṃ manasikarotha, bhāsissāmī"ti. — "Evaṃ, bhante"ti kho te bhikkhū bhagavato paccassosuṃ. Bhagavā etadavoca:

"Dependent-origination-and to you, monks, I will teach, dependently-originated and phenomena. That listen-to, well attend, I will speak." — "Yes, Bhante," those monks to the Blessed One replied. The Blessed One this-said:

"I will teach you, monks, dependent origination and dependently originated phenomena. Listen to that and attend well. I will speak." — "Yes, Bhante," those monks replied to the Blessed One. The Blessed One said this:

"Katamo ca, bhikkhave, paṭiccasamuppādo? Jātipaccayā, bhikkhave, jarāmaraṇaṃ. Uppādā vā tathāgatānaṃ anuppādā vā tathāgatānaṃ, ṭhitā'va sā dhātu dhammaṭṭhitatā dhammaniyāmatā idappaccayatā. Taṃ tathāgato abhisambujjhati abhisameti. Abhisambujjhitvā abhisametvā ācikkhati deseti paññāpeti paṭṭhapeti vivarati vibhajati uttānīkaroti. 'Passathā'ti cāha: 'Jātipaccayā, bhikkhave, jarāmaraṇaṃ.'

"What and, monks, dependent-origination? Through birth-condition, monks, old-age-death. Through arising or of tathāgatas, through non-arising or of tathāgatas, has stood indeed that element, dhamma-stability, dhamma-fixity, this-conditionality. That the Tathāgata awakens to, breaks through to. Having awakened to, having broken through to, explains, teaches, points out, establishes, discloses, analyzes, elucidates. 'See' and-says: 'Through birth-condition, monks, old-age-death.'

"And what, monks, is dependent origination? With birth as condition, [there is] old-age-and-death: whether there is an arising of tathāgatas or no arising of tathāgatas, that element still persists, the stability [of the nature of] phenomena, the fixed lawfulness of phenomena, specific conditionality. The Tathāgata awakens to this and breaks through to it. Having awakened to it, having broken through to it, he explains it, teaches it, points it out, establishes it, discloses it, analyzes it, elucidates it. And he says: 'See! With birth as condition, monks, [there is] old-age-and-death.'

"Bhavapaccayā, bhikkhave, jāti . . . Avijjāpaccayā, bhikkhave, saṅkhārā. Uppādā vā tathāgatānaṃ anuppādā vā tathāgatānaṃ, ṭhitā'va sā dhātu dhammaṭṭhitatā dhammaniyāmatā idappaccayatā. Taṃ tathāgato abhisambujjhati abhisameti. Abhisambujjhitvā abhisametvā ācikkhati deseti paññāpeti paṭṭhapeti vivarati vibhajati uttānīkaroti. 'Passathā'ti cāha: 'Avijjāpaccayā, bhikkhave, saṅkhārā.'

"Through existence-condition, monks, birth . . . Through ignorance-condition, monks, volitional-activities. Through arising or of tathāgatas, through non-arising or of tathāgatas, has stood indeed that element, dhamma-stability, dhamma-fixity, this-conditionality. That the Tathāgata awakens to, breaks through to. Having awakened to, having broken through to, explains, teaches, points out, establishes, discloses, analyzes, elucidates. 'See' and-says: 'Through ignorance-condition, monks, volitional-activities.'

"With existence as condition, [there is] birth . . . With ignorance as condition, [there are] volitional activities: whether there is an arising of tathāgatas or no arising of tathāgatas, that element still persists, the stability [of the nature of] phenomena, the fixed lawfulness of phenomena, specific conditionality. The Tathāgata awakens to this and breaks through to it. Having awakened to it, having broken through to it, he explains it, teaches it, points it out, establishes it, discloses it, analyzes it, elucidates it. And he says: 'See! With ignorance as condition, monks, [there are] volitional activities.'

"Iti kho, bhikkhave, yā tatra tathatā avitathatā anaññathatā idappaccayatā: ayaṃ vuccati, bhikkhave, 'paṭiccasamuppādo.'

"Thus, monks, what there reality, not-unreality, not-otherwiseness, this-conditionality: this is called, monks, 'dependent-origination.'

"Thus, monks, the reality in that, the lack of unreality, the not-being otherwise, specific conditionality: this is called 'dependent origination.'

"Katame ca, bhikkhave, paṭiccasamuppannā dhammā? Jarāmaraṇaṃ, bhikkhave, aniccaṃ saṅkhataṃ paṭiccasamuppannaṃ khayadhammaṃ vayadhammaṃ virāgadhammaṃ nirodhadhammaṃ. Jāti . . . Avijjā, bhikkhave, aniccā saṅkhatā paṭiccasamuppannā khayadhammā vayadhammā virāgadhammā nirodhadhammā. Ime vuccanti, bhikkhave, 'paṭiccasamuppannā dhammā.'"

"What and, monks, dependently-originated phenomena? Old-age-death, monks, impermanent, conditioned, dependently-originated, destruction-subject, vanishing-subject, fading-subject, cessation-subject. Birth . . . Ignorance, monks, impermanent, conditioned, dependently-originated, destruction-subject, vanishing-subject, fading-subject, cessation-subject. These are called, monks, 'dependently-originated phenomena.'"

"And what, monks, are dependently originated phenomena? Old-age-and-death, monks, is impermanent, conditioned, dependently originated, subject to destruction, subject to vanishing, subject to fading away, subject to cessation. Birth . . . Ignorance is impermanent, conditioned, dependently originated, subject to destruction, subject to vanishing, subject to fading away, subject to cessation. These, monks, are called 'dependently originated phenomena.'"

Grammatical explanations

paṭiccasamuppanne ca dhamme: "and dependently originated phenomena." *Paṭiccasamuppanne* is a syntactical compound composed of the absolutive *paṭicca* and the past participle *samuppanne* (see p. 45). The compound qualifies the masculine plural accusative *dhamme*, the object of *desessāmi*.

uppādā vā tathāgatānaṃ anuppādā vā tathāgatānaṃ: "whether there is an arising of tathāgatas or no arising of tathāgatas." *Uppādā* and *anuppādā* are ablatives. The Saṃyutta commentary first glosses the ablative *uppādā* with the locative *uppāde*, and then paraphrases the clause with a locative absolute construction.[165]

165. Spk II 40,16–17: *Uppādā vā tathāgatānan ti tathāgatānaṃ uppādepi, buddhesu uppannesu anuppannesupi jātipaccayā jarāmaraṇaṃ, jātiyeva jarāmaraṇassa paccayo.*

ṭhitā'va sā dhātu dhammaṭṭhitatā dhammaniyāmatā: "that element still persists, the stability [of the nature of] phenomena, the fixed lawfulness of phenomena." *Ṭhitā* is a past participle qualifying *dhātu*, a feminine noun, with emphatic *'va* (= *eva*, abridged through sandhi). The three nouns that follow, in apposition to *sā dhātu*, are all formed with the abstract suffix *-tā*. In the two expressions, *dhammaṭṭhitatā dhammaniyāmatā*, it is uncertain whether *dhamma* is intended as a singular, as "the Dhamma," or as a plural. I have taken it in the latter sense. At AN I 286 a similar statement is made with regard to the three marks of impermanence, suffering, and non-self.

idappaccayatā: "specific conditionality"; from *idaṃ*, "this," joined to *paccaya*, with assimilation of *-ṃ* to the following *-p-* and addition of the suffix *-tā*; thus it literally means "the state of having this as condition."

'passathā'ti cāha: "and he says: 'See!'" *Passatha* is the second-person plural imperative of *passati*, addressed to the monks; *cāha* is a sandhi of *ca* and *āha*, an archaic perfect form used either with a present or past sense. The plural is *āhu*.

yā tatra tathatā avitathatā anaññathatā: "the reality in that, the lack of unreality, the not-being otherwise." These are three more abstract nouns. The first is formed by adding the abstract suffix *-tā* to the adjective *tatha*, "real, true"; the second, a negation of the negative abstraction *vitathatā*, "voidness of reality"; the third, a negative abstraction based on the indeclinable *aññathā*, "otherwise." For these terms as adjectives, see p. 108.

aniccaṃ saṅkhataṃ paṭiccasamuppannaṃ khayadhammaṃ vayadhammaṃ virāgadhammaṃ nirodhadhammaṃ: "impermanent, conditioned, dependently originated, subject to destruction, subject to vanishing, subject to fading away, subject to cessation." These descriptive terms all agree in gender with the noun they qualify. Here they are neuter as describing *jarāmaraṇaṃ*, but just below they become feminine when describing *avijjā*. The four compounds ending in *-dhammaṃ* are bahubbīhis. On *-dhamma* as the last term in a compound, see p. 154.

6. Dasabalasutta

Ten Powers (SN 12:22; II 28–29)

[1. The lion's roar]

"Dasabalasamannāgato, bhikkhave, tathāgato catūhi ca vesārajjehi samannāgato āsabhaṃ ṭhānaṃ paṭijānāti, parisāsu sīhanādaṃ nadati, brahmacakkaṃ pavatteti: 'Iti rūpaṃ, iti rūpassa samudayo, iti rūpassa atthaṅgamo; iti vedanā, iti vedanāya samudayo, iti vedanāya atthaṅgamo; iti saññā, iti saññāya samudayo, iti saññāya atthaṅgamo; iti saṅkhārā, iti saṅkhārānaṃ samudayo, iti saṅkhārānaṃ atthaṅgamo; iti viññāṇaṃ, iti viññāṇassa samudayo, iti viññāṇassa atthaṅgamo.'

"Ten-powers-possessed, monks, the Tathāgata, with four and self-confidences possessed, chief-bull place claims, in assemblies lion-roar roars, brahma-wheel rolls: 'Such form, such of form origin, such of form passing away; such feeling, such of feeling origin, such of feeling passing away; such perception, such of perception origin, such of perception passing away; such volitional-activities, such of volitional-activities origin, such of volitional-activities passing away; such consciousness, such of consciousness origin, such of consciousness passing away.'

"The Tathāgata, monks, possessing the ten powers and possessing the four kinds of self-confidence, claims the place of the chief bull, roars a lion's roar in the assemblies, and rolls the Brahma-wheel: 'Such is form, such its origin, such its passing away; such is feeling, such its origin, such its passing away; such is perception, such its origin, such its passing away; such are volitional activities, such their origin, such their passing away; such is consciousness, such its origin, such its passing away.'

"Iti imasmiṃ sati idaṃ hoti; imass'uppādā idaṃ uppajjati. Imasmiṃ asati idaṃ na hoti; imassa nirodhā idaṃ nirujjhati, yadidaṃ: avijjāpaccayā saṅkhārā; saṅkhārapaccayā viññāṇaṃ. . . . Evametassa kevalassa dukkhakkhandhassa samudayo hoti. Avijjāya tveva asesavirāganirodhā saṅkhāranirodho; saṅkhāranirodhā viññāṇanirodho. . . . Evametassa kevalassa dukkhakkhandhassa nirodho hoti.

"Thus when this existing, that occurs; of this through arising, that arises. When this not existing, that not occurs; of this through cessation, that ceases.

That is: Through ignorance-condition, volitional-activities; through volitional-activities consciousness. . . . Thus-of this whole suffering-mass origin is. Of ignorance but-indeed through remainderless-fading-cessation, volitional-activities cessation; through volitional-activities-cessation, consciousness-cessation. . . . Thus-of this whole suffering-mass cessation is.

"Thus when this exists, that occurs; with the arising of this, that arises. When this does not exist, that does not occur; with the cessation of this, that ceases. That is, with ignorance as condition, volitional activities [occur]; with volitional activities as condition, consciousness. . . . Such is the origin of this whole mass of suffering. But with the remainderless fading away and cessation of ignorance [there occurs] cessation of volitional activities; with the cessation of volitional activities, cessation of consciousness. . . . Such is the cessation of this whole mass of suffering.

[2. Strive with heedfulness]

"Evaṃ svākkhāto, bhikkhave, mayā dhammo uttāno vivaṭo pakāsito chinnapilotiko. Evaṃ svākkhāte kho, bhikkhave, mayā dhamme uttāne vivaṭe pakāsite chinnapilotike alameva saddhāpabbajitena kulaputtena viriyaṃ ārabhituṃ: 'Kāmaṃ taco ca nahāru ca aṭṭhi ca avasissatu, sarīre upasussatu maṃsalohitaṃ, yaṃ taṃ purisathāmena purisaviriyena purisaparakkamena pattabbaṃ, na taṃ apāpuṇitvā viriyassa saṇṭhānaṃ bhavissatī'ti.

"Thus well expounded, monks, by me the Dhamma, elucidated, disclosed, revealed, stripped-patchwork. Thus when well expounded, monks, by me the Dhamma, elucidated, disclosed, revealed, stripped-patchwork, enough-indeed by a faith-gone-forth family-son energy to arouse: 'Willingly, skin and sinews and bones and let remain, in body let dry up the flesh-blood. Which that by man-strength, by man-energy, by man-exertion to be attained, not that without having attained, of energy standing-still will be.'

"The Dhamma, monks, has thus been well expounded by me, elucidated, disclosed, revealed, stripped of patchwork. When, monks, the Dhamma has thus been well expounded by me, elucidated, disclosed, revealed, stripped of patchwork, this is surely enough for a young person who has gone forth out of faith to arouse energy thus: 'Willingly, let [only] my skin, sinews, and bones remain; let the flesh and blood in my body dry up, but so long as I have not attained whatever is to be attained by human strength, by human energy, by human exertion, there will be no stagnation of energy.'

"Dukkhaṃ, bhikkhave, kusīto viharati vokiṇṇo pāpakehi akusalehi dhammehi, mahantañca sadatthaṃ parihāpeti. Āraddhaviriyo ca kho, bhikkhave, sukhaṃ viharati pavivitto pāpakehi akusalehi dhammehi, mahantañca sadatthaṃ paripūreti. Na, bhikkhave, hīnena aggassa patti hoti. Aggena ca kho, bhikkhave, aggassa patti hoti. Maṇḍapeyyam idaṃ, bhikkhave, brahmacariyaṃ, satthā sammukhībhūto.

"Painfully, monks, a lazy one dwells, mixed with bad unwholesome qualities, great-and own-good discards. Aroused-energy-one but, monks, happily dwells, secluded from bad unwholesome qualities, great-and own-good fulfills. Not, monks, by inferior of the foremost the attainment is. By the foremost but, monks, of the foremost attainment is. Cream-beverage this, monks, spiritual life, the Teacher present-become.

"A lazy person, monks, dwells painfully, mixed with bad unwholesome qualities, and he discards great personal good. But an energetic person dwells happily, secluded from bad unwholesome qualities, and he fulfills great personal good. It is not by the inferior that there is the attainment of the foremost, but it is by the foremost that there is the attainment of the foremost. This spiritual life, monks, is a beverage of cream; the Teacher is present before you.

"Tasmātiha, bhikkhave, viriyaṃ ārabhatha appattassa pattiyā, anadhigatassa adhigamāya, asacchikatassa sacchikiriyāya. 'Evaṃ no ayaṃ amhākaṃ pabbajjā avañjhā bhavissati saphalā saudrayā. Yesaṃ mayaṃ paribhuñjāma cīvara-piṇḍapāta-senāsana-gilānappaccayabhesajjaparikkhāraṃ tesaṃ te kārā amhesu mahapphalā bhavissanti mahānisaṃsā'ti. Evaṃ hi vo, bhikkhave, sikkhitabbaṃ.

"Therefore, monks, energy arouse of unattained for attainment, of unachieved for achievement, of unrealized for realization. 'Thus for us this our going-forth not-barren will be, with-fruit, with-value. Whose we use robe-almsfood-lodging-illness-support-medicine-requisite, for them those deeds in us great-fruit will be, great-benefit.' Thus indeed by you, monks, should-be-trained.

"Therefore, monks, arouse energy for the attainment of the as-yet-unattained, for the achievement of the as-yet-unachieved, for the realization of the as-yet-unrealized, [with the thought]: 'In such a way this going forth of ours will not be barren for us, but fruitful and valuable. As for those whose [gifts of] robes, almsfood, lodgings, and medicinal requisites we use, these services of theirs for us will be of great fruit and benefit [for them].' In such a way, monks, you should train.

"Attatthaṃ vā hi, bhikkhave, sampassamānena alameva appamādena sampādetuṃ; paratthaṃ vā hi, bhikkhave, sampassamānena alameva appamādena sampādetuṃ; ubhayatthaṃ vā hi, bhikkhave, sampassamānena alameva appamādena sampādetun"ti.

"Self-good or for, monks, by one considering, enough-indeed with heedfulness to strive; others-good or for, monks, by one considering, enough-indeed with heedfulness to strive; both-good or for, monks, by one considering enough-indeed with heedfulness to strive."

"For by considering your own good, monks, it is enough to strive with heedfulness; by considering the good of others, monks, it is enough to strive with heedfulness; by considering the good of both, monks, it is enough to strive with heedfulness."

Grammatical explanations

[1. The lion's roar]

dasabalasamannāgato: "possessing the ten powers"; an instrumental tappurisa qualifying *tathāgato*. On the ten powers and four kinds of self-confidence, see MN I 69–72.

catūhi ca vesārajjehi samannāgato: "possessing the four kinds of self-confidence." Here, *samannāgato* takes the things possessed in the instrumental case.

āsabhaṃ ṭhānaṃ paṭijānāti: "claims the place of the chief bull." According to PED, *āsabha* means "a bull, peculiar to a bull, bull-like." Here it is an adjective qualifying the accusative noun *ṭhānaṃ*.

sīhanādaṃ nadati: "roars a lion's roar"; a verb taking its cognate noun as its own object. See p. 186.

brahmacakkaṃ: "the Brahma-wheel"; equivalent in denotation to *dhammacakkaṃ*.[166]

iti rūpaṃ, iti rūpassa samudayo, etc.: see p. 217.

[2. Strive with heedfulness]

svākkhāto: "well expounded"; a kammadhāraya compound of the prefix *su-*, meaning "good, well," and the past participle *akkhāto*, with *su-* changing to *sv-* before the vowel, which is lengthened by sandhi (see Geiger §7).

chinnapilotiko: "stripped of patchwork"; a bahubbīhi modifying *dhammo*. The commentary (Spk II 48,15–19) explains *pilotikā* as an old cloth that has been sewn and stitched together here and there, and *chinnapilotika* as one whose clothes have not been sewn and stitched together.

evaṃ svākkhāte kho, bhikkhave, mayā dhamme . . . chinnapilotike: "when, monks, the Dhamma has thus been well expounded by me . . . stripped of patchwork"; a locative absolute with *dhamme* as the subject and the other words as its qualifiers.

alameva saddhāpabbajitena kulaputtena viriyaṃ ārabhituṃ: "this is surely enough for a young person who has gone forth out of faith to arouse energy"; a passive construction in which the agent, *saddhāpabbajitena kulaputtena*, occurs in the instrumental case. *Kulaputtena* is "a young man of good family" (PED), here qualified by *saddhāpabbajitena*, a tappurisa of the ablative type. The action enjoined by *alaṃ*, "enough," is in the infinitive, *ārabhituṃ*, and the object, *viriyaṃ*, in the accusative. On the use of the infinitive with *alaṃ*, see Perniola §287(i).

kāmaṃ: an adverb meaning "willingly," often (as here) used with a third-person imperative.

taco ca nahāru ca aṭṭhi ca avasissatu: "let [only] my skin, sinews, and bones remain"; three bodily constituents each taken individually as the subject of the singular third-person imperative, *avasissatu*, "let remain."

sarīre upasussatu maṃsalohitaṃ: "let the flesh and blood in my body dry up"; a locative, *sarīre*, followed by the singular third-person imperative,

166. While the compound appears to be a tappurisa, "the wheel of Brahmā," the commentary (Spk II 46,24–25) explains it as "the best wheel" and thus as a kammadhāraya: "*Brahma* means best, supreme; this is a designation for the pure Dhamma-wheel" (*brahman ti seṭṭhaṃ uttamaṃ, visuddhassa dhammacakkass'etaṃ adhivacanaṃ*).

upasussatu, followed next by the subject, *maṃsalohitaṃ*, a dvanda of the collective singular type.

yaṃ taṃ: "which that"—that is, "whatever." The two, respectively relative and demonstrative, qualify *pattabbaṃ*, a future passive participle functioning as a noun.

taṃ apāpuṇitvā: "without having attained that"; a negative absolutive of *pāpuṇāti*, with *taṃ* referring back to *pattabbaṃ*.

na . . . viriyassa saṇṭhānaṃ bhavissati: "there will be no standing-still of energy." It is rare, though not impossible, for the absolutive to have a different subject from the subject of the clause. Here *saṇṭhānaṃ* is the grammatical subject, while the logical subject, merely implicit, is the monk who is making this determination. According to PED, *saṇṭhāna* "seems to be used [in this passage] in the sense of 'end, stopping, cessation.'"

dukkhaṃ: "painfully"; an adverb qualifying the verb *viharati*, with *kusīto* functioning as a substantive, "a lazy one."

sadatthaṃ: "the personal good." The Saṃyutta commentary explains it in two ways: as a compound of *sad* = "good, excellent," and *attha*, "good, goal," and of *sa-* (Skt *sva-*), "one's own," and *attha*, "good, goal," with *-d-* as a liaison consonant.[167]

āraddhaviriyo: "an energetic person"; a bahubbīhi composed of the past participle *āraddha*, "started, aroused," and *viriya*, "energy," representing the person who has aroused energy.

sukhaṃ: "happily"; an adverb qualifying *viharati*.

na . . . hīnena aggassa patti hoti: "It is not by the inferior that there is the attainment of the foremost." The instrumental *hīnena* signifies the means, here dwelling lazily, and *aggassa* the foremost goal, arahantship. Just below *aggena* is again the means, in that case, dwelling diligently.

maṇḍapeyyaṃ: "to be drunk [like] cream," a beverage of cream—that is, of the finest quality. *Maṇḍapeyyaṃ* here functions as a description of *brahmacariyaṃ*. *Maṇḍa* is "the best part of milk or butter" (PED) and *peyyaṃ* a future passive participle of *pivati*, "drinks," used here either as an adjective or a noun.

167. Spk II 49,30: *Sadatthan ti sobhanaṃ vā atthaṃ sakaṃ vā atthaṃ, ubhayenāpi arahattameva adhippetaṃ* ("*Sadattha* is an excellent good or one's own good; by both arahantship itself is intended.")

satthā sammukhībhūto: "the Teacher is present before you." *Satthā* is nominative of the agent noun, *satthar*. *Sammukhībhūto*, a tappurisa compound that agrees with *satthā*, is from *sammukha*, "before one's face," conjoined with *-bhūto*, past participle of *bhavati*.

ārabhatha: the second-person plural imperative.

appattassa pattiyā, etc.: "for the attainment of the unattained." Each phrase consists of the genitive of the negative past participle followed by the dative of the corresponding noun.

avañjhā bhavissati saphalā saudrayā: "will not be barren, but fruitful and valuable." The three feminine adjectives describe *pabbajjā*. *Saphalā* and *saudrayā* are bahubbīhis formed from *sa-*, "with," and respectively *phala*, "fruit," and *udraya*, "outcome."

yesaṃ . . . tesaṃ: plural genitive pronouns, correlated as relative and demonstrative, representing the donors of the four requisites, whose deeds (*kārā*) of generosity become of great fruit and great benefit (*mahapphalā, mahānisaṃsā*) by virtue of being offered "to us." *Amhesu* is a first-person plural pronoun in the locative case, since in Pāli the recipient of a gift occurs in the locative. *Mahapphalā* and *mahānisaṃsā* are bahubbīhis modifying *kārā*.

vo, bhikkhave, sikkhitabbaṃ: *Vo* is the enclitic second-person pronoun, here instrumental, "by you," and *sikkhitabbaṃ*, the future passive participle. In English, the sentence is best rendered in an active voice.

attatthaṃ: a tappurisa compound of *atta*, "self, own," and *attha*, "good." The case is accusative, as object of the instrumental present participle *sampassamānena*.

paratthaṃ: a tappurisa compound of *para*, "other," and *attha*, "good."

ubhayatthaṃ: a tappurisa compound of *ubhaya*, "both," and *attha*, "good."

alameva appamādena sampādetuṃ: "it is enough to strive with heedfulness." For this kind of expression, see p. 322 on *alameva saddhāpabbajitena kulaputtena viriyaṃ ārabhituṃ*.

7. Pañcaverabhayasutta

Five Enemies and Perils (SN 12:41; II 68–69)

[1. Opening statement]

Atha kho anāthapiṇḍiko gahapati yena bhagavā ten'upasaṅkami. Upasaṅkamitvā bhagavantaṃ abhivādetvā ekamantaṃ nisīdi. Ekamantaṃ nisinnaṃ kho anāthapiṇḍikaṃ gahapatiṃ bhagavā etadavoca:

Then Anāthapiṇḍika the householder where the Blessed One, there approached. Having approached, the Blessed One having paid homage to, one-side sat down. One-side seated, to Anāthapiṇḍika the householder the Blessed One this-said:

Then the householder Anāthapiṇḍika approached the Blessed One. Having approached, he paid homage to the Blessed One and sat down to one side. The Blessed One then said this to the householder Anāthapiṇḍika as he was seated to one side:

"Yato kho, gahapati, ariyasāvakassa pañca bhayāni verāni vūpasantāni honti,[168] *catūhi ca sotāpattiyaṅgehi samannāgato hoti, ariyo c'assa ñāyo paññāya sudiṭṭho hoti suppaṭividdho, so ākaṅkhamāno attanā'va attānaṃ vyākareyya: 'Khīṇanirayo'mhi khīṇatiracchānayoni khīṇapettivisayo khīṇāpāyaduggativinipāto, sotāpanno'hamasmi avinipātadhammo niyato sambodhiparāyano'ti.*

"When, householder, for a noble-disciple five perils enemies subsided are, with four and stream-entry factors possessed is, noble and of him method with wisdom well-seen is, well-penetrated, he wishing by himself just, himself might declare: 'Finished-hell I am, finished-animal-realm, finished-spirit-domain, finished-misery-plane-bad-destinations-lower-world, stream-enterer I am, not-lower-world-subject-to, fixed, enlightenment-destination.'

"When, householder, for a noble disciple five perils and enemies have subsided, and he possesses the four factors of stream-entry, and the noble

168. Although in the title of this sutta *vera*, "enmity," precedes *bhaya*, "peril," in the exposition the order is inverted, with *bhaya* preceding *vera*. The commentary does not give a reason for this inversion.

method has been well seen and well penetrated by him with wisdom, then, if he wishes he could even by himself declare himself thus: 'I am one finished with hell, finished with the animal realm, finished with the domain of spirits, finished with the plane of misery, the bad destinations, the lower world. I am a stream-enterer, no longer subject to the lower world, fixed [in destiny], with enlightenment as destination.'

[2. The five enemies and perils]

"Katamāni pañca bhayāni verāni vūpasantāni honti? Yaṃ, gahapati, pāṇātipātī pāṇātipātapaccayā diṭṭhadhammikampi bhayaṃ veraṃ pasavati, samparāyikampi bhayaṃ veraṃ pasavati, cetasikampi dukkhaṃ domanassaṃ paṭisaṃvedayati, pāṇātipātā paṭiviratassa evaṃ taṃ bhayaṃ veraṃ vūpasantaṃ hoti.

"What five perils enemies subsided are? Which, householder, a life-destroyer through life-destruction-condition present-life-too peril enemy engenders, future-life-too peril enemy engenders, mental-too pain dejection experiences, from life-destruction for one abstained, thus that peril enemy subsided is.

"What are the five perils and enemies that have subsided? Householder, one who destroys life, with the destruction of life as condition, engenders a peril and enemy pertaining to the present life and a peril and enemy pertaining to the future life, and he experiences mental pain and dejection. Thus for one who abstains from the destruction of life, this peril and enemy has subsided.

"Yaṃ, gahapati, adinnādāyī . . . kāmesu micchācārī . . . musāvādī . . . surāmerayamajjapamādaṭṭhāyī surāmerayamajjapamādaṭṭhānapaccayā diṭṭhadhammikampi bhayaṃ veraṃ pasavati, samparāyikampi bhayaṃ veraṃ pasavati, cetasikampi dukkhaṃ domanassaṃ paṭisaṃvedayati, surāmerayamajjapamādaṭṭhānā paṭiviratassa evaṃ taṃ bhayaṃ veraṃ vūpasantaṃ hoti. Imāni pañca bhayāni verāni vūpasantāni honti.

"Which, householder, not-given taker . . . in sensual pleasures one-of-misconduct . . . a falsehood-speaker . . . liquor-wine-intoxicant-heedlessness-basis-[user], through liquor-wine-intoxicant-heedlessness-basis-condition, present-life-too peril enemy engenders, future-life-too peril enemy engenders, mental-too pain dejection experiences, from wine-liquor-intoxicant-heedlessness-basis for one abstained, thus that peril enemy subsided is. These five perils enemies subsided are.

"One who takes what is not given . . . One who engages in sexual misconduct . . . One who speaks falsely . . . One who [uses] liquor, wine, and intoxicants, a basis for heedlessness, with [the use of] liquor, wine, and intoxicants, a basis for heedlessness, as condition, engenders a peril and enemy pertaining to the present life and a peril and enemy pertaining to the future life, and he experiences mental pain and dejection. Thus for one who abstains from [the use of] liquor, wine, and intoxicants, a basis for heedlessness, this peril and enemy has subsided. These are the five perils and enemies that have subsided.

[3. The four factors of stream-entry]

"Katamehi catūhi sotāpattiyaṅgehi samannāgato hoti? Idha, gahapati, ariyasāvako buddhe aveccappasādena samannāgato hoti: 'Itipi so bhagavā arahaṃ sammāsambuddho vijjācaraṇasampanno sugato lokavidū anuttaro purisadammasārathi satthā devamanussānaṃ buddho bhagavā'ti.

"With what four stream-entry-factors possessed is? Here, householder, a noble-disciple in the Buddha with confirmed-confidence possessed is: 'So-too that Blessed One, arahant, perfectly-enlightened, knowledge-conduct-accomplished, fortunate, world-knower, unsurpassed persons-tamable-charioteer, teacher of devas-humans, enlightened one, blessed one.'

"What are the four factors of stream-entry that he possesses? Here, householder, the noble disciple possesses confirmed confidence in the Buddha thus: 'The Blessed One is an arahant, perfectly enlightened, accomplished in clear knowledge and conduct, fortunate, knower of the world, unsurpassed trainer of persons to be tamed, teacher of devas and humans, the Enlightened One, the Blessed One.'

"Dhamme aveccappasādena samannāgato hoti: 'Svākkhāto bhagavatā dhammo sandiṭṭhiko akāliko ehipassiko opanayiko paccattaṃ veditabbo viññūhī'ti.

"In the Dhamma with confirmed-confidence possessed is: 'Well expounded by the Blessed One the Dhamma, directly-visible, not-temporal, a come-see-thing, applicable, personally to-be-understood by the wise.'

"He possesses confirmed confidence in the Dhamma thus: 'The Dhamma is well expounded by the Blessed One, directly visible, immediate, asking one to come and see, applicable, to be personally understood by the wise.'

"Saṅghe aveccappasādena samannāgato hoti: 'Suppaṭipanno bhagavato sāvakasaṅgho, ujuppaṭipanno bhagavato sāvakasaṅgho, ñāyappaṭipanno bhagavato sāvakasaṅgho, sāmīcippaṭipanno bhagavato sāvakasaṅgho, yad-idaṃ cattāri purisayugāni aṭṭha purisapuggalā, esa bhagavato sāvakasaṅgho āhuneyyo pāhuneyyo dakkhiṇeyyo añjalikaraṇīyo anuttaraṃ puññak-khettaṃ lokassā'ti.

"In the Sangha with confirmed-confidence possessed is: 'Well-practiced of the Blessed One disciples-sangha, straight-practiced of the Blessed One disciples-sangha, method-practiced of the Blessed One disciples-sangha, proper-practiced of the Blessed One disciples-sangha, that is: four persons-pairs, eight persons-individuals, this of the Blessed One disciples-sangha, gift-worthy, hospitality-worthy, offerings-worthy, salutation-to-be-done, unsurpassed merits-field of the world.'

"He possesses confirmed confidence in the Sangha thus: 'The Sangha of the Blessed One's disciples is practicing well, practicing in a straight way, practicing methodically, practicing properly—that is, the four pairs of persons, the eight types of individuals, this Sangha of the Blessed One's disciples is worthy of gifts, worthy of hospitality, worthy of offerings, worthy of salutation, the unsurpassed field of merit for the world.'

"Ariyakantehi sīlehi samannāgato hoti akhaṇḍehi acchiddehi asabalehi akammāsehi bhujissehi viññuppasatthehi aparāmaṭṭhehi samādhisaṃvat-tanikehi. Imehi catūhi sotāpattiyaṅgehi samannāgato hoti.

"With nobles-loved good-behaviors possessed is, unbroken, untorn, unblemished, unmottled, freeing, wise-praised, ungrasped, concentration-leading. With these four stream-entry-factors possessed is.

"He possesses the kinds of good behavior loved by the noble ones—unbroken, untorn, unblemished, unmottled, freeing, praised by the wise, ungrasped, leading to concentration. These are the four factors of stream-entry that he possesses.

[4. The noble method]

"Katamo c'assa ariyo ñāyo paññāya sudiṭṭho hoti suppaṭividdho? Idha, gahapati, ariyasāvako paṭiccasamuppādaññeva sādhukaṃ yoniso manasikaroti: 'Iti imasmiṃ sati idaṃ hoti; imass'uppādā idaṃ uppajjati. Imasmiṃ asati idaṃ na hoti; imassa nirodhā idaṃ nirujjhati.'[169]

"What and of him the noble method with wisdom well-seen is, well-penetrated? Here, householder, the noble-disciple dependent-origination itself well thoroughly attends to: 'Thus when this existing, that occurs; of this through arising, that arises. When this not existing, that does not occur; of this through cessation, that ceases.'

"And what is the noble method that he has well seen and well penetrated with wisdom? Here, householder, the noble disciple well attends thoroughly to dependent origination itself thus: 'When this exists, that occurs; with the arising of this, that arises. When this does not exist, that does not occur; with the cessation of this, that ceases.'

"'Yadidaṃ avijjāpaccayā saṅkhārā; saṅkhārapaccayā viññāṇaṃ . . . Evametassa kevalassa dukkhakkhandhassa samudayo hoti. Avijjāya tveva asesavirāganirodhā saṅkhāranirodho; saṅkhāranirodhā viññāṇanirodho. . . . Evametassa kevalassa dukkhakkhandhassa nirodho hotī'ti. Ayamassa ariyo ñāyo paññāya sudiṭṭho hoti suppaṭividdho.

"'That is, through ignorance-condition, volitional-activities; through volitional-activities consciousness. . . . Thus-of this whole suffering-mass origin is. Of ignorance but-indeed, through remainderless-fading-cessation, volitional-activities cessation; through volitional-activities-cessation, consciousness-

169. I here follow the reading of Ce. Be and Ee pair the two statements in terms of existence and the two in terms of arising and ceasing: *Iti imasmiṃ sati idaṃ hoti, imasmiṃ asati idaṃ na hoti; imass'uppādā idaṃ uppajjati, imassa nirodhā idaṃ nirujjhati.*

cessation. . . . Thus-of this whole suffering-mass cessation is.' This-of him the noble method with wisdom well-seen is, well-penetrated.

"'That is, with ignorance as condition, volitional activities [occur]; with volitional activities as condition, consciousness. . . . Such is the origin of this whole mass of suffering. But with the remainderless fading away and cessation of ignorance [there occurs] cessation of volitional activities; with the cessation of volitional activities, cessation of consciousness. . . . Such is the cessation of this whole mass of suffering.' This is the noble method that he has well seen and well penetrated with wisdom.

"Yato kho, gahapati, ariyasāvakassa imāni pañca bhayāni verāni vūpasantāni honti, imehi catūhi ca sotāpattiyaṅgehi samannāgato hoti, ayañc'assa ariyo ñāyo paññāya sudiṭṭho hoti suppaṭividdho, so ākaṅkhamāno attanā'va attānaṃ vyākareyya: 'Khīṇanirayo'mhi khīṇatiracchānayoni khīṇapettivisayo khīṇāpāyaduggativinipāto, sotāpanno'hamasmi avinipātadhammo niyato sambodhiparāyano'"ti.

"When, householder, of a noble-disciple these five perils enemies subsided are, with these four and stream-entry factors possessed is, this-and-of him noble method with wisdom well seen is, well penetrated, he wishing by himself-just himself might declare: 'Finished-hell I am, finished-animal-realm, finished-spirit-domain, finished-misery-plane-bad-destinations-lower-world, stream-enterer I am, not-lower-world-subject-to, fixed, enlightenment-destination.'"

"When, householder, these five perils and enemies have subsided in a noble disciple, and he possesses these four factors of stream-entry, and he has well seen and well penetrated with wisdom this noble method, if he wishes he could even by himself declare himself thus: 'I am one finished with hell, finished with the animal realm, finished with the domain of spirits, finished with the plane of misery, the bad destinations, the lower world. I am a stream-enterer, no longer subject to the lower world, fixed [in destiny], with enlightenment as destination.'"

Grammatical explanations

[1. Opening statement]

ariyasāvakassa pañca bhayāni verāni vūpasantāni honti: "for a noble disciple five perils [and] enemies have subsided." The clauses in the opening sentence employ a variety of constructions. The first is a passive formation in which the logical subject, *ariyasāvakassa*, is dative (or genitive), and the grammatical subject, *pañca bhayāni verāni*, is nominative (see pp. 74–75). The action is described by a past participle and auxiliary verb, *vūpasantāni honti*. The relationship between *bhayāni* and *verāni* is not clear from the sutta itself, but they appear to be used synonymously.[170]

catūhi ca sotāpattiyaṅgehi samannāgato hoti: "and he possesses the four factors of stream-entry." Here, the noble disciple is the grammatical subject qualified by the nominative past participle, *samannāgato*, which takes the qualities possessed, *sotāpattiyaṅgehi*, in the instrumental case. The latter is a tappurisa compound of *sotāpatti* and *aṅgehi*, with *-y-* inserted for euphony.[171]

ariyo c'assa ñāyo paññāya sudiṭṭho hoti suppaṭividdho: "and the noble method has been well seen and well penetrated by him with wisdom." Here the logical subject is a genitive with an instrumental sense, *assa*, "of him," designating the noble disciple; the grammatical subject, *ariyo ñāyo*, "noble method," is the object of the action performed by the agent (see p. 105). *Ariyo ñāyo* is described as *sudiṭṭho* and *suppaṭividdho*, each formed from a past participle with the prefix *su-*. Though I follow the passive syntax of the Pāli, a translation in more natural English would use the active voice: "and he has well seen and well penetrated the noble method with wisdom."

so ākaṅkhamāno attanā'va attānaṃ vyākareyya: "if he wishes (= wishing) he could even by himself declare himself thus." The middle-voice present participle, *ākaṅkhamāno*, is nominative in agreement with the subject *so*; *attanā* is instrumental, followed by the emphatic *va* (= *eva*); *attānaṃ* is the accusative object of the optative verb, *vyākareyya*.

170. The Saṃyutta commentary (Spk II 72–73) explains the terms jointly as "peril-enemy-volitions" (*bhayaveracetanāyo*) and says the two are one in meaning (*atthato ekaṃ*).

171. Perniola (§9) cites this compound as an example of "the insertion of a consonant." Most grammarians, however, speak of *y* as a semivowel or glide.

khīṇanirayo'mhi: "I am one finished with hell." *Khīṇanirayo* is a bahubbīhi composed of the past participle *khīṇa*, "destroyed, exhausted, finished," and the noun *nirayo*, "hell," with the auxiliary verb *'mhi* (= *amhi*). Each of the nominative compounds to follow is constructed in the same way, with *amhi* implicit.

'hamasmi: a sandhi of *ahaṃ* and *asmi*. *Amhi* and *asmi* are alternative forms of the first-person singular of *atthi*.

avinipātadhammo: "no longer subject to the lower world." *Vinipāta* (literally "the downfall") refers to the three bad destinations; here, it is negated by *a-*, with *-dhammo* as final member of the compound meaning "subject to." The compound is a bahubbīhi. On this form, see too the explanation of *viparināmadhammo* on p. 154.

niyato: He is "fixed [in destiny]" because, having entered the path, he is bound to reach liberation in a maximum of seven more lives.

sambodhiparāyano: "with enlightenment as destination"; another bahubbīhi describing *ariyasāvako*.

[2. The five enemies and perils]

yaṃ: the relative adjective, to be taken with *bhayaṃ veraṃ* and correlated with the demonstrative *taṃ* in the last clause of the sentence.

pāṇātipātī: "one who commits *pāṇātipāta*," the taking of life. The compound seems to be an accusative tappurisa in the nominative case (based on the stem *pāṇātipātin*). So too for *adinnādāyī* and the others that follow.

diṭṭhadhammikaṃ: "pertaining to the present life, this visible state," composed from *diṭṭha* + *dhamma*, with the adjectival suffix *-ika*. It is contrasted with *samparāyikaṃ*, "pertaining to the future state." Both describe *bhayaṃ veraṃ*.

cetasikaṃ: an adjective describing *dukkhaṃ*. In the suttas the word does not mean "a mental factor," as it does in the Abhidhamma.

pāṇātipātā paṭiviratassa: "for one who abstains from the destruction of life"; an ablative followed by a dative.

surāmerayamajjapamādaṭṭhānā: "from [using] liquor, wine, and intoxicants, a basis for heedlessness." I translate according to the intended sense rather than in accordance with the grammatical structure. Taken literally, the statement is urging abstinence from "a state of heedlessness on account of liquor, wine, and intoxicants," but it is clear from other sources (such as Sn 400 and Dhp 247) that the training rule calls for total abstinence.

[3. The four factors of stream-entry]

aveccappasādena: "confirmed confidence"; a syntactical compound of *avecca*, the absolutive of *aveti* (see DOP), and *pasādena*, an instrumental. *Avecca* probably originally meant "having undergone," that is, having directly realized the Dhamma. The commentaries consistently gloss the compound with *avigatena acalappasādena*, "unvanished unwavering confidence," apparently taking *avecca* as resolvable into *a* + *vecca*, the latter an absolutive of *veti*, "vanished."[172]

cattāri purisayugāni aṭṭha purisapuggalā: "the four pairs of persons, the eight types of individuals"; the four who have attained the fruits and the four practicing for each of those fruits.

añjalikaraṇīyo: "worthy of salutation"; a compound of *añjali*, the traditional Indian gesture of reverence, and the future passive participle, *karaṇīyo*, "to be done."

anuttaraṃ puññakkhettaṃ lokassa: "the unsurpassed field of merit for the world." With *lokassa* at the end, normal word order is inverted. *Puññakkhettaṃ* is a genitive tappurisa in the nominative case.

akhaṇḍehi, etc.: Each of these is an adjective describing *sīlehi*.

[4. The noble method]

paṭiccasamuppādaññeva: = *paṭiccasamuppādaṃ* + *eva*, where *eva* is a mere emphatic.

ayamassa = *ayaṃ* + *assa*, where the demonstrative *ayaṃ* agrees with *ariyo ñāyo* and the genitive pronoun *assa* (again with an instrumental sense) designates the *ariyasāvaka*.

imāni: the nominative demonstrative plural agreeing with *pañca bhayāni verāni*.

imehi: the instrumental demonstrative plural agreeing with *catūhi sotāpattiyaṅgehi*.

172. See for instance Spk II 74,4.

8. Parivīmaṃsanasutta

Investigation (SN 12:51; II 80–84)

[1. The investigation]

"Idha, bhikkhave, bhikkhu parivīmaṃsamāno parivīmaṃsati: 'Yaṃ kho idaṃ anekavidhaṃ nānappakārakaṃ dukkhaṃ loke uppajjati jarāmaraṇaṃ, idaṃ nu kho dukkhaṃ kiṃnidānaṃ kiṃsamudayaṃ kiṃjātikaṃ kiṃpabhavaṃ? Kismiṃ sati jarāmaraṇaṃ hoti; kismiṃ asati jarāmaraṇaṃ na hotī'ti?

"Here, monks, a monk investigating investigates: 'Which this manifold different-kind suffering in the world arises old-age-death: this suffering what-cause, what-origin, what-genesis, what-source? What existing, old-age-death occurs; what not existing, old-age-death not occurs?'

"Here, monks, when investigating, a monk investigates thus: 'The manifold different kinds of suffering that arise in the world [headed by] old-age-and-death: what is the cause of this suffering, what is its origin, what is its genesis, what is its source? When what exists does old-age-and-death occur? When what does not exist does old-age-and-death not occur?'

"So parivīmaṃsamāno evaṃ pajānāti: 'Yaṃ kho idaṃ anekavidhaṃ nānappakārakaṃ dukkhaṃ loke uppajjati jarāmaraṇaṃ, idaṃ kho dukkhaṃ jātinidānaṃ jātisamudayaṃ jātijātikaṃ jātippabhavaṃ. Jātiyā sati jarāmaraṇaṃ hoti; jātiyā asati jarāmaraṇaṃ na hotī'ti.

"He investigating thus understands: 'Which this manifold different-kind suffering in the world arises old-age-death: this suffering birth-cause, birth-origin, birth-genesis, birth-source. Birth existing, old-age-death occurs; birth not existing, old-age-death not occurs.'

"As he investigates he understands thus: 'The manifold different kinds of suffering that arise in the world [headed by] old-age-and-death: this suffering has birth as its cause, birth as its origin, birth as its genesis, birth as its source. When there is birth, old-age-and-death occurs; when there is no birth, old-age-and-death does not occur.'

"So jarāmaraṇañca pajānāti, jarāmaraṇasamudayañca pajānāti, jarāmaraṇanirodhañca pajānāti, yā ca jarāmaraṇanirodhasāruppagāminī paṭipadā tañca pajānāti, tathā paṭipanno ca hoti anudhammacārī. Ayaṃ vuccati, bhikkhave, 'bhikkhu sabbaso sammā dukkhakkhayāya paṭipanno jarāmaraṇanirodhāya.'

"He old-age-death-and understands, old-age-death-origin-and understands, old-age-death-cessation-and understands, which and old-age-death-cessation-conformity-going way, that-and understands, so practicing and is, according-to-Dhamma-acting. This is called, monks, 'a monk entirely completely for suffering-destruction practicing, for old-age-death-cessation.'

"He understands old-age-and-death, its origin, its cessation, and the way going in conformity with its cessation. He practices in that way and acts in accordance with the Dhamma. This is called 'a monk who is practicing for the entirely complete destruction of suffering, for the cessation of old-age-and-death.'

"Athāparaṃ parivīmaṃsamāno parivīmaṃsati: 'Jāti panāyaṃ kiṃnidānā . . . Bhavo panāyaṃ kiṃnidāno . . . Upādānaṃ . . . Taṇhā . . . Vedanā . . . Phasso . . . Saḷāyatanaṃ . . . Nāmarūpaṃ . . . Viññāṇaṃ . . . Saṅkhārā pan'ime kiṃnidānā kiṃsamudayā kiṃjātikā kiṃpabhavā. Kismiṃ sati saṅkhārā honti; kismiṃ asati saṅkhārā na hontī'ti?

"Then-further investigating, he investigates: "Birth but-this what-cause . . . Existence but-this what cause . . . Clinging . . . Craving . . . Feeling . . . Contact . . . Six-sense-base . . . Name-form . . . Consciousness . . . Volitional-activities but these what-cause, what-origin, what-genesis, what-source? What existing, volitional-activities occur; what not existing, volitional-activities not occur?'

"Then, further investigating, he investigates thus: 'But what is the cause of this birth?. . . But what is the cause of this existence?. . . this clinging?. . . this craving?. . . this feeling?. . . this contact?. . . these six sense bases?. . . this name-and-form?. . . this consciousness?. . . But what is the cause of these volitional activities, what is their origin, what is their genesis, what is their source? When what exists do volitional activities occur? When what does not exist do volitional activities not occur?'

"So parivīmaṃsamāno evaṃ pajānāti: 'Saṅkhārā avijjānidānā avijjāsamudayā avijjājātikā avijjāpabhavā. Avijjāya sati saṅkhārā honti; avijjāya asati saṅkhārā na hontī'ti.

"He investigating thus understands: 'Volitional-activities ignorance-cause, ignorance-origin, ignorance-genesis, ignorance-source. Ignorance existing, volitional-activities occur; ignorance not existing, volitional-activities not occur.'

"As he investigates he understands thus: 'Volitional activities have ignorance as their cause, ignorance as their origin, ignorance as their genesis, ignorance as their source. When there is ignorance, volitional activities occur; when there is no ignorance, volitional activities do not occur.'

"So saṅkhāre ca pajānāti, saṅkhārasamudayañca pajānāti, saṅkhāranirodhañca pajānāti, yā ca saṅkhāranirodhasāruppagāminī paṭipadā tañca pajānāti, tathā paṭipanno ca hoti anudhammacārī. Ayaṃ vuccati, bhikkhave, 'bhikkhu sabbaso sammā dukkhakkhayāya paṭipanno saṅkhāranirodhāya.'

"He volitional-activities and understands, volitional-activities-origin-and understands, volitional-activities-cessation-and understands, which and volitional-activities-cessation-conformity-going way, that-and understands, so practicing and is according-to-Dhamma-acting. This is called, monks, a monk entirely completely for suffering-destruction practicing, for volitional-activities-cessation.

"He understands volitional activities, their origin, their cessation, and the way going in conformity with their cessation. He practices in that way and acts in accordance with the Dhamma. This is called 'a monk who is practicing for the entirely complete destruction of suffering, for the cessation of volitional activities.'

[2. Liberation]

"Avijjāgato'yaṃ, bhikkhave, purisapuggalo puññaṃ ce saṅkhāraṃ abhisaṅkharoti, puññūpagaṃ hoti viññāṇaṃ. Apuññaṃ ce saṅkhāraṃ abhisaṅkharoti, apuññūpagaṃ hoti viññāṇaṃ. Āneñjaṃ ce saṅkhāraṃ abhisaṅkharoti āneñjūpagaṃ hoti viññāṇaṃ.

"Ignorance-gone this, monks, person-individual merit if volitional-activity generates, merit-approached is consciousness. Demerit if volitional-activity generates, demerit-approached is consciousness. Imperturbable if volitional-activity generates, imperturbable-approached is consciousness.

"If, monks, this ignorant person generates a meritorious volitional activity, consciousness approaches the meritorious. If he generates a demeritorious volitional activity, consciousness approaches the demeritorious. If he generates an imperturbable volitional activity, consciousness approaches the imperturbable.

"Yato kho, bhikkhave, bhikkhuno avijjā pahīnā hoti, vijjā uppannā, so avijjāvirāgā vijjuppādā n'eva puññābhisaṅkhāraṃ abhisaṅkharoti, na apuññābhisaṅkhāraṃ abhisaṅkharoti, na āneñjābhisaṅkhāraṃ abhisaṅkharoti.

"When, monks, for a monk ignorance abandoned is, clear-knowledge arisen, he through ignorance-fading, through clear-knowledge-arising, not merit-volitional-activity generates, not demerit-volitional-activity generates, not imperturbable-volitional-activity generates.

"But, monks, when for a monk ignorance is abandoned and clear knowledge has arisen, then, with the fading away of ignorance, with the arising of clear knowledge, he does not generate a meritorious volitional activity, does not generate a demeritorious volitional activity, does not generate an imperturbable volitional activity.

"Anabhisaṅkharonto anabhisañcetayanto na kiñci loke upādiyati. Anupādiyaṃ na paritassati. Aparitassaṃ paccattaññeva parinibbāyati. 'Khīṇā jāti, vusitaṃ brahmacariyaṃ, kataṃ karaṇīyaṃ, nāparaṃ itthattāyā'ti pajānāti.

"One-not-generating-volitional-activity, one-not-volitionally-producing, not anything in the world clings. Not-clinging, not thirsts. Not-thirsting, personally-indeed attains-nibbāna. 'Finished birth, lived the spiritual-life, done what-is-to-be-done, not-further for such-a-state,' understands.

"One not volitionally generating or volitionally producing does not cling to anything in the world. Not clinging, he does not thirst. Not thirsting, he personally attains nibbāna. He understands: 'Finished is birth, the spiritual life has been lived, what had to be done has been done, there is no more for this state of being.'

[3. Nibbāna with residue]
"So sukhaṃ ce vedanaṃ vedayati, 'sā aniccā'ti pajānāti, 'anajjhositā'ti pajānāti, 'anabhinanditā'ti pajānāti. Dukkhaṃ ce vedanaṃ vedayati, 'sā aniccā'ti pajānāti, 'anajjhositā'ti pajānāti, 'anabhinanditā'ti pajānāti. Adukkhamasukhaṃ ce vedanaṃ vedayati, 'sā aniccā'ti pajānāti, 'anajjhositā'ti pajānāti, 'anabhinanditā'ti pajānāti. So sukhaṃ ce vedanaṃ vedayati, visaṃyutto naṃ vedanaṃ vedayati. Dukkhaṃ ce vedanaṃ vedayati, visaṃyutto naṃ vedanaṃ vedayati. Adukkhamasukhaṃ ce vedanaṃ vedayati, visaṃyutto naṃ vedanaṃ vedayati.

"He pleasant if a feeling feels, 'That impermanent' understands; 'not held to,' understands; 'not delighted in' understands. Painful if a feeling feels, 'That impermanent' understands; 'not held to,' understands; 'not delighted in' understands. Not-painful-not-pleasant if a feeling feels, 'That impermanent' understands; 'not held to,' understands; 'not delighted in' understands. He pleasant if a feeling feels, detached that feeling feels. Painful if a feeling feels, detached that feeling feels. Not-painful-not-pleasant if a feeling feels, detached that feeling feels.

"If he feels a pleasant feeling, he understands: 'It is impermanent'; he understands: '[It's] not held to'; he understands: '[It's] not delighted in.' If he feels a painful feeling, he understands: 'It is impermanent'; he understands: '[It's] not held to'; he understands: '[It's] not delighted in.' If he feels a neither-painful-nor-pleasant feeling, he understands: 'It is impermanent'; he understands: '[It's] not held to'; he understands: '[It's] not delighted in.' If he feels a pleasant feeling, he feels it detached; if he feels a painful feeling, he feels it detached; if he feels a neither-painful-nor-pleasant feeling, he feels it detached.

"So kāyapariyantikaṃ vedanaṃ vedayamāno 'kāyapariyantikaṃ vedanaṃ vedayāmī'ti pajānāti; jīvitapariyantikaṃ vedanaṃ vedayamāno 'jīvitapariyantikaṃ vedanaṃ vedayāmī'ti pajānāti. 'Kāyassa bhedā uddhaṃ

jīvitapariyādānā idh'eva sabbavedayitāni anabhinanditāni sītībhavissanti, sarīrāni avasissantī'ti pajānāti.

"He a body-limited feeling when feeling, 'A body-limited feeling I feel' understands; a life-limited feeling when feeling, 'A life-limited feeling I feel' understands. 'Of the body through breakup, following life-exhaustion, here itself all-felt not-delighted-in cool-will-become, bodily-remnants will remain,' understands.

"When he feels a feeling limited by the body, he understands: 'I feel a feeling limited by the body.' When he feels a feeling limited by life, he understands: 'I feel a feeling limited by life.' He understands: 'With the breakup of the body, following the exhaustion of life, all that is felt, not being delighted in, will become cool right here; bodily remnants will remain.'

"Seyyathāpi, bhikkhave, puriso kumbhakārapākā uṇhaṃ kumbhaṃ uddharitvā same bhūmibhāge paṭiviseyya. Tatra yāyaṃ usmā sā tatth'eva vūpasameyya, kapallāni avasisseyyuṃ. Evameva kho, bhikkhave, bhikkhu kāyapariyantikaṃ vedanaṃ vedayamāno 'kāyapariyantikaṃ vedanaṃ vedayāmī'ti pajānāti, jīvitapariyantikaṃ vedanaṃ vedayamāno 'jīvitapariyantikaṃ vedanaṃ vedayāmī'ti pajānāti. 'Kāyassa bhedā uddhaṃ jīvitapariyādānā idh'eva sabbavedayitāni anabhinanditāni sītībhavissanti, sarīrāni avasissantī'ti pajānāti.

"Suppose, monks, a man from a potter-oven a hot pot having removed, on even ground-portion would place. There which-this heat, that there-itself would subside, shards would remain. Just-so, monks, a monk a body-limited feeling when feeling, 'A body-limited feeling I feel' understands; a life-limited feeling when feeling, 'A life-limited feeling I feel' understands. 'Of the body through breakup, following life-exhaustion, here itself all-felt not-delighted-in cool-will-become, bodily-remnants will remain,' understands.

"Suppose, monks, a man would remove a hot clay pot from a potter's oven and set it down on even ground. Its heat would subside right there and shards would remain. So too, when he feels a feeling limited by the body, he understands: 'I feel a feeling limited by the body.' When he feels a feeling limited by life, he understands: 'I feel a feeling limited by life.' He understands: 'With the breakup of the body, following the exhaustion of life, all that is felt, not being delighted in, will become cool right here; bodily remnants will remain.'

[4. Nibbāna without residue]

"Taṃ kiṃ maññatha, bhikkhave, api nu kho khīṇāsavo bhikkhu puññābhisaṅkhāraṃ vā abhisaṅkhareyya, apuññābhisaṅkhāraṃ vā abhisaṅkhareyya, āneñjābhisaṅkhāraṃ vā abhisaṅkhareyyā"ti? — "No h'etaṃ, bhante." — "Sabbaso vā pana saṅkhāresu asati, saṅkhāranirodhā api nu kho viññāṇaṃ paññāyethā"ti? — "No h'etaṃ, bhante."

"That what you think, monks, is it the case that a destroyed-influxes monk a merit-volitional-activity or would generate, a demerit-volitional-activity or would generate, an imperturbable-volitional-activity or would generate?" — "Not indeed this, Bhante." — "Completely or volitional-activities not existing, through volitional-activities-cessation, is it the case that consciousness would be discerned?" — "Not indeed this, Bhante."

"What do you think, monks? Would a monk whose influxes are destroyed generate a meritorious volitional activity, or would he generate a demeritorious volitional activity, or would he generate an imperturbable volitional activity?" — "Surely not, Bhante." — "When volitional activities completely do not exist, with the cessation of volitional activities, would consciousness be discerned?" — "Surely not, Bhante."

"Sabbaso vā pana viññāṇe asati, viññāṇanirodhā api nu kho nāmarūpaṃ paññāyethā"ti? — "No h'etaṃ, bhante." — "Sabbaso vā pana nāmarūpe asati . . . saḷāyatane asati . . . phasse asati . . . vedanāya asati . . . taṇhāya asati . . . upādāne asati . . . bhave asati, bhavanirodhā api nu kho jāti paññāyethā"ti? — "No h'etaṃ, bhante." — "Sabbaso vā pana jātiyā asati, jātinirodhā api nu kho jarāmaraṇaṃ paññāyethā"ti? — "No h'etaṃ, bhante."

"Completely or consciousness not existing, through consciousness-cessation, is it the case that name-form would be discerned?" — "Not indeed this, Bhante." — "Completely or name-form not existing . . . six-sense-base not existing . . . contact not existing . . . feeling not existing . . . craving not existing . . . clinging not existing . . . existence not existing, through existence-cessation, is it the case that birth would be discerned?" — "Not indeed this,

Bhante." — "Completely or birth not existing, through birth-cessation, is it the case that old-age-death would be discerned?" — "Not indeed this, Bhante."

"When consciousness completely does not exist, with the cessation of consciousness, would name-and-form be discerned?" — "Surely not, Bhante." — "When name-and-form completely does not exist... When the six sense bases completely do not exist... When contact completely does not exist... When feeling completely does not exist... When craving completely does not exist... When clinging completely does not exist... When existence completely does not exist, with the cessation of existence, would birth be discerned?" — "Surely not, Bhante." — "When birth completely does not exist, with the cessation of birth, would old-age-and-death be discerned?" — "Surely not, Bhante."

"Sādhu sādhu, bhikkhave! Evametaṃ, bhikkhave, n'etaṃ aññathā. Saddahatha me taṃ, bhikkhave, adhimuccatha. Nikkaṅkhā ettha hotha nibbicikicchā. Es'ev'anto dukkhassā"ti.

"Good, good, monks! Thus-this, monks, not this otherwise. Have-faith of me that, monks, be convinced. Without-perplexity here be, without-doubt. This itself the end of suffering."

"Good, good, monks! So it is, monks, and not otherwise. Have faith in me about that, monks, be convinced. Be without perplexity about this, without doubt. This itself is the end of suffering."

Grammatical explanations

[1. The investigation]

parivīmaṃsamāno parivīmaṃsati: "when investigating, [he] investigates"; the nominative present participle followed by the cognate finite verb.

anekavidhaṃ nānappakārakaṃ: "manifold different kinds." *Aneka*, "many," is the negation of *eka*, "one," *-vidhaṃ* a suffix similar in meaning to "-fold." *Nānā*, "different," is joined with *pakāra*, "kind, aspect," hence the adjective *nānappakāraka*, "of different kinds" (*nānā* becomes *nāna* before the following double consonant, with *-pp-* representing the *-pr-* of the Skt). Both *anekavidhaṃ* and *nānappakārakaṃ* qualify *dukkhaṃ*.

idaṃ nu kho dukkhaṃ kiṃnidānaṃ: "What is the cause of this suffering?" *Kiṃnidānaṃ* is an interrogative bahubbīhi agreeing with *dukkhaṃ*. So too for *kiṃsamudayaṃ* and the following interrrogatives.

kismiṃ sati, kismiṃ asati: "When what exists? . . . When what does not exist?" These are interrogative locative absolutes, in positive and negative modes; see the explanation of *kimhi nu kho sati* on p. 302. *Kismiṃ* and *kimhi* are alternative forms of the locative interrogative pronoun.

idaṃ kho dukkhaṃ jātinidānaṃ . . . jātippabhavaṃ: "this suffering has birth as its cause . . . birth as its source." The bahubbīhis are in agreement with *dukkhaṃ*.

jātiyā sati, jātiyā asati: see p. 302.

jarāmaraṇanirodhasāruppagāminī paṭipadā: "the way going in conformity with the cessation of old-age-and-death." The Saṃyutta commentary explains: "The meaning is that it goes, having become similar to the cessation of old-age-and-death through its conformity to it, because of its purity through its undefiled nature."[173]

tathā paṭipanno: "practices in that way"; an adverb of manner followed by a past participle used to describe a continuous action occurring in the present.

anudhammacārī: "acts in accordance with the Dhamma"; a kammadhāraya compound composed of the prefix *anu-*, "in accord with," *dhamma*, and the suffix *-cārī*, from the verb *carati*. The commentary explains this to mean: "One acts upon—fulfills—the *dhamma* of practice that is in accord with the *dhamma* of nibbāna."[174]

sabbaso sammā dukkhakkhayāya paṭipanno jarāmaraṇanirodhāya: "practicing for the entirely complete destruction of suffering, for the cessation of old-age-and-death." *Sabbaso* is an adverb derived from *sabba*. I take *sammā* to qualify *dukkhakkhayāya*.[175] *Dukkhakkhayāya* and

173. Spk II 77,6–8: *Jarāmaraṇanirodhassa sāruppabhāvena nikkilesatāya parisuddhatāya sadisāva hutvā gāminī ti attho.*

174. Spk II 77,9–11: *Anudhammacārī ti nibbānadhammaṃ anugataṃ paṭipattidhammaṃ carati, pūretī ti attho.*

175. Although *sammā* might have been taken to qualify *paṭipanno*, "rightly practicing," in support of the present rendering I would cite the many occasions where *sammā dukkhakkhayāya* occurs without *paṭipanno*, for instance at SN III 144,18–20: *Yasmā ca kho, bhikkhu, ettakopi attabhāvapaṭilābho natthi nicco dhuvo sassato avipariṇāmadhammo, tasmā brahmacariyavāso paññāyati sammā dukkhakkhayāya.*

jarāmaraṇanirodhāya are tappurisa compounds in the dative case, the latter with a dvanda, *jarāmaraṇa*, as the prior member.
athāparaṃ: a sandhi of *atha*, "then," and *aparaṃ*, "further."
panāyaṃ: a sandhi of *pana* and *ayaṃ*.

[2. Liberation]
avijjāgato'yaṃ: *Avijjāgato*—literally, "gone to ignorance," but rendered more simply as "ignorant"—is a tappurisa compound qualifying *purisa-puggalo*. Both words, *purisa* and *puggala*, signify "a person, an individual," but they are often joined in a compound. When contrasted with *itthi*, "a woman," *purisa* means "a man."
puññaṃ ce saṅkhāraṃ abhisaṅkharoti: "if [he] generates a meritorious volitional activity." *Ce* is the enclitic conditional particle, "if." *Puññaṃ* functions here as an adjective describing *saṅkhāraṃ*. In the expression *saṅkhāraṃ abhisaṅkharoti* the verb takes its cognate noun as its own object, a construction hard to replicate in translation.
puññūpagaṃ: "consciousness approaches the meritorious"; an accusative tappurisa compound describing *viññāṇaṃ*. *Upaga*, from *upagacchati*, is used only at the end of a tappurisa (Perniola §135c). The initial vowel is lengthened by sandhi.
yato kho, bhikkhave, bhikkhuno avijjā pahīnā hoti, vijjā uppannā: "But, monks, when for a monk ignorance is abandoned and clear knowledge has arisen." For this kind of construction, see p. 75.
avijjāvirāgā vijjuppādā: "with the fading away of ignorance, with the arising of clear knowledge." Both these genitive tappurisa compounds are in the ablative case indicating causation.
anabhisaṅkharonto anabhisañcetayanto: "not generating or producing [volitional activities]"; two negative present participles, almost synonymous. The subject "one" is implicit in the participles.
anupādiyaṃ: "not clinging"; the nominative present participle.
na paritassati: The verb *paritassati* combines nuances of craving and fear. I give precedence to the former, which is probably more original, and thus render it "does not thirst." The commentary explains: "He does not thirst either through the *paritassanā* of craving or through the *paritassanā* of fear. This means he does not crave and does not fear."[176]

176. Spk II 78,20–21: *N'eva taṇhāparitassanāya, na bhayaparitassanāya paritassati, na taṇhāyati na bhāyatī ti attho.*

aparitassaṃ: the nominative present participle.

paccattaññeva (= *paccattaṃ*, "personally," + emphatic *eva*). The commentary explains: "He attains nibbāna himself through himself, not through the spiritual power of another."[177]

parinibbāyati: the verb designating the attainment of nibbāna, here evidently the attainment of the nibbāna element "with residue," that is, nibbāna during life.

[3. Nibbāna with residue]

vedanaṃ vedayati: "he feels a feeling," the verb taking an object cognate with itself.

sā aniccā, etc. The nominative feminine pronoun *sā* refers back to *vedanā* (now the subject); the adjectives describing the feeling—*aniccā*, *anajjhositā*, *anabhinanditā*—are also feminine nominatives.

naṃ vedanaṃ: *Naṃ* is an alternative to *taṃ* (Duroiselle §295; Perniola §40b); here it is feminine accusative, in agreement with *vedanaṃ*, object of *vedayati*.

kāyapariyantikaṃ vedanaṃ: "a feeling limited by the body." The commentary explains: "As long as the body with its five sense doors continues, feeling continues through the five sense doors."[178] On this interpretation the expression does not mean "a feeling at the end of the body."

jīvitapariyantikaṃ vedanaṃ: "a feeling limited by life." The commentary explains: "As long as life continues, feeling continues through the mind door.'"[179] Again, on this interpretation the expression does not mean "a feeling at the end of life."

kāyassa bhedā: "with the breakup of the body"; a genitive followed by an ablative.

uddhaṃ jīvitapariyādānā: "following the exhaustion of life"; an indeclinable followed by a genitive tappurisa in the ablative case.

sabbavedayitāni: "all that is felt"; a neuter plural. *Vedayita*, originally a past participle, is used as a neuter noun equivalent in sense to *vedanā*.

177. Spk II 78,22: *Sayameva attanā'va parinibbāyati, na aññassa ānubhāvena.*

178. Spk II 78,32–33: *Yāva pañcadvārakāyo pavattati, tāva pavattaṃ pañcadvārikavedanan ti attho.*

179. Spk II 79,1–2: *Yāva jīvitaṃ pavattati, tāva pavattaṃ manodvārikavedanan ti attho.*

sītībhavissanti: "will become cool"; a verbal compound of the adjective *sīta*, "cool," and *bhavati*, plural in the future tense (Duroiselle §556–57; Perniola §145).

sarīrāni: *Sarīra* usually means "body," but here, in the plural, it refers to bodily remains.

yāyaṃ: = *yā* + *ayaṃ*, both qualifying *usmā*, "heat."

[4. Nibbāna without residue]

khīṇāsavo bhikkhu: "a monk whose influxes are destroyed." *Khīṇāsavo* is a bahubbīhi composed of the past participle *khīṇa*, "destroyed, finished," and *āsava*, "influx." In the commentaries, *khīṇāsavo* is used as an independent noun meaning "arahant."

saṅkhāresu asati: "when volitional activities do not exist." In this locative absolute, the singular present participle, *asati*, occurs with the plural subject, *saṅkhāresu*, probably for consistency with the parallel passages. Similarly, in what follows, masculine *asati* is always used even when the locative subject is a feminine (for instance, *vedanāya asati*); the normal feminine locative participle would be *asatiyā*.

api nu kho: "is it the case that?" An indeclinable formation expressing doubt or introducing a question.

paññāyetha: "would be discerned"; the middle-voice optative in the third-person singular.

saddahatha me taṃ: "have faith in me about that." I take *taṃ* to represent the present teaching and to serve as the direct object of the second-person plural imperative verb, *saddahatha*, with the enclitic genitive pronoun *me* as the indirect object.

nikkaṅkhā, nibbicikicchā: "without perplexity, without doubt." The prefix *nir-* has a privational sense; in both words *r-* is assimilated to the following consonant, with *r* + *v* > *bb*. Both words modify the plural "you" (the monks) implicit in the verb *hotha*.

9. Mahārukkhasutta

The Great Tree (SN 12:55; II 87–88)

[1. Contemplating enjoyment]

"Upādāniyesu, bhikkhave, dhammesu assādānupassino viharato taṇhā pavaḍḍhati. Taṇhāpaccayā upādānaṃ; upādānapaccayā bhavo. . . . Evametassa kevalassa dukkhakkhandhassa samudayo hoti.

"In clingable, monks, things for enjoyment-contemplating-one dwelling, craving increases. Through craving-condition, clinging; through clinging-condition, existence. . . . Thus-of this whole suffering-mass origin is.

"For one who dwells, monks, contemplating enjoyment in things that can be clung to, craving increases. With craving as condition, clinging [occurs]; with clinging as condition, existence. . . . Such is the origin of this whole mass of suffering.

"Seyyathāpi, bhikkhave, mahārukkho. Tassa yāni c'eva mūlāni adhogamāni, yāni ca tiriyaṅgamāni, sabbāni tāni uddhaṃ ojaṃ abhiharanti. Evaṃ hi so, bhikkhave, mahārukkho tadāhāro tadupādāno ciraṃ dīghamaddhānaṃ tiṭṭheyya. Evameva kho, bhikkhave, upādāniyesu dhammesu assādānupassino viharato taṇhā pavaḍḍhati. Taṇhāpaccayā upādānaṃ . . . Evametassa kevalassa dukkhakkhandhassa samudayo hoti.

"Suppose, monks, a great-tree. Its which and roots down-going, which and across-going, all those upward the sap convey. Thus indeed that, monks, great-tree, that-nutriment that-sustenance, long long-time would stand. Just so, monks, in clingable things for enjoyment-contemplating-one dwelling, craving increases. Through craving-condition, clinging. . . . Thus-of this whole suffering-mass origin is.

"Suppose, monks, there were a great tree. Its downward-going roots and those going across would all convey the sap upward. Thus, monks, that great tree, with that [sap] as nutriment, with that [sap] as sustenance, would stand for a very long time. Just so, monks, for one who dwells contemplating enjoyment in things that can be clung to, craving increases. With craving as condition, clinging [occurs]. . . . Such is the origin of this whole mass of suffering.

[2. Contemplating danger]
"Upādāniyesu, bhikkhave, dhammesu ādīnavānupassino viharato taṇhā nirujjhati. Taṇhānirodhā upādānanirodho; upādānanirodhā bhava-nirodho. . . . Evametassa kevalassa dukkhakkhandhassa nirodho hoti.

"In clingable, monks, things for danger-contemplating-one dwelling, craving ceases. Through craving-cessation, clinging-cessation; through clinging-cessation, existence-cessation. . . . Thus-of this whole suffering-mass cessation is.

"For one, monks, who dwells contemplating danger in things that can be clung to, craving ceases. With the cessation of craving [there is] cessation of clinging; with the cessation of clinging, cessation of existence. . . . Such is the cessation of this whole mass of suffering.

"Seyyathāpi, bhikkhave, mahārukkho. Atha puriso āgaccheyya kuddālapiṭakaṃ ādāya. So taṃ rukkhaṃ mūle chindeyya; mūle chetvā palikhaṇeyya; palikhaṇitvā mūlāni uddhareyya antamaso usīranāḷimattānipi.

"Suppose, monks, a great-tree. Then a person would come, shovel-basket having taken. He that tree at the root would cut; at the root having cut, would dig around; having dug around, roots would pull up, even *usīra*-fibers-size-too.

"Suppose, monks, there were a great tree. Then a person would come, having taken a shovel and a basket. He would cut that tree at the root; having cut it at the root, he would dig around it; having dug around it, he would pull up the roots, even those the size of *usīra* fibers.

"So taṃ rukkhaṃ khaṇḍākhaṇḍikaṃ chindeyya; khaṇḍākhaṇḍikaṃ chinditvā phāleyya; phāletvā sakalikaṃ sakalikaṃ kareyya. Sakalikaṃ sakalikaṃ karitvā vātātape visoseyya; vātātape visosetvā agginā ḍaheyya; agginā ḍahetvā masiṃ kareyya.

"He that tree piece-piece would cut; piece-piece having cut, would split; having split, splinter splinter would make. Splinter splinter having made, in the wind-sun-heat would dry; in the wind-sun-heat having dried, with fire would burn; with fire having burned, ash would make.

"He would cut that tree into pieces; having cut it into pieces, he would split them; having split them, he would make splinters. Having made splinters, he would dry them in the wind and the sun's heat; having dried them in the wind and the sun's heat, he would burn them with fire; having burned them with fire, he would make ashes.

"Masiṃ karitvā mahāvāte vā opuneyya nadiyā vā sīghasotāya pavāheyya. Evaṃ hi so, bhikkhave, mahārukkho ucchinnamūlo assa tālāvatthukato anabhāvakato āyatiṃ anuppādadhammo.

"Ash having made, in a great-wind or would winnow, by river or swift-current would have-carried-off. Thus indeed that, monks, great-tree cut-off-root would be, palm-base-made, obliteration-made, future not-arising-subject.

"Having made ashes, he would winnow them in a strong wind or have them carried off by a river with a swift current. Thus indeed, monks, that great tree would be cut off at the root, made like a palm stump, obliterated, not subject to future arising.

"Evameva kho, bhikkhave, upādāniyesu dhammesu ādīnavānupassino viharato taṇhā nirujjhati. Taṇhānirodhā upādānanirodho; upādānanirodhā bhavanirodho. . . . Evametassa kevalassa dukkhakkhandhassa nirodho hoti."

"Just so, monks, in clingable things for danger-contemplating-one dwelling, craving ceases. Through craving-cessation, clinging-cessation; through clinging-cessation, existence-cessation. . . . Thus-of this whole suffering-mass cessation is."

"Just so, monks, for one who dwells contemplating danger in things that can be clung to, craving increases. With the cessation of craving [there is] cessation of clinging; with the cessation of clinging, cessation of existence. . . . Such is the cessation of this whole mass of suffering."

Grammatical explanations

[1. Contemplating enjoyment]

upādāniyesu: "things that can be clung to"; the future passive participle of *upādiyati*, here locative plural in agreement with *dhammesu*. In Pāli the locative is used for objects of knowledge and contemplation.

assādānupassino viharato: "for one who dwells contemplating enjoyment." Both are singular datives, with *viharato* a present participle. In the compound *assādānupassino*, *assāda* can be seen as an accusative in relation to *anupassino*, which functions almost like a present participle with the subject "one" inherent in it.[180] This expression may also have been rendered: "When one dwells contemplating enjoyment. . . ."

tadāhāro tadupādāno: "with that [sap] as nutriment, with that [sap] as sustenance"; two bahubbīhis qualifying *mahārukkho*, where *tad* (= *taṃ* in sandhi with the following vowel) represents *ojaṃ*.

ciraṃ dīghamaddhānaṃ: "a very long time." *Dīghamaddhānaṃ* = *dīghaṃ* + *addhānaṃ*, the accusative used adverbially to represent a period of time. The two expressions, *ciraṃ* and *dīghamaddhānaṃ*, seem redundant.

[2. Contemplating danger]

ādīnavānupassino viharato: "for one who dwells contemplating danger." Both are singular datives, as above. Again, this might have also been rendered: "When one dwells contemplating danger. . . ."

kuddālapiṭakaṃ ādāya: "having taken a shovel and a basket." *Kuddālapiṭakaṃ* is a dvanda compound of the singular collective type, followed by an absolutive of *ādiyati*, "takes."

usīranāḷimattāni: PED defines *usīra* as "the fragrant root of Andropogon Muricatum." The expression here is a bahubbīhi qualifying *mūlāni*, "roots the size of *usīra* fibers."

khaṇḍākhaṇḍikaṃ chindeyya: "would cut into pieces." The duplication of *khaṇḍa* (with elongation of the middle vowel) suggests a repetitive

180. Spk II 81,29–30 glosses *assādānupassino* as if it were a present participle taking an accusative object: *Assādānupassino ti assādaṃ anupassantassa*. Whitney at §1230c remarks that derivatives of this form [with suffix *-in*] "often have a value equivalent to that of present participles." At §271 he cites such forms as taking their object in the accusative.

action. DOP takes *khaṇḍākhaṇḍikaṃ* to be an adverb. So too for *sakalikaṃ sakalikaṃ kareyya*, "would make splinters."

nadiyā vā sīghasotāya pavāheyya: see p. 279.

ucchinnamūlo . . . anuppādadhammo: "cut off at the root . . . not subject to future arising"; bahubbīhis describing *mahārukkho*. On this use of *dhamma* at the end of a compound, see p. 154.

assa: the third-person singular optative of *atthi*.

tālāvatthukato: "made [like] a palm stump." The Saṃyutta commentary, commenting on the expression at SN II 63,12, says: "Made like the base of a palm tree in the sense of not growing again. The meaning is: 'Made like a palm tree whose top has been cut off, and made like its base after the palm tree has been extricated along with its root.'"[181]

10. Assutavāsutta

Unlearned (SN 12:61; II 94–95)

[1. The worldling grasps the mind]

"Assutavā, bhikkhave, puthujjano imasmiṃ cātummahābhūtikasmiṃ kāyasmiṃ nibbindeyyapi virajjeyyapi vimucceyyapi. Taṃ kissa hetu? Dissati hi, bhikkhave, imassa cātumahābhūtikassa kāyassa ācayopi apacayopi ādānampi nikkhepanampi. Tasmā tatra assutavā puthujjano nibbindeyyapi virajjeyyapi vimucceyyapi.

"The unlearned, monks, worldling in this four-great-element body might become disenchanted-too, might become dispassionate-too, might be liberated-too. That for what reason? Is seen because, monks, of this four-great-element body growth-too, decline-too, taking up-too, putting down-too. Therefore there the unlearned worldling might become disenchanted-too, might become dispassionate-too, might be liberated-too.

"The unlearned worldling, monks, might become disenchanted with this body [composed of] the four great elements, might become dispassionate toward it and be liberated from it. For what reason? Because there is seen in

181. Spk II 69,28–30: *Tālāvatthukatānī ti tālavatthu viya katāni, puna aviruhaṇaṭṭhena matthakacchinnatālo viya samūlaṃ tālaṃ uddharitvā tassa patiṭṭhitaṭṭhānaṃ viya ca katānī ti attho.*

this body [composed of] the four great elements growth and decline, taking up and putting down. Therefore the unlearned worldling might become disenchanted with this body [composed of] the four great elements, might become dispassionate toward it and be liberated from it.

"Yañca kho etaṃ, bhikkhave, vuccati cittaṃ itipi, mano itipi, viññāṇaṃ itipi, tatra assutavā puthujjano nālaṃ nibbindituṃ nālaṃ virajjituṃ nālaṃ vimuccituṃ. Taṃ kissa hetu? Dīgharattaṃ h'etaṃ, bhikkhave, assutavato puthujjanassa ajjhositaṃ mamāyitaṃ parāmaṭṭhaṃ: 'Etaṃ mama, eso'hamasmi, eso me attā'ti. Tasmā tatra assutavā puthujjano nālaṃ nibbindituṃ nālaṃ virajjituṃ nālaṃ vimuccituṃ.

"Which-but this, monks, is called 'mind' thus-too, 'thought' thus-too, 'consciousness' thus-too, there the unlearned worldling not-able to become disenchanted, not-able to become dispassionate, not-able to be liberated. That for what reason? A long time because this, monks, of the unlearned worldling held to, appropriated, grasped: 'This mine, this I-am, this my self.' Therefore there the unlearned worldling not-able to become disenchanted, not-able to become dispassionate, not-able to be liberated.

"But, monks, as to that which is called 'mind' and 'thought' and 'consciousness'—the unlearned worldling is unable to become disenchanted with it, unable to become dispassionate toward it, unable to be liberated from it. For what reason? Because for a long time, monks, this has been held by the unlearned worldling, appropriated, and grasped thus: 'This is mine, this I am, this is my self.' Therefore the unlearned worldling is unable to become disenchanted with it, unable to become dispassionate toward it, unable to be liberated from it.

[2. Better to grasp the body than the mind]
"Varaṃ, bhikkhave, assutavā puthujjano imaṃ cātummahābhūtikaṃ kāyaṃ attato upagaccheyya, na tveva cittaṃ. Taṃ kissa hetu? Dissatāyaṃ, bhikkhave, cātummahābhūtiko kāyo ekampi vassaṃ tiṭṭhamāno dvepi vassāni tiṭṭhamāno tīṇipi vassāni tiṭṭhamāno cattāripi vassāni tiṭṭhamāno pañcapi vassāni tiṭṭhamāno dasapi vassāni tiṭṭhamāno vīsatipi vassāni tiṭṭhamāno tiṃsampi vassāni tiṭṭhamāno cattārīsampi vassāni tiṭṭhamāno

paññāsampi vassāni tiṭṭhamāno vassasatampi tiṭṭhamāno, bhiyyopi tiṭṭhamāno.

"Better, monks, the unlearned worldling this four-great-element body as self should approach, not but the mind. That for what reason? Is seen-this, monks, four-great-element body one-too year standing, two-too years standing, three-too years standing, four-too years standing, five-too years standing, ten-too years standing, twenty-too years standing, thirty-too years standing, forty-too years standing, fifty-too years standing, years-hundred-too standing, more-too standing.

"It would be better, monks, for the unlearned worldling to take as self this body [composed of] the four great elements rather than the mind. For what reason? Because this body [composed of] the four great elements is seen standing for one year, for two years, for three, four, five, or ten years, for twenty, thirty, forty, or fifty years, for a hundred years, or even more.

"Yañca kho etaṃ, bhikkhave, vuccati cittaṃ itipi, mano itipi, viññāṇaṃ itipi, taṃ rattiyā ca divasassa ca aññadeva uppajjati aññaṃ nirujjhati. Seyyathāpi, bhikkhave, makkaṭo araññe pavane caramāno sākhaṃ gaṇhati, taṃ muñcitvā aññaṃ gaṇhati, taṃ muñcitvā aññaṃ gaṇhati; evameva kho, bhikkhave, yamidaṃ vuccati cittaṃ itipi, mano itipi, viññāṇaṃ itipi, taṃ rattiyā ca divasassa ca aññadeva uppajjati aññaṃ nirujjhati.

"Which-but this, monks, is called 'mind' thus-too, 'thought' thus-too, 'consciousness' thus-too, that of night and of day and other-indeed arises, other ceases. Just as, monks, a monkey in a forest in a grove roaming, a branch grabs, that having released another grabs, that having released another grabs, just so, monks, which this, monks, is called 'mind' thus-too, 'thought' thus-too, 'consciousness' thus-too, that of night and of day and other-indeed arises, other ceases.

"But that which is called 'mind' and 'thought' and 'consciousness' by day and by night arises as one thing and ceases as another. Just as, monks, a monkey roaming in a forest grove grabs hold of one branch, releases it and grabs another, then releases it and grabs still another, so too that which is called 'mind' and 'thought' and 'consciousness' by day and by night arises as one thing and ceases as another.

[3. Contemplating dependent origination]

"Tatra, bhikkhave, sutavā ariyasāvako paṭiccasamuppādaññeva sādhukaṃ yoniso manasikaroti: 'Iti imasmiṃ sati idaṃ hoti, imass'uppādā idaṃ uppajjati; imasmiṃ asati idaṃ na hoti, imassa nirodhā idaṃ nirujjhati, yadidaṃ avijjāpaccayā saṅkhārā; saṅkhārapaccayā viññāṇaṃ . . . evametassa kevalassa dukkhakkhandhassa samudayo hoti. Avijjāya tveva asesavirāganirodhā saṅkhāranirodho; saṅkhāranirodhā viññāṇanirodho . . . Evametassa kevalassa dukkhakkhandhassa nirodho hotī'ti.

"There, monks, the learned noble-disciple to dependent-origination-itself well thoroughly attends: 'Thus this existing, that occurs; of this through arising, that arises. This not existing, that not occurs; of this through cessation, that ceases, that is: Through ignorance-condition, volitional-activities; through volitional-activities consciousness. . . . Thus-of this whole suffering-mass origin is. Of ignorance but-indeed, through remainderless-fading-cessation, volitional-activities cessation; through volitional-activities-cessation, consciousness-cessation. . . . Thus-of this whole suffering-mass cessation is.'

"In regard to that, monks, the learned noble disciple well attends thoroughly to dependent origination itself thus: 'When this exists, that occurs; with the arising of this, that arises. When this does not exist, that does not occur; with the cessation of this, that ceases—that is, with ignorance as condition, volitional activities [occur]; with volitional activities as condition, consciousness. . . . Such is the origin of this whole mass of suffering. But with the remainderless fading away and cessation of ignorance [there occurs] cessation of volitional activities; with the cessation of volitional activities, cessation of consciousness. . . . Such is the cessation of this whole mass of suffering.'

"Evaṃ passaṃ, bhikkhave, sutavā ariyasāvako rūpasmimpi nibbindati, vedanāyapi nibbindati, saññāyapi nibbindati, saṅkhāresupi nibbindati, viññāṇasmimpi nibbindati. Nibbindaṃ virajjati. Virāgā vimuccati. Vimuttasmiṃ vimuttamiti ñāṇaṃ hoti. 'Khīṇā jāti, vusitaṃ brahmacariyaṃ, kataṃ karaṇīyaṃ, nāparaṃ itthattāyā'ti pajānātī ti."

"Thus seeing, monks, the learned noble-disciple in regard to form-too is disenchanted, in regard to feeling-too is disenchanted, in regard to perception-too is disenchanted, in regard to volitional-activities-too is disenchanted, in regard to consciousness-too is disenchanted. Being disenchanted, becomes dispassionate. Through dispassion is liberated. In liberated, 'liberated' thus knowledge occurs. 'Finished birth, lived the spiritual-life, done what-is-to-be-done, not-further for such-a-state,' understands."

"Seeing thus, monks, the learned noble disciple becomes disenchanted with form, disenchanted with feeling, disenchanted with perception, disenchanted with volitional activities, disenchanted with consciousness. Being disenchanted, he becomes dispassionate. Through dispassion he is liberated. In regard to what is liberated, the knowledge occurs thus: 'Liberated.' He understands: 'Finished is birth, the spiritual life has been lived, what had to be done has been done, there is no more for this-state-of being.'"

Grammatical explanations

[1. The worlding grasps the mind]

imasmiṃ cātummahābhūtikasmiṃ kāyasmiṃ: "with this body [composed of] the four great elements." All are locatives, with *cātummahābhūtikasmiṃ* a bahubbīhi describing *kāyasmiṃ*, the body, derived from *catur*, "four," and *mahābhūta*, "great elements." To form the adjective, the initial vowel is strengthened, the *-r-* assimilated to the following consonant, and the adjectival suffix *-ika* added, here in the locative in agreement with *kāyasmiṃ*.

dissati: "is seen"; the third-person singular passive of the verb **dassati*.

yañca etaṃ: a sandhi of *yaṃ* and *ca*. Both *yaṃ* and *etaṃ* refer to *cittaṃ*.

itipi: the quotation marker *iti* followed by the conjunction *pi*.

nālaṃ: "not able"; a sandhi of *na* and *alaṃ*, used with the infinitives of the verbs (see Perniola §287(i)).

dīgharattaṃ: "a long time," literally, "long night." The word is a kammadhāraya compound used as an adverb (see Perniola §132).

etaṃ: the neuter pronoun representing *cittaṃ*, *mano*, and *viññāṇaṃ*. Grammatically it is the nominative subject but serves in a passive role as an object in relation to the agent and the actions (see the following).

assutavato puthujjanassa: "by the unlearned worldling"; the logical subject, the agent of the action, in the genitive case with an instrumental sense.

ajjhositaṃ mamāyitaṃ parāmaṭṭhaṃ: "held, appropriated, grasped"; past participles agreeing with *etaṃ*, hence nominatives signifying how the genitive agent acts upon "this," the *citta*.

[2. Better to grasp the body than the mind]

varaṃ: an indeclinable meaning "better," going along with the optative verb, *upagaccheyya*, which is used here and elsewhere in a metaphoric sense, "to view, to consider."

attato: an ablative, "as self." On *-to* forms, see pp. 154–55.

tveva: a sandhi of *tu*, "but," and emphatic *eva*.

dissatāyaṃ: a sandhi of *dissati* and *ayaṃ*.

rattiyā ca divasassa ca: Though the case is genitive, in English this would correspond to the expression "by night and by day."

aññadeva uppajjati aññaṃ nirujjhati: "arises as one thing and ceases as another"; an idiomatic way of saying that it constantly undergoes change. *Aññadeva* is a sandhi of *aññaṃ* and *eva*.

11. Nagarasutta

The City (SN 12:65; II 104–7)

In the earlier part of this discourse, the Buddha relates how, before his enlightenment, he investigated dependent origination in a manner similar to that described in SN 12:10 (see pp. 298–99), but here culminating in the mutual dependence of consciousness and name-and-form. The discourse continues as follows.

[1. The simile of the city]

"Tassa mayhaṃ, bhikkhave, etadahosi: 'Adhigato kho myāyaṃ maggo bodhāya, yadidaṃ nāmarūpanirodhā viññāṇanirodho; viññāṇanirodhā nāmarūpanirodho; nāmarūpanirodhā saḷāyatananirodho; saḷāyatana-nirodhā phassanirodho. . . . Evametassa kevalassa dukkhakkhandhassa nirodho hoti.'

"'Nirodho, nirodho'ti kho me, bhikkhave, pubbe ananussutesu dhammesu cakkhuṃ udapādi, ñāṇaṃ udapādi, paññā udapādi, vijjā udapādi, āloko udapādi.

"To that me, monks, this-occurred: 'Discovered by me-this path to enlightenment, which-this, through name-form-cessation, consciousness-cessation; through consciousness-cessation, name-form-cessation; through name-form-cessation, six-sense-base cessation; through six-sense-base cessation, contact-cessation . . . Thus-of this whole suffering-mass cessation occurs.'

"'Cessation, cessation,' for me, monks, in the past in unheard things the eye arose, knowledge arose, wisdom arose, clear-knowledge arose, light arose.

"This occurred to me, monks: 'I have discovered this path to enlightenment—that is, with the cessation of name-and-form [there occurs] cessation of consciousness; with the cessation of consciousness [there occurs] cessation of name-and-form. With the cessation of name-and-form, cessation of the six sense bases; with the cessation of the six sense bases, cessation of contact. . . . Such is the cessation of this whole mass of suffering.'

"'Cessation, cessation'—thus, monks, for me, in regard to things unheard before, the eye arose, knowledge arose, wisdom arose, clear knowledge arose, light arose.

"Seyyathāpi, bhikkhave, puriso araññe pavane caramāno passeyya purāṇaṃ maggaṃ purāṇañjasaṃ pubbakehi manussehi anuyātaṃ. So tam-anugaccheyya. Tamanugacchanto passeyya purāṇaṃ nagaraṃ purāṇaṃ rājadhāniṃ pubbakehi manussehi ajjhāvutthaṃ ārāmasampannaṃ vanasampannaṃ pokkharaṇīsampannaṃ uddāpavantaṃ ramaṇīyaṃ.

"Suppose, monks, a man in a forest in grove wandering would see an ancient path, an ancient-road, by past people traveled. He that-would follow. That-following, would see an ancient city, an ancient capital, by past people inhabited, parks-possessing, groves-possessing, ponds-possessing, mounds-possessing, delightful.

"Suppose, monks, a man wandering in a forest grove would see an ancient path, an ancient road, traveled along by people in the past. He would follow it. Following it, he would see an ancient city, an ancient capital, inhabited by people in the past, possessing parks, groves, ponds, and mounds, delightful.

"Atha kho so, bhikkhave, puriso rañño vā rājamahāmattassa vā āroceyya: 'Yagghe, bhante, jāneyyāsi ahaṃ addasaṃ araññe pavane caramāno purāṇaṃ maggaṃ purāṇañjasaṃ pubbakehi manussehi anuyātaṃ. Tamanugacchiṃ. Tamanugacchanto addasaṃ purāṇaṃ nagaraṃ purāṇaṃ rājadhāniṃ pubbakehi manussehi ajjhāvutthaṃ ārāmasampannaṃ vanasampannaṃ pokkharaṇīsampannaṃ uddhāpavantaṃ ramaṇīyaṃ. Taṃ, bhante, nagaraṃ māpehī'ti.

"Then that, monks, man to the king or to the king-great-minister or would report: 'Here, sire, you should know I saw, in a forest in a grove wandering, an ancient path, an ancient-road, by past people traveled. That-I followed. That-following, I saw an ancient city, an ancient capital, by past people inhabited, parks-possessing, groves-possessing, ponds-possessing, mounds-possessing, delightful. That, sire, city build up.'

"Then the man would report to the king or to the king's chief minister: 'Sire, you should know that while wandering through a forest grove I saw an ancient path, an ancient road, traveled along by people in the past. I followed it, and following it, I saw an ancient city, an ancient capital, inhabited by people in the past, possessing parks, groves, ponds, and mounds, delightful. Build up that city, sire!'

"Atha kho so, bhikkhave, rājā vā rājamahāmatto vā taṃ nagaraṃ māpeyya. Tadassa nagaraṃ aparena samayena iddhañc'eva phītañca bāhujaññaṃ ākiṇṇamanussaṃ vuddhivepullappattaṃ.

"Then that, monks, king or king-great-minister or that city would build up. That-would be city by a later time successful-and prosperous-and, populated, filled-people, to growth-expansion-attained.

"Then, monks, that king or the king's chief minister would build up that city. Some time later that city would become successful and prosperous, populated, filled with people, attained to growth and expansion.

[2. The ancient path]

"Evameva khvāhaṃ, bhikkhave, addasaṃ purāṇaṃ maggaṃ purāṇañjasaṃ pubbakehi sammāsambuddhehi anuyātaṃ. Katamo ca so, bhikkhave, purāṇamaggo purāṇañjaso pubbakehi sammāsambuddhehi anuyāto? Ayameva ariyo aṭṭhaṅgiko maggo, seyyathīdaṃ: sammādiṭṭhi . . . sammāsamādhi. Ayaṃ kho so, bhikkhave, purāṇamaggo purāṇañjaso pubbakehi sammāsambuddhehi anuyāto.

"Just so I, monks, saw the ancient path, the ancient-road, by past perfectly-enlightened ones traveled. What and that, monks, ancient path, ancient-road, by past perfectly-enlightened ones traveled? This-just noble eightfold path, that is, right-view . . . right-concentration. This that, monks, ancient path, ancient-road, by past perfectly-enlightened ones traveled.

"So too, monks, I saw the ancient path, the ancient road, traveled along by the perfectly enlightened ones of the past. And what is that ancient path, that ancient road? It is just this noble eightfold path—that is, right view . . . right concentration. This is the ancient path, the ancient road, traveled along by the perfectly enlightened ones of the past.

"Tamanugacchiṃ. Tamanugacchanto jarāmaraṇaṃ abbhaññāsiṃ, jarāmaraṇasamudayaṃ abbhaññāsiṃ, jarāmaraṇanirodhaṃ abbhaññāsiṃ, jarāmaraṇanirodhagāminiṃ paṭipadaṃ abbhaññāsiṃ. Tamanugacchiṃ. Tamanugacchanto jātiṃ abbhaññāsiṃ . . . saṅkhāre abbhaññāsiṃ, saṅkhārasamudayaṃ abbhaññāsiṃ, saṅkhāranirodhaṃ abbhaññāsiṃ, saṅkhāranirodhagāminiṃ paṭipadaṃ abbhaññāsiṃ.

"That-I followed. That-following, old-age-death I directly-knew; old-age-death-origin I directly-knew; old-age-death-cessation I directly-knew; old-age-death-cessation-going way I directly knew. That-I followed. That-following, birth I directly-knew . . . volitional-activities I directly-knew; volitional-activities-origin I directly-knew; volitional-activities-cessation I directly-knew; volitional-activities-cessation-going way I directly knew.

"I followed it, and following it I have directly known old-age-and-death, its origin, its cessation, and the way leading to its cessation. I followed it, and following it I have directly known birth . . . existence . . . clinging . . . craving . . . feeling . . . contact . . . the six sense bases . . . name-and-form . . .

consciousness . . . volitional activities, their origin, their cessation, and the way leading to their cessation.

"Tadabhiññā ācikkhiṃ bhikkhūnaṃ bhikkhunīnaṃ upāsakānaṃ upāsikānaṃ. Tayidaṃ, bhikkhave, brahmacariyaṃ iddhañc'eva phītañca vitthārikaṃ bāhujaññaṃ puthubhūtaṃ yāva devamanussehi suppakāsitan"ti.

"That-having directly known, I pointed out to the monks, to the nuns, to the male-lay-followers, to the female-lay-followers. That-this, monks, spiritual life successful-and prosperous-and, extensive, popular, widespread, among devas-humans well proclaimed."

"Having directly known that, I have pointed that out to the monks, the nuns, the male lay followers, and the female lay followers. This spiritual life, monks, has become successful and prosperous, extensive, popular, widespread, well proclaimed among devas and humans."

Grammatical explanations

[1. The simile of the city]

myāyaṃ: a sandhi of the enclitic pronoun *me*, "by me," and *ayaṃ*, "this," which qualifies *maggo* (Duroiselle §27).

bodhāya: "to enlightenment"; a dative indicating the destination of the path.

udapādi: "arose"; an aorist of *uppajjati*. See p. 23.

anuyātaṃ: "traveled along": a past participle of *anuyāti*, here in agreement with *maggaṃ*, the accusative object of *passeyya*.

ajjhāvutthaṃ: a past participle of *ajjhāvasati*, in agreement with *rājadhāniṃ*.

ārāmasampannaṃ . . . ramaṇīyaṃ: "possessing parks . . . delightful"; all in agreement with *rājadhāniṃ*.

yagghe: a vocative interjection used in addressing a superior person. It is followed by *jāneyyāsi*, a second-person singular optative of *jānāti*.

addasaṃ: "saw"; a first-person singular a-aorist of **dassati*.

māpehi: a second-person imperative of *māpeti*, itself a causative, "builds, makes, creates (also by supernormal power)."

tadassa nagaraṃ: *Tadassa* is a sandhi of *taṃ* and *assa*, the third-person singular optative of *atthi*. Although *assa* might have been taken to be the masculine genitive pronoun ("of his"—that is, the king's), the commentary glosses the phrase with *taṃ aparena samayena iddhañceva assa phītañca*,[182] where *assa* can only be the optative verb.

[2. The ancient path]
khvāhaṃ: a sandhi of *kho* and *ahaṃ*.
abbhaññāsiṃ: see p. 155.
tadabhiññā: a sandhi of *taṃ* and *abhiññā*, the latter a truncated absolutive (= *abhiññāya*). See p. 180.
ācikkhiṃ: a first-person aorist of *ācikkhati*.
tayidaṃ: see p. 105.
yāva devamanussehi suppakāsitaṃ: *Devamanussehi* appears to be a plural instrumental, but it is likely that *-ehi* is here a vestigial Eastern locative plural termination. On this, see Geiger §80.3.

12. Sammasanasutta
Exploration (SN 12:66; II 107–12)

[1. Inward exploration]
Evaṃ me sutaṃ. Ekaṃ samayaṃ bhagavā kurūsu viharati kammāsadammaṃ nāma kurūnaṃ nigamo. Tatra kho bhagavā bhikkhū āmantesi: "Bhikkhavo"ti. — "Bhadante"ti te bhikkhū bhagavato paccassosuṃ. Bhagavā etadavoca:

Thus by me heard. One occasion the Blessed One among the Kurus was dwelling, Kammāsadamma named of Kurus town. There the Blessed One the monks addressed: "Monks!" — "Bhadante!" those monks to the Blessed One replied. The Blessed One this-said:

Thus have I heard. On one occasion the Blessed One was dwelling among the Kurus, [where there was] a town of the Kurus named Kammāsadamma. There the Blessed One addressed the monks: "Monks!" — "Bhadante!" those monks replied to the Blessed One. The Blessed One said this:

182. At Spk II 117,1.

"Sammasatha no tumhe, bhikkhave, antaraṃ sammasanan"ti.[183] *Evaṃ vutte, aññataro bhikkhu bhagavantaṃ etadavoca: "Ahaṃ kho, bhante, sammasāmi antaraṃ sammasanan"ti.*

"Yathākathaṃ pana tvaṃ, bhikkhu, sammasasi antaraṃ sammasanan"ti? Atha kho so bhikkhu vyākāsi. Yathā so bhikkhu vyākāsi, na so bhikkhu bhagavato cittaṃ ārādhesi.

"Explore you, monks, inward exploration?" Thus said, a certain monk to the Blessed One this-said: "I, Bhante, explore inward exploration."

"How but you, monk, explore inward exploration?" Then that monk explained. How that monk explained, not that monk the Blessed One's mind satisfied.

"Do you, monks, engage in inward exploration?" When this was said, a certain monk said to the Blessed One: "Bhante, I engage in inward exploration."

"But how, monk, do you engage in inward exploration?" The monk then explained, but the way that monk explained did not satisfy the Blessed One's mind.

Evaṃ vutte āyasmā ānando bhagavantaṃ etadavoca: "Etassa, bhagavā, kālo! Etassa, sugata, kālo, yaṃ bhagavā antaraṃ sammasanaṃ bhāseyya. Bhagavato sutvā bhikkhū dhāressantī"ti. — "Tena h'ānanda, suṇātha, sādhukaṃ manasikarotha, bhāsissāmī"ti. — "Evaṃ, bhante"ti kho te bhikkhū bhagavato paccassosuṃ. Bhagavā etadavoca:

Thus said, the Venerable Ānanda to the Blessed One this-said: "For this, Blessed One, the time! For this, Fortunate One, the time, which the Blessed One inward exploration should state. Of the Blessed One having heard, the monks will retain." — "In that case, Ānanda, listen, well attend. I will speak." — "Yes, Bhante," those monks to the Blessed One replied. The Blessed One this-said:

Then the Venerable Ānanda said this to the Blessed One: "Now is the time for this, Blessed One! Now is the time for this, Fortunate One, that the Blessed One should speak of inward exploration. Having heard it from the Blessed One, the monks will retain it [in mind]." — "In that case, Ānanda,

183. I follow Ce and Ee here. Be has *sammasaṃ* throughout.

listen and attend well. I will speak." — "Yes, Bhante," those monks replied to the Blessed One. The Blessed One said this:

[2. Exploring old age and death]

"Idha, bhikkhave, bhikkhu sammasamāno sammasati antaraṃ sammasanaṃ: 'Yaṃ kho idaṃ anekavidhaṃ nānappakārakaṃ dukkhaṃ loke uppajjati jarāmaraṇaṃ: idaṃ kho dukkhaṃ kiṃnidānaṃ kiṃsamudayaṃ kiṃjātikaṃ kiṃpabhavaṃ. Kismiṃ sati jarāmaraṇaṃ hoti; kismiṃ asati jarāmaraṇaṃ na hotī'ti?

"Here, monks, a monk exploring explores inward exploration: 'Which this manifold different-kind suffering in the world arises, old-age-death: this suffering what-cause, what-origin, what-genesis, what-source? What existing, old-age-death occurs? What not existing, old-age-death not occurs?'

"Here, monks, when engaged in inward exploration, a monk explores thus: 'The manifold different kinds of suffering that arise in the world [headed by] old-age-and-death: what is the source of this suffering, what is its origin, what is its genesis, what is its source? When what exists does old-age-and-death occur? When what does not exist does old-age-and-death not occur?'

"So sammasamāno evaṃ jānāti: 'Yaṃ kho idaṃ anekavidhaṃ nānappakārakaṃ dukkhaṃ loke uppajjati jarāmaraṇaṃ, idaṃ kho dukkhaṃ upadhinidānaṃ upadhisamudayaṃ upadhijātikaṃ upadhipabhavaṃ. Upadhismiṃ sati jarāmaraṇaṃ hoti; upadhismiṃ asati jarāmaraṇaṃ na hotī'ti.

"He exploring thus knows: 'Which this manifold different-kind suffering in the world arises, old-age-death: this suffering acquisition-cause, acquisition-origin, acquisition-genesis, acquisition-source. Acquisition existing, old-age-death occurs; acquisition not existing, old-age-death not occurs.'

"As he is exploring he knows thus: 'The manifold different kinds of suffering that arise in the world [headed by] old-age-and-death: this suffering has acquisition as its cause, acquisition as its origin, acquisition as its genesis, acquisition as its source. When there is acquisition, old-age-and-death occurs; when there is no acquisition, old-age-and-death does not occur.'

"So jarāmaraṇañca pajānāti, jarāmaraṇasamudayañca pajānāti, jarāmaraṇanirodhañca pajānāti, yā ca jarāmaraṇanirodhasāruppagāminī paṭipadā tañca pajānāti, tathāpaṭipanno ca hoti anudhammacārī. Ayaṃ vuccati, bhikkhave, 'bhikkhu sabbaso sammā dukkhakkhayāya paṭipanno jarāmaraṇanirodhāya.'

"He old-age-death-and understands, old-age-death-origin-and understands, old-age-death-cessation-and understands, which and old-age-death-cessation-conformity-going way, that-and understands, so practicing and is according-to-Dhamma-acting. This is called, monks, 'a monk entirely completely for suffering-destruction practicing, for old-age-death-cessation.'

"He understands old-age-and-death, its origin, its cessation, and the way leading on that is in conformity with its cessation. He practices in that way and acts in accordance with the Dhamma. This is called 'a monk who is practicing for the entirely complete destruction of suffering, for the cessation of old-age-and-death.'

[3. Exploring acquisition]

"Athāparaṃ sammasamāno sammasati antaraṃ sammasanaṃ: 'Upadhi panāyaṃ kiṃnidāno kiṃsamudayo kiṃjātiko kiṃpabhavo. Kismiṃ sati upadhi hoti; kismiṃ asati upadhi na hotī'ti?

"Then-further exploring explores inward exploration: "Acquisition but-this what-cause, what-origin, what-genesis, what-source? What existing, acquisition occurs? What not existing, acquisition not occurs?'

"Then, engaging further in inward exploration, he explores thus: 'What is the cause of this acquisition, what is its origin, what is its genesis, what is its source? When what exists does acquisition occur; when what does not exist does acquisition not occur?'

"So sammasamāno evaṃ jānāti: 'Upadhi taṇhānidāno taṇhāsamudayo taṇhājātiko taṇhāpabhavo. Taṇhāya sati upadhi hoti; taṇhāya asati upadhi na hotī'ti.

"He exploring thus knows: 'Acquisition craving-cause, craving-origin, craving-genesis, craving-source. Craving existing, acquisition occurs; craving not existing, acquisition not occurs.'

"As he is exploring he knows thus: 'Acquisition has craving as its cause, craving as its origin, craving as its genesis, craving as its source. When there is craving, acquisition occurs; when there is no craving, acquisition does not occur.'

"So upadhiñca pajānāti, upadhisamudayañca pajānāti, upadhinirodhañca pajānāti, yā ca upadhinirodhasāruppagāminī paṭipadā tañca pajānāti, tathā paṭipanno ca hoti anudhammacārī. Ayaṃ vuccati, bhikkhave, 'bhikkhu sabbaso sammā dukkhakkhayāya paṭipanno upadhinirodhāya.'

"He acquisition-and understands, acquisition-origin-and understands, acquisition-cessation-and understands, which and acquisition-cessation-conformity-going way, that-and understands, so practicing and is according-to-Dhamma-acting. This is called, monks, 'a monk entirely completely for suffering-destruction practicing, for acquisition-cessation.'

"He understands acquisition, its origin, its cessation, and the way leading on that is in conformity with its cessation. He practices in that way and acts in accordance with the Dhamma. This is called 'a monk who is practicing for the entirely complete destruction of suffering, for the cessation of acquisition.'

[4. Exploring craving]

"Athāparaṃ sammasamāno sammasati antaraṃ sammasanaṃ: 'Taṇhā panāyaṃ kattha uppajjamānā uppajjati, kattha nivisamānā nivisatī'ti?

"Then-further exploring explores an inward exploration: 'Craving but-this where arising arises, where settling settles?'

"Then, engaging further in inward exploration, he explores thus: 'When this craving is arising, where does it arise? When it is settling down, where does it settle?'

"So sammasamāno evaṃ jānāti: 'Yaṃ kho loke piyarūpaṃ sātarūpaṃ, etth'esā taṇhā uppajjamānā uppajjati, ettha nivisamānā nivisati.'

"He exploring thus knows: 'Which in the world pleasant-nature agreeable-nature, here this craving arising arises, here settling settles.'

"As he explores he understands thus: 'Whatever in the world has a pleasant nature, an agreeable nature: here this craving, when arising, arises; here when settling down, it settles down.'

"Kiñca loke piyarūpaṃ sātarūpaṃ? Cakkhuṃ loke piyarūpaṃ, sātarūpaṃ; etth'esā taṇhā uppajjamānā uppajjati, ettha nivisamānā nivisati. Sotaṃ loke piyarūpaṃ sātarūpaṃ . . . Ghānaṃ loke piyarūpaṃ sātarūpaṃ . . . Jivhā loke piyarūpaṃ sātarūpaṃ . . . Kāyo loke piyarūpaṃ sātarūpaṃ . . . Mano loke piyarūpaṃ sātarūpaṃ; etth'esā taṇhā uppajjamānā uppajjati, ettha nivisamānā nivisati.

"What-and in the world pleasant-nature agreeable-nature? The eye in the world pleasant-nature agreeable-nature; here this craving arising arises, here settling settles. The ear in the world pleasant-nature agreeable-nature . . . The nose in the world pleasant-nature agreeable-nature . . . The tongue in the world pleasant-nature agreeable-nature . . . The body in the world pleasant-nature agreeable-nature . . . The mind in the world pleasant-nature agreeable-nature; here this craving arising arises, here settling settles.

"And what in the world has a pleasant nature, an agreeable nature? The eye has a pleasant nature, an agreeable nature in the world; here this craving, when arising, arises; here when settling down, it settles down. The ear has a pleasant nature, an agreeable nature. . . . The nose has a pleasant nature, an agreeable nature. . . . The tongue has a pleasant nature, an agreeable nature. . . . The body has a pleasant nature, an agreeable nature. . . . The mind has a pleasant nature, an agreeable nature in the world; here this craving, when arising, arises; here when settling down, it settles down.

[5. Those not freed from suffering]
"Ye hi keci, bhikkhave, atītamaddhānaṃ samaṇā vā brāhmaṇā vā yaṃ loke piyarūpaṃ sātarūpaṃ taṃ niccato addakkhuṃ, sukhato addakkhuṃ,

attato addakkhuṃ, ārogyato addakkhuṃ, khemato addakkhuṃ, te taṇhaṃ vaḍḍhesuṃ. Ye taṇhaṃ vaḍḍhesuṃ, te upadhiṃ vaḍḍhesuṃ. Ye upadhiṃ vaḍḍhesuṃ, te dukkhaṃ vaḍḍhesuṃ. Ye dukkhaṃ vaḍḍhesuṃ, te na parimucciṃsu jātiyā jarāya maraṇena sokehi paridevehi dukkhehi domanassehi upāyāsehi. 'Na parimucciṃsu dukkhasmā'ti vadāmi.

"Those who, monks, past-period ascetics or brahmins or which in the world pleasant-nature agreeable-nature, that as permanent saw, as pleasant saw, as self saw, as health saw, as security saw, they craving increased. Who craving increased, they acquisition increased. Who acquisition increased, they suffering increased. Who suffering increased, they not were freed from birth, from old age, from death, from sorrows, from lamentations, from pains, from dejections, from miseries. 'Not were freed from suffering,' I say.

"Monks, whatever ascetics and brahmins in the past regarded that in the world having a pleasant nature, an agreeable nature, as permanent, as happiness, as self, as healthy, as secure: they increased craving. Those who increased craving increased acquisition. Those who increased acquisition increased suffering. Those who increased suffering were not freed from birth, old age, and death, from sorrow, lamentation, pain, dejection, and misery. 'They were not freed from suffering,' I say.

"Yepi hi keci, bhikkhave, anāgatamaddhānaṃ samaṇā vā brāhmaṇā vā yaṃ loke piyarūpaṃ sātarūpaṃ taṃ niccato dakkhissanti, sukhato dakkhissanti, attato dakkhissanti, ārogyato dakkhissanti, khemato dakkhissanti, te taṇhaṃ vaḍḍhissanti. Ye taṇhaṃ vaḍḍhissanti, te upadhiṃ vaḍḍhissanti. Ye upadhiṃ vaḍḍhissanti, te dukkhaṃ vaḍḍhissanti. Ye dukkhaṃ vaḍḍhissanti, te na parimuccissanti jātiyā jarāya maraṇena sokehi paridevehi dukkhehi domanassehi upāyāsehi. 'Na parimuccissanti dukkhasmā'ti vadāmi.

"Those-too who, monks, future-period ascetics or brahmins or which in the world pleasant-nature agreeable-nature, that as permanent will see, as pleasant will see, as self will see, as health will see, as security will see, they craving will increase. Who craving will increase, they acquisition will increase. Who acquisition will increase, they suffering will increase. Who suffering will increase, they not will be freed from birth, from old age, from death, from sorrows, from lamentations, from pains, from dejections, from miseries. 'Not will be freed from suffering,' I say.

"Whatever ascetics and brahmins in the future, too, will regard that in the world having a pleasant nature, an agreeable nature, as permanent, as happiness, as self, as healthy, as secure: they will increase craving. Those who will increase craving will increase acquisition. Those who will increase acquisition will increase suffering. Those who will increase suffering will not be freed from birth, old age, and death, from sorrow, lamentation, pain, dejection, and misery. 'They will not be freed from suffering,' I say.

"Yepi hi keci, bhikkhave, etarahi samaṇā vā brāhmaṇā vā yaṃ loke piyarūpaṃ sātarūpaṃ taṃ niccato passanti, sukhato passanti, attato passanti, ārogyato passanti, khemato passanti, te taṇhaṃ vaḍḍhenti. Ye taṇhaṃ vaḍḍhenti, te upadhiṃ vaḍḍhenti. Ye upadhiṃ vaḍḍhenti, te dukkhaṃ vaḍḍhenti. Ye dukkhaṃ vaḍḍhenti, te na parimuccanti jātiyā jarāya maraṇena sokehi paridevehi dukkhehi domanassehi upāyāsehi. 'Na parimuccanti dukkhasmā'ti vadāmi.

"Those-too who, monks, now ascetics or brahmins or which in the world pleasant-nature agreeable-nature, that as permanent see, as pleasant see, as self see, as health see, as security see, they craving increase. Who craving increase, they acquisition increase. Who acquisition increase, they suffering increase. Who suffering increase, they not are freed from birth, from old age, from death, from sorrows, from lamentations, from pains, from dejections, from miseries. 'Not are freed from suffering,' I say.

"Whatever ascetics and brahmins at present, too, regard that in the world having a pleasant nature, an agreeable nature, as permanent, as happiness, as self, as healthy, as secure: they increase craving. Those who increase craving increase acquisition. Those who increase acquisition increase suffering. Those who increase suffering are not freed from birth, old age, and death, from sorrow, lamentation, pain, dejection, and misery. 'They are not freed from suffering,' I say.

[6. Drinking the poisoned beverage]
"Seyyathāpi, bhikkhave, āpānīyakaṃso vaṇṇasampanno gandhasampanno rasasampanno, so ca kho visena saṃsaṭṭho. Atha puriso āgaccheyya ghammābhitatto ghammapareto kilanto tasito pipāsito. Tamenaṃ evaṃ vadeyyuṃ:

"Suppose, monks, a goblet color-possessing, fragrance-possessing, flavor-possessing, that but with poison mixed. Then a person would come heat-oppressed, heat-afflicted, tired thirsty parched. To that-him thus they would say:

"Suppose, monks, there was a goblet [filled with a beverage] having a fine color, fragrance, and flavor, but it was mixed with poison. Then a man would come along, oppressed by the heat, afflicted by the heat, tired, thirsty, and parched. They would tell him:

'Ayaṃ te, ambho purisa, āpānīyakaṃso vaṇṇasampanno gandhasampanno rasasampanno, so ca kho visena saṃsaṭṭho. Sace ākaṅkhasi piva. Pivato hi kho taṃ chādessati vaṇṇenapi gandhenapi rasenapi, pivitvā ca pana tatonidānaṃ maraṇaṃ vā nigacchasi maraṇamattaṃ vā dukkhan'ti. So taṃ āpānīyakaṃsaṃ sahasā appaṭisaṅkhā piveyya, nappaṭinissajjeyya. So tatonidānaṃ maraṇaṃ vā nigaccheyya maraṇamattaṃ vā dukkhaṃ.

'This for you, good man, goblet color-possessing, fragrance-possessing, flavor-possessing, that but with poison mixed. If you wish, drink. For one drinking indeed that will please with color-too, with fragrance-too, with flavor-too, having drunk however from-that-cause death or will undergo, death-measure or suffering.' He that goblet suddenly, without having reflected, would drink, not would relinquish. He from-that-cause death or would undergo, death-measure or suffering.

'Good man, this goblet for you [is filled with a beverage] having a fine color, fragrance, and flavor, but it is mixed with poison. Drink it if you wish. For if you drink it, it will please you with its color, fragrance, and flavor, but having drunk it, on that account you will undergo death or deadly suffering.' Suddenly, without having reflected, he would drink [the beverage in] the goblet—he would not relinquish it—and on that account he would undergo death or deadly suffering.

"Evameva kho, bhikkhave, ye hi keci atītamaddhānaṃ samaṇā vā brāhmaṇā vā yaṃ loke piyarūpaṃ . . . anāgatamaddhānaṃ . . . etarahi samaṇā vā brāhmaṇā vā yaṃ loke piyarūpaṃ sātarūpaṃ taṃ niccato passanti,

sukhato passanti, attato passanti, ārogyato passanti, khemato passanti, te taṇhaṃ vaḍḍhenti. Ye taṇhaṃ vaḍḍhenti, te upadhiṃ vaḍḍhenti. Ye upadhiṃ vaḍḍhenti, te dukkhaṃ vaḍḍhenti. Ye dukkhaṃ vaḍḍhenti, te na parimuccanti jātiyā jarāya maraṇena sokehi paridevehi dukkhehi domanassehi upāyāsehi. 'Na parimuccanti dukkhasmā'ti vadāmi.

"Just so, monks, those who past-period ascetics or brahmins or, which in the world pleasant-nature agreeable-nature . . . future-period . . . now ascetics or brahmins or, which in the world pleasant-nature agreeable-nature, as permanent see, as pleasant see, as self see, as health see, as security see, they craving increase. Who craving increase, they acquisition increase. Who acquisition increase, they suffering increase. Who suffering increase, they not are freed from birth, from old age, from death, from sorrows, from lamentations, from pains, from dejections, from miseries. 'Not are freed from suffering,' I say.

"So too, monks, whatever ascetics and brahmins in the past . . . in the future . . . at present regard that in the world having a pleasant nature, an agreeable nature, as permanent, as happiness, as self, as healthy, as secure: they are increasing craving. Those who increase craving increase acquisition. Those who increase acquisition increase suffering. Those who increase suffering are not freed from birth, old age, and death, from sorrow, lamentation, pain, dejection, and misery. 'They are not freed from suffering,' I say.

[7. Those freed from suffering]

"Ye ca kho keci, bhikkhave, atītamaddhānaṃ samaṇā vā brāhmaṇā vā yaṃ loke piyarūpaṃ sātarūpaṃ taṃ aniccato addakkhuṃ, dukkhato addakkhuṃ, anattato addakkhuṃ, rogato addakkhuṃ, bhayato addakkhuṃ, te taṇhaṃ pajahiṃsu. Ye taṇhaṃ pajahiṃsu, te upadhiṃ pajahiṃsu. Ye upadhiṃ pajahiṃsu, te dukkhaṃ pajahiṃsu. Ye dukkhaṃ pajahiṃsu, te parimucciṃsu jātiyā jarāya maraṇena sokehi paridevehi dukkhehi domanassehi upāyāsehi. 'Parimucciṃsu dukkhasmā'ti vadāmi.

"Those but who, monks, past-period ascetics or brahmins or, which in the world pleasant-nature agreeable-nature, that as impermanent saw, as suffering saw, as non-self saw, as illness saw, as peril saw, they craving abandoned. Who craving abandoned, they acquisition abandoned. Who acquisition abandoned, they suffering abandoned. Who suffering abandoned, they were freed from birth, from old age, from death, from sorrows, from lamentations, from pains, from dejections, from miseries. 'They were freed from suffering,' I say.

"But, monks, whatever ascetics and brahmins in the past regarded that in the world having a pleasant nature, an agreeable nature, as impermanent, as suffering, as non-self, as an illness, as perilous: they abandoned craving. Those who abandoned craving abandoned acquisition. Those who abandoned acquisition abandoned suffering. Those who abandoned suffering were freed from birth, old age, and death, from sorrow, lamentation, pain, dejection, and misery. 'They were freed from suffering,' I say.

"Yepi hi keci, bhikkhave, anāgatamaddhānaṃ samaṇā vā brāhmaṇā vā yaṃ loke piyarūpaṃ sātarūpaṃ taṃ aniccato dakkhissanti, dukkhato dakkhissanti, anattato dakkhissanti, rogato dakkhissanti, bhayato dakkhissanti, te taṇhaṃ pajahissanti. Ye taṇhaṃ pajahissanti . . . 'Parimuccissanti dukkhasmā'ti vadāmi.

"Those-too who, monks, future-period ascetics or brahmins or, what in the world pleasant-nature agreeable-nature, that as impermanent will see, as suffering will see, as non-self will see, as illness will see, as peril will see, they craving will abandon. Who craving will abandon . . . 'They will be freed from suffering,' I say.

"Whatever ascetics and brahmins in the future, too, will regard that in the world having a pleasant nature, an agreeable nature, as impermanent, as suffering, as non-self, as an illness, as perilous: they will abandon craving. Those who will abandon craving . . . 'They will be freed from suffering,' I say.

"Yepi hi keci, bhikkhave, etarahi samaṇā vā brāhmaṇā vā yaṃ loke piyarūpaṃ sātarūpaṃ taṃ aniccato passanti, dukkhato passanti, anattato passanti, rogato passanti, bhayato passanti, te taṇhaṃ pajahanti. Ye taṇhaṃ pajahanti . . . 'Parimuccanti dukkhasmā'ti vadāmi.

"Those who, monks, now ascetics or brahmins or, what in the world pleasant-nature agreeable-nature, that as impermanent see, as suffering see, as non-self see, as illness see, as peril see, they craving abandon. Who craving abandon . . . 'They are freed from suffering,' I say.

"Whatever ascetics and brahmins at present, too, regard that in the world having a pleasant nature, an agreeable nature, as impermanent, as suffering, as non-self, as an illness, as perilous: they abandon craving. Those who abandon craving . . . 'They are freed from suffering,' I say.

[8. Rejecting the poisoned beverage]

"Seyyathāpi, bhikkhave, āpānīyakaṃso vaṇṇasampanno gandhasampanno rasasampanno, so ca kho visena saṃsaṭṭho. Atha puriso āgaccheyya ghammābhitatto ghammapareto kilanto tasito pipāsito. Tamenaṃ evaṃ vadeyyuṃ:

"Suppose, monks, a goblet color-possessing, fragrance-possessing, flavor-possessing, that but with poison mixed. Then a person would come heat-oppressed, heat-afflicted, tired, thirsty, parched. To that-him thus they would say:

"Suppose, monks, there was a goblet [filled with a beverage] having a fine color, fragrance, and flavor, but it was mixed with poison. Then a man would come along, oppressed by the heat, afflicted by the heat, tired, thirsty, and parched. They would tell him:

'Ayaṃ te, ambho purisa, āpānīyakaṃso vaṇṇasampanno gandhasampanno rasasampanno so ca kho visena saṃsaṭṭho. Sace ākaṅkhasi piva. Pivato hi kho taṃ chādessati vaṇṇenapi gandhenapi rasenapi; pivitvā ca pana tatonidānaṃ maraṇaṃ vā nigacchasi maraṇamattaṃ vā dukkhan'ti.

'This for you, good man, goblet color-possessing fragrance-possessing flavor-possessing, that but with poison mixed. If you wish, drink. For one drinking indeed that will please with color-too, with fragrance-too, with flavor-too, having drunk but from-that-cause death or will undergo, death-measure or suffering.'

'Good man, this goblet for you [is filled with a beverage] having a fine color, fragrance, and flavor, but it is mixed with poison. Drink it if you wish. For if you drink it, it will gratify you with its color, fragrance, and flavor, but having drunk it, on that account you will undergo death or deadly suffering.'

"Atha kho, bhikkhave, tassa purisassa evamassa: 'Sakkā kho me ayaṃ surāpipāsitā[184] *pānīyena vā vinetuṃ dadhimaṇḍakena vā vinetuṃ maṭṭhaloṇikāya vā vinetuṃ loṇasovīrakena vā vinetuṃ, na tvevāhaṃ taṃ piveyyaṃ, yaṃ mama assa dīgharattaṃ ahitāya dukkhāyā'ti.*[185] *So taṃ āpānīyakaṃsaṃ paṭisaṅkhā na piveyya, paṭinissajjeyya. So tatonidānaṃ na maraṇaṃ vā nigaccheyya maraṇamattaṃ vā dukkhaṃ.*

"Then, monks, to that man such-would occur: 'It's possible for me this thirst with water or to remove, with whey or to remove, with porridge or to remove, with soup or to remove, not but I that should drink, since for me would be long-time to harm to suffering.' He that goblet, having reflected, not would drink, would relinquish. He from-that-cause not death or would undergo, death-measure or suffering.

"Then it would occur to that man: 'I can quench my thirst with water, with whey, with porridge, or with soup, but I should not drink that [beverage], since to do so would lead to my harm and suffering for a long time.' Having reflected, he would not drink [the beverage in] the goblet but would relinquish it, and on that account he would not undergo death or deadly suffering.

"Evameva kho, bhikkhave, ye hi keci atītamaddhānaṃ samaṇā vā brāhmaṇā vā . . . anāgatamaddhānaṃ samaṇā vā brāhmaṇā vā . . . etarahi samaṇā vā brāhmaṇā vā yaṃ loke piyarūpaṃ sātarūpaṃ taṃ aniccato passanti, dukkhato passanti, anattato passanti, rogato passanti, bhayato passanti, te taṇhaṃ pajahanti. Ye taṇhaṃ pajahanti, te upadhiṃ pajahanti. Ye upadhiṃ pajahanti, te dukkhaṃ pajahanti. Ye dukkhaṃ pajahanti, te parimuccanti jātiyā jarāya maraṇena sokehi paridevehi dukkhehi domanassehi upāyāsehi. 'Parimuccanti dukkhasmāti vadāmī'"ti.

"Just so, monks, those who past-period ascetics or brahmins or . . . future-period ascetics or brahmins or . . . now ascetics or brahmins or, which in the world pleasant-nature agreeable-nature, that as impermanent see, as suffer-

184. *Surā* normally means "liquor," but it is hard to see how thirst for liquor makes sense in this passage. I have therefore rendered *surāpipāsitā* simply as "thirst."

185. I follow Ce and Ee here, both of which have *ahitāya dukkhāyā ti*, as against Be *hitāya sukhāyā ti*, which is clearly contrary to the required sense.

ing see, as non-self see, as illness see, as peril see, they craving abandon. Who craving abandon, they acquisition abandon. Who acquisition abandon, they suffering abandon. Who suffering abandon, they are freed from birth, from old age, from death, from sorrows, from lamentations, from pains, from dejections, from miseries. 'They are freed from suffering,' I say."

"So too, monks, whatever ascetics and brahmins in the past . . . whatever ascetics and brahmins in the future . . . whatever ascetics and brahmins at present regard that in the world having a pleasant nature, an agreeable nature, as impermanent, as suffering, as non-self, as an illness, as perilous: they abandon craving. Those who abandon craving abandon acquisition. Those who abandon acquisition abandon suffering. Those who abandon suffering are freed from birth, from old age, from death, from sorrow, lamentation, pain, dejection, and misery. 'They are freed from suffering,' I say."

Grammatical explanations

[1. Inward exploration]

evaṃ me sutaṃ: "thus have I heard"; an indeclinable, *evaṃ*, followed by the enclitic first-person singular pronoun, *me*, probably instrumental (or genitive with an instrumental sense), followed by *sutaṃ*, "heard," the past participle of *suṇāti*, "hears."

kurūsu viharati kammāsadammaṃ nāma kurūnaṃ nigamo: "was dwelling among the Kurus, [where there was] a town of the Kurus named Kammāsadamma." The sentence designates the place where the Buddha was staying with a nominative rather than a locative, as is usually done.[186]

sammasatha no: "do you explore?"; a second-person plural interrogative, with *no* an interrogative particle similar to *nu*. The verb *sammasati* takes its corresponding noun, *sammasanaṃ*, as object.[187]

antaraṃ: probably an adjective qualifying accusative *sammasanaṃ*, but possibly an indeclinable used in an adverbial sense, "internally."

186. Sv II 483,21–26, explains that the locative is not used because there was no proper dwelling place for the Buddha; rather, he went some distance from the town and there set up camp in a delightful forest grove, relying on the town as his alms resort.

187. The word *sammasana* is rare in the suttas but becomes more common in later exegetical works and the commentaries, where it denotes a stage in the development of insight. See especially Vism 607–11, which relies heavily on the Paṭisambhidāmagga.

[2. Exploring old age and death]

yaṃ kho idaṃ anekavidhaṃ nānappakārakaṃ dukkhaṃ loke uppajjati: For this and the following, see p. 341.

upadhinidānaṃ upadhisamudayaṃ upadhijātikaṃ upadhipabhavaṃ: a series of bahubbīhis qualifying *idaṃ dukkhaṃ*. The commentary explains *upadhi* here as the five aggregates.[188] Otherwise, the rest of this section echoes the corresponding passage of SN 12:51; see pp. 334–36.

[4. Exploring craving]

taṇhā panāyaṃ kattha uppajjamānā uppajjati, kattha nivisamānā nivisati: "When this craving is arising, where does it arise? When it is settling down, where does it settle?" *Panāyaṃ* is a sandhi of *pana* and *ayaṃ*. *Kattha* is an interrogative of location. As is common in Pāli, the present participle and the finite verb are cognates of the same verb, with the present participle, *uppajjamānā*, here agreeing in gender and case with *taṇhā*. The two verbs, it seems, indicate two stages in the manifestation of craving, *uppajjati* its initial arising and *nivisati* its habitual recurrence.

yaṃ kho loke piyarūpaṃ sātarūpaṃ: "Whatever in the world has a pleasant nature, an agreeable nature." In these compounds, *-rūpa* is glossed by the commentary with *-sabhāva*, "nature." On the varied meanings of *rūpa*, see p. 143.

[5. Those not freed from suffering]

taṃ niccato addakkhuṃ: *Taṃ* here refers back to *yaṃ loke piyarūpaṃ sātarūpaṃ*. *Niccato* and the other terms with the *-to* suffix are ablatives in the sense of "as"; see pp. 154–55. *Addakkhuṃ* is a third-person plural s-aorist based on **dassati* (Duroiselle §426; Perniola §86; Geiger §164).

vaḍḍhesuṃ: "increased": a third-person plural s-aorist of the causative transitive verb *vaḍḍheti*.

parimucciṃsu: "were freed"; a third-person plural aorist of *parimuccati*.

jātiyā jarāya maraṇena, etc.: These are ablatives, though *maraṇena* has the form of an instrumental.

dakkhissanti: a third-person plural future of **dassati*.

188. Spk II 119,25: *Khandhapañcakaṃ h'ettha upadhī ti adhippetaṃ*.

[6. Drinking the poisoned beverage]

āpānīyakaṃso: According to PED, this is "a drinking-bowl, a goblet," apparently made of bronze. It seems the beverage inside the goblet is implicit.

piva: "drink"; a second-person singular imperative.

pivato: "for one drinking"; the present participle, dative case, of *pivati*.

chādessati: "will please"; a third-person singular future of *chādeti*, taking its object, the person pleased, in the dative case.

ca pana: used in the disjunctive sense, "however."

tatonidānaṃ: an indeclinable meaning "because of, on account of."

nigacchasi: "will undergo"; a present tense form with a future sense. See too the use of *upagacchati* at pp. 264–65.

maraṇamattaṃ dukkhaṃ: an idiom roughly equivalent to "deadly suffering." *Maraṇamattaṃ*, literally "suffering whose measure is death," is a bahubbīhi describing *dukkhaṃ*.

appaṭisaṅkhā: "without having reflected": a negative truncated absolutive, equivalent to *appaṭisaṅkhāya*. The commentary glosses it with *apaccavekkhitvā*.

nappaṭinissajjeyya: "would not relinquish." There is sandhi of *na* and *paṭinissajjeyya*.

[7. Those freed from suffering]

pajahiṃsu: "abandoned"; a third-person plural aorist of *pajahati*.

[8. Rejecting the poisoned beverage]

sakkā kho me: "it's possible for me." PED classifies *sakkā* (= Vedic *śakyāt*) as an indeclinable, originally an optative of *sakkoti* but "later reduced to an adverb with the infinitive."

vinetuṃ: infinitive of *vineti*, "removes."

tvevāhaṃ: a sandhi of *tu*, *eva*, and *ahaṃ*.

5. The Path and the Way: The Practices Leading to the End of Suffering

Introduction

Since dependent origination shows that ignorance and craving are the roots of the round of repeated existence, this entails that to reach the goal of the Dhamma, the cessation of suffering, ignorance and craving must be extricated. To extricate them is the task of the path. In his first discourse, the Buddha described the noble eightfold path as "the way to the cessation of suffering." However, while the noble eightfold path is the best-known system of practice for reaching the end of *dukkha*, the suttas offer various entry points to the practice, partly overlapping the eightfold path, as alternative formulations of the way to the attainment of the goal.

These are grouped into seven sets comprising a total of thirty-seven constituents:

- the four establishments of mindfulness (*cattāro satipaṭṭhānā*)
- the four right kinds of striving (*cattāro sammappadhānā*)
- the four bases for spiritual potency (*cattāro iddhipādā*)
- the five faculties (*pañc'indriyāni*)
- the five powers (*pañca balāni*)
- the seven factors of enlightenment (*satta bojjhaṅgā*)
- the noble eightfold path (*ariya aṭṭhaṅgika magga*)

The seven sets are not totally distinct, for a single factor may appear multiple times in the list among different groups. Mindfulness, for instance, appears in the four establishments of mindfulness; as a faculty, power, and factor of enlightenment; and as the right mindfulness of the eightfold path. Energy appears as the four right strivings; a basis for spiritual potency; a faculty, power, and enlightenment factor; and as the right effort of the eightfold path. Concentration and wisdom, too, appear in several sets, the latter under different designations. The different sets were probably designed to meet the aptitudes and inclinations of different practitioners, but eventually they all converge into a single highway leading to liberation.

The Mahāvagga, the last volume of the Saṃyutta Nikāya, contains separate chapters on each of these groups. Since including suttas from each group would have swelled the present chapter to excessive size, I have selected suttas from only three groups, taking them to represent the entire collection. I have also changed the order of presentation, in effect inverting the order in which they appear in the Mahāvagga. I take the four establishments of mindfulness first, as the fundamental contemplative practice. These are followed by the seven factors of enlightenment, which are in turn followed by the noble eightfold path.

This change is justified in view of the fact that mindfulness—developed through the four contemplations (see just below)—serves as the first enlightenment factor. From mindfulness, the other six factors of enlightenment are said to emerge. The seven factors of enlightenment might be seen either as culminating in the world-transcending noble eightfold path or as offering an alternative course of development complementary to and congruent with the noble eightfold path.

The primary textual source for the four establishments of mindfulness is the *Satipaṭṭhāna Sutta*, which occurs twice in the Nikāyas: in a more concise version as MN 10 (probably more original) and in an expanded version as DN 22. The latter differs from the former only in providing detailed definitions of the four noble truths. The Satipaṭṭhānasaṃyutta might be considered a supplement to the primary text, reinforcing the importance of *satipaṭṭhāna* and depicting a variety of contexts in which the practice is commended.

The expression *satipaṭṭhāna* is usually rendered "foundation of mindfulness," but the term is likely to be a compound of *sati*, "mindfulness," and *upaṭṭhāna*, "setting up" or "establishing," in which case the rendering "establishment of mindfulness" would be more accurate. I have adopted the latter, for which I believe there is canonical support. The four are contemplation of the body, contemplation of feelings, contemplation of mind, and contemplation of *dhammas*, a word I render somewhat inadequately as "phenomena." The formula that describes the practice shows that the practitioner must not only be mindful but also "ardent," which represents the factor of energy or effort, and "clearly comprehending," which suggests incipient wisdom. For the endeavor to succeed, one must also remove—or be intent on removing—"longing and dejection" in regard to worldly conditions.

In **5.1.1**, as in the *Satipaṭṭhāna Sutta*, the Buddha describes the four establishments of mindfulness as *ekāyana magga*. The expression has sometimes been rendered "the only way" or "the sole way," but it seems unlikely that this was the original meaning. Literally the expression means "one-going path," which I take to mean a path going in one direction—that is, heading directly toward the destinations that follow, from "the purification of beings" through "the realization of nibbāna." The dative case used for those expressions in the opening declaration supports this interpretation.

The cultivation of mindfulness is almost invariably coupled with *sampajañña*, which I render as "clear comprehension." Others have rendered this term as "full awareness" or "alertness." The word is based on the root *ñā*, meaning "to know," with two prefixes, *sam-* and *pa-*. As mentioned above, the standard formula for the establishments of mindfulness says that the meditator engaged in each of the four contemplations should be "clearly comprehending" (*sampajāno*), which entails that clear comprehension is integral to the contemplative process initiated by mindfulness. But clear comprehension is sometimes singled out as a distinct practice, as in **5.1.2**. In such cases, it is said that one should bring clear comprehension to bear on all the familiar activities of daily life: walking, looking around, bending and stretching the limbs, dressing, eating, speaking, going to the toilet, and so forth. We might suppose that in the meditative development of mindfulness, clear comprehension is ever-present in a background role, while in performing the tasks of daily life, clear comprehension is dominant, with mindfulness now relegated to a background role.

The suttas selected for this chapter do not provide a detailed explanation of the cultivation of mindfulness but rather highlight different contexts for the practice, which is treated at length in the primary sutta on the subject. Thus **5.1.3** states that the four establishments of mindfulness are to be adopted by monastics at different stages of maturity—novices, trainees, and arahants—each for a different purpose. It is significant that in the first two cases the cultivation of mindfulness contributes to the arising of insight or understanding; it does not pertain merely to the development of concentration, as is sometimes alleged. In **5.1.5** we encounter the story of the Buddha's grave illness near the end of his life, a narrative also related in the

Mahāparinibbāna Sutta (at DN II 98–101). Aware that his end is near, he instructs the monks to be islands and refuges for themselves, which they can do by practicing the four establishments of mindfulness. Text **5.1.8** shows that the four establishments of mindfulness should be cultivated even in times of illness; the subject of the discourse is a layman who at the end proclaims himself a non-returner. Several suttas offer memorable similes: of the monkey that gets stuck in glue (**5.1.4**), of the acrobats who protect each other by protecting themselves (**5.1.6**), and of the man ordered to carry a bowl of oil through a raucous crowd under threat of decapitation (**5.1.7**).

Properly cultivated, the four establishments of mindfulness naturally give rise to the *satta bojjhaṅgā*, the seven factors of enlightenment. The standard formula for the enlightenment factors says, with regard to each, that it is "based on seclusion, based on dispassion, based on cessation, evolving toward release." We might see "seclusion, dispassion, and cessation" as representing the goal of aspiration one sets up when undertaking the practice, and "evolving toward release" as pointing to the inherent capacity of these factors to culminate in that goal. In **5.2.4** the Buddha explains that these seven factors of enlightenment are so called because they lead to enlightenment. While this seems obvious, the explanation is noteworthy because the commentarial tradition takes the seven *bojjhaṅgā* to be primarily *constituents* of the enlightenment experience rather than as factors leading to enlightenment; but here they are said to be the qualities that conduce to enlightenment.

This interpretation is confirmed by **5.2.3**, which shows how the seven factors unfold in a graded sequence, each one coming to prominence when its predecessor reaches a sufficient degree of strength. Text **5.2.5** again highlights the instrumental role of the enlightenment factors as well as their place in the sequential development of the practice. The seven factors culminate in "clear knowledge and liberation"; they do not constitute clear knowledge as such. The seven factors in turn arise through the development of the four establishments of mindfulness, which depend on the three kinds of good conduct, which in turn require the exercise of sense restraint.

The seven factors of enlightenment are sometimes paired in an antithetical relationship with the five hindrances, the obstacles to progress. Text **5.2.2** explains the "nutriments" both for the five hindrances, which are to be overcome by "starving" them of their nutriments, and the nutriments for the seven factors of enlightenment, which have to be properly nourished.

Although it is not expressly mentioned in the suttas, this positing of a conditional relationship between the hindrances and enlightenment factors and their respective nutriments illustrates another application of the principle of conditionality that underlies the teaching of dependent origination.

Cultivation of the seven factors requires skill. The seven factors fall into two groups—three arousing factors and three calming factors. As 5.2.7 shows with its simile of kindling and extinguishing a fire, a proficient meditator must know the right occasions for developing the appropriate factors. But mindfulness does not fall into either group for, as the sutta says, it is useful everywhere.

The third subsection of this chapter introduces the noble eightfold path, with 5.3.3 providing formal definitions of the individual path factors. From these definitions, it can be seen that the path has a wider scope than the seven factors of enlightenment. Whereas the latter operate almost entirely in the domain of meditative practice, the eightfold path includes a cognitive factor, right view; a motivational factor, right intention; and three ethical factors: right speech, right action, and right livelihood. These all precede and support the three meditative factors—right effort, right mindfulness, and right concentration—though when the path matures, all eight operate in unison.

The suttas of the Maggasaṃyutta attach two alternative descriptions to each path factor. One is the "based on seclusion" formula also used in relation to the enlightenment factors. The other describes each path factor as culminating in the removal of lust, the removal of hatred, and the removal of delusion. Often in this collection duplicate versions of a sutta appear, differing only in the description they attach to the path factors. We find instances of this duplication here in 5.3.5 and 5.3.6.

Three suttas included in this anthology connect the eightfold path to good friendship. In 5.3.1 the Buddha corrects Ānanda's assertion that half the spiritual life consists in good friendship; for the Buddha, the entire spiritual life is good friendship. He goes on to declare that he himself is the good friend of beings who helps to liberate them from birth, old age, and death. The two suttas combined in 5.3.5, which differ only in the formula they attach to the path factors, state that good friendship is the forerunner of the noble eightfold path. The last sutta included here, 5.3.7, declares that just as the Ganges River, which flows to the east, cannot be made to flow to the west, so a monk who has taken up the noble eightfold path cannot be persuaded to give up the training and revert to the lay life. With a sureness of direction like a river, the eightfold path carries that monk irreversibly toward nibbāna.

1. The Four Establishments of Mindfulness

1. Ambapālisutta

Ambapāli (SN 47:1; V 141)

Evaṃ me sutaṃ. Ekaṃ samayaṃ bhagavā vesāliyaṃ viharati ambapālivane. Tatra kho bhagavā . . . etadavoca: "Ekāyano ayaṃ, bhikkhave, maggo sattānaṃ visuddhiyā sokaparidevānaṃ samatikkamāya dukkhadomanassānaṃ atthaṅgamāya ñāyassa adhigamāya nibbānassa sacchikiriyāya, yadidaṃ cattāro satipaṭṭhānā.

Thus by me heard. One occasion the Blessed One at Vesālī was dwelling, in Ambapālī-grove. There the Blessed One . . . this-said: "One-going this, monks, path, of beings for purification, of sorrow-lamentation for overcoming, of pain-dejection for passing-away, of method for achievement, of nibbāna for realization, that-is, the four mindfulness-establishments.

Thus have I heard. On one occasion the Blessed One was dwelling at Vesālī in Ambapālī's grove. There . . . the Blessed One said this: "This one-way path, monks, is for the purification of beings, for the overcoming of sorrow and lamentation, for the passing away of pain and dejection, for the achievement of the method, for the realization of nibbāna, that is, the four establishments of mindfulness.

"Katame cattāro? Idha, bhikkhave, bhikkhu kāye kāyānupassī viharati ātāpī sampajāno satimā, vineyya loke abhijjhādomanassaṃ; vedanāsu vedanānupassī viharati ātāpī sampajāno satimā, vineyya loke abhijjhādomanassaṃ; citte cittānupassī viharati ātāpī sampajāno satimā, vineyya loke abhijjhādomanassaṃ; dhammesu dhammānupassī viharati ātāpī sampajāno satimā, vineyya loke abhijjhādomanassaṃ.

"What four? Here, monks, a monk in the body body-contemplating dwells, ardent, clearly-comprehending, mindful, having removed in the world longing-dejection; in feelings feeling-contemplating dwells, ardent, clearly-comprehending, mindful, having removed in the world longing-dejection; in the mind mind-contemplating dwells, ardent, clearly-comprehending, mindful, having removed in the world longing-dejection; in phenomena phenomena-contemplating dwells, ardent, clearly-comprehending, mindful, having removed in the world longing-dejection.

"What four? Here, monks, a monk dwells contemplating the body in the body, ardent, clearly comprehending, mindful, having removed longing and dejection in regard to the world; contemplating feelings in feelings, ardent, clearly comprehending, mindful, having removed longing and dejection in regard to the world; contemplating the mind in the mind, ardent, clearly comprehending, mindful, having removed longing and dejection in regard to the world; contemplating phenomena in phenomena, ardent, clearly comprehending, mindful, having removed longing and dejection in regard to the world.

"Ekāyano ayaṃ, bhikkhave, maggo sattānaṃ visuddhiyā sokaparidevānaṃ samatikkamāya dukkhadomanassānaṃ atthaṅgamāya ñāyassa adhigamāya nibbānassa sacchikiriyāya, yadidaṃ cattāro satipaṭṭhānā"ti.

"One-going this, monks, path, of beings for purification, of sorrow-lamentation for overcoming, of pain-dejection for passing-away, of method for achievement, of nibbāna for realization, that is, the four mindfulness-establishments."

"This one-way path, monks, is for the purification of beings, for the overcoming of sorrow and lamentation, for the passing away of pain and dejection, for the achievement of the method, for the realization of nibbāna, that is, the four establishments of mindfulness."

Grammatical explanations

evaṃ me sutaṃ: see p. 373.

ekāyano: literally, "one-going, one-way"; a compound qualifying *maggo*, composed of *eka*, "one," and *ayana*, "going, motion, path, road." Though often translated "the only path" or "the sole path," the purport of *ekāyano maggo* is probably that the path goes in one direction, namely, toward "the purification of beings . . . the realization of nibbāna."[189]

visuddhiyā, samatikkamāya, atthaṅgamāya, adhigamāya, sacchikiriyāya: "for purification, for overcoming, for the passing away, for achievement, for realization." Each of these is a singular dative in relation to a preceding genitive. The first and last are feminine, the middle three masculine.

satipaṭṭhānā: The preferred resolution in the commentaries is *sati* + *paṭṭhāna*, hence "a foundation of mindfulness,"[190] but it is likely that the compound should be resolved *sati* + *upaṭṭhāna*, "the establishment (or setting up) of mindfulness."[191] The Skt texts have *smṛtyupasthāna*, indicating a preference for the second derivation.

kāye kāyānupassī: "contemplating the body in the body." *Kāye* is a locative, *kāyānupassī* modifies *bhikkhu*. Derivatives ending in *-in* (such as *anupassin*) function in such compounds like a present participle, with its prior member accusative in sense.[192] Vibh 194,25–29 defines *anupassanā* in relation to the *satipaṭṭhāna* passage with the string of terms for wisdom: "That which is wisdom, understanding . . . non-delusion, discrimination of phenomena, right view—this is called contemplation" (*yā paññā pajānanā . . . amoho dhammavicayo sammādiṭṭhi, ayaṃ vuccati anupassanā*). One who possesses this contemplation is said to be "contemplating" (*imāya anupassanāya upeto hoti . . . vuccati "anupassī"ti*).

189. The only other use of the expression *ekāyana* in the Nikāyas occurs in a long passage at MN I 74–77, where it describes literally a path going in a single direction. For instance at I 74,14: *Seyyathāpi, sāriputta, aṅgārakāsu sādhikaporisā pūrā aṅgārānaṃ vītaccikānaṃ vītadhūmānaṃ. Atha puriso āgaccheyya ghammābhitatto ghammapareto kilanto tasito pipāsito ekāyanena maggena tameva aṅgārakāsuṃ paṇidhāya.* "Suppose, Sāriputta, there was a pit full of coals exceeding a man's height, without flame or smoke. Then a man afflicted and oppressed by the heat, tired and thirsty, would come along *by a path going in one direction* straight toward that pit of coals."

190. Spk III 178,29: *Satiyā paṭṭhānaṃ satipaṭṭhānaṃ.*

191. This seems supported by the common expressions found in the suttas, *upaṭṭhitassati*, "with mindfulness established" (at SN V 331,10, etc.) and *parimukhaṃ satiṃ upaṭṭhapetvā*, "having established mindfulness in front" (at SN V 311,13, etc.).

192. Spk III 179,27–28 glosses *kāyānupassī* in just such a way: *kāyaṃ anupassanasīlo, kāyaṃ vā anupassamāno*, "one whose habit is contemplating the body, or one contemplating the body." See too p. 349, note 180.

ātāpī sampajāno satimā: "ardent, clearly comprehending, mindful"; the three words are nominative singulars qualifying *bhikkhu*. *Sampajāno* is a middle-voice present participle (Duroiselle §448; Perniola §95); *satimā* is a masculine singular nominative of the possessive, *satimat*.

vineyya loke abhijjhādomanassaṃ: "having removed longing and dejection in regard to the world." *Vineyya* is an absolutive of *vineti*; the normal word order is inverted, with the accusative *abhijjhādomanassaṃ*, a dvanda of the collective singular type, placed after the absolutive.

dhammānupassī: *Dhamma*, as can be seen from the *Satipaṭṭhāna Sutta*, has in this context a broad sense, comprising five groups relevant to the process of mind cultivation and the development of insight: the five hindrances, the five aggregates, the twelve sense bases, the seven enlightenment factors, and the four noble truths.

2. Satisutta

Mindfulness (SN 47:2; V 142)

"Sato, bhikkhave, bhikkhu vihareyya sampajāno. Ayaṃ vo amhākaṃ anusāsanī. Kathañca, bhikkhave, bhikkhu sato hoti? Idha, bhikkhave, bhikkhu kāye kāyānupassī viharati ātāpī sampajāno satimā, vineyya loke abhijjhādomanassaṃ; vedanāsu vedanānupassī . . . citte cittānupassī . . . dhammesu dhammānupassī viharati ātāpī sampajāno satimā, vineyya loke abhijjhādomanassaṃ. Evaṃ kho, bhikkhave, bhikkhu sato hoti.

"Mindful, monks, a monk should dwell clearly-comprehending. This to you our instruction. How-and, monks, a monk mindful is? Here, monks, a monk in the body body-contemplating dwells, ardent, clearly-comprehending, mindful, having removed in the world longing-dejection; in feelings feeling-contemplating . . . in the mind mind-contemplating . . . in phenomena phenomena-contemplating dwells, ardent, clearly-comprehending, mindful, having removed in the world longing-dejection. Thus, monks, a monk mindful is.

"Monks, a monk should dwell mindful and clearly comprehending. This is our instruction to you. And how, monks, is a monk mindful? Here, monks, a monk dwells contemplating the body in the body, ardent, clearly comprehending, mindful, having removed longing and dejection in regard to the world; he dwells contemplating feelings in feelings . . . contemplating the mind in the mind . . . contemplating phenomena in phenomena, ardent, clearly comprehending, mindful, having removed longing and dejection in regard to the world.

"Kathañca, bhikkhave, bhikkhu sampajāno hoti? Idha, bhikkhave, bhikkhu abhikkante paṭikkante sampajānakārī hoti, ālokite vilokite sampajānakārī hoti, samiñjite pasārite sampajānakārī hoti, saṅghāṭipattacīvaradhāraṇe sampajānakārī hoti, asite pīte khāyite sāyite sampajānakārī hoti, uccāra-passāvakamme sampajānakārī hoti, gate ṭhite nisinne sutte jāgarite bhāsite tuṇhībhāve sampajānakārī hoti. Evaṃ kho, bhikkhave, bhikkhu sampajānakārī hoti. Sato, bhikkhave, bhikkhu vihareyya sampajāno. Ayaṃ vo amhākaṃ anusāsanī"ti.

"How-and, monks, a monk clearly-comprehending is? Here, monks, a monk in-gone-out in-returned a clearly-comprehending-doer is, in-looked-ahead in-looked-aside a clearly-comprehending-doer is, in-bent in-stretched a clearly-comprehending-doer is, in-cloak-bowl-robe-wearing a clearly-comprehending-doer is, in-eaten in-drunk in-chewed in-tasted a clearly-comprehending-doer is, in-defecation-urination-act a clearly-comprehending-doer is, in-gone in-stood in-sat in-slept in-awakened in-spoken in-silence a clearly-comprehending-doer is. Thus, monks, a monk a clearly-comprehending-doer is. Mindful, monks, a monk should dwell clearly-comprehending. This to you our instruction."

"And how, monks, is a monk clearly comprehending? Here, monks, in going out and returning, a monk is one who acts with clear comprehension; in looking ahead and looking aside, he is one who acts with clear comprehension; in bending and stretching, he is one who acts with clear comprehension; in wearing the cloak and robe and [holding] the bowl, he is one who acts with clear comprehension; in eating, drinking, chewing, and tasting, he is one who acts with clear comprehension; in defecation and urination, he is one who acts with clear comprehension; in going, in standing, in sitting, in going to sleep, in waking up, in speaking, and in keeping silent, he is one who acts with clear comprehension. Thus, monks, a monk is one who acts with clear comprehension. Monks, a monk should dwell mindful and clearly comprehending. This is our instruction to you."

Grammatical explanations

sato: "mindful." In this passage two adjectives are used to describe one who is mindful: the past participle *sato* (of the verb *sarati*) and the possessive *satimā* (see p. 385). There is no difference in sense.

abhikkante paṭikkante: "in going out [and] in returning." Each of these words (and those that follow, *ālokite vilokite* and so forth) is a past participle in the locative case, used to represent the action itself. Hence the commentary glosses these words with action nouns, which is how I render them in English.[193]

sampajānakārī: "one who acts with clear comprehension." The commentary explains this to mean "one who does all tasks with clear comprehension, or one who practices clear comprehension itself."[194]

saṅghāṭipattacīvaradhāraṇe: The commentary explains: "*Dhāraṇa* means 'using' by way of putting on and wearing the cloak and robe, and receiving almsfood with the bowl."[195] The word *dhāraṇa* can mean both wearing and holding.

3. Sālasutta

At Sāla (SN 47:4; V 144–45)

[1. Juniors]

"Ye te, bhikkhave, bhikkhū navā acirapabbajitā adhunāgatā imaṃ dhammavinayaṃ, te vo, bhikkhave, bhikkhū catunnaṃ satipaṭṭhānānaṃ bhāvanāya samādapetabbā nivesetabbā patiṭṭhāpetabbā.

"Who those, monks, monks juniors, not-long-gone-forth, recently-come-to this Dhamma-discipline, those by you, monks, monks of four mindfulness-establishments in the development should-be-enjoined, should-be-settled, should-be-established.

193. Spk III 181,29–30: *Ettha abhikkantaṃ vuccati gamanaṃ, paṭikkantaṃ nivattanaṃ.*

194. Spk III 182,7–8: *Sampajaññena sabbakiccakārī, sampajaññass'eva vā kārī. Sampajānakārī* is an example of the upapada compound. See Duroiselle §552.

195. Spk III 194,19–21: *Ettha saṅghāṭicīvarānaṃ nivāsanapārupanavasena, pattassa bhikkhāpaṭiggahaṇādivasena paribhogo dhāraṇaṃ nāma.*

"Monks, those monks who are juniors, not long gone forth, recently come to this Dhamma and discipline, should be enjoined, settled, and established by you in the development of the four establishments of mindfulness.

"Katamesaṃ catunnaṃ? Etha tumhe, āvuso, kāye kāyānupassino viharatha ātāpino sampajānā ekodibhūtā vippasannacittā samāhitā ekaggacittā, kāyassa yathābhūtaṃ ñāṇāya. Vedanāsu vedanānupassino viharatha ātāpino sampajānā ekodibhūtā vippasannacittā samāhitā ekaggacittā, vedanānaṃ yathābhūtaṃ ñāṇāya. Citte cittānupassino viharatha ātāpino sampajānā ekodibhūtā vippasannacittā samāhitā ekaggacittā, cittassa yathābhūtaṃ ñāṇāya. Dhammesu dhammānupassino viharatha ātāpino sampajānā ekodibhūtā vippasannacittā samāhitā ekaggacittā, dhammānaṃ yathābhūtaṃ ñāṇāya.

"Of which four? 'Come you, friends, in the body body-contemplating dwell, ardent, clearly comprehending, unified, tranquil-minds, concentrated, one-pointed-minds, of body as-really-is for knowledge. In feelings feelings-contemplating dwell, ardent, clearly comprehending, unified, tranquil-minds, concentrated, one-pointed-minds, of feelings as-really-is for knowledge. In the mind mind-contemplating dwell, ardent, clearly comprehending, unified, tranquil-minds, concentrated, one-pointed-minds, of mind as-really-is for knowledge. In phenomena phenomena-contemplating dwell, ardent, clearly comprehending, unified, tranquil-minds, concentrated, one-pointed-minds, of phenomena as-really-is for knowledge.'

"What four? 'Come, friends, dwell contemplating the body in the body, ardent, clearly comprehending, unified, with tranquil minds, concentrated, with one-pointed minds, for knowledge of the body as it really is. Dwell contemplating feelings in feelings, ardent, clearly comprehending, unified, with tranquil minds, concentrated, with one-pointed minds, for knowledge of feelings as they really are. Dwell contemplating the mind in the mind, ardent, clearly comprehending, unified, with tranquil minds, concentrated, with one-pointed minds, for knowledge of the mind as it really is. Dwell contemplating phenomena in phenomena, ardent, clearly comprehending, unified, with tranquil minds, concentrated, with one-pointed minds, for knowledge of phenomena as they really are.'

[2. Trainees]

"Yepi te, bhikkhave, bhikkhū sekhā appattamānasā anuttaraṃ yogakkhemaṃ patthayamānā viharanti, tepi kāye kāyānupassino viharanti ātāpino sampajānā ekodibhūtā vippasannacittā samāhitā ekaggacittā, kāyassa pariññāya; vedanāsu vedanānupassino viharanti ātāpino sampajānā ekodibhūtā vippasannacittā samāhitā ekaggacittā, vedanānaṃ pariññāya; citte cittānupassino viharanti ātāpino sampajānā ekodibhūtā vippasannacittā samāhitā ekaggacittā, cittassa pariññāya; dhammesu dhammānupassino viharanti ātāpino sampajānā ekodibhūtā vippasannacittā samāhitā ekaggacittā, dhammānaṃ pariññāya.

"Who-too those, monks, monks trainees, not-reached-ideal, unsurpassed bonds-security yearning-for dwell, they-too in the body body-contemplating dwell, ardent, clearly comprehending, unified, tranquil-minds, concentrated, one-pointed-minds, of body for full-understanding. In feelings feelings-contemplating dwell, ardent, clearly comprehending, unified, tranquil-minds, concentrated, one-pointed-minds, of feelings for full-understanding. In the mind mind-contemplating dwell, ardent, clearly comprehending, unified, tranquil-minds, concentrated, one-pointed-minds, of mind for full-understanding. In phenomena phenomena-contemplating dwell, ardent, clearly comprehending, unified, tranquil-minds, concentrated, one-pointed-minds, of phenomena for full-understanding.

"Monks, those monks who are trainees, who have not reached their mind's ideal, who dwell yearning for unsurpassed security from the bonds, they too dwell contemplating the body in the body, ardent, clearly comprehending, unified, with tranquil minds, concentrated, with one-pointed minds, for full understanding of the body. They dwell contemplating feelings in feelings, ardent, clearly comprehending, unified, with tranquil minds, concentrated, with one-pointed minds, for full understanding of feelings. They dwell contemplating the mind in the mind, ardent, clearly comprehending, unified, with tranquil minds, concentrated, with one-pointed minds, for full understanding of the mind. They dwell contemplating phenomena in phenomena, ardent, clearly comprehending, unified, with tranquil minds, concentrated, with one-pointed minds, for full understanding of phenomena.

[3. Arahants]

"Yepi te, bhikkhave, bhikkhū arahanto khīṇāsavā vusitavanto katakaraṇīyā ohitabhārā anuppattasadatthā parikkhīṇabhavasaṃyojanā sammadaññā vimuttā, tepi kāye kāyānupassino viharanti ātāpino sampajānā ekodibhūtā vippasannacittā samāhitā ekaggacittā, kāyena visaṃyuttā; vedanāsu vedanānupassino viharanti ātāpino sampajānā ekodibhūtā vippasannacittā samāhitā ekaggacittā, vedanāhi visaṃyuttā; citte cittānupassino viharanti ātāpino sampajānā ekodibhūtā vippasannacittā samāhitā ekaggacittā, cittena visaṃyuttā; dhammesu dhammānupassino viharanti ātāpino sampajānā ekodibhūtā vippasannacittā samāhitā ekaggacittā, dhammehi visaṃyuttā.

"Who-too those, monks, monks arahants, destroyed-influxes, lived, done-what-should-be-done, dropped-burden, reached-own-good, fully-destroyed-existence-fetters, completely-having finally known liberated, they-too in the body body-contemplating dwell, ardent, clearly comprehending, unified, tranquil-minds, concentrated, one-pointed-minds, by body detached. In feelings feelings-contemplating dwell, ardent, clearly comprehending, unified, tranquil-minds, concentrated, one-pointed-minds, by feelings detached. In the mind mind-contemplating dwell, ardent, clearly comprehending, unified, tranquil-minds, concentrated, one-pointed-minds, by mind detached. In phenomena phenomena-contemplating dwell, ardent, clearly comprehending, unified, tranquil-minds, concentrated, one-pointed-minds, by phenomena detached.

"Monks, those monks who are arahants, whose influxes are destroyed, who have lived [the spiritual life], done what had to be done, dropped the burden, reached their own good, fully destroyed the fetters of existence, and are completely liberated by final knowledge, they too dwell contemplating the body in the body, ardent, clearly comprehending, unified, with tranquil minds, concentrated, with one-pointed minds, detached from the body. They dwell contemplating feelings in feelings, ardent, clearly comprehending, unified, with tranquil minds, concentrated, with one-pointed minds, detached from feelings. They dwell contemplating the mind in the mind, ardent, clearly comprehending, unified, with tranquil minds, concentrated, with one-pointed minds, detached from the mind. They dwell contemplating phenomena in phenomena, ardent, clearly comprehending, unified, with tranquil minds, concentrated, with one-pointed minds, detached from phenomena.

"Yepi te, bhikkhave, bhikkhū navā acirapabbajitā adhunāgatā imaṃ dhammavinayaṃ, te vo, bhikkhave, bhikkhū imesaṃ catunnaṃ satipaṭṭhānānaṃ bhāvanāya samādapetabbā nivesetabbā patiṭṭhāpetabbā"ti.

"Who-too those, monks, monks juniors, not-long-gone-forth, recently-come-to this Dhamma-discipline, those by you, monks, monks of these four mindfulness-establishments in the development should-be-enjoined, should-be-settled, should-be-established."

"Monks, those monks who are juniors, not long gone forth, recently come to this Dhamma and discipline, should be enjoined, settled, and established by you in the development of these four establishments of mindfulness."

Grammatical explanations

[1. Juniors]

ye te: "those who"; masculine plural pronouns qualifying *bhikkhū*, completed by *te* in the main clause.

acirapabbajitā adhunāgatā: "not long gone forth, recently come"; kammadhāraya compounds describing *bhikkhū*, nominative plurals in agreement with their subject. The first is composed of the adjective *acira* and the past participle of *pabbajati*, the second by the adverb *adhunā* and the past participle of *āgacchati*.

vo: "by you"; the enclitic pronoun, second-person plural in the instrumental case.

samādapetabbā nivesetabbā patiṭṭhāpetabbā: "should be enjoined, settled, [and] established"; future passive participles of the causative verbs *samādapeti*, *niveseti*, and *patiṭṭhapeti*. The sentence exemplifies the penchant of the suttas for passive constructions (see p. 77).

etha tumhe: "come, you"; a second-person plural imperative of *eti* followed by the second-person plural pronoun. This imperative is usually a mere call to attention, followed by another more pertinent imperative, here *viharatha*.

ātāpino sampajānā ekodibhūtā vippasannacittā samāhitā ekaggacittā: "ardent, clearly comprehending, unified, with tranquil minds, concentrated, with one-pointed minds." These all serve as adjectives qualifying *tumhe*, "you," the junior monks. *Vippasannacittā* and *ekaggacittā* are bahubbīhis based on kammadhārayas.

ñāṇāya: "for knowledge"; a dative of the neuter noun *ñāṇa*, with its object in the genitive.

[2. Trainees]

sekhā appattamānasā anuttaraṃ yogakkhemaṃ patthayamānā: "trainees, who have not reached their ideal, who dwell yearning for unsurpassed security from the bonds." *Sekhā* are those who have reached the irreversible path to liberation but have not yet attained the final fruit—technically, those from the path of stream-entry through the path of arahantship. *Appattamānasā* is a bahubbīhi composed of the negative prefix *a* + *patta*, "attained," and *mānasa*, a derivative of *manas*, which I thus render freely as "mind's ideal."[196] *Patthayamānā*, "yearning," is the present participle of *pattheti*; *anuttaraṃ yogakkhemaṃ*, "unsurpassed security from the bonds," an epithet of nibbāna, is its object. *Yogakkhemaṃ* is an ablative tappurisa compound.

[3. Arahants]

khīṇāsavā . . . vimuttā: This is a stock description of arahants. On *khīṇāsava*, see p. 345. *Vusitavanto*, "who have lived [the spiritual life]," is a past active participle (see pp. 30–31) composed of *vusita* (a past participle of *vasati*, "lives") and the suffix *-vat*, here in the nominative plural; see the description of the arahant as *vusitaṃ brahmacariyaṃ* (p. 144). On *katakaraṇīyā*, see *kataṃ karaṇīyaṃ* (also on p. 144). *Ohitabhārā* is a bahubbīhi composed of *ohita*, "dropped," and *bhāra*, "burden." *Anuppattasadatthā* is another bahubbīhi composed of *anuppatta*, "reached, attained," and *sadattha*, "own good," on which see p. 323. *Parikkhīṇabhavasaṃyojanā* is still another bahubbīhi composed of *parikkhīṇa*, "fully destroyed," *bhava*, "existence," and *saṃyojana*, "fetter." *Sammadaññā vimuttā*, "completely liberated by final knowledge," is constructed from *sammā*, a truncated absolutive *aññā* (from *aññāya*, absolutive of *ājānāti*), and the past participle, *vimuttā*.[197]

196. Following the negative prefix *a-*, *p-* is doubled to represent the consonant cluster *pr-* of Skt *prāpta*. The Skt consonant cluster *-pt-* is represented in Pāli by *-tt-*, with shortening of the long vowel.

197. To conform to normal English diction, I find it more convenient to translate *aññā* as if it were a truncated instrumental.

kāyena visaṃyuttā: "detached from the body." Although *kāyena* is an instrumental, in connection with *visaṃyuttā*, it should be translated as ablative in sense.

4. Makkaṭasutta

The Monkey (SN 47:7; V 148–49)

[1. The monkey trap]

"Atthi, bhikkhave, himavato pabbatarājassa duggā visamā desā, yattha n'eva makkaṭānaṃ cārī na manussānaṃ. Atthi, bhikkhave, himavato pabbatarājassa duggā visamā desā, yattha makkaṭānaṃ hi kho cārī na manussānaṃ. Atthi, bhikkhave, himavato pabbatarājassa samā bhūmibhāgā ramaṇīyā, yattha makkaṭānañc'eva cārī manussānañca. Tatra, bhikkhave, luddā makkaṭavīthīsu lepaṃ oḍḍenti makkaṭānaṃ bādhanāya.

"There are, monks, of the Himalaya the mountain-king impassable uneven places, where not of monkeys traveling, not of human beings. There are, monks, of the Himalaya the mountain-king impassable uneven places, where of monkeys traveling, not of human beings. There are, monks, of the Himalaya the mountain-king even ground-regions delightful, where of monkeys traveling, of human beings-and. There, monks, hunters on monkey-trails glue set out of monkeys for trapping.

"There are, monks, impassable uneven places in the Himalaya, the king of mountains, that are not fit for traveling either by monkeys or human beings. There are, monks, impassable uneven places in the Himalaya, the king of mountains, that are fit for traveling by monkeys but not by human beings. There are, monks, in the Himalaya, the king of mountains, even regions that are delightful, fit for traveling both by monkeys and human beings. There, monks, on the monkey trails hunters set out glue for trapping monkeys.

"Tatra, bhikkhave, ye te makkaṭā abālajātikā alolajātikā, te taṃ lepaṃ disvā ārakā parivajjanti. Yo pana so hoti makkaṭo bālajātiko lolajātiko, so taṃ lepaṃ upasaṅkamitvā hatthena gaṇhāti; so tattha bajjhati.

"There, monks, which those monkeys not-foolish-nature not-frivolous-nature, they that glue having seen, from afar avoid. Which but that is monkey foolish-nature frivolous-nature, he that glue having approached, with a hand grabs; he there is bound.

"When, monks, those monkeys there that are not foolish and frivolous see that glue, they avoid it from afar. But there is a monkey, foolish and frivolous, who approaches that glue and grabs it with his hand; he is bound there.

"'Hatthaṃ mocessāmī'ti dutiyena hatthena gaṇhāti; so tattha bajjhati. 'Ubho hatthe mocessāmī'ti pādena gaṇhāti; so tattha bajjhati. 'Ubho hatthe mocessāmi pādañcā'ti dutiyena pādena gaṇhāti; so tattha bajjhati. 'Ubho hatthe mocessāmi pāde cā'ti tuṇḍena gaṇhāti; so tattha bajjhati.

"'Hand I will release,' with a second hand grabs; he there is bound. 'Both hands I will release,' with a foot grabs; he there is bound. 'Both hands I will release foot-and,' with the second foot grabs; he there is bound. 'Both hands I will release feet and,' with snout grabs; he there is bound.

"Thinking, 'I will release my hand,' he grabs it with his second hand; he is bound there. Thinking, 'I will release both hands,' he grabs it with his foot; he is bound there. Thinking, 'I will release both hands and the foot,' he grabs it with his second foot; he is bound there. Thinking, 'I will release both hands and feet,' he grabs it with his snout; he is bound there.

"Evaṃ hi so, bhikkhave, makkaṭo pañcoḍḍito thunaṃ seti, anayaṃ āpanno vyasanaṃ āpanno yathākāmakaraṇīyo luddassa. Tamenaṃ, bhikkhave, luddo vijjhitvā tasmiṃyeva makkaṭaṃ uddharitvā avassajjetvā[198] *yenakāmaṃ pakkamati. Evaṃ so taṃ, bhikkhave, hoti yo agocare carati paravisaye.*

"Thus indeed that, monks, monkey five-trapped screeching lies, misery has incurred, disaster has incurred, according-to-desire-to-be-done-with of the hunter. That-him, monks, the hunter having speared, on that-itself the mon-

198. I have adopted the reading of Ce. Be has *tasmiṃ yeva kaṭṭhakataṅgāre avissajjetvā*. Possibly the readings in all editions are corrupt. My rendering is thus partly a conjecture, but the general point is clear.

key having raised, having suspended, where-desire departs. Thus one that, monks, becomes who into not-range wanders, into others-domain.

"Thus, monks, that monkey, trapped in five places, lies there screeching; he has incurred misery, incurred disaster, to be done with by the hunter as he desires. Having speared him, monks, having raised the monkey on that [spear] itself, having suspended [him from it], the hunter departs where he desires. Thus that happens to him, monks, who wanders into what is not one's own range, into the domain of others.

[2. The proper range for a monk]

"Tasmātiha, bhikkhave, mā agocare carittha paravisaye. Agocare, bhikkhave, caratam̩ paravisaye lacchati māro otāram̩, lacchati māro ārammaṇam̩.

"Therefore, monks, do not into not-range wander, into others-domain. Into not-range, monks, of those wandering, into others-domain, will gain Māra an opening, will gain Māra a basis.

"Therefore, monks, do not wander into what is not your range, into the domain of others. For those wandering into what is not their range, into the domain of others, Māra will gain an opening, Māra will gain a basis.

"Ko ca, bhikkhave, bhikkhuno agocaro paravisayo? Yadidam̩ pañca kāmaguṇā. Katame pañca? Cakkhuviññeyyā rūpā iṭṭhā kantā manāpā piyarūpā kāmūpasam̩hitā rajanīyā, sotaviññeyyā saddā . . . ghānaviññeyyā gandhā . . . jivhāviññeyyā rasā . . . kāyaviññeyyā phoṭṭhabbā iṭṭhā kantā manāpā piyarūpā kāmūpasam̩hitā rajanīyā. Ayam̩, bhikkhave, bhikkhuno agocaro paravisayo.

"What and, monks, of a monk not-range, others-domain? Which-this five sensual-pleasure-objects. What five? Eye-cognizable forms, wished-for, desired, agreeable, pleasing-nature, sensuality-connected, enticing; ear-cognizable sounds . . . nose-cognizable odors . . . tongue-cognizable tastes . . . body-cognizable tactiles wished-for, desired, agreeable, pleasing-nature, sensuality-connected, enticing. This, monks, of a monk not-range, others-domain.

"And what, monks, is not the range of a monk but the domain of others? It is the five objects of sensual pleasure. What five? Forms cognizable by the eye that are wished for, desired, agreeable, of a pleasing nature, connected with sensuality, enticing; sounds cognizable by the ear . . . odors cognizable by the nose . . . tastes cognizable by the tongue . . . tactiles cognizable by the body that are wished for, desired, agreeable, of a pleasing nature, connected with sensuality, enticing. This, monks, is not the range of a monk but the domain of others.

"Gocare, bhikkhave, caratha sake pettike visaye. Gocare, bhikkhave, carataṃ sake pettike visaye na lacchati māro otāraṃ, na lacchati māro ārammaṇaṃ.

"In range, monks, wander, in own ancestral domain. In range, monks, of those wandering, in own ancestral domain, not will gain Māra an opening, not will gain Māra a basis.

"Wander in your range, monks, in your own ancestral domain. For those wandering in their range, monks, in their own ancestral domain, Māra will not gain an opening, Māra will not gain a basis.

"Ko ca, bhikkhave, bhikkhuno gocaro sako pettiko visayo? Yadidaṃ cattāro satipaṭṭhānā. Katame cattāro? Idha, bhikkhave, bhikkhu kāye kāyānupassī viharati ātāpī sampajāno satimā, vineyya loke abhijjhādomanassaṃ; vedanāsu . . . citte . . . dhammesu dhammānupassī viharati ātāpī sampajāno satimā, vineyya loke abhijjhādomanassaṃ. Ayaṃ, bhikkhave, bhikkhuno gocaro sako pettiko visayo"ti.

"What and, monks, of a monk range, own ancestral domain? Which-this four mindfulness-establishments. What four? Here, monks, a monk in the body body-contemplating dwells, ardent, clearly-comprehending, mindful, having removed in the world longing-dejection; in feelings . . . in the mind . . . in phenomena phenomena-contemplating dwells, ardent, clearly-comprehending, mindful, having removed in the world longing-dejection. This, monks, of a monk range, own ancestral domain."

"And what, monks, is the range of a monk, his own ancestral domain? It is the four establishments of mindfulness. What four? Here, monks, a monk dwells contemplating the body in the body, ardent, clearly comprehending, mindful, having removed longing and dejection in regard to the world; contemplating feelings in feelings . . . contemplating the mind in the mind . . . contemplating phenomena in phenomena, ardent, clearly comprehending, mindful, having removed longing and dejection in regard to the world. This, monks, is the range of a monk, his own ancestral domain."

Grammatical explanations

[1. The monkey trap]

cārī (or *cāri*): The word in this sense may be unique to this passage. The Saṃyutta commentary glosses it with *sañcāro*, "traveling."[199]

abālajātikā alolajātikā: "not foolish, not frivolous." The word *-jāta* at the end of a compound conveys the sense "having [such] a nature, of [such] a kind." The compounds here are bahubbīhis, with the suffix *-kā* enabling them to function as adjectives. And so just below for the opposites, *bālajātiko lolajātiko*.

mocessāmi: "I will release"; causative of *muñcati*, first-person singular in the future tense.

ubho: see p. 313.

pañcoḍḍito: "trapped in five [places]"; a numerical compound qualifying *makkaṭo*.

thunaṃ: "screeching"; a present participle, masculine singular, of *thunati*. The other form of the present participle is *thunanto*.

anayaṃ āpanno vyasanaṃ āpanno yathākāmakaraṇīyo luddassa: see p. 253.

yenakāmaṃ pakkamati: "departs where he desires." *Yenakāmaṃ* may be an adverbial compound (Duroiselle §549) or perhaps a syntactical compound (Perniola §142).

evaṃ so taṃ, bhikkhave, hoti: The structure is unusual and my rendering, "Thus that happens to him," is uncertain. It seems that *so* is correlated with the following *yo*, as demonstrative pronoun and relative pronoun, but the grammatical function of *taṃ* here is problematic. Possibly the text has been corrupted. The commentary offers no help here.

199. Spk III 201,7.

yo agocare carati paravisaye: "who wanders into what is not one's own range, into the domain of others." *Agocare* and *paravisaye* are locatives.

[2. The proper range for a monk]

mā . . . carittha: "do not wander." *Mā* is the prohibitive particle often used with the second-person aorist, here the plural *carittha*. With *mā* the aorist does not have a past tense but issues a prohibition (Duroiselle §612,iii; Perniola §273b).

caratam̩: "for those wandering"; the plural dative of the present participle.

lacchati māro otāram̩, lacchati māro ārammaṇam̩: "Māra will gain an opening, Māra will gain a basis." *Lacchati* is a third-person singular future of *labhati* (see Geiger §150, §152). The verb is placed before the subject (*māro*) for emphasis.

caratha: the second-person plural imperative of *carati*.

5. Gilānasutta

Ill (SN 47:9; V 152–54)

[1. The Buddha falls ill]

Evam̩ me sutam̩. Ekam̩ samayam̩ bhagavā vesāliyam̩ viharati beḷuvagāmake. Tatra kho bhagavā bhikkhū āmantesi: "Etha tumhe, bhikkhave, samantā vesāliyā yathāmittam̩ yathāsandiṭṭham̩ yathāsambhattam̩ vassam̩ upetha. Idh'evāham̩ beḷuvagāmake vassam̩ upagacchāmī"ti.

Thus by me heard. One occasion the Blessed One at Vesālī was dwelling, at Beḷuva-village. There the Blessed One the monks addressed: "Come you, monks, around Vesālī according-friend, according-acquaintance, according-intimates, the rains enter. Here itself-I in Beḷuva-village the rains enter."

Thus have I heard. On one occasion the Blessed One was dwelling at Vesālī in Beḷuva village. There the Blessed One addressed the monks: "Come, monks, enter the rains around Vesālī, wherever you have friends, acquaintances, and intimates. I myself will enter the rains right here in Beḷuva village."

"Evam̩, bhante"ti kho te bhikkhū bhagavato paṭissutvā samantā vesāliyā yathāmittam̩ yathāsandiṭṭham̩ yathāsambhattam̩ vassam̩ upagacchum̩. Bhagavā pana tatth'eva beḷuvagāmake vassam̩ upagañchi.

"Yes, Bhante," those monks to the Blessed One having replied, around Vesālī according-friend, according-acquaintance, according-intimates, the rains entered. The Blessed One but there itself in Beḷuva-village the rains entered.

Having replied to the Blessed One, "Yes, Bhante," those monks entered the rains around Vesālī, wherever they had friends, acquaintances, and intimates. But the Blessed One entered the rains right there in Beḷuva village.

Atha kho bhagavato vassūpagatassa kharo ābādho uppajji, bāḷhā vedanā vattanti māraṇantikā. Tatra sudaṃ bhagavā sato sampajāno adhivāsesi avihaññamāno.

Then to the Blessed One rains-entered a terrible affliction arose, severe pains occurring death-bordering. There the Blessed One, mindful, clearly-comprehending, endured, not-being-distressed.

Then, when the Blessed One had entered the rains, a terrible affliction arose in him, with severe pains occurring bordering on death. There the Blessed One endured them, mindful and clearly comprehending, without being distressed.

Atha kho bhagavato etadahosi: "Na kho me taṃ patirūpaṃ, yo'haṃ anāmantetvā upaṭṭhāke anapaloketvā bhikkhusaṅghaṃ parinibbāyeyyaṃ. Yaṃnūnāhaṃ imaṃ ābādhaṃ viriyena paṭipaṇāmetvā jīvitasaṅkhāraṃ adhiṭṭhāya vihareyyan"ti. Atha kho bhagavā taṃ ābādhaṃ viriyena paṭipaṇāmetvā jīvitasaṅkhāraṃ adhiṭṭhāya vihāsi.

Then to the Blessed One this-occurred: "Not for me that proper, which I not-having-addressed attendants, not-having-taken-leave-of monk-Sangha, would-attain-final-nibbāna. Let me, this affliction with energy having suppressed, life-condition having determined, should dwell." Then the Blessed One that affliction with energy having suppressed, life-condition having determined, dwelled.

Then this occurred to the Blessed One: "It is not proper for me that I should attain final nibbāna without having addressed my attendants and without having taken leave of the monastic Sangha. Surely I should suppress this affliction by means of energy, determine [to maintain] the life condition, and live on." Then the Blessed One, having suppressed that illness by means of energy, having determined [to maintain] the life condition, lived on.

[2. Ānanda's hope]

Atha kho bhagavā gilānā vuṭṭhito. Aciravuṭṭhito gelaññā vihārā nikkhamitvā vihārapacchāyāyaṃ[200] *paññatte āsane nisīdi. Atha kho āyasmā ānando yena bhagavā ten'upasaṅkami. Upasaṅkamitvā bhagavantaṃ abhivādetvā ekamantaṃ nisīdi. Ekamantaṃ nisinno kho āyasmā ānando bhagavantaṃ etadavoca:*

Then the Blessed One from illness recovered. Not-long-recovered from illness, from dwelling having come-out, in dwelling-shade in prepared seat sat down. Then the Venerable Ānanda where the Blessed One, there approached. Having approached, to the Blessed One having paid homage, one-side sat down. One-side seated, the Venerable Ānanda to the Blessed One this-said:

Then the Blessed One recovered from illness. Not long after he had recovered from illness, having come out from his dwelling, he sat down in the seat prepared for him in the shade of his dwelling. Then the Venerable Ānanda approached the Blessed One. Having approached, he paid homage to the Blessed One and sat down to one side. Seated to one side, the Venerable Ānanda said this to the Blessed One:

"Diṭṭhā[201] *me, bhante, bhagavato phāsu; diṭṭhā, bhante, bhagavato khamanīyaṃ; diṭṭhā, bhante, bhagavato yāpanīyaṃ. Api ca me, bhante, madhurakajāto viya kāyo, disāpi me na pakkhāyanti, dhammāpi maṃ nappaṭibhanti bhagavato gelaññena.*

"Fortunate for me, Bhante, of the Blessed One comfort; fortunate, Bhante, of the Blessed One bearing-up; fortunate, Bhante, of the Blessed One getting-

200. PED defines *pacchāyā* as "a place in the shade, shaded part." *Pacchāyāyaṃ* is the locative. Some editions read *vihārapacchāchāyāyaṃ*, "in the shade at the back of the dwelling."

201. DOP derives *diṭṭhā* from Skt *diṣṭyā*, which SED explains as the instrumental of *diṣṭi*, "auspicious juncture, good fortune, happiness." It appears to have been an idiomatic expression, and should not be confused with the past participle *diṭṭha*, though several editions of the text conflate them.

along. However, for me, Bhante, drugged-become like the body, directions-too to me not appear, teachings-too me not occur, the Blessed One's by illness.

"It's fortunate for me, Bhante, that the Blessed One is comfortable; it's fortunate that the Blessed One is bearing up; it's fortunate that the Blessed One is healthy. However, Bhante, my body had been as if drugged, even the directions did not appear clearly to me, even the teachings did not occur to me because of the Blessed One's illness.

"Api ca me, bhante, ahosi kācideva assāsamattā: 'Na tāva bhagavā parinibbāyissati, na yāva bhagavā bhikkhusaṅghaṃ ārabbha kiñcideva udāharatī'"ti.

"However to me, Bhante, occurred some consolation-measure: 'Not so long the Blessed One will attain-final-nibbāna, not as long as the Blessed One the monk-Sangha concerning something-just pronounces.'"

"However, Bhante, I had at least some consolation: 'The Blessed One will not attain final nibbāna so long as he has not pronounced something concerning the monastic Sangha.'"

[3. The Buddha's rejoinder]
"Kiṃ pana dāni, ānanda, bhikkhusaṅgho mayi paccāsiṃsati? Desito, ānanda, mayā dhammo anantaraṃ abāhiraṃ karitvā. Natth'ānanda, tathāgatassa dhammesu ācariyamuṭṭhi.

"What but now, Ānanda, the monk-sangha in me expects? Taught, Ānanda, by me the Dhamma, not-inside not-outside having made. There is not, Ānanda, of the Tathāgata in teachings a teacher-fist.

"What now, Ānanda, does the monastic Sangha expect of me? I have, Ānanda, taught the Dhamma without making [distinctions of] an inside and an outside. The Tathāgata, Ānanda, does not have a teacher's [closed] fist in regard to the teachings.

"Yassa nūna, ānanda, evamassa: 'Ahaṃ bhikkhusaṅghaṃ pariharissāmī'ti vā, 'mam'uddesiko bhikkhusaṅgho'ti vā, so nūna, ānanda, bhikkhusaṅghaṃ ārabbha kiñcideva udāhareyya. Tathāgatassa kho, ānanda, na evaṃ hoti: 'Ahaṃ bhikkhusaṅghaṃ pariharissāmī'ti vā, 'mam'uddesiko bhikkhusaṅgho'ti vā. Sa kiṃ, ānanda, tathāgato bhikkhusaṅghaṃ ārabbha kiñcideva udāharissati?

"To whom surely, Ānanda, such-may occur: 'I the monk-sangha will lead' or 'Of me dependent the monk-sangha' or, he surely, Ānanda, the monk-sangha concerning something-just might pronounce. To the Tathāgata, Ānanda, not thus occurs: 'I the monk-sangha will lead' or, 'Of me dependent the monk-sangha' or. He why, Ānanda, Tathāgata the monk-sangha concerning something-just will pronounce?

"Surely, Ānanda, one to whom such occurs: 'I will lead the monastic Sangha,' or 'The monastic Sangha is dependent on me'—he surely might pronounce something concerning the monastic Sangha. To the Tathāgata, Ānanda, such does not occur: 'I will lead the monastic Sangha,' or 'The monastic Sangha is dependent on me.' Why, Ānanda, should he, the Tathāgata, pronounce something concerning the monastic Sangha?

"Etarahi kho panāhaṃ, ānanda, jiṇṇo vuddho mahallako addhagato vayoanuppatto. Āsītiko me vayo vattati. Seyyathāpi, ānanda, jajjarasakaṭaṃ veṭhamissakena[202] *yāpeti, evameva kho, ānanda, veṭhamissakena maññe tathāgatassa kāyo yāpeti.*

"Now but-I, Ānanda, old, aged, elderly, journey-gone, life-(end)-arrived. Eighty my life occurs. Just as, Ānanda, a dilapidated-cart by straps-assortment keeps-going, just so, Ānanda, by straps-assortment, as it were, the Tathāgata's body keeps-going.

202. There are various readings of this expression, unique to this passage. Be has *veḷamissakena* and cites as variants *vegamissakena* (Ce), *vedhamissakena* (Ee). The commentary explains: "*With an assortment of straps*: With an assortment of straps, by repairing it with arm bands, wheel bands, and so forth" (*veṭhamissakenā ti bāhabandhacakkabandhādinā paṭisaṅkharaṇena veṭhamissakena*). This is according to the reading of the VRI at Spk III 238 (= Ee III 204,10–12, which differs only in having *vekha* for *veṭha*).

"Now, Ānanda, I am old, aged, elderly, reached the end of my journey, arrived at [the end of] life. I am eighty years of age. Just as, Ānanda, a dilapidated cart keeps going by means of an assortment of straps, just so the Tathāgata's body keeps going, as it were, by an assortment of straps.

"Yasmiṃ, ānanda, samaye tathāgato sabbanimittānaṃ amanasikārā ekaccānaṃ vedanānaṃ nirodhā animittaṃ cetosamādhiṃ upasampajja viharati, phāsutaro, ānanda, tasmiṃ samaye tathāgatassa kāyo hoti.

"On which, Ānanda, occasion the Tathāgata of all-marks through non-attention, of some feelings through cessation, markless mind-concentration having entered dwells, more comfortable, Ānanda, on that occasion the Tathāgata's body is.

"On whatever occasion, Ānanda, the Tathāgata, through non-attention to all marks, through the cessation of some feelings, enters and dwells in the markless concentration of mind, on that occasion the Tathāgata's body is more comfortable.

[4. The Buddha's instruction]
"Tasmātih'ānanda, attadīpā viharatha attasaraṇā anaññasaraṇā, dhammadīpā dhammasaraṇā anaññasaraṇā. Kathañcānanda, bhikkhu attadīpo viharati attasaraṇo anaññasaraṇo, dhammadīpo dhammasaraṇo anaññasaraṇo?

"Therefore, Ānanda, self-island dwell, self-refuge, not-another-refuge, Dhamma-island, Dhamma-refuge, not-another-refuge. How-and-Ānanda, a monk self-island dwells, self-refuge, not-another-refuge, Dhamma-island, Dhamma-refuge, not-another-refuge?

"Therefore, Ānanda, dwell with yourselves as an island, with yourselves as a refuge, with no other refuge, with the Dhamma as an island, with the Dhamma as a refuge, with no other refuge. And how, Ānanda, does a monk dwell with himself as an island, with himself as a refuge, with no other refuge, with the Dhamma as an island, with the Dhamma as a refuge, with no other refuge?

"Idh'ānanda, bhikkhu kāye kāyānupassī viharati ātāpī sampajāno satimā, vineyya loke abhijjhādomanassaṃ; vedanāsu vedanānupassī . . . citte cittānupassī . . . dhammesu dhammānupassī viharati ātāpī sampajāno satimā, vineyya loke abhijjhādomanassaṃ. Evaṃ kho, ānanda, bhikkhu attadīpo viharati attasaraṇo anaññasaraṇo, dhammadīpo dhammasaraṇo anaññasaraṇo.

"Here, Ānanda, a monk in the body body-contemplating dwells, ardent, clearly-comprehending, mindful, having removed in the world longing-dejection; in feelings feeling-contemplating . . . in the mind mind-contemplating . . . in phenomena phenomena-contemplating dwells, ardent, clearly-comprehending, mindful, having removed in the world longing-dejection. Thus, Ānanda, a monk self-island dwells, self-refuge, not-another-refuge, Dhamma-island, Dhamma-refuge, not-another-refuge.

"Here, Ānanda, a monk dwells contemplating the body in the body, ardent, clearly comprehending, mindful, having removed longing and dejection in regard to the world; he dwells contemplating feelings in feelings . . . contemplating the mind in the mind . . . contemplating phenomena in phenomena, ardent, clearly comprehending, mindful, having removed longing and dejection in regard to the world. It is in such a way, Ānanda, that a monk dwells with himself as an island, with himself as a refuge, with no other refuge, with the Dhamma as an island, with the Dhamma as a refuge, with no other refuge.

"Ye hi keci, ānanda, etarahi vā mam'accaye vā attadīpā viharissanti attasaraṇā anaññasaraṇā, dhammadīpā dhammasaraṇā anaññasaraṇā; tamatagge m'ete, ānanda, bhikkhū bhavissanti ye keci sikkhākāmā"ti.

"Those who, Ānanda, now or of me passing or, self-island will dwell, self-refuge, not-another-refuge, Dhamma-island, Dhamma-refuge, not-another-refuge, topmost for me these, Ānanda, monks will be whoever training-desire."

"Those who, either now or after my passing, will dwell with themselves as an island, with themselves as a refuge, with no other refuge, with the Dhamma as an island, with the Dhamma as a refuge, with no other refuge—for me, Ānanda, these monks will be topmost of those who desire the training."

GRAMMATICAL EXPLANATIONS

[1. The Buddha falls ill]

beḷuvagāmake: a village on the outskirts of the large city of Vesālī.

etha tumhe: see p. 391.

samantā vesāliyā: "around Vesālī." *Samantā* is an indeclinable. Here *vesāliyā* seems to be a locative, though the parallel at DN II 99,31 has the accusative *vesāliṃ*.

yathāmittaṃ yathāsandiṭṭhaṃ yathāsambhattaṃ: an unusual construction occurring, it seems, only in this passage. The commentary explains *mittā* as "simply friends," *sandiṭṭhā* as "acquaintances but not close friends," and *sambhattā* as "close friends."[203] *Yathāmittaṃ*, etc., may be considered adverbial compounds. I translate in accordance with the commentary's paraphrase: "Wherever there are such monks (those who are one's friends, etc.), enter the rains there."[204]

vassaṃ upetha: "enter the rains." *Vassa* is the three-month rains retreat during which monastics must remain in a fixed residence and avoid traveling except under extenuating circumstances.

upagacchāmi: the third-person singular present tense, here used with a future sense (see p. 270).

upagacchuṃ, upagañchi: These are aorists, the former third-person plural, the latter first-person singular.

vassūpagatassa: a tappurisa qualifying *bhagavato*. The case is dative, depicting the Blessed One as the passive subject of the illness.

bāḷhā vedanā vattanti māraṇantikā: "severe pains occurring bordering on death." The verb *vattanti* is present tense, probably the historical present used to show an action continuing to occur in the past. *Māraṇantikā* is a bahubbīhi qualifying *vedanā*, derived from *maraṇa*, "death" (with strengthening of the initial vowel), and *anta*, "end," with the adjectival suffix *-ikā*.

sudaṃ: a particle used in narration as a mere connective, not translatable.

203. Spk III 201,29–31: *Sandiṭṭhā ti tattha tattha saṅgamma diṭṭhamattā nātidaḷhamittā. Sambhattā ti suṭṭhu bhattā sinehavanto daḷhamittā.*

204. Spk III 201,31–33: *Yesaṃ yattha yattha evarūpā bhikkhū atthi, te tattha tattha vassaṃ upethā ti attho.*

adhivāsesi: "endured"; an s-aorist of *adhivāseti*. Depending on context, the verb can also mean "consents," as at p. 417.

avihaññamāno: "without being distressed"; a negative passive present participle agreeing with *bhagavā* (in forming the passive base, *han* + *ya* > *hañña*).

anāmantetvā upaṭṭhāke anapaloketvā bhikkhusaṅghaṃ: "without having addressed [my] attendants, without having taken leave of the monastic Sangha." Both absolutives here precede their respective accusative objects, an inversion of normal syntax.

parinibbāyeyyaṃ: "should attain final nibbāna." The verb is a first-person singular optative used in the sense of passing away.

yaṃnūnāhaṃ (= *yaṃ* + *nūna* + *ahaṃ*): a construction that typically introduces reflection on a future course of action.

paṭipaṇāmetvā: "having suppressed"; the absolutive of *paṭipaṇāmeti*.

jīvitasaṅkhāraṃ adhiṭṭhāya: literally, "having determined the life-activity," apparently meaning: "having determined to live on." Later in this narrative (at DN II 106,22), when the Buddha decides to let his life take its course, the narrator says: *āyusaṅkhāraṃ ossaji*, "he relinquished the vital activity."

[2. Ānanda's request]

aciravuṭṭhito: "not long after he had recovered"; a kammadhāraya compound qualifying *bhagavā* and with *gelaññā* in the ablative.

bhagavato khamanīyaṃ, bhagavato yāpanīyaṃ: "the Blessed One is bearing up, the Blessed One is healthy." *Khamanīyaṃ* and *yāpanīyaṃ* are originally future passive participles, respectively from *khamati*, "bears patiently," and *yāpeti*, "keeps going." They function as nouns in the nominative case, as states possessed by the Blessed One (*bhagavato* as a genitive or dative). The expression is an idiomatic way of saying that someone is enduring an illness and regaining health.

madhurakajāto viya kāyo: "my body had been as if drugged." *Madhura* is a sweet drink, probably with intoxicating properties; the suffix *-jāto* has the sense of "become, was." The commentary explains *madhurakajāto* to mean: "the body becomes heavy and stiff, like that of a person impaled on a stake."[205]

205. Spk III 203,12–13: *Sañjātagarubhāvo sañjātathaddhabhāvo sūle uttāsitapuriso viya.*

dhammāpi maṃ nappaṭibhanti: "even the teachings (or things) did not occur to me." *Nappaṭibhanti* = *na* + *paṭibhanti*, a plural. *Paṭibhanti* and *pakkhāyanti*, in the preceding phrase, are present-tense forms, though apparently referring to the recent past. On the use of *paṭibhanti* with the accusative, see the comment on *paṭibhātu* on p. 166.

kācideva assāsamattā: Since the suffix *-mattā* is a feminine nominative, the pronoun qualifying it, *kāci* (with emphatic *eva* and *-d-* as a liaison consonant), is feminine.

na tāva bhagavā parinibbāyissati, na yāva . . . kiñcideva udāharati: "The Blessed One will not attain final nibbāna so long as he has not pronounced something." *Yāva* and *tāva* are correlated as relative and demonstrative. For emphasis, the sentence inverts normal syntax, putting the main clause before the relative. *Kiñcideva* is the neuter form corresponding to *kācideva*, but here it is an independent pronoun in the accusative as object of *udāharati*.

ārabbha: originally an absolutive of *ārabhati*, "begins, undertakes," but with an acquired meaning: "concerning, referring to."

[3. The Buddha's rejoinder]

anantaraṃ abāhiraṃ karitvā: "without making [distinctions of] an inside and an outside." Both *anantaraṃ* and *abāhiraṃ* are accusatives apparently used adverbially.

nūna: see p. 133.

mam'uddesiko bhikkhusaṅgho: "The monastic Sangha is dependent on me." DOP defines *uddesika* as "(what) looks to, is concerned with, a specific person." Here *mam'uddesiko* qualifies *bhikkhusaṅgho*.

sa kiṃ, ānanda, tathāgato: "Why, Ānanda, should he, the Tathāgata. . . ." The commentary glosses *sa kiṃ* with *so kiṃ*. Apparently, this unusual locution serves for emphasis.

kiñcideva udāharissati: The verb is in the future tense, but with an optative sense: "Why should he pronounce something?"

jiṇṇo vuddho mahallako addhagato vayoanuppatto: "old, aged, elderly, reached the end of my journey, arrived at [the end of] life." Pāli has a rich string of synonyms describing old age, for which it is hard to find a sufficient number of English counterparts. Here all these terms qualify *ahaṃ*.

āsītiko me vayo vattati: "I am eighty years of age," literally, "my life occurs at eighty." *Āsītiko* is an adjective derived from *asīti*, "eighty." It modifies *vayo*, which though originally neuter (Vedic *vayas*) is here treated as masculine.

maññe: Originally a first-person singular optative of *maññati*, *maññe* takes on an independent meaning. PED explains: "*maññe* is used like an adverb, as affirmative particle, and is inserted without influencing the grammatical or syntactical construction of the sentence; meaning: methinks, for certain, surely, indeed, I guess, presumably."

amanasikārā, nirodhā: ablatives used in conjunction with genitives to show the conditions for entering the "markless mental concentration."

animittaṃ cetosamādhiṃ: "markless mental concentration." The commentary identifies this with fruition attainment (*phalasamāpatti*).

attadīpā viharatha attasaraṇā anaññasaraṇā: "dwell with yourselves as an island, with yourselves as a refuge, with no other refuge." The compounds are bahubbīhis qualifying an implicit *tumhe*, indicated by the second-person plural imperative verb, *viharatha*. Some translators have rendered *attadīpā viharatha* as "be a light (or lamp) unto yourselves." *Dīpa* is a homonym, representing both Skt *dvīpa*, "island," and Skt *dīpa*, "lamp." While either can work, other contexts suggest that "island" is intended here.[206]

tamatagge: The meaning of this expression is obscure. Even DOP hesitantly offers alternative explanations—"in the highest degree" and "at the end of ignorance"—both with question marks. I follow the commentary, which glosses: "these monks of mine will be at the top, in the highest position."[207]

ye keci sikkhākāmā: The commentary glosses this as if the words are genitive plural in sense: "As for those who desire the training, those monks

206. The commentary explains: "Dwell having made yourself an island, a support, as an island is for those who have entered the ocean." See too Dhp 25: *uṭṭhānen'appamādena saṃyamena damena ca, dīpaṃ kayirātha medhāvī, yaṃ ogho nābhikīrati*. Here the *dīpa* that a wise man creates, which a flood does not overwhelm, is surely an island, not a lamp. The Skt version edited by Waldschmidt has *dvīpa*, island: "*tasmād ānandaitarhi mama vātyayād ātmadvīpair vihartavyam ātmaśaraṇair dharmadvīpair dharmaśaraṇair ananyadvīpair ananyaśaraṇaiḥ*" (https://suttacentral.net/sf245/san/waldschmidt#1.1--33.3).

207. Spk III 205,2–3: *Agge uttamabhāve ete, ānanda, mama bhikkhū bhavissanti.*

whose range is the four establishments of mindfulness will be at the top of all of them."[208]

6. Sedakasutta

Sedaka (SN 47:19; V 168–69)

[1. The parable]

Ekaṃ samayaṃ bhagavā sumbhesu viharati sedakaṃ nāma sumbhānaṃ nigamo. Tatra kho bhagavā bhikkhū āmantesi: "Bhūtapubbaṃ, bhikkhave, caṇḍālavaṃsiko caṇḍālavaṃsaṃ ussāpetvā medakathālikaṃ antevāsiṃ āmantesi: 'Ehi tvaṃ, samma medakathālike, caṇḍālavaṃsaṃ abhiruhitvā mama uparikhandhe tiṭṭhāhī'ti. 'Evaṃ, ācariyā'ti kho, bhikkhave, medakathālikā antevāsī[209] *caṇḍālavaṃsikassa paṭissutvā caṇḍālavaṃsaṃ abhiruhitvā ācariyassa uparikhandhe aṭṭhāsi.*

One occasion the Blessed One among the Sumbhas was dwelling, Sedaka named of the Sumbhas town. There the Blessed One the monks addressed: "Become-past, monks, an acrobat a bamboo-pole having set up, Medakathālikā the apprentice addressed: 'Come you, dear Medakathālikā, bamboo-pole having climbed, my above-shoulders stand.' — 'Yes, teacher,' monks, Medakathālikā the apprentice to the acrobat having replied, the bamboo-pole having climbed, teacher's above-shoulders stood.

On one occasion the Blessed One was dwelling among the Sumbhas [where there was] a town of the Sumbhas named Sedaka. There the Blessed One addressed the monks: "In the past, monks, an acrobat, having set up his bamboo pole, addressed his apprentice Medakathālikā: 'Come, dear Medakathālikā, having climbed up the bamboo pole, stand upon my shoulders.' Having replied to the acrobat, 'Yes, teacher,' the apprentice Medakathālikā climbed up the bamboo pole and stood upon the teacher's shoulders.

208. Spk III 205,3–5: *Ye keci sikkhākāmā, sabbesaṃ tesaṃ catusatipaṭṭhānagocarā'va bhikkhū agge bhavissanti.*

209. Although Medakathālikā is a feminine name, *antevāsī* (apprentice) is a masculine form. Thus the gender of the apprentice is unclear. Spk III 226,8 says: "Thus the name is obtained by way of the feminine gender" (*evaṃ itthiliṅgavasena laddhanāmaṃ*), but the commentary uses masculine pronouns when referring to the apprentice.

"Atha kho, bhikkhave, caṇḍālavaṃsiko medakathālikaṃ antevāsiṃ etadavoca: 'Tvaṃ, samma medakathālike, mamaṃ rakkha, ahaṃ taṃ rakkhissāmi. Evaṃ mayaṃ aññamaññaṃ guttā aññamaññaṃ rakkhitā sippāni c'eva dassessāma, lābhañca lacchāma, sotthinā ca caṇḍālavaṃsā orohissāmā'ti.

"Then, monks, the acrobat to Medakathālikā the apprentice this-said: 'You, dear Medakathālikā, me protect, I you will protect. Thus we other-other guarded, other-other protected, skills and will display, profit-and will gain, safely and from the bamboo-pole will descend.'

"Then, monks, the acrobat said this to the apprentice Medakathālikā: 'Dear Medakathālikā, you protect me, and I will protect you. Thus guarded by one another, protected by one another, we will display our skills, and will gain a profit, and will safely descend from the bamboo pole.'

"Evaṃ vutte, bhikkhave, medakathālikā antevāsī caṇḍālavaṃsikaṃ etadavoca: 'Na kho pan'etaṃ, ācariya, evaṃ bhavissati. Tvaṃ, ācariya, attānaṃ rakkha, ahaṃ attānaṃ rakkhissāmi. Evaṃ mayaṃ attaguttā attarakkhitā sippāni c'eva dassessāma, lābhañca lacchāma, sotthinā ca caṇḍālavaṃsā orohissāmā'ti.

"Such said, monks, Medakathālikā the apprentice to the acrobat this-said: 'Not but this, teacher, thus will be. You, teacher, self protect, I self will protect. Thus we self-guarded, self-protected, skills and will show, profit-and will gain, safely and from the bamboo-pole will descend.'

"When such was said, monks, the apprentice Medakathālikā said this to the acrobat: 'That, teacher, won't be the way [to do it]. You, teacher, protect yourself; I will protect myself. Thus self-guarded and self-protected, we will display our skills, and will gain a profit, and will safely descend from the bamboo pole.'

[2. The application]

"So tattha ñāyo"ti bhagavā etadavoca, "yathā medakathālikā antevāsī ācariyaṃ avoca. 'Attānaṃ rakkhissāmī'ti, bhikkhave, satipaṭṭhānaṃ sevitabbaṃ;

'paraṃ rakkhissāmī'ti satipaṭṭhānaṃ sevitabbaṃ. Attānaṃ, bhikkhave, rakkhanto paraṃ rakkhati; paraṃ rakkhanto attānaṃ rakkhati.

"That there the method," the Blessed One this-said, "as Medakathālikā the apprentice to the teacher said. 'Self I will protect,' monks, mindfulness-establishment should-be-practiced; 'other I will protect,' mindfulness-establishment should-be-practiced. Self, monks, protecting, other protects; other protecting, self protects.

"That is the method there," the Blessed One said, "as the apprentice Medakathālikā said to the teacher. 'I will protect myself,' monks, thus the establishment of mindfulness should be practiced; 'I will protect others,' thus the establishment of mindfulness should be practiced. Protecting oneself, monks, one protects others; protecting others, one protects oneself.

"Kathañca, bhikkhave, attānaṃ rakkhanto paraṃ rakkhati? Āsevanāya bhāvanāya bahulīkammena:[210] *evaṃ kho, bhikkhave, attānaṃ rakkhanto paraṃ rakkhati. Kathañca, bhikkhave, paraṃ rakkhanto attānaṃ rakkhati? Khantiyā avihiṃsāya mettacittatāya anudayatāya: evaṃ kho, bhikkhave, paraṃ rakkhanto attānaṃ rakkhati.*

"How-and, monks, self protecting, other protects? By regular-practice, by development, by cultivation: thus, monks, self protecting other protects. How-and, monks, other protecting, self protects? By patience, by harmlessness, by loving-kindness-mind, by sympathy: thus, monks, other protecting, self protects.

"And how, monks, by protecting oneself does one protect others? By regular practice, by development, by cultivation [of the four establishments of mindfulness]: thus, monks, by protecting oneself, one protects others. And how, monks, by protecting others does one protect oneself? By patience, by harmlessness, by a mind of loving-kindness, by sympathy: thus, monks, by protecting others, one protects oneself.

210. It seems that this sentence should have begun with *catunnaṃ satipaṭṭhānānaṃ*. Otherwise there is no explicit mention that the practice of the four establishments of mindfulness is intended.

"'Attānaṃ rakkhissāmī'ti, bhikkhave, satipaṭṭhānaṃ sevitabbaṃ. 'Paraṃ rakkhissāmī'ti satipaṭṭhānaṃ sevitabbaṃ. Attānaṃ, bhikkhave, rakkhanto paraṃ rakkhati; paraṃ rakkhanto attānaṃ rakkhatī"ti.

"'Self I will protect,' monks, mindfulness-establishment should-be-practiced. 'Other I will protect,' mindfulness-establishment should-be-practiced. Self, monks, protecting, other protects; other protecting, self protects."

"'I will protect myself,' monks, thus the establishment of mindfulness should be practiced. 'I will protect others,' thus the establishment of mindfulness should be practiced. Protecting oneself, monks, one protects others; protecting others, one protects oneself."

Grammatical explanations

[1. The parable]

sedakaṃ nāma sumbhānaṃ nigamo: On a parallel construction, see p. 373.

bhūtapubbaṃ: an adverb introducing a story of the past, composed of the past participle of *bhavati* and the indeclinable *pubbaṃ*.

uparikhandhe: "upon [my] shoulders"; a kammadhāraya composed of an adverb and a noun (Perniola §132), here in the locative case.

aññamaññaṃ guttā aññamaññaṃ rakkhitā: "guarded by one another, protected by one another." The indeclinable *aññamaññaṃ* (*añña* + *aññāṃ*, with *-m-* as a liaison consonant) indicates mutuality.

lābhañca lacchāma: "will gain a profit." *Lacchāma* is a future form of *labhati*, first-person plural. See p. 398. The verb takes its cognate noun as its object.

tvaṃ, ācariya, attānaṃ rakkha, ahaṃ attānaṃ rakkhissāmi: "You, teacher, protect yourself; I will protect myself." *Attānaṃ*, the accusative of *attan*, is being used here in a reflexive sense, not to posit a metaphysical self.

attaguttā attarakkhitā: "self-guarded, self-protected." These are tappurisas modifying *mayaṃ*.

[2. The application]

sevitabbaṃ: "should be practiced"; a future passive participle in agreement with *satipaṭṭhānaṃ*.

attānaṃ, bhikkhave, rakkhanto paraṃ rakkhati; paraṃ rakkhanto, attānaṃ rakkhati: "protecting oneself, monks, one protects others; protecting others, one protects oneself." In each clause, *rakkhanto* is the present participle, masculine singular, of *rakkhati*.

āsevanāya, bhāvanāya, bahulīkammena: "by regular practice, by development, by cultivation." These are instrumentals, the first two feminine, the last neuter.

khantiyā, avihiṃsāya, mettacittatāya, anudayatāya: "by patience, by harmlessness, by a mind of loving-kindness, by sympathy." These too are instrumentals, all feminine.

7. Janapadakalyāṇīsutta

The Country Belle (SN 47:20; V 169–70)

"Seyyathāpi, bhikkhave, 'janapadakalyāṇī, janapadakalyāṇī'ti kho, bhikkhave, mahājanakāyo sannipateyya. Sā kho pan'assa janapadakalyāṇī paramapāsāvinī nacce, paramapāsāvinī gīte. 'Janapadakalyāṇī naccati gāyatī'ti kho, bhikkhave, bhiyyosomattāya mahājanakāyo sannipateyya.

"Suppose, monks, 'the country-belle, the country-belle,' monks, a great-people-crowd would assemble. That but would be country-belle supreme-performer in dancing, supreme-performer in singing, 'The country-belle dances sings,' monks, to-a-greater-extent great-people-crowd would assemble.

"Suppose, monks, [having heard] 'the country belle, the country belle,' a great crowd of people would assemble. That country belle would be a supreme performer in dancing, a supreme performer in singing. [Having heard] 'the country belle is dancing [and] singing,' an even greater crowd of people would assemble.

"Atha puriso āgaccheyya jīvitukāmo amaritukāmo sukhakāmo dukkhappaṭikūlo. Tamenaṃ evaṃ vadeyyuṃ: 'Ayaṃ te, ambho purisa, samatittiko telapatto antarena mahāsamajjaṃ antarena janapadakalyāṇiyā pariharitabbo. Puriso ca te ukkhittāsiko piṭṭhito piṭṭhito anubandhissati. Yatth'eva naṃ thokampi chaḍḍessasi, tatth'eva te siro pātessatī'ti.

"Then a man would come to-live-desire not-to-die-desire, happiness-desire suffering-averse. To that-him thus they would say: 'This by you, good man, even-brim oil-bowl between the great-assembly between the country-belle to-be-carried-around. A man and of you uplifted-sword from back from back will follow. Wherever just that a little-even will spill, there just your head he will fell.'

"Then a man would come along who desires to live and does not desire to die, who desires happiness and is averse to suffering. They would say thus to him: 'This bowl of oil, filled to the brim, must be carried around by you between the great assembly and the country belle. A man with uplifted sword will follow right behind you. Wherever you spill even a little of this, just there he will fell your head.'

"Taṃ kiṃ maññatha, bhikkhave, api nu so puriso amuṃ telapattaṃ amanasikaritvā bahiddhā pamādaṃ āhareyyā"ti? — "No h'etaṃ, bhante."

"That what do you think, monks, that man that oil-bowl not having attended to, externally heedlessness would bring?" — "No indeed, Bhante."

"What do you think about this, monks? Would that man stop paying attention to that bowl of oil and direct [attention] outwardly due to heedlessness?" — "Certainly not, Bhante."

"Upamā kho myāyaṃ, bhikkhave, katā atthassa viññāpanāya. Ayaṃ c'ev'ettha attho: 'Samatittiko telapatto'ti kho, bhikkhave, kāyagatāya satiyā etaṃ adhivacanaṃ. Tasmātiha, bhikkhave, evaṃ sikkhitabbaṃ: 'Kāyagatā sati no bhāvitā bhavissati bahulīkatā yānīkatā vatthukatā anuṭṭhitā paricitā susamāraddhā'ti. Evaṃ hi kho, bhikkhave, sikkhitabban"ti.

"Simile by me-this, monks, made of meaning for communicating. This and just here the meaning: 'Even-brim oil-bowl,' monks, of body-gone mindfulness this a designation. Therefore, monks, thus should-be-trained: 'Body-gone mindfulness by us developed will be, cultivated, vehicle-made, basis-made, stabilized, repeated, well undertaken.' Thus indeed, monks, should-be-trained."

"This simile has been made by me, monks, for the purpose of communicating a meaning. And this is the meaning here: 'The bowl of oil filled to the brim'—this, monks, is a designation for mindfulness directed to the body. Therefore, monks, you should train thus: 'Mindfulness directed to the body will be developed and cultivated by us, made a vehicle, made a basis, stabilized, repeated, and well undertaken.' Thus indeed, monks, you should train."

Grammatical explanations

"janapadakalyāṇī, janapadakalyāṇī"ti: *Janapadakalyāṇī* seems to have been an epithet for a beauty queen. The repetition and use of *ti* to indicate a direct quotation implies that this expression was being proclaimed by those in the crowd.

paramapāsāvinī nacce, paramapāsāvinī gīte: "a supreme performer in dancing, a supreme performer in singing." The word *pāsāvinī* is unique to this passage. The compound *paramapāsāvinī*, qualifying *janapadakalyāṇī*, is feminine singular. The meaning is obscure and my rendering is conjectural, governed by the context.

jīvitukāmo amaritukāmo: "who desires to live, does not desire to die." These compounds are composed by adding *kāmo* to the infinitive ending in *-tuṃ*, with the infinitive losing its niggahīta.[211]

te: the enclitic pronoun, here instrumental singular "by you."

ambho: see p. 278.

samatittiko: "filled to the brim"; a bahubbīhi composed of *sama*, "even with, equal to," and *titti*, "brim," with the suffix *-iko* turning it into an adjective qualifying *telapatto*.

antarena: "between"; an instrumental used adverbially. It is placed before both points between which the bowl is to be carried, the first in the accusative and the second in an indirect case, probably the genitive.

ukkhittāsiko: "with uplifted sword"; a bahubbīhi composed of *ukkhitta*, "raised up, lifted," and *asi*, "sword," with the adjectival suffix *-iko*. The *te* preceding this compound suggests that the sword is raised "against you."

piṭṭhito piṭṭhito anubandhissati: "will follow right behind." *Piṭṭhi* is the back; the duplicated ablative means "right at your back."

211. According to Duroiselle §545 (iii)(b), "compounds formed by adding *kāmo*, 'desirous of,' to an infinitive are considered to be tappurisas in the dative relation."

te siro pātessati: "will fell your head," that is, will decapitate you. *Siro* is an accusative of the neuter noun *siras*; *pātessati* is future of *pāteti*, a causative of *patati*, "falls."

bahiddhā pamādaṃ āhareyya: The construction here is odd and I've had to take liberties in translation.

atthassa viññāpanāya: "for the purpose of communicating a meaning." *Viññāpanāya* is dative of *viññāpana*, "causing to know."

yānīkatā vatthukatā: see p. 290.

8. Sirivaḍḍhasutta

Sirivaḍḍha (SN 47:29; V 176–77)

[1. Sirivaḍḍha's request]

Ekaṃ samayaṃ āyasmā ānando rājagahe viharati, veḷuvane kalandakanivāpe. Tena kho pana samayena sirivaḍḍho gahapati ābādhiko hoti dukkhito bāḷhagilāno.

One occasion the Venerable Ānanda at Rājagaha was dwelling, in the bamboo-grove in the squirrel-feeding-ground. By that occasion Sirivaḍḍha the householder afflicted was, sick, severely-ill.

On one occasion the Venerable Ānanda was dwelling at Rājagaha in the bamboo grove, in the squirrels' feeding ground. Now on that occasion the householder Sirivaḍḍha was afflicted, sick, severely ill.

Atha kho sirivaḍḍho gahapati aññataraṃ purisaṃ āmantesi: "Ehi tvaṃ, ambho purisa, yen'āyasmā ānando ten'upasaṅkama. Upasaṅkamitvā mama vacanena āyasmato ānandassa pāde sirasā vanda: 'Sirivaḍḍho, bhante, gahapati ābādhiko dukkhito bāḷhagilāno. So āyasmato ānandassa pāde sirasā vandatī'ti. Evañca vadehi: 'Sādhu kira, bhante, āyasmā ānando yena sirivaḍḍhassa gahapatissa nivesanaṃ ten'upasaṅkamatu anukampaṃ upādāyā'"ti.

Then Sirivaḍḍha the householder a certain man addressed: "Come you, good man, where the Venerable Ānanda, there approach. Having approached, my by word the Venerable Ānanda's at feet with head venerate: 'Sirivaḍḍha, Bhante, the householder afflicted, sick, severely-ill. He the Venerable Ānanda's at feet with head venerates.' Thus-and say: 'Good indeed, Bhante, the Venerable Ānanda where Sirivaḍḍha the householder's residence, there let him approach compassion out of.'"

Then the householder Sirivaḍḍha addressed a man: "Come, man, approach the Venerable Ānanda. Having approached, on my behalf venerate the Venerable Ānanda's feet with your head [and say]: 'The householder Sirivaḍḍha, Bhante, is afflicted, sick, severely ill. He venerates the Venerable Ānanda's feet with his head.' And then say thus: 'Please, Bhante, let the Venerable Ānanda come to the householder Sirivaḍḍha's residence out of compassion.'"

"Evaṃ, bhante"ti kho so puriso sirivaḍḍhassa gahapatissa paṭissutvā yen'āyasmā ānando ten'upasaṅkami. Upasaṅkamitvā āyasmantaṃ ānandaṃ abhivādetvā ekamantaṃ nisīdi. Ekamantaṃ nisinno kho so puriso āyasmantaṃ ānandaṃ etadavoca: "Sirivaḍḍho, bhante, gahapati ābādhiko dukkhito bāḷhagilāno. So āyasmato ānandassa pāde sirasā vandati. Evañca vadeti: 'Sādhu kira, bhante, āyasmā ānando yena sirivaḍḍhassa gahapatissa nivesanaṃ ten'upasaṅkamatu anukampaṃ upādāyā'"ti. Adhivāsesi kho āyasmā ānando tuṇhībhāvena.

"Yes, Bhante," that man to Sirivaḍḍha the householder having replied, where the Venerable Ānanda, there approached. Having approached, the Venerable Ānanda having paid homage to, one-side sat. One-side seated, that man to the Venerable Ānanda this-said: "Sirivaḍḍha, Bhante, the householder afflicted, sick, severely-ill. He the Venerable Ānanda's at feet with head venerates. Thus-and says: 'Good indeed, Bhante, the Venerable Ānanda where Sirivaḍḍha the householder's residence, there let him approach compassion-out of.'" Consented the Venerable Ānanda by silence.

"Yes, Bhante," that man replied to the householder Sirivaḍḍha. Then he approached the Venerable Ānanda. Having approached, having paid homage to the Venerable Ānanda, he sat down to one side. Seated to one side, that man said this to the Venerable Ānanda: "Bhante, the householder Sirivaḍḍha is afflicted, sick, severely ill. He venerates the Venerable Ānanda's feet with his head. And he says this: 'Please, Bhante, let the Venerable Ānanda come to the householder Sirivaḍḍha's residence out of compassion.'" The Venerable Ānanda consented by silence.

[2. The conversation]

Atha kho āyasmā ānando pubbaṇhasamayaṃ nivāsetvā pattacīvaramādāya yena sirivaḍḍhassa gahapatissa nivesanaṃ ten'upasaṅkami. Upasaṅkamitvā paññatte āsane nisīdi. Nisajja kho āyasmā ānando sirivaḍḍhaṃ gahapatiṃ etadavoca: "Kacci te, gahapati, khamanīyaṃ, kacci yāpanīyaṃ, kacci dukkhā vedanā paṭikkamanti, no abhikkamanti; paṭikkamosānaṃ paññāyati, no abhikkamo"ti?

Then the Venerable Ānanda morning-time having dressed, bowl-robe-having taken, where Sirivaḍḍha the householder's residence, there approached. Having approached, in prepared seat sat down. Having sat down, the Venerable Ānanda to Sirivaḍḍha the householder this-said: "Is it the case by you, householder, bearing-up? Is it the case getting-along? Is it the case painful feelings retreating, not advancing, retreat is discerned, not advance?"

Then in the morning the Venerable Ānanda dressed, took his bowl and [outer] robe, and went to the householder Sirivaḍḍha's residence. Having gone there, he sat down in the prepared seat. Having sat down, the Venerable Ānanda said this to the householder Sirivaḍḍha: "Are you bearing up, householder? Are you getting healthy? Are your painful feelings retreating, not advancing, [so that] their retreat, not their advance, is discerned?"

"Na me, bhante, khamanīyaṃ, na yāpanīyaṃ. Bāḷhā me dukkhā vedanā abhikkamanti, no paṭikkamanti; abhikkamosānaṃ paññāyati, no paṭikkamo"ti.

"Not by me, Bhante, bearing-up, not getting-along. Severe of me painful feelings are advancing, not retreating, advance is discerned, not retreat."

"I am not bearing up, Bhante, not getting healthy. My severe painful feelings are advancing, not retreating, [so that] their advance, not their retreat, is discerned."

"Tasmātiha te, gahapati, evaṃ sikkhitabbaṃ: 'Kāye kāyānupassī viharissāmi ātāpī sampajāno satimā, vineyya loke abhijjhādomanassaṃ; vedanāsu vedanānupassī . . . citte cittānupassī . . . dhammesu dhammānupassī viharissāmi ātāpī sampajāno satimā, vineyya loke abhijjhādomanassan'ti. Evaṃ hi te, gahapati, sikkhitabban"ti.

"Therefore by you, householder, thus should-be-trained: 'In the body body-contemplating I will dwell, ardent, clearly-comprehending, mindful, having removed in the world longing-dejection; in feelings feeling-contemplating . . . in the mind mind-contemplating . . . in phenomena phenomena-contemplating I will dwell, ardent, clearly-comprehending, mindful, having removed in the world longing-dejection.' Thus by you, householder, should-be-trained."

"Therefore, householder, you should train thus: 'I will dwell contemplating the body in the body, ardent, clearly comprehending, mindful, having removed longing and dejection in regard to the world; I will dwell contemplating feelings in feelings . . . contemplating the mind in the mind . . . contemplating phenomena in phenomena, ardent, clearly comprehending, mindful, having removed longing and dejection in regard to the world.' It is in such a way, householder, that you should train."

"Ye ime, bhante, bhagavatā cattāro satipaṭṭhānā desitā, saṃvijjanti te dhammā mayi, ahañca tesu dhammesu sandissāmi. Ahaṃ hi, bhante, kāye kāyānupassī viharāmi ātāpī sampajāno satimā, vineyya loke abhijjhādomanassaṃ; vedanāsu vedanānupassī . . . citte cittānupassī . . . dhammesu dhammānupassī viharāmi ātāpī sampajāno satimā, vineyya loke abhijjhādomanassaṃ.

"Which these, Bhante, by the Blessed One the four mindfulness-establishments taught, are found those things in me, I-and in those things am seen. I because, Bhante, in the body body-contemplating dwell, ardent, clearly-comprehending, mindful, having removed in the world longing-dejection; in feelings feeling-contemplating . . . in the mind mind-contemplating . . . in phenomena phenomena-contemplating dwell, ardent, clearly-comprehending, mindful, having removed in the world longing-dejection.

"Bhante, as to these four establishments of mindfulness that have been taught by the Blessed One, those things are found in me and I am seen [engaging] in those things. For, Bhante, I dwell contemplating the body in the body, ardent, clearly comprehending, mindful, having removed longing and dejection in regard to the world; I dwell contemplating feelings in feelings . . . contemplating the mind in the mind . . . contemplating phenomena in phenomena, ardent, clearly comprehending, mindful, having removed longing and dejection in regard to the world.

"Yāni c'imāni, bhante, bhagavatā pañc'orambhāgiyāni saṃyojanāni desitāni, nāhaṃ, bhante, tesaṃ kiñci attani appahīnaṃ samanupassāmī"ti.

"Which and these, Bhante, by the Blessed One five lower-portion fetters taught, not-I, Bhante, of those any in self not abandoned perceive."

"And, Bhante, as to those five lower fetters taught by the Blessed One, I do not perceive in myself any of them that has not been abandoned."

"Lābhā te, gahapati, suladdhaṃ te, gahapati! Anāgāmiphalaṃ tayā, gahapati, vyākatan"ti.

"Gains for you, householder, well gained by you, householder! Non-returner-fruit by you, householder, have declared."

"[Those are] gains for you, householder, [it is] well gained by you, householder! The fruit of a non-returner, householder, has been declared by you."

Grammatical explanations

[1. Sirivaḍḍha's request]

sirasā: "with the head"; the instrumental of the neuter noun *siras.*

tena kho pana samayena: see p. 196.

anukampaṃ upādāya: "out of compassion." *Upādāya*, an absolutive of *upādiyati*, "clings to," is used with an idiomatic sense: "on account of, for the sake of."

adhivāsesi: "consented"; an s-aorist. The verb *adhivāseti* also means "patiently endures" (as at p. 406 above).

[2. The conversation]

nisajja: "having sat down"; the absolutive of *nisīdati*, with palatalization of *nisad + ya > nisajja* (see Geiger §55, Collins p. 9).

kacci te, gahapati, khamanīyaṃ, kacci yāpanīyaṃ: "Are you bearing up, householder? Are you getting healthy?"; the stock way of inquiring about the condition of one who has been ill. See p. 406 above.

paṭikkamosānaṃ paññāyati, no abhikkamo: "their retreat, not their advance, is discerned." I cannot account for *osānaṃ* here and in *abhikkamosānaṃ* just below and thus render the two expressions simply as "retreat" and "advance," respectively.[212]

pañc'orambhāgiyāni saṃyojanāni: the "five lower fetters": the view of a self, doubt, wrong grasp of rules and observances, sensual lust, and ill will (see MN I 432–34). Their abandonment marks attainment of the stage of a non-returner.

lābhā te, gahapati, suladdhaṃ te, gahapati!: "[Those are] gains for you, householder, [it is] well gained by you, householder!" This is a stock expression of congratulations. While *lābhā* is nominative plural and *suladdhaṃ* a past participle with prefix *su-*, the expression is used even when the gain is singlefold.[213]

anāgāmiphalaṃ tayā, gahapati, vyākataṃ: "You have declared, householder, the fruit of a non-returner." See p. 76.

2. The Seven Factors of Enlightenment

1. Himavantasutta

The Himalaya (SN 46:1; V 63–64)

"Seyyathāpi, bhikkhave, himavantaṃ pabbatarājānaṃ nissāya nāgā kāyaṃ vaḍḍhenti, balaṃ gāhenti. Te tattha kāyaṃ vaḍḍhetvā balaṃ gāhetvā kusobbhe otaranti. Kusobbhe otaritvā mahāsobbhe otaranti. Mahāsobbhe otaritvā kunnadiyo otaranti. Kunnadiyo otaritvā mahānadiyo otaranti. Mahānadiyo otaritvā mahāsamuddasāgaraṃ otaranti. Te tattha mahantattaṃ vepullattaṃ āpajjanti kāyena.

"Just as, monks, the Himalaya the mountain-king based on, nāgas the body increase, strength make it acquire. They there the body having increased, strength having made it acquire, the little-pools enter. The little-pools having entered, the large-pools enter. The large-pools having entered, the little-rivers

212. Levman suggests (in a personal communication) that *osāna* may mean "limit," the limit of their retreat being a cure and the limit of their advance being death. But the meaning is far from settled.

213. For commentarial elaborations, see Spk I 182,9–15 and Mp II 344,14–23.

enter. The little-rivers having entered, the large-rivers enter. The large-rivers having entered, the great-ocean-sea enter. They there greatness vastness achieve with the body.

"Monks, based on the Himalaya, the king of mountains, nāgas grow their bodies and acquire strength. Having grown their bodies and acquired strength there, they enter the little pools. Having entered the little pools, they enter the large pools. Having entered the large pools, they enter the little rivers. Having entered the little rivers, they enter the large rivers. Having entered the large rivers, they enter the great ocean. There they achieve greatness and vastness with respect to the body.

"Evameva kho, bhikkhave, bhikkhu sīlaṃ nissāya sīle patiṭṭhāya satta bojjhaṅge bhāvento satta bojjhaṅge bahulīkaronto mahantattaṃ vepullattaṃ pāpuṇāti dhammesu.

"Just so, monks, a monk good-behavior based on, in good-behavior having been established, seven enlightenment-factors developing, seven enlightenment-factors cultivating, greatness vastness acquire in qualities.

"Just so, monks, based on good behavior, established in good behavior, developing the seven factors of enlightenment, cultivating the seven factors of enlightenment, a monk acquires greatness and vastness in [wholesome] qualities.

"Kathañca, bhikkhave, bhikkhu sīlaṃ nissāya sīle patiṭṭhāya satta bojjhaṅge bhāvento satta bojjhaṅge bahulīkaronto mahantattaṃ vepullattaṃ pāpuṇāti dhammesu? Idha, bhikkhave, bhikkhu satisambojjhaṅgaṃ bhāveti vivekanissitaṃ virāganissitaṃ nirodhanissitaṃ vossaggapariṇāmiṃ; dhammavicayasambojjhaṅgaṃ bhāveti . . . viriyasambojjhaṅgaṃ bhāveti . . . pītisambojjhaṅgaṃ bhāveti . . . passaddhisambojjhaṅgaṃ bhāveti . . . samādhisambojjhaṅgaṃ bhāveti . . . upekkhāsambojjhaṅgaṃ bhāveti vivekanissitaṃ virāganissitaṃ nirodhanissitaṃ vossaggapariṇāmiṃ.

"How-and, monks, a monk good-behavior based on, in good-behavior having been established, seven enlightenment-factors developing, seven enlightenment-factors cultivating, greatness vastness acquires in qualities?

Here, monks, a monk mindfulness-enlightenment-factor develops, seclusion-based, dispassion-based, cessation-based, release-evolving-toward; qualities-discrimination-enlightenment-factor develops . . . energy-enlightenment-factor develops . . . rapture-enlightenment-factor develops . . . tranquility-enlightenment-factor develops . . . concentration-enlightenment-factor develops . . . equanimity-enlightenment-factor develops, seclusion-based, dispassion-based, cessation-based, release-evolving-toward.

"And how, monks, does a monk, based on good behavior, established in good behavior, developing the seven factors of enlightenment, cultivating the seven factors of enlightenment, acquire greatness and vastness in [wholesome] qualities? Here, monks, a monk develops the enlightenment factor of mindfulness, which is based on seclusion, based on dispassion, based on cessation, evolving toward release. He develops the enlightenment factor of discrimination of qualities . . . the enlightenment factor of energy . . . the enlightenment factor of rapture . . . the enlightenment factor of tranquility . . . the enlightenment factor of concentration . . . the enlightenment factor of equanimity, which is based on seclusion, based on dispassion, based on cessation, evolving toward release.

"Evaṃ kho, bhikkhave, bhikkhu sīlaṃ nissāya sīle patiṭṭhāya satta bojjhaṅge bhāvento satta bojjhaṅge bahulīkaronto mahantattaṃ vepullattaṃ pāpuṇāti dhammesū"ti.

"Thus, monks, a monk good-behavior based on, in good-behavior having been established, seven enlightenment-factors developing, seven enlightenment-factors cultivating, greatness vastness acquires in qualities."

"It is in such a way, monks, that a monk, based on good behavior, established in good behavior, developing the seven factors of enlightenment, cultivating the seven factors of enlightenment, acquires greatness and vastness in [wholesome] qualities."

Grammatical explanations

nissāya: "based on, by means of"; an absolutive of *nissayati*, used adverbially with the accusative.

vaḍḍhenti: "increase, cause to increase"; a third-person plural causative of *vaḍḍhati*, "increases, grows." The former is transitive, the latter intransitive.

gāhenti: "acquire"; a third-person plural causative of *gaṇhāti*, "takes, grasps."

mahantattaṃ vepullattaṃ: "greatness [and] vastness." Both are abstract nouns formed by adding the neuter abstract suffix *-tta* (Skt *-tva*) respectively to *mahanta*, an adjective, and *vepulla*, a noun from the adjective *vipula*, "vast."

patiṭṭhāya: "established in"; an absolutive of *patiṭṭhāti*, used with the locative.

satta bojjhaṅge bhāvento: "developing the seven factors of enlightenment." SN 46:5 (see p. 442) best expresses the original meaning of the term: "They are called *bojjhaṅgā* because they lead to enlightenment." On this explanation *bojjhaṅga* is a dative tappurisa. The word is compounded from *bodhi* + *aṅga*, with palatalization of *bodhyaṅga* to *bojjhaṅga*.

satisambojjhaṅgaṃ bhāveti: "develops the enlightenment factor of mindfulness." There does not seem to be any difference in sense between *bojjhaṅga* and *sambojjhaṅga*. *Satisambojjhaṅga* is a complex compound, with the tappurisa *sambojjhaṅga* embedded within a kammadhāraya: "the enlightenment factor that is mindfulness." The commentary says: "mindfulness itself is the enlightenment factor."[214]

vivekanissitaṃ virāganissitaṃ nirodhanissitaṃ vossaggapariṇāmiṃ: "based on seclusion, based on dispassion, based on cessation, evolving toward (or maturing in) release"; a stock description of the enlightenment factors, also used for the path factors (see p. 469 below). All the terms are masculine accusatives, in agreement with *sambojjhaṅgaṃ*.

2. Kāyasutta

Body (SN 46:2; V 64–67)

[1. The nutriments for the hindrances]

"Seyyathāpi, bhikkhave, ayaṃ kāyo āhāraṭṭhitiko, āhāraṃ paṭicca tiṭṭhati, anāhāro no tiṭṭhati; evameva kho, bhikkhave, pañca nīvaraṇā āhāraṭṭhitikā, āhāraṃ paṭicca tiṭṭhanti, anāhārā no tiṭṭhanti.

214. Spk III 139,2: *Satiyeva sambojjhaṅgo ti.*

"Just as, monks, this body nutriment-subsisting, nutriment in dependence on subsists, without-nutriment not subsists, just so, monks, the five hindrances nutriment-subsistent, nutriment in dependence on subsist, without-nutriment not subsist.

"Just as, monks, this body is subsistent on nutriment, subsists in dependence on nutriment, and does not subsist without nutriment; just so, monks, the five hindrances are subsistent on nutriment, subsist in dependence on nutriment, and do not subsist without nutriment.

(1) "Ko ca, bhikkhave, āhāro anuppannassa vā kāmacchandassa uppādāya, uppannassa vā kāmacchandassa bhiyyobhāvāya vepullāya? Atthi, bhikkhave, subhanimittaṃ. Tattha ayonisomanasikārabahulīkāro: ayamāhāro anuppannassa vā kāmacchandassa uppādāya, uppannassa vā kāmacchandassa bhiyyobhāvāya vepullāya.

"What and, monks, the nutriment of unarisen or sensual-desire for arising, of arisen or sensual-desire for increase, for expansion? There is, monks, a beautiful-object. There non-thorough-attention-cultivation: this-nutriment of unarisen or sensual-desire for arising, of arisen or sensual desire for increase, for expansion.

"And what, monks, is the nutriment for the arising of unarisen sensual desire and for the increase and expansion of arisen sensual desire? There is, monks, a beautiful object. The cultivation of superficial attention to it: this is the nutriment for the arising of unarisen sensual desire and for the increase and expansion of arisen sensual desire.

(2) "Ko ca, bhikkhave, āhāro anuppannassa vā vyāpādassa uppādāya, uppannassa vā vyāpādassa bhiyyobhāvāya vepullāya? Atthi, bhikkhave, paṭighanimittaṃ. Tattha ayonisomanasikārabahulīkāro: ayamāhāro anuppannassa vā vyāpādassa uppādāya, uppannassa vā vyāpādassa bhiyyobhāvāya vepullāya.

"What and, monks, the nutriment of unarisen or ill-will for arising, of arisen or ill-will for increase, for expansion? There is, monks, an aversion-object. There non-thorough-attention-cultivation: this-nutriment of unarisen or ill-will for arising, of arisen or ill-will for increase, for expansion.

"And what, monks, is the nutriment for the arising of unarisen ill will and for the increase and expansion of arisen ill will? There is, monks, an object of aversion. The cultivation of superficial attention to it: this is the nutriment for the arising of unarisen ill will and for the increase and expansion of arisen ill will.

(3) "Ko ca, bhikkhave, āhāro anuppannassa vā thinamiddhassa uppādāya, uppannassa vā thinamiddhassa bhiyyobhāvāya vepullāya? Atthi, bhikkhave, arati tandi vijambhitā bhattasammado cetaso ca līnattaṃ. Tattha ayonisomanasikārabahulīkāro: ayamāhāro anuppannassa vā thinamiddhassa uppādāya, uppannassa vā thinamiddhassa bhiyyobhāvāya vepullāya.

"What and, monks, the nutriment of unarisen or dullness-drowsiness for arising, of arisen or dullness-drowsiness for increase, for expansion? There is, monks, discontent, lethargy, yawning, meals-tiredness, of mind and sluggishness. There non-thorough-attention-cultivation: this-nutriment of unarisen or dullness-drowsiness for arising, of arisen or dullness-drowsiness for increase, for expansion.

"And what, monks, is the nutriment for the arising of unarisen dullness and drowsiness and for the increase and expansion of arisen dullness and drowsiness? There is, monks, discontent, lethargy, yawning, tiredness after meals, and sluggishness of mind. The cultivation of superficial attention to these: this is the nutriment for the arising of unarisen dullness and drowsiness and for the increase and expansion of arisen dullness and drowsiness.

(4) "Ko ca, bhikkhave, āhāro anuppannassa vā uddhaccakukkuccassa uppādāya, uppannassa vā uddhaccakukkuccassa bhiyyobhāvāya vepullāya? Atthi, bhikkhave, cetaso avūpasamo. Tattha ayonisomanasikārabahulīkāro: ayamāhāro anuppannassa vā uddhaccakukkuccassa uppādāya, uppannassa vā uddhaccakukkuccassa bhiyyobhāvāya vepullāya.

"What and, monks, the nutriment of unarisen or restlessness-regret for arising, of arisen or restlessness-regret for increase, for expansion? There is, monks, of mind disquietude. There non-thorough-attention-cultivation: this-nutriment of unarisen or restlessness-regret for arising, of arisen or restlessness-regret for increase, for expansion.

"And what, monks, is the nutriment for the arising of unarisen restlessness and regret and for the increase and expansion of arisen restlessness and regret? There is, monks, disquietude of mind. The cultivation of superficial attention to this: this is the nutriment for the arising of unarisen restlessness and regret and for the increase and expansion of arisen restlessness and regret.

(5) "Ko ca, bhikkhave, āhāro anuppannāya vā vicikicchāya uppādāya, uppannāya vā vicikicchāya bhiyyobhāvāya vepullāya? Atthi, bhikkhave, vicikicchāṭṭhānīyā dhammā. Tattha ayonisomanasikārabahulīkāro: ayamāhāro anuppannāya vā vicikicchāya uppādāya, uppannāya vā vicikicchāya bhiyyobhāvāya vepullāya.

"What and, monks, the nutriment of unarisen or doubt for arising, of arisen or doubt for increase, for expansion? There are, monks, doubt-basis things. There non-thorough-attention-cultivation: this-nutriment of unarisen or doubt for arising, of arisen or doubt for increase, for expansion.

"And what, monks, is the nutriment for the arising of unarisen doubt and for the increase and expansion of arisen doubt? There are, monks, things that are the basis for doubt. The cultivation of superficial attention to this: this is the nutriment for the arising of unarisen doubt and for the increase and expansion of arisen doubt.

"Seyyathāpi, bhikkhave, ayaṃ kāyo āhāraṭṭhitiko, āhāraṃ paṭicca tiṭṭhati, anāhāro no tiṭṭhati; evameva kho, bhikkhave, ime pañca nīvaraṇā āhāraṭṭhitikā, āhāraṃ paṭicca tiṭṭhanti, anāhārā no tiṭṭhanti.

"Just as, monks, this body nutriment-subsisting, nutriment in dependence on subsists, without-nutriment not subsists, just so, monks, these five hindrances nutriment-subsisting, nutriment in dependence on subsist, without-nutriment not subsist.

"Just as, monks, this body is subsistent on nutriment, subsists in dependence on nutriment, and does not subsist without nutriment, just so, monks, these five hindrances are subsistent on nutriment, subsist in dependence on nutriment, and do not subsist without nutriment.

[2. The nutriments for the factors of enlightenment]

"Seyyathāpi, bhikkhave, ayaṃ kāyo āhāraṭṭhitiko, āhāraṃ paṭicca tiṭṭhati, anāhāro no tiṭṭhati; evameva kho, bhikkhave, satta bojjhaṅgā āhāraṭṭhitikā, āhāraṃ paṭicca tiṭṭhanti, anāhārā no tiṭṭhanti.

"Just as, monks, this body nutriment-subsisting, nutriment in dependence on subsists, without-nutriment not subsists, just so, monks, seven enlightenment-factors nutriment-subsistent, nutriment in dependence on subsist, without-nutriment not subsist.

"Just as, monks, this body is subsistent on nutriment, subsists in dependence on nutriment, and does not subsist without nutriment, just so, monks, the seven factors of enlightenment are subsistent on nutriment, subsist in dependence on nutriment, and do not subsist without nutriment.

(1) "Ko ca, bhikkhave, āhāro anuppannassa vā satisambojjhaṅgassa uppādāya, uppannassa vā satisambojjhaṅgassa bhāvanāya pāripūriyā? Atthi, bhikkhave, satisambojjhaṅgaṭṭhānīyā dhammā. Tattha yonisomanasikāra-bahulīkāro: ayamāhāro anuppannassa vā satisambojjhaṅgassa uppādāya, uppannassa vā satisambojjhaṅgassa bhāvanāya pāripūriyā.

"What and, monks, the nutriment of unarisen or mindfulness-enlightenment-factor for arising, of arisen or mindfulness-enlightenment-factor by development for fulfillment? There are, monks, mindfulness-enlightenment-factor-basis things. There thorough-attention-cultivation: this-nutriment of unarisen or mindfulness-enlightenment-factor for arising, of arisen or mindfulness-enlightenment-factor by development for fulfillment.

"And what, monks, is the nutriment for the arising of the unarisen enlightenment factor of mindfulness and for the fulfillment by development of the arisen enlightenment factor of mindfulness? There are, monks, things that are the basis for the enlightenment factor of mindfulness. The cultivation of thorough attention to them: this is the nutriment for the arising of the unarisen enlightenment factor of mindfulness and for the fulfillment by development of the arisen enlightenment factor of mindfulness.

(2) "Ko ca, bhikkhave, āhāro anuppannassa vā dhammavicayasambojjhaṅgassa uppādāya, uppannassa vā dhammavicayasambojjhaṅgassa bhāvanāya pāripūriyā? Atthi, bhikkhave, kusalākusalā dhammā, sāvajjānavajjā dhammā, hīnapaṇītā dhammā, kaṇhasukkasappaṭibhāgā dhammā. Tattha yonisomanasikārabahulīkāro: ayamāhāro anuppannassa vā dhammavicayasambojjhaṅgassa uppādāya, uppannassa vā dhammavicayasambojjhaṅgassa bhāvanāya pāripūriyā.

"What and, monks, the nutriment of unarisen or qualities-discrimination-enlightenment-factor for arising, of arisen or qualities-discrimination-enlightenment-factor by development for fulfillment? There are, monks, wholesome-unwholesome qualities, blameworthy-blameless qualities, inferior-superior qualities, dark-bright-with-counterparts qualities. There thorough-attention-cultivation: this-nutriment of unarisen or qualities-discrimination-enlightenment-factor for arising, of arisen or qualities-discrimination-enlightenment-factor by development for fulfillment.

"And what, monks, is the nutriment for the arising of the unarisen enlightenment factor of discrimination of qualities and for the fulfillment by development of the arisen enlightenment factor of discrimination of qualities? There are, monks, wholesome and unwholesome qualities, blameworthy and blameless qualities, inferior and superior qualities, qualities dark and bright with their counterparts. The cultivation of thorough attention to them: this is the nutriment for the arising of the unarisen enlightenment factor of discrimination of qualities and for the fulfillment by development of the arisen enlightenment factor of discrimination of qualities.

(3) "Ko ca, bhikkhave, āhāro anuppannassa vā viriyasambojjhaṅgassa uppādāya, uppannassa vā viriyasambojjhaṅgassa bhāvanāya pāripūriyā? Atthi, bhikkhave, ārambhadhātu nikkamadhātu parakkamadhātu. Tattha yonisomanasikārabahulīkāro: ayamāhāro anuppannassa vā viriyasambojjhaṅgassa uppādāya, uppannassa vā viriyasambojjhaṅgassa bhāvanāya pāripūriyā.

"What and, monks, the nutriment of unarisen or energy-enlightenment-factor for arising, of arisen or energy-enlightenment-factor by development for fulfillment? There are, monks, the arousal-element, the endeavor-element, the exertion-element. There thorough-attention-cultivation: this-nutriment of unarisen or energy-enlightenment-factor for arising, of arisen or energy-enlightenment-factor by development for fulfillment.

"And what, monks, is the nutriment for the arising of the unarisen enlightenment factor of energy and for the fulfillment by development of the arisen enlightenment factor of energy? There are, monks, the element of arousal, the element of endeavor, the element of exertion. The cultivation of thorough attention to them: this is the nutriment for the arising of the unarisen enlightenment factor of energy and for the fulfillment by development of the arisen enlightenment factor of energy.

(4) "Ko ca, bhikkhave, āhāro anuppannassa vā pītisambojjhaṅgassa uppādāya, uppannassa vā pītisambojjhaṅgassa bhāvanāya pāripūriyā? Atthi, bhikkhave, pītisambojjhaṅgaṭṭhānīyā dhammā. Tattha yonisomanasikāra-bahulīkāro: ayamāhāro anuppannassa vā pītisambojjhaṅgassa uppādāya, uppannassa vā pītisambojjhaṅgassa bhāvanāya pāripūriyā.

"What and, monks, the nutriment of unarisen or rapture-enlightenment-factor for arising, of arisen or rapture-enlightenment-factor by development for fulfillment? There are, monks, rapture-enlightenment-factor-basis things. There thorough-attention-cultivation: this-nutriment of unarisen or rapture-enlightenment-factor for arising, of arisen or rapture-enlightenment-factor by development for fulfillment.

"And what, monks, is the nutriment for the arising of the unarisen enlightenment factor of rapture and for the fulfillment by development of the arisen enlightenment factor of rapture? There are, monks, things that are the basis for the enlightenment factor of rapture. The cultivation of thorough attention to them: this is the nutriment for the arising of the unarisen enlightenment factor of rapture and for the fulfillment by development of the arisen enlightenment factor of rapture.

(5) "Ko ca, bhikkhave, āhāro anuppannassa vā passaddhisambojjhaṅgassa uppādāya, uppannassa vā passaddhisambojjhaṅgassa bhāvanāya pāripūriyā? Atthi, bhikkhave, kāyapassaddhi, cittapassaddhi. Tattha yonisomanasikārabahulīkāro: ayamāhāro anuppannassa vā passaddhisambojjhaṅgassa uppādāya, uppannassa vā passaddhisambojjhaṅgassa bhāvanāya pāripūriyā.

"What and, monks, the nutriment of unarisen or tranquility-enlightenment-factor for arising, of arisen or tranquility-enlightenment-factor by development for fulfillment? There are, monks, body-tranquility, mind-tranquility. There thorough-attention-cultivation: this-nutriment of unarisen or tranquility-enlightenment-factor for arising, of arisen or tranquility-enlightenment-factor by development for fulfillment.

"And what, monks, is the nutriment for the arising of the unarisen enlightenment factor of tranquility and for the fulfillment by development of the arisen enlightenment factor of tranquility? There are, monks, tranquility of body and tranquility of mind. The cultivation of thorough attention to them: this is the nutriment for the arising of the unarisen enlightenment factor of tranquility and for the fulfillment by development of the arisen enlightenment factor of tranquility.

(6) "Ko ca, bhikkhave, āhāro anuppannassa vā samādhisambojjhaṅgassa uppādāya, uppannassa vā samādhisambojjhaṅgassa bhāvanāya pāripūriyā? Atthi, bhikkhave, samathanimittaṃ avyagganimittaṃ. Tattha yonisomanasikārabahulīkāro: ayamāhāro anuppannassa vā samādhisambojjhaṅgassa uppādāya, uppannassa vā samādhisambojjhaṅgassa bhāvanāya pāripūriyā.

"What and, monks, the nutriment of unarisen or concentration-enlightenment-factor for arising, of arisen or concentration-enlightenment-factor by development for fulfillment? There is, monks, serenity-object, non-diffusion-object. There thorough-attention-cultivation: this-nutriment of unarisen or concentration-enlightenment-factor for arising, of arisen or concentration-enlightenment-factor by development for fulfillment.

"And what, monks, is the nutriment for the arising of the unarisen enlightenment factor of concentration and for the fulfillment by development of the arisen enlightenment factor of concentration? There is, monks, an object of serenity, an object of non-diffusion. The cultivation of thorough attention to this: this is the nutriment for the arising of the unarisen enlightenment factor of concentration and for the fulfillment by development of the arisen enlightenment factor of concentration.

(7) "Ko ca, bhikkhave, āhāro anuppannassa vā upekkhāsambojjhaṅgassa uppādāya, uppannassa vā upekkhāsambojjhaṅgassa bhāvanāya pāripūriyā? Atthi, bhikkhave, upekkhāsambojjhaṅgaṭṭhānīyā dhammā. Tattha yonisomanasikāṛabahulīkāro: ayamāhāro anuppannassa vā upekkhāsambojjhaṅgassa uppādāya, uppannassa vā upekkhāsambojjhaṅgassa bhāvanāya pāripūriyā.

"What and, monks, the nutriment of unarisen or equanimity-enlightenment-factor for arising, of arisen or equanimity-enlightenment-factor by development for fulfillment? There are, monks, equanimity-enlightenment-factor-basis things. There thorough-attention-cultivation: this-nutriment of unarisen or equanimity-enlightenment-factor for arising, of arisen or equanimity-enlightenment-factor by development for fulfillment.

"And what, monks, is the nutriment for the arising of the unarisen enlightenment factor of equanimity and for the fulfillment by development of the arisen enlightenment factor of equanimity? There are, monks, things that are the basis for the enlightenment factor of equanimity. The cultivation of thorough attention to them: this is the nutriment for the arising of the unarisen enlightenment factor of equanimity and for the fulfillment by development of the arisen enlightenment factor of equanimity.

"Seyyathāpi, bhikkhave, ayaṃ kāyo āhāraṭṭhitiko, āhāraṃ paṭicca tiṭṭhati, anāhāro no tiṭṭhati; evameva kho, bhikkhave, ime satta bojjhaṅgā āhāraṭṭhitikā, āhāraṃ paṭicca tiṭṭhanti, anāhārā no tiṭṭhantī ti."

"Just as, monks, this body nutriment-subsisting, nutriment in dependence on subsists, without-nutriment not subsists, just so, monks, these seven enlightenment-factors nutriment-subsistent, nutriment in dependence on subsist, without-nutriment not subsist."

"Just as, monks, this body is subsistent on nutriment, subsists in dependence on nutriment, and does not subsist without nutriment, just so, monks, these seven factors of enlightenment are subsistent on nutriment, subsist in dependence on nutriment, and do not subsist without nutriment."

Grammatical explanations

[1. The nutriment for the hindrances]

āhāraṭṭhitiko: "subsistent on nutriment": a bahubbīhi compound describing the masculine singular *kāyo*; it is composed of *āhāra* + *ṭhiti*, with the adjectival suffix *-iko*. Just below the masculine plural, *āhāraṭṭhitikā*, describes *pañca nīvaraṇā*.

anuppannassa vā kāmacchandassa uppādāya, uppannassa vā kāmacchandassa bhiyyobhāvāya vepullāya: "for the arising of unarisen sensual desire and for the increase and expansion of arisen sensual desire." Each alternative uses a dative—*uppādāya* and *bhiyyobhāvāya vepullāya* (a double dative)—in relation to a genitive, *kāmacchandassa*, which is distinguished as unarisen and as arisen. And so for the remaining hindrances.

subhanimittaṃ: The commentary explains this as beauty or an object grasped as beautiful.[215]

ayonisomanasikārabahulīkāro: "cultivation of superficial attention." *Ayonisomanasikāra* is interpreted as attention to the impermanent as permanent, to the painful as pleasant, to what is non-self as a self, and to the unbeautiful as beautiful. On *yonisomanasikāra*, see p. 302.

paṭighanimittaṃ: The commentary explains this as aversion itself or an object of aversion.[216]

thinamiddhassa: "dullness and drowsiness"; a dvanda of the collective singular type, here in the genitive. So too for *uddhaccakukkuccassa* just below.

vicikicchāṭṭhānīyā dhammā: "things that are the basis for doubt." PED defines *ṭhānīya* as "founded on or caused by," but DOP has "being a source or cause (for)." The latter better fits the context. And so too in relation to the *bojjhaṅga* just below.

215. Spk III 139,22–23: *Subhanimittan ti subhampi subhanimittaṃ, subhassa ārammaṇampi subhanimittaṃ.*

216. Spk III 139,30–31: *Paṭighopi paṭighanimittaṃ paṭighārammaṇampi.*

[2. The nutriments for the factors of enlightenment]

anuppannassa vā satisambojjhaṅgassa uppādāya, uppannassa vā satisambojjhaṅgassa bhāvanāya pāripūriyā: "for the arising of the unarisen enlightenment factor of mindfulness and for the fulfillment by development of the arisen enlightenment factor of mindfulness." Since *bhāvanā* is a feminine noun, and since the instrumental and dative cases of the feminine nouns of this class are identical, both *bhāvanāya* and *pāripūriyā* might have been taken as datives, "for development [and] fulfillment." However, in the line of the *Satipaṭṭhāna Sutta*, *yathā ca uppannassa satisambojjhaṅgassa bhāvanāya pāripūrī hoti tañca pajānāti*, it is necessary to take *bhāvanāya* as an instrumental in relation to *pāripūrī*, and it seems the same relationship should obtain here.[217]

kusalākusalā: a dvanda of *kusala* and *akusala* functioning as an adjective in relation to *dhammā*. And so for *sāvajjānavajjā*. Both are dvanda compounds.

kaṇhasukkasappaṭibhāgā dhammā: "qualities dark and bright with their counterparts." *Kaṇhasukkasappaṭibhāgā* is a bahubbīhi qualifying *dhammā*, with the first part the dvanda *kaṇhasukka* and the second part the kammadhāraya *sappaṭibhāgā*. The commentary gives three explanations of the compound: (1) the dark and bright qualities are "with counterparts" because each yields its corresponding result, dark and bright respectively; (2) the bright is the counterpart of the dark and the dark the counterpart of the bright because they are opposites; (3) the dark and bright are counterparts because each excludes the other in yielding its result.[218]

ārambhadhātu nikkamadhātu parakkamadhātu: "the element of arousal, the element of endeavor, the element of exertion." The commentary explains these as three stages in the development of energy, each subsequent one stronger than its predecessor. The compounds should probably be taken as kammadhārayas ("the element that is arousal" and so forth).

217. See DN II 303–4, MN I 62,3. Spk III 126,8, commenting on *bhāvanāya pāripūriyā* at SN V 9,24, says: "by development for the sake of fulfillment" (*bhāvanāya paripūraṇatthaṃ*), which further supports this interpretation.

218. See Spk III 141,11–18.

samathanimittaṃ avyagganimittaṃ: "an object of serenity, an object of non-diffusion." The commentary takes these as synonymous.

3. Sīlasutta
Good Behavior (SN 46:3; V 67–70)

[1. Right association]
"Ye te, bhikkhave, bhikkhū sīlasampannā samādhisampannā paññāsampannā[219] *vimuttisampannā vimuttiñāṇadassanasampannā: dassanampāhaṃ, bhikkhave, tesaṃ bhikkhūnaṃ bahukāraṃ vadāmi; savanampāhaṃ, bhikkhave, tesaṃ bhikkhūnaṃ bahukāraṃ vadāmi; upasaṅkamanampāhaṃ, bhikkhave, tesaṃ bhikkhūnaṃ bahukāraṃ vadāmi; payirupāsanampāhaṃ, bhikkhave, tesaṃ bhikkhūnaṃ bahukāraṃ vadāmi; anussatimpāhaṃ, bhikkhave, tesaṃ bhikkhūnaṃ bahukāraṃ vadāmi; anupabbajjampāhaṃ, bhikkhave, tesaṃ bhikkhūnaṃ bahukāraṃ vadāmi.*

"Those who, monks, monks good-behavior-accomplished, concentration-accomplished, wisdom-accomplished, liberation-accomplished, liberation-knowledge-vision-accomplished: sight-too-I, monks, of those monks helpful I say; listening-too-I, monks, of those monks helpful I say; approaching-too-I, monks, of those monks helpful I say; attending-too-I, monks, of those monks helpful I say; recollection-too-I, monks, of those monks helpful I say; going-forth-after-too-I, monks, of those monks helpful I say.

"Monks, as to those monks who are accomplished in good behavior, accomplished in concentration, accomplished in wisdom, accomplished in liberation, accomplished in the knowledge and vision of liberation: I say, monks, that the sight of those monks is helpful; I say, monks, that listening to those monks too is helpful; I say, monks, that approaching those monks too is helpful; I say, monks, that attending on those monks too is helpful; I say, monks, that recollecting those monks too is helpful; I say, monks, that following those monks in going forth too is helpful.

219. I follow the Ce and Ee reading here. Be has *ñāṇasampannā*, which seems to be an editorial error.

"Taṃ kissa hetu? Tathārūpānaṃ, bhikkhave, bhikkhūnaṃ dhammaṃ sutvā dvayena vūpakaṭṭho viharati kāyavūpakāsena ca cittavūpakāsena ca. So tathā vūpakaṭṭho viharanto taṃ dhammaṃ anussarati anuvitakketi.

"That for what reason? Of such-kind, monks, of monks Dhamma having heard, by dyad withdrawn one dwells: by body-withdrawal and by mind-withdrawal and. He thus withdrawn dwelling, that Dhamma recollects, thinks over.

"For what reason? Because, monks, having heard the Dhamma of such kind of monks, one dwells withdrawn in two ways: by withdrawal of body and by withdrawal of mind. Dwelling thus withdrawn, one recollects and thinks over that Dhamma.

[2. The factors of enlightenment]

(1) "*Yasmiṃ samaye, bhikkhave, bhikkhu tathā vūpakaṭṭho viharanto taṃ dhammaṃ anussarati anuvitakketi, satisambojjhaṅgo tasmiṃ samaye bhikkhuno āraddho hoti; satisambojjhaṅgaṃ tasmiṃ samaye bhikkhu bhāveti; satisambojjhaṅgo tasmiṃ samaye bhikkhuno bhāvanāpāripūriṃ gacchati.*

"On which occasion, monks, a monk thus withdrawn dwelling that Dhamma recollects thinks over, the mindfulness-enlightenment-factor on that occasion of the monk aroused is; the mindfulness-enlightenment-factor on that occasion the monk develops; the mindfulness-enlightenment-factor on that occasion for the monk development-fulfillment goes.

"When, monks, a monk dwelling thus withdrawn recollects and reflects on that Dhamma, on that occasion the enlightenment factor of mindfulness is aroused by the monk; on that occasion the monk develops the enlightenment factor of mindfulness; on that occasion the enlightenment factor of mindfulness goes to fulfillment by development for the monk.

(2) "So tathā sato viharanto taṃ dhammaṃ paññāya pavicinati pavicarati parivīmaṃsaṃ āpajjati. Yasmiṃ samaye, bhikkhave, bhikkhu tathā sato viharanto taṃ dhammaṃ paññāya pavicinati pavicarati parivīmaṃsaṃ āpajjati, dhammavicayasambojjhaṅgo tasmiṃ samaye bhikkhuno āraddho hoti; dhammavicayasambojjhaṅgaṃ tasmiṃ samaye bhikkhu bhāveti; dhammavicayasambojjhaṅgo tasmiṃ samaye bhikkhuno bhāvanāpāripūriṃ gacchati.

"He thus mindful dwelling that Dhamma with wisdom discriminates, examines, investigation embarks upon. On which occasion, monks, a monk thus mindful dwelling that Dhamma with wisdom discriminates, examines, investigation embarks upon, the qualities-discrimination-enlightenment-factor on that occasion of the monk aroused is; the qualities-discrimination-enlightenment-factor on that occasion the monk develops; the qualities-discrimination-enlightenment-factor on that occasion for the monk development-fulfillment goes.

"Dwelling thus mindful, he discriminates that Dhamma with wisdom, examines it, and embarks upon an investigation into it. When, monks, a monk, dwelling thus mindful, discriminates that Dhamma with wisdom, examines it, and embarks upon an investigation into it, on that occasion the enlightenment factor of discrimination of qualities is aroused by the monk; on that occasion the monk develops the enlightenment factor of discrimination of qualities; on that occasion the enlightenment factor of discrimination of qualities goes to fulfillment by development for the monk.

(3) "Tassa taṃ dhammaṃ paññāya pavicinato pavicarato parivīmaṃsamāpajjato āraddhaṃ hoti viriyaṃ asallīnaṃ. Yasmiṃ samaye, bhikkhave, bhikkhuno taṃ dhammaṃ paññāya pavicinato pavicarato parivīmaṃsamāpajjato āraddhaṃ hoti viriyaṃ asallīnaṃ, viriyasambojjhaṅgo tasmiṃ samaye bhikkhuno āraddho hoti; viriyasambojjhaṅgaṃ tasmiṃ samaye bhikkhu bhāveti; viriyasambojjhaṅgo tasmiṃ samaye bhikkhuno bhāvanāpāripūriṃ gacchati.

"Of him that Dhamma with wisdom discriminating, examining, investigation embarking upon, aroused is energy unsluggish. On which occasion, monks, of a monk that Dhamma with wisdom discriminating, examining, investigation embarking upon, aroused is energy unsluggish, the energy-enlightenment-factor on that occasion of the monk aroused is; the energy-enlightenment-factor on that occasion the monk develops; the energy-enlightenment-factor on that occasion for the monk development-fulfillment goes.

"As he is discriminating that Dhamma with wisdom, examining it, and embarking upon an investigation into it, unsluggish energy is aroused. When, monks, unsluggish energy is aroused in a monk as he is discriminating that

Dhamma with wisdom, examining it, and embarking upon an investigation into it, on that occasion the enlightenment factor of energy is aroused by the monk; on that occasion the monk develops the enlightenment factor of energy; on that occasion the enlightenment factor of energy goes to fulfillment by development for the monk.

(4) "Āraddhaviriyassa uppajjati pīti nirāmisā. Yasmiṃ samaye, bhikkhave, bhikkhuno āraddhaviriyassa uppajjati pīti nirāmisā, pītisambojjhaṅgo tasmiṃ samaye bhikkhuno āraddho hoti; pītisambojjhaṅgaṃ tasmiṃ samaye bhikkhu bhāveti; pītisambojjhaṅgo tasmiṃ samaye bhikkhuno bhāvanāpāripūriṃ gacchati.

"For one aroused-energy arises rapture non-carnal. On which occasion, monks, for a monk who has aroused-energy arises rapture non-carnal, the rapture-enlightenment-factor on that occasion of the monk aroused is; the rapture-enlightenment-factor on that occasion the monk develops; the rapture-enlightenment-factor on that occasion for the monk development-fulfillment goes.

"For one with energy aroused there arises non-carnal rapture. When, monks, for a monk with energy aroused there arises non-carnal rapture, on that occasion the enlightenment factor of rapture is aroused by the monk; on that occasion the monk develops the enlightenment factor of rapture; on that occasion the enlightenment factor of rapture goes to fulfillment by development for the monk.

(5) "Pītimanassa kāyopi passambhati, cittampi passambhati. Yasmiṃ samaye, bhikkhave, bhikkhuno pītimanassa kāyopi passambhati cittampi passambhati, passaddhisambojjhaṅgo tasmiṃ samaye bhikkhuno āraddho hoti; passaddhisambojjhaṅgaṃ tasmiṃ samaye bhikkhu bhāveti; passaddhisambojjhaṅgo tasmiṃ samaye bhikkhuno bhāvanāpāripūriṃ gacchati.

"For one rapture-mind, body-too becomes tranquil, mind-too becomes tranquil. On which occasion, monks, of a monk rapture-mind body-too becomes tranquil, mind-too becomes tranquil, the tranquility-enlightenment-factor on that occasion of the monk aroused is; the tranquility-enlightenment-factor on that occasion the monk develops; the tranquility-enlightenment-factor on that occasion for the monk development-fulfillment goes.

"For one with a mind of rapture, the body becomes tranquil and the mind becomes tranquil. When, monks, for a monk with a mind of rapture the body becomes tranquil and the mind becomes tranquil, on that occasion the enlightenment factor of tranquility is aroused by the monk; on that occasion the monk develops the enlightenment factor of tranquility; on that occasion the enlightenment factor of tranquility goes to fulfillment by development for the monk.

(6) "Passaddhakāyassa sukhino cittaṃ samādhiyati. Yasmiṃ samaye, bhikkhave, bhikkhuno passaddhakāyassa sukhino cittaṃ samādhiyati, samādhisambojjhaṅgo tasmiṃ samaye bhikkhuno āraddho hoti; samādhisambojjhaṅgaṃ tasmiṃ samaye bhikkhu bhāveti; samādhisambojjhaṅgo tasmiṃ samaye bhikkhuno bhāvanāpāripūriṃ gacchati.

"Of one tranquil-body, a happy one, the mind is concentrated. On which occasion, monks, of a monk tranquil-body, a happy one, the mind is concentrated, the concentration-enlightenment-factor on that occasion of the monk aroused is; the concentration-enlightenment-factor on that occasion the monk develops; the concentration-enlightenment-factor on that occasion for the monk development-fulfillment goes.

"For one tranquil in body, one who is happy, the mind becomes concentrated. When, monks, for a monk tranquil in body, one who is happy, the mind becomes concentrated, on that occasion the enlightenment factor of concentration is aroused by the monk; on that occasion the monk develops the enlightenment factor of concentration; on that occasion the enlightenment factor of concentration goes to fulfillment by development for the monk.

(7) "So tathāsamāhitaṃ cittaṃ sādhukaṃ ajjhupekkhitā hoti. Yasmiṃ samaye, bhikkhave, bhikkhu tathāsamāhitaṃ cittaṃ sādhukaṃ ajjhupekkhitā hoti, upekkhāsambojjhaṅgo tasmiṃ samaye bhikkhuno āraddho hoti;

upekkhāsambojjhaṅgaṃ tasmiṃ samaye bhikkhu bhāveti; upekkhāsambojjhaṅgo tasmiṃ samaye bhikkhuno bhāvanāpāripūriṃ gacchati."

"He thus-concentrated mind well equanimous-observer is. On which occasion, monks, of a monk thus-concentrated mind well equanimous-observer is, the equanimity-enlightenment-factor on that occasion of the monk aroused is; the equanimity-enlightenment-factor on that occasion the monk develops; the equanimity-enlightenment-factor on that occasion for the monk development-fulfillment goes."

"He is one who observes well with equanimity the mind thus concentrated. When, monks, a monk is one who observes well with equanimity the mind thus concentrated, on that occasion the enlightenment factor of equanimity is aroused by the monk; on that occasion the monk develops the enlightenment factor of equanimity; on that occasion the enlightenment factor of equanimity goes to fulfillment by development for the monk."

[*The final section of the sutta states that one who develops the seven factors of enlightenment in such a way may expect one or another of seven benefits. These are: the attainment of arahantship during life, its attainment at the time of death, or the attainment of the fruit of a non-returner in any of five ways, graded by degrees of superiority.*]

Grammatical explanations

sīlasampannā . . . vimuttiñāṇadassanasampannā: "accomplished in good behavior . . . accomplished in the knowledge and vision of liberation." These are all tappurisa compounds qualifying *bhikkhū*. The last is a complex tappurisa that contains an internal dvanda, *ñāṇadassana*, "knowledge and vision," standing in a genitive tappurisa relation to *vimutti*, "liberation."

dassanampāhaṃ: to be resolved into *dassanaṃ + pi + ahaṃ*. The last, the first-person pronoun, is the subject of the verb *vadāmi*, which takes *dassanaṃ* as object. *Savanampāhaṃ* and the following should be similarly resolved. *Anupabbajjaṃ* is accusative of *anupabbajjā*, which DOP defines as "adopting the wanderer's life after or in imitation (of another)."

bahukāraṃ: "helpful," literally, "doing much."

tathārūpānaṃ: "of such kind"; a bahubbīhi modifying *bhikkhūnaṃ*, genitive plural, composed of the adverb of manner, *tathā*, and the noun *rūpa*.

kāyavūpakāsena ca cittavūpakāsena ca: "by withdrawal of body and by withdrawal of mind." PED derives *vūpakāsa* from *vūpakāseti*, of which *vūpakaṭṭha* is the corresponding past participle. The case is instrumental, expressing the manner in which the action is performed (Perniola §253d).

[2. The factors of enlightenment]

satisambojjhaṅgo tasmiṃ samaye bhikkhuno āraddho hoti: "on that occasion the enlightenment factor of mindfulness is aroused by the monk." *Bhikkhuno* is another instance of the logical subject—the agent of the action—occurring in the genitive case with an instrumental sense; the object of the action, *satisambojjhaṅgo*, serves as the grammatical subject in the nominative case. The action performed is represented by the past participle (*āraddho*), a nominative agreeing with the grammatical subject. See the comment on *tumhākaṃ* on p. 105.

bhāvanāpāripūriṃ: "to fulfillment by development." For my reason in taking this compound as an instrumental tappurisa, see p. 434.

asallīnaṃ: "unsluggish"; the negation of *sallīnaṃ* (< *sam* + *līnaṃ*), originally a past participle with the literal sense "contracted, compressed."

āraddhaviriyassa: "for one with energy aroused"; a bahubbīhi qualifying *bhikkhuno*, implicit in the first sentence and specified in the second. The compound joins the past participle *āraddha* and the noun *viriya*. Sections (5) and (6) use the same structure, again with the bahubbīhi qualifying *bhikkhuno*.

nirāmisā: "non-carnal"; an adjective qualifying the feminine noun *pīti*. The word is a negation (by the prefix *nir-*) of *āmisa*, "flesh, bait, carnal thing."

pītimanassa: "one with a mind of rapture"; a bahubbīhi composed of two nouns, *pīti* and *mana*; the compound again qualifies *bhikkhuno*.

passaddhakāyassa: "for one tranquil in body"; still another bahubbīhi composed of the past participle *passaddha*, "calmed down," and the noun *kāya*.

so tathāsamāhitaṃ cittaṃ sādhukaṃ ajjhupekkhitā hoti: "He is one who observes well with equanimity the mind thus concentrated." *Tathāsamāhitaṃ* is a kammadhāraya compound that joins the adverb *tathā* and the past participle *samāhitaṃ*; it qualifies *cittaṃ*, an accusative object in relation to the agent noun *ajjhupekkhitā*, the nominative singular of *ajjhupekkhitar* (Duroiselle §163; Perniola §37), from the verb *ajjhupekkhati* (*adhi* + *upa* + *ikkhati*), "observes (with equanimity)." *Sādhukaṃ* is an adverb qualifying the act of observation. Here the agent noun takes an object, *cittaṃ*, in the accusative case.

4. Bhikkhusutta

A Monk (SN 46:5; V 72)

Atha kho aññataro bhikkhu yena bhagavā ten'upasaṅkami. . . . Ekamantaṃ nisinno kho so bhikkhu bhagavantaṃ etadavoca: "'Bojjhaṅgā, bojjhaṅgā'ti, bhante, vuccanti. Kittāvatā nu kho, bhante, 'bojjhaṅgā'ti vuccantī"ti?

Then a certain monk where the Blessed One, there approached. . . . One-side seated, that monk to the Blessed One this-said: "'Enlightenment-factors, enlightenment-factors,' Bhante, are called. In what way, Bhante, 'enlightenment-factors' are called?"

Then a certain monk approached the Blessed One. . . . Seated to one side, that monk said this to the Blessed One: "They are called, Bhante, 'factors of enlightenment, factors of enlightenment.' In what way, Bhante, are they called 'factors of enlightenment'?"

"'Bodhāya saṃvattantī'ti kho, bhikkhu, tasmā 'bojjhaṅgā'ti vuccanti. Idha, bhikkhu, bhikkhu satisambojjhaṅgaṃ bhāveti vivekanissitaṃ virāganissitaṃ nirodhanissitaṃ vossaggapariṇāmiṃ . . . upekkhāsambojjhaṅgaṃ bhāveti vivekanissitaṃ virāganissitaṃ nirodhanissitaṃ vossaggapariṇāmiṃ.

"To enlightenment they lead, monk, therefore 'enlightenment-factors' are called. Here, monk, a monk mindfulness-enlightenment-factor develops, seclusion-based, dispassion-based, cessation-based, release-evolving-toward . . . equanimity-enlightenment-factor develops, seclusion-based, dispassion-based, cessation-based, release-evolving-toward.

"They lead to enlightenment, monk, therefore they are called 'factors of enlightenment.' Here, monks, a monk develops the enlightenment factor of mindfulness, which is based on seclusion, based on dispassion, based on cessation, evolving toward release. . . . He develops the enlightenment factor of equanimity, which is based on seclusion, based on dispassion, based on cessation, evolving toward release.

"Tass'ime satta bojjhaṅge bhāvayato kāmāsavāpi cittaṃ vimuccati, bhavāsavāpi cittaṃ vimuccati, avijjāsavāpi cittaṃ vimuccati. Vimuttasmiṃ vimuttamiti ñāṇaṃ hoti. 'Khīṇā jāti, vusitaṃ brahmacariyaṃ, kataṃ karaṇīyaṃ, nāparaṃ itthattāyā'ti pajānāti. 'Bodhāya saṃvattantī'ti, bhikkhu, tasmā 'bojjhaṅgā'ti vuccantī"ti.

"For him these seven enlightenment-factors developing, from the sensuality-influx-too the mind is liberated, from the existence-influx-too the mind is liberated, from the ignorance-influx-too the mind is liberated. In liberated 'liberated,' thus the knowledge occurs. 'Finished birth, lived the spiritual-life, done what-is-to-be-done, not-further for such-a-state,' understands. 'To enlightenment they lead,' monk, therefore 'enlightenment-factors' are called."

"For one developing these seven factors of enlightenment, the mind is liberated from the influx of sensuality, liberated from the influx of existence, liberated from the influx of ignorance. In regard to what is liberated, the knowledge occurs thus: 'Liberated.' He understands: 'Finished is birth, the spiritual life has been lived, what had to be done has been done, there is no more for this state of being.' They lead to enlightenment, monk, therefore they are called 'factors of enlightenment.'"

Grammatical explanations

tass'ime satta bojjhaṅge bhāvayato: "for him developing these seven factors of enlightenment"; *bhāvayato* is the present participle of *bhāveti*, in the singular dative, qualifying the dative subject *tassa*.

kāmāsavā: "from the influx of sensuality." The case is ablative, expressing separation. And so for *bhavāsavā* and *avijjāsavā*. The commentaries explain *kāmāsava* as lust connected with the five sensual objects; *bhavāsava* as desire for form and formless existence and attachment to jhāna associated with the eternalist view; and *avijjāsava* as ignorance of the four noble truths.[220]

220. Ps I 67,27–31: *Kāmāsavo ti pañcakāmaguṇiko rāgo. Bhavāsavo ti rupārūpabhave*

5. Kuṇḍaliyasutta

Kuṇḍaliya (SN 46:6; V 73–75)

[1. The wanderer's questions]

Ekaṃ samayaṃ bhagavā sākete viharati añjanavane migadāye. Atha kho kuṇḍaliyo paribbājako yena bhagavā ten'upasaṅkami. Upasaṅkamitvā bhagavatā saddhiṃ sammodi. Sammodanīyaṃ kathaṃ sāraṇīyaṃ vītisāretvā ekamantaṃ nisīdi. Ekamantaṃ nisinno kho kuṇḍaliyo paribbājako bhagavantaṃ etadavoca:

One occasion the Blessed One at Sākata was dwelling in the añjana-grove[221] in the deer-park. Then Kuṇḍaliya the wanderer where the Blessed One, there approached. Having approached, with the Blessed One together greeted. Greeting talk cordial having concluded, one-side sat. One-side seated, Kuṇḍaliya the wanderer to the Blessed One this-said:

On one occasion the Blessed One was dwelling at Sāketa in the añjana grove in the deer park. Then the wanderer Kuṇḍaliya approached the Blessed One. Having approached, he exchanged greetings with the Blessed One. When they had concluded their greetings and cordial talk, he sat down to one side. Seated to one side, the wanderer Kuṇḍaliya said this to the Blessed One:

"Ahamasmi, bho gotama, ārāmanisādī[222] parisāvacaro. Tassa mayhaṃ, bho gotama, pacchābhattaṃ bhuttapātarāsassa ayamācāro hoti: ārāmena ārāmaṃ uyyānena uyyānaṃ anucaṅkamāmi anuvicarāmi. So tattha passāmi eke samaṇabrāhmaṇe itivādappamokkhānisaṃsañc'eva kathaṃ kathente upārambhānisaṃsañca. Bhavaṃ pana gotamo kimānisaṃso viharatī"ti?

"I-am, Master Gotama, park-sitter assembly-sphere. Of that me, Master Gotama, after-meal, eaten-breakfast, this-custom is: by park to park, by garden to garden, I walk around, wander around. That there I see some

---

chandarāgo, jhānanikanti ca sassatucchedadiṭṭhisahagatā. . . . Avijjāsavo ti catūsu saccesu aññāṇaṃ.

221. According to DOP, *añjana* is "the name of a tree or plant." This is distinct from another kind of *añjana*, defined as "ointment, esp. a collyrium for the eyes, used for decoration or as a medication."

222. I follow Ce and Ee here, as against Be *ārāmanissayī*, "one who depends on parks."

ascetics-brahmins debate-freedom-benefit-and, talk talking, refutation-benefit-and. Master but Gotama what-benefit lives?"

"Master Gotama, I am one who sits down in parks and frequents assemblies. After the meal, Master Gotama, when I have eaten breakfast, this is my custom: I walk and wander from park to park, from garden to garden. There I see some ascetics and brahmins engaging in talk for the benefit of freeing [their doctrines from criticism] in debate and for the benefit of refuting [the doctrines of others]. But [having] what benefit does Master Gotama live?"

"Vijjāvimuttiphalānisaṃso kho, kuṇḍaliya, tathāgato viharatī"ti

"Clear-knowledge-liberation-fruit-benefit, Kuṇḍaliya, the Tathāgata lives."

"The Tathāgata, Kuṇḍaliya, lives [having] the fruit and benefit of clear knowledge and liberation."

"Katame pana, bho gotama, dhammā bhāvitā bahulīkatā vijjāvimuttiṃ paripūrentī"ti?

"Satta kho, kuṇḍaliya, bojjhaṅgā bhāvitā bahulīkatā vijjāvimuttiṃ paripūrentī"ti.

"What but, Master Gotama, things developed cultivated clear-knowledge-liberation fulfill?"

"Seven, Kuṇḍaliya, enlightenment-factors developed cultivated clear-knowledge-liberation fulfill."

"But, Master Gotama, what things, developed and cultivated, fulfill clear knowledge and liberation?"

"The seven factors of enlightenment, Kuṇḍaliya, when developed and cultivated, fulfill clear knowledge and liberation."

"Katame pana, bho gotama, dhammā bhāvitā bahulīkatā satta bojjhaṅge paripūrentī"ti?

"Cattāro kho, kuṇḍaliya, satipaṭṭhānā bhāvitā bahulīkatā satta bojjhaṅge paripūrentī"ti.

"What but, Master Gotama, things developed cultivated seven enlightenment-factors fulfill?"

"Four, Kuṇḍaliya, mindfulness-establishments developed cultivated seven enlightenment-factors fulfill."

"But, Master Gotama, what things, when developed and cultivated, fulfill the seven factors of enlightenment?"

"The four establishments of mindfulness, Kuṇḍaliya, when developed and cultivated, fulfill the seven factors of enlightenment."

"Katame pana, bho gotama, dhammā bhāvitā bahulīkatā cattāro satipaṭṭhāne paripūrentī"ti?

"Tīṇi kho, kuṇḍaliya, sucaritāni bhāvitāni bahulīkatāni cattāro satipaṭṭhāne paripūrentī"ti.

"What but, Master Gotama, things developed cultivated four mindfulness-establishments fulfill?"

"Three, Kuṇḍaliya, good-conducts developed cultivated four mindfulness-establishments fulfill."

"But, Master Gotama, what things, when developed and cultivated, fulfill the four establishments of mindfulness?"

"The three kinds of good conduct, Kuṇḍaliya, when developed and cultivated, fulfill the four establishments of mindfulness."

"Katame pana, bho gotama, dhammā bhāvitā bahulīkatā tīṇi sucaritāni paripūrentī"ti?

"Indriyasaṃvaro kho, kuṇḍaliya, bhāvito bahulīkato tīṇi sucaritāni paripūretī"ti.

"What but, Master Gotama, things developed cultivated three good-conducts fulfill?"

"Faculties-restraint, Kuṇḍaliya, developed cultivated three good-conducts fulfill."

"But, Master Gotama, what things, developed and cultivated, fulfill the three kinds of good conduct?"

"Restraint of the [sense] faculties, Kuṇḍaliya, when developed and cultivated, fulfills the three kinds of good conduct."

[2. Restraint of the senses]

"Kathaṃ bhāvito ca, kuṇḍaliya, indriyasaṃvaro kathaṃ bahulīkato tīṇi sucaritāni paripūreti? Idha, kuṇḍaliya, bhikkhu cakkhunā rūpaṃ disvā manāpaṃ nābhijjhati nābhihaṃsati na rāgaṃ janeti. Tassa ṭhito ca kāyo hoti ṭhitaṃ cittaṃ ajjhattaṃ susaṇṭhitaṃ suvimuttaṃ.

"How developed and, Kuṇḍaliya, faculties-restraint, how cultivated, three good-conducts fulfills? Here, Kuṇḍaliya, a monk with the eye a form having seen, agreeable not-longs-for, not-rejoices, not lust generates. His steady and body is, steady mind, inwardly well-composed, well-liberated.

"And how, Kuṇḍaliya, is restraint of the [sense] faculties developed, how cultivated, so that it fulfills the three kinds of good conduct? Here, Kuṇḍaliya, having seen a form with the eye, a monk does not long for one that is agreeable, does not rejoice in it, does not generate lust for it. His body is steady and his mind is steady, inwardly well composed, well liberated.

"Cakkhunā kho pan'eva rūpaṃ disvā amanāpaṃ na maṅku hoti appatiṭṭhīnacitto[223] *adīnamānaso avyāpannacetaso. Tassa ṭhito ca kāyo hoti ṭhitaṃ cittaṃ ajjhattaṃ susaṇṭhitaṃ suvimuttaṃ.*

"With the eye but a form having seen, disagreeable not dismayed is, undaunted-mind, undejected-mind, without-ill-will-mind. His steady and body is, steady mind, inwardly well-composed, well-liberated.

"But having seen a form with the eye, he is not dismayed by one that is disagreeable, not daunted in mind, not dejected in mind, without ill will. His body is steady and his mind is steady, inwardly well composed and well liberated.

223. I follow the reading suggested by DOP, which explains *appatiṭṭhīna* or *appatitthīna* as the negative past participle of *patiṭṭhīyati*. Ce has *apatitthinacitto*. Be and Ee *appatiṭṭhitacitto* is surely a mistake.

"Puna caparaṃ, kuṇḍaliya, bhikkhu sotena saddaṃ sutvā . . . ghānena gandhaṃ ghāyitvā. . . jivhāya rasaṃ sāyitvā. . . kāyena phoṭṭhabbaṃ phusitvā . . . manasā dhammaṃ viññāya manāpaṃ nābhijjhati nābhihaṃsati, na rāgaṃ janeti. Tassa ṭhito ca kāyo hoti ṭhitaṃ cittaṃ ajjhattaṃ susaṇṭhitaṃ suvimuttaṃ. Manasā kho pan'eva dhammaṃ viññāya amanāpaṃ na maṅku hoti appatitthīnacitto adīnamānaso avyāpannacetaso. Tassa ṭhito ca kāyo hoti, ṭhitaṃ cittaṃ ajjhattaṃ susaṇṭhitaṃ suvimuttaṃ.

"Again further, Kuṇḍaliya, a monk with the ear a sound having heard . . . with the nose an odor having smelled . . . with the tongue a taste having tasted . . . with the body a tactile having felt . . . with the mind a mental-object having cognized, agreeable not-longs-for, not rejoices, not lust generates. His steady and body is, steady mind, inwardly well-composed well-liberated. With the mind but a mental-object having cognized, disagreeable not dismayed is, undaunted-mind, undejected-mind, without-ill-will-mind. His steady and body is, steady mind, inwardly well-composed, well-liberated.

"Further, Kuṇḍaliya, having heard a sound with the ear . . . having smelled an odor with the nose . . . having tasted a taste with the tongue . . . having felt a tactile object with the body . . . having cognized a mental object with the mind, a monk does not long for one that is agreeable, does not rejoice in it, does not generate lust for it. His body is steady and his mind is steady, inwardly well composed and well liberated. But having cognized a mental object with the mind, he is not dismayed by one that is disagreeable, not daunted in mind, not dejected in mind, without ill will. His body is steady and his mind is steady, inwardly well composed and well liberated.

"Yato kho, kuṇḍaliya, bhikkhuno cakkhunā rūpaṃ disvā manāpāmanāpesu rūpesu ṭhito ca kāyo hoti ṭhitaṃ cittaṃ ajjhattaṃ susaṇṭhitaṃ suvimuttaṃ; sotena saddaṃ sutvā . . . ghānena gandhaṃ ghāyitvā . . . jivhāya rasaṃ sāyitvā . . . kāyena phoṭṭhabbaṃ phusitvā . . . manasā dhammaṃ viññāya manāpāmanāpesu dhammesu ṭhito ca kāyo hoti ṭhitaṃ cittaṃ ajjhattaṃ susaṇṭhitaṃ suvimuttaṃ, evaṃ bhāvito kho, kuṇḍaliya, indriyasaṃvaro evaṃ bahulīkato tīṇi sucaritāni paripūreti.

"When, Kuṇḍaliya, of a monk with the eye a form having seen, in regard to agreeable-disagreeable forms steady and body is, steady mind, inwardly well-composed, well-liberated; with the ear a sound having heard . . . with the nose an odor having smelled . . . with the tongue a taste having tasted . . . with the body a tactile having felt . . . with the mind a mental-object having cognized, in regard to agreeable-disagreeable mental-objects steady and body is, steady mind, inwardly well-composed, well-liberated, thus developed, Kuṇḍaliya, faculties-restraint, thus cultivated, three good-conducts fulfills.

"When, Kuṇḍaliya, after he has seen a form with the eye, a monk's body is steady and his mind is steady, inwardly well composed and well liberated in regard to agreeable and disagreeable forms; when, after he has heard a sound with the ear . . . smelled an odor with the nose . . . tasted a taste with the tongue . . . felt a tactile object with the body . . . cognized a mental object with the mind, a monk's body is steady and his mind is steady, inwardly well composed and well liberated in regard to agreeable and disagreeable mental objects, then his restraint of the [sense] faculties has been developed and cultivated in such a way that it fulfills the three kinds of good conduct.

[3. From good conduct to liberation]

"Kathaṃ bhāvitāni ca, kuṇḍaliya, tīṇi sucaritāni kathaṃ bahulīkatāni cattāro satipaṭṭhāne paripūrenti? Idha, kuṇḍaliya, bhikkhu kāyaduccaritaṃ pahāya kāyasucaritaṃ bhāveti; vacīduccaritaṃ pahāya vacīsucaritaṃ bhāveti; manoduccaritaṃ pahāya manosucaritaṃ bhāveti. Evaṃ bhāvitāni kho, kuṇḍaliya, tīṇi sucaritāni evaṃ bahulīkatāni cattāro satipaṭṭhāne paripūrenti.

"How developed and, Kuṇḍaliya, three good-conducts, how cultivated, four mindfulness-establishments fulfill? Here, Kuṇḍaliya, a monk body-misconduct having abandoned, body-good-conduct develops; speech-misconduct having abandoned, speech-good-conduct develops; mind-misconduct having abandoned, mind-good-conduct develops. Thus developed, Kuṇḍaliya, three good-conducts, thus cultivated, four mindfulness-establishments fulfill.

"And how, Kuṇḍaliya, are the three kinds of good conduct developed, how cultivated, so that they fulfill the four establishments of mindfulness? Here, Kuṇḍaliya, having abandoned misconduct of body, a monk develops good conduct of body; having abandoned misconduct of speech, he develops good conduct of speech; having abandoned misconduct of mind, he develops good conduct of mind. When the three kinds of good conduct have been developed and cultivated in such a way, they fulfill the four establishments of mindfulness.

"Kathaṃ bhāvitā ca, kuṇḍaliya, cattāro satipaṭṭhānā kathaṃ bahulīkatā satta bojjhaṅge paripūrenti? Idha, kuṇḍaliya, bhikkhu kāye kāyānupassī viharati ātāpī sampajāno satimā, vineyya loke abhijjhādomanassaṃ; vedanāsu vedanānupassī viharati . . . citte cittānupassī viharati . . . dhammesu dhammānupassī viharati ātāpī sampajāno satimā, vineyya loke abhijjhādomanassaṃ. Evaṃ bhāvitā kho, kuṇḍaliya, cattāro satipaṭṭhānā evaṃ bahulīkatā satta bojjhaṅge paripūrenti.

"How developed and, Kuṇḍaliya, four mindfulness-establishments, how cultivated, seven enlightenment-factors fulfill? Here, Kuṇḍaliya, a monk in the body body-contemplating dwells, ardent, clearly-comprehending, mindful, having removed in the world longing-dejection; in feelings feeling-contemplating dwells . . . in the mind mind-contemplating dwells . . . in phenomena phenomena-contemplating dwells, ardent, clearly-comprehending, mindful, having removed in the world longing-dejection. Thus developed, Kuṇḍaliya, four mindfulness-establishments, thus cultivated, seven enlightenment-factors fulfill.

"And how, Kuṇḍaliya, are the four establishments of mindfulness developed, how cultivated, so that they fulfill the seven factors of enlightenment? Here, Kuṇḍaliya, a monk dwells contemplating the body in the body, ardent, clearly comprehending, mindful, having removed longing and dejection in regard to the world; he dwells contemplating feelings in feelings . . . contemplating the mind in the mind . . . contemplating phenomena in phenomena, ardent, clearly comprehending, mindful, having removed longing and dejection in regard to the world. When the four establishments of mindfulness have been developed and cultivated in such a way, they fulfill the seven factors of enlightenment.

"Kathaṃ bhāvitā ca, kuṇḍaliya, satta bojjhaṅgā kathaṃ bahulīkatā vijjāvimuttiṃ paripūrenti? Idha, kuṇḍaliya, bhikkhu satisambojjhaṅgaṃ bhāveti vivekanissitaṃ virāganissitaṃ nirodhanissitaṃ vossaggapariṇāmiṃ . . . upekkhāsambojjhaṅgaṃ bhāveti vivekanissitaṃ virāganissitaṃ nirodhanissitaṃ vossaggapariṇāmiṃ. Evaṃ bhāvitā kho, kuṇḍaliya, satta bojjhaṅgā evaṃ bahulīkatā vijjāvimuttiṃ paripūrenti"ti.

"How developed and, Kuṇḍaliya, seven enlightenment-factors, how cultivated, clear-knowledge-liberation fulfill? Here, Kuṇḍaliya, a monk mindfulness-enlightenment-factor develops, seclusion-based, dispassion-based, cessation-based, release-evolving-toward . . . equanimity-enlightenment-factor develops, seclusion-based, dispassion-based, cessation-based, release-evolving-toward. Thus developed, Kuṇḍaliya, seven enlightenment-factors, thus cultivated, clear-knowledge-liberation fulfill."

"And how, Kuṇḍaliya, are the seven factors of enlightenment developed, how cultivated, so that they fulfill clear knowledge and liberation? Here, Kuṇḍaliya, a monk develops the enlightenment factor of mindfulness based on seclusion, based on dispassion, based on cessation, evolving toward release. . . . He develops the enlightenment factor of equanimity, which is based on seclusion, based on dispassion, based on cessation, evolving toward release. When the seven factors of enlightenment have been developed and cultivated in such a way, they fulfill clear knowledge and liberation."

[4. Going for refuge]

Evaṃ vutte kuṇḍaliyo paribbājako bhagavantaṃ etadavoca: "Abhikkantaṃ, bho gotama, abhikkantaṃ, bho gotama! Seyyathāpi, bho gotama, nikkujjitaṃ vā ukkujjeyya, paṭicchannaṃ vā vivareyya, mūḷhassa vā maggaṃ ācikkheyya, andhakāre vā telapajjotaṃ dhāreyya, 'Cakkhumanto rūpāni dakkhantī'ti, evameva bhotā gotamena anekapariyāyena dhammo pakāsito.

Thus said, Kuṇḍaliya the wanderer to the Blessed One this-said: "Excellent, Master Gotama, excellent, Master Gotama! Just as, Master Gotama, over-turned or would turn upright, concealed or would reveal, to one lost or the path would point out, in darkness or oil-lamp would hold, 'Eye-possessors forms will see,' just so by Master Gotama by many-way the Dhamma revealed.

When such was said, the wanderer Kuṇḍaliya said this to the Blessed One: "Excellent, Master Gotama, excellent, Master Gotama! Just as, Master Gotama, one would turn upright what had been overturned, or would reveal what was concealed, or would point out the path to one who is lost, or would hold up an oil lamp in the darkness, [thinking,] 'Those with eyes will see forms,' just so the Dhamma has been revealed in many ways by Master Gotama.

"Esāhaṃ bhavantaṃ gotamaṃ saraṇaṃ gacchāmi dhammañca bhikkhu-saṅghañca. Upāsakaṃ maṃ bhavaṃ gotamo dhāretu ajjatagge pāṇupetaṃ saraṇaṃ gatan"ti.

"This-I Master Gotama refuge go, the Dhamma-and the monk-sangha-and. Lay-disciple me Master Gotama let consider today-onward life-endowed refuge gone."

"I go to Master Gotama as a refuge, to the Dhamma, and to the monastic Sangha. Let Master Gotama consider me a lay disciple who from today, as long as he is endowed with life, has gone for refuge."

Grammatical explanations

[1. The wanderer's questions]

bho: the vocative of the honorific form of address, *bhavat* in the stem form. The nominative singular *bhavaṃ* occurs just below.

ārāmanisādī parisāvacaro: "one who sits down in parks and frequents assemblies." The two compounds, which occur only in this passage, qualify the first-person pronoun *ahaṃ*.[224]

bhuttapātarāsassa: "when I have eaten breakfast"; a bahubbīhi composed of the past participle *bhutta*, "eaten," and *pātarāsa*, "breakfast," in the genitive case, agreeing with *tassa mayhaṃ*.

ārāmena ārāmaṃ uyyānena uyyānaṃ: "from park to park, from garden to garden." The instrumental is used here in an ablative sense.

itivādappamokkhānisaṃsañc'eva kathaṃ kathente upārambhānisaṃsañca: "engaging in talk for the benefit of freeing [their doctrines from criticism] in debate and for the benefit of refuting [the doctrines of others]." The present participle *kathente* is a plural accusative in agreement with *samaṇabrāhmaṇe*, "ascetics and brahmins." It takes a cognate accusative object, *kathaṃ*, which is described by two bahubbīhis, *itivādappamokkhānisaṃsaṃ* and *upārambhānisaṃsaṃ*. My rendering of these obscure expressions follows the explanation in the commentary.[225] DOP defines

224. The second compound, composed of two nouns and qualifying the speaker, is clearly a bahubbīhi. The first appears to be a tappurisa.

225. Spk III 145,17–21: *Itivādappamokkhānisaṃsan ti "evaṃ pucchā hoti, evaṃ vissajjanaṃ, evaṃ gahaṇaṃ, evaṃ nibbeṭhanan"ti iminā nayena itivādo hoti itivādappamokkho ti etaṃ*

itivāda as "discussion, debate" and "criticism," but the former seems to agree better with the commentarial explanation.

bhavaṃ: nominative singular of the honorific, here qualifying *gotamo*.

kimānisaṃso: "[having] what benefit"; a bahubbīhi composed of an interrogative pronoun and a noun, here qualifying *gotamo*.

vijjāvimuttiphalānisaṃso: "[having] the fruit and benefit of clear knowledge and liberation." A complex bahubbīhi compound in agreement with *tathāgato*. It contains two subordinate dvandas, *vijjāvimutti* and *phalānisaṃso*, joined in a kammadhāraya relationship: "the fruit and benefit that is knowledge and liberation." Yet as qualifying *tathāgato*, the whole compound is a bahubbīhi.

bhāvitā bahulīkatā: "developed [and] cultivated"; past participles respectively of *bhāveti* and *bahulīkaroti*, here masculine plural nominatives qualifying *dhammā*. The pair recur throughout this series, taking on the number and gender of the nouns they qualify.

[2. Restraint of the senses]

appatitthīnacitto adīnamānaso avyāpannacetaso: "not daunted in mind, not dejected in mind, without a mind of ill will." The three bahubbīhis qualify *bhikkhu*, mentioned just above.

[4. Going for refuge]

evaṃ vutte: "when such was said"; a locative absolute, with *evaṃ*, an adverb of manner in place of a locative noun or pronoun.

nikkujjitaṃ: "overturned"; a past participle used as a noun, in the accusative case as the object of *ukkujjeyya*.

paṭicchannaṃ: "hidden"; another past participle used as a noun, also accusative.

mūḷhassa: "one confused"; a past participle of *muyhati*, in the dative.

cakkhumanto: "those with eyes"; nominative plural of *cakkhumat*.

dakkhanti: "will see"; a third-person plural future of **dassati*.

ānisaṃsaṃ. Upārambhānisaṃsan ti "ayaṃ pucchāya doso, ayaṃ vissajjane"ti evaṃ vādadosānisaṃsaṃ. ("*The benefit of freeing* [*their doctrines*] *in debate*: 'Such is the question, such is the answer, such is the critique, such is the disentangling [of one's position from the critique].' In such a way there is a debate and this benefit—the freeing [of one's doctrine from criticism] in debate. *The benefit of refuting*: 'This is the fault in the question, this [is the fault] in the reply': such is the benefit of [ascribing] faults to a doctrine.")

bhotā gotamena anekapariyāyena dhammo pakāsito: "the Dhamma has been revealed in many ways by Master Gotama." *Bhotā* is the instrumental singular of *bhavat*, in apposition to *gotamena*. Note the passive syntax, with *dhammo* being at once the object of the action but the grammatical subject in the nominative case. The action is indicated by the past participle *pakāsito* qualifying *dhammo*; the logical subject, or effective agent, is represented by the instrumental *bhotā gotamena*.

esāhaṃ: a sandhi of *eso* and *ahaṃ*, both referring to the wanderer himself. The duplication is again for emphasis.

bhavantaṃ gotamaṃ saraṇaṃ gacchāmi: "I go to Master Gotama as a refuge." *Bhavantaṃ* is the accusative singular of *bhavat*, here agreeing with *gotamaṃ*. In the formula for refuge, both the word for refuge, *saraṇaṃ*, and the object of refuge, *bhavantaṃ gotamaṃ* (and *dhammaṃ* and *saṅghaṃ*) are accusatives of the verb *gacchāmi*. This contrasts with the usual English rendering: "I go *for* refuge *to* the Buddha." The fact that the wanderer addresses the Buddha as *bho gotama* and goes for refuge to *bhavantaṃ gotamaṃ* rather than to *bhagavantaṃ* suggests he was a brahmin. Such was the way brahmins spoke to and about the Buddha, whereas non-brahmins would use *bhagavat* in its various cases.

upāsakaṃ maṃ bhavaṃ gotamo dhāretu: "Let Master Gotama remember me as a lay disciple." Here both the pronoun *maṃ* by which the wanderer refers to himself and the condition entered, that of being an *upāsaka*, are accusatives in relation to the polite third-person singular imperative *dhāretu*, "let [him] remember."

ajjatagge: "starting from today." DOP explains this indeclinable as either *ajjato* + *agge*, or *ajja-t-agge*, with *-t-* as a liaison consonant.[226]

pāṇupetaṃ: "endowed with life"; an instrumental tappurisa composed of *pāṇa* and *upetaṃ*, in the accusative case as qualifying *maṃ*.

226. Both Duroiselle §28 and Collins 5 cite *ajjatagge* as an example of *-t-* used as a liaison consonant.

6. Gilānasutta
Ill (SN 46:14; V 79–80)

Ekaṃ samayaṃ bhagavā rājagahe viharati veḷuvane kalandakanivāpe. Tena kho pana samayena āyasmā mahākassapo pipphaliguhāyaṃ viharati ābādhiko dukkhito bāḷhagilāno. Atha kho bhagavā sāyanhasamayaṃ paṭisallānā vuṭṭhito yen'āyasmā mahākassapo ten'upasaṅkami. Upasaṅkamitvā paññatte āsane nisīdi. Nisajja kho bhagavā āyasmantaṃ mahākassapaṃ etadavoca: "Kacci te, kassapa, khamanīyaṃ kacci yāpanīyaṃ? Kacci dukkhā vedanā paṭikkamanti, no abhikkamanti, paṭikkamosānaṃ paññāyati, no abhikkamo"ti?

One occasion the Blessed One at Rājagaha was dwelling in the bamboo grove, in the squirrel-feeding-ground. By that occasion the Venerable Mahākassapa in the pipphali-cave[227] was dwelling, afflicted, sick, severely-ill. Then the Blessed One evening-time from seclusion emerged, where the Venerable Mahākassapa, there approached. Having approached, in a prepared seat sat down. Having sat down, the Blessed One to the Venerable Mahākassapa this-said: "Is it the case by you, Kassapa, bearing-up? Is it the case getting-along? Is it the case painful feelings retreating, not advancing, retreat is discerned, not advance?"

On one occasion the Blessed One was dwelling at Rājagaha in the bamboo grove, in the squirrels' feeding ground. Now on that occasion the Venerable Mahākassapa was dwelling in the pipphali cave, afflicted, sick, severely ill. Then in the evening, when he emerged from seclusion, the Blessed One approached the Venerable Mahākassapa. Having approached, he sat down in the prepared seat. Having sat down, the Blessed One said this to the Venerable Mahākassapa: "Are you bearing up, Kassapa? Are you getting healthy? Are your painful feelings retreating, not advancing, [so that] their retreat, not their advance, is discerned?"

227. PED defines *pipphalī* as "long pepper." However, according to the Pāli commentaries, Mahākassapa's name in lay life was "Pipphali," so the cave may have been named after him.

"Na me, bhante, khamanīyaṃ, na yāpanīyaṃ. Bāḷhā me dukkhā vedanā abhikkamanti, no paṭikkamanti, abhikkamosānaṃ paññāyati, no paṭikkamo"ti.

"Not by me, Bhante, bearing-up, not getting-along. Severe of me painful feelings are advancing, not retreating, advance is discerned, not retreat."

"I am not bearing up, Bhante, not getting healthy. My severe painful feelings are advancing, not retreating, [so that] their advance, not their retreat, is discerned."

"Satt'ime, kassapa, bojjhaṅgā mayā sammadakkhātā bhāvitā bahulīkatā abhiññāya saṃbodhāya nibbānāya saṃvattanti. Katame satta? Satisambojjhaṅgo kho, kassapa, mayā sammadakkhāto bhāvito bahulīkato abhiññāya sambodhāya nibbānāya saṃvattati. . . . Upekkhāsambojjhaṅgo kho, kassapa, mayā sammadakkhāto bhāvito bahulīkato abhiññāya sambodhāya nibbānāya saṃvattati. Ime kho, kassapa, satta bojjhaṅgā mayā sammadakkhātā bhāvitā bahulīkatā abhiññāya sambodhāya nibbānāya saṃvattantī"ti.

"Seven these, Kassapa, enlightenment-factors by me rightly-expounded, developed cultivated, to direct-knowledge, to enlightenment, to nibbāna lead. What seven? The mindfulness-enlightenment-factor, Kassapa, by me rightly-expounded, developed cultivated, to direct-knowledge, to enlightenment, to nibbāna leads. . . . The equanimity-enlightenment-factor, Kassapa, by me rightly-expounded, developed cultivated, to direct-knowledge, to enlightenment, to nibbāna leads. These, Kassapa, seven enlightenment-factors by me rightly expounded, developed cultivated, to direct-knowledge, to enlightenment, to nibbāna lead."

"These seven factors of enlightenment, Kassapa, rightly expounded by me, when developed and cultivated, lead to direct knowledge, to enlightenment, to nibbāna. What seven? The enlightenment factor of mindfulness, Kassapa, rightly expounded by me, when developed and cultivated, leads to direct knowledge, to enlightenment, to nibbāna. . . . The enlightenment factor of equanimity, Kassapa, rightly expounded by me, when developed and cultivated, leads to direct knowledge, to enlightenment, to nibbāna. These seven factors of enlightenment, Kassapa, rightly expounded by me, when developed and cultivated, lead to direct knowledge, to enlightenment, to nibbāna."

"Taggha, bhagavā, bojjhaṅgā! Taggha, sugata, bojjhaṅgā!"ti.

"Certainly, Blessed One, enlightenment-factors. Certainly, Fortunate One, enlightenment-factors."

"Certainly, Blessed One, [they are] enlightenment factors! Certainly, Fortunate One, [they are] enlightenment factors!"

Idamavoca bhagavā. Attamano āyasmā mahākassapo bhagavato bhāsitaṃ abhinandi. Vuṭṭhahi c'āyasmā mahākassapo tamhā ābādhā. Tathāpahīno c'āyasmato mahākassapassa so ābādho ahosī ti.

This-said the Blessed One. Elated the Venerable Mahākassapa the Blessed One's statement delighted in. Recovered and the Venerable Mahākassapa from that affliction. Thus-abandoned and of the Venerable Mahākassapa that affliction was.

This is what the Blessed One said. Elated, the Venerable Mahākassapa delighted in the Blessed One's statement. And the Venerable Mahākassapa recovered from that affliction. And thus that affliction was abandoned by the Venerable Mahākassapa.

Grammatical explanations

kacci te, kassapa, khamanīyaṃ kacci yāpanīyaṃ: see p. 420.

sammadakkhātā: a kammadhāraya compound with *-d-* serving as a liaison consonant between the indeclinable *sammā* and the past participle *akkhātā*, "expounded." The compound is nominative plural because all seven factors are being referred to, but when each is taken individually the number changes to singular.

abhiññāya sambodhāya nibbānāya: "to direct knowledge, to enlightenment, to nibbāna." These are datives of purpose or direction; the nouns are respectively feminine, masculine, and neuter.

taggha: an exclamatory particle indicating affirmation, "surely, certainly, indeed."

vuṭṭhahi: "recovered" (literally, "rose up"); a third-person singular aorist (of *vuṭṭhahati* or *vuṭṭhāti*), taking its dependent words in the ablative, here *tamhā ābādhā*, "from that affliction."

tathāpahīno: "thus abandoned." I am reading this as a kammadhāraya compound made up of an adverb and past participle (see Perniola §129), but it is also possible to separate the two words, with *tathā* an adverb of manner modifying *pahīno*.

7. Aggisutta

Fire (SN 46:53; V 112–15)

[*At the beginning of the discourse a number of monks, out on their alms round, visit the park where the wanderers of other sects dwell. The wanderers tell the monks that they too, just like the Buddha, teach their disciples to abandon the five hindrances and develop the seven factors of enlightenment. So, they ask, what is the difference between the ascetic Gotama and themselves with respect to their manner of teaching? Without responding, the monks return to the Buddha after their alms round and ask this question. The Buddha answers as follows:*]

[1. The challenge]

"Evaṃvādino, bhikkhave, aññatitthiyā paribbājakā evamassu vacanīyā: 'Yasmiṃ, āvuso, samaye līnaṃ cittaṃ hoti, katamesaṃ tasmiṃ samaye bojjhaṅgānaṃ akālo bhāvanāya, katamesaṃ tasmiṃ samaye bojjhaṅgānaṃ kālo bhāvanāya? Yasmiṃ panāvuso, samaye uddhataṃ cittaṃ hoti, katamesaṃ tasmiṃ samaye bojjhaṅgānaṃ akālo bhāvanāya, katamesaṃ tasmiṃ samaye bojjhaṅgānaṃ kālo bhāvanāyā'ti?

"Thus-speakers, monks, other-sect wanderers thus should-be-told: 'On which, friends, occasion sluggish the mind is, of which on that occasion enlightenment-factors not-time for development, of which on that occasion enlightenment-factors time for development? On which but-friends, occasion excited the mind is, of which on that occasion enlightenment-factors not-time for development, of which on that occasion enlightenment-factors time for development?'

"Wanderers of other sects who speak thus should be told thus: 'On an occasion, friends, when the mind is sluggish, on that occasion which factors of enlightenment is it not the time to develop, and which factors of enlightenment is it the time to develop? But, friends, on an occasion when the mind is excited, on that occasion which factors of enlightenment is it not the time to develop, and which factors of enlightenment is it the time to develop?'

"Evaṃ puṭṭhā, bhikkhave, aññatitthiyā paribbājakā na c'eva sampāyissanti, uttariñca vighātaṃ āpajjissanti. Taṃ kissa hetu? Yathā taṃ, bhikkhave, avisayasmiṃ.

"Thus asked, monks, other-sect wanderers not and will succeed, further-and distress will incur. That for what reason? As that, monks, not-in-domain.

"Asked thus, monks, wanderers of other sects will not succeed [in replying], and further, they will incur distress. For what reason? Because, monks, that is not in their domain.

"Nāhaṃ taṃ, bhikkhave, passāmi sadevake loke samārake sabrahmake, sassamaṇabrāhmaṇiyā pajāya sadevamanussāya, yo imesaṃ pañhānaṃ veyyākaraṇena cittaṃ ārādheyya aññatra tathāgatena vā tathāgatasāvakena vā ito vā pana sutvā.

"Not-I him, monks, see in with-devas world, with-Māra with-Brahmā, in with-ascetics-brahmins population, with-devas-humans, who of these questions with answer the mind could satisfy, apart by the Tathāgata or by a Tathāgata-disciple or from here or having heard.

"I do not see anyone, monks, in the world with its devas, with Māra, with Brahmā, in this population with its ascetics and brahmins, with its devas and humans, who could satisfy the mind with an answer to these questions apart from the Tathāgata or a disciple of the Tathāgata or one who has heard it from here.

[2. Stimulating the sluggish mind: not the time]
"Yasmiṃ, bhikkhave, samaye līnaṃ cittaṃ hoti, akālo tasmiṃ samaye passaddhisambojjhaṅgassa bhāvanāya, akālo samādhisambojjhaṅgassa bhāvanāya, akālo upekkhāsambojjhaṅgassa bhāvanāya. Taṃ kissa hetu? Līnaṃ, bhikkhave, cittaṃ; taṃ etehi dhammehi dussamuṭṭhāpayaṃ hoti.

"On which, monks, occasion sluggish the mind is, not-time, on that occasion, of tranquility-enlightenment-factor for development, not-time of concentration-enlightenment-factor for development, not-time of equanimity-enlightenment-factor for development. That for what reason? Sluggish, monks, the mind; that by these things hard-arousing is.

"On an occasion, monks, when the mind is sluggish, on that occasion it is not the time to develop the enlightenment factor of tranquility; it is not the time to develop the enlightenment factor of concentration; it is not the time to develop the enlightenment factor of equanimity. For what reason? Because, monks, the mind is sluggish; it is hard to arouse it with these things.

"Seyyathāpi, bhikkhave, puriso parittaṃ aggiṃ ujjāletukāmo assa. So tattha allāni c'eva tiṇāni pakkhipeyya, allāni ca gomayāni pakkhipeyya, allāni ca kaṭṭhāni pakkhipeyya, udakavātañca dadeyya, paṃsukena ca okireyya. Bhabbo nu kho so puriso parittaṃ aggiṃ ujjāletun"ti? — "No h'etaṃ, bhante."

"Suppose, monks, a person a small fire to-blaze-up-desire would be. He there wet and grass would throw, wet and cow-dung would throw, wet and sticks would throw, water-wind-and would give, with soil and would sprinkle. Capable that person a small fire to blaze up?" — "Not indeed this, Bhante."

"Suppose, monks, a person would desire to cause a small fire to blaze up. He would throw wet grass upon it, and would throw wet cow dung upon it, and would throw wet sticks upon it, and would give it a wet wind, and would sprinkle it with soil. Would that person be capable of causing a small fire to blaze up?" — "Certainly not, Bhante."

"Evameva kho, bhikkhave, yasmiṃ samaye līnaṃ cittaṃ hoti, akālo tasmiṃ samaye passaddhisambojjhaṅgassa bhāvanāya, akālo samādhisambojjhaṅ-

gassa bhāvanāya, akālo upekkhāsambojjhaṅgassa bhāvanāya. Taṃ kissa hetu? Līnaṃ, bhikkhave, cittaṃ; taṃ etehi dhammehi dussamuṭṭhāpayaṃ hoti.

"Just so, monks, on which occasion sluggish the mind is, not-time, on that occasion, of tranquility-enlightenment-factor for development, not-time of concentration-enlightenment-factor for development, not-time of equanimity-enlightenment-factor for development. That for what reason? Sluggish, monks, the mind; that by these things hard-arousing is.

"Just so, monks, on an occasion when the mind is sluggish, on that occasion it is not the time to develop the enlightenment factor of tranquility; it is not the time to develop the enlightenment factor of concentration; it is not the time to develop the enlightenment factor of equanimity. For what reason? Because, monks, the mind is sluggish; it is hard to arouse it with these things.

[3. Stimulating the sluggish mind: the time]

"Yasmiñca kho, bhikkhave, samaye līnaṃ cittaṃ hoti, kālo tasmiṃ samaye dhammavicayasambojjhaṅgassa bhāvanāya, kālo viriyasambojjhaṅgassa bhāvanāya, kālo pītisambojjhaṅgassa bhāvanāya. Taṃ kissa hetu? Līnaṃ, bhikkhave, cittaṃ; taṃ etehi dhammehi susamuṭṭhāpayaṃ hoti.

"On which-and, monks, occasion sluggish the mind is, time, on that occasion, of qualities-discrimination-enlightenment-factor for development, time of energy-enlightenment-factor for development, time of rapture-enlightenment-factor for development. That for what reason? Sluggish, monks, the mind; that by these things easy-arousing is.

"On an occasion, monks, when the mind is sluggish, on that occasion it is the time to develop the enlightenment factor of discrimination of qualities; it is the time to develop the enlightenment factor of energy; it is the time to develop the enlightenment factor of rapture. For what reason? Because, monks, the mind is sluggish; it is easy to arouse it with these things.

"Seyyathāpi, bhikkhave, puriso parittaṃ aggiṃ ujjāletukāmo assa. So tattha sukkhāni c'eva tiṇāni pakkhipeyya, sukkhāni gomayāni pakkhipeyya,

sukkhāni kaṭṭhāni pakkhipeyya, mukhavātañca dadeyya, na ca paṃsukena okireyya. Bhabbo nu kho so puriso parittaṃ aggiṃ ujjāletun"ti? — "Evaṃ, bhante."

"Suppose, monks, a person a small fire to-blaze-up-desire would be. He there dry and grass would throw, dry and cow-dung would throw, dry and sticks would throw, mouth-wind-and would give, not and with soil would sprinkle. Capable that person a small fire to blaze up?" — "Yes, Bhante."

"Suppose, monks, a person would desire to cause a small fire to blaze up. He would throw dry grass upon it, and would throw dry cow dung upon it, and would throw dry sticks upon it, and would blow on it with his mouth, and would not sprinkle it with soil. Would that person be capable of causing a small fire to blaze up?" — "Yes, Bhante."

"Evameva kho, bhikkhave, yasmiṃ samaye līnaṃ cittaṃ hoti, kālo tasmiṃ samaye dhammavicayasambojjhaṅgassa bhāvanāya, kālo viriyasambojjhaṅgassa bhāvanāya, kālo pītisambojjhaṅgassa bhāvanāya. Taṃ kissa hetu? Līnaṃ, bhikkhave, cittaṃ; taṃ etehi dhammehi susamuṭṭhāpayaṃ hoti.

"Just so, monks, on which occasion sluggish the mind is, time, on that occasion, of qualities-discrimination-enlightenment-factor for development, time of energy-enlightenment-factor for development, time of rapture-enlightenment-factor for development. That for what reason? Sluggish, monks, the mind; that by these things easy-arousing is.

"Just so, monks, on an occasion when the mind is sluggish, on that occasion it is the time to develop the enlightenment factor of discrimination of qualities; it is the time to develop the enlightenment factor of energy; it is the time to develop the enlightenment factor of rapture. For what reason? Because, monks, the mind is sluggish; it is easy to arouse it with these things.

[4. Calming the excited mind: not the time]

"Yasmiṃ, bhikkhave, samaye uddhataṃ cittaṃ hoti, akālo tasmiṃ samaye dhammavicayasambojjhaṅgassa bhāvanāya, akālo viriyasambojjhaṅgassa bhāvanāya, akālo pītisambojjhaṅgassa bhāvanāya. Taṃ kissa hetu? Uddhataṃ, bhikkhave, cittaṃ; taṃ etehi dhammehi duvūpasamayaṃ hoti.

"On which, monks, occasion excited the mind is, not-time, on that occasion, of qualities-discrimination-enlightenment-factor for development, not-time of energy-enlightenment-factor for development, not-time of rapture-enlightenment-factor for development. That for what reason? Excited, monks, the mind; that by these things hard-calming is.

"On an occasion, monks, when the mind is excited, on that occasion it is not the time to develop the enlightenment factor of discrimination of qualities; it is not the time to develop the enlightenment factor of energy; it is not the time to develop the enlightenment factor of rapture. For what reason? Because, monks, the mind is excited; it is hard to calm it down with these things.

"Seyyathāpi, bhikkhave, puriso mahantaṃ aggikkhandhaṃ nibbāpetukāmo assa. So tattha sukkhāni c'eva tiṇāni pakkhipeyya, sukkhāni ca gomayāni pakkhipeyya, sukkhāni ca kaṭṭhāni pakkhipeyya, mukhavātañca dadeyya, na ca paṃsukena okireyya. Bhabbo nu kho so puriso mahantaṃ aggikkhandhaṃ nibbāpetun"ti? — "No h'etaṃ, bhante."

"Suppose, monks, a person a large fire-mass to-extinguish-desire would be. He there dry and grass would throw, dry and cow-dung would throw, dry and sticks would throw, mouth-wind-and would give, not and with soil would sprinkle. Capable that person a large fire-mass to extinguish?" — "Not indeed this, Bhante."

"Suppose, monks, a person would desire to extinguish a large bonfire. He would throw dry grass upon it, and would throw dry cow dung upon it, and would throw dry sticks upon it, and would blow on it with his mouth, and would not sprinkle it with soil. Would that person be capable of extinguishing a large bonfire?" — "Certainly not, Bhante."

"Evameva kho, bhikkhave, yasmiṃ samaye uddhataṃ cittaṃ hoti, akālo tasmiṃ samaye dhammavicayasambojjhaṅgassa bhāvanāya, akālo viriyasambojjhaṅgassa bhāvanāya, akālo pītisambojjhaṅgassa bhāvanāya. Taṃ kissa hetu? Uddhataṃ, bhikkhave, cittaṃ; taṃ etehi dhammehi duvūpasamayaṃ hoti.

"Just so, monks, on which occasion excited the mind is, not-time, on that occasion, of qualities-discrimination-enlightenment-factor for development, not-time of energy-enlightenment-factor for development, not-time of rapture-enlightenment-factor for development. That for what reason? Excited, monks, the mind; that by these things hard-calming is.

"Just so, monks, on an occasion when the mind is excited, on that occasion it is not the time to develop the enlightenment factor of discrimination of qualities; it is not the time to develop the enlightenment factor of energy; it is not the time to develop the enlightenment factor of rapture. For what reason? Because, monks, the mind is excited; it is hard to calm it down with these things.

[5. Calming the excited mind: the time]
"Yasmiñca kho, bhikkhave, samaye uddhataṃ cittaṃ hoti, kālo tasmiṃ samaye passaddhisambojjhaṅgassa bhāvanāya, kālo samādhisambojjhaṅgassa bhāvanāya, kālo upekkhāsambojjhaṅgassa bhāvanāya. Taṃ kissa hetu? Uddhataṃ, bhikkhave, cittaṃ; taṃ etehi dhammehi suvūpasamayaṃ hoti.

"On which, monks, occasion excited the mind is, time, on that occasion, of tranquility-enlightenment-factor for development, time of concentration-enlightenment-factor for development, time of equanimity-enlightenment-factor for development. That for what reason? Excited, monks, the mind; that by these things easy-calming is.

"On an occasion, monks, when the mind is excited, on that occasion it is the time to develop the enlightenment factor of tranquility; it is the time to develop the enlightenment factor of concentration; it is the time to develop the enlightenment factor of equanimity. For what reason? Because, monks, the mind is excited; it is easy to calm it down with these things.

"Seyyathāpi, bhikkhave, puriso mahantaṃ aggikkhandhaṃ nibbāpetukāmo assa. So tattha allāni c'eva tiṇāni pakkhipeyya, allāni ca gomayāni pakkhipeyya, allāni ca kaṭṭhāni pakkhipeyya, udakavātañca dadeyya, paṃsukena ca okireyya. Bhabbo nu kho so puriso mahantaṃ aggikkhandhaṃ nibbāpetun"ti? — "Evaṃ, bhante."

"Suppose, monks, a person a large fire-mass to-extinguish-desire would be. He there wet and grass would throw, wet and cow-dung would throw, wet and sticks would throw, water-wind-and would give, with soil and would sprinkle. Capable that person a large fire-mass to extinguish?" — "Yes, Bhante."

"Suppose, monks, a person would desire to extinguish a large bonfire. He would throw wet grass upon it, and would throw wet cow dung upon it, and would throw wet sticks upon it, and would give it a wet wind, and would sprinkle it with soil. Would that person be capable of extinguishing a large bonfire?" — "Yes, Bhante."

"Evameva kho, bhikkhave, yasmiṃ samaye uddhataṃ cittaṃ hoti, kālo tasmiṃ samaye passaddhisambojjhaṅgassa bhāvanāya, kālo samādhisambojjhaṅgassa bhāvanāya, kālo upekkhāsambojjhaṅgassa bhāvanāya. Taṃ kissa hetu? Uddhataṃ, bhikkhave, cittaṃ; taṃ etehi dhammehi suvūpasamayaṃ hoti.

"Just so, monks, on which occasion excited the mind is, time, on that occasion, of tranquility-enlightenment-factor for development, time of concentration-enlightenment-factor for development, time of equanimity-enlightenment-factor for development. That for what reason? Excited, monks, the mind; that by these things easy-calming is.

"Just so, monks, on an occasion when the mind is excited, on that occasion it is the time to develop the enlightenment factor of tranquility; it is the time to develop the enlightenment factor of concentration; it is the time to develop the enlightenment factor of equanimity. For what reason? Because, monks, the mind is excited; it is easy to calm it down with these things.

[6. The Place of Mindfulness]
"Satiñca khvāhaṃ, bhikkhave, sabbatthikaṃ vadāmī"ti.

"Mindfulness-but I, monks, everywhere-useful say."

"But mindfulness, monks, I say is useful everywhere."

Grammatical explanations

[1. The challenge]

evaṃvādino: "who speak thus"; a compound of *evaṃ* and *vādin*, "speaker," here an adjective in the nominative plural in agreement with *paribbājakā*.

aññatitthiyā paribbājakā: "wanderers [belonging to] other sects." *Aññatitthiyā* is a bahubbīhi composed of *añña*, "other," and *tittha*, a spiritual sect, with the adjectival suffix *-iyā*. The *aññatitthiyā paribbājakā* were rivals of the Buddha and his Sangha.

evamassu vacanīyā: "should be told thus." *Assu* is the third-person plural optative of *atthi*, used as an auxiliary verb of the future passive participle *vacanīyā*, which is nominative plural in agreement with *paribbājakā*. See too p. 100. In the latter passage, the impersonal neuter *vacanīyaṃ* is used in relation to an assertion, and thus was rendered: "(it) should be said." Here, however, *vacanīyā* qualifies persons, the nominative plural *paribbājakā*, and thus should be rendered: "(they) should be told."

yasmiṃ samaye, tasmiṃ samaye: These are correlated as relative and demonstrative: "on which occasion" and "on that occasion." The word *kālo* just below carries the nuance, not simply of time, but of the *right* time, as opposed to *akālo*, the *wrong* time.

bhāvanāya: "for development"; a dative of purpose.

na . . . sampāyissanti: "will not succeed." On this rare verb, I follow the explanation of the commentary to SN 46:52: "*Will not succeed*: having made the effort, they will not be able to explain."[228]

yathā taṃ, bhikkhave, avisayasmiṃ: "Because, monks, that is not in their domain." My rendering follows the paraphrase in the commentary, which explains *taṃ* as "a mere indeclinable" and *yathā* as a causal term: "because the question asked is not in their domain."[229]

nāhaṃ taṃ, bhikkhave, passāmi: "I do not see anyone, monks." The sentence inverts normal syntax by putting the main clause before the relative clause. Here, *taṃ*, the accusative object of *passāmi*, is the demonstrative pronoun correlated with the relative *yo* just below.

228. Spk III 169,20–21: *Na c'eva sampāyissantī ti sampādetvā kathetuṃ na sakkhissanti.*

229. Spk III 169,24–25: *Yathā taṃ, bhikkhave, avisayasmin ti ettha tan ti nipātamattaṃ, yathā ti kāraṇavacanaṃ, yasmā avisaye pañho pucchito ti attho.*

sadevake loke . . . sadevamanussāya: "in the world with its devas . . . with its devas and humans"; see pp. 109–10.

aññatra: "apart from," usually with the instrumental (as here) or the ablative.

ito vā pana sutvā: "or one who has heard it from here." The commentary paraphrases: "Or having heard it from my teaching."[230]

[2. Stimulating the sluggish mind: not the time]

dussamuṭṭhāpayaṃ: "hard to arouse"; a compound of the prefix *dur-* and *samuṭṭhāpaya*, "arousing," from the causative verb *samuṭṭhāpeti*. In sandhi the *-r-* of *dur-* is assimilated to the following consonant. The compound modifies *cittaṃ*.

ujjāletukāmo: "one who desires to cause to blaze up." On compounds formed from *kāma* and the infinitive, see the comment on *jīvitukāmo* on p. 415. The compound modifies *puriso*.

bhabbo: "capable"; see p. 149. It is here used with the infinitive *ujjālituṃ*.

[3. Stimulating the sluggish mind: the time]

susamuṭṭhāpayaṃ: "easy to arouse"; the opposite of *dussamuṭṭhāpayaṃ*, from *su-* and *samuṭṭhāpayaṃ*.

[4. Calming the excited mind: not the time]

duvūpasamayaṃ: "hard to calm down"; a compound of *dur-* and the noun **vūpasamaya*, from the causative verb *vūpasameti*, "calms down, allays, pacifies." Its opposite, *suvūpasamayaṃ*, "easy to calm down," is in section 5.

nibbāpetukāmo: "one who desires to extinguish"; the opposite of *ujjāletukāmo* just above. The full infinitive *nibbāpetuṃ* occurs below.

[6. The Place of Mindfulness]

satiñca khvāhaṃ, bhikkhave, sabbatthikaṃ vadāmi: "But mindfulness, monks, I say is useful everywhere." *Sabbatthikaṃ*, an adjective qualifying *satiṃ*, is ambiguous and may even have been intended to convey a double meaning. The commentary takes it to be based on the indeclinable *sabbattha*, "everywhere," because "it is desirable everywhere" (*sabbattha icchitabbaṃ*), both in restraining the mind when it is excited and

230. Spk III 169,30–31: *Ito vā pana sutvā ti ito vā pana mama sāsanato sutvā.*

in rousing it when it is sluggish. But the word might also be taken as a compound of *sabba* and *attha*, with the suffix *-ika*, "all-useful," good on all occasions.

3. The Noble Eightfold Path

1. Upaḍḍhasutta
Half (SN 45:2; V 2–3)

[1. Good friendship is the whole spiritual life]
Ekaṃ samayaṃ bhagavā sakyesu viharati nāgarakaṃ nāma sakyānaṃ nigamo. Atha kho āyasmā ānando yena bhagavā ten'upasaṅkami. Upasaṅkamitvā bhagavantaṃ abhivādetvā ekamantaṃ nisīdi. Ekamantaṃ nisinno kho āyasmā ānando bhagavantaṃ etadavoca: "Upaḍḍhamidaṃ, bhante, brahmacariyassa,[231] *yadidaṃ kalyāṇamittatā kalyāṇasahāyatā kalyāṇasampavaṅkatā"ti.*

One occasion the Blessed One among the Sakyans was dwelling, Nāgaraka named of the Sakyans town. Then the Venerable Ānanda where the Blessed One, there approached. Having approached, the Blessed One having paid homage to, one-side sat down. One-side seated, the Venerable Ānanda to the Blessed One this-said: "Half-this, Bhante, of spiritual-life, that is, good-friendship, good-companionship, good-comradeship."

On one occasion the Blessed One was dwelling among the Sakyans, [where there was] a town of the Sakyans named Nāgaraka. Then the Venerable Ānanda approached the Blessed One. Having approached, he paid homage to the Blessed One and sat down to one side. Seated to one side, the Venerable Ānanda said this to the Blessed One: "This is half of the spiritual life, Bhante—that is, good friendship, good companionship, good comradeship."

231. I follow the Ce reading. Be and Ee have *brahmacariyaṃ* here but *brahmacariyassa* in their reading of the parallel passage at SN 3:18.

"Mā h'evaṃ, ānanda! Mā h'evaṃ, ānanda! Sakalamev'idaṃ, ānanda, brahmacariyaṃ, yadidaṃ kalyāṇamittatā kalyāṇasahāyatā kalyāṇa-sampavaṅkatā. Kalyāṇamittass'etaṃ, ānanda, bhikkhuno pāṭikaṅkhaṃ kalyāṇasahāyassa kalyāṇasampavaṅkassa ariyaṃ aṭṭhaṅgikaṃ maggaṃ bhāvessati, ariyaṃ aṭṭhaṅgikaṃ maggaṃ bahulīkarissati.

"Not indeed so, Ānanda! Not indeed so, Ānanda! Whole-indeed this, Ānanda, spiritual-life, that is, good-friendship, good-companionship, good-comradeship. Of good-friend this, Ānanda, of a monk, to-be-expected, of good-companion, of good-comrade, noble eightfold path will develop, noble eightfold path will cultivate.

"Do not [speak] thus, Ānanda! Do not [speak] thus, Ānanda![232] This is indeed the whole spiritual life, Ānanda—that is, good friendship, good companionship, good comradeship. Of a monk who has a good friend, a good companion, a good comrade, Ānanda, this is to be expected: that he will develop the noble eightfold path, will cultivate the noble eightfold path.

"Kathañc'ānanda, bhikkhu kalyāṇamitto kalyāṇasahāyo kalyāṇasam-pavaṅko ariyaṃ aṭṭhaṅgikaṃ maggaṃ bhāveti, ariyaṃ aṭṭhaṅgikaṃ maggaṃ bahulīkaroti? Idh'ānanda, bhikkhu sammādiṭṭhiṃ bhāveti vivekanissitaṃ virāganissitaṃ nirodhanissitaṃ vossaggapariṇāmiṃ; sammāsaṅkappaṃ bhāveti . . . sammāvācaṃ bhāveti . . . sammākam-mantaṃ bhāveti . . . sammāājīvaṃ bhāveti . . . sammāvāyāmaṃ bhāveti . . . sammāsatiṃ bhāveti . . . sammāsamādhiṃ bhāveti vivekanissitaṃ virāganissitaṃ nirodhanissitaṃ vossaggapariṇāmiṃ. Evaṃ kho, ānanda, bhikkhu kalyāṇamitto kalyāṇasahāyo kalyāṇasampavaṅko ariyaṃ aṭṭhaṅgikaṃ maggaṃ bhāveti, ariyaṃ aṭṭhaṅgikaṃ maggaṃ bahulīkaroti.

"How-and-Ānanda, a monk good-friend, good-companion, good-comrade, noble eightfold path develops, noble eightfold path cultivates? Here, Ānanda, a monk right-view develops, seclusion-based, dispassion-based, cessation-based, release-evolving-toward; right-intention develops . . . right-speech

232. I follow the commentarial gloss at Spk I 157,11, which adds an aorist in the prohibitive sense: *Ānanda, mā evaṃ abhaṇi*. See DN II 55,12, where we find the same admonition but with the prohibitive aorist *avaca* in the text itself: *Mā h'evaṃ, ānanda, avaca, mā h'evaṃ, ānanda, avaca.*

develops . . . right-action develops . . . right-livelihood develops . . . right-effort develops . . . right-mindfulness develops . . . right-concentration develops, seclusion-based, dispassion-based, cessation-based, release-evolving-toward. Thus, Ānanda, a monk good-friend good-companion good-comrade, noble eightfold path develops, noble eightfold path cultivates.

"And how, Ānanda, does a monk who has a good friend, a good companion, a good comrade, develop the noble eightfold path, cultivate the noble eightfold path? Here, Ānanda, a monk develops right view, which is based on seclusion, based on dispassion, based on cessation, evolving toward release; he develops right intention . . . right speech . . . right action . . . right livelihood . . . right effort . . . right mindfulness . . . right concentration, which is based on seclusion, based on dispassion, based on cessation, evolving toward release. It is in such a way, Ānanda, that a monk who has a good friend, a good companion, a good comrade develops the noble eightfold path, cultivates the noble eightfold path.

[2. The Buddha as the good friend]

"Tadaminā'p'etaṃ, ānanda, pariyāyena veditabbaṃ yathā sakalamev'idaṃ brahmacariyaṃ, yadidaṃ kalyāṇamittatā kalyāṇasahāyatā kalyāṇa-sampavaṅkatā. Mamañhi, ānanda, kalyāṇamittaṃ āgamma jātidhammā sattā jātiyā parimuccanti; jarādhammā sattā jarāya parimuccanti; maraṇadhammā sattā maraṇena parimuccanti; soka-parideva-dukkha-domanass'upāyāsadhammā sattā soka-parideva-dukkha-domanass'upāyāsehi parimuccanti. Iminā kho etaṃ, ānanda, pariyāyena veditabbaṃ yathā sakalamev'idaṃ brahmacariyaṃ, yadidaṃ kalyāṇamittatā kalyāṇasahāyatā kalyāṇasampavaṅkatā"ti.

"That-by this-too this, Ānanda, by way can-be-understood how whole-indeed this spiritual-life, that is, good-friendship, good-companionship, good-comradeship. Me-indeed, Ānanda, good-friend relying-on, birth-nature beings from birth are freed; old-age-nature beings from old-age are freed; death-nature beings from death are freed; sorrow-lamentation-pain-dejection-misery-nature beings from sorrow-lamentation-pain-dejection-misery are freed. By this, this, Ānanda, by way can-be-understood how whole-indeed this spiritual-life, that is, good-friendship, good-companionship, good-comradeship."

"In this way, too, Ānanda, it can be understood how this is indeed the whole spiritual life—that is, good friendship, good companionship, good comradeship. By relying on me as a good friend, Ānanda, beings subject to birth are freed from birth; beings subject to old age are freed from old age; beings subject to death are freed from death; beings subject to sorrow, lamentation, pain, dejection, and misery are freed from sorrow, lamentation, pain, dejection, and misery. In this way, too, Ānanda, it can be understood how this is the whole spiritual life—that is, good friendship, good companionship, good comradeship."

Grammatical explanations

[1. Good friendship is the whole spiritual life]

upaḍḍhamidaṃ, bhante, brahmacariyassa: "this [is] half of the spiritual life." *Upaḍḍhamidaṃ* = *upaḍḍhaṃ* + *idaṃ*. *Upaḍḍhaṃ*, "half," can be either an adjective or a neuter noun. Here it is a neuter noun, taking genitive *brahmacariyassa* as its dependent term (but see note 231 above).

kalyāṇamittatā kalyāṇasahāyatā kalyāṇasampavaṅkatā: "good friendship, good companionship, good comradeship." These are abstract nouns formed by adding the suffix *-tā* to each of the corresponding concrete nouns, *kalyāṇamitta* and so forth.

sakalamev'idaṃ, ānanda, brahmacariyaṃ: "This is indeed the whole spiritual life." *Sakalaṃ* is an adjective qualifying *brahmacariyaṃ*, the nominative subject.

kalyāṇamittass'etaṃ, ānanda, bhikkhuno pāṭikaṅkhaṃ kalyāṇasahāyassa kalyāṇasampavaṅkassa: "Of a monk who has a good friend, a good companion, a good comrade, Ānanda, this is to be expected." Here, *kalyāṇamittassa* and the parallel terms that follow are bahubbīhis qualifying *bhikkhuno*. Thus the sense is "a monk who *has* a good friend," not "a monk who *is* a good friend." *Pāṭikaṅkhaṃ*, qualified by *etaṃ*, is a future passive participle, here impersonal neuter and referring to the clause that follows about developing the eightfold path.

aṭṭhaṅgikaṃ: "eightfold"; see p. 102.

sammādiṭṭhiṃ: The terms for the path factors are all kammadhāraya compounds composed of the adverb *sammā* and a noun. Here, as objects of *bhāveti*, they are accusatives.

tadaminā p'etaṃ, ānanda, pariyāyena veditabbaṃ: (1) *Tad* (= *taṃ*, with *-ṃ* > *-d* before the initial vowel of *aminā*) and *etaṃ* are paired pronouns referring to the statement that is to be understood—namely, that the whole of the spiritual life is good friendship. (2) *Aminā* qualifies *pariyāyena*, "by this method, in this way,"[233] the way being the Buddha's role in liberating beings from birth, old age, and death. (3) And *-p-* is a contraction of *pi*, "too."

mamañhi, ānanda, kalyāṇamittaṃ āgamma: "Relying on me [as] a good friend." *Mamaṃ* is accusative, a variant on *maṃ* (Duroiselle §289), here belonging with *kalyāṇamittaṃ*. *Āgamma*, an absolutive of *āgacchati*, is used with an adverbial sense: "relying on, owing to, thanks to," taking *mamaṃ* as its accusative object.

jātidhammā sattā: "beings subject to birth." On this use of *dhamma* to form a bahubbīhi, see p. 154.

iminā kho etaṃ, ānanda, pariyāyena veditabbaṃ: "In this way, too, Ānanda, it can be understood"—that is, in the way just stated (Perniola §253d).

2. Kimatthiyasutta

For What Purpose? (SN 45:5; V 6–7)

[1. The encounter with the wanderers]

Atha kho sambahulā bhikkhū yena bhagavā ten'upasaṅkamiṃsu. . . . Ekamantaṃ nisinnā kho te bhikkhū bhagavantaṃ etadavocuṃ: "Idha no,[234] bhante, aññatitthiyā paribbājakā amhe evaṃ pucchanti: 'Kimatthiyaṃ, āvuso, samaṇe gotame brahmacariyaṃ vussatī'ti? Evaṃ puṭṭhā mayaṃ, bhante, tesaṃ aññatitthiyānaṃ paribbājakānaṃ evaṃ vyākaroma: 'Dukkhassa kho, āvuso, pariññatthaṃ bhagavati brahmacariyaṃ vussatī'ti.

Then several monks where the Blessed One, there approached. . . . One-side seated, those monks to the Blessed One this-said: "Here, Bhante, other-sect wanderers us thus ask: 'What-purpose, friends, under the ascetic Gotama

233. Geiger §108.1 explains that *aminā* is a variant on *iminā* based on the *a-*, *ana-* pronominal stem rather than the *ima-* stem

234. Spk II 370,20 commenting on a parallel passage, explains that *no* in the text is "a mere indeclinable" (*ettha no-kāro nipātamattameva*). I thus do not translate it. While *no* can also be the enclitic accusative of the first-person plural pronoun *mayaṃ*, since the accusative pronoun *amhe* occurs in the text, it is unlikely that this is the meaning of *no* here.

the spiritual-life is lived?' Thus asked we, Bhante, to those other-sect wanderers thus answer: 'Of suffering, friends, full-understanding-purpose under the Blessed One the spiritual-life is lived.'

Then several monks approached the Blessed One. . . . Seated to one side, those monks said this to the Blessed One: "Here, Bhante, wanderers belonging to other sects ask us thus: 'For what purpose, friends, is the spiritual life lived under the ascetic Gotama?' When we are asked thus, Bhante, we answer those wanderers belonging to other sects thus: 'For the purpose of full understanding of suffering, friends, the spiritual life is lived under the Blessed One.'

"Kacci mayaṃ, bhante, evaṃ puṭṭhā evaṃ vyākaramānā vuttavādino c'eva bhagavato homa, na ca bhagavantaṃ abhūtena abbhācikkhāma, dhammassa cānudhammaṃ vyākaroma, na ca koci sahadhammiko vādānuvādo gārayhaṃ ṭhānaṃ āgacchatī"ti?

"Is it the case we, Bhante, thus asked, thus answering, of-what-was-spoken-speakers and of the Blessed One are, not and the Blessed One falsely misrepresent, of the Dhamma and-according-to-Dhamma answer, not and any reasonable assertion-consequence reproachable ground comes upon?"

"Is it the case, Bhante, that when we are asked thus and answer thus, we are stating what has been said by the Blessed One and do not falsely misrepresent the Blessed One; that we answer in accordance with the Dhamma, and no reasonable consequence of our assertion comes upon a ground for reproach?"

[2. The Buddha's response]
"Taggha tumhe, bhikkhave, evaṃ puṭṭhā evaṃ vyākaramānā vuttavādino c'eva me hotha, na ca maṃ abhūtena abbhācikkhatha, dhammassa cānudhammaṃ vyākarotha, na ca koci sahadhammiko vādānuvādo gārayhaṃ ṭhānaṃ āgacchati. Dukkhassa hi pariññatthaṃ mayi brahmacariyaṃ vussati.

"Certainly you, monks, thus asked thus answering of-what-was-spoken-speakers and of me are, not and me falsely misrepresent, of the Dhamma and-according-to-Dhamma answer, not and any reasonable assertion-consequence reproachable ground comes upon. Of suffering because full-understanding-purpose under me the spiritual-life is lived.

"Certainly, monks, when you are asked thus and answer thus, you state what has been said by me and do not falsely misrepresent me; you answer in accordance with the Dhamma, and no reasonable consequence of your assertion comes upon a ground for reproach. Because it is for the purpose of full understanding of suffering that the spiritual life is lived under me.

"Sace vo, bhikkhave, aññatitthiyā paribbājakā evaṃ puccheyyuṃ: 'Atthi pan'āvuso, maggo, atthi paṭipadā etassa dukkhassa pariññāyā'ti, evaṃ puṭṭhā tumhe, bhikkhave, tesaṃ aññatitthiyānaṃ paribbājakānaṃ evaṃ vyākareyyātha: 'Atthi kho, āvuso, maggo, atthi paṭipadā etassa dukkhassa pariññāyā'ti.

"If you, monks, other-sect wanderers thus would ask, 'Is there but, friends, a path, is there a way, of this suffering for full-understanding,' thus asked you, monks, to those other-sect wanderers thus should answer: 'There is, friends, a path, there is a way, of this suffering for full-understanding.'

"If, monks, wanderers belonging to other sects would ask you, 'But is there, friends, a path, is there a way, for the full understanding of this suffering?' being asked thus, monks, you should answer those wanderers belonging to other sects thus: 'There is, friends, a path, there is a way, for the full understanding of this suffering.'

"Katamo ca, bhikkhave, maggo, katamā paṭipadā etassa dukkhassa pariññāya? Ayameva ariyo aṭṭhaṅgiko maggo, seyyathīdaṃ: sammādiṭṭhi . . . sammāsamādhi. Ayaṃ, bhikkhave, maggo, ayaṃ paṭipadā etassa dukkhassa pariññāyā ti. Evaṃ puṭṭhā tumhe, bhikkhave, tesaṃ aññatitthiyānaṃ paribbājakānaṃ evaṃ vyākareyyāthā"ti.

"What and, monks, the path, what the way, of this suffering for full-understanding? This-just noble eightfold path, that is, right-view . . . right-concentration. This, monks, the path, this the way, of this suffering for full-understanding. Thus asked you, monks, to those other-sect wanderers thus should answer."

"And what, monks, is the path, what is the way, for the full understanding of this suffering? It is just this noble eightfold path—that is, right view... right concentration. This, monks, is the path, this is the way, for the full understanding of this suffering. When you are asked thus, monks, you should thus answer those wanderers belonging to other sects."

Grammatical explanations

aññatitthiyā paribbājakā: see p. 466.
amhe: "us"; a personal pronoun, first-person plural.
kimatthiyaṃ: "what purpose"; an interrogative bahubbīhi compound formed from *kiṃ*, "what?" and *attha*, "purpose," with the adjectival suffix *-iya*. The compound qualifies *brahmacariyaṃ*.
samaṇe gotame: "under the ascetic Gotama"; the case is locative, and so too for *bhagavati*, which the monks use in their reply.
pariññatthaṃ: "for the purpose of full understanding"; another bahubbīhi qualifying *brahmacariyaṃ*, composed of *pariññā* + *atthaṃ*.[235]
kacci: an interrogative that conveys a sense of doubt, "Is it the case?"
evaṃ puṭṭhā evaṃ vyākaramānā: "thus asked, thus answering." *Puṭṭhā* is the past participle of *pucchati*, *vyākaramānā* the present participle of *vyākaroti*; both are masculine plural nominatives in agreement with *mayaṃ*.
vuttavādino c'eva bhagavato homa: "we are stating what has been said by the Blessed One." The inquiry is about the account the monks gave of the Blessed One's teaching. The compound *vuttavādino*, qualifying *mayaṃ*, is composed of the past participle *vutta*, which represents what was said by the Blessed One, and *vādino*, "speakers." *Bhagavato* is a genitive used with an instrumental sense. *Homa* is the first-person plural of *hoti*, and *hotha* (just below) is the second-person plural of *hoti*.
sahadhammiko vādānuvādo: "reasonable consequence of an assertion." The compound *sahadhammiko*, qualifying *vādānuvādo*, is composed of *saha*, "with," and *dhammiko*, in the sense of "reasonable, justifiable." For *vādānuvādo* there is an alternative reading *vādānupāto*. The Saṃyutta commentary (commenting on SN 22:2) explains: "*Sahadhammiko*

235. On this use of *atthaṃ* at the end of a compound to mean "for the sake of," see Perniola (§247f) and DOP *attha*².

means 'with reason.' *Vādānuvādo* means 'an assertion that follows from an assertion made by the Blessed One.' There is also the reading *anupāto*, a consequence of an assertion of the Teacher, meaning 'an entailment.' By this word too just an assertion that follows from an assertion is indicated."[236] Elsewhere *anuvāda* means "criticism," but that does not seem to be the sense intended here.

gārayhaṃ ṭhānaṃ: "a ground for reproach." *Gārayhaṃ* is a future passive participle, "to be reproached, deserving criticism," with metathesis—transposition of letters—such that *gārahyaṃ* > *gārayhaṃ* (Duroiselle §78; Geiger §49.1).

3. Vibhaṅgasutta

Analysis (SN 45:8; V 8–10)

"Ariyaṃ vo, bhikkhave, aṭṭhaṅgikaṃ maggaṃ desessāmi vibhajissāmi. Taṃ suṇātha, sādhukaṃ manasikarotha, bhāsissāmī"ti. — "Evaṃ, bhante"ti kho te bhikkhū bhagavato paccassosuṃ. Bhagavā etadavoca:

"The noble to you, monks, eightfold path I will teach, I will analyze. That listen to, well attend, I will speak." — "Yes, Bhante," those monks to the Blessed One replied. The Blessed One this-said:

"I will teach you, monks, the noble eightfold path and I will analyze it. Listen to that and attend well. I will speak." — "Yes, Bhante," those monks replied to the Blessed One. The Blessed One said this:

"Katamo ca, bhikkhave, ariyo aṭṭhaṅgiko maggo? Seyyathīdaṃ: sammādiṭṭhi . . . sammāsamādhi.

"What and, monks, the noble eightfold path? That is: right-view . . . right-concentration.

"And what, monks, is the noble eightfold path? It is this: right view . . . right concentration.

236. Spk II 258,5–8: *Sahadhammiko ti sakāraṇo. Vādānuvādo ti bhagavatā vuttavādassa anuvādo. Vādānupāto ti pi pāṭho, satthu vādassa anupāto anupatanaṃ, anugamanan ti attho. Iminā pi vādaṃ anugato vādoyeva dīpito hoti.*

"Katamā ca, bhikkhave, sammādiṭṭhi? Yaṃ kho, bhikkhave, dukkhe ñāṇaṃ, dukkhasamudaye ñāṇaṃ, dukkhanirodhe ñāṇaṃ, dukkhanirodhagāminiyā paṭipadāya ñāṇaṃ: ayaṃ vuccati, bhikkhave, 'sammādiṭṭhi.'

"What and, monks, right-view? Which, monks, in suffering knowledge, in suffering-origin knowledge, in suffering-cessation knowledge, in suffering-cessation-going way knowledge: this is called, monks, 'right-view.'

"And what, monks, is right view? That which, monks, is knowledge of suffering, knowledge of the origin of suffering, knowledge of the cessation of suffering, knowledge of the way leading to the cessation of suffering: this is called, monks, 'right view.'

"Katamo ca, bhikkhave, sammāsaṅkappo? Yo kho, bhikkhave, nekkhamma-saṅkappo, avyāpādasaṅkappo, avihiṃsāsaṅkappo: ayaṃ vuccati, bhikkhave, 'sammāsaṅkappo.'

"What and, monks, right-intention? Which, monks, renunciation-intention, non-ill-will-intention, harmlessness-intention: this is called, monks, 'right-intention.'

"And what, monks, is right intention? That which, monks, is the intention of renunciation, the intention of non-ill will, the intention of harmlessness: this is called, monks, 'right intention.'

"Katamā ca, bhikkhave, sammāvācā? Yā kho, bhikkhave, musāvādā veramaṇī, pisuṇāya vācāya veramaṇī, pharusāya vācāya veramaṇī, samphappalāpā veramaṇī: ayaṃ vuccati, bhikkhave, 'sammāvācā.'

"What and, monks, right-speech? Which, monks, from false-speech abstinence, from divisive speech abstinence, from harsh speech abstinence, from idle-chatter abstinence: this is called, monks, 'right-speech.'

"And what, monks, is right speech? That which, monks, is abstinence from false speech, abstinence from divisive speech, abstinence from harsh speech, abstinence from idle chatter: this is called, monks, 'right speech.'

"Katamo ca, bhikkhave, sammākammanto? Yā kho, bhikkhave, pāṇātipātā veramaṇī, adinnādānā veramaṇī, abrahmacariyā veramaṇī:[237] *ayaṃ vuccati, bhikkhave, 'sammākammanto.'*

"What and, monks, right-action? Which, monks, from life-destruction abstinence, from not-given-taking abstinence, from impure-conduct abstinence: this is called, monks, 'right-action.'

"And what, monks, is right action? That which, monks, is abstinence from the destruction of life, abstinence from taking what is not given, abstinence from impure [sexual] conduct: this is called, monks, 'right action.'

"Katamo ca, bhikkhave, sammāājīvo? Idha, bhikkhave, ariyasāvako micchāājīvaṃ pahāya sammāājīvena jīvitaṃ kappeti: ayaṃ vuccati, bhikkhave, 'sammāājīvo.'

"What and, monks, right-livelihood? Here, monks, a noble-disciple wrong-livelihood having abandoned, by right-livelihood living makes: this is called, monks, 'right-livelihood.'

"And what, monks, is right livelihood? Here a noble disciple, having abandoned wrong livelihood, earns his living by right livelihood: this is called, monks, 'right livelihood.'

"Katamo ca, bhikkhave, sammāvāyāmo? Idha, bhikkhave, bhikkhu anuppannānaṃ pāpakānaṃ akusalānaṃ dhammānaṃ anuppādāya chandaṃ janeti vāyamati viriyaṃ ārabhati cittaṃ paggaṇhāti padahati. Uppannānaṃ pāpakānaṃ akusalānaṃ dhammānaṃ pahānāya chandaṃ janeti. . . . Anuppannānaṃ kusalānaṃ dhammānaṃ uppādāya chandaṃ janeti. . . . Uppannānaṃ kusalānaṃ dhammānaṃ ṭhitiyā asammosāya bhiyyobhāvāya vepullāya bhāvanāya pāripūriyā chandaṃ janeti vāyamati

237. All editions read here *abrahmacariyā veramaṇī*, which signifies total sexual abstinence. However, the definition of *sammākammanta* at DN II 312,13, MN III 74,22, and MN III 251,24 has *kāmesu micchācārā veramaṇī*, "abstinence from misconduct in sensual pleasures," that is, abstaining from sexual misconduct. Vibh 235,19 also has *kāmesu micchācārā veramaṇī*. Perhaps the definition by way of total abstinence was formulated with specific reference to monastics, whereas the more common reading is intended for lay disciples.

viriyaṃ ārabhati cittaṃ paggaṇhāti padahati. Ayaṃ vuccati, bhikkhave, 'sammāvāyāmo.'

"What and, monks, right-effort? Here, monks, a monk of unarisen bad unwholesome qualities for the non-arising desire generates, makes-effort, energy arouses, mind applies, strives. Of arisen bad unwholesome qualities for abandoning desire generates. . . . Of unarisen wholesome qualities for arising desire generates. . . . Of arisen wholesome qualities for continuation, for non-decline, for increase, for expansion, by development for fulfillment desire generates, makes-effort, energy arouses, mind applies, strives. This is called, monks, 'right-effort.'

"And what, monks, is right effort? Here, monks, a monk generates desire for the non-arising of unarisen bad unwholesome qualities; he makes an effort, arouses energy, applies his mind, and strives. He generates desire for the abandoning of arisen evil unwholesome qualities. . . . He generates desire for the arising of unarisen wholesome qualities. . . . He generates desire for the continuation of arisen wholesome qualities, for their non-decline, increase, expansion, and fulfillment by development; he makes an effort, arouses energy, applies his mind, and strives. This is called, monks, 'right effort.'

"Katamā ca, bhikkhave, sammāsati? Idha, bhikkhave, bhikkhu kāye kāyānupassī viharati ātāpī sampajāno satimā, vineyya loke abhijjhādomanassaṃ; vedanāsu vedanānupassī viharati ātāpī sampajāno satimā, vineyya loke abhijjhādomanassaṃ; citte cittānupassī viharati ātāpī sampajāno satimā, vineyya loke abhijjhādomanassaṃ; dhammesu dhammānupassī viharati ātāpī sampajāno satimā, vineyya loke abhijjhādomanassaṃ: ayaṃ vuccati, bhikkhave, 'sammāsati.'

What and, monks, right-mindfulness? Here, monks, a monk in the body body-contemplating dwells, ardent, clearly-comprehending, mindful, having removed in the world longing-dejection; in feelings feeling-contemplating dwells, ardent, clearly-comprehending, mindful, having removed in the world longing-dejection; in the mind mind-contemplating dwells, ardent, clearly-comprehending, mindful, having removed in the world longing-dejection; in phenomena phenomena-contemplating dwells, ardent, clearly-comprehending, mindful, having removed in the world longing-dejection. This is called, monks, 'right-mindfulness.'

"And what, monks, is right mindfulness? Here, monks, a monk dwells contemplating the body in the body, ardent, clearly comprehending, mindful, having removed longing and dejection in regard to the world; contemplating feelings in feelings, ardent, clearly comprehending, mindful, having removed longing and dejection in regard to the world; contemplating the mind in the mind, ardent, clearly comprehending, mindful, having removed longing and dejection in regard to the world; contemplating phenomena in phenomena, ardent, clearly comprehending, mindful, having removed longing and dejection in regard to the world. This is called, monks, 'right mindfulness.'

"Katamo ca, bhikkhave, sammāsamādhi? Idha, bhikkhave, bhikkhu vivicc'-eva kāmehi vivicca akusalehi dhammehi savitakkaṃ savicāraṃ vivekajaṃ pītisukhaṃ paṭhamaṃ jhānaṃ upasampajja viharati.

"What and, monks, right-concentration? Here, monks, a monk, having become secluded indeed from sensual-pleasures, having become secluded from unwholesome qualities, with-thought, with-examination, seclusion-born rapture-pleasure first jhāna having entered dwells.

"And what, monks, is right concentration? Here, monks, having become secluded from sensual pleasures, having become secluded from unwholesome qualities, a monk enters and dwells in the first jhāna, which is accompanied by thought, accompanied by examination, [having] rapture and pleasure born of seclusion.

"Vitakkavicārānaṃ vūpasamā ajjhattaṃ sampasādanaṃ cetaso ekodi-bhāvaṃ avitakkaṃ avicāraṃ samādhijaṃ pītisukhaṃ dutiyaṃ jhānaṃ upasampajja viharati.

"Of thought-examination through subsiding, internal placidity, of mind unification, without-thought, without-examination, concentration-born rapture-pleasure second jhāna having entered dwells.

"Through the subsiding of thought and examination, he enters and dwells in the second jhāna, [which is marked by] internal placidity and unification of mind, which is without thought, without examination, [having] rapture and pleasure born of concentration.

"Pītiyā ca virāgā upekkhako ca viharati sato ca sampajāno, sukhañca kāyena paṭisaṃvedeti, yaṃ taṃ ariyā ācikkhanti: 'Upekkhako satimā sukhavihārī'ti tatiyaṃ jhānaṃ upasampajja viharati.

"Of rapture and with fading away, equanimous and he dwells, mindful and clearly comprehending, pleasure-and with the body experiences, which that the noble ones declare: 'Equanimous, mindful, pleasant-dwelling,' the third jhāna having entered dwells.

"And with the fading away of rapture, he dwells equanimous, mindful and clearly comprehending, and he experiences pleasure with the body; he enters and dwells in the third jhāna on account of which the noble ones declare of him: '[He is] equanimous, mindful, dwelling pleasantly.'

"Sukhassa ca pahānā dukkhassa ca pahānā pubbeva somanassa-domanassānaṃ atthaṅgamā adukkhamasukhaṃ upekkhāsatipārisuddhiṃ catutthaṃ jhānaṃ upasampajja viharati. Ayaṃ vuccati, bhikkhave, 'sammāsamādhī'"ti.

"Of pleasure and through the abandoning, of pain and through the abandoning, previously of joy-dejection through the passing away, not-painful-not-pleasant, equanimity-mindfulness-purification fourth jhāna having entered dwells. This is called, monks, 'right-concentration.'"

"Through the abandoning of pleasure and through the abandoning of pain, and through the passing away previously of joy and dejection, he enters and dwells in the fourth jhāna, which is neither painful nor pleasant and has the purification of mindfulness by equanimity. This is called, monks, 'right concentration.'"

Grammatical explanations

dukkhe ñāṇaṃ, etc.: "knowledge of suffering." *Ñāṇaṃ* usually takes its dependent term in the locative case. Perhaps the sense can be formulated in English as "knowledge in regard to suffering."

musāvādā veramaṇī, etc.: *Veramaṇī* takes its dependent term in the ablative case. In the first and fourth abstinences, *musāvādā* and *samphappalāpā* are masculine ablatives, both kammadhārayas; in the second and third, *vācāya* is a feminine ablative.

pāṇātipātā veramaṇī, etc.: *Pāṇātipātā* is a masculine ablative; *adinnādānā* and *abrahmacariyā* neuter ablatives. Both *pāṇātipātā* and *adinnādānā* are tappurisas.

anuppādāya, pahānāya, uppādāya, ṭhitiyā, pāripūriyā: "for the non-arising, for the abandoning, for the arising, for the continuation, for the fulfillment." These are all datives of purpose, with the dependent *dhammānaṃ* a genitive plural. On my reason for taking *bhāvanāya pāripūriyā* as "for fulfillment by development," see p. 434.

vivicc'eva kāmehi vivicca akusalehi dhammehi: "having become secluded from sensual pleasures, having become secluded from unwholesome qualities." *Vivicca* is the absolutive of the passive verb *viviccati*, "becomes secluded," with assimilation such that *vivicya* > *vivicca*. It takes its dependent terms—*kāmehi* and *akusalehi dhammehi*—in the ablative.

savitakkaṃ savicāraṃ: "with thought, with examination." These are bahubbīhis (Duroiselle §551) qualifying *paṭhamaṃ jhānaṃ*.

vivekajaṃ pītisukhaṃ: "[having] rapture and pleasure born of seclusion." *Vivekajaṃ* is used adjectivally to describe *pītisukham*, which is itself a bahubbīhi qualifying *paṭhamaṃ jhānaṃ*, an accusative in relation to the absolutive *upasampajja*.

vitakkavicārānaṃ vūpasamā: "through the subsiding of thought and examination." *Vūpasamā* is an ablative, the condition for entering the second jhāna.

ajjhattaṃ sampasādanaṃ cetaso ekodibhāvaṃ: "internal placidity [and] unification of mind." Each of the two phrases functions adjectivally in relation to *dutiyaṃ jhānaṃ*. *Ekodibhāvaṃ* is a bahubbīhi.

avitakkaṃ avicāraṃ samādhijaṃ pītisukhaṃ: "without thought, without examination, [having] rapture and pleasure born of concentration." The first, second, and fourth terms are bahubbīhis describing *dutiyaṃ jhānaṃ*; *samādhijaṃ* is a tappurisa qualifying *pītisukhaṃ*.

pītiyā ca virāgā: "and with the fading away of rapture"; an ablative clause describing the condition for entering the third jhāna.

yaṃ taṃ: Vism paraphrases this in such a way that *yaṃ* qualifies the third jhāna as the cause or reason and *taṃ* denotes the person who attains the third jhāna.[238] I follow this explanation in my translation, but it is also possible that both pronouns refer to the third jhāna itself.

238. Vism 163,22–25: *Ettha yaṃjhānahetu yaṃjhānakāraṇā taṃ tatiyajjhānasamaṅgipug-*

sukhassa ca pahānā dukkhassa ca pahānā pubbeva somanassadomanassānaṃ atthaṅgamā: "through the abandoning of pleasure and through the abandoning of pain, and through the passing away previously of joy and dejection." The sentence contains three ablative clauses describing the conditions for entering the fourth jhāna.

adukkhamasukhaṃ upekkhāsatipārisuddhiṃ: "which is neither painful nor pleasant and has the purification of mindfulness by equanimity"; both compounds describe *catutthaṃ jhānaṃ*. *Adukkhamasukhaṃ* is originally a negative dvanda, here used as a bahubbīhi; *upekkhāsatipārisuddhiṃ* is a complex tappurisa used as a bahubbīhi.[239] I construe the sense of the latter in accordance with the explanation given at Vism 167,30–35, which is based on the canonical Abhidhamma treatise, the Vibhaṅga.[240] Alternatively, the phrase might have been construed as "the purification of equanimity and mindfulness," but this does not agree with the commentaries.

4. Paṭipadāsutta

Practice (SN 45:24; V 18–19)

[1. Wrong practice]

"Gihino vāhaṃ, bhikkhave, pabbajitassa vā micchāpaṭipadaṃ na vaṇṇemi. Gihi vā, bhikkhave, pabbajito vā micchāpaṭipanno micchāpaṭipattādhikaraṇahetu na ārādhako hoti ñāyaṃ dhammaṃ kusalaṃ.

"Of a layperson or-I, monks, of one-gone-forth or, wrong-practice not I praise. A layperson or, monks, one-gone-forth or, wrong-practicing, wrong-practice-undertaking-cause, not achiever is the method, the Dhamma, the wholesome.

---

galaṃ buddhādayo ariyā ācikkhanti desenti paññapenti paṭṭhapenti vivaranti vibhajanti uttānīkaronti pakāsenti, pasaṃsantī ti adhippāyo.

239. The tappurisa is of the genitive type (*satipārisuddhi* = *satiyā pārisuddhi*, "purification of mindfulness") with the first member functioning as an instrumental (that is, as an implicit *upekkhāya*, "by equanimity"). Because it describes *catutthaṃ jhānaṃ*, the entire tappurisa becomes a bahubbīhi.

240. The passage reads: *Upekkhāya janitasatiyā pārisuddhiṃ. Imasmiñhi jhāne suparisuddhā sati, yā ca tassā satiyā pārisuddhi, sā upekkhāya katā, na aññena. Tasmā etaṃ "upekkhāsatipārisuddhin"ti vuccati. Vibhaṅgepi vuttaṃ "ayaṃ sati imāya upekkhāya visadā hoti parisuddhā pariyodātā. Tena vuccati upekkhāsatipārisuddhī"ti.*

"I do not, monks, praise wrong practice, whether of a layperson or of one gone forth. One practicing wrongly, monks, whether a layperson or one gone forth, because of their undertaking of wrong practice, is not one who achieves the method, the Dhamma, the wholesome.

"Katamā ca, bhikkhave, micchāpaṭipadā? Seyyathīdaṃ micchādiṭṭhi . . . micchāsamādhi. Ayaṃ vuccati, bhikkhave, 'micchāpaṭipadā.' Gihino vāhaṃ, bhikkhave, pabbajitassa vā micchāpaṭipadaṃ na vaṇṇemi. Gihi vā, bhikkhave, pabbajito vā micchāpaṭipanno micchāpaṭipattādhikaraṇahetu na ārādhako hoti ñāyaṃ dhammaṃ kusalaṃ.

"What and, monks, wrong-practice? That is: wrong-view . . . wrong-concentration. This is called, monks, 'wrong practice.' Of a layperson or-I, monks, of one-gone-forth or, wrong-practice not I praise. A layperson or, monks, one-gone-forth or, wrong-practicing, wrong-practice-undertaking-cause, not-achiever is the method, the Dhamma, the wholesome.

"And what, monks, is wrong practice? It is this: wrong view . . . wrong concentration. This, monks, is called 'wrong practice.' I do not, monks, praise wrong practice, whether of a layperson or of one gone forth. One practicing wrongly, monks, whether a layperson or one gone forth, because of their undertaking of wrong practice, is not one who achieves the method, the Dhamma, the wholesome.

[2. Right practice]

"Gihino vāhaṃ, bhikkhave, pabbajitassa vā sammāpaṭipadaṃ vaṇṇemi. Gihi vā, bhikkhave, pabbajito vā sammāpaṭipanno sammāpaṭipattādhikaraṇahetu ārādhako hoti ñāyaṃ dhammaṃ kusalaṃ.

"Of a layperson or-I, monks, of one-gone-forth or, right-practice I praise. A layperson or, monks, one-gone-forth or, right-practicing, right-practice-undertaking-cause, achiever is the method, the Dhamma, the wholesome.

"I praise, monks, right practice, whether of a layperson or of one gone forth. One practicing rightly, monks, whether a layperson or one gone forth, because of their undertaking of right practice, is one who achieves the method, the Dhamma, the wholesome.

"Katamā ca, bhikkhave, sammāpaṭipadā? Seyyathīdaṃ sammādiṭṭhi . . . sammāsamādhi. Ayaṃ vuccati, bhikkhave, 'sammāpaṭipadā.' Gihino vāhaṃ, bhikkhave, pabbajitassa vā sammāpaṭipadaṃ vaṇṇemi. Gihi vā, bhikkhave, pabbajito vā sammāpaṭipanno sammāpaṭipattādhikaraṇahetu ārādhako hoti ñāyaṃ dhammaṃ kusalan"ti.

"What and, monks, right-practice? That is, right-view . . . right-concentration. This is called, monks, 'right practice.' Of a layperson or-I, monks, of one-gone-forth or, right-practice I praise. A layperson or, monks, one-gone-forth or, right-practicing right-practice-undertaking-cause, achiever is the method, the Dhamma, the wholesome."

"And what, monks, is right practice? It is this: right view . . . right concentration. This, monks, is called 'right practice.' I praise, monks, right practice, whether of a layperson or of one gone forth. One practicing rightly, monks, whether a layperson or one gone forth, because of their undertaking of right practice, is one who achieves the method, the Dhamma, the wholesome."

Grammatical explanations

micchāpaṭipanno: "practicing wrongly"; a kammadhāraya consisting of an adverb (*micchā*, and *sammā* just below) and a past participle, *paṭipanno*, used with a present sense.

micchāpaṭipattādhikaraṇahetu: "because of their undertaking of wrong practice."[241] My construing of the relationship between *adhikaraṇa* and *hetu* is hypothetical. They may be synonymous, but *adhikaraṇa* can also mean "supervision" (as well as "litigation" in other contexts). There is sandhi between the final and initial vowels of *paṭipatti* and *adhikaraṇa*, with lengthening of the latter's initial vowel.

ārādhako: "one who achieves"; the noun, standing in relation to an accusative object, is from the verb *ārādheti*, "achieves, succeeds." The accusative objects are *ñāyaṃ dhammaṃ kusalaṃ*. I see here three nouns: the method, the Dhamma, and the wholesome (or the good), but it is also possible to treat *kusalaṃ* as an adjective modifying *dhammaṃ*. The Saṃyutta commentary takes *ñāyaṃ* and *dhammaṃ* jointly as "the noble path *dhamma*."[242]

241. Levman (in a personal note) suggests the compound is a tappurisa used adverbially.

242. Spk III 132,1–2: *Ñāyaṃ dhamman ti ariyamaggadhammaṃ*. The Aṅguttara commentary

5. Kalyāṇamittasutta

Good Friend (SN 45:49, 45:56 combined; V 29–30, V 31)

"Suriyassa, bhikkhave, udayato etaṃ pubbaṅgamaṃ etaṃ pubbanimittaṃ, yadidaṃ aruṇuggaṃ. Evameva kho, bhikkhave, bhikkhuno ariyassa aṭṭhaṅgikassa maggassa uppādāya etaṃ pubbaṅgamaṃ etaṃ pubbanimittaṃ, yadidaṃ kalyāṇamittatā. Kalyāṇamittass'etaṃ, bhikkhave, bhikkhuno pāṭikaṅkhaṃ: ariyaṃ aṭṭhaṅgikaṃ maggaṃ bhāvessati, ariyaṃ aṭṭhaṅgikaṃ maggaṃ bahulīkarissati.

"Of the sun, monks, rising this the forerunner, this the sign, which this: the dawn-break. Just so, monks, for a monk, of the noble eightfold path for the arising, this the forerunner, this the sign, which this: good-friendship. Of a good-friend this, monks, of a monk, to-be-expected: the noble eightfold path will develop, the noble eightfold path will cultivate.

"This, monks, is the forerunner, this is the sign for the rising of the sun—that is, the break of dawn. Just so, monks, for a monk, this is the forerunner, this is the sign for the arising of the noble eightfold path—that is, good friendship. Of a monk who has a good friend, monks, this is to be expected, that he will develop the noble eightfold path, that he will cultivate the noble eightfold path.

(45:49) "Kathañca, bhikkhave, bhikkhu kalyāṇamitto ariyaṃ aṭṭhaṅgikaṃ maggaṃ bhāveti, ariyaṃ aṭṭhaṅgikaṃ maggaṃ bahulīkaroti? Idha, bhikkhave, bhikkhu sammādiṭṭhiṃ bhāveti . . . sammāsamādhiṃ bhāveti vivekanissitaṃ virāganissitaṃ nirodhanissitaṃ vossaggapariṇāmiṃ. Evaṃ kho, bhikkhave, bhikkhu kalyāṇamitto ariyaṃ aṭṭhaṅgikaṃ maggaṃ bhāveti, ariyaṃ aṭṭhaṅgikaṃ maggaṃ bahulīkarotī ti.

"How-and, monks, a monk a good-friend the noble eightfold path develops, the noble eightfold path cultivates? Here, monks, a monk right-view develops . . . right-concentration develops, seclusion-based, dispassion-based, cessation-based, release-evolving-toward. Thus, monks, a monk a good-friend the noble eightfold path develops, the noble eightfold path cultivates.

(Mp II 143,5–6) explains *ñāyaṃ dhammaṃ kusalaṃ* as "the path together with insight" (*sahavipassanakaṃ maggaṃ*).

"And how, monks, does a monk who has a good friend develop the noble eightfold path, cultivate the noble eightfold path? Here, monks, a monk develops right view . . . develops right concentration, which is based on seclusion, based on dispassion, based on cessation, evolving toward release. It is in such a way, monks, that a monk who has a good friend develops the noble eightfold path, cultivates the noble eightfold path.

(45:56) "Kathañca, bhikkhave, bhikkhu kalyāṇamitto ariyaṃ aṭṭhaṅgikaṃ maggaṃ bhāveti, ariyaṃ aṭṭhaṅgikaṃ maggaṃ bahulīkaroti? Idha, bhikkhave, bhikkhu sammādiṭṭhiṃ bhāveti . . . sammāsamādhiṃ bhāveti rāgavinayapariyosānaṃ dosavinayapariyosānaṃ mohavinayapariyosānaṃ. Evaṃ kho, bhikkhave, bhikkhu kalyāṇamitto ariyaṃ aṭṭhaṅgikaṃ maggaṃ bhāveti, ariyaṃ aṭṭhaṅgikaṃ maggaṃ bahulīkarotī"ti.

"How-and, monks, a monk a good-friend the noble eightfold path develops, the noble eightfold path cultivates? Here, monks, a monk right-view develops . . . right-concentration develops, lust-removal-culmination, hatred-removal-culmination, delusion-removal-culmination. Thus, monks, a monk a good-friend the noble eightfold path develops, the noble eightfold path cultivates."

"And how, monks, does a monk who has a good friend develop the noble eightfold path, cultivate the noble eightfold path? Here, monks, a monk develops right view . . . develops right concentration, which has as its culmination the removal of lust, which has as its culmination the removal of hatred, which has as its culmination the removal of delusion. It is in such a way, monks, that a monk who has a good friend develops the noble eightfold path, cultivates the noble eightfold path."

Grammatical explanations

suriyassa . . . aruṇuggaṃ: see p. 119.

vivekanissitaṃ, etc.: see p. 424.

rāgavinayapariyosānaṃ, etc.: "which has as its culmination the removal of lust"; a bahubbīhi qualifying each of the path factors. And so for the following two compounds, with *dosa* and *moha* in the place of *rāga*.

6. Pācīnaninnasutta

Slants to the East (SN 45:91, 45:103 combined; V 38, V 40)

"Seyyathāpi, bhikkhave, gaṅgā nadī pācīnaninnā pācīnapoṇā pācīnapabbhārā, evameva kho, bhikkhave, bhikkhu ariyaṃ aṭṭhaṅgikaṃ maggaṃ bhāvento ariyaṃ aṭṭhaṅgikaṃ maggaṃ bahulīkaronto nibbānaninno hoti nibbānapoṇo nibbānapabbhāro.

"Just as, monks, Ganges river east-slanting, east-sloping, east-inclining, just so, monks, a monk noble eightfold path developing, noble eightfold path cultivating, nibbāna-slanting is, nibbāna-sloping, nibbāna-inclining.

"Just as, monks, the Ganges River slants to the east, slopes to the east, inclines to the east, just so, monks, a monk developing the noble eightfold path, cultivating the noble eightfold path, slants to nibbāna, slopes to nibbāna, inclines to nibbāna.

(45:91) "Kathañca, bhikkhave, bhikkhu ariyaṃ aṭṭhaṅgikaṃ maggaṃ bhāvento ariyaṃ aṭṭhaṅgikaṃ maggaṃ bahulīkaronto nibbānaninno hoti nibbānapoṇo nibbānapabbhāro? Idha, bhikkhave, bhikkhu sammādiṭṭhiṃ bhāveti . . . sammāsamādhiṃ bhāveti vivekanissitaṃ virāganissitaṃ nirodhanissitaṃ vossaggapariṇāmiṃ. Evaṃ kho, bhikkhave, bhikkhu ariyaṃ aṭṭhaṅgikaṃ maggaṃ bhāvento ariyaṃ aṭṭhaṅgikaṃ maggaṃ bahulīkaronto nibbānaninno hoti nibbānapoṇo nibbānapabbhāro ti.

"How-and, monks, a monk noble eightfold path developing, noble eightfold path cultivating, nibbāna-slanting is, nibbāna-sloping, nibbāna-inclining? Here, monks, a monk right-view develops . . . right-concentration develops, seclusion-based, dispassion-based, cessation-based, release-evolving-toward. Thus, monks, a monk the noble eightfold path developing, the noble eightfold path cultivating, nibbāna-slanting is, nibbāna-sloping, nibbāna-inclining.

"And how, monks, does a monk developing the noble eightfold path, cultivating the noble eightfold path, slant to nibbāna, slope to nibbāna, incline to nibbāna? Here, monks, a monk develops right view . . . develops right concentration, which is based on seclusion, based on dispassion, based on cessation, evolving toward release. It is in such a way, monks, that a monk developing the noble eightfold path, cultivating the noble eightfold path, slants to nibbāna, slopes to nibbāna, inclines to nibbāna.

(45:103) "Kathañca, bhikkhave, bhikkhu ariyaṃ aṭṭhaṅgikaṃ maggaṃ bhāvento ariyaṃ aṭṭhaṅgikaṃ maggaṃ bahulīkaronto nibbānaninno hoti nibbānapoṇo nibbānapabbhāro? Idha, bhikkhave, bhikkhu sammādiṭṭhiṃ bhāveti . . . sammāsamādhiṃ bhāveti rāgavinayapariyosānaṃ dosavinayapariyosānaṃ mohavinayapariyosānaṃ. Evaṃ kho, bhikkhave, bhikkhu ariyaṃ aṭṭhaṅgikaṃ maggaṃ bhāvento ariyaṃ aṭṭhaṅgikaṃ maggaṃ bahulīkaronto nibbānaninno hoti nibbānapoṇo nibbānapabbhāro"ti.

"How-and, monks, a monk noble eightfold path developing, noble eightfold path cultivating, nibbāna-slanting is, nibbāna-sloping, nibbāna-inclining? Here, monks, a monk right-view develops . . . right-concentration develops, lust-removal-culmination, hatred-removal-culmination, delusion-removal-culmination. Thus, monks, a monk the noble eightfold path developing, the noble eightfold path cultivating, nibbāna-slanting is, nibbāna-sloping, nibbāna-inclining."

"And how, monks, does a monk developing the noble eightfold path, cultivating the noble eightfold path, slant to nibbāna, slope to nibbāna, incline to nibbāna? Here, monks, a monk develops right view . . . develops right concentration, which has as its culmination the removal of lust, which has as its culmination the removal of hatred, which has as its culmination the removal of delusion. It is in such a way, monks, that a monk developing the noble eightfold path, cultivating the noble eightfold path, slants to nibbāna, slopes to nibbāna, inclines to nibbāna."

Grammatical explanations

pācīnaninnā pācīnapoṇā pācīnapabbhārā: "slants to the east, slopes to the east, inclines to the east." On this type of compound with *samudda*, "ocean," see p. 270.

7. Nadīsutta

The River (SN 45:160; V 53–54)

[1. The Ganges does not flow westward]

"Seyyathāpi, bhikkhave, gaṅgā nadī pācīnaninnā pācīnapoṇā pācīnapabbhārā. Atha mahājanakāyo āgaccheyya kuddālapiṭakaṃ ādāya: 'Mayaṃ imaṃ gaṅgaṃ nadiṃ pacchāninnaṃ karissāma pacchāpoṇaṃ pacchāpabbhāran'ti. Taṃ kiṃ maññatha, bhikkhave, api nu so mahājanakāyo gaṅgaṃ nadiṃ pacchāninnaṃ kareyya pacchāpoṇaṃ pacchāpabbhāran"ti?

"Suppose, monks, the Ganges River east-slanting, east-sloping, east-inclining. Then great-people-crowd would come, shovel-basket having taken: 'We this Ganges River west-slanting will make, west-sloping, west-inclining.' That what you think, monks, that great-people-crowd the Ganges River west-slanting can make, west-sloping, west-inclining?"

"Monks, the Ganges River slants to the east, slopes to the east, inclines to the east. Suppose now a great crowd of people would come, having taken a shovel and a basket, [thinking:] 'We will make this Ganges River slant to the west, slope to the west, incline to the west.'[243] What do you think, monks, can that great crowd of people make the Ganges River slant to the west, slope to the west, incline to the west?"

"No h'etaṃ, bhante. Taṃ kissa hetu? Gaṅgā, bhante, nadī pācīnaninnā pācīnapoṇā pācīnapabbhārā. Sā na sukarā pacchāninnaṃ kātuṃ pacchāpoṇaṃ pacchāpabbhāraṃ. Yāvadeva pana so mahājanakāyo kilamathassa vighātassa bhāgī assā"ti.

"Not indeed this, Bhante. That for what reason? The Ganges, Bhante, River east-slanting, east-sloping, east-inclining. That not easily-done west-slanting to make, west-sloping, west-inclining. So much only that great-people-crowd of fatigue, of distress, partaker would be."

243. In the Pāli text the word *seyyathāpi*, introducing a simile, precedes the factual statement about the Ganges River. However, the imaginary situation to be described begins with the statement about the arrival of a group of people who want to reverse the river's flow. Hence in translation I put "Suppose now" before this statement rather than before the factual statement about the river's eastward flow.

"Certainly not, Bhante. For what reason? As the Ganges River slants to the east, slopes to the east, inclines to the east, it is not easy to make it slant to the west, slope to the west, incline to the west. In the end that great crowd of people would only reap fatigue and distress."

[2. A monk on the path will not revert]

"Evameva kho, bhikkhave, bhikkhuṃ ariyaṃ aṭṭhaṅgikaṃ maggaṃ bhāventaṃ ariyaṃ aṭṭhaṅgikaṃ maggaṃ bahulīkarontaṃ rājāno vā rāja-mahāmattā vā mittā vā amaccā vā ñātī vā sālohitā vā bhogehi abhihaṭṭhuṃ pavāreyyuṃ: 'Ehi ambho purisa, kiṃ te ime kāsāvā anudahanti, kiṃ muṇḍo kapālaṃ anusaṃcarasi? Ehi, hīnāyāvattitvā bhoge ca bhuñjassu, puññāni ca karohī'ti.

"Just so, monks, a monk the noble eightfold path developing, the noble eightfold path cultivating, kings or king-ministers or friends or associates or relatives or kinsfolk or, with wealths to partake-of might invite: 'Come, good man, why for you these dyed-robes burn, why shaven-headed begging-bowl you roam-around? Come, to the low-having reverted, wealths and enjoy, merits and do.'

"Just so, monks, kings or royal ministers, friends or associates, relatives or kinsfolk, might invite a monk who is developing the noble eightfold path, cultivating the noble eightfold path, to partake of wealth, [saying:] 'Come, good man, why should these dyed robes burn you? Why do you roam around with a shaved head [carrying] a begging bowl? Come, having reverted to the low state, enjoy wealth and do meritorious deeds.'

"So vata, bhikkhave, bhikkhu ariyaṃ aṭṭhaṅgikaṃ maggaṃ bhāvento ariyaṃ aṭṭhaṅgikaṃ maggaṃ bahulīkaronto sikkhaṃ paccakkhāya hīnāyā-vattissatī ti, n'etaṃ ṭhānaṃ vijjati. Taṃ kissa hetu? Yaṃ hi taṃ, bhikkhave, cittaṃ dīgharattaṃ vivekaninnaṃ vivekapoṇaṃ vivekapabbhāraṃ, taṃ vata hīnāyāvattissatī ti, n'etaṃ ṭhānaṃ vijjati.

"That indeed, monks, a monk the noble eightfold path developing, the noble eightfold path cultivating, the training having rejected, to the low-will revert, not this case exists. That for what reason? Because that, monks, mind long-night seclusion-slanting, seclusion-sloping, seclusion-inclining, 'That indeed to the low-will revert,' not this case exists.

"Monks, that a monk who is developing the noble eightfold path, cultivating the noble eightfold path, will reject the training and revert to the low state, there is no possibility of this. For what reason? Because, monks, that mind [of his] for a long time has slanted to seclusion, sloped to seclusion, inclined to seclusion, there is no possibility that he will revert to the low state.

"Kathañca, bhikkhave, bhikkhu ariyaṃ aṭṭhaṅgikaṃ maggaṃ bhāveti ariyaṃ aṭṭhaṅgikaṃ maggaṃ bahulīkaroti? Idha, bhikkhave, bhikkhu sammādiṭṭhiṃ bhāveti . . . sammāsamādhiṃ bhāveti vivekanissitaṃ virāganissitaṃ nirodhanissitaṃ vossaggapariṇāmiṃ. Evaṃ kho, bhikkhave, bhikkhu ariyaṃ aṭṭhaṅgikaṃ maggaṃ bhāveti, ariyaṃ aṭṭhaṅgikaṃ maggaṃ bahulīkarotī"ti.

"How-and, monks, a monk the noble eightfold path develops, the noble eightfold path cultivates? Here, monks, a monk right-view develops . . . right-concentration develops, seclusion-based, dispassion-based, cessation-based, release-evolving-toward. Thus, monks, a monk the noble eightfold path develops, the noble eightfold path cultivates."

"And how, monks, does a monk develop the noble eightfold path, cultivate the noble eightfold path? Here, monks, a monk develops right view . . . develops right concentration, which is based on seclusion, based on dispassion, based on cessation, evolving toward release. It is in such a way, monks, that a monk develops the noble eightfold path, cultivates the noble eightfold path."

Grammatical explanations

sukarā: "easily done"; an adjective agreeing with the pronoun *sā*, standing for *gaṅgā nadī*.

yāvadeva = *yāva* + *eva*, with *-d-* as a liaison consonant. The term is used in the sense of "only, nothing but."

kilamathassa vighātassa: "of fatigue [and] of distress"; genitives in relation to the nominative *bhāgī*, "one who partakes of."

bhāventaṃ, bahulīkarontaṃ: "developing, cultivating"; both are singular accusative present participles qualifying *bhikkhuṃ*.

hīnāyāvattitvā (= *hīnāya āvattitvā*): "having reverted to the low state"; a dative followed by an absolutive. The expression means leaving the monastic life to return to lay life.

bhuñjassu: a second-person singular of the middle voice of *bhuñjati*, "eats, enjoys."

sikkhaṃ paccakkhāya: "having rejected the training." *Paccakkhāya* is an absolutive of *paccakkhāti*, taking an accusative as object.

dīgharattaṃ: see p. 354.

6. The Unconditioned: The Goal

Introduction

The theme of this chapter is the unconditioned (*asaṅkhata*), a word often used as a designation for nibbāna. Whereas the cessation aspect of dependent origination included in chapter 4 shows the goal of the Dhamma through a series of negations, the present chapter shows the goal more directly and explicitly under thirty-two epithets, including nibbāna. As is characteristic of the Nikāyas, the goal is still described largely in negative terms: as the unconditioned, uninclined, unaging, undisintegrating, and so forth. Even the definition of the unconditioned as "the destruction of lust, the destruction of hatred, the destruction of delusion" has a negative ring.

When nibbāna is described as the destruction of lust, hatred, and delusion, this naturally gives rise to the question whether it is simply the eradication of defilements or some transcendent state or dimension. A sutta in the Itivuttaka (§44) speaks of two "elements of nibbāna." The element of nibbāna with residue remaining (*saupādisesā nibbānadhātu*) is defined as the arahant's destruction of lust, hatred, and delusion. And about the element of nibbāna without residue remaining (*anupādisesā nibbānadhātu*), the text merely says that for the arahant, "all feelings, not being delighted in, will become cool right here."[244] These two nibbāna elements are considered to represent nibbāna during life and nibbāna attained with the passing away of the arahant, and in both cases their characterization here seems negative. But other suttas speak of nibbāna as a state that is unborn, unproduced, unbecome, and unconditioned, or as a base where none of the conditioned phenomena of the world are to be found.[245] Such descriptions, while cryptic and still expressed by way of negations, point to nibbāna as a transcendent,

244. It 38,19-20: *Sabbavedayitāni anabhinanditāni sītībhavissanti.*

245. See Ud 80–81.

ever-existent state that makes possible liberation from the round of birth and death.

In any case, in the suttas that constitute this chapter of the Saṃyutta Nikāya, the stress is not on a theoretical understanding of nibbāna but on the path that leads to the final goal. The path is shown by taking first the term "unconditioned" to represent the aim of practice and then highlighting the path from different angles. The opening sutta proclaims mindfulness of the body to constitute the path. This sutta is then expanded upon in two steps. At the first step, it is elaborated upon by taking ten other sets of factors collectively as the way to the unconditioned. The ten are: (1) serenity and insight; (2) three kinds of concentration—that associated with thought and examination, that partly dissociated from them, and that fully dissociated from them;[246] (3) the emptiness, signless, and wishless concentrations; (4) the four establishments of mindfulness; (5) the four right strivings; (6) the four bases for spiritual power; (7) the five spiritual faculties; (8) the five powers; (9) the seven factors of enlightenment; and (10) the noble eightfold path. Each set constitutes a separate sutta.

Hence, including mindfulness directed to the body, we obtain eleven suttas, SN 43:1–11. The next sutta, SN 43:12, contains forty-five subdivisions. Here, serenity and insight are treated *separately* as the path to the unconditioned, and then each factor within the above-mentioned groups is treated as a distinct path to the unconditioned. Thus serenity and insight constitute two suttas, while the two sets of three concentrations give us six more. When we add these to the thirty-seven aids to enlightenment bundled into the seven groups, we obtain a total of forty-five suttas laying out the way to the unconditioned.

This entire pattern is then applied to the goal described by thirty-one other epithets, from the uninclined (*anata*) down to the destination (*parāyaṇa*). Since the path leading to the destination begins with mindfulness directed to the body, this means that fifty-six versions of the path (the eleven of 45:1–11 plus the forty-five of 45:12) are to be conjoined with each of the following thirty-one epithets of nibbāna for a total of 1,736 suttas. All printed editions of this chapter severely compress the presentation of

246. The first represents the first jhāna and the third the jhānas from the second on up. The middle term points to a kind of concentration midway between the first and the second jhānas but not included in the scheme of four jhānas.

the material, but it is possible that in the era when oral recitation prevailed, reciters would recite each sutta in full.

1. Asaṅkhatasutta
The Unconditioned (SN 43:1; IV 359)

"Asaṅkhatañca vo, bhikkhave, desessāmi asaṅkhatagāmiñca maggaṃ. Taṃ suṇātha. Katamañca, bhikkhave, asaṅkhataṃ? Yo, bhikkhave, rāgakkhayo dosakkhayo mohakkhayo, idaṃ vuccati, bhikkhave, 'asaṅkhataṃ.' Katamo ca, bhikkhave, asaṅkhatagāmī maggo?[247] *Kāyagatā sati. Ayaṃ vuccati, bhikkhave, 'asaṅkhatagāmī maggo.'*

"The unconditioned-and to you, monks, I will teach, the unconditioned-going-and path. That listen to. What-and, monks, the unconditioned? Which, monks, lust-destruction, hatred-destruction, delusion-destruction: this is called, monks, 'the unconditioned.' What and, monks, the unconditioned-going path? Body-gone mindfulness. This is called, monks, 'the unconditioned-going path.'

"I will teach you, monks, the unconditioned and the path leading to the unconditioned. Listen to that. And what, monks, is the unconditioned? The destruction of lust, the destruction of hatred, the destruction of delusion: this is called the 'unconditioned.' And what, monks, is the path leading to the unconditioned? Mindfulness directed to the body: this is called 'the path leading to the unconditioned.'

"Iti kho, bhikkhave, desitaṃ vo mayā asaṅkhataṃ, desito asaṅkhatagāmī maggo. Yaṃ, bhikkhave, satthārā karaṇīyaṃ sāvakānaṃ hitesinā anukampakena anukampaṃ upādāya, kataṃ vo taṃ mayā. Etāni, bhikkhave, rukkhamūlāni, etāni suññāgārāni. Jhāyatha, bhikkhave, mā pamādattha. Mā pacchā vippaṭisārino ahuvattha. Ayaṃ vo amhākaṃ anusāsanī"ti.

"Thus, monks, taught to you by me the unconditioned, taught the unconditioned-going path. What, monks, by a teacher should-be-done for

247. Here and below I adopt the Ce reading *asaṅkhatagāmī maggo*. Be has *asaṅkhatagāmimaggo*, Ee *asaṅkhatagāmi maggo*. The meaning is not affected.

disciples by-one-seeking-welfare, by a compassionate one, compassion out of, done for you that by me. These, monks, tree-roots, these empty-huts. Meditate, monks, do not be heedless. Do not later regretful be. This to you our instruction."

"Thus, monks, I have taught you the unconditioned, I have taught the path leading to the unconditioned. Whatever should be done, monks, by a teacher out of compassion for his disciples—by one desiring their welfare, by one who is compassionate—that I have done for you. These are the roots of trees, monks, these are empty huts. Meditate, monks, do not be heedless. Do not be regretful later. This is our instruction to you."

Grammatical explanations

asaṅkhatañca vo, bhikkhave, desessāmi asaṅkhatagāmiñca maggaṃ: "I will teach you, monks, the unconditioned and the path leading to the unconditioned." *Asaṅkhataṃ* and *maggaṃ* are both accusative objects of *desessāmi*. *Asaṅkhatagāmiṃ* is an accusative tappurisa compound qualifying *maggaṃ* (see p. 91), here masculine accusative in agreement with *maggaṃ*. The enclitic pronoun *vo* is a second-person plural, "to you." The sentence exemplifies a common Pāli syntactical structure when a single verb takes multiple objects: the first object (here *asaṅkhataṃ*) precedes the verb, the second (here *maggaṃ*) follows it. If there were additional objects, they too would likely follow the verb.

yo, bhikkhave, rāgakkhayo dosakkhayo mohakkhayo, idaṃ vuccati, bhikkhave, "asaṅkhataṃ." "The destruction of lust, the destruction of hatred, the destruction of delusion: this is called the 'unconditioned.'" The pronominal adjective in the relative clause is in the gender appropriate for the term it qualifies—here the masculine *yo* qualifying *rāgakkhayo dosakkhayo mohakkhayo*—while the corresponding demonstrative in the main clause is in the gender appropriate for the word it qualifies, here neuter *idaṃ* qualifying *asaṅkhataṃ*.

hitesinā anukampakena: "by one desiring welfare, by one who is compassionate." Both these instrumentals are in agreement with *satthārā*, instrumental of the agent noun *satthar*. *Hitesin* is compounded of *hita*, "welfare," and the suffix *-esin*, "one who seeks."

anukampaṃ upādāya: "out of compassion." See p. 420.

mā pamādattha: "do not be heedless." The prohibitive particle *mā* with the aorist used in the prohibitive sense. See p. 398. Here the aorist is the second-person plural of *pamajjati*.[248]

mā pacchā vippaṭisārino ahuvattha: "do not be regretful later." Again, the prohibitive particle *mā* is used, here with *ahuvattha*, a second-person plural aorist of *hoti*. *Vippaṭisārino* is a plural possessive in the nominative case derived from the noun *vippaṭisāra*, regret or remorse. It thus means those who possess, or who are overcome by, *vippaṭisāra*.

2. Anatasutta, Etc.

The Uninclined, Etc. (SN 43:13–43; IV 368–73)

"Anatañca vo, bhikkhave, desessāmi, anatagāmiñca maggaṃ. Taṃ suṇātha. Katamañca, bhikkhave, anataṃ?. . . Anāsavañca . . . Saccañca . . . Pārañca . . . Nipuṇañca . . . Sududdasañca . . . Ajajjarañca . . . Dhuvañca . . . Apalokitañca . . . Anidassanañca . . . Nippapañcañca . . . Santañca . . . Amatañca . . . Paṇītañca . . . Sivañca . . . Khemañca . . . Taṇhākkhayañca . . . Acchariyañca . . . Abbhutañca . . . Anītikañca . . . Anītikadhammañca . . . Nibbānañca . . . Avyāpajjhañca . . . Virāgañca . . . Muttiñca . . . Anālayañca . . . Dīpañca . . . Leṇañca . . . Tāṇañca . . . Saraṇañca . . . Parāyaṇañca vo, bhikkhave, desessāmi parāyaṇagāmiñca maggaṃ. Taṃ suṇātha. Katamañca, bhikkhave, parāyaṇaṃ? Yo, bhikkhave, rāgakkhayo dosakkhayo mohakkhayo, idaṃ vuccati, bhikkhave, 'parāyaṇaṃ.' Katamo ca, bhikkhave, parāyaṇagāmī maggo? Kāyagatā sati. Ayaṃ vuccati, bhikkhave, 'parāyaṇagāmī maggo.'

"The uninclined-and to you, monks, I will teach, the uninclined-going-and path. That listen to. What-and, monks, the uninclined?. . . The influx-free-and . . . Truth-and . . . The beyond-and . . . The subtle-and . . . The very-hard-sight-and . . . The unaging-and . . . The everlasting-and . . . The undisintegrating-and . . . The invisible-and . . . The unproliferated-and . . . The peaceful-and . . . The deathless-and . . . The sublime-and . . . The auspicious-and . . . The secure-and . . . Craving-destruction-and . . . The wondrous-and . . . The marvelous-and

248. Perniola (§84) cites *pamādattha* as an example of an a-aorist built up on the pattern of the s-aorist.

. . . The unailing-and . . . The unailing-nature-and . . . Nibbāna-and . . . The unafflicted-and . . . Dispassion-and . . . Freedom-and . . . Non-attachment-and . . . The island-and . . . The cavern-and . . . The shelter-and . . . The refuge-and . . . The destination-and to you, monks, I will teach, the destination-going-and path. That listen to. What-and, monks, the destination? Which, monks, lust-destruction, hatred-destruction, delusion destruction: this is called, monks, 'the destination.' What and, monks, the destination-going path? Body-gone mindfulness. This is called, monks, 'the destination-going path.'

"I will teach you, monks, the uninclined and the path leading to the uninclined. Listen to that. And what, monks, is the uninclined?. . . I will teach you, monks, the influx-free and . . . truth and . . . the beyond and . . . the subtle and . . . the very hard to see and . . . the unaging and . . . the everlasting and . . . the undisintegrating and . . . the invisible and . . . the unproliferated and . . . the peaceful and . . . the deathless and . . . the sublime and . . . the auspicious and . . . the secure and . . . the destruction of craving and . . . the wondrous and . . . the marvelous and . . . the unailing and . . . that not subject to ailing and . . . nibbāna and . . . the unafflicted and . . . dispassion and . . . freedom and . . . non-attachment and . . . the island and . . . the cavern and . . . the shelter and . . . the refuge and . . . the destination and the path leading to the destination. Listen to that. And what, monks, is the destination? The destruction of lust, the destruction of hatred, the destruction of delusion: this is called 'the destination.' And what, monks, is the path leading to the destination? Mindfulness directed to the body: this is called 'the path leading to the destination.'

"Iti kho, bhikkhave, desitaṃ vo mayā parāyaṇaṃ, desito parāyaṇagāmī maggo. Yaṃ, bhikkhave, satthārā karaṇīyaṃ sāvakānaṃ hitesinā anukampakena anukampaṃ upādāya, kataṃ vo taṃ mayā. Etāni, bhikkhave, rukkhamūlāni, etāni suññāgārāni. Jhāyatha, bhikkhave, mā pamādattha; mā pacchā vippaṭisārino ahuvattha. Ayaṃ vo amhākaṃ anusāsanī"ti.

"Thus, monks, taught to you by me the destination, taught the destination-going path. What, monks, by a teacher should-be-done for disciples by-one-seeking-welfare, by a compassionate one, compassion on account of, done for you that by me. These, monks, tree-roots, these empty-huts. Meditate, monks, do not be heedless. Do not later regretful be. This to you our instruction."

"Thus, monks, I have taught the destination, I have taught the path leading to the destination. Whatever should be done, monks, by a teacher out of compassion for his disciples—by one desiring their welfare, by one who is compassionate—that I have done for you. These are the roots of trees, monks, these are empty huts. Meditate, monks, do not be heedless. Do not be regretful later. This is our instruction to you."

Grammatical explanations

anataṃ: "the uninclined." The commentary explains: "Uninclined because of the absence of inclination through craving."[249]

sududdasaṃ: "the very hard to see." The stem of the word is *dasa*, based on **dassati*, "sees." It is prefixed with *su-*, "very," and *dur-*, "hard," with assimilation of *-r-* to the initial consonant of *dasaṃ*.

ajajjaraṃ: "the unaging." The word is formed from *jajjarati*, the intensive of *jarati*, "grows old," which is then negated by the initial *a-*.

nippapañcaṃ: "the unproliferated." The commentary explains that it is called thus because of the absence of proliferation through craving, conceit, and views.[250]

anītikadhammaṃ: "that not subject to ailing." It is hard to see why this should have been included, since it does not add anything to the preceding term in the series.

249. Spk III 112,5: *Anatan ti ādīsu taṇhānatiyā abhāvena anataṃ.*

250. Spk III 112,11–12: *Taṇhāmānadiṭṭhipapañcānaṃ abhāvena nippapañcaṃ.*

Pāli-English Glossary

Organized according to the order of the Pāli alphabet

aṃsa, m. a shoulder

akālika, mfn. non-temporal, immediate

akuppa, mfn. unshakable

akusala, mfn. unwholesome

akkhāta, mfn. expounded, declared

akkhātar, m. an expounder

agāra, n. (1) home, house; (2) the household life

agga, n. the top, the end; mfn. foremost, best

aggi, m. fire

agghati, vb. is worth

aṅga, n. a factor

acakkhuka, mfn. sightless

acira, mfn. not long after

accaya, m. a passage, a lapse, passing away, death

accuggamma, absol. having emerged from, having risen above (< *ati* + *uggacchati*)

acchariya, mfn. wondrous

ajjatagge, ind. from today onward

ajjhattaṃ, ind. internal(ly)

ajjhattika, mfn. internal

ajjhāvuttha, mfn. inhabited

ajjhupekkhitar, mfn. an equanimous observer

ajjhokāse, ind. in the open

ajjhosāya, absol. having held to

ajjhosita, mfn. held to

añjali, m. salutation [with joined palms]

añjasa, n. a road

añña, mfn. other

aññatara, mfn. one, a certain one

aññatitthiya, mfn. belonging to other sects (said of non-Buddhist wanderers)

aññatra, ind. elsewhere, apart from

aññatha, mfn. otherwise

aññathatā, f. otherwiseness

aññathābhāvin, mfn. becoming otherwise

aññamaññaṃ, ind. one another

aññā, f. final knowledge

aññāta, mfn. understood (pp of *ājānāti*)

aṭṭha, num. eight

aṭṭhaṅgika, mfn. eightfold

aṭṭhi, n. a bone

aṇṇava, m. a flood

ativelaṃ, ind. excessively, extremely

atīta, mfn. the past [period of time]

attan, m. (1) the self (as a metaphysical entity); (2) oneself (in reflexive sense)

attaniya, n. what belongs to a self; mfn. belonging to a self

attamana, mfn. elated, satisfied

attha, m. (1) good, benefit; (2) meaning; (3) need

atthaṅgama, m. passing away

atthi, vb. there is, there exists

atthika, mfn. in need of (< *attha*)

atthitā, f. existence

atha, ind. then, but

adukkhamasukha, mfn. neither painful nor pleasant [feeling]

addhan, m. a period of time

addhamāsa, m. a half-month

addhāna, n. a journey [through *saṃsāra*]

adhikaraṇa, n. a reason, a cause

adhigacchati, vb. finds, achieves

adhigata, mfn. found, achieved, attained

adhigama, m. achievement

adhiṭṭhāti, vb. (1) takes a stand upon; (2) determines, resolves on

adhiṭṭhāna, n. a standpoint

adhippāya (*adhippāyāsa*?), m. disparity

adhimatta, mfn. extraordinary, exceptional

adhimuccati, vb. (1) is intent on; (2) is convinced of

adhivacana, n. a designation

adhivāseti, vb. (1) patiently endures; (2) consents

adhunā, ind. recently, newly

adho, ind. downward, below

anagāriya, n. homelessness

anata, n. uninclined, unbent

anabhāva, m. obliteration

anamatagga, mfn. without knowable beginning (said of *saṃsāra*; etymology uncertain)

anaya, m. misery

anavajja, mfn. blameless

anāgata, mfn. the future [period of time]

anāgāmin, m.f., a non-returner

anālaya, m. non-attachment

anāsava, mfn. without influxes

anicca, mfn. impermanent

anītika, mfn. unailing

anukampaka, mfn. compassionate

anukampā, f. compassion

anuga, mfn. one following

anugacchati, vb. follows

anuggaha, m. assistance

anucaṅkamati, vb. walks around

anuṭṭhita, mfn. stabilized

anuttara, mfn. unsurpassed

anudayatā, f. sympathy, kindness

anudahati, anuḍahati, vb. burns

anudhamma: in accordance with [the Dhamma] (at beginning of compounds)

anupagamma, ind. not having approached (neg. absol. of *upagacchati*)

anupabbajjā, f. going forth after

anuparidhāvati, vb. runs around

anuparivattati, vb. revolves around

anupassin, mfn. contemplating (ifc)

anupāta, m. a consequence [of an assertion]

anupādā, anupādāya, ind. without having clung, without clinging (neg. absol. of *upādiyati*)

anuppatta, mfn. reached

anubandhati, vb. follows

anubuddha, mfn. understood (pp of *anubujjhati*)

anubodha, m. understanding

anumodati, vb. rejoices in

anuyāta, mfn. traveled

anuvattati, vb. follows

anuvicarati, vb. wanders around

anuvitakketi, vb. thinks over

anuvidhīyati, vb. submits to, conforms to

anuviloketi, vb. looks around, surveys

anusañcarati, vb. wanders around

anusaya, m. a tendency

anusāsanī, f. instruction

anussati, f. recollection

anussarati, vb. recollects

anussuta, mfn. heard, learned about (usually neg. *ananussuta*, unheard, unlearned)

aneka, mfn. many, numerous

anta, m. (1) end; (2) extreme; (3) side

antamaso, ind. even, even so much as

antara, mfn. internal

antarena, ind. in between, in the midst of

antima, mfn. final

antevāsin, m.f. an apprentice

anto, ind. inside, within, inwardly

andha, n. blindness; mfn. blind

andhakāra, m. darkness

apacaya, m. decline, decrease

apara, mfn. (1) further, another, again; (2) later

aparisesa, mfn. without remainder

apaloketi, vb. takes leave of

apāya, m. misery (collective name for the bad realms of rebirth)

appaṭivānī, f. persistence (not giving up, not turning away)

appamatta, mfn. heedful

appamattaka, mfn. few, trifling

appamāṇa, mfn. measureless

abbhācikkhati, vb. misrepresents

abbhuta, mfn. marvelous

abbhussakkati, abbhussukkati, vb. rises (said of sun)

abhikkanta, mfn. gone forward, advanced (pp of *abhikkamati*)

abhikkama, m. advance

abhikkamati, vb. advances

abhijānāti, vb. directly knows (aor. *abbhaññāsi*)

abhijjhati, vb. longs for

abhijjhā, f. longing

abhiññā[1], f. direct knowledge, higher knowledge

abhiññā[2], ind. having directly known (absol. of *abhijānāti*)

abhitatta, mfn. scorched

abhinandati, vb. delights in

abhinandita, mfn. delighted in

abhinandin, mfn. delighting in (ifc)

abhinibbatti, f. production
abhinivesa, m. adherence
abhibhavati, vb. overcomes
abhiramati, vb. delights in
abhiruhati, vb. climbs up
abhivadati, vb. welcomes
abhivādeti, vb. pays homage to
abhivihacca, ind. having dispersed, having destroyed (absol. of *abhivihanati*)
abhisaṅkhata, mfn. volitionally generated
abhisaṅkharoti, vb. generates (through volitional activity); instigates volitional activity
abhisañcetayita, mfn. volitionally produced
abhisañceteti, vb. volitionally produces
abhisamaya, m. breakthrough, realization
abhisameta, mfn. broken through, realized
abhisameti, vb. makes a breakthrough, realizes
abhisambujjhati, vb. becomes fully enlightened, fully awakens to
abhisambuddha, mfn. fully enlightened
abhihaṃsati, vb. rejoices in
abhiharati, vb. carries, conveys
amacca, m. a companion
amata, n. the deathless
amanussa, m. non-human (usually referring to a spirit or demon)
ambho, ind. exclamatory particle used to attract attention, often followed by voc.
arati, f. discontent
arahat, m. "a worthy one," one liberated from all defilements (untranslated)
arahati, vb. is worthy
ariya, mfn. noble, a noble one
aru, n. a wound
aruṇa, m. the dawn
alaṃ, ind. fitting, suitable, enough, sufficient
alla, mfn. wet
avacara, m. a sphere, a domain
avasiṭṭha, mfn. remained, left over
avasissati, vb. remains
avijjā, f. ignorance
avidūre, ind. not far, near
avihiṃsā, f. harmlessness
avecca, ind. having confirmed, having penetrated; unshakable
avoca, avocuṃ, aor. vb. said
avyagga, m. non-diffusion
asaṅkhata, n. unconditioned
asāraka, mfn. insubstantial
asi, m. a sword
asita, mfn. eaten
asuci, mfn. impure
asesa, mfn. without remainder, remainderless
asmimāna, m. the conceit "I am"
assāda, m. enjoyment
assāsa, m. comfort
assutavat, mfn. unlearned
aha (*aho*), n. a day
ahaṅkāra, m. I-making
ahi, m. a snake

ākaṅkhati, vb. wishes, desires

ākiṇṇa, mfn. filled with, full of

ākāsa, m. space, the sky

āgata, mfn. come

āgamma, ind. relying upon, owing to (absol. of *āgacchati*)

ācaya, m. growth, increase

ācariya, m. a teacher

ācāra, m. behavior, conduct, custom

ācikkhaṇā, f. pointing out, explaining

ācikkhati, vb. points out, explains

ājānāti, vb. understands

ājīva, m. livelihood

ātapa, m. the sun's heat

ātāpin, mfn. ardent

ādāna, n. [act of] taking

ādāya, absol. having taken

ādi, m. beginning, basis

ādicca, m. the sun

āditta, mfn. burning

ādīnava, m. a danger

ānisaṃsa, m. a benefit

āneñja, n. imperturbable state; mfn. imperturbable

āpajjati, vb. enters upon, incurs, attains, falls into

āpas, n. water

āpānīyakaṃsa, m. a goblet [filled with a beverage]

ābādha, m. an affliction

ābādhika, mfn. afflicted

āmanteti, vb. addresses

āmisa, n. (1) carnal pleasure; (2) bait

āyatiṃ, ind. in the future

āyasmat, m. venerable (respectful appellation of a monk)

āyu, n. life, vitality

ārakā, ind. from afar

āraddha, mfn. aroused

ārabbha, ind. with reference to, concerning (absol. of *ārabhati*)

ārabhati, vb. arouses

ārambha, m. arousal

ārammaṇa, n. a basis

ārādhaka, m. one who achieves

ārādheti, vb. satisfies

ārāma, m. (1) delight; (2) a park, a monastery; (3) mfn. delights in (ifc)

ārogya, n. health

āroceti, vb. reports, informs

āropeti, vb. picks up, lifts up

āloka, m. light

ālokita, mfn. looked ahead

āvaṭṭa, m. a whirlpool, a vortex

āvattati, vb. reverts

āvahati, vb. carries along

āviñjati, vb. pulls

āvuso, m. sg. and pl. voc. "friend" (polite but friendly form of address)

āsana, n. a seat

āsabha, m. a bull; mfn. bull-like

āsaya, m. a lair, an abode

āsava, m. an influx

āsiñcati, vb. pours, sprinkles

āsītika, mfn. eighty (said of person's age)

āsevanā, f. regular practice

āha, vb. says

āharati, vb. brings

āhāra, m. nutriment

āhāreti, vb. consumes [food]

āhuneyya, mfn. worthy of gifts
iṭṭha, mfn. wished for
iti, ind. thus
ito, ind. from here
ittha, ind. thus
itthatta, n. this state of being (the state of being thus, existence in this form)
idappaccayatā, f. specific conditionality
idāni, ind. now
iddha, mfn. successful, powerful
idha, ind. here, now
inda, m. a lord, a ruler
indriya, n. a faculty
ukkhitta, mfn. uplifted
ucca, mfn. high, tall, grand
uccāra, m. feces
ucchinna, mfn. cut off (pp of *ucchindati*)
uju, mfn. straight
ujjāleti, vb. to cause to blaze
uṭṭhāya, ind. having risen, having gotten up (absol. of *uṭṭhahati*, *uṭṭhāti*)
uṇha, mfn. hot
utu, m. a season
uttariṃ, ind. further, beyond, above
uttāna, mfn. elucidated
uttānīkamma, n. elucidation
uttānīkaroti, vb. elucidates
udāharati, vb. utters, pronounces
udeti, vb. rises
uddāpa, m. a mound
uddesika, mfn. dependent on
uddhaṃ, ind. upward, after
uddhacca, n. restlessness
uddhata, mfn. excited, agitated
uddharati, vb. removes, raises
udraya, mfn. outcome (usually ifc)
upaga, mfn. approached
upagacchati, vb. approaches, considers
upaṭṭhāka, m. an attendant
upaṭṭhita, mfn. established, set up
upaḍḍha, n., mfn. half
upatiṭṭhati, vb. stands near
upadhi, m. an acquisition
upanikkhitta, mfn. placed, put down (pp of *upanikkhipati*)
upanikkhipati, vb. places, puts down
upanidhā, f. comparison
upanidhāya, ind. compared with
upanipajjati, vb. lies down near
upanibaddha, mfn. bound
upanibandhati, vb. ties, binds
upanisīdati, vb. sits near
upapajjati, vb. is reborn
upaparikkhati, vb. investigates
upamā, f. a simile
upaya, m. involvement
upari, ind. above, upward
upalitta, mfn. tainted
upasaṃhita, mfn. connected with (ifc)
upasaṅkamati, vb. approaches
upasaṅkamana, n. approaching
upasama, m. peace, calming down
upasampajjati, vb. enters, attains
upasampadā, f. ordination [into the monastic Sangha]
upasussati, vb. dries up
upahāra, m. presentation, provision

upādāna, n. (1) clinging; (2) sustenance, support
upādāya, ind. on account of, for the sake of, in dependence on (absol. of *upādiyati*)
upādiyati, vb. clings
upāyāsa, m. misery
upārambha, m. condemnation
upekkhā, f. equanimity
upeti, vb. approaches, becomes involved, enters upon
uposatha, m. the religious observance day (untranslated)
uppajjati, vb. arises (aor. *udapādi*)
uppanna, mfn. arisen
uppala, n. a blue lotus
uppāda, m. arising
uppādetar, m. an originator
ubhaya, n., mfn. both
ummagga, m. a wrong path
ummujjati, vb. emerges, comes to the surface
uyyāna, n. a garden
usīra, n. a particular kind of grass, esp. its roots
usmā, f. heat
ussāda, m. being cast up
ussāpeti, vb. sets up
ussāha, m. zeal
ussīdati, vb. is cast up
ussussati, vb. dries up
ussoḷhī, f. enthusiasm
ūmi, f. a wave
eka, num., mfn. one
ekagga, mfn. one-pointed
ekacca, mfn. some, someone
ekodibhūta, mfn. unified
etarahi, ind. now, at present
eti, vb. comes
ettaka, mfn. this much
ettāvatā, ind. in this way, to this extent
ettha, ind. here, about this, in relation to this
eva, ind. just, indeed, actually, the very same, exactly (term of emphasis)
evaṃ, ind. thus, such, in such a way
esin, mfn. seeking (ifc)
ehipassika, mfn. inviting one to come and see
okāsa, m. (1) an open space; (2) an opportunity, a chance, a favor
okirati, vb. sprinkles
oja, m. sap, nutritive essence
oḍḍita, mfn. trapped
oḍḍeti, vb. sets up a trap, lays a snare
otarati, vb. descends into, enters
otāra, m. an opening, an opportunity
odāta, mfn. white
opanayika, mfn. applicable, fit for making use of
opunāti, vb. winnows
obhāsa, m. radiance
orambhāgiya, mfn. lower, pertaining to this world
orima, mfn. near [shore or bank of a river]
orohati, vb. descends
oḷārika, mfn. gross
ossajjati, vb. lets go, lets loose
ohita, mfn. laid down

kaṅkhati, vb. is perplexed, has doubt

kacci, ind. an interrog. particle expressing doubt

kaṭṭha, n. a log, wood

kaṇṭaka, m. a thorn

kaṇha, mfn. dark

kata, mfn. done

katama, mfn., interrog. what? which?

kathaṃ, ind., interrog. how?

kathā, f. talk, discussion

kathika, mfn. a speaker

katheti, vb. talks, speaks

kadali, f. a plantain

kadāci, ind. rarely, hardly ever, if at all (with *karahaci*)

kanta, mfn. desired

kapalla, n. shard, potsherd

kapāla, m. a begging bowl

kappeti, vb. arranges, makes [a living]

kabaliṅkāra, mfn. "made into a ball," edible food (with *āhāra*)

kamanīya, mfn. lovely

kamma, n. action, a deed; also untranslated

kammanta, m. action

kammāsa, mfn. mottled

karaṇīya, mfn. should be done, should be made

karīsa, n. feces

karoti, vb. does, makes

kalandaka, m. a squirrel

kalā, f. a fraction (often a sixteenth part)

kalyāṇa, mfn. good

kalyāṇī, f. a beautiful woman

kalla, n. what is fit, what is proper; mfn. fit, proper

kasati, vb. plows

kassaka, m. a plowman

kāma, m. sensuality, sensual desire, desire; mfn. desiring, wishing (ifc)

kāmaṃ, ind. willingly

kāya, m. the body

kāra, m. a deed [of service]

kārin, mfn. one who acts (ifc)

kāla, m. time

kāḷa, mfn. black

kāsāva, n. an ochre robe

kiṃ, n., interrog. what? why?

kiccha, n. trouble

kiñci, ind. something, anything

kittāvatā, ind., interrog. in what way? to what extent?

kinti, ind., interrog. why indeed? precisely how?

kira, ind. indeed, it seems, it is said

kiriyā, f. activity

kilanta, mfn. fatigued

kilamatha, m. fatigue

kukkucca, n. regret

kukkura, m. a dog

kuṭhārī, f. an axe

kuto, ind., interrog. how?

kudāssu, ind., interrog. when indeed? when will?

kuddāla, m. a shovel

kumbha, m. a pot

kumbhakāra, m. a potter

kummagga, m. a bad path

kusa, m. kusa grass

kusala, mfn. wholesome

kusīta, mfn. lazy

kūṭa, m. a peak

kevala, mfn. whole, entire

koṭi, f. a point

kovida, mfn. skilled

khaṇḍa, n. a piece; mfn. broken; *khaṇḍākhaṇḍikaṃ*, ind. [broken] into pieces

khattuṃ, ind. "times" (ifc with num.)

khanti, f. patience

khandha, m. (1) aggregate; (2) mass; (3) trunk (of tree), stem (of plant), log; (4) shoulder

khamanīya, n. bearing up

khaya, m. destruction

khara, mfn. terrible

khāyati, vb. appears

khāyita, mfn. eaten, chewed

khitta, mfn. thrown

khippaṃ, ind. quickly

khīṇa, mfn. destroyed, finished

khīla, m. a post

khetta, n. a field

khema, n. security

kho, ind. (1) a mere expletive; (2) marker of a change of subject or a further stage in a narrative, often in the expressions *atha kho* and *kho pana*

gaṇṭhi, m. a knot

gaṇhāti, vb. grasps, grabs, takes

gata, mfn. gone

gati, f. range, movement, destination

gatta, n. body, limbs

gaddula, m. a leash

gandha, m. odor, fragrance

gambhīra, mfn. deep

gavesin, mfn. seeking (ifc)

gahana, n. a thicket

gahapati, m. a householder

gahita, mfn. taken, grasped

gāma, m. a village

gāmin, mfn. going (to), leading (to) (ifc)

gāyati, vb. sings

gārayha, mfn. deserving criticism, blameworthy

gāvo, m. pl. cows

gāha, m.n. (1) seizing, holding, grasp; (2) m. a dangerous water-creature, perhaps a shark or crocodile

gāheti, vb. acquires (caus. of *gaṇhāti*)

giddhin, mfn. having a longing for, greedy for (ifc)

gimhāna, n. the hot season; mfn. of the hot season

gilati, vb. swallows

gilāna, m. illness; m.f. an ill person, a patient

gilita, mfn. swallowed

gihin, m. a layman

gīta, n. singing

gīva, n. the neck

guṇa, m. quality, aspect, object

gutta, mfn. guarded

gelañña, n. an illness

go, m. a cow; pl. *gāvo*

gocara, m. a range, a feeding ground

gopālaka, m. a cowherd

gomaya, n. cow dung

ghamma, m. heat, hot weather

ghāna, n. the nose

ca, ind. (1) and (conjunctive particle); (2) but (disjunctive particle)

cakka, n. a wheel

cakkhu, n. the eye

cakkhumat, mfn. clear-sighted

cajati, vb. (1) gives up, renounces; (2) discharges (urine and feces)

caṇḍālavaṃsa, m. a bamboo pole (used in an acrobatic feat)

caṇḍālavaṃsika, m. an acrobat

catuttha, mfn. fourth

catummahāpatha, m. a crossroads

catur, num. four (*cattāro*, m.; *cattāri*, n.; *catasso*, f.)

canda, m. the moon

candima, m. the moon

caraṇa, n. conduct, esp. good conduct

cariyā, f. conduct (ifc)

cala, mfn. moving

cavati, vb. passes away

cāga, m. giving up, generosity

cātummahābhūtika, mfn. consisting of the four great elements

cārī, m. or f. traveling, accessibility

citta, n. the mind

cira, mfn. long (of time); *ciraṃ* (ind.) for a long time

cīvara, n. a robe

ce, ind. if

cetanā, f. volition, intention

cetas, n. the mind

cetasika, mfn. mental

ceteti, vb. intends

cela, n. a cloth, a turban

chaḍḍeti, vb. throws away, spills [a liquid]

chanda, m. desire

chādeti, vb. pleases

chidda, mfn. torn

chindati, vb. cuts

jajjara, mfn. dilapidated, aged

jana, m. people, a person

janapada, m. a country, a province

janeti, vb. generates

jarā, f. old age

jalati, vb. burns

jāgarita, mfn. awake, wakeful

jāta, n. kind, class; mfn. born, produced

jāti, f. birth, genesis

jātika, mfn. of such a kind (ifc)

jānāti, vb. knows

jāyati, vb. is born, arises

jiṇṇa, mfn. old

jivhā, f. the tongue

jīyati, vb. grows old

jīvati, vb. lives

jīvita, n. life, living

jhatta, mfn. weakened (pp of *jhāyati*, consumed, dried up)

jhāna, n. a meditative absorption (untranslated)

jhāyati[1], vb. meditates

jhāyati[2], vb. burns

ñāṇa, n. knowledge

ñāti, m. a relative

ñāya, m. a method

ṭhāti, vb. stands (also *tiṭṭhati*)

ṭhāna, n. a place, position, possibility

ṭhānīya, mfn. basis for (ifc)

ṭhita, mfn. stood, steady

ṭhitatā, f. stability

ṭhiti, f. (1) stability, duration, continuation; (2) a support

ṭhitika, mfn. subsistent on, supported by (ifc)

ḍayhati, vb. is burnt

ḍahati, vb. burns

taggha, ind. surely, certainly, indeed

taca, m. skin

tajja, mfn. appropriate, corresponding

taṇhā, f. craving

tatiya, mfn. third

tato, ind. from that, because of that

tatonidānaṃ, ind. because of that, on that account

tattha, ind. there

tatra, ind. there

tatha, mfn. real, true

tathatā, f. reality, truth

tathā, ind. thus, in such a way

tathāgata, m. an honorific designation of the Buddha (untranslated)

tathārūpa, mfn. such kind of

tandī, f. lethargy

tapati, vb. beams, shines

tama, n. darkness

tasati, vb. craves, thirsts

tasita, mfn. thirsty

tasmā, ind. therefore; *tasmātiha*, ind. therefore (often followed by an injunction)

tāṇa, n. a shelter

tārakā, f. a star

tāla, m. a palm tree

ti, num. three (*tayo*, m.; *tīṇi*, n.; *tisso*, f.)

ti, ind. marker for the end of an emphatic statement or a direct quotation

tiṇa, n. grass, weed

tiṇṇa, mfn. crossed over (pp of *tarati*)

tiṇha, mfn. sharp

tiṭṭhati, vb. stands, lasts, endures (also *ṭhāti*)

titti, f. the brim [of a bowl]

timisā, f. gloom

tiracchānagata, m. an animal

tiriyaṃ, ind. across

tīra, n. a bank [of a river], the shore [of a lake or ocean]

tucchaka, mfn. hollow

tuṇḍa, n. a beak [of a bird], a snout [of an animal]

tuṇhībhāva, m. silence

tumhākaṃ, gen. pl. pron. yours

tena hi, ind. in that case

tela, n. oil

thambha, m. a pillar

thala, n. high ground, dry land

thāma, m. strength

thīna, n. dullness

thunati, vb. moans, groans

thulla, mfn. big

thoka, mfn. a little, a few

daka [= *udaka*], n. water

dakkhiṇeyya, mfn. worthy of offerings

daṭṭhabba, mfn. should be seen, to be seen

daṇḍa, m. a stick

dadhi, n. curds; *dadhimaṇḍaka*, m. whey

damma, mfn. tamable, to be tamed

daḷha, mfn. firm, tight, strong

**dassati*, vb. sees

dassana, n. vision, seeing

dassāvin, mfn. a seer (one who sees)

dāni [= *idāni*], ind. now

dāma, n. a harness

dāya, m. a forest, a park

dāru, n. wood

diṭṭha, mfn. seen

diṭṭhadhammika, mfn. pertaining to this present life

diṭṭhā, ind. fortunate, lucky

diṭṭhi, f. a view

dinna, mfn. given

diva, m. a day

divasa, m. a day

disā, f. a quarter, a direction

dissati, vb. is seen

dīgha, mfn. long

dīgharatta, n. a long time

dīna, mfn. disappointed

dīpa, n. an island

dukkha, n. pain, suffering; mfn. painful

dukkhita, mfn. miserable, sick

dugga, mfn. impassable

duggati, f. a bad destination [of rebirth]

duccarita, n. misconduct

dutiya, mfn. second

duddasa, mfn. hard to see

dūre, ind. far, at a distance

deva, m. (1) a celestial being (untranslated); (2) the sky

desa, m. (1) a place; (2) a point [of doctrine]

desanā, f. teaching

desita, mfn. taught

deseti, vb. teaches

domanassa, n. dejection

dosa, m. hatred

dvaya, n. a dyad, duality

dhamma, m. (1) the Buddha's teaching; (2) any teaching or doctrine; (3) what is righteous; (4) mental object; (5) a thing; (6) a quality

dhātu, f. an element

dhāraṇa, n. (1) retaining in mind, remembering; (2) wearing; (3) carrying

dhāreti, vb. retains in mind, remembers

dhuva, mfn. lasting, stable, everlasting

na, ind. not, no

nakha, m. nail [of finger or toe]

nagara, n. a city

naṅgala, n. a plow

nacca, n. dancing

naccati, vb. dances

natthi, vb. there is not, does not exist

natthitā, f. non-existence

nadati, vb. roars

nadī, f. a river

nandi, nandī, f. delight

nabha, n. the sky, the firmament

nava, mfn. new, young, fresh

nahāru, m. a sinew

nāga, m. a serpent-like spirit (untranslated)

nāda, m. a roar

nānā, ind. different, differently

nānākaraṇa, n. difference

nāma[1], ind. (1) by name, called; (2) a marker of emphasis

nāma[2], n. "name" (the set of mental factors invariably associated with consciousness)

nikkaṅkha, mfn. without perplexity

nikkama, m. endeavor

nikkhamati, vb. comes out

nikkhepana, n. putting down, laying down

nigacchati, vb. undergoes

nigama, m. a town

nicca, mfn. permanent

nijjhāyati, vb. ponders, meditates on

nidassana, mfn. invisible

nidāna, n. a cause

ninna, mfn. slanting toward (ifc)

nipatati, vb. falls, drops

nipuṇa, mfn. subtle

nibbāna, n. the ultimate goal of the Dhamma (untranslated)

nibbāpana, n. [act of] extinguishing

nibbāpeti, vb. extinguishes

nibbicikiccha, mfn. without doubt

nibbidā, f. disenchantment

nibbindati, vb. becomes disenchanted

nimitta, n. an object, a mark, a feature

niyata, m.f. fixed [in destiny]

niyāmatā, f. orderliness

niyyādita, mfn. returned, given back

niyyādeti, vb. returns, gives back

niraya, m. hell

nirāmisa, mfn. non-sensual

nirujjhati, vb. ceases

nirodha, m. cessation

nivāpa, m. fodder, feeding ground

nivāreti, vb. restrains, reins in

nivisati, vb. settles down

nivuta, mfn. hindered

nivesana, n. a residence

niveseti, vb. settles in, establishes in

nisinna, mfn. seated

nisīdati, vb. sits down

nissaṭa, mfn. escaped

nissaraṇa, n. an escape

nissarati, vb. escapes

nissāya, ind. based on (absol. of *nissayati*)

nissita, mfn. supported by, dependent upon (ifc)

nīvaraṇa, m. a hindrance

nu, ind. an interrog. particle (often followed by *kho*)

nūna, ind. (1) surely, indeed; (2) perhaps

nekkhamma, n. renunciation

netti, f. a guide; *nettika*, mfn. guided by

no[1], 1st person pl. pron. us, by us, to us, our

no[2], ind. no, not (emphatic)

paṃsu, m. soil, dust

pakāraka, mfn. of kinds (ifc)

pakāsita, mfn. revealed, proclaimed

pakkamati, vb. departs

pakkhāyati, vb. clearly appears

pakkhin, m. a bird

pakkhipati, vb. throws

paggaṇhāti, vb. applies [the mind]

paccakkhāya, ind. having disavowed (absol. of *paccakkhāti*)

paccattaṃ, ind. personally

paccaya, m. (1) a condition; (2) a support, a requisite

paccāsiṃsati, vb. expects

paccuppanna, mfn. present

pacchā, ind. (1) later, afterward; (2) westward

pacchima, mfn. last

pajahati, vb. abandons

pajā, f. population, people

pajānāti, vb. understands

pañca, num. five

paññatta, mfn. (1) made known; (2) prepared (said of a seat)

paññā, f. wisdom

paññāpanā, f. making known

paññāpeti, vb. makes known

paññāyati, vb. is discerned

pañha, m. a question

paṭikūla, mfn. repulsive; repelled by, averse to (ifc)

paṭikkanta, mfn. returned (pp of paṭikkamati)

paṭikkama, m. retreat, subsiding

paṭikkamati, vb. retreats, subsides

paṭigha, m. aversion

paṭicca, ind. in dependence on (absol. of *pacceti*)

paṭijānāti, vb. claims

paṭinissagga, m. relinquishment

paṭinissajjati, vb. rejects, relinquishes

paṭipaṇāmeti, vb. suppresses

paṭipadā, f. way, practice

paṭipanna, mfn. practicing

paṭibhaya, n. danger

paṭibhāga, m. counterpart

paṭibhāti, vb. occurs to, shines upon

paṭividdha, mfn. penetrated (pp of *paṭivijjhati*)

paṭivirata, mfn. abstained from

paṭivedha, m. penetration

paṭisaṃvedeti, paṭisaṃvediyati, vb. experiences

paṭisaṃvedin, mfn. one who experiences

paṭisaṅkhā, absol. having reflected

paṭisaraṇa, n. recourse

paṭisallāna, n. seclusion

paṭisalliyati, vb. is in seclusion

paṭissuṇāti, vb. replies (usually as aor. *paccassosi, paccassosuṃ*)

paṭṭhapanā, f. establishing

paṭṭhapeti, vb. establishes

paṭhama, mfn. first

paṭhavī, f. the earth

paṇāmeti, vb. salutes, bends down

paṇīta, mfn. superior, excellent

paṇḍita, m. a wise person; mfn. wise

paṇṇa, n. a leaf

patiṭṭhāpeti, vb. establishes in

patitthīna, mfn. obdurate

patirūpa, mfn. proper

patta[1], mfn. attained, reached (usually ifc)

patta[2], n. a leaf

patta[3], n. an almsbowl
pattabba, mfn. to be attained
patti, f. attainment
pattheti, vb. yearns for
padakkhiṇa, n. circumambulation
padahati, vb. strives
padīpa, m. a lamp
paduma, n. a lotus
pana, ind. adversative and interrog. particle, a narrative connective: but, now then, and (often untranslatable)
pannarasa, mfn. the fifteenth [of the lunar fortnight]
papāta, m. a precipice
pabbajati, vb. goes forth [into homelessness]
pabbajjā, f. the going forth [into homelessness]
pabbata, m. a mountain
pabbhāra, m. incline [of a mountain]; mfn. inclining toward (ifc)
pabhava, m. source, origin
pabhā, f. radiance
pamajjati, vb. is heedless
pamatta, mfn. heedless
pamāda, m. heedlessness
payirupāsana, n. attending on
para, mfn. other, another
parakkama, m. exertion
parama, mfn. supreme, maximum
parāmaṭṭha, mfn. grasped
parāyana, n. destination; mfn. having as destination (ifc)
parikkhīṇa, mfn. fully destroyed
paricita, mfn. repeatedly practiced
parijānāti, vb. fully understands
pariññā, f. full understanding
pariññāta, mfn. fully understood
pariññeyya, mfn. to be fully understood
pariṇāmin, mfn. evolving toward, maturing in (ifc)
paritassati, vb. thirsts [on account of craving]
paritta, mfn. a few, little, limited
parideva, m. lamentation
parinibbāyati, vb. attains [final] *nibbāna*
paripūreti, vb. fulfills
paribbājaka, m. a wanderer
paribhuñjati, vb. uses, enjoys
parimuccati, vb. is freed
pariyantika, mfn. limited by
pariyādāna, n. exhaustion, elimination
pariyādinna, mfn. eliminated
pariyādiyati, vb. eliminates
pariyāpanna, mfn. included in (ifc)
pariyāya, m. a method, a way
pariyesanā, f. quest
pariyosāna, n. goal
parivajjati, vb. avoids
parivīmaṃsati, vb. investigates
parivīmaṃsā, f. an investigation
parivuta, mfn. surrounded by
parisā, f. an assembly
pariharati, vb. (1) carries around; (2) leads [a community]
parihāpeti, vb. discards, abandons
pareta, mfn. afflicted
palaḷita, mfn. deceived

palāsa, n. foliage

palāyati, paleti, vb. flees

palikhaṇati, vb. digs around

palokita, mfn. disintegrating

pavaḍḍhati, vb. increases

pavatteti, vb. rolls, sets in motion

pavana, n. a forest

pavāreti, vb. invites

pavāheti, vb. causes to be carried away

pavicarati, vb. examines

pavicinati, vb. discriminates

pavivitta, mfn. secluded from

pavisati, vb. enters

paveseti, vb. inserts (caus. of *pavisati*)

pasattha, mfn. praised

pasavati, vb. engenders, produces

pasāda, m. confidence

pasārita, mfn. stretched out [of the limbs]

passati, vb. sees

passaddha, mfn. tranquil

passaddhi, f. tranquility

passambhati, vb. becomes tranquil

passāva, m. urine

pahātabba, mfn. to be abandoned

pahāna, n. abandoning

pahitatta, mfn. resolute

pahīna, mfn. abandoned

pahīyati, vb. is abandoned

pāka, m. an oven

pācīna, mfn. eastward

pāṭikaṅkha, mfn. to be expected

pāṇa, pāṇaka, m. a living being, a creature

pāṇātipāta, m. destruction of life

pāṇi, m. a hand

pāṇin, m. a living being

pātarāsa, m. breakfast

pātubhāva, m. manifestation

pāteti, vb. fells (caus. of *patati*)

pāda, m. a foot

pānīya, n. water

pāpaka, mfn. bad, evil

pāpimā, m. the Evil One (an epithet of Māra)

pāpuṇāti, vb. attains, reaches

pāra, n. the beyond, the far shore

pāripūrī, f. fulfillment

pārima, mfn. far [shore or bank of a river]

pārisuddhi, f. purification

pāsāṇa, m. a rock, a stone

pāsāda, m. a mansion

pāsāvin, mfn. a performer

pāhuneyya, mfn. worthy of hospitality

pi, ind. also, too, even, although

piṭaka, n. a basket

piṭṭhi, f. the back

piṇḍa, n. a lump

piṇḍapāta, m. almsfood

pipāsita, mfn. thirsty, parched

pipāsitā, f. thirst

piya, mfn. pleasing, dear

pilotikā, f. a patch of cloth, rag, bandage

pivati, vb. drinks

pisuṇa, mfn. divisive [speech]

pīta, mfn. drunk

pīti, f. rapture

puggala, m. a person, an individual

pucchati, vb. asks

puñña, n. merit; mfn. meritorious

puṇḍarīka, n. a white lotus

puṇṇa, mfn. full

puṇṇamā, f. the day or night of the full moon

puthujjana, m. a worldling, an ordinary person

puthubhūta, mfn. widespread

punabbhava, m. renewed existence

pubba, mfn. (1) former, first, the past; (2) eastern

pubbaka, mfn. former, of the past

pubbaṅgama, n. a forerunner

pubbaṇha, m. the morning

pubbanimitta, n. a sign

pubbe, ind. in the past, prior to

purāṇa, mfn. old

purima, mfn. former, previous

purisa, m. a man, a person

pūti, pūtika, mfn. rotten

pettika, mfn. ancestral

pettivisaya, m. the domain of spirits

peyya, n. a beverage

pokkharaṇī, f. a pond

poṇa, mfn. sloping toward (ifc)

ponobhavika, mfn. causing renewed existence

phandati, vb. shimmers

pharusa, mfn. harsh [speech]

phala, n. a fruit

phassa, m. contact

phāleti, vb. splits

phāsu, m. comfort; mfn. comfortable

phīta, mfn. prosperous

phuṭṭha, mfn. contacted, touched

phusati, vb. touches, reaches, contacts

phusita, n. a raindrop

pheggu, n. softwood

pheṇa, n. foam

phoṭṭhabba, m. a tactile object

bajjhati, vb. is bound

baddha, mfn. bound, tied up

bandha, m. a bond

bandhati, vb. binds, ties

bandhana, n. bondage

bandhanīya, mfn. captivating

bala, m. power, strength

balavat, mfn. strong

balivadda, m. an ox

balisa (*baḷisa*), m.n. a fish hook

bahiddhā, ind. external(ly)

bahu, mfn. many

bahukāra, mfn. helpful

bahula, mfn. abounding in (ifc)

bahulīkata, mfn. cultivated

bahulīkamma, n. cultivation

bahulīkaroti, vb. cultivates

bahulīkāra, m. cultivation

bādhana, n. trapping, catching

bāla, m. a fool; mfn. foolish

bālisika (*bāḷisika*), m. a fisherman

bāḷha, mfn. severe

bāhira, mfn. external

bāhujañña, mfn. populated

bila, n. a hole

buddha, m. an enlightened one; mfn. enlightened

bubbuḷa, n. a bubble

bojjhaṅga, m. a factor of enlightenment

bodhisatta, m. a future buddha, a seeker of enlightenment (untranslated)

brahma, mfn. holy, spiritual

brahmacariya, n. (1) the spiritual life; (2) pure conduct (celibacy)

brāhmaṇa, m. a brahmin

bhagavā, m. the Blessed One

bhaññati, vb. is spoken

bhatta, n. a meal

bhadante, voc. respectful term of address for the Buddha or a senior monk

bhante, voc. contraction of *bhadante*

bhabba, mfn. capable

bhaya, n. (1) fear; (2) peril

bhava, m. existence

bhavaṃ, m. an honorific designation used by the brahmins when speaking about other brahmins or other distinguished persons (voc. bho)

bhavati, vb. is, becomes, comes to be, occurs

bhāga, m. a portion, a part

bhāgin, mfn. one who partakes of

bhāra, m. a burden

bhāvita, mfn. developed

bhāvetabba, mfn. to be developed

bhāveti, vb. develops (caus. of *bhavati*)

bhāsati[1], vb. speaks, states

bhāsati[2], vb. shines

bhāsita, n. a statement; mfn. stated, spoken

bhikkhu, m. a Buddhist monk

bhikkhunī, f. a Buddhist nun

bhiyyo, ind. more

bhiyyobhāva, m. increase

bhiyyosomattāya, ind. to a greater extent, even more so

bhīta, mfn. frightened

bhujissa, m.f. a freeman, a freed slave; mfn. freeing

bhuñjati, vb. (1) eats; (2) enjoys

bhutta, mfn. eaten

bhūta, mfn. (1) come to be; (2) real, genuine

bhūtapubbaṃ, ind. in the past

bhūmi, f. the ground, the earth

bheda, m. breakup

bhesajja, n. medicine

bho, voc. of *bhavaṃ*

bhoga, m. wealth

maṃsa, n. flesh

makkaṭa. m. a monkey

magga, m. a path

maṅku, mfn. dismayed

maccha, m. a fish

majja, n. an intoxicant

majjha, m. the middle

majjhanhika, mfn. pertaining to midday

maññati, vb. thinks

maññe, ind. "one would think," it seems, as it were

maṇḍa, m. cream

matta, mfn. by amount, by measure (usually ifc)

madanīya, mfn. intoxicating

madhuraka, mfn. drugged

mana, manas, m.n. the mind
manasikaroti, vb. attends
manasikāra, m. attention
manāpa, mfn. agreeable
manussa, m. a human being
manussatta, n. the human state
mamaṅkāra, m. mine-making
mamāyita, mfn. appropriated
maya, mfn. made of, consisting of (ifc)
maraṇa, n. death
marati, vb. dies
marīcikā, f. a mirage
masi, m. ash
mahat, mfn. great
mahantatta, n. greatness
mahallaka, mfn. old, elderly
mahānubhāva, m. might; mfn. mighty
mahābhūta, m. great element
mahāmatta, m. a minister [of government]
mahiddhika, mfn. powerful
mahesakkha, mfn. commanding, influential
mā, neg. particle, do not
mātar, f. a mother
māna, m. conceit
mānasa, n. mind's ideal, purpose, intention
māpeti, vb. builds
māyā, f. a magical illusion
māyākāra, m. a magician
māsa, m. a month
micchā, ind. wrong
miga, m. (1) a beast; (2) a deer
mitta, m. a friend
middha, n. drowsiness
missaka, n. mixture, combination
mīyati, vb. dies
mukha, m. the mouth
mugga, m. a mung bean
mucchanīya, mfn. infatuating
muñcati, vb. lets go
muṭṭhi, f. a fist
muṇḍa, mfn. shaven-headed
mutta[1], n. urine
mutta[2], mfn. freed
mutti, f. freedom
musāvāda, m. false speech
mūla, n. root, bottom
mūlaka, mfn. rooted in
meraya, n. wine
moceti, vb. frees
moha, m. delusion

yagghe, ind. particle used in addressing a superior person
yato, ind. when, since
yathā, ind. as, like, according to, in accordance with
yathābhūtaṃ, ind. as it really is, correctly
yadā, ind. when
yadi, ind. if
yadidaṃ, ind. that is, namely
yasmā, ind. because, since
yānīkata, mfn. made a vehicle
yāpanīya, n. getting along [in good health]
yāpeti, vb. gets along, keeps going

yāva, ind. as long as, as far as; often completed by *tāva*, for just so long, just so far

yuga, n. (1) a yoke; (2) a pair

yebhuyyena, ind. mostly, for the most part

yoga, m. exertion

yotta, n. a yoke

yoni, f. (1) origin; (2) womb; (3) realm of existence

yoniso, ind. thoroughly

rakkhati, vb. protects

rakkhasa, m. a kind of demon that haunts the ocean

rakkhita, mfn. protected

rajanīya, mfn. enticing, arousing lust

rajju, f. a rope

rata, mfn. delighted with (ifc)

ratti, f. night

ramaṇīya, mfn. delightful

rasa, m. taste, flavor

rahada, m. a lake

rāga, m. lust

rājadhānī, f. a royal city

rājan, m. a king

rāsi, m. a mass, a heap

rittaka, mfn. void

rukkha, m. a tree

rūpa, m.n. (1) material form; (2) a visible form; (3) mfn. nature (ifc)

roga, m. illness

lakkhaṇa, n. a characteristic

labhati, vb. gets, gains

lābha, m. gain, profit

līna, mfn. sluggish

līnatta, n. sluggishness

ludda, m. a hunter

leṇa, n. a cavern

lepa, n. paste, glue

loka, m. the world

lola, mfn. frivolous

lohita, n. blood

vagga, m. a group

vaggiya, mfn. belonging to a group (ifc)

vacana, n. word, teaching

vacanīya, mfn. should be said, should be told

vaccha, m. a calf

vañjha, mfn. barren

vaṭṭi, f. a coil of leaves

vaḍḍheti, vb. increases, causes to grow (caus. of *vaḍḍhati*)

vaṇṇeti, vb. praises

vaṇṇa, n. (1) color, beauty; (2) praise

vata, ind. indeed (often untranslatable)

vattati, vb. occurs

vattar, m. one who speaks

vatthukata, mfn. made a basis

vadati, vadeti, vb. says

vana, n. a grove, woods, forest

vandati, vb. venerates

vammika, m. an anthill

vaya[1], n. vitality, life

vaya[2], m. vanishing

varaṃ, ind. better

varatta, n. a thong

valāhaka, m. a cloud

vasa, m. control, authority

vassa, n. (1) a year; (2) the rainy season
vassati, vb. rains
vā, ind. or
vācā, f. speech
vāta, m. a wind
vādin, mfn. a speaker of, an exponent of (ifc)
vāyamati, vb. makes an effort
vāyāma, m. effort
vāsa, m. living (ifc)
vigata, mfn. rid of, devoid of
vighāta, m. distress
vicaya, m. discrimination, examination
vicāra, m. examination
vicikicchati, vb. doubts
vicikicchā, f. doubt
vighāta, m. distress
vijambhati, vb. stretches
vijambhitā, n. stretching
vijānāti, vb. is conscious of, knows, cognizes
vijjā, f. clear knowledge
vijjhati, vb. pierces
viññāṇa, n. consciousness
viññāpana, n. conveying, communicating
viññāya, ind. having known (absol. of *vijānāti*)
viññu, mfn. wise; *viññū*, m. a wise person
viññeyya, mfn. cognizable, to be cognized
vitakka, m. a thought
vitakketi, vb. thinks
vitatha, mfn. unreal
vitathatā, f. unreality
vitthārena, ind. in detail, extensively
vitthārika, mfn. extended
vidaṃsati, vb. displays
viditvā, ind. having known, having understood (absol. of *vindati*)
vidū, m. a knower
viddha, mfn. clear
vidha, mfn. kind, type (ifc)
vinaya, m. (1) removal; (2) monastic discipline
vinassati, vb. perishes
vinipāta, m. the lower world
vinibbhujati, vb. unrolls, unravels
vinīta, mfn. trained
vineti, vb. removes, trains
vipariṇāma, m. change
vippaṭisāra, m. regret
vippaṭisārin, mfn. regretful
vippamutta, mfn. freed
vippasanna, mfn. tranquil
vibhajati, vb. analyzes
vibhajanā, f. analyzing
vibhava, m. non-existence
vimariyādīkata, mfn. unbounded
vimāna, m. a celestial palace
vimuccati, vb. is liberated
vimutta, mfn. liberated
vimutti, f. liberation
vimokkha, m. emancipation
viya, ind. like, as
virajjati, vb. becomes dispassionate
virāga, m. (1) dispassion; (2) fading away
virājeti, vb. removes passion

viriya, n. energy

virūḷhi, f. increase, growth

virocati, vb. shines, radiates

vilikhati, vb. scratches

vilokita, mfn. looked aside

vivaṭa, mfn. revealed

vivadati, vb. disputes

vivaraṇā, f. disclosing

vivarati, vb. discloses

vivicca, ind. having become secluded from, detached from (absol. of *viviccati*)

viveka, m. seclusion

visa, n. poison

visaṃyutta, mfn. detached

visama, mfn. (1) uneven, unequal; (2) unrighteous

visaya, m. a domain

visuddhi, f. purification

visussati, vb. evaporates, dries up

visesa, m. (1) distinction; (2) excellence

visoseti, vb. causes to dry up

vihaññati, vb. is distressed

viharati, vb. dwells

vihāra, m. a dwelling

vihiṃsā, f. harm, injury

vīṇā, f. the Indian lute

vītisāretvā, absol. having concluded

vīthi, f. a road, a trail

vuccati, vb. is called

vuṭṭhāti, vb. (1) emerges, rises up; (2) recovers [from illness]

vuṭṭhita, mfn. (1) emerged, risen up; (2) recovered [from illness]

vuddha, mfn. (1) increased; (2) mature, aged

vuddhi, f. increase, growth

vuyhati, vb. is swept along

vusita, mfn. lived

vūpakaṭṭha, mfn. withdrawn

vūpasanta, mfn. subsided

vūpasama, m. quiescence, subsiding

vūpasamati, vb. settles down, subsides

vūpasameti, vb. calms down

vega, m. a current

veṭha, m. a band, a strap

vedanā, f. feeling

vedaniya, vedanīya, mfn. (1) to be felt; (2) to be understood

vedayita, n. feeling; mfn. what is felt

vedayati, vedeti, vediyati, vb. feels

veditabba, mfn. to be understood

vepulla, n. maturity, expansion

vemattatā, f. diversity

veyyākaraṇa, n. (1) a discourse, exposition; (2) an explanation, answer (to a question)

vera, n. enmity

veramaṇī, f. abstinence

veḷu, m. bamboo

vesārajja n. self-confidence

vehāsa, m. the air, the sky

vokiṇṇa, mfn. soiled by, mixed with

vossagga, m. release, giving up

vyasana, n. disaster

vyākata, mfn. explained, answered, declared

vyākaroti, vb. explains, answers, declares

vyāpajjati, vb. is annoyed

vyāpanna, mfn. annoyed

vyāpāda, m. ill will

vyābādha, m. harm, injury

sa-, together with (at beginning of compounds)

saṃkhittena, ind. briefly, in brief

saṃyutta, mfn. connected, attached, yoked, fettered

saṃyojana, n. a fetter

saṃyojaniya, mfn. able to fetter

saṃvacchara, m. a year

saṃvaḍḍha, mfn. grown up

saṃvattati, vb. leads to

saṃvattanika, mfn. leading to (ifc)

saṃvara, n. restraint

saṃvijjati, vb. exists, is found

saṃvega, m. sense of urgency

saṃsaṭṭha, mfn. mixed

saṃsarati, vb. roams through

saṃsāda, m. sinking

saṃsāra, m. the "roaming" through successive rebirths (untranslated)

saṃsīdati, vb. sinks

saṃhita, mfn. connected with (ifc)

saka, mfn. one's own

sakaṭa, n. a cart

sakala, mfn. entire, whole

sakalikā, f. a splinter

sakiṃ, ind. once

sakkā, vb. is possible

sakkāya, m. "the personal-collection" (the set of five clinging-aggregates)

sakkhara, m. a grain, a pebble

saṅkappa, m. intention

saṅkhata, mfn. conditioned

saṅkhā, f. calculation

saṅkhāra, m. (1) volitional activity; (2) a conditioned thing

saṅgati, f. a meeting

saṅgha, m. (1) the monastic community; (2) the community of disciples (untranslated)

saṅghāṭi, f. a cloak (double-layered monastic robe)

sace, ind. if

sacca, n. truth

sacchikaroti, vb. realizes

sacchikātabba, mfn. to be realized

sacchikiriyā, f. realization

sañcetanā, f. volition

sañchindati, vb. cuts, bursts

sañjanetar, m. a producer

sañjāta, mfn. produced

sañjānāti, vb. perceives

saññā, f. perception

saṇṭhāna, n. relaxation, settling down

saṇṭhita, mfn. composed

sata[1], n. a hundred

sata[2], mfn. mindful

sati, f. mindfulness

satipaṭṭhāna, m. establishment of mindfulness

satimat, mfn. mindful

satta,[1] m. a [sentient] being

satta,[2] num. seven

satthar, m. a teacher

sadattha, m. personal good

sadda, m. a sound

saddahati, vb. has faith in, believes

saddhā, f. faith

saddhiṃ, ind. together with (used with instrumental)

san (*sā*), m. a dog

santānaka, n. a filament

santāsa, m. terror

santa, pres. p., existing

santi, vb. pl., there are

santike, ind. near, in the presence of

santiṭṭhati, vb. is composed, is steady

sandiṭṭha, m. an acquaintance

sandiṭṭhika, mfn. directly visible

sandissati, vb. is seen

sandhāvati, vb. runs on

sannipatati, vb. assembles

sannipāta, m. an encounter

sannisīdati, vb. settles down

sappurisa, m. a good person

sabala, mfn. blemished

sabba, n. the all (everything); mfn. all

sabbaso, ind. entirely

sama, mfn. (1) even, smooth; (2) righteous; (3) equal to, the same as (ifc)

samajja, n. an assembly, a gathering

samaṇa, m. an ascetic

samatikkama, m. overcoming

samatha, m. serenity

samanupassati, vb. considers, regards, perceives

samantā, ind. all around

samannāgata, mfn. possessing

samanvesati (*samannesati*), vb. investigates

samaya, m. an occasion, a time

samavāya, m. concurrence

samācāra, m. behavior

samādapeti, vb. enjoins

samādhi, m. concentration

samādhiyati, vb. becomes concentrated

samāraddha, mfn. undertaken

samāhita, mfn. concentrated

samiñjita, mfn. bent in [of the limbs]

samuṭṭhāpeti, vb. arouses

samudaya, m. origin, origination

samudāgata, mfn. arisen

samudda, m. the ocean

samuppanna, mfn. arisen

samuppāda, m. origination

samūhanati, vb. removes

sampajāna, mfn. clearly comprehending

sampadāleti, vb. splits

sampanna, mfn. accomplished in, possessed of, endowed with

samparāyika, mfn. pertaining to future lives

sampavaṅka, m. a comrade, a friend

sampassati, vb. sees, considers

sampādeti, vb. strives

sampāyati, vb. succeeds

samphappalāpa, m. idle chatter

samphassa, m. contact

sambahula, mfn. several

sambuddha, m. an enlightened one; mfn. enlightened

sambojjhaṅga, m. a factor of enlightenment (= *bojjhaṅga*)

sambodha, m. enlightenment

sambodhi, f. enlightenment

sambhatta, m. a companion

sambhavati, vb. comes to be

sambhavesin, mfn. approaching existence (about to come-to-be)

sambhāra, m. a component

sambhūta, mfn. originated (ifc)

sambhoti, vb. comes to be (= *sambhavati*)

samma, ind. a term of familiar address, "dear"

sammata, mfn. agreed upon (ifc)

sammada, m. sloth, languor

sammasati, vb. explores

sammasana, n. exploration

sammosa, m. decline

sammā, ind. right, correct(ly), complete(ly), perfect(ly)

sammukhībhūta, mfn. personally present

sammudita, mfn. rejoicing in (ifc)

sammodati, vb. exchanges greetings with

sammodanīya, mfn. related to greetings

sayaṃ, ind. by oneself, for oneself

sayita, mfn. (1) laid down; (2) planted

sara, n. a sharp reed

saraṇa, n. a refuge

sarada, m. autumn

sarīra, n. the body

sallīna, mfn. sluggish

saḷāyatana, n. the six sense bases

savana, n. listening

sassata, mfn. eternal

sassati, f. eternity

sahagata, mfn. accompanied by (ifc)

sahati, vb. (1) endures; (2) overcomes

sahadhammika, mfn. reasonable, legitimate

sahasā, ind. suddenly

sahassa, n. a thousand

sahāya, m. a companion

sākhā, f. a branch

sāgara, m. the ocean

sāta, mfn. agreeable

sādhu, mfn. (1) good; (2) well; (3) please (preceding a request)

sādhukaṃ, ind. well

sāmika, m. an owner

sāmīci, f. propriety

sāyanha (*sāyaṇha*), m. the evening

sāyita, mfn. tasted

sāra, m. (1) heartwood; (2) substance

sārajjati, vb. becomes attached to

sāraṇīya, mfn. cordial

sārathi, m. a trainer, a charioteer

sārāda, mfn. fertile

sāruppa, mfn. in conformity with, suitable for

sālohita, m. kinsfolk

sāvaka, m. a disciple

sāvajja, mfn. blameworthy

siṃsapā, f. a kind of tree (untranslated)

sikkhā, f. the training

sikhā, f. the top, tip

siṅgāla, m. a jackal

sippa, n. art, craft, skill

siras, n. the head

siva, mfn. auspicious

sīgha, mfn. swift

sīla, n. good behavior

sīvathikā, f. a charnel ground

sīha, m. a lion

su–, a prefix implying well, good, thorough, easy

suṃsumāra, m. a crocodile

sukara, mfn. easy to do

sukka, mfn. bright

sukkha, mfn. dry

sukha, n. pleasure, happiness; mfn. pleasant

sukhin, mfn. happy

sukhuma, mfn. subtle

sugata, m. a fortunate one (epithet of the Buddha); mfn. fortunate

sucarita, n. good conduct

suñña, mfn. empty

suṇāti, vb. listens

sutavat, mfn. learned

sutta[1], mfn. slept

sutta[2], n. a discourse

sudaṃ, ind. a connective particle used in narration (untranslatable)

subha, mfn. beautiful

surā, f. liquor

suriya, m. the sun

sekha, m. a trainee, a disciple in higher training

seti, vb. lies down

senāsana, n. a lodging [of a monk]

seyyathāpi, ind. suppose, just as

seyyathīdaṃ, ind. that is

sevita, mfn. practiced

sevitabba, mfn. to be practiced

soka, m. sorrow

sota[1], n. the ear

sota[2], m.n. a stream

sotāpatti, f. stream-entry

sotāpanna, m.f., a stream-enterer

sotthi, f. safety

sobbha, n. a pool of water

somanassa, n. joy

soḷasī, f. a sixteenth

hata, mfn. damaged

hattha, m. a hand

harati, vb. takes

hi, ind. (1) for, because; (2) indeed

hita, n. welfare

himavat, m. the Himālaya Mountains

hīna, n. inferior state, low state; mfn. inferior

hetu, m. a cause, a reason

hoti, vb. is, becomes, comes to be, occurs (= *bhavati*)

Bibliography

Bodhi, Bhikkhu. 2000. *The Connected Discourses of the Buddha: A Translation of the Saṃyutta Nikāya*. Somerville, MA: Wisdom Publications.

———. 2007. *Discourse on the All-Embracing Net of Views*. Kandy, Sri Lanka: Buddhist Publication Society.

Collins, Steven. 2006. *A Pali Grammar for Students*. Chiang Mai, Thailand: Silkworm Books.

Cone, Margaret. 2001, 2010. *A Dictionary of Pali*. Oxford: Pali Text Society. Part 1 (a–kh): 2001. Part 2 (g–n): 2010.

Coomaraswamy, Ananda. 1930. "The Parts of the Vīṇā." *Journal of the American Oriental Society* 50: 244–53.

De Silva, Lily. 2008. *Pāli Primer*. Available online at http://www.pratyeka.org/Silva/. Originally published in 1994 by the Vipassana Research Institute.

Duroiselle, Charles. 1997. *A Practical Grammar of the Pāli Language*. 3rd ed. Buddha Dharma Education Association. Available online at http://www.buddhanet.net/pdf_file/paligram.pdf. Originally published in 1906 in Rangoon.

Gair, James, and W. S. Karunatillake. 1998. *A New Course in Reading Pāli*. Delhi: Motilal Banarsidass.

Geiger, Wilhelm. 1994. *A Pāli Grammar*. Revised and edited by K. R. Norman. Oxford: Pali Text Society.

Gombrich, Richard. 2018. *Buddhism and Pali*. Oxford: Mud Pie Books.

Macdonell, Arthur A. 1927. *A Sanskrit Grammar for Students*. 3rd ed. Oxford: Oxford University Press.

Monier-Williams, Monier. 2003. *A Sanskrit-English Dictionary*. Delhi: Motilal Banarsidass. First published in 1899 by Oxford University Press.

Norman, K. R. 1993. *Collected Papers*. vol. 4. Oxford: Pali Text Society.

———. 2006. *A Philological Approach to Buddhism*. 2nd ed. Lancaster, UK: Pali Text Society.

Oberlies, Thomas. 2019. *Pāli Grammar: The Language of the Canonical Texts of Theravāda Buddhism*. vol. 1. Bristol, UK: Pali Text Society.

Perniola, Vito. 1997. *Pali Grammar*. Oxford: Pali Text Society.

Rhys Davids, T. W., and William Stede. 1999. *Pali-English Dictionary*. Oxford: Pali Text Society. First published in 1921–25.

Sujato, Bhikkhu, and Bhikkhu Brahmali. 2014. *The Authenticity of the Early Buddhist Texts*. Kandy, Sri Lanka: Buddhist Publication Society.

Von Hinüber, Oskar. 1996. *A Handbook of Pali Literature*. Berlin: Walter de Gruyter.

Warder, A. K. 2005. *Introduction to Pali*. 3rd ed. Oxford: Pali Text Society. First published in 1963.

Whitney, William Dwight. 1879. *Sanskrit Grammar*. Leibzig: Breitkopf and Härtel.

Wijesekera, O. H. de A. 1993. *Syntax of the Cases in the Pāli Nikāyas*. Colombo, Sri Lanka: Postgraduate Institute of Pāli and Buddhist Studies.

About the Author

VEN. BHIKKHU BODHI is an American Buddhist monk from New York City, born in 1944. He obtained a BA in philosophy from Brooklyn College and a PhD in philosophy from Claremont Graduate School. After completing his university studies he traveled to Sri Lanka, where he received novice ordination in 1972 and full ordination in 1973, both under the leading Sri Lankan scholar-monk Ven. Balangoda Ananda Maitreya (1896–1998). From 1984 to 2002 he was the editor for the Buddhist Publication Society in Kandy, where he lived for ten years with the senior German monk Ven. Nyanaponika Thera (1901–1994) at the Forest Hermitage. He returned to the United States in 2002. He currently lives and teaches at Chuang Yen Monastery in Carmel, New York. Ven. Bodhi has many important publications to his credit, either as author, translator, or editor. These include *The Middle Length Discourses of the Buddha* (*Majjhima Nikaya*, 1995), *The Connected Discourses of the Buddha* (*Samyutta Nikaya*, 2000), and *The Numerical Discourses of the Buddha* (*Anguttara Nikaya*, 2012). In 2008, together with several of his students, Ven. Bodhi founded Buddhist Global Relief, a nonprofit supporting hunger relief, sustainable agriculture, and education in countries suffering from chronic poverty and malnutrition.

What to Read Next from Wisdom Publications

The Connected Discourses of the Buddha
A Translation of the Saṃyutta Nikāya
Bhikkhu Bodhi

"To hold a copy of *The Connected Discourses of the Buddha* is like holding treasure in your hands." —*Eastern Horizon*

In the Buddha's Words
An Anthology of Discourses from the Pāli Canon
Bhikkhu Bodhi

"It will rapidly become the sourcebook of choice for both neophyte and serious students alike." —*Buddhadharma*

The Middle Length Discourses of the Buddha
A Translation of the Majjhima Nikāya
Bhikkhu Ñāṇamoli and Bhikkhu Bodhi

"As close as we'll get to the original teachings and account of the life of the Buddha." —*Tricycle*

The Numerical Discourses of the Buddha
A Translation of the Aṅguttara Nikāya
Bhikkhu Bodhi

"A priceless gift." —Joseph Goldstein, author of *A Heart Full of Peace* and *One Dharma*

About Wisdom Publications

Wisdom Publications is the leading publisher of classic and contemporary Buddhist books and practical works on mindfulness. To learn more about us or to explore our other books, please visit our website at wisdomexperience.org or contact us at the address below.

Wisdom Publications
199 Elm Street
Somerville, MA 02144 USA

We are a 501(c)(3) organization, and donations in support of our mission are tax deductible.

Wisdom Publications is affiliated with the Foundation for the Preservation of the Mahayana Tradition (FPMT).